WATERLOO
1815

About the Author

Gregory Fremont-Barnes holds a doctorate in Modern History from the University of Oxford and has served as a Senior Lecturer in War Studies at the Royal Military Academy, Sandhurst. A prolific author, his other books on this period include *The French Revolutionary Wars*, *The Peninsular War, 1807–14*, *The Fall of the French Empire, 1813–15*, *Nile 1798* and *Trafalgar 1805*. He also edited *Armies of the Napoleonic Wars* and the three-volume *Encyclopedia of the French Revolutionary and Napoleonic Wars*. As an academic advisor, Dr Fremont-Barnes has accompanied several groups of British Army officers and senior NCOs in their visits to the battlefields of the Peninsula and to Waterloo. In addition to the Napoleonic period, he specialises in the study of insurgency and counter-insurgency, his wider work for the UK Ministry of Defence on these subjects regularly taking him to Africa, the Middle East and South America.

WATERLOO 1815

THE BRITISH ARMY'S DAY OF DESTINY

GREGORY FREMONT-BARNES

Front cover illustration: Lieutenant Colonel James Macdonell with a party of Coldstream and 3rd Foot Guards shutting the North Gate of Hougoumont, by Robert Gibb. (National War Museum, Edinburgh Castle)

First published 2014
This edition first published 2022

The History Press
97 St George's Place, Cheltenham,
Gloucestershire, GL50 3QB
www.thehistorypress.co.uk

British Library Cataloguing in Publication Data.
A catalogue record for this book is available from the British Library.

ISBN 978 1 80399 010 1

Typesetting and origination by The History Press
Printed and bound in Great Britain by TJ Books Limited, Padstow, Cornwall.

Trees for LYfe

CONTENTS

TIMELINE

The French Revolutionary and Napoleonic Wars

20 April 1792: France declares war on Austria, thereby initiating the Revolutionary Wars.

1 February 1793: France declares war on Britain and Holland. In the course of the coming months the Allies form the First Coalition.

5 April 1795: By the Treaty of Basle, Prussia leaves the First Coalition.

17 October 1797: France and Austria conclude the Treaty of Campo Formio, effectively ending all continental resistance to Revolutionary France and marking the end of the Second Coalition.

25 March 1802: Britain concludes the Treaty of Amiens with France, ending the Revolutionary Wars.

18 May 1803: After a brief hiatus, hostilities between Britain and France resume, so marking the beginning of the Napoleonic Wars.

11 April 1805: Russia and Britain conclude an alliance, later joined by Austria (9 August) and Sweden (3 October), which results in the formation of the Third Coalition.

21 October 1805: Vice Admiral Nelson decisively defeats the Franco-Spanish fleet under Villeneuve.

2 December 1805: Napoleon decisively defeats combined Austro-Russian Army at Austerlitz, thereby destroying the Third Coalition.

14 October 1806: The French decisively defeat the Prussians in the twin battles of Jena and Auerstädt.

7–9 July 1807: France, Prussia and Russia conclude the Treaties of Tilsit, effectively acknowledging Napoleon's extensive dominion west of the River Niemen.

14 July 1807: The Battle of Friedland, fought in East Prussia, puts paid to the last vestiges of Prussian as well as, more importantly, Russian resistance to French control of most of the European mainland.

2 May 1808: A popular uprising in Spain marks the beginning of open resistance throughout Iberia against French control.

1 August 1808: Forces under Sir Arthur Wellesley (the future Duke of Wellington) land in Portugal, marking the beginning of British participation in the Peninsular War.

5–6 July 1809:	Battle of Wagram, the decisive battle of Napoleon's campaign against a resurgent Austria, which concludes peace on 14 October at Schönbrunn.
22 June 1812:	Napoleon leads the Grande Armée of over half a million men into Russia.
22 July 1812:	Wellington defeats the French at Salamanca in central Spain opening the way for a major Anglo-Portuguese offensive to clear Iberia.
19 October 1812:	Having failed to bring the Russians to terms, Napoleon abandons Moscow and begins to retreat west, with disastrous consequences.
21 June 1813:	At Vitoria, Wellington inflicts a decisive defeat on the main French Army in Spain.
16–19 October 1813:	A colossal Allied force consisting of Austrians, Prussians, Russians and Swedes decisively defeats Napoleon's army at Leipzig, in Saxony, forcing it to abandon Germany and cross back into France.
6 April 1814:	After failing to hold back the Allies in a remarkable but ultimately unsuccessful campaign on home soil, Napoleon abdicates.
30 April 1814:	(First) Treaty of Paris concluded between France and the Allies.
1 November 1814:	The Congress of Vienna convenes to redraw the map of Europe after a generation of war led to the abolition of some states, the creation of others and the shifting of the frontiers of practically all the rest.
26 February 1815:	Napoleon leaves exile on Elba for France.
1 March 1815:	Napoleon lands on the south coast of France.
19 March 1815:	King Louis XVIII leaves Paris for the safety of Ghent in Belgium.
20 March 1815:	Napoleon arrives in Paris and returns to power, marking the beginning of his 'Hundred Days'.
25 March 1815:	The Allies declare Napoleon an outlaw and form the Seventh Coalition.
16 June 1815:	Battles of Ligny and Quatre Bras.
18 June 1815:	Battles of Waterloo and Wavre.
22 June 1815:	Napoleon abdicates.
20 November 1815:	(Second) Treaty of Paris concluded between France and the Allies.

The Battle of Waterloo

Early Phases: Furious French Attacks on the Anglo–Allied Right and Centre

6 a.m.:   Bülow's IV Corps begins to move through Wavre in the direction of the Waterloo battlefield.

8.30–9 a.m.:   Anglo-Allied Army takes up final positions at Mont St Jean; Napoleon rides forward to La Belle Alliance to examine Wellington's position.

11 a.m.:   French cannonade begins.

11.30 a.m.:   French commence attack on Hougoumont.

12.30–1.15 p.m.: British guardsmen drive off French from the north side of Hougoumont and reinforce the garrison; at 1 p.m. Napoleon's 'grand battery' of eighty guns opens fire.

1.15 p.m.:   Napoleon receives intelligence from a Prussian prisoner that Bülow's corps is en route.

1.30 p.m.:   Main bombardment by grand battery ceases and d'Erlon's corps advances; Uxbridge orders the Household and Union Brigades to charge d'Erlon's corps; Prussian I Corps under Ziethen begins its march along a northern route in order to join Wellington's left flank.

2.15–3 p.m.:   Anglo-German garrison continues to defend Hougoumont; Household Brigade fights French heavy cavalry west of La Haye Sainte and Union Brigade repulses d'Erlon's infantry; both Allied cavalry formations continue their charge into the grand battery and sabre the gunners, but suffer heavy losses from flank and frontal attacks by French cavalry; King's German Legion garrison continues to defend La Haye Sainte.

Developments in the Afternoon: Ney's Cavalry Assault and Prussian Approach

3–4 p.m.:   Buildings in Hougoumont are set on fire; La Haye Sainte reinforced by three companies of King's German Legion infantry, but French make renewed assault on this position; remnants of d'Erlon's corps reassemble; gunner casualties from grand battery replaced and guns returned to action; at approximately 3.30 p.m. the leading elements of Bülow's corps enter the Bois to Paris; at about 4 p.m. Ney interprets movement towards the Allied rear as a sign of general withdrawal and orders a major assault with his cavalry.

4–5 p.m.:   Wellington's infantry under attack from cavalry and forms square; repeated French cavalry assaults fail amid heavy losses from Anglo-Allied guns and defending infantry; Lobau's VI Corps, encountering Prussians emerging from the Bois de Paris, is gradually pushed back to Plancenoit; French attacks continue against Hougoumont and La Haye Sainte.

5–6 p.m.: Notwithstanding the progressive introduction of reinforcements, French cavalry continue their fruitless attempts to break Anglo-Allied squares, though artillery inflicts some damage on Wellington's troops during periods of quiet between charges; by 5.30 p.m. all of Prussian IV Corps is engaged against Lobau.

Evening Phases: Fall of La Haye Sainte, Crisis in the Anglo-Allied Centre and at Plancenoit

6–6.30 p.m.: Fighting around Hougoumont continues, with the French controlling the woods and orchard but British and Nassauer garrison continuing to hold the buildings.

6.30 p.m.: The remnants of the garrison at La Haye Sainte, having exhausted their ammunition supply, abandon the position; Prussians take Plancenoit, obliging Napoleon to dispatch the Young Guard to retake it.

6.30–7.30 p.m.: With the loss of La Haye Sainte the Anglo-Allied centre stands in mortal danger; French artillery continues to inflict heavy damage in this sector; Wellington begins to reinforce his centre with Dutch-Belgians and British cavalry; by around 6.45 p.m. the Young Guard manages to retake Plancenoit, temporarily neutralising the threat to the French right and rear; Prussians then recapture the village, which two battalions of the Old Guard retake; leading brigade of Ziethen's I Corps links up with Wellington's left flank.

7.30–8.30 p.m.: A false message stating that Grouchy has arrived is distributed along the French line to raise French morale; just after 7.30 p.m. Napoleon launches eight battalions of the Imperial Guard against the Anglo-Allied centre, where heavy artillery fire inflicts serious losses on the attackers; fire from British infantry repulses the Imperial Guard; at about 8 p.m. infantry from the Prussian II Corps begin assault on Plancenoit from which French are at last permanently driven out.

8.30–10 p.m.: French rout begins around 8.30 p.m.; Wellington signals a general advance; squares of the Old Guard retire slowly in fighting retreat; Prussians assume responsibility for pursuing the fleeing French; Blücher and Wellington meet south of La Belle Alliance.

INTRODUCTION

Producing yet another account of the Battle of Waterloo – about which more ink has been spilt than any other single clash of arms in history – confronts the historian with a number of salient problems, not least the fact that the task defies all attempts to render a truly accurate and comprehensive treatment of a complex series of events confined to a single day and involving over 150,000 participants. Writing home three weeks after Waterloo, Ensign Edward Macready of the 30th Foot penned a great truism of military historiography in general, but more than particularly apt for Waterloo: 'I am endeavouring to do an impossibility,' he said, 'to describe a battle.'[1] In short, no single account can truly grasp the scale, complexity – the simultaneity of events – much less the horror, elation, pain, excitement and the extraordinary range of other human emotions and other sensations of battle involving both sight and sound. The limitations of space alone preclude adequate treatment of so vast a subject as Waterloo. Struggling to report home the day's drama, Private John Lewis, 95th Foot, wrote: 'my pen cannot explain to you nor twenty sheets of paper would not contain what I could say about it'.[2]

Of course, in the final analysis any battle can be explained, albeit to an imperfect degree, and many historians have done just that with respect to Waterloo.[3] Yet the feasibility of the task alone does not justify one in adding further to the mountain of knowledge already acquired. Having said this, the large collection of new primary source material gathered in the last decade, when examined in conjunction with previously published eyewitness accounts, offers the appealing possibility of shedding new light on an old subject matter. This work has sought to exploit such material and to present the battle from a new perspective – exclusively from that of the British soldier.

Inevitably, some shortcomings thereby arise; for instance the absence, by definition, of coverage from the perspective of the various German and Dutch-Belgian forces who fought in Wellington's army – hence the Hanoverians' defence of La Haye Sainte or the part played by the Nassauers at Hougoumont must necessarily receive but limited coverage here – yet, without implying by the absence of their voices the important contribution which they and the other non-British contingents of Wellington's army made towards victory. This approach of course also excludes the French and Prussian perspectives, though readers wishing to examine those may consult the relevant scholarship devoted specifically to those subjects,[4] quite apart from material contained in every standard work on Waterloo. In short, while the benefits of adopting a multinational approach to the battle must be recognised, much may be gleaned by focusing on a single perspective and examining it in detail. The present work, therefore, devotes careful attention to the parts played by individual units or commanders. In short, the battle is viewed from the eyewitness perspectives of officers and men in order to provide an impression of the conditions and experience of battle, as well as close examination of of troop movements – including in many cases the precise positioning of British units – and analysis of episodes and phases of battle.

Eyewitness sources provide exceedingly valuable new insights into our understanding of Waterloo; yet they are by no means authoritative: every source suffers from innate weaknesses in terms of reliability and the limited scope of the author's perspective, consigning to the military historian the not inconsiderable task of separating fact from fiction and exaggeration from understatement. In short, one must piece together the complex mosaic of battle from myriad sources of varying length and quality and seek, in so doing, to furnish a reasonably clear and accurate version of events. No definitive account is, of course, ever possible, for the reason provided in a letter written a few weeks after Waterloo by Lieutenant Colonel Sir Robert Gardiner, Royal Artillery:

> You will observe my dear sir, that I can only offer what you will consider general outlines of the occurrences of this most glorious day. I have noticed them as nearly as I have been able, under the impressions which they effected at the time. It is a task for which few have adequate powers, to enter on what I should consider a perfect narrative of its events, they can *only* be traced in the individual testimony of every man whose fortune it was to bear a part in its achievement …[5]

Yet even when blessed with a treasure trove of primary sources, there remain the issues of accuracy and reliability. Some correspondents and diarists confidently assert the veracity of their accounts, such as Major General Sir Hussey Vivian, commander of the 6th Cavalry Brigade who, writing in 1837, more than twenty years after Waterloo, confidently stated that he could provide an accurate account of the events in which his formation took part. 'I do not know how or why it was,' he wrote:

> but I felt on that day so perfectly cool & collected that I have the most exact recollection of everything that occurred immediately about where I was placed & most especially as to what occurred to those under my orders as far as it came under my observation.[6]

Ensign J.P. Dirom was equally confident of his powers of recollection: 'With regard to our formation, that of the Imperial Guard, and what took place, I feel as certain as if it had only occurred yesterday.'[7] Another officer, in 1842, wrote of his 'personal observation and recollections [being] as vivid to me at the present moment as they were on the 18th June [1815].'[8]

These officers may be correct insofar as their own memory and field of vision are concerned. Yet the fact remains that notwithstanding the benefits of eyewitness accounts written in the immediate wake of battle, or accounts recorded by participants long after the event but nonetheless penned by those with the sharpest of recollections, no single participant in a battle of any significant scale can furnish anything but a very superficial and localised account of his experiences. As Captain Alexander Mercer, commander of a battery of horse artillery, very perceptively observed in his memoirs, short of enjoying a vantage point with a commanding view over the whole of the battlefield, a single observer possesses but a very limited perspective on the events unfolding around him. 'Depend upon it,' said Mercer:

> he who pretends to give a general account of a great battle from his own observation deceives you – believe him not. He can see no farther (that is, if he be personally engaged in it) than the length of his nose; and how is he to tell what is passing two or three miles off, with hills and trees and buildings intervening, and all enveloped in smoke?[9]

Captain John Kincaid of the 95th Foot, positioned near La Haye Sainte, noted similarly that: 'the higher ground near us, prevented our seeing anything of what was going on', a situation only exacerbated by the fact that the 'smoke hung so thick about, that, although not more than eighty yards asunder, we could only distinguish each other by the flashes of the pieces'.[10] Lieutenant Brown of the 4th Foot echoed his views:

> [I] fancy that Regimental Officers, and more particularly Company Officers, have little time or opportunity of knowing anything beyond their own Division or Brigade, and that the smoke, the bustle, which I fear is almost inseparable to Regiments when close to the Enemy, and more particularly the attention which is required from the Company Officers to their men, intercepts all possibility of their giving any correct account of the battles in which they may be engaged.[11]

Major Dawson Kelly, 73rd Foot, recalled that, with respect to gleaning an understanding of the circumstances surrounding the attack of the Imperial Guard:

The fog and smoke lay so heavy upon the ground that we could only ascertain the approach of the Enemy by the noise and clashing of arms which the French usually make in their advance to attack, and it has often occurred to me from the above circumstance (the heavy fog), that the accuracy and the particulars with which the Crisis has been so frequently and so minutely discussed, must have had a good deal of fancy in the narrative.[12]

Smoke proved the biggest problem, Lieutenant William Ingilby, Royal Horse Artillery, noting that around 8.30 p.m. 'the smoke was so dense we could for a time see nothing immediately before us…'[13] John Scott, a 10-year-old triangle player attached to the 42nd Foot, recalled how 'the smoke hung so thick around us that we could see little'.[14] Commissary Tupper Carey watched smoke spread from right to left as the cannonade intensified, enveloping the whole position in dense smoke, obscuring all observation.[15]

Fortunately for the historian, most British units at Waterloo occupied more or less the same positions throughout the course of the day, a fact that lends a degree of accuracy to the numerous letters and journal extracts relevant to the battle. Still, exceptions remain, not least with some of the cavalry whose position, as noted by an unknown officer of the 18th Hussars, 'was so varied, that I hardly know how to define the exact one …'[16]

The limited physical view of participants in combat constitutes but one of the many potential shortcomings that plague eyewitness accounts, obliging the military historian always to remain somewhat circumspect when examining primary sources. In short, one faces a veritable minefield of problems: some letters and memoirs are written with self-serving motives, exaggerating or embellishing facts; others inadvertently oversimplify a series of events or, conversely, assign disproportionate significance to events important only to the writer and the recipient of his communication. Still others fabricate experiences or statistics or simply exclude information which may be vital for the historian but not worthy of notice – or at least recording – by a participant, thereby rendering their correspondence incomplete or fragmentary. Finally, of course, the accuracy of memoirs written long after the fact may fall victim to fading memories or distorted recollections. Private Thomas Playford's memoir is a case in point:

The occurrences of the 18th of June have a place in my memory like a dreadful dream; like some fearful vision of the night when gloomy horrors brood over the [mind?]. Scenes of frightful destructions flit before my mind as shadows and yet I know that they represent awful realities. I have a confused, disjointed recollection of many things; yet no clear, comprehensive idea of them as a whole.[17]

Other challenges confound the work of anyone attempting to produce an account of Waterloo, above all one based primarily on first-hand accounts. These may be written with a personal agenda in mind, as an apologia in defence of one's conduct in the hopes of preserving or retrieving a sullied reputation or impugned character; or they may appear in print with some other motivation – perhaps merely the desire to 'improve' a story to lend it drama. This tends to be more prevalent amongst those who write in hope of publishing their memoirs, diaries or other forms of reportage. But even those inclined to an honest approach to their subject may draw upon the perspectives of others the veracity of whose accounts must be subjected to scrutiny. Captain Rees Howell Gronow, 1st Foot Guards, said of the sources he drew upon in producing his memoirs:

> Though I took but a humble part in this great contest, yet I had opportunities of seeing and hearing much, both during and after the battle. My anecdotes are derived either from personal experience and observation, from the conversation of those to whom they refer, or from the common talk of the army at the time; and many of these anecdotes may be new to my readers.[18]

Errors and omission also arise owing to the sheer confusion of battle or to contradictions between the accounts of eyewitnesses, as Major George De Lacy Evans, an aide-de-camp to Major General Sir William Ponsonby, observed:

> You speak of the difficulties you have in reconciling different accounts of eye-witnesses. This is only what invariably occurs. There is scarcely an instance, I think, of two persons, even though only fifty yards distant from each other, who give of such events a concurring account.[19]

John Davy, a hospital assistant writing from Brussels three weeks after the battle, summed the problem associated with rendering a clear picture out of chaos:

> I will try to give you a sketch of what I have seen: it will be very imperfect, for a scene of confusion scarcely allows of accurate observation and those engaged in it are usually those who remember least, individual matters occupying their attention, they know little or nothing of the general state of things.[20]

Such confusion manifests itself in print in various ways, such as with respect to the numbers of combatants engaged – a statistic seldom accurately known except by those on the headquarters staff. Gronow, for instance, wildly over-estimated the number of Imperial Guardsmen attacking the Anglo-Allied position at the close of the day – 'about 20,000' he claimed – while Ross-Lewin stated it as only half as many, a figure still too high.[21] Lieutenant Colonel Sir John May joined this chorus when he exaggerated the numbers of both infantry and artillery: 'In his [Napoleon's] last effort he is said to have assembled 20,000 infantry of his Guards, 96 pieces of can[n]on and with cavalry on the flanks, advanced to pierce our centre.'[22] Captain Gronow also inflated – almost certainly inadvertently – the number of attackers involved in this particular phase of the battle.[23] Captain Courtenay Ilbert, Royal Artillery, wrongly estimated overall French strength at 125,000 men – about 50,000 in excess of the true figure,[24] while Lieutenant Standish O'Grady, 7th Hussars, went further, claiming the French outnumbered the Anglo-Allies by two to one,[25] as did Sir John May.[26] 'The very lowest estimate of the enemy's force on that day I have heard made puts it at 95,000 men' wrote Lieutenant Colonel Lord Greenock, inadvertently adding 20,000 men to the true total. If on the other hand his figures for Wellington's forces are incorrect, his qualitative observation on the troops is not far from the truth: '[M]any of the troops had scarcely ever seen a shot fired.'[27] Lieutenant Colonel James Stanhope, 1st Foot Guards, reckoned the French possessed over 100,000 men – an overestimate of about 30,000, although if one included Grouchy's detached corps at Wavre (unknown to British troops at Waterloo) this figure is remarkably accurate.[28] A high number of British participants, like Lord Saltoun, also of the 1st Foot Guards, greatly overestimated French strength at 120,000 men – an exaggeration of more than 40,000.[29]

Some contemporaries provided fairly accurate figures for Anglo-Allied strength. Ross-Lewin, for instance, in stating Wellington's army as having a strength of 70,000 men, came very close to the mark.[30] Still, even when Sir John May correctly estimated that 'The Duke had about 70,000 infantry, 10,000 cavalry and about 150 pieces of cannon', he was quite incorrect when describing, at least in overall strength, Napoleon's force as 'very much greater'.[31] The French were indeed much superior in cavalry and artillery, but almost identical to their adversaries in overall numbers. Colonel Sir George Wood, a fellow artillery officer, proved almost exactly right when estimating the army's strength at about 80,000, half of it British, though overly harsh in describing it as 'a very bad army'.[32]

Still, in general, the great majority of contemporaries who offer up statistics concerning troop strengths do so across a bewildering range of sometimes wild and speculative numbers – especially respecting French forces, which they invariably inflate. Numerous letters, for instance, make reference to the numbers of French killed and the number of guns captured. In many cases these

statistics are entirely unreliable. 'The enemy doubled our number', claimed
Lieutenant William Chapman, 95th Foot. 'I have no doubt of his losing more
men that day than we had in the field ...'[33] When Ensign Thomas Wedgwood
of the 3rd Foot Guards stated that '[t]he French have lost about 90 pieces of
cannon and an immense number of killed and wounded',[34] he was certainly
right about the latter statistic, but under-reported the former. Sir John May
reckoned the French abandoned 122 pieces of artillery and approximately 300
ammunition caissons and wagons – another underestimate.[35] Gunner John
Edwards came closer to the true figure when he claimed the French abandoned 210 guns and several hundred wagons, 'the ground covered with men
and horses four or five miles' – doubtless a reference to those who fell during
the retreat across the area extending south of the battlefield rather than to
those wounded and killed across its very much narrower breadth.[36]

Other exaggerated claims litter contemporary correspondence. An
unknown sergeant of the Scots Greys claimed that at the Battle of Quatre
Bras, fought two days before Waterloo, British artillery 'mowed the French
like grass', killing thousands[37] – a patently false assertion. Colonel Sir George
Wood, commanding the artillery at Waterloo, toured the Waterloo battlefield
on the 19th and calculated that of the 19,000 troops he estimated as killed
at least 17,000 died from artillery fire, concluding: 'The battle in fact was a
battle of artillery altogether, and decided by the guns.'[38] Quite apart from the
fact that his casualty figures are woefully too small, he wrongly assigns too
much credit to his own arm of service for the outcome of the battle, as did a
cavalry officer, Captain George Luard, 18th Hussars, who farcically claimed
that 'Towards the close of the evening our turn came, and I do not hesitate
in saying that our gallant and desperate charge decided the fate of the day.'[39]
Paymaster James Cocksedge, 15th Hussars, greatly exaggerated losses amongst
Anglo-Allied cavalry when claiming a 50 per cent casualty rate.[40]

A number of errors also arise in primary sources in connection with the
massed French cavalry charges in the afternoon, by far the most common
constituting numerous participants' mistaken belief that the cuirassiers comprised units of the Imperial Guard.[41] These splendidly armoured cavalry did
indeed enjoy an elite status, yet they nevertheless formed part of the regular
mounted formations of the army. Nor did they carry lances, as claimed by
Lieutenant James Crummer, though no other source appears to have committed this very obvious error, the cuirassiers being famous for their long,
straight swords.[42] Lieutenant Richard Eyre of the 95th Foot advanced the
grossly exaggerated claim that '30,000 cavalry charged on a single occasion',[43]
while Captain George Barlow, 69th Foot, claimed that Marshal Murat led
the cavalry[44] – a perhaps forgivable sin in light of the fact that Murat had
commanded Napoleon's cavalry in most of the principal campaigns of the

previous decade and did in fact unsuccessfully apply for a command in the campaign of the Hundred Days. Other errors contained in several British letters and diaries with respect to the French cavalry attacks include Gunner John Edwards' recording of those assaults having begun at 10.30 a.m., when in fact they did not commence until well into the afternoon.[45]

Historians must also confront a range of various other inaccuracies and falsehoods, some concerning specific commanders in the field. Colonel Colin Campbell claimed Major General Sir William Ponsonby was taken prisoner, when in fact he died leading the charge of his heavy cavalry brigade.[46] False rumours spread throughout Allied lines that Jérôme Bonaparte had died of wounds and a number of correspondents recorded this as fact.[47] Another officer reported that Napoleon was wounded in the arm, had had two horses killed under him, and that both Prince Jérôme, commander of the French 6th Division, and Comte Vandamme, commander of III Corps, were dead.[48] Captain Thomas Wildman, 7th Hussars, heard reports of Jérôme and Marshal Murat being dead and General Bertrand having his leg, while Chaplain George Stonestreet wrongly claimed Jérôme was a prisoner; in fact, not only were Jérôme and Bertrand not dead – or even wounded for that matter – but Murat was not even present.[49] Other false reports include that of Courtenay Ilbert, a captain in the Royal Artillery, who stated that 'Bonaparte was in front of his troops the whole day and in every part where the greatest slaughter was going on',[50] when in fact Napoleon remained idle at Rossomme, well behind the front line, for practically the whole of the action.

Several accounts, moreover, misidentify friendly units, like one soldier's belief that due to severe losses the Black Watch combined with the 77th Foot, when in reality the latter unit was not present at Waterloo; it was the 44th to which John Scott was actually referring.[51] Other soldiers misidentify enemy units or wrongly connect them with events in which they took no part, the most common of these constituting the contention that the Old Guard attacked up the ridge at the close of the battle,[52] when in fact the Middle Guard mounted the slope. One British officer mistakenly believed that the final French attack consisted of the Young, rather than the Middle, Guard,[53] while Gronow wrongly stated in his memoirs that it was the Young Guard that advanced against Hougoumont at the outset of the battle,[54] when in fact the attackers consisted of ordinary regiments of line and light infantry from d'Erlon's I Corps. The Young Guard, as is well known, engaged the Prussians in the village of Plancenoit on the extreme French right and consequently took no part in the fighting against Wellington's centre. Other errors connected with the Imperial Guard abound: in 1846, Private Thomas Patton, 28th Foot, claimed that his battalion was responsible for repulsing the Imperial Guard[55] when in fact his battalion played no part whatsoever in that episode.

Lieutenant General Sir Henry Clinton, commander of the 2nd Division, mistakenly believed that troops from Brunswick assisted in the defence of the farm complex of Hougoumont, when in reality the foreign troops to which he referred were Nassauers.[56] Ensign Thomas Wedgwood, 3rd Foot Guards, a participant in the defence of the same place and consequently in a position to speak with authority, nevertheless wrongly asserted that the French knocked down part of the walls of the Hougoumont enclosure with artillery.[57]

Some errors concern the Prussians, such as the common assertion amongst British soldiers – ignorant of the fighting raging in Plancenoit between the French and Prussians on the extreme French right – that the Anglo-Allies had fought entirely unassisted on 18 June, with the Prussian arrival on the battlefield only coinciding with the British repulse of the Imperial Guard during the final moments of the battle. 'The Prussians were not attacked,' wrote a colonel of artillery, 'but all the weight of the French fell on us.'[58] Another officer claimed the late arrival of the Prussians 'was occasioned by the circumstance of a house so near the Bridge of Wavre having taken fire, that it was not safe for artillery to pass, a bridge was therefore to be constructed'.[59] No such event took place. Further, while he may have been only 10 at Waterloo, and by his own admission as a man in his 80s remembered very little of the action in his capacity as a triangle player attached to the Black Watch (his father's regiment), John Scott's sweeping assertion about the conduct of Dutch-Belgian troops is patently inaccurate, though some, as we shall see, did behave disgracefully. 'They never fired a shot,' Scott recalled, 'for as soon as the first crack was heard they were off as hard as they could go.'[60] Further examples include a greatly exaggerated version of an incident at Quatre Bras penned by the Assistant Quartermaster General: 'The French lancers drove the 42nd into the river and the battle lasted between them, breast high in the water two hours, the English pulling the lancers off their horses into the water, and drowning them.'[61]

Other problems associated with first-hand accounts present themselves, such as wide variations in timings. Under the confusing circumstances associated with battle men are seldom concerned with the passage of time and regularly contradict each other's accounts on this question and even, on some occasions, the sequence of events. Ordinary soldiers did not carry pocket-watches and their officers did not as a rule synchronise theirs with their fellows; indeed, as late as the Crimean War half a century later, the practice had yet to attain universal acceptance. The dozens of memoirs and hundreds of letters written by British officers and men present at Waterloo reveal them as largely unconcerned with or unaware of the time during which a particularly noteworthy moment in the fighting occurred – a fact reflected by the very infrequent references made to these matters in their correspondence and journals.

Indeed, this is so much the case that few accounts even agree on as simple an issue as the time at which fighting commenced on the morning of battle. Examples are legion. Troop Sergeant Major James Page, 1st Dragoon Guards, claimed the battle started at 'day break'.[62] Gunner John Edwards recorded the action as starting at 8 a.m.,[63] while Wheeler put it an hour later.[64] The Duke of Wellington himself stated in his dispatch to the War Office that the battle began at 10 a.m.,[65] which conforms to information contained in the letters written by Ensign Thomas Wedgwood, 3rd Foot Guards,[66] Ensign Charles Short, Coldstream Guards,[67] Lieutenant Colonel Sir Robert Gardiner, Royal Artillery,[68] Cornet James Gape, Scots Greys[69] and Sergeant William Dewar, 1/79th.[70] On the other hand, in his memoirs written many years later, Ross-Lewin recorded the fighting as beginning a few minutes past ten,[71] whereas Sergeant Archibald Johnston, Scots Greys, and Ensign William Thain, 33rd Foot asserted it as 10.30 a.m.[72] Colonel Sir George Wood recorded the battle as beginning around 10.30 or 10.45 a.m.[73] The majority of correspondents and diarists state that the battle began at 11 a.m.; these include such varied individuals as Private Joseph Lord, 2nd Life Guards,[74] Lady De Lancey, wife of Colonel Sir William De Lancey, Deputy Quartermaster General of the army,[75] Sir Richard Henegan,[76] Lieutenant General Sir Henry Clinton,[77] Sergeant William Tennant, 1st Foot Guards,[78] Major General Sir Hussey Vivian, commander of the 6th Cavalry Brigade,[79] Lieutenant Colonel Henry Murray, 18th Hussars,[80] Lieutenant Richard Cocks Eyre, 2/95th,[81] Captain George Barlow, 69th Foot,[82] Lieutenant Henry Lane, 15th Hussars,[83] Colonel Colin Campbell, Commandant at Headquarters,[84] Lieutenant George Gunning, 1st Dragoons,[85] Captain Edward Kelly, 1st Life Guards,[86] Lieutenant John Sperling, Royal Engineers,[87] and Major John Oldfield, also of the Engineers.[88] On the other hand, Lieutenant Colonel Francis Home, 3rd Foot Guards, and an officer in the 52nd Foot recorded the battle as beginning at 11.20 a.m.,[89] whereas Captain Orlando Bridgeman, 1st Foot Guards and aide-de-camp to Lieutenant General Lord Hill, indicated a time ten minutes later, at half past the hour,[90] as did Ensign Edward Macready, 30th Foot,[91] giving the time agreed by most historians – but in light of the weight of evidence almost certainly incorrect. Yet conflicting evidence does not end there: Major General Lord Edward Somerset, Commander of the brigade of Household Cavalry, stated the battle to have begun at 11.50 a.m.,[92] whereas numerous participants thought the battle commenced at noon, including Captain Peter Bowlby, 1/4th,[93] Captain Horace Churchill, 1st Foot Guards,[94] and Sir John May, Royal Artillery,[95] together with Private John Marshall, 10th Hussars,[96] Sir John May, in a second letter,[97] Ensign William Thain, 33rd Foot,[98] Lieutenant Colonel Frederick Ponsonby, commander of the 12th Light Dragoons,[99] Captain James Nixon, 1st Foot Guards,[100] Captain Joseph Logan of the

95th Foot,[101] Lieutenant John Pratt, 30th Regiment,[102] Commissary Tupper Carey,[103] Private John Abbott, 1/51st,[104] Lieutenant Colonel Lord Saltoun, 3/1st Foot Guards,[105] Lieutenant William Ingilby, Royal Horse Artillery,[106] Captain Henry Grove, 23rd Light Dragoons,[107] Captain Thomas Wildman, 7th Hussars,[108] and Captain James Naylor, 1st Dragoon Guards.[109] Remarkably, Captain Courtenay Ilbert, Royal Artillery, recorded the battle as having begun at 1 p.m.,[110] fully two hours after it actually occurred. One must also note that the timings of particular events also vary greatly between participants' accounts. Kincaid, for instance, indicates in his memoirs that the defenders of La Haye Sainte lost control of their position not later than 4 p.m., when in fact the garrison held out for another two and a half hours,[111] while various sources disagree as to the timing of the attack of the Imperial Guard or the arrival of the Prussians on Wellington's left flank. Lieutenant Robert Winchester of the 92nd reckoned the Imperial Guard advanced to the attack at 7 p.m.,[112] whereas Captain Clark Kennedy, Royal Dragoons, recalled the general Allied advance occurring at the same time, when of course the latter actually followed the former.[113]

Confronted by such contradictory accounts one must approach all records – whether written in the immediate aftermath of the battle or decades later – with a certain degree of circumspection. Nonetheless, most of the first-hand sources on which this work depends constitute letters written at the time of the campaign. Many were written the day after the battle – under circumstances in which the writer possessed no agenda for deliberate deception or inaccuracy, no eye on future publication, and with an intended readership usually confined to a single recipient, almost invariably a close member of his family. Nor must one discount sources written with the perspective of a significant passage of time, for some bear a ring of truth on the basis of the writer's particularly valuable insight, especially when corroborated by other evidence. Sergeant Major Edward Cotton, for instance, although writing years after the campaign, did so with probably a uniquely informed perspective of the Waterloo battlefield, having taken up long-term residence in the village of Mont St Jean, where he died in June 1849. In that capacity Cotton acquired an intimate acquaintance of the ground well before its alteration by the construction of the Lion Mound that stands upon it today and spoke with, and acted as a guide to, dozens of veterans who returned over the years to visit the site.[114]

It therefore behoves today's historian to endeavour to refine and, where appropriate, revise our understanding of Waterloo in light of any fresh material which, drawing conclusions based on the most logical interpretation of those primary sources. The present work – albeit having examined most of the secondary literature – therefore relies almost exclusively on original sources, some previously published, but most the product of the extraordinary efforts made by Gareth Glover, who has painstakingly compiled six volumes (four of these exclusively British sources) of almost entirely unpublished letters and jour-nal extracts connected with the Waterloo campaign. The present work draws extensively upon this new and extremely valuable research, not least with an eye to correct the inconsistencies and contradictions repeated over time and without challenge, by historians relying on the versions of events originally committed to paper in the nineteenth century.

Writing home a fortnight after Waterloo, Captain Arthur Kennedy, 18th Hussars, noted that the importance of the victory over the French 'will give more employment to the pen of … future historians than probably any 14 days ever did since the commencement of the world'.[115] One certainly need not have waited two centuries to prove the profound truth of that asser-tion. The fact is, Waterloo holds an enduring international appeal, with greater attention than ever focusing on the event as the bicentenary approaches. Accounting for this fascination amongst scholars, students, lay readers, histori-cal re-enactors and war gamers poses little challenge, for few battles combine so many separate, but each compelling, struggles within a greater struggle: the stubborn defence of Hougoumont, – a position 'as vigorously fought for by the enemy', wrote Henegan, 'as valiantly defended by the allies';[116] – the fight for the little farm of La Haye Sainte, the charge of the French heavy cavalry against Wellington's centre, the bitter street fighting in Plancenoit, the attack of Napoleon's Imperial Guard and a host of other remarkable episodes whose outcomes in nearly every case remained in the balance until evening. Waterloo offers a glimpse into the events of a single day whose salient fea-tures appear to bear little resemblance to the experience of combat familiar to us today. The 'invisible battlefield' – that eerie environment shaped by the lethality of fire that so often separates combatants to the extent that they become effectively unseen – has brought a cold, impersonal detachment to what the soldiers of 1815 understood as a very intimate business of killing. The pathos associated with men deployed shoulder-to-shoulder, following a strict evolution of drill in order to load and fire their muskets in volley at their geometrically arranged opposites from harrowingly short distances; and the dramatic spectacle of horsemen, resplendent in impractical but superbly colourful uniforms, wielding sword or lance, holds a particularly romantic appeal to some who, with considerable justice, believe that war since 1914 has reduced mankind to new depths of inhumanity – even barbarism – sullied by the substitution of machines for men, by the horrors associated with the mass destruction of civilians from 20,000ft and by conflicts waged for less honour-able motives than those of an apparently lost, halcyon age. The sheer spectacle of Waterloo – undoubtedly dreadful in its own sanguinary nature – neverthe-less distinguishes it from all such modern, mechanised horrors. Lieutenant William Ingilby Royal Artillery described the battle as:

… the greatest of all sights I have ever yet witnessed … I believe the veterans of the veterans hardly could form an idea of the struggle we had for the victory. The continued and incessant roar of the cannon during the whole of the day, accompanied by the regular rolls of musketry, and [the] perfect view I had of all the different charges of the cavalry, certainly rendered it the grandest and most awful scene I had ever been present in, in my life.[117]

Ensign Edmund Wheatley was equally descriptive:

Nothing could equal the splendour and terror of the scene. Charge after charge succeeded in constant succession. The clashing of swords, the clattering of musketry, the hissing of balls, and shouts and clamours produced a sound, jarring and confounding the senses, as if hell and the Devil were in evil contention.[118]

Lieutenant John Sperling's account is equally compelling about the chaos of battle:

Sometimes we were enveloped in smoke; shells bursting on all sides, cannon balls and bullets flying about. Nevertheless, every movement was effected with that order and precision which excited admiration, even in such a terrific scene of desolation, in which were continually multiplying the dead and dying. Horses were galloping about, having lost their riders; others were maimed. Wounded men were limping or creeping to the rear; others, more severely [wounded], were being assisted.[119]

'What a glorious day was yesterday', declared Lieutenant Colonel John Woodford, 1st Foot Guards. '[M]y imagination is still full of squares & cavalry & charging & melees.'[120] Lieutenant George Horton, 71st Foot, called it 'the most beautiful sight I ever saw'.[121]

The act of men standing opposite one another and blazing away like rival firing squads until the steadiness of one side or the other broke under the pressure of fire or the impact of a bayonet assault somehow sparks the imagination, reminding us of the extraordinary courage required of soldiers who, quite literally, could see the whites of the enemy's eyes. 'Never,' recorded Ross-Lewin in his memoirs, 'were positions more furiously attacked or more obstinately defended.'[122] Captain William Bowles, a naval officer in Brussels, summed up the views of many of his contemporaries: 'Nothing could exceed the desperation of the French attacks except the determination of the British infantry not to be beaten.'[123] To Sergeant Major Cotton, Waterloo constituted 'as noble a display of valour and discipline, as is to be found either in our own military annals, or in those of any other nation',[124] a sentiment echoed by Henegan: '[B]oth armies displayed a desperate valour, that has never been surpassed.'[125] Lieutenant Colonel John Fremantle, one of Wellington's aides-de-camp, said of the four-day campaign that it was 'as severe [an] operation as ever were known I suppose in the annals of military history',[126] while Lieutenant Colonel Lord Saltoun, commander of the 3rd Battalion 1st Foot Guards, described Quatre Bras and Waterloo as 'two of the sharpest actions ever fought by men'.[127] Private Samuel Boulter of the Scots Greys wrote of 'the dreadful yet glorious battle of Waterloo'.[128] The extraordinary toll of dead inspired practically every correspondent to comment on the fearful losses, like Ensign Jack Barnett of the 71st. '... I can say nothing of the battle,' he wrote three days later, 'further than that all the old soldiers say, they never saw so great a slaughter.'[129] Captain George Bowles of the Coldstream Guards, the day after the carnage, wrote of 'the glorious (though dearly earned) laurels of yesterday; a day which will always stand proudly pre-eminent in the annals of the British Army. A more desperate, and probably a more important, battle for the interest of Europe has hardly occurred even during the great events of the last three campaigns.'[130] Captain Henry Grove, 23rd Light Dragoons, like so many of his comrades, fully appreciated the significance of the day, recording that:

> The Battle of Waterloo will not be soon forgotten, as having determined the fate of Europe, and fought under the Great Wellington, defeating the French army under Bonaparte in person, in the severest fight ever detailed in history.[131]

Little wonder Waterloo continues to grip the imagination.

On a grand strategic level, it signified the end of an era – of over a century of conflict with France, with whom Britain would never again cross swords. Indeed, the two nations would co-operate in the Crimea forty years later and, of course, again in the two World Wars. It also marked the end of any further French attempts at territorial aggrandisement in Europe – hence Henegan's description of the Waterloo campaign as 'this glorious struggle for Europe's freedom'.[132] Captain George Barlow, 69th Foot, also recognised the magnitude of the event: 'So decisive was the tremendous blow struck,' he wrote the day after the fighting, 'that tyranny [will] never be able to recover from its effects.'[133] A fellow officer described the battle as a 'mighty struggle which was to determine the fate of Europe'.[134] Such observations rightly underscore the extraordinary significance of Waterloo, whose outcome signified the end of the long period of Anglo-French hostility that dated from the great conflict against Louis XIV commencing in 1689 – though some may trace it back to the Hundred Years War if not to the Norman invasion. Moreover, the comprehensive nature of Waterloo led to Napoleon's final downfall and the redrawing of the map of Europe, with central Europe rationalised into a few dozen, instead of a few hundred, states – thereby setting the stage for German unification later in the century. Thus could Captain Arthur Kennedy, 18th Hussars, accurately assert:

> Posterity ought to be much obliged to the British army of the present day for having terminated in so short a space of time what all Europe have been fighting for these 20 years. They will not have much more war I should think for the next 100 years at least if the cause of it is now (as he, I hope will be) put completely hors de combat and rendered for ever incapable of again disturbing the peace of civilised Society.[135]

Waterloo not only ended a generation of conflict, it put paid to such a blood-letting as Europe had not experienced since the religious wars of the seventeenth century and ushered in a hundred years of comparative peace. True, there were wars yet to be fought – the Crimean and those of Italian and German unification; but these paled into insignificance as compared with the sheer scale of the conflicts unleashed on Europe by the French revolutionaries in 1792, belatedly but definitively crushed in Belgium twenty-three years later. It was not for nothing that contemporary Britons referred to this period as 'The Great War' a century before the term was applied again in another, far more horrifying context.

Waterloo is not significant as representing a passing era of warfare and the beginning of a new phase, for the weaponry arrayed there bore a great deal in common with that deployed by the Duke of Marlborough's army over a century earlier, and warfare on land would not undergo any genuinely significant change until the 1850s, with the application of rifling to small arms and, later, artillery, followed rapidly by the advent of breech-loading technology. But if the subtle differences between the weapons employed on either side at Waterloo did not palpably contribute to its outcome, the tactics employed there certainly did. In the absence of any great flanking movements on the battlefield, the battle amounted to a great slogging match, with the balance between victory and defeat depending heavily upon the degree of French determination to press home the attack and the stubbornness with which the Anglo-Allies were prepared to meet that attack. The fact that both sides fought with remarkable energy and spirit contributes all the more to the appeal of a subject that remains a great epic in the history of the British Army.

Contemporary accounts of Waterloo reveal several consistent themes which explain the longevity of interest in the battle. A paragraph from a letter written by Colonel Colin Campbell, Commandant at Headquarters, refers to several such themes:

> We have gained a great and most glorious victory yesterday evening and totally defeated Bonaparte's army … it was the severest and most bloody action ever fought and the British infantry has surpassed anything ever before known … this victory has saved Europe, it was frequently all but lost; but the Duke alone, by his extraordinary perseverance and example, saved the day.[136]

Therein lay a series of compelling points of interest: a dramatic, decisive event whose outcome hung in the balance throughout the day, with far-reaching political repercussions, only achieved after monumental exertion, determination and the costly expenditure of human life, with the leadership of a single man playing an instrumental role in the outcome of the contest.

British soldiers seldom highlighted in their correspondence or journals the particular significance of the engagements in which they participated in the Iberian Peninsula during the campaigns that immediately preceded those in Belgium. This is not to claim that the battles in Iberia were not hard-fought; merely that soldiers frequently drew distinctions between the severity of the fighting in Spain and Portugal with that characteristic of the Waterloo campaign, a fact reflected in the praise they heaped upon their comrades: 'Nothing could exceed the gallantry both of the officers and men', wrote Major General Peregrine Maitland when reporting the result of the fighting at Waterloo.[137] Lieutenant Colonel the Hon. James Stanhope, 1st Foot Guards, writing about the bitter struggle for possession of the farm complex at Hougoumont, offered well-deserved praise to its defenders: 'The steadiness and unconquerable obstinacy with which the Second Brigade held a wood & house in the front of our right excited the admiration of all & saved us.'[138] The Assistant Adjutant General concluded that the troops 'behaved well and showed the greatest steadiness under the most tremendous cannonade and most persevering attacks of a very superior force of cavalry and infantry'.[139] As far as Captain James Nixon, 1st Foot Guards, was concerned, the 'steadiness and great endurance of privations for yesterday's total victory, are equalled by none of modern days, excepting Leipzig'.[140] Elizabeth Ord, a civilian in Brussels at the time of the battle, rightly declared that 'there is no end of the instances of heroism that were displayed from the Duke down to the common men on this tremendous & glorious day'.[141] Lieutenant Colonel Sir Henry Willoughby Rooke, Assistant Adjutant General, described the battle as 'one of the hardest fought',[142] while Colonel Felton Hervey, 14th Light Dragoons, used more colourful language to express the same sentiment:

'The French fought like madmen and the English like devils.'[143] For Sergeant Thomas Critchley, Royal Dragoons, the battle was 'dreadful and difficult to gain, I can assure you, although we made a complete victory of it with hard fighting, by the double courage of our British heroes'.[144] An ordinary soldier, Gunner John Edwards, stated it more simply, but with equal expression: 'Every man that never [saw] a bullet would [h]a[ve] thought that the world was at an end.'[145]

Contemporary British accounts also abound with admiration for the fighting spirit of the French – again, not a characteristic frequently encountered in letters and diaries associated with the Iberian experience of 1808 to 1814: 'No troops could fight more desperately or with greater courage than the French', declared Captain Orlando Bridgeman, 1st Foot Guards,[146] while Sir John May claimed 'the charges of cavalry, principally of the Imperial Guards and cuirassiers were terrific and would probably have shaken the nerves and solid squares of any other infantry but our own; and their infantry was led on with great spirit and determination'.[147] Lieutenant Henry McMillan felt the same: 'The heavy cavalry was the admiration of the whole army, they bore down everything that came in their way.'[148] Lieutenant Colonel Sir Alexander Dickson expressed a similar sentiment: 'You know I have seen a good deal of works, but such a day as this of close fighting and duration I never witnessed. The conduct of the French cavalry was brilliant, and no one but the Duke of Wellington could have resisted such impetuosity.'[149]

Lieutenant Colonel Sir John May paid specific tribute to the methods employed by the French: 'The battle of the 18th,' he wrote five days after the fighting, 'was a most complete lesson in the art of war, and accounts for most satisfactorily to my mind of the causes why Bonaparte had such brilliant and decisive success over the allies until they were beaten into the same system.'[150] Many observers heaped particular praise on the exploits of the French cavalry, the determination of which they had never witnessed before.[151] 'The cuirassiers did wonders', wrote one officer. Another found the French attacking 'with such impetuosity as we had never experienced in the Peninsula', which he attributed to the personal presence of Napoleon.[152] Hospital Assistant Isaac James claimed that '[t]he French fought better than ever they were known [to] and were not the British Army almost invincible it must have been beaten. The French were not defeated till evening and before it was doubtful as to our success.'[153]

It is for these reasons that Waterloo remains one of history's greatest battles and the object of so much scholarship.

PART 1

1

HISTORICAL BACKGROUND

In seeking to understand the Allies' motives in wishing to defeat Napoleon one must examine, if only briefly, the wars spawned in 1792 by the French Revolution which, apart from a brief period of peace between March 1802 and May 1803, finally came to an end in the spring of 1814. The first phase of this fighting, known as the French Revolutionary Wars, arose principally out of two requirements of the new republic, one ideological and the other strategic. In the case of the former, the French sought to spread the principles of the Revolution abroad, specifically by appealing to the populations of the Low Countries, Switzerland, the Rhineland and northern Italy to throw off, as the revolutionaries characterised it, the yoke of monarchical tyranny, which represented the corrupt system of privilege the French themselves had cast off in the first years of social and political turmoil following the fall of the Bastille in 1789. Having seized that great fortress and prison – the very symbol of monarchical oppression – the revolutionaries established a national assembly. The powers of the king were curbed. Later, a republic was declared and a series of constitutions adopted. Finally, Louis was executed in January 1793 – as much to hail the triumphs of the Revolution as to offend the crowned heads of Europe, many of whom, by that time, had already seen the Revolution for what it was – a threat to their ideological well-being and the principle of legitimacy. Appreciating, too, that so much power as that gathered in the hands of men constituted a grave danger to European security – quite apart from the obvious threat to monarchical rule – Austria, Prussia, Holland, Spain and numerous smaller states went to war with France as early as April 1792.

The combined strength of this, the First Coalition, ought to have crushed the Revolution in short order; but through bungled strategy, competing war aims, indecisiveness and military incompetence in the face of the new, energetic and above all massive conscripted armies of the French republic, the Allied powers repeatedly failed to bring the revolutionaries to heel, forming in fact two impressive coalitions in the decade between 1792 and 1802 without accomplishing more than enabling France to expand her borders to an extent never even dreamed of by Louis XIV: the whole of the Low Countries, the west bank of the Rhine, the Alps (thus including parts of north-west Italy) and the Pyrenees – the so-called natural frontiers. In fact, there was nothing 'natural' about them at all, apart from the southern frontier with Spain, which had remained more or less unchanged for centuries. The French, not content merely to defend their own soil against, admittedly, those bent on the destruction of what amounted to wholesale improvements in the political, social and economic lives of millions of French citizens, took possession by force of arms these vast swathes of new territory, justifying these extraordinary conquests on the cynical basis that annexation, occupation or the imposition of some form of dependent status on the conquered inevitably benefited them all. Who, the argument ran, could fail to appreciate the advantages bestowed by the Revolution? Accordingly, where neighbouring lands escaped outright annexation, they found themselves controlled either directly or indirectly from Paris – not quite akin to the eastern European experience of Soviet control in the wake of the Second World War – but something of a precursor of that phenomenon. Those states with the temerity to oppose the 'liberators' paid a heavy price: military intervention, forced requisitioning, the imposition of indemnities and, in many cases, outright annexation.

Disagreements within the Allied camp strongly contributed to the collapse of the First Coalition, a process begun as early as 1795 when Spain and Prussia, demoralised by failure to make progress against the growing strength of the republic, unilaterally abandoned their allies, which now included Britain since February 1793. After Austria suffered a series of humiliating defeats in her former Belgian possessions, along the Rhine and, above all, across northern Italy between 1796 and 1797, she concluded the Treaty of Campo Formio, which sounded the death knell for the First Coalition. A resurgent Austria, still supported by Britain and joined by Russia, Turkey and others, formed the Second Coalition in 1798, with some initial success. Most of northern Italy was retaken from the French, Russian forces managed to penetrate as far west as Switzerland and even co-operated with the British in Holland in 1799, but they withdrew from the fighting, leaving Britain practically on her own in 1801 once Austria concluded a separate peace with France at Lunéville. Thus, with an impasse created by French dominance on land and British supremacy at sea, the two sides agreed to peace at Amiens in the spring of 1802. No one could deny that, in standing utterly triumphant on the Continent – with the consequent radical shift in the balance of power – France reaped the lion's share of the benefits.

French claims that she required buffer states to protect her from her ideological rivals rang hollow during the interlude of peace created at Amiens.

If Britain could grudgingly accept by 1803 that the principles of the Revolution – admirable though most of them were – had been thrust upon France's neighbours at the point of the bayonet and remained an incontestable fact of life in western Europe, it could not long tolerate the strategic imbalance which French occupation represented or the control of the belt of satellite states created to enhance and extend French power beyond historically accepted bounds. The renewal of war was inevitable even before the ink had dried at Amiens. Accordingly, hostilities resumed in May 1803, first in the form of a strictly Anglo-French conflict, but by the summer of 1805 to expand into a full-fledged coalition – the Third. By this time the Allies had ceased to insist upon the restoration of the Bourbon monarchy and concentrated simply on deposing Napoleon and restraining the overarching power of an expansive, now imperial, France. France no longer represented an ideological threat – the fact that Napoleon had reined in constitutionalism and established himself as virtual dictator confirmed the fact. Yet again, the Allies' endeavour to re-establish a degree of strategic equilibrium on the Continent failed – and in shorter order than ever before – thanks to the capitulation of an entire Austrian army at Ulm in October 1805, followed swiftly by Napoleon's decisive victory at Austerlitz, near Vienna, in December, which led to the coalition's collapse. Napoleon, flushed with victory, renewed his nation's bid for further territorial gain, a process rendered all the more permanent when he placed various members of his family on the thrones of some of his dependencies.

By establishing the Confederation of the Rhine in 1806, Napoleon could levy financial contributions as well as troops from a host of German states – some large like Bavaria and Saxony, some small like Hesse-Darmstadt and Mecklenburg. In his efforts to extend French influence well beyond central Europe, Napoleon also created a Polish satellite state known as the Duchy of Warsaw and redrew the map of Italy to consolidate his control, such that when, upon crushing the resurgent Russians at Friedland in June 1807, the Emperor concluded accords with Russia and Prussia at Tilsit, he controlled virtually the whole of the Continent from the Atlantic in the west to Denmark and the Prussian coast in the north, to Naples and the Adriatic coast in the south and to the Russian frontier in the east. In three short years the Napoleonic armies had cowed the three great continental powers of Austria, Russia and Prussia – a military feat not repeated again until Germany's stunning successes in the early years of the Second World War. A resurgent Austria struck again in 1809, only to be cowed and further weakened by a punitive peace settlement. Britain, though supreme at sea, particularly after Trafalgar in October 1805, could only operate on land in a limited fashion, initially by seizing French colonies in the West Indies and mounting largely ineffectual expeditionary forces to the Continent. From 1805, however, she could and did fund her allies generously with subsidies; but in the wake of such catastrophes as Austerlitz, Jena and Friedland, financial aid proved woefully insufficient in reversing the hegemony imposed by France in the remarkable string of victories which marked out the Napoleonic heydays of 1805–07. Britain's greatest contribution came in Iberia, in a struggle known as the Peninsular War – not the sideshow which some historians have dubbed it – where between 1808 and 1814 British, in conjunction chiefly with Portuguese but also Spanish, forces engaged the French, eventually driving them back over the Pyrenees.

With Napoleon's 'Spanish ulcer', followed by his disastrous campaign in Russia in 1812, the Empire began to unravel. Three more coalitions followed, with the sixth (1813–14) finally successful in April 1814 in subduing France, forcing Napoleon's abdication and exile to the tiny Mediterranean island of Elba and restoring the Bourbon dynasty in the person of Louis XVIII, with whom came a new charter designed not as a reactionary doctrine to return an exhausted France to the status quo antebellum – which even the monarchists understood to be both unrealistic and unworkable – but to provide for a parliamentary government which, at least in principle and appearance, would rival any found elsewhere in Europe. The king's rule was to be established on a limited basis, including consultation with ministers and assistance provided by a bicameral legislature composed of a House of Peers nominated by Louis, as well as an assembly selected by electors eligible by virtue of their annual tax contribution.

Very sensibly, the king agreed that the very sizeable tracts of land once the property of the Crown and Church, which the Revolutionaries had sold off in the course of the 1790s, must remain in the hands of their new owners, many of whom could trace their new acquisitions back more than two decades. The new constitution guaranteed civil liberties, while many of the institutions and much of the bureaucracy of the Imperial years the royalist government retained with little amendment. The Restoration amounted, in effect, to a compromise, with the upper middle class accepting, albeit with some disgruntled protest, a new order that limited the power of the franchise while according to them, via a conservative legislature, the responsibility for enacting laws and levying taxes. If the broad public no longer enjoyed the influence upon politics which had constituted their new right from the earliest days of the Revolution, that memory now appeared a distant one in any event, for Napoleon's seizure of power as First Consul in 1799 had largely put paid to the notion that the Revolution must remain in a state of perpetual change.

Yet in less than a year this system began to break down, so creating the widespread atmosphere of discontent by which Napoleon could profit by plotting his return to power. The government of Louis XVIII revealed itself much less sympathetic to liberal constitutionalism than the rhetoric of its first days in power implied, in so doing alienating not merely individuals on a broad scale, but whole sectors of society wielding varying degrees of power and whose voices and sentiments the new regime could only ignore at its peril. In practice, the Bourbons accepted no genuine admission of responsibility for rule based on cabinet government. Ministers advised and reported to the king on an individual basis and could – and regularly did – ignore the legislature, particularly the chambers. Many former courtiers, returned from exile or at the very least from obscurity within France, gathered in the Tuileries in a manner alarmingly reminiscent of the days prior to the fall of the Bastille.

In the army, much of the Napoleonic officer corps was retired on half-pay and replaced with sycophants and much of the breed of aristocrats whom the republicans had long ago, and with entire justification, removed from their posts on grounds ranging from simple incompetence to disloyalty to the new political realities of republicanism which had demanded their removal. To compound matters, an increasing number of elements lobbied for a restoration of their former privileged status, including émigré officers, priests and nobles. The ultra-royalists, in particular, sought a wholesale reversal of political affairs and made no attempt to conceal their contempt for a charter which they connived to replace with a restored, absolutist order. Personally, in his nonchalant attitude to the affairs of state and general neglect of business, Louis exhibited every sign of sympathy with the ultras, who therefore looked optimistically upon the prospect of achieving their objectives of reversing many features of political and social progress whose retention practically everyone else – that is, widely different spectra of French society – could agree upon.

Moreover, just as the royalists revelled in restoring the old order, so many former officers and civil servants, jettisoned from their positions upon the fall of the Empire in April 1814, longed for the return of Napoleonic rule. Many wished to re-establish the nation's military prowess and thus extinguish the humiliation of defeat; others opposed the new regime on the ideological grounds that, notwithstanding the restrictions imposed on civil rights by the Napoleonic state, many of the gains achieved during the Revolution had remained down to the fall of the Empire; indeed, the introduction of the Napoleonic Code in 1802 had built upon these sweeping, often egalitarian reforms. This is not to claim that the nation as a whole enthusiastically longed for the Emperor's return; the only truly reliable base of support was to be found amongst much, though by no means all, of the peasantry and former soldiers. No one longed for a return to the blood-letting that had left nearly a million French soldiers dead since 1792; but nor did they wish to return to pre-revolutionary conditions for whose destruction the nation had paid so high a price over the course of a generation.

Napoleon had never been resigned to managing the internal affairs of Elba – hardly surprising for a man who had controlled a vast empire and dreamed of pursuing his destiny once again. Determined to return to power, he sailed for France on the evening of 26 February, accompanied by a small flotilla and about 1,100 soldiers – all loyal followers who had remained with him on Elba. Three vessels, one French and the others British, failed to intercept Napoleon, who landed on 1 March near Antibes, in southern France, where the garrison offered no resistance. He then proceeded north, gathering adherents as he went, particularly at Laffrey, where whole units defected to his cause, leaving the Bourbon authorities in Paris paralysed by a situation in which the army revealed its true allegiances by refusing to stop the usurper's progress towards the capital. At Lyon, thought to be a royalist stronghold, support for the king faltered and the city welcomed the prodigal emperor, thereby increasing his forces still further. Marshal Ney, one of the greatest commanders of the Imperial era but now in royal employ, initially pledged to capture the 'Corsican ogre' and return him to Paris in a cage; but, like thousands of others, he cast aside his allegiance to the king and gave further impetus to Napoleon's momentum. Thus, entering the Tuileries Palace in triumph on 20 March, without so much as a shot being fired to oppose him, the Emperor re-established political and military authority over most of the country with minimal objection, apart from the Vendée and traditional royalist parts of the south; troops suppressed the uprising in the former, while the advance of Napoleonic forces against Marseille and Toulon brought them to heel without recourse to violence. There appeared a certain inevitability to the whole course of events, for Louis had accomplished little to attract popularity in the brief period of the Restoration and failed to summon the arguments required to oppose the return of a man whose promises to protect France from external threats met with wide popularity.

Napoleon ensured his popularity by promising reforms meant to reverse some of the reactionary measures implemented by the Bourbons. He abolished feudal titles and authorised public works, promised constitutional government in the style of the 1790s and liberal concessions like freedom of the press and the preservation of the constitutional assemblies established by Louis, but on a more democratic basis. At the same time, Napoleon hoped to placate the crowned heads of Europe by promising to honour existing treaties and declaring himself committed to peaceful co-existence with all Europe. All the while, however, he put out diplomatic feelers to some of the minor states of Iberia, Germany and Italy in pursuit of allies, appealing as well to foreigners who had served the Napoleonic cause to return to the fold.

The Allied governments, whose diplomatic representatives had sat in Vienna since the peace in order to re-establish some semblance of territorial logic out of the Continent's radical redrawn borders, immediately declared their determination to oppose Napoleon personally – for this, the Seventh Coalition, was not to constitute a war waged against France as such, but a struggle against an illegitimate regime. Cries of righteous indignation from Napoleon in Paris that he intended to pursue a policy of peace towards his neighbours; that internal reform would mark his reign; and that he desired no territorial gains – and thus renounced all claims on foreign soil – fell on deaf ears – or rather on those for whom the Emperor's past record of conquest rendered his promises very hollow indeed. Perhaps Napoleon genuinely sought to live in harmony with his neighbours and that the dispatch of Allied armies towards the French frontier accounted for the Emperor's immediate decision to mobilise his resources; yet whatever the truth of the matter, the historical record comprehensively failed to assuage the anxieties of those who branded Napoleon an international pariah bent on re-imposing French hegemony over the whole of Europe.

2

BRITISH TROOPS
AT WATERLOO

Whilst this study focuses chiefly on the experience of the British soldier at Waterloo, exhaustive material on the rival armies at Waterloo is available.[1] Thus, on both counts, merely a brief outline of the French and Prussians armies should suffice here.

Immediately at Napoleon's disposal stood the 200,000 men of Louis' army, whose loyalty to the returned emperor carried over from the numerous previous campaigns in which many such troops had participated. Napoleon at once set about supplementing this force by recalling men from leave, drafting in repatriated prisoners and discharged veterans, inducting sailors into the army and appealing for volunteers. Potential manpower stood high, but the rapidity of events denied him the use of the nearly 50,000 men furnished by the class of 1815, who did not reach the army in the field before Waterloo. The emperor renamed his principal force l'Armée du Nord, which numbered 123,000 men and 350 guns at the outset of the campaign, and consisted of six corps, positioned in early June as follows: I Corps under the Comte d'Erlon at Lille; II Corps under Comte Reille at Valenciennes; III Corps under General Vandamme at Mézières; IV Corps under General Gérard at Metz; and VI Corps under Comte Lobau at Laon. The Imperial Guard stood at this time in Paris. The reserve cavalry, consisting of divisions under Generals Pajol, Exelmans, Milhaud and Kellermann, stood in camps between the rivers Aisne, the Meuse and the Sambre.

Smaller contingents, but totalling 104,800 troops, were deployed along various frontiers, for consolidating the whole disposable force – even if time enabled such an ambitious and vast enterprise – would have left the borders totally exposed. Besides, forces were also required to discourage unrest and suppress actual rebellion. In due course, Napoleon could confidently expect his field army to rise above 200,000 men. Apart from limited numbers, his army suffered from serious shortages of weapons, horses and equipment as a consequence of the previous regime's neglect. Napoleon began to remedy these deficiencies from the moment he returned to power, such that by the time l'Armée du Nord took the field it possessed the requisite amount of materiel and represented a formidable, highly motivated fighting force.

In 1815, many of the veteran Prussian units that had fought in the campaigns of 1813–14 to clear not only their own country but all of central Europe of French forces were back on home soil or had undergone reductions as a consequence of large-scale demobilisation. These measures seriously affected Prussia's state of preparedness, a circumstance exacerbated by financial problems that affected supply and equipment. Nevertheless, upon Napoleon's departure from Elba, King Frederick William III ordered the full-scale mobilisation of regular forces and called out the militia, known as the *Landwehr*, so that by the start of the campaign Field Marshal Gebhard von Blücher commanded just over 130,000 troops and 304 pieces of artillery, organised into four corps.

As an island nation, Britain naturally devoted a far greater proportion of its resources to the Royal Navy (the responsibilities of which extended beyond the defence of the nation to wider strategic interests) than to the army. When war with France began in 1793, the army, which numbered a mere 45,000 men, had not fought in a major conflict in the decade since the end of the War of American Independence (1775–83), from which it emerged with a respectable battlefield record but a bruised sense of inadequacy as a result of the disastrous capitulations at Saratoga and Yorktown, in 1777 and 1781 resectively.

The army's main responsibilities lay in the colonies and in the maintenance of order in restless Ireland. A massive two-thirds of the nation's troops were serving abroad at the outbreak of war with Revolutionary France, leaving a tiny disposable force available for amphibious operations on the European continent. Even had the bulk of the army remained at home, it would still have paled in comparison to its larger continental counterparts, which in some cases numbered over 200,000 men. Thus, the main burden of the war on land for the first two coalitions (1792–97, 1798–1802) stood squarely on the shoulders of Austria and Russia, with Prussia, Spain and a host of smaller powers in support. This would remain so until 1808, when, with the rising in Spain against French occupation, an expeditionary force sent to Portugal under Lieutenant General Sir Arthur Wellesley (by the time of Waterloo, the Duke of Wellington) would begin the gradual build-up of British forces in the Iberian Peninsula. Under Wellington the army would ultimately oust the French from Portugal and Spain and invade France itself even before Britain's allies crossed the Rhine in January 1814.

Recruitment focused largely on the lowest classes – those who sought an alternative to prison, a quest for adventure or, most commonly, release from poverty, as Moyle Sherer observed:

Wander where he will, a regiment is ever, to a single man, the best of homes
... For him, who by the want of fortune or other controlling circumstances,
is debarred the exquisite happiness of reposing his aching heart on that
blessed resting-place, the bosom of a wife – for such a man there is no life,
save one of travel or military occupation, which can excite feelings of interest or consolation. The hazard of losing life, which a soldier is often called
on to encounter, gives to his existence, as often as it is preserved, a value it
would, otherwise, soon cease to possess ... if it is painful at a certain age,
to think that, when you fall, no widow, no child, will drop a tear over your
grave – it is, on the other hand, a comfort to know, that none are dependent
upon your existence; that none will be left unprotected and in misery at
your death.[2]

Others were drawn to the ranks out of more patriotic motives, like Sergeant
Charles Wood, 1st Foot Guards, who:

... felt it my duty to go in search of that enemy of peace, the Tyrant of the
World; and, if it were required, to die in the cause; for I was fully sensible we
were defending truth and justice. Our object was Europe's peace and happiness; and I was confident that God had only permitted the evil to bring
about the greatest blessing, which I hope is nearly accomplished, though it
has cost much blood.[3]

The record of the British Army during the war with Revolutionary France
was mixed. Like his other eighteenth-century predecessors, especially his
father, William Pitt (Prime Minister, 1783–1801, 1804–6) dispatched numerous
minor expeditions – such as to Flanders in 1793–95 and to North Holland in
1799 – in order to divert French attention from the main theatre of war, but
none of these made much of an impact on the greater strategic aims sought by
Allied nations such as Austria, Prussia and Russia, who contributed far more
substantial troops. The British Army also had a poor record of co-operation
with the navy, on which it obviously depended for its transport and supply,
and unlike the continental armies lacked a permanent system for organising
regiments into formations higher than brigades, though a divisional system
was later employed during the Peninsular War and in the Waterloo campaign.

Certainly the army enjoyed a number of successes in the West Indies in the
1790s, but this was by no means universal, with setbacks particularly notable
on St Domingue (now Haiti). But far greater enemies awaited the army there:
yellow fever, malaria and other tropical diseases ravaged the forces sent to
that theatre, possibly accounting for as many as 100,000 deaths or invalid discharges. The most significant success enjoyed by the army during this period

was Sir Ralph Abercromby's expedition to Egypt in 1801, but by then the French Army there had been isolated for over two years and no longer posed a serious threat to the strategic interests of the Second Coalition (apart from the Ottoman Empire, of course) – and certainly no longer to British interests in India, as had been the case when Napoleon first arrived in 1798.

By the time the Napoleonic Wars began in 1803, the Commander-in-Chief, the Duke of York – an ineffective field commander but a superb administrator – had instituted a number of important reforms, while Sir John Moore had introduced light infantry and new training methods for the infantry as a whole. The government had by then begun to realise the folly of an under-strength army and had raised its capacity to over 200,000 men, though many of these were still required for home defence and colonial policing; thus, the forces sent to Hanover and Naples in 1805 were again merely diversionary (and not terribly effective at that) and extremely small compared to the massive armies fielded by Austria and Russia in the main theatre of operations. Having said this, from 1808 onward the army's role in Portugal and Spain would grow year by year, so that in the comparatively short space of four years it would become a first-rate fighting force second to none in Europe. The crucial – some would say decisive – role played by British troops at Waterloo, albeit as part of a larger Anglo-Allied and Prussian effort, would offer proof of the enormous progress achieved by the army in the preceding decade.

At the outset of the Napoleonic Wars the army possessed no larger unit than a brigade, consisting of two or more infantry battalions, all under the command of a 'brigadier', which constituted an appointment rather than a rank, since he might in fact not be a Général de Brigade but rather the senior battalion commander, in which case his battalion was led by the second in command. The staff of a brigade comprised only a handful of individuals, above the brigadier's aide-de-camp and his brigade major. If more than one brigade served together, the senior brigadier held command. No higher structure was implemented until 1807, during the expedition against Copenhagen, when Sir John Moore structured his army based on four divisions of two infantry brigades and one cavalry brigade. The division became the standard higher formation when Sir Arthur Wellesley was given independent command in the summer of 1809, and maintained this system for the remainder of the war. Naturally, army organisation varied according to circumstances, but each division comprised two, three or four infantry brigades and their commissariat. Initially, with artillery available in short supply, no permanent allocations were made, although companies tended to be assigned to specific divisions.

If divisions appeared more or less uniform on paper with respect to their structure, their constituent parts tended to vary qualitatively, though

Wellington sought to alleviate this disparity by intermingling stronger and weaker units, as well as green and veteran troops, so that quality remained fairly uniform across divisions, while at the same time less reliable units benefited from the presence of those with greater field experience. This was particularly necessary during the Waterloo campaign, where the Duke commanded regiments most of which either contained new recruits and therefore lacked Iberian experience, or which had not served in Spain and Portugal at all – many of the veteran battalions being then in America, Ireland and Canada. This left Wellington with forces of mixed quality as compared to the first-rate army he had led only a year before. As Kincaid rightly observed: 'If Lord Wellington had been at the head of his old Peninsula army, I am confident that he would have swept his opponents off the face of the earth immediately after their first attack; but with such a heterogeneous mixture under his command, he was obliged to submit to a longer day.'[4] Indeed, Wellington himself is said to have described his army during the Waterloo campaign as 'The most infamous I ever commanded'.

Nor was Wellington's army truly 'British', for it contained a mixture of nationalities, including Dutch and Belgian troops, many having fought for the French in recent years and whose loyalty therefore stood under suspicion. The fact that Wellington's command consisted of troops from across the Low Countries and parts of Germany gave rise to the term, 'Anglo-Allied Army', which represents a far more accurate description of his force, since fewer than half his men hailed from across the Channel. Specifically, of the 73,200 troops under Wellington's command at Waterloo, only 36 per cent were British, with the remainder composed thusly: 10 per cent King's German Legion, i.e. Hanoverians in British service; 10 per cent Nassauer; 8 per cent Brunswicker; 17 per cent Hanoverian; 13 per cent Dutch; and 6 per cent Belgian. As a result approximately 45 per cent of the army spoke German as its primary language. The polyglot nature of the Anglo-Allied Army necessarily affected its quality. The British and a particular portion of the Duke's Hanoverian contingent constituted by far the better-trained and more reliable troops. Hanoverians – north Germans – of two kinds fought at Waterloo: those, effectively raw militia, serving the re-established kingdom of Hanover by dint of the hereditary patrimony held by George III; and, by contrast, the highly reliable and competent troops of the King's German Legion – a component of the British Army – composed of volunteers who went into exile when the French invaded Hanover in 1803, supplemented two years later when a British expedition landed at the Elbe and Weser rivers, whereupon the ranks swelled and an émigré force keen to fight the French in any theatre of operations thereafter served very effectively in the Peninsula and southern France between 1808 and 1814. Finally, the tiny German states of Nassau and Brunswick supplied small contingents of their own. To compensate for the varying quality of this international force, Wellington reorganised his army along the pattern adopted in the Peninsula, whereby he brigaded together formations of different nationalities with differing degrees of experience and training, thereby stiffening divisions of otherwise green troops – such as the Dutch-Belgians – by mixing them with veteran British battalions.

Infantry

Although British infantry of the 1790s were not of impressive material, by the time of the Peninsular War (1808–14) great improvements had been made in training and morale. Under Wellington's command the infantry became one of the finest in Europe: extremely reliable, dogged and stalwart in battle, and capable of issuing a disciplined fire the French found themselves utterly incapable of matching.

According to the unofficial doctrine of the day, soldiers did not assume the initiative and although officers were increasingly expected to treat them humanely, many still regarded them as automata. According to Gleig: 'Soldiers are, as every person knows, mere machines; they cannot think for themselves, or act for themselves in any point of duty.'[5]

Regular infantry regiments were numbered up to 104 by 1815. In addition to these were three regiments of Foot Guards. Most regiments held titles as well as a number, indicating an affiliation with a county or territory from which most of the ranks were recruited, though in many cases these designations did not reflect the true geographical origins of the men at all. From 1805 onward, however, regulations allowed men from the militia to join the regular army, thus raising the local composition or recruits who normally enlisted in their county formation. Regiments from the Highlands and Ireland were drawn from those places for the most part, the former in particular characterised by distinct uniforms including a kilt, sporran and feather bonnet. Scottish regiments had proud martial traditions, and most had distinguished themselves in battle.

Theoretically, the basic unit of organisation was the regiment, usually consisting of two battalions, but because these rarely served together in the field, it was the battalion that actually functioned as the basic administrative unit. Thus, the two operated independently, with the second battalion frequently serving in a completely different theatre, often on another continent. One battalion of a regiment might, for instance, be stationed (or on operations) as far away as Gibraltar or India. Sometimes one battalion remained at home, where it served for recruitment purposes and sent out drafts to keep up the strength of its sister battalion on campaign. Nearly all infantry regiments composed units of the line, about two-thirds of which consisted of two battalions and a few with three or four. There were also two rifle regiments, one of which, the 95th Foot, served at Waterloo, with two of its under-strength battalions. Units designated as fusiliers were actually no different from the ordinary line regiments except in minor variations in uniform (but particularly in headdress, for they wore fur caps instead of leather shakos) and the fact that they descended from regiments that had once carried a fusil – a lighter form of musket.

The Foot Guards, together with the Household Cavalry, made up the elite of the army. In the case of the infantry, their normal established strength was much larger than ordinary regiments of the line, and their conduct and per-formance in battle was also generally higher. The 1st Foot Guards had three battalions, and the other two Foot Guards regiments had two battalions each. Guardsmen were better paid, and their officers held double rank, which meant that, for instance, a lieutenant in the Foot Guards was the equivalent to a captain in a line regiment.

Officers could rise through the ranks via the normal course of seniority or through distinguished battlefield performance, but the quickest route to promotion was through the purchase of a commission, by which an officer paid for a rank sold to him by another, more senior, officer. On the mere transfer of funds came a promotion in rank, irrespective of other considera-tions – including ability. Wellington generally favoured the system with a staunch conservatism. On the other hand, during his years on active service he condemned the fact that he had little power to promote officers of genu-ine ability, so entrenched had the purchase system become. In fury he wrote:

> It would be desirable, certainly, that the only claim to promotion should be military merit; but this is a degree of perfection to which the disposal of military patronage has never been, and cannot be, I believe, brought in any military establishment. The Commander-in-Chief must have friends, officers on the staff attached to him, etc., who will press him to promote their friends and relations, all doubtless very meritorious, and no man will at times resist these applications; but ... I, who command the largest British army that has been employed against the enemy for many years, and who have upon my hands certainly the most extensive and difficult concern that was ever imposed on any British officer, have not the power of making even a corporal!!![6]

This, of course, meant that the higher ranks were beyond the reach of any but the most affluent members of society, a fact that preserved the social exclu-sivity of the officer corps and accounted for the very high proportion of aristocrats and landed gentry in senior command, particularly in the Guards and Household Cavalry regiments, where commissions were more expensive than those in the line. Although the purchase of commissions continued until abolition occurred under Cardwell's reforms in the 1870s, many of Wellington's contemporaries decried the system for its failure to reward those worthy by dint of merit. J.F. Neville, who served in the Peninsula, observed that in the opening years of that conflict, in addition to the injustices of competent men going unnoticed, the system enabled the downright inept and, as he saw it, the socially unqualified to occupy all levels of command:

It would be fulsome flattery to give the name of 'AN ARMY' to an unwieldy concourse of men, necessarily ill-disciplined, from the fatal circumstance of their being ill-officered … the most barefaced profligacy prevailed throughout every military department. Whatever was connected with the army-establishment was, more or less, a dirty job, and a public robbery. Commissions were thrown away on persons unworthy of bearing them, or incapable of performing the duties which the letter and spirit of them religiously enjoined. Boys at school, smarting under the wholesome application of birch [i.e. beaten by schoolmasters wielding sticks], were field-officers in the British army, and regularly received their daily pay, as a just remuneration for the important services which they were rendering to the State! The brother or relative of a petty prostitute, was complimented with the command of a regiment, while the son of a low, but opulent mechanic, by the means of a bribe, saw himself at the head of a troop of horse, which he had neither the courage nor the abilities to lead …[7]

Still, in the course of the Peninsular War Wellington had weeded out the idle and inefficient, leaving a strong officer corps on whose reliable character the ordinary soldier in the ranks could count for steadiness and confidence under fire bordering on the nonchalant, and many other qualities besides. 'The subaltern officers of our army are its mainstring,' argued Lieutenant George Gunning of the Royal Dragoons:

and I hope to see their services more justly rewarded. Like the working clergy, they want their merits brought fairly before the public, and I hope the reformed parliament will take into their consideration the case of the subalterns of the army, for without them an army could not be moved.[8]

As Sergeant Charles Wood, 1st Foot Guards, described of his company commander five weeks after Waterloo:

As for [Lieutenant] Colonel [William] Miller's attention to his company, none excelled. He was continually enquiring what could be done to make them more comfortable. On the close of a day's march, his first care was to see his men comfortable, and then he considered himself; and after an absence of any time, his first enquiry was concerning their health and conduct. Before the enemy he was cool and deliberate, vigilant and brave, firm and determined; and on the 16th of June, at the head of his company in very close action, cheering his men, he received a wound in his breast, which proved mortal. As he passed to the rear, borne by four men, he said, 'Let me see the Colours'. The last office I could do for him was to place the Colour in Ensign Batty's hand, to pay him his funeral honours, while living. He then said, 'I thank you, that will do, I am satisfied.' His meaning was, that he died for his country, and in a just cause.[9]

Indeed, duty and patriotism prominently marked this era, and many brothers, fathers and sons served in the army at the same time, with Waterloo providing multiple examples of this phenomenon. While Lord Edward Somerset commanded the Heavy Cavalry brigade, his brother, Lord Fitzroy Somerset, served as Wellington's secretary. Brothers Captain Peter Bowlby and Lieutenant Edward Bowlby served together in the 4th Foot.[10] Captain Thomas Wildman, 7th Hussars, fought on the same field as his two brothers.[11] Lieutenant Arthur Gore and Captain Richard Gore, both of the 33rd Foot, fought in the Waterloo campaign, the former being killed at Quatre Bras.[12]

More than 80 per cent of Wellington's army consisted of musket-armed infantry, organised into battalions, each consisting of ten companies, eight of which were 'centre' companies (so named from the position they held in line formation); the other two were 'flank' companies. The company positioned on the right flank consisted of grenadiers, in theory the biggest men of the battalion, while the left-flank company was made up of light infantry – usually the smallest and quickest men. In the light infantry and the rifle regiments all the companies were identical, with no grenadiers. A full-service line regiment theoretically consisted of about 1,000 rank and file, or about ten companies of 100 men each. With officers, non-commissioned officers and drummers, this would bring the total up to about 1,100 men. However, this figure was rarely attained on campaign, though numbers in one battalion could be bolstered by drawing men from the second battalion. At Waterloo the average strength of a British battalion numbered 640 all ranks as compared to 520 for the French.

The musket – what most British soldiers popularly referred to as a 'firelock'[13] – served as the basic weapon of the infantry, which was known as 'line' (in French, 'ligne') or 'foot' regiments owing to the ordinary functions they performed in the line of battle. Officers carried a pistol and sword in lieu

of a musket. Muskets were notoriously inaccurate; even a trained infantryman would be fortunate to strike his target at 100 yards. Hitting a specifically
targeted individual man was practically impossible except at very short range.
In theory, while a musket ball could strike a man at 200 yards, actual effective
range was under 100, as Colonel George Hanger noted at the time:

> A soldier's musket, if not exceedingly ill bored and very crooked, as many
> are, will strike the figure of a man at 80 yards; it may even at a hundred; but a
> soldier must be very fortunate indeed who shall be wounded by a common
> musket at 150 yards, provided his antagonist aims at him; and, as to firing at
> a man at 200 yards with a common musket, you may just as well fire at the
> moon and have the same hope of hitting your object. I do maintain, and
> will prove, whenever called on, that no man was ever killed, at two hundred
> yards, by a common soldier's musket, by the person who aimed at him.[14]

Exceptions, of course, may be found in contemporary records: Gronow
reckoned the British infantryman's 'Brown Bess' rather underrated, with
'some good solid merits of her own … and when held straight was not to be
despised even at a long range', recalling one instance during the investment
of Bayonne when he observed a picket kill a French soldier with an ordinary
musket at no less than 400 yards.[15] A soldier's chances of striking his target
naturally increased as the distance shortened, which accounted for the regular exchange of volleys at 50–75 yards. Great destruction was caused at such
ranges, or even when closer, which therefore left the advantage in the hands
of better trained, better disciplined infantry, who typically fired by company
or platoon when deployed in column or line.

Light infantry, less heavily burdened with equipment – Gleig recorded
that in the Peninsula an infantryman carried a load of about 50lb[16] – and
more agile on their feet, were more adept in the use of the musket than
were ordinary line infantrymen, partly as a result of lessons painfully learned
during the War of American Independence. Skirmishing, scouting, flank
cover and screening had often been more crucial in the broken ground and
forests of North America than they were in the open fields of Flanders and
the Rhineland. Light infantry regiments proved to be all the more necessary
when ordinary line regiments found themselves confronted by the annoying
fire of the French voltigeurs and tirailleurs, who normally screened friendly
units moving inexorably forward in column. The British had lost some of
these skills by the 1790s, but through the limited efforts of officers such as
Sir David Dundas, who reformed methods of infantry manoeuvre, and above
all Sir John Moore, light infantry eventually came into its own as an elite force
of divisional strength in the Peninsula under Major General Robert Craufurd

and could match its opposite numbers in the field, utilising skills of an entirely different ilk to the virtual automatons of the line regiments, who generally fired by half-companies; rather, the light infantryman exhibited intelligence and self-reliance, since he had to employ his initiative and make the best use of natural cover. A contemporary training manual explained:

> Vigilance, activity, and intelligence, are particularly requisite ... The intelligence chiefly required in a light infantry man is that he should know how to take advantage of every circumstance of good ground which can enable him to harass and annoy an enemy, without exposing himself ... In some situations they must conceal themselves by stopping, in others they must kneel, or lie flat ... Against regular infantry they must hover round these continually ... In such a situation light infantry can be opposed not otherwise than by men acting in the same manner with themselves ... To fire seldom and always with effect should be their chief study ... Noise and smoke is not sufficient to stop the advance of soldiers accustomed to war ... a considerable proportion of their [light infantry] force should at all times be kept in reserve. The men who are scattered in front ought to be supported by small parties a little way in the rear; and these again should depend upon, and communicate with stronger bodies, further removed from the point of attack ... In advancing the reserves must not be too eager to press forward ... In retiring, the skirmishers must keep a good countenance, and avoid hurry. They must endeavour to gall the enemy from every favourable situation, and make him pay dearly for the ground he acquires ...[17]

Light infantry served most effectively when spread out as individual sharpshooters firing in a skirmish line as a screen for their formed comrades, who stood shoulder to shoulder to maximise firepower and to facilitate the already difficult process of exercising command and control and maintaining unit cohesion in an age of bugles, trumpets and shouting as large blocks of opposing infantry blazed away at one another amidst a terrible – and terrifying – cacophony.

The muskets carried by the infantry of all nationalities at Waterloo were remarkably similar to one another, although light infantry weapons were slightly shorter (and consequently lighter) and in the British Army had backsights to aid in aiming. All consisted of a smooth bore (i.e. no specialised grooves producing a rifling effect) with a flintlock mechanism firing a lead ball of approximately an ounce in weight. Black powder served as the propellant, with the ball rammed down the muzzle. Any infantryman at Waterloo could load and fire a musket belonging to that of another nationality so long as he had the ammunition specific to that weapon. Thus, all that fundamentally distinguished muskets were their differing calibres, the Prussians using the Potsdam musket with a calibre of 19.5mm, his British ally the 18.7mm 'Brown Bess' and the French the 17.2mm Charleville. Firing a musket required a sequenced drill, which for British infantry consisted of eleven movements. Weight of fire – that is, the frequency with which an infantryman could discharge his musket – generally determined the victor, so long as one excludes other factors such as numbers or any role played by artillery or cavalry. All well-trained infantrymen could fire two, sometimes three shots a minute. The British generally achieved this rate of fire, while the French and Prussians probably fired two rounds per minute at best.

Space precludes discussion of all types of muskets, but the bare specifications of the 'India Pattern' musket, better known as the 'Brown Bess', carried by British infantry provides a general impression. Its 39in barrel accommodated a triangular 17in spike bayonet, the whole weapon weighing 11lb. Soldiers carried sixty cartridges consisting of greased paper packets containing ball and powder.

At Waterloo, two battalions of British infantry and a number of their German allies carried rifles. Rifle-armed detachments and sometimes whole units had existed for some time on the Continent, particularly in the German states, where the utility of the weapon, first appreciated by hunters and estate managers, was eventually grasped by the more forward-thinking continental tacticians of the era of the Seven Years War (1756–63). The rifle, though slower to load than the musket and requiring more training, proved significantly more accurate, and an adept rifleman, taking advantage of available cover on the battlefield, could sometimes pick off mounted officers and gunners with impunity. The 95th Foot, which would attain great fame in Iberia, was formed in 1800 and equipped with the Baker rifle, which could be fired from a prone position (unlike a musket) and whose grooved rifling on the inside of the barrel offered superb accuracy – 200 yards or more. With this advantage riflemen could oppose French skirmishers, whose inferior weapons could not reply in kind. They also excelled at exploiting cover and sniping, as Wheeler relates of an incident at Waterloo:

> I was ordered with two men to post ourselves behind a rock or large stone, well studded with brambles. This was somewhat to our right and in advance [of the battalion's position at La Haye Sainte]. About an hour after we were posted we saw an officer of Huzzars [*sic*; a type of light cavalry] sneaking down to get a peep at our position. One of my men was what we term a dead shot, [and] when he was within point blank distance I asked him if he could make sure of him … When Chipping fired, down he fell and in a minute we had his body with the horse in our possession behind the rock.[18]

Kincaid related another incident in which the Baker rifle proved its exceptional value: 'They immediately brought up two guns ... and began serving out some grape [*sic*: canister] to us; but they were so very near, that we destroyed their artillerymen before they could give us a second round.'[19] The rifle proved so accurate that individual horsemen risked death if they ventured too close, as a sergeant of the Scots Greys described after his regiment was dogged by a foolhardy opposing lancer wielding his own, inaccurate firearm:

> One individual ... sallied out occasionally from his rank and advanced nearly half way where he presented his carbine and fired upon us, after which he waved it round his head and called out in broken English 'Come on you English buggers', this was several times repeated when some of our brave riflemen discovered the brave adventurer, crawled upon their hands and knees until they were within reach of him, and when he came out again brought him down off his horse like a rook![20]

On the other hand, the rifle was less robust than the musket, more expensive to manufacture and required far more practice to master; hence, the British Army's reliance on the musket as the standard infantry weapon. The 95th wore distinctive dark-green uniforms and black (as opposed to white) cross-belts and lace to aid in camouflage and to render them visibly distinct from the line and light regiments.

Infantry also carried socket bayonets which when not in use hung in a sheath suspended from a belt. As a close-order weapon, the bayonet saw less use than popularly believed, although the bitter fighting in and around the fortified structures of Hougoumont and La Haye Sainte as well as in the village of Plancenoit to the south-east saw its extensive use. The bayonet's principal benefit lay in its psychological effect since infantry and cavalry generally did not charge into the defensive hedge of steel thus created and only steady troops were likely to stand up to a determined attack by infantry advancing with the bayonet at the ready. Instead, a unit normally only charged with the bayonet once its intended target began to waver as a consequence of heavy losses inflicted by musket or artillery fire. The approach of an enemy, shouting menacingly and advancing at a rapid pace with bayonets levelled, tended to drive off untried or unsteady defenders before a clash of steel ever took place. George Gleig related a typical example of this from an encounter in Spain – and repeated with minor variations in the accounts of many other Peninsular veterans: 'We poured in one volley, and then rushed on with the bayonet. The enemy would not stand it; their ranks were broken, and they fled in utter confusion. We followed, without giving them a moment to recover from their panic ...'[21]

Infantry officers carried swords and at least one flintlock pistol. In his memoirs Kincaid recalled the facility with which one officer wielded his bladed weapon in hand–to–hand combat:

> A French officer rushed out of their ranks and made a dash at one of ours, but neglecting the prudent precaution of calculating the chances of success before striking the first blow, it cost him his life. The officer he stormed happened to be a gigantic Highlander about six feet and a half – and, like most big men, slow to wrath, but a fury when roused. The Frenchman held ... in his hand ... a good small sword – but as he had forgotten to put on his spectacles, his first (and last) thrust passed by the body and lodged in the Highlander's left arm. Saunders's blood was now up (as well as down), and with our then small regulation half-moon sabre, better calculated to shave a lady's maid than a French-man's head, he made it descend on the pericranium of his unfortunate adversary with a force which snapped it at the hilt. His next dash was with his fist (and the hilt in it) smack in his adversary's face, which sent him to the earth; and though I grieve to record it, yet as the truth must be told, I fear ... that the chivalrous Frenchman died an ignominious death, viz. by a kick. But where one's own life is at stake, we must not be too particular.[22]

All line infantry and light battalions carried two flags, known as the Colours, which held a status akin to that of holy relics, used to symbolise the attachment of the men to their regiment, and through it to the sovereign and nation. Each battalion possessed a King's Colour, in the form of a large Union flag, and a Regimental Colour, distinguished by a shade of the regimental facings, with a small Union in the upper corner nearest the pole, with a large St George's Cross embroidered on it for regiments with white or black facings so that the flag could not be mistaken for one of surrender in the case of the former, or be obscured amidst the smoke of battle in the case of the latter. Both bore the regiment's number and name, and any badges associated with that regiment and its battle honours, though most were not granted these until after Waterloo. As the Colours possessed a somewhat mythical status, they naturally became the focus of attention in battle, partly as an identifier for members of the regiment keen to maintain unit cohesion, but also by the enemy, who sought to capture them. The Colours and the Colour party frequently came under fire, making the task of escorting them an extremely hazardous one, as William Lawrence, 40th Foot, recalled of action on the afternoon of Waterloo:

> I was ordered to the colours. This, although I was used to warfare as much as any, was a job I did not at all like; but still I went as boldly to work as

I could. There had been before me that day fourteen sergeants already killed and wounded while in charge of those colours, with officers in proportion, and the staff and colours were almost cut to pieces. This job will never be blotted from my memory: although I am now an old man, I remember it as if it had been yesterday. I had not been there more than a quarter of an hour when a cannon-shot came and took the captain's head clean off ...[23]

As the Anglo-Allies stood on the defensive during the entire course of the battle, their tactics naturally reflected this circumstance – though localised counter-attacks did occur. Most units remained more or less in the same position for much or all of the fighting since Wellington required them simply to hold the ground on which they stood. Tactics were based on fire and movement, the first to inflict casualties on the enemy and the second to place units in a position in which to fire. Infantry which could deliver two or three shots a minute and alter formation efficiently stood a good chance of success at Waterloo. British infantry were organised around the battalion as the basic fighting unit (itself subdivided into companies) with an average strength at Waterloo of 640 all ranks, 615 for the Prussians. When deployed in line the battalion stood in two ranks, which allowed every weapon to bear on a target at any one time, whereas the French and Prussians fought in ranks of three, whose advantage lay in the narrower frontage and ease of manoeuvre.

Infantry adopted one of three tactical formations: column, line and square. Each offered benefits and drawbacks, leaving officers to decide which formation to adopt and when to execute the various drills required to alter their unit's formation in order to meet a specific requirement in attack or defence. Adopting the correct formation and choosing the timing when circumstances dictated such change could profoundly affect unit effectiveness – or even its survival on the battlefield. By dint of its extended frontage, the line offered the greatest firepower, though space might preclude its feasibility. Fire issued by infantry in line, normally in volleys of half-platoons, left a distinct impression not only on those in the immediate area, but amongst combatants across the battlefield, leaving most contemporaries to describe the sound of small-arms fire as a 'roar',[24] with others suggesting a 'whizzing' sound.[25] In a similar vein, Gronow wrote of 'the incessant rattling echoes of musketry' at Waterloo.[26]

General Bugeaud's description of British defensive tactics in the Peninsula reveals much about the power of steady infantry deployed in line receiving an approaching enemy:

The English generally occupied well chosen defensive positions having a certain command, and they showed only a portion of their forces. The

usual artillery action first took place. Soon, in great haste, without study-
ing the position, without taking time to examine if there were means to
make a flank attack, we marched straight on, taking the bull by the horns.
About 1,000 yards from the English line the men became excited, spoke
to one another and hurried their march; the column began to be a little
confused. The English remained quite silent with ordered arms, and from
their steadiness appeared to be a long red wall. This steadiness invariably produced an effect on the young soldiers. Very soon we got nearer, shouting
Vive l'Empereur! En avant! à la baionnette! [Long live the emperor! Forward!
Bayonets ready!] Shakos were raised on the muzzles of the muskets; the
column began to double, the ranks got into confusion, the agitation produced
a tumult; shots were fired as we advanced. The English line remained silent,
still and immovable, with ordered arms, even when we were only 300 yards
distant, and it appeared to ignore the storm about to break. The contrast was
striking; in our inmost thoughts each felt that the enemy was a long time in
firing, and this fire reserved for so long, would be very unpleasant when it
did come. Our ardour cooled. The moral power of steadiness, which nothing
shakes (even if it be only appearance), over disorder which stupefies itself
with noise, overcame our minds. At this moment of intense excitement, the
English wall shouldered arms; an indescribable feeling rooted many of our
men to the spot; they began to fire. The enemy's steady concentrated volleys
swept our ranks; decimated, we turned round seeking to recover our equilibrium; then three deafening cheers broke the silence of our opponents; at the
third they were on us, pushing our disorganised flight.[27]

The line also functioned perfectly well in the charge, as Gleig related in an
encounter in Spain in 1813:

We wheeled into line and advanced. Not a word was spoken, nor a shot
fired, till our troops had reached about half way across the little hollow,
when the French, raising one of their discordant yells – a sort of shout, in
which every man halloos for himself, without regard to the tone or time of
those about him – fired a volley. It was well directed, and did considerable
execution; but it checked not our approach for a moment. Our men replied
to it with a hearty British cheer, and, giving them back their fire, rushed on
to the charge.

In this they were met with great spirit by the enemy … nor was it
without very considerable difficulty, and after having exchanged several discharges of musketry, that we succeeded in getting within charging distance.
Then, indeed, another cheer was given, and the French, without waiting for
the rush, once more broke their ranks and fled.[28]

The column was employed for speed of movement or when circumstances did not immediately reveal the best formation required, since infantry could change formation from column to line or to square with relative ease. The column offered a narrow front and substantial depth and enabled an attacker so deployed to concentrate its force to drive off a defender. At Waterloo, French columns stood with a frontage of about 200 yards. While rapid movement towards the enemy – thus subjecting the men in this formation to less time under fire – bestowed certain virtues, failure to prepare the target with sufficient fire by artillery and skirmishers generally left the column unable to dislodge the object of its attack. Moreover, once a column began to move it could not fire, and success depended much more on the fire of, for instance, artillery in a supporting role to enable the infantry to drive off the defender. As proved repeatedly in the Peninsula, when French artillery or clouds of skirmishers failed to inflict heavy casualties on British infantry prior to an attack in column, the assault invariably foundered under the withering fire of the defender. Still, a French column constituted a formidable sight and had consistently defeated various Continental foes in the more than two decades of warfare afflicting Europe prior to Waterloo. In his memoirs Gleig described a typical attack by the French in 1814:

> Nothing can be more spirited or impetuous than the first attack of French troops. They come on, for a while slowly, and in silence; till, having reached within a hundred yards or two of the point to be assaulted, they raise a loud but discordant yell, and rush forward. The advance of their columns is, moreover, covered by a perfect cloud of tirailleurs, who press on, apparently in utter confusion, but with every demonstration of courage; who fire irregularly, it is true, but with great rapidity and precision; and who are as much at home in the art of availing themselves of every species of cover, as any light troops in the world. The ardour of the French is, however, admirably opposed by the coolness and undaunted deportment of Britons. On the present occasion, for instance, our people met their assailants exactly as if the whole affair had been a piece of acting, no man quitting his ground, but each deliberately waiting till the word of command was given, and then discharging his piece.[29]

Lieutenant Colonel William Tomkinson's description of a French column in the attack adds further detail to this phenomenon:

> This is the system they have gone upon with every other nation, and have succeeded. They move an overawing column or two to one point. It comes up with the greatest regularity, and on arriving at close quarters with their opponents, they carry so steady and determined an appearance that those

hitherto opposed to them have generally abandoned their positions without being beaten out of them. The nearer this column gets to the enemy the greater will be its loss from grape and a fire of musketry concentr[at]ed on it; and if the troops holding the position are inclined to use the bayonet, they have the advantage in being able to move quickly against it, whilst the column must receive the charge from not being able to move at such a quick pace as troops acting in line.[30]

Although difficult to form, the square rendered itself all but impervious to cavalry by presenting an all-round defence in four ranks with all sides facing outwards, thereby offering an impenetrable hedge of bayonets. On the other hand, thus deployed, the battalion found its firepower greatly reduced since many fewer soldiers could bring their weapons to bear. Moreover, where enemy infantry or artillery lay close at hand, the square found itself extremely vulnerable, since its reduced firepower, inability to move at any appreciable speed and, above all, its compactness rendered it a prime target for artillery. Tight ranks were critical to a square's survival against cavalry, but if attacking horsemen benefited from supporting artillery, infantry in square endured terrible punishment and could in theory be driven off, leaving the fleeing infantry at the mercy of pursuing troopers. If time did not permit the formation of a square, the infantry had to fend as best they could with a makeshift formation, as Gleig noted in the Peninsula:

> Several troops of French dragoons were advancing; their horses were already in speed. There was no time to collect or form a square; so we threw ourselves, as we best could, into compact circles, and stood to receive them. They came on with the noise of thunder. One circle wavered – some of the men abandoned their ranks – the cavalry rode through it in an instant. That in which I was stood more firm. We permitted them to approach, till the breasts of the horses almost touched our bayonets, when a close and well-directed volley was poured in, and numbers fell beneath it.[31]

Cavalry

As with infantry, cavalry in the three armies at Waterloo were clothed and armed in a similar fashion to one another and fought using largely similar weapons and tactics. British cavalry were divided into several types: the Household regiments, of which there were two; the dragoons, of which the senior version were the Dragoon Guards, which with the ordinary dragoon regiments were designated as 'heavy', as were the regiments in the Household Brigade; and the light cavalry, consisting of light dragoons and hussars.

The difference between the heavy dragoons and the light cavalry was that the former were intended for use on the battlefield to execute the charge, whereas the latter, while also able to fight in pitched battles, could also perform duties like scouting, screening the army's movement from the enemy, skirmishing, pursuing a defeated foe and protecting baggage trains and lines of communications. Heavy cavalry, which in the French Army consisted of helmeted and breast-plated cuirassiers and carabiniers, served as the principal shock weapon, often kept in reserve to deliver a great, decisive blow.

Private Smithies, 1st Dragoon Guards, recorded this account of hand-to-hand fighting with cuirassiers:

> The cuirassiers, you will recollect, had coats of steel, whilst we had no such protection; and then again their swords were much longer ... On we rushed at each other, and when we met the shock was terrific. We wedged ourselves between them as much as possible, to prevent them from cutting, and the noises of the horses, the clashing of swords against their steel armour, can be imagined only by those who heard it. There were some riders who had caught hold of each other's bodies – wrestling fashion – and fighting for life, but the superior physical strength of our regiment soon showed itself ... it was desperate work indeed, cutting through their steel armour.[32]

As cavalry cannot hold ground like infantry, its only means of defence is to attack. Standing to receive a charge surrendered impetus to the enemy and almost invariably led to defeat. Even light cavalry therefore operated on the basis that it must use the weight and momentum of its movement – even if not actually charging – to achieve some sort of success over an opponent, whether mounted or otherwise. The charge proceeded at a gradually increasing rate of advance, starting from about 600 paces at a trot, rising to a canter at 400, to a gallop at 150 paces, and the final rush at 50 paces. Cavalry carried swords, sabres or lances, depending on the type and function of the regiment. British heavy cavalry carried a long, heavy, unwieldy straight sword with both edges and its point sharpened, which proved unreliable in combat. If it made contact with its target in a downward stroke it caused dreadful injury, though it was less likely to kill an adversary than a thrust delivered by a French cavalryman. If this were not difficult enough, the French cavalry commander, General Exelmans, noted how the tight-fitting uniforms of British cavalry seriously impaired their ability to wield their swords.[33] Light cavalry carried a light, curved weapon known as a sabre, capable of inflicting dreadful wounds. On a Spanish battlefield Gleig discovered a French soldier with a head 'cloven asunder, the sword of his adversary having fairly divided it as far as the eyes; whilst another lay upon his back, with his face absolutely split into two parts, across the line of the nose.'[34]

Cavalry also carried a carbine, a lighter and shorter version of an infantry-man's musket – though these were even less effective. Cumbersome and adding unnecessary additional weight to already heavily equipped troops, such weapons seldom benefited the heavy regiments, which rarely per-formed picket duty or fought as skirmishers as did their comrades in the light regiments. 'The use of fire arms on horseback had not attained much perfection,' observed Private Thomas Playford, 2nd Life Guards, 'for on one occasion I watched the mounted skirmishers of the French and English armies, firing at each other for more than twenty minutes, and not one man or horse fell on either side.'[35] All officers and troopers also carried a pistol or a pair of pistols, though with such a short range these weapons were practically useless except when nearly within arm's length of an opponent. Success in the field also depended heavily on the robustness of a cavalry-man's mount; a strong charger could sustain itself in the course of many charges in an engagement; a weak one, easily blown, could prove a fatal handicap to its rider. Captain Edward Kelly of the 1st Life Guards noted how at Waterloo he 'owed his life to the excellence of his charger, which was well bred, very well broke, and of immense power ... with an ordinary horse [I] would have been killed a hundred times in the numerous encoun-ters which [we] had to sustain.'[36]

The regiment, subdivided into squadrons and then into troops, formed the basic tactical unit for cavalry, with an average strength for both French and British regiments of 460 all ranks. Tactics and formation varied depending on circumstances. Ideally, cavalry hoped to catch infantry unprepared to receive them – especially skirmishers, who possessed virtually no defence against formed cavalry; but more usually they might also strike a column or line, or a battery of guns. At Waterloo, fully fledged charges at a gallop or better were rare owing to the confined space caused by the very high density of combat-ants. This is not to assert that cavalry did not attack; they frequently did, but seldom did they carry out an assault at great speed, especially considering the various obstacles that stood in their way, including troops, guns, ammunition wagons, sunken roads, hedges, slopes, and wet ground. In most instances cav-alry at Waterloo seldom advanced more quickly than at a trot, operating most effectively when accompanied by horse artillery, which usually consisted of batteries of six 6-pounders which moved into the best position of support before unlimbering and bombarding a particular target, hopefully causing it to waver or, better still, break just before the cavalry pressed home its attack, thus enabling the horsemen to inflict maximum casualties on a unit incapable of offering a proper defence.

It must be borne in mind, of course, that for the great majority of the time, cavalry simply stood in anticipation of orders to move or attack, accepting whatever volume of fire the enemy might send in its direction. 'There were trying moments indeed,' declared Sergeant Matthew Colgan, 18th Hussars:

> Who can describe the change of feelings that now take place after view-ing the havoc around in breasts that but for an hour before were swelling with enthusiasm at the prospect before them? Sitting as we were, motionless on our horses, each awaiting the fate of his companion, expecting every instant to be swept off without the liberty to make any exertion, with the deafening thunder of small arms, coming, as it seemed, from a shower bath, strained and loosened our nerves.
>
> It was painfully apparent, from the groans which escaped from some, and the agonised expressions on the countenances of others, how greatly we were tried, waiting so long for the striking point, and how much our cour-age was taxed. A man's temperament is indeed changeable, one moment drooping in spirits and the next acting with savage bravery, yet a man does not really know himself until he has experienced these things. He is an animal that requires to be thrown on its mettle, as will hereafter be seen. While undergoing these painful sensations, we were at last released by the sight of Brigade Major Harris, who galloped up with a 'brief' to us, with these or similar words. 'Eighteenth, you are about to charge; the general trusts to past experience that you will act as soldiers, and I know you will, Eighteenth.' What a relief to our feelings to be taken thus from the scaffold (as I must term the position we were then in) to fight our way to death or glory, which henceforth was to be the motto for all. The elements, the thun-dering of cannon and small arms on all quarters, proclaimed the necessity of a desperate effort at this moment.[37]

Major T. W. Taylor, 10th Hussars, recalled similar circumstances for his own regiment standing under galling small-arms fire:

> A cloud of tirailleurs being close up to our Infantry, behind which we were, and keeping up a heavy fire, we had many casualties here, particu-larly numbers of horses hit, some in two or three places. Captain Gurwood, of my right half-Squadron, was struck in the knee, the shot wounding his horse, which was killed as he was going to the rear. Captain Wood was shot through the thigh, and I think Captain Grey was wounded here. The men behaved with great steadiness in a position rather trying for Cavalry.[38]

In action cavalry tended to restrict itself to two basic formations: column and line, although light cavalry sometimes extended into skirmish order such as when acting as vedettes or while scouting. As with infantry, circumstances dictated formation and a regiment very much depended on the skill of its commander to choose the most suitable manner of deploying his unit, based usually on such factors as the enemy's formation, the space available to deploy the unit and timing. Cavalry experienced many of the same benefits and drawbacks as infantry deployed in like formation. The column facilitated quick movement since it was easier to control than a line, which required constant dressing to keep the ranks from becoming ragged. Mounted units in column also suffered from fewer problems when encountering obstacles and, owing to their narrower frontage, left the enemy ignorant of their strength unless they could be viewed from an elevated position. The column also enabled a regiment to deploy quickly into the formation most popularly used in the attack: the line, which owing to its narrower depth left the regiment less vulnerable to artillery fire as it approached its target and positioned the largest possible number of troopers on the broadest possible front. The column had the disadvantage of being particularly vulnerable to artillery fire, since while its density and depth furnished it greater 'shock' value than a line, it effectively guaranteed that a round shot would wreak havoc against file after file of man and beast.

British cavalry was famous for its dash, with well mounted and well trained troopers, but the officers possessed the exasperating habit of regularly failing to execute a disciplined charge, which often led to disastrous consequences when their regiments, carried away by the excitement and impetus of the attack, proved hopelessly incapable of extricating themselves from enemy lines after troopers galloped on through the enemy's position until the horses were blown and their formation's cohesion broken. Finding the cavalry now vulnerable, the enemy counter-charged with their mounted reserve, drove back the attackers and thus reversed the initial success, not least because no reserve had been maintained to counter such an eventuality. This inability to maintain control over the men in the course of a charge, to rally and withdraw them safely to friendly lines, repeated itself on several occasions in the Peninsula, amongst these involving heavy cavalry under Général de Brigade Slade during a small skirmish at Maguilla in June 1812, which prompted Wellington to write sourly to one of his divisional commanders, Sir Rowland (later Lord) Hill:

> I have never been more annoyed than by Slade's affair ... It is occasioned entirely by the trick our officers have acquired of galloping at everything and their galloping back as fast as they galloped on the enemy. They never consider their situation, never think of manoeuvring before an enemy – so little that one would think they cannot manoeuvre except on Wimbledon Common; and when they use their arm as it ought to be used, viz offensively, they never keep nor provide for a reserve.[39]

His observation was hardly an isolated example, Gronow noting of British units that 'It has been my misfortune to witness oft-repeated blunders in the employment of the best-mounted regiments in the world.'[40]

Even the French commented on this indiscipline. After the Waterloo campaign General Exelmans, commander of a French cavalry corps, observed that although British cavalry possessed the finest horses in Europe and pronounced their riders better than any on the Continent, their commanders consistently squandered these advantages. 'The great deficiency,' he explained to Gronow:

> is in your officers, who have nothing to recommend them but their dash and sitting well in their saddles; indeed, as far as my experience goes, your English generals have never understood the use of cavalry: they have undoubtedly frequently misapplied that important arm of a grand army, and have never, up to the battle of Waterloo, employed the mounted soldier at the proper time and in the proper place. The British cavalry officer seems to be impressed with the conviction that he can dash and ride over everything; as if the art of war were precisely the same as that of fox-hunting. I need not remind you of the charge of your two heavy brigades at Waterloo: this charge was utterly useless, and all the world knows they came upon a masked battery, which obliged a retreat, and entirely disconcerted Wellington's plans during the rest of the day.[41]

Artillery

Field artillery fell into two categories: 'foot' and 'horse', indicating the speed with which a battery was conveyed. As the Royal Artillery was a very small enterprise within the army as a whole, and especially in comparison with its French counterpart, no British field commander could ever assemble massed batteries in the manner of the French (or the Russians). This was a consequence of limited resources and a shortage of trained personnel; the artillery, being a technical arm, required considerably more advanced training for its officers and gunners and hence the sale of commissions was not permitted, as it was in the infantry and cavalry. Other factors account for limitations on the size of the artillery. Whereas militia and yeomanry units could provide ready trained men for the infantry and cavalry, no such equivalent existed with respect to artillery, since virtually no formation possessed ordnance. Even for those fit and keen to learn gunnery, places at the instructional college at Woolwich were limited, and thus however many guns the Royal Artillery might procure from government arsenals there was never a large enough corps of trained officers and men to make use of them all. In practical terms this all meant than an army in the field possessed relatively few, albeit well-served, guns. Nevertheless, the artillery was well officered and crewed and pains were taken to deploy the guns carefully and select the most suitable targets for the tactical situation in question.

Artillery at Waterloo varied in type according to the armies involved but, again as with the other arms – infantry and cavalry – it did not differ substantially in technological terms from one army to another. Heavy guns provided greater striking power, which meant that a heavier ball travelled further, losing its kinetic energy at a slower rate than its lighter-calibre counterpart. Guns were organised into batteries, generally of six pieces. Like small arms, guns were smooth-bore and muzzle-loading, with the type of gun identified by the weight of the shot it fired; hence a 6-pounder fired a 6lb iron shot. A gun (technically, seldom referred to by contemporaries as 'cannon') fired with direct line of sight, which required that the crew actually see the target, using round shot, which consisted of a simple iron sphere that smashed its way through ranks of man and beast alike. This was as opposed to the howitzer, an indirect fire weapon that lobbed its ordnance – a hollow sphere containing gunpowder – over the crests of slopes or walls in a high trajectory with a fuse that exploded after a timed delay. 'Shrapnel' or 'spherical case' was a similar form of ammunition to the shell, fired from a howitzer and timed (if the gunner calculated the correct range and elevation) to shower the target with musket balls from above. This form of ordnance was unique to the British Army.

Extraordinarily, according to Gleig, not only could some soldiers recognise – presumably by the sound of the discharge – the type of projectile being fired before it struck its target, but could with careful attention also track its path through the air:

> The unmilitary reader may perhaps question whether it be possible to tell the nature of the missile which is coming against you, when as yet it has barely escaped from the muzzle of the gun, and is still a mile or two distant; but he who has been in the habit of attending to these matters will entertain no such doubt. Not to mention the fact, that an experienced eye can trace, by means of the burning fuse, the whole journey of a shell through the air, from its expulsion till its fall … I have heard men assert, that they can trace, not only a shell, but a cannon ball through the air. This may be possible; but if it be, it is possible only to those whose sense of sight is far more acute than mine.[42]

Range depended on the size of shot but, for instance, a Prussian 6-pounder could project its shot a maximum range of 1,500m, though its most effective range consisted of about half that distance. A British 6-pounder's most effective range fell between 600m and 700m, while a French 12-pounder could fire as far as 1,800m, but ideally struck its target at half that distance. Anti-personnel ammunition, such as canister shot, consisted of a thin tin container filled with lead balls which upon leaving the barrel spread with the effect of a giant shotgun, though the inaccuracy of this method meant that it could be used only at the closest ranges. Thus, a French 6-pounder firing canister enjoyed a range of 400–450m; a British 9-pounder 450m and a Prussian 12-pounder 550m. Canister shot – often mistakenly referred to by contemporaries as 'grape shot', its naval equivalent – caused horrific damage to targets at such ranges, particularly attacking columns of infantry or cavalry or, above all, squares of static infantry which, if positioned beyond 150 yards, posed no danger to the gunners, who could pummel a square fixed in position by the presence nearby of cavalry. On the other hand, artillery crews stood no chance against cavalry if they found their batteries overrun, and thus depended on reaching the safety of nearby infantry if they chose to abandon their guns until the danger passed.

Despite all that may be said about the soft ground at Waterloo impeding the progress of round shot on its first contact with the ground, eyewitness accounts abound with stories of heavy losses and horrendous injuries inflicted by artillery, particularly by the French, who brought 246 pieces to the field, as opposed to Wellington's 157 and the Prussians' (eventual) 134. Corporal John Bingley, Royal Horse Guards, wrote of a fellow trooper, two or three files on his right, decapitated by a round shot,[43] while Ensign George Keppel, a 16-year-old in the 14th Foot, observed the same fate befalling a bugler of the 51st Foot:

> … a round shot took off his head and spattered the whole battalion [deployed in square] with his brains, the colours and the ensigns in charge of them coming in for an extra share. One of them, Ensign Charles Fraser, a fine gentleman in speech and manner, raised a laugh by drawing out, 'How extremely disgusting!' A second shot carried off six of the men's bayonets, a third broke the breastbone of a Lance-Sergeant, whose piteous cries were anything but encouraging to his youthful comrades.[44]

Gleig observed how a round shot struck a sergeant in his company on the crown of the head, noting how the lethal projectile 'smashed him to atoms',[45] while Gronow recalled that the first soldier he ever saw killed, in Spain, was cut in two by a round shot.[46] Even if the shot didn't kill a man, the noise alone could shake his nerves and impair his hearing, at least temporarily; Sergeant William Dewar, 1/79th recorded that he remained deaf for three days after Waterloo.[47]

The Royal Artillery also employed rockets, an innovative weapon which, like shrapnel, was peculiar to the British Army. The Mounted Rocket Corps, associated with the Royal Horse Artillery, fired small tripod-mounted projectiles with an explosive head, invented by Sir William Congreve and first used in action in 1804. Wellington was sceptical of their efficacy, though rockets were employed in the attack on Copenhagen in 1807, in the Peninsula, and at New Orleans in January 1815. At Waterloo, Major Whinyates commanded a rocket troop consisting of five 6lb guns and thirteen rocket sections, each section carrying eight 6lb rockets.[48]

The rockets' main disadvantage was obvious for even a lay observer to see: their flight was wildly erratic, it was impossible to predict where they would land, and their explosive effect was minimal. Yet despite all these shortcomings, these unorthodox weapons could seriously affect enemy morale, causing otherwise steady troops to become disordered and sometimes flee. Gleig described the effect of one such battery in the Peninsula:

> The rocket men, throwing in their diabolical engines with extraordinary precision, simultaneously with a well-directed volley from the infantry, the confusion created in the ranks of the enemy beggars all description. I saw and conversed with a French sergeant who was taken in this affair. He assured me, that he had been personally engaged in twenty battles, and that he had never known the sensation of fear till to-day. But a rocket, it appeared, had passed harmlessly through his knapsack, and such was the violence with which it flew, that he fell upon his face, not stunned but stupefied – so frightful in his ears was the hissing sound which the missile sends forth in its progress. Nor is it the least appalling incident in a rocket's eccentricities, that you see it coming, yet know not how to avoid it. It skips and starts about from place to place, in so strange a manner, that the chances are, when you are running to the right or left, to get out of the way, that you run directly against it; and hence the absolute rout which a fire of ten or twelve rockets can create, provided they take effect. But it is a very uncertain weapon. It may, indeed, spread havoc among the enemy, but it may also turn back upon the people who use it, causing, like the elephant of other days, the defeat of those whom it was designed to protect.[49]

The Duke initially refused to allow a rocket troop to accompany the army in 1815. On the appeal of an artillery officer, however, he relented, such that a troop served at both Quatre Bras and Waterloo.

The Commissariat

The commissariat functioned to supply soldiers with their daily ration, a responsibility that of course ultimately rested with the government to furnish.

The British service contrasted strongly with that of the French, the latter of whom sought wherever possible to 'live off the land' or to requisition, usually by forcible means, supplies, whereas in the British Army the acquisition of food without proper compensation to the supplier constituted plundering and carried a severe penalty. All purchases were made either in cash or with a ticket that amounted to a promissory note for future payment. For the most part the army met its obligations and the local peasantry did not suffer from false promises or unpaid bills.

The daily ration for ordinary ranks consisted of hard biscuit, not unlike its counterpart in the navy, and thus required either softening by being soaked in water or broken to bits by pounding. A typical daily ration for a soldier consisted of 1½lb of flour or bread (or 1lb of biscuit), 1lb of beef or ½lb of pork, ¼ pint of peas, 1oz of butter or cheese and 1oz of rice. Horses on home service received 14lb of hay, 10lb of oats and 4lb of straw per day. Infestation by weevils or maggots was not uncommon and the men largely pooled their food and cooked it in a common pot, with boiling the most common method. Notwithstanding the fact that the Anglo-Allied Army was operating on friendly soil during the Waterloo campaign – and with lines of supply close to home – the commissariat faced a serious task in meeting the supply needs of an army of over 85,000 men. A division of 7,000 men, for instance, required for its daily consumption 10,500lb of bread, 7,000lb of meat and 7,000 pints of wine. Alcohol was supplied in large quantities, with a quart of beer for each man constituting the standard issue and more available for private purchase. As will be shown, breakdowns in supply could leave the troops with little or no food for days.

The commissariat fell under the jurisdiction of the Treasury, and thus its staff were civilians, free from military discipline and standards. Commissaries received no formal training and could be grossly inefficient, often supplementing their meagre incomes through corrupt practices. Treasury officials could appoint friends and family members through patronage, and qualifications were not imposed until 1810, which even then only required a commissary to have reached the age of 16 and to have spent a year as a clerk. Even the most efficient and conscientious commissaries found their task daunting, not least owing to excessive administration in the form of red tape and regulations.

Medical Services

Ignorance of medical science rendered the medical services rudimentary at best and woefully inadequate at worst. The failure of doctors to understand the necessity of practising basic hygiene meant that wounded soldiers enjoyed little

prospect of survival if wounded, for death from infection often followed any sur-
gical procedure owing to the use of unsterilised instruments or unclean hands.

Army medical services came under the superintendence of the Medical
Board, which consisted of the Surgeon General, the Physician General and
the Inspector General of Hospitals, all of whom were civilians with their own
practices, and thus did not always devote sufficient time to the needs of the
service. Each of these men controlled his own department, with provision
of medical supplies the responsibility of the Apothecary General and non-
medical supplies for hospitals the task of the Purveyor General. Fitness for the
former post was not an issue, for it had remained a hereditary office for six
decades by the time of the Waterloo campaign.

In most cases the medical services did not direct matters as a whole, obliging
officers within individual regiments largely to manage their own affairs. Each
battalion had a surgeon with the equivalent rank of a captain and two assistant surgeons, holding the equivalent ranks of lieutenant, who received their
appointment directly by the battalion's or regiment's colonel, for no overarching medical corps existed at this time. With chronic shortages of (necessarily
inadequately trained) staff surgeons and with apothecaries often standing in
their stead, the medical services amounted to a lamentable institution even by
early nineteenth-century standards, notwithstanding the conscientious efforts
of most personnel who laboured under immense disadvantages, including
the total absence of any form of organised evacuation of, or procedure for
treating, the wounded. Typically, buglers and drummer boys acted as stretcher-
bearers, but with no established system in place for such fundamental tasks,
the wounded often lay for hours, overnight or even days on the battlefield
before receiving attention. Surgeons not only had to purchase their instruments out of their own funds, but received no trained assistance in the form
of orderlies or attendants unless they took it upon themselves to explain basic
first aid to whoever had been assigned to them.

During action, a battalion surgeon might erect a makeshift 'aid post' somewhere in the rear, but he had no means of following his unit if it moved
elsewhere and possessed limited means of conveying the wounded, with most
being expected to shift themselves further to the rear, usually without any
help, for fit men from the parent unit were not to be detached for this task lest
they weaken the fighting capability of the formation. If they could not move
themselves, the wounded had no choice but to remain *in situ* until someone
came to their assistance.

Even if they received some form of first aid and survived the ordeal, the
wounded, removed from the field by blanket, had little to look forward to in
the form of the 'hospital' to which they would be conveyed by cart, which
without springs caused untold agony to the occupants and left many to die

from the bleeding caused by jolting. Buildings termed 'hospitals' amounted to little more than a locally requisitioned structure where patients were fortunate to occupy a bed, but might share space on the floor in unventilated corridors with virtually nothing in the way of sanitation. Damaged limbs required amputation, for contemporary doctors knew no better method of preventing the onset of gangrene, whereas wounds to the abdomen were probed and the ball or shrapnel removed with unsanitised forceps.

George Napier described how, having been hit in the arm with a canister shot during a siege in 1812, he underwent the standard medical procedure for such a wound:

> I must confess that I did not bear the amputation of my arm as well as I ought to have done, for I made noise enough when the knife cut through my skin and flesh. It is no joke I assure you, but still it was a shame to say a word, as it is of no use … Staff Surgeon Guthrie cut it off. However, for want of light, and from the number of amputations he had already performed, and other circumstances, his instruments were blunted, so it was a long time before the thing was finished, at least twenty minutes, and the pain was great. I then thanked him for his kindness, having sworn at him like a trooper while he was at it, to his great amusement …[50]

Surgery such as that described above consisted of primitive means – bone saws and knives – with amputation conducted without the benefit of anaesthetic, many patients dying either from excessive blood loss or simple shock.

3

OPPOSING STRATEGIES

None of the Allied forces that had taken Paris and deposed Napoleon in 1814 still remained in France, but the diplomats still assembled at Vienna and tasked with forging a political and territorial settlement for Europe appreciated the necessity of setting aside their differences – particularly over the question of allocating Polish and Saxon territory to Russia and Prussia, respectively – and on 13 March duly declared Napoleon an outlaw, with no legitimate claim to the French crown, and offered help to Louis XVIII. Two days later Lord Liverpool's government summoned the Duke of Wellington, acting on behalf of Britain, back from Vienna to assume command of the Anglo-Allied forces in Belgium. On the 25th the major European powers represented at the Austrian capital, together with many minor powers besides, resuscitated the alliance of 1814, with Austria, Prussia, Russia and Britain each committing to the coming campaign contingents of 150,000 men, with the caveat that Britain could supply a smaller force in return for subsidies paid to other powers who could furnish proportionally greater numbers of troops. In the event, units from some of the minor German states which joined this, the Seventh Coalition, pledged themselves to serve under Wellington's command.

All told, the Allies mustered 700,000 troops, but most of these, consisting of Austrians and Russians, required months to reach France. The only Allied forces immediately available stood in Belgium, consisting of 95,000 British, Dutch-Belgian and Hanoverian troops under the Prince of Orange in the west and 120,000 Prussians under Lieutenant General Gneisenau in the valley of the Meuse to the east. Wellington maintained that the campaign should open once the Allies could field 450,000 men, confident that Napoleon could deploy no more than a third of that number. The Emperor, for his part, reckoned that time was of the essence; if he was to succeed against superior numbers his only chance lay in striking first, defeating the separate elements of the Allies' forces in Belgium before the overwhelming numbers en route for the Rhine could be brought to bear against him. Whereas the bulk of his

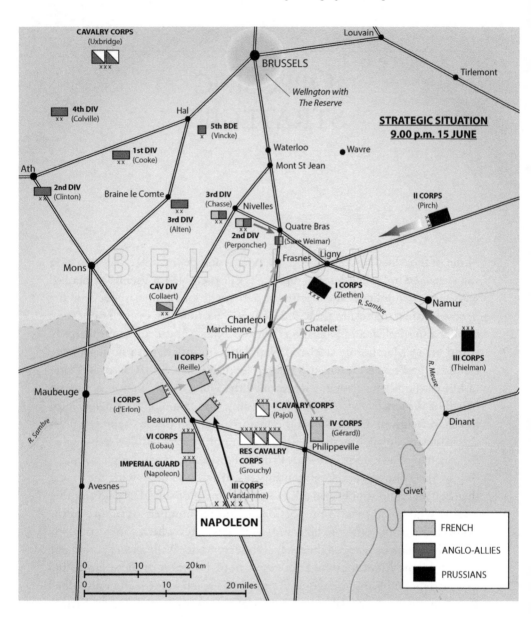

opponents' forces still lay far to the east, operating on exterior lines of communication, France could operate close to home soil with the added benefit of the geographical protection partly afforded by the Alps and Pyrenees. By launching an offensive, moreover, Napoleon hoped to galvanise domestic political support, forestall opposition in Paris and disrupt the coalition ranged against him. In short, if he could defeat the Allies in detail, there stood a reasonable prospect of disabling the coalition altogether while consolidating his hold at home.

Strategically, the key to French success required local superiority in numbers, without exposing Paris. Striking east into Germany against the slowly approaching Austrians and Russians would not offer Napoleon such advantages, for his forces remained relatively small and the proximity of the Anglo-Allies and Prussians to the north offered them the opportunity to threaten Napoleon's left flank as well as the French capital. Thus, military logic dictated that the Emperor strike north, into Belgium, with all possible speed.

Wellington arrived in Brussels on 4 April and assumed command of the Anglo-Allied forces, thus succeeding the Prince of Orange. Unable in the short term to rely on aid from the Russians and Austrians, the Allied armies in Belgium (now, formally, the United Netherlands, which included Holland) necessarily adopted a defensive posture. Ignorance of the probable axis of French advance moreover obliged the Allies to deploy their forces over a wide area of Belgium, a task complicated by the large number of roads, paved and unpaved, available to the French, not only on the line of march south of the border, but in southern Belgium as well, particularly via Lille. Such routes led to key cities such as Antwerp, Brussels, Ostend and Ghent, any one of which the French might have good reason to capture. The Allies' conundrum lay in the fact that they could not defend them all simultaneously, and covering more than one would leave the Allies dangerously dispersed. Anticipating French objectives proved problematical: both Ostend and Antwerp provided vital lines of communication across the Channel for Wellington; Ghent constituted the refuge of the exiled court of Louis XVIII; Brussels, as the capital of Belgium, represented a key strategic position of much psychological value, particularly in light of the dubious allegiance of the Dutch-Belgian troops, many of whom had previously served Napoleon; and the fortresses along the Meuse, notably Namur, Liège and Maastricht, provided protection to the Low Countries against invasion.

Yet despite each city's inherent merits, the capture of all such places lay subordinate to Napoleon's prime objective: the defeat in succession of the two Allied armies, in whichever order circumstances dictated. In turn, the Allies' success could be measured in terms of their ability to maintain them as operationally viable – that is, effectively intact and capable of fighting – thus denying

Napoleon the separate victories he required before the massive Russian and Austrian armies could bring truly palpable force to bear. In short, both sides understood two fundamental points: first, the existence of the Allied armies represented their centre of gravity; and second, their preservation depended on their uniting or, at the very least, operating on a co-operative basis, thus preventing the French from isolating and defeating them in succession. It was therefore incumbent upon the two Allied commanders to ascertain as quickly as possible the French axis of advance and respond accordingly, concentrating their forces so as to engage Napoleon with superior numbers.

From the outset Wellington and Blücher proposed different strategies for the campaign, the former advocating deployment south of Brussels and the latter wishing to shift all forces to Tirlemont, approximately 25 miles east of Brussels, thus connecting the Prussians more closely to their logistical tail – their lines of supply. The Duke opposed the idea on the grounds that it would expose Brussels to French occupation, thus imperilling the alliance with the Netherlands and risking the defection of its politically suspect forces. Moreover, the fall of the capital would sever Wellington's links with Ostend – which secured his line of communication across the Channel – and open the way to the vital port of Antwerp. Gneisenau, the temporary commander of Prussian forces, awaiting the arrival of Field Marshal Blücher, bowed to the Duke's objections; accordingly, the two armies – with Wellington's by mid-June increased to approximately 112,000 troops and 203 guns, of whom 95,000 served in the field army – proceeded on separate routes to positions south of Brussels, in so doing placing them closer to the French border and therefore exposing them to more immediate contact with Napoleon's Armée du Nord – a circumstance beneficial only if the Allies could concentrate beforehand lest they risk separation and defeat in detail. Yet, to do so – to concentrate components within their respective armies as well as to unite as a whole – required their moving across the path of Napoleon's thrust north-wards. The Allies would merely await Napoleon, who intended to occupy a central position, thereby poised to defeat the two Allied armies separately before taking Brussels. In the event, the Prussian I Corps occupied a position which blocked the road to Brussels via Charleroi – the route of advance Napoleon chose.

PART 2

4

OPENING MOVES

Without intelligence of enemy movements in northern France, the Allies remained ignorant of the axis of principal attack and consequently found themselves caught partly by surprise, notwithstanding the fact that Blücher (replacing Gneisenau, who remained as Chief of Staff) knew – partly as a consequence of the defection of General Bourmont, a divisional commander – that the French were concentrating forces south-west of Charleroi. As it happened, Bourmont's supposition that the Prussians could expect to be attacked on the morning of 15 June proved correct; before dawn on the 15th the French crossed the frontier and descended upon Charleroi, straddling the River Sambre and held by a small Prussian force. Strongly outnumbered, the Prussians briefly defended the bridge before withdrawing, leaving the French in possession of the town and the way north clear. Meanwhile, Ziethen, commander of I Corps, retreated in order to concentrate with other formations and to avoid substantial losses. Simultaneously, II and III Corps moved to oppose the French advance, while Wellington, as yet unaware of the direction of Napoleon's main thrust – and erroneously predicting an advance further west, via Mons – failed to react promptly, despite receiving word from Ziethen, via Major General von Müffling, the Prussian military liaison officer at Wellington's headquarters, of the French advance through Charleroi and the direction of their subsequent advance. Having promised Blücher on 3 June to shift his forces towards the Prussians in the event of French attack, Wellington now failed to do so in a timely manner, thus throwing into doubt the possibility of the Allies linking up and opposing Napoleon together.

While the Allies sought to take up mutually supporting positions south of Brussels, Marshal Ney, commanding the French left wing, sought out Wellington by moving north from Charleroi along the Brussels road, an advance which betrayed the lack of eagerness to engage the enemy so characteristic of the marshal's previous years in command. As a consequence, he failed to seize the important crossroads of Quatre Bras, 2 miles north of Charleroi, partly owing to the lacklustre manner in which he sought to clear the road of a small blocking force of Nassauers at Frasnes. Nevertheless, by nightfall on the 15th, Napoleon had managed to interpose his forces between those of Wellington and Blücher, leaving both to be engaged separately, with the Duke's forces yet to concentrate. Had he been in a position to strike these scattered forces on the 15th, Napoleon might have prevented Wellington from establishing any substantial field force; but faulty administration by Marshal Soult, the Chief of Staff, resulted in much of the Emperor's forces remaining on the wrong side of the River Sambre by evening, thereby preventing Napoleon from profiting by Wellington's own difficulties in assembling his scattered forces.

There can be no question that Napoleon's rapid advance into Belgium caught Wellington entirely unprepared, for he and a large number of senior and regimental officers spent the evening of the 15th at a ball thrown in Brussels by the Duchess of Richmond, with a few Scottish soldiers included to provide a 'Highland Fling'.[1] Meanwhile, the Duke remained oblivious of the French incursion over the border into Belgium, much less the engagement with the Prussians earlier that day. Assistant Surgeon John Haddy James, 1st Life Guards, described the circumstances: 'We were all in a state of sleep when Bonaparte first attacked our lines. Nothing showed the least apprehension of an attack, the greater part of the cavalry and artillery were at the distance of nearly 56 miles from the infantry in front.'[2] According to Sir Hussey Vivian, commander of the 6th (Light) Cavalry Brigade, Wellington had so little inkling of French intentions to invade Belgium that he planned himself to throw a ball on 21 June, marking the second anniversary of the Battle of Vitoria, the most decisive engagement of his various campaigns in the Peninsula.[3] 'It will no doubt be known,' admitted Ensign Charles Dallas, 32nd Foot, 'that we were as completely surprised by Napoleon as ever men were ... We had not ten days ago the slightest idea of the campaign commencing and three days afterwards Bonaparte was three leagues from Brussels.'[4] Hospital Assistant John Davy confirms the truth of these assertions:

> The war ... burst suddenly upon us, on the evening of the 15th of June, all was perfectly quiet at Brussels, I recollect walking in the park that evening, it was crowded with officers and ladies. I remember well the various conjectures respecting the beginning of hostilities. In less than 3 hours the trumpets sounded, at midnight the troops marched and in less than 12 hours were engaged [at Quatre Bras] and cannonading was heard from the ramparts [of the city]. Napoleon surprised the allies and was at the head of his army, when supposed to be in Paris.[5]

Elizabeth Ord, attending the Duchess of Richmond's ball, confirms the view that Wellington was caught unawares, and even when apprised of developments displayed no great sense of urgency:

> We went to the Duchess of Richmond's Ball that night, more to hear news than with the expectation of seeing any of our friends. The room however was full of officers of all ranks, some not knowing the news, others making light of it that their friends spirits might be kept up and all of them except at the moment of taking leave of those they loved, looking forward as if they were delighted the moment for action was come & that they were sure of success. Lord Wellington walking about with Lady F[rancis] Webster on his arm sometimes talking nonsense to her and sometimes reading reports and giving orders but not seeming as if he had more than usual on his mind. Lord Uxbridge received his orders to go and collect the cavalry, just as he was going down to supper and so did General Ponsonby. The young officers insisted on our dancing but it was with such an effort that of course it did not last long. Little parties with pale cheeks and red eyes were to be seen in many parts of the room. Those on the Staff belonging to Headquarters told us they had no doubt they should take a ride the next day but they should most likely return in the evening. As we came home about 2 o'clock the streets were full of regiments collecting to march and of officers' baggage horses. Two of the Highland regiments assembled in the Place Royal with their bagpipes playing cheerful tunes were affecting …[6]

Captain Digby Mackworth, 7th Foot, gave the most detailed account of the events of the evening of the 15th:

> The greater part of our staff went yesterday evening to a ball given by the Duchess of Richmond, which was of course attended by 'Everybody' at Brussels. We had heard during the day that the French had begun to advance and we knew that Bonaparte had joined them; still it was thought that, as the Prussian army was nearer to them than we were, we should have quite sufficient notice of their approach to make the necessary preparations to give them a warm and hearty reception. About eleven o'clock, however, while the dancing was yet going with great spirit, we learned from the Duke that the Prussians had suffered severely that same evening, and that our Belgian outposts had given notice that the enemy was in sight of them; it was consequently necessary to start immediately and rejoin as quick as possible our several corps. In vain did the charms of music, the persuasions, and even in some instances the tears, of beauty tempt us to remain; in vain did the afflicted Duchess of Richmond, placing herself at the entrance of the hall

room, pray and entreat that we would not 'go before supper'; that we would wait 'one little hour more' and 'not spoil her ball'. Ungentle hard-hearted cavaliers, we resisted all and departed … In our ball costumes, brilliant with gold lace and embroidery, exulting in the assurance that our long tiresome days of inactivity were at an end, and that we were on the point of meeting this celebrated *loup-garou* [werewolf] Bonaparte, so long our anxious wish, we spurred our chargers and soon covered the thirty miles which separated us from our corps.[7]

At last, armed with news of the French thrust across the border and the defeat of the Prussians at Charleroi, Wellington's headquarters issued orders to all units to converge on the crossroads at Quatre Bras. Captain John Whale, 1st Life Guards, described the circumstances which jolted the army into motion:

> The drums beat to arms and the trumpets loud call was heard from every part of the city. It is impossible to describe the effect of those sounds, heard in the silence of the night … [A] courier had arrived from Blucher, the attack had become serious, the enemy were in considerable force, they had taken Charleroi and had gained some advantage over the Prussians and our troops were ordered to march immediately to support them. Instantly every place resounded with martial preparations. There was not a house in which military were not quartered and consequently the whole town was one scene of bustle. The soldiers were assembling from all parts in the Place Royale with their knapsacks on their backs, some taking leave of their wives and children, others sitting waiting for their comrades, others sleeping upon packs of straw, surrounded by all the din of war, while baggage wagons were loading artillery, trains tramping, officers riding in all directions, carts clattering, chargers neighing, bugles sounding, drums beating and colours flying.[8]

The French advance had effectively caught Wellington entirely by surprise, with Anglo-Allied formations scattered not only across Brussels, but across central and southern Belgium as a whole, as a result of which various regiments and corps received their marching orders at various times. In the capital itself, drums beat and trumpets and bugles blared, ordering all the troops to 'turn out' to their respective parade grounds. Private John Lewis, 95th Foot, reckoned this to have occurred around midnight, with one hour's notice to march: 'There we was, all of a bustle, so off we goes & it was not light as there was no moon.'[9] Private James Gunn of the 42nd states that the Highlanders of his unit received their orders around 2 a.m. on the 17th.[10] At 11 p.m. the 1/32nd received orders to move at a moment's notice, which came an hour later: 'About 12,' Ensign John Dallas wrote, 'the bugles sounded and about 2 we marched off …'" Some units did not move until even later: 'I made haste to the parade and we were soon under arms,' wrote Lieutenant John Black, 3/1st. 'Four days biscuit [*sic*] was immediately served to the men then we had orders to lay [*sic*] down in the street till four in the morning when we were to march, God knows where, for we did not [know].' Black remained behind for two hours, along with subalterns from all the other regiments, with the object of ensuring that anyone not with the Colours could be accounted for. About thirty men of the 1st Foot had failed to appear by 4 a.m., but by dawn all had mustered and marched to join the regiment on the road.[12] According to Hospital Assistant Isaac James, the Duke himself did not leave Brussels until 7 a.m.[13] According to Sir Hussey Vivian, most of the officers with regiments outside Brussels left the capital around midnight or 1 a.m. on the 16th, with his own regiment receiving orders to march for Enghien at dawn.[14]

In ordering the whole of his forces to converge on Quatre Bras, Wellington hoped to rectify his vulnerable position, for by controlling these strategic crossroads he could block the route to Brussels while at the same time either move to assist the Prussians if the French attacked Blücher or, conversely, benefit from the Prussians' presence in the event the French attacked the Anglo-Allies. With this in mind, on the afternoon of the 16th, both commanders met, the Duke offering to aid Blücher with 20,000 men if the French engaged the Prussians, provided of course that the Anglo-Allies had not themselves encountered a substantial body of the enemy. In fact, such a promise was rather disingenuous, not because Ney actually attacked Wellington later that day and therefore spared him from honouring his promise, but on the grounds that the Duke misled his Prussian counterpart by failing to admit that many Anglo-Allied formations remained scattered – and indeed would remain so for most of the 16th. In the event, Napoleon chose to attack both Allied armies simultaneously, sending Ney with the left wing to confront Wellington at Quatre Bras,[15] while the Emperor engaged the Prussians at the village of Ligny,[16] where Blücher concentrated three out of his four corps.

Action commenced around 2.30 p.m., with the Prussians foolishly deployed on a forward slope, thereby exposing them to devastating French artillery fire. Still, with 83,000 men – outnumbering the French by a quarter – they could endure heavy losses, but owing to vaguely worded orders the Prussian IV Corps, under Bülow, failed to join the main body and thus played no part at Ligny, where his absence was keenly felt. Still, Napoleon suffered from his own problems of concentration, including the failure to make use of VI Corps, under Comte Lobau, who arrived late to the fighting. Worse still, when both Ney and Napoleon ordered Comte d'Erlon's I Corps to march to their assistance, the resulting confusion left that exasperated commander unable to

appear at either battlefield. Accordingly, lacking the manpower required to turn
Blücher's right flank, Napoleon simply launched his troops forward in a series
of expensive frontal assaults that resulted in separate, desperate struggles to seize
and hold the village, as each side ejected the other in succession at great cost to
both sides. By nightfall, largely thanks to co-ordinated efforts by artillery and
cavalry against the Prussian centre, the French at last drove their opponents
from the field with heavy casualties: 13,700 French killed and wounded to
19,000 Prussians. Vitally, the Prussians – though badly mauled, with their commander bruised after a fall from his horse under which he lay trapped for some
minutes – managed to extricate themselves from the field intact. In this respect,
though Ligny constituted a tactical victory for the French, it represented a
strategic defeat, for the Prussians stood ready, after a brief period of recovery,
to fight another day – a situation which, two days later at Waterloo, Napoleon
thought unlikely though not altogether out of the question.

At precisely the time Napoleon launched his attack against Blücher at
Ligny, Ney pressed forward against Wellington only 6 miles to the north-west
at Quatre Bras. At the outset the French marshal enjoyed a healthy numerical
advantage of 28,000 to only 8,000 Anglo-Allies, for the Duke not only had
issued his orders for concentration very late on the 15th, but himself set out
late from Brussels on the morning of the 16th with the forces he commanded
there, as a consequence of which he spent the afternoon perilously fending
off waves of French attacks as more and more friendly formations filtered
onto the battlefield. In the meantime, particularly before Lieutenant General
Sir Thomas Picton's 5th Division reached the crossroads, Wellington's troops,
in particular his Nassauers and Dutch-Belgians, tenaciously hung on with
the issue only decided by reinforcements gradually bolstering Wellington's
force to about 30,000. Although Wellington had not, contrary to his practice stretching back to his first campaign in the Peninsula, chosen his own
ground, his infantry took what advantage it could from hedges and other
natural obstacles and managed to hold off repeated French assaults through
the disciplined firepower for which British infantry, deployed in two-rank
lines, had become famous. Similarly, while French cavalry briefly stood upon
the crossroads, they could not hold them without support from their infantry,
which failed to materialise, and efforts to break British infantry in squares met
with total failure. Both sides suffered about 4,000–5,000 casualties.

Much of the French failure to break Wellington's tenuous hold on the
crossroads may be attributed to the absence of I Corps. While Allied units
arrived piecemeal, hastily deployed and fed into the battle the moment they
arrived, what Ney needed most was the additional 20,000 men contained
in d'Erlon's absent formation. To Ney's extreme aggravation, Napoleon had
overridden his plea for assistance, the Emperor instead insisting that I Corps

operate against the Prussian right flank at Ligny, so withholding from Ney the numbers which might very well have driven Wellington from his position and denying him the ability to take up a far more defensible one near Waterloo two days later. Napoleon's plan for Ney rapidly to defeat Wellington before aiding the Emperor at Ligny on the same day also went awry, not only owing to the late dispatch of orders to this effect, but by the Emperor's robbing Ney of d'Erlon's men. Ironically, through this astonishing mismanagement and confusion, I Corps reached neither battlefield on the 16th and consequently left Napoleon little option but to abandon any notion of outflanking Blücher and instead to rely on the more costly alternative of direct assaults and bitter house-to-house fighting. Moreover, although Wellington could not spare troops to assist Blücher, by engaging Ney and the left wing he thus prevented their appearance at Ligny – though in truth he cannot be credited with deliberately seeking contact, since the initiative lay with the French. Thus, while the distraction created by Quatre Bras certainly did not compensate for Blücher's failure to maintain his own position, the Allies nonetheless remained intact, albeit still separated. Crucially, moreover, the Prussians remained close at hand – at Wavre, 11 miles east of Waterloo.

If Quatre Bras did not constitute the decisive victory Napoleon desired, it did oblige Wellington to make a hasty retreat in order to protect Brussels. Similarly, although the Prussians suffered heavily at Ligny, they remained intact and retreated in sufficiently sound order to reorganise and fight another day. In this respect, while both battles of the 16th constituted tactical victories for the French, in fact, in light of the events of just two days later, they may be seen as strategic failures.

On the other hand, Napoleon remained in the central position he sought and could still achieve his strategic aim, whereas on the 17th the Allies remained just beyond mutual support. Had the French either fixed Wellington at the crossroads or in any event pursued him with greater vigour than they did during the Anglo-Allied retreat of 16–17 June, they might have lengthened the distance between the two Allied armies – either scenario made all the more feasible when d'Erlon linked up again with Ney on the 17th, thereby strengthening his numbers. Similarly, Napoleon ought to have pressed home in pursuit of the Prussians, exploiting his victory at Ligny and denying Blücher the opportunity to recover from that serious blow. Instead, he was allowed to retreat north from Ligny towards Wavre, at the same time recalling Bülow's IV Corps and concentrating it with the other three. Napoleon, for his part, belatedly issued orders late on the morning of the 17th both to fix Wellington in place and to dispatch a corps of 33,000 men and ninety-six guns under Marshal Grouchy to stay in contact with the Prussians and prevent them from supporting Wellington.

Napoleon's late orders, combined with foul weather in the form of a torrential downpour, left his plans in tatters, for Wellington's retreat north was
conducted with sufficient speed not entirely to outpace his pursuers, but to
enable him to disengage from them after the engagement that day at Quatre
Bras, followed by a successful rearguard action that prevented the French from
pinning Wellington in place.

Wellington's army retreated from Quatre Bras through various villages and
towns including Braine-le-Comte and Nivelles. The march proved a lengthy
and exhausting affair through darkness, rain and mud, the Coldstream Guards,
for instance, reaching Braine-le-Comte at 3 a.m. on the 18th, where they
halted for four hours before continuing on to Nivelles.[17]

While the bulk of his forces proceeded to Mont St Jean and anxious lest
the French turn his right and occupy Brussels by a *coup de main*, Wellington
detached 18,000 troops and twenty-eight guns 5 miles to the west at the small
villages of Hal and Tubize. His retreat north left his forces fatigued but still
fully capable of engaging the French a second time. Moreover, the Duke now
knew the direction of Napoleon's main thrust and could deploy his forces
accordingly for the next engagement. With this is mind Wellington withdrew
to ground which, in marked contrast to that at Quatre Bras, he had studied
previously and intended to occupy for the purpose of making a stand – so
long as he could rely on Blücher's support.

The Prussians' situation therefore bears some consideration. By failing to
outflank them at Ligny, Napoleon failed to dictate the direction of their
retreat, which common sense would suggest as east, toward Liège, thus
tempting Blücher to continue along his lines of communication towards
the Rhine and consequently away from Wellington. Instead, the two Allied
armies remained within a realistic supporting distance of one another, allowing at the very minimum the ability of Wellington to maintain contact with
Blücher by courier, informing him on the morning of the 17th, of the new
position the Duke intended to assume and of his determination to give
battle there if Blücher could offer a minimum of a single corps to assist him.
Blücher replied at 6 p.m. that he would do better than that: the Duke could
depend on the Prussian Army. Accordingly – and crucially – on receiving
this message late on the night of the 17th, Wellington determined to fight
rather than continue his withdrawal beyond Brussels – a course which would
have put a very different complexion on the remainder of the campaign if he
had declined to defend the Belgian capital, which lay only 12 miles north of
Waterloo/Mont St Jean.

On reaching the area around Mont St Jean – Lieutenant George Maule,
Royal Artillery, recorded that the whole army had taken their positions on
Mont St Jean by 6.30 p.m.[18] Anglo-Allied units had settled themselves on

and around a ridge just south of the village of that name, with the larger village of Waterloo – a place in fact not destined to witness any fighting later
that day – immediately to the north. Napoleon followed up, positioning his
troops immediately opposite the Duke, minus the corps of 33,000 men under
Marshal Grouchy, detached, as previously mentioned, to follow and observe
the Prussians, now camped in and around Wavre, 11 miles east of Mont St Jean.
The French offered desultory artillery fire against those Anglo-Allied units
who reached the ridge before darkness, but the firing petered out by sunset.[19]

Practically all contemporaries agree on the hardships suffered by
Wellington's army while on the move during the 17th, which was conducted
in excessive heat,[20] and while encamped from about dusk until the early hours
of the 18th. Private Thomas Jeremiah, Royal Welch Fusiliers, summed up well
the three elements which afflicted upon the troops the greatest suffering: torrential rain, the fatigue associated with the lengthy march from Quatre Bras,
and the hunger induced by the shortage of – and in many instances the complete absence of – food:

> By the evening of the 17th we were greatly fatigued from the extreme
> inclemency of this day's weather and from marching nearly 8 French leagues
> [24 miles] since 6 o'clock in the morning in the greatest rain that ever I saw,
> the heavens seemed to have opened their sluices and the celestial floodgates
> bursted open, so showered the 17th on us. I need not mention that all we
> had about us was completely soaked; by the same our blankets which was
> on the back of our knapsacks were completely drenched. Then where was
> our dried beds, but that was not the greatest of our thoughts, for hunger
> bites harder than a wet shirt.[21]

Numerous accounts speak of the tremendous volume of rain which fell on the
night of the 17th. 'We had the most tremendous rain I ever beheld,' recalled
Major General Sir Hussey Vivian, 'and were soaked to the skin without
anything to change, and the canopy of heaven for our covering.'[22] Sergeant
Matthew Colgan, 18th Hussars, related the same degree of discomfort:

> We fell back on Waterloo in one of the most severe tempests and thunder-
> storms it has ever been my lot to behold. So bad was the weather that on
> arriving at the position we were to take up for the night, approached as it
> was by bye and cross roads choked by mud, we resembled drowned rats
> more than anything else. The men were ordered to cut green forage for the
> horses, and take what rest they could, as well as circumstances would permit,
> without unsaddling. The poor fellows huddled together as well as possible,
> rolling themselves in their wet cloaks, the only comfort which was then

possible for them, many of them without breaking their fast at the time, for if they had had anything to cook, it was impossible to do so, placed as they were. When we awakened in the morning we found ourselves a few yards lower down, owing to the current that passed under our cot, and which had completely wetted every article of clothing as if it had been dragged through the mire of mud and water which was floating around us.[23]

According to Lieutenant Edward Byam, 15th Hussars, his regiment as well as the 18th established a rudimentary bivouac around sunset, in a field of rye, 'on the right and close to Mont St Jean, a perfect swamp, horses up to their hocks. Torrents of rain during the night, no rations or supplies of any kind, in fact in every respect a bad bivouac',[24] while Sergeant Major James Page, 1st Dragoon Guards, wrote of:

… one of the heaviest storms of rain ever known, accompanied with thunder and lightning. The fall of rain was so very heavy on the 17th that in the fields, which were covered with corn, our horses sunk in every step up to near the hock, therefore our cavalry could do but little this day [and] ended when darkness commenced and we remained in the open fields, our horses saddled and bridled the whole night for fear of an attack before morning. It is out of my power herein to express our situation, our boots were filled with water, and as our arms hung down by our side the water ran off a stream at our finger ends. We remained in the situation the whole of the night halfway up to our knees in mud.[25]

Lieutenant John Black of the 1st (King's) Regiment camped in a ploughed field of rye on the bare ground without the benefit of a fire, he and many others with their swords drawn in the expectation that on this moonless night the French would attack under cover of darkness. 'It was dreadful beyond description,' he reported, 'we had double allowance of gin and we poured it down our throats while we lay on our backs till we dropped off asleep, for we were so very cold and shaking for intoxication it could not hurt us on that [night]'.[26] The wounded suffered the most, Lieutenant Richard Eyre of the 95th describing them as 'like so many half drowned and half starved rats', while Lieutenant Donald Mackenzie of the 42nd Highlanders observed that many of the men in his unit had undressed wounds.[27]

Most of Wellington's army went without rations that night; indeed, some units had had nothing since before the fighting at Quatre Bras on the 16th.[28] Captain Orlando Bridgeman, 1st Foot Guards, for instance, noted that the whole of Hill's corps went hungry on the 17th. An unknown officer of the 95th echoed complaints about the shortage of food:

The whole of the 17th, and indeed until late the next morning, the weather continued dreadful; and we were starving with hunger, no provision having been served out since the march from Brussels. While five officers who composed our mess were looking at each other with the most deplorable faces imaginable, one of the men brought us a fowl he had plundered, and a handful of biscuits, which though but little, added to some tea we boiled in a camp kettle, made us rather more comfortable; and we huddled up together, covered ourselves with straw, and were soon as soundly asleep as though reposing on beds of down.[29]

Gunner John Edwards, Royal Artillery, recorded that he and his comrades had empty haversacks,[30] with Lieutenant William Turner, 13th Light Dragoons, reporting the same: 'a dreadful rainy night, every man in the cavalry wet to the skin and nearly all the infantry as bad; nothing to eat all day, being without rations and our baggage at Brussels.'[31] Simmons of the 95th echoed these travails:

We were as wet as if we had gone through a river. I now picked up a blanket, leaving a third of it as a cape & fixing it round my neck with a strap, so that I was wet & warm. A blanket used in this way was an old peninsular trick … We arrived at Waterloo about dark, where our army got into position for the night. The French fired a few cannon shot which ceased with the darkness. The ground we now occupied was in the morning a corn field in full bloom, now squashed into clay & mud. The rain still coming down heavily … I pitched upon a bit of rising ground to locate upon for the night. A soldier brought me a little straw, a valuable present, poor young Smith tired & jaded, crouched down upon it. I gave him some biscuit & wine …[32]

This breakdown in the logistics chain is more easily explained than excused: the army retreated from Quatre Bras so rapidly as to out-march the commissariat,[33] leaving the troops with virtually nothing precisely when they needed it most – in the course of a long march. Thus, under these extreme circumstances and despite the army's exceptional record of conduct in the Peninsula, where officers generally condemned looting, some now turned a blind eye to it as their men went in search of food and firewood, disregarding the normal strict regulations against the practice.[34] This process had begun as early as following Quatre Bras, for Lieutenant George Simmons of the 95th wrote of his foragers bringing in chickens, eggs, bacon, tea and sugar. In the absence of a frying pan the men improvised with the back plate of a cuirass described as 'perfect, the edges were embossed with silver; the skewered fowls & bacon were hissing and spluttering upon it in gravy …'[35]

Simmons observed infantry of another regiment butchering a bull – clearly an instance of looting, since livestock did not accompany specific units.[36] A fellow officer in the Rifles, Lieutenant Richard Eyre, recorded that Major General Adam, commander of the 3rd (British) Brigade in Lieutenant General Sir Henry Clinton's 2nd Division, granted permission for his men to plunder three farmhouses nearby, almost certainly in the village of Mont St Jean. Accordingly, the men gathered all manner of objects and built a fire before proceeding to their post in the line of battle:

> Chairs, tables, sofas, cradles, churns, barrels and all manner of combustibles were soon cracking in the flames, our fellows then proceeded to the slaughter of all the living stock the yard contained, and in less than an hour we had as delicious a breakfast of beef, pork, veal, duck, chicken, potatoes and other delicacies as I ever made an attack upon. This repast was just finished and our fellows had got themselves thoroughly dry when we were ordered to fall in and proceed as fast as possible with the 52nd and 71st Regiments (which comprised our brigade) to the front to protect three brigades of artillery which were ordered out to the edge of the hill on which the British and Belgic armies had taken up their position.[37]

Sergeant Archibald Johnston of the Scots Greys wrote how:

> Preparations were made for cooking, by lighting up large bonfires &c &c, the materials for which we had recourse to a large farm house to the rear of our brigade; from which we carried away ploughs, harrows, corn fanners, doors off the hinges, gates &c &c with any other consumable article we could lay our hands on, and bore them down in military triumph to our lines. Articles for cooking were of course the next consideration of which we were completely destitute; the pig sties, hen roosts &c supplied this exigency. No ceremony was observed either in killing or dressing these poor creatures which fell a prey to the half famished intruders; some of the pigs put to the fire without either skinning or singeing; others were made handsomely dressed; one of these after being put on the fire got away but was soon recaptured.[38]

Private Thomas Playford, 2nd Life Guards, offers further proof that British troops resorted to plunder before the battle. 'The morning was clear, the rain gradually abated and Shaw, myself and several others were sent in search of food for our regiment. We each took a sack full of loaves, and then went to a large farm house in search for cheese, butter, or bacon, to be eaten with the bread …'[39] Apart from cleaning their weapons, a few of the Royal Welch

Fusiliers managed to produce cakes fashioned from flour and brandy, cooked on fires, and for which officers offered substantial sums.[40]

The 2/95th left Quatre Bras at 10 a.m. on the 17th and did not reach Mont St Jean until 4 p.m. Wellington ordered the riflemen to collect wood, establish large fires to dry themselves and to render their rifles ready for action by dawn,[41] but various eyewitnesses agree that the heavy rain rendered this all but impossible,[42] Cornet Robert Bullock of the 11th Light Dragoons constituting a rare exception. In spite of marching through 'the heaviest tempest I ever saw' and enduring a night which 'proved the wettest and most uncomfortable I ever passed', he and his comrades managed to generate some heat: 'We made a large fire and by that means were not quite frozen.'[43] Private Thomas Playford, 2nd Life Guards, similarly recorded:

> Although midsummer was near, we passed an uncomfortable night exposed to a cold wind and heavy rain. There we stood on soaked ploughed ground, shivering, wet, and hungry; for there was neither food for man nor horse. Some soldiers complained of the hardship, some jested at their sufferings, and others tried to guess at what would take place on the morrow; and some hinted at the probability that not many of us would see the 19th of June. But no one believed in gloomy prognostications. We pulled down a fence and made a fire, but we gained little good by standing round it, for while one side was warming the other was cold and wet.[44]

One trooper of the 16th Light Dragoons returned from the village of Waterloo with a clock on his back, which he then proceeded to set alight.[45]

Some units rose well before dawn, like the 13th Light Dragoons, whose troopers mounted their horses while still wet at 3 a.m. and with little or nothing to eat. Lieutenant George Packe had only a small piece of sour bread – his only food in two days – which in his famished condition tasted 'as good as the most delicate fricassee'.[46]

According to Private George Hemingway, 33rd Foot, the sun began to warm the troops around seven,[47] but Private John Marshall, 10th Hussars, reckoned the clouds did not disperse until around nine, when the rain ceased. The French began to draw up in order of battle, most of the Allies already having taken up their positions for the expected contest.[48] Gronow related the scene:

> On the morning of the 18th the sun shone most gloriously, and so clear was the atmosphere that we could see the long, imposing lines of the enemy most distinctly … The whole of the British infantry not actually engaged were at that time formed into squares; and as you looked along our lines, it seemed as if we formed a continuous wall of human beings.[49]

The Life Guards gathered wood, built fires and dried their clothes. 'At day break,' Private Joseph Lord wrote, 'we got a little beer and victuals one way or another and was quite refreshed by 10 o'clock when we mounted & moved our place a few hundred yards to better ground.'[50] Senior officers did not sit idle, either. Captain Orlando Bridgeman, aide-de-camp to Lord Hill, recorded that at least one senior Allied commander began reconnoitring the field at 2.40 a.m., to be precise. His party appears to have ridden extensively over the ground, not returning for breakfast until around 10 a.m.[51] In the camp of the 32nd Foot, the men received biscuits and spirits, rubbed dry their muskets, put in new flints and watched as the French appeared on the heights to the south.[52] Sergeant Matthew Colgan, 18th Hussars, found inadequate time with which to dry – much less feed – himself:

> We rose and endeavoured to dry our clothing by the sun, hanging it on the branches of the young trees, when a sudden order was given to mount and fall in. I hastened to put on the only dry shirt I possessed, and bridling my horse I bundled up all my kit before me on my horse, put on my overalls, mounted, finishing my dressing there and crying out to those I had charge of to mount also.[53]

As the sun broke through the clouds, Lieutenant Donald Mackenzie of the 42nd Foot noted how 'the kindly heat and brightness did much to cheer and enliven us, the more so as it was evident we were to have warm enough work to make us forget the chills and depression of the previous night.'[54] Still, some units proved unable to dry themselves before action began, for Sergeant Major James Page, 1st Dragoon Guards, recorded how his regiment's troopers wrung out their uniforms before putting them back on.[55] Archibald Johnston observed the same phenomenon, the sunshine 'hailed with gratitude by every individual, as it served to get our clothes &c which were very wet upon us, well dried.'[56] Lieutenant Byam, 15th Hussars, failed to obtain part of the supply of bread meant for the 11th Light Dragoons, but they may have suffered less than other units, since he noted that on the morning of the battle the regiment turned loose some cattle, which suggests they had at least some supply of meat.[57] Apparently the 33rd did possess some rations on the morning of the 18th, as Assistant Surgeon Donald Finlayson referred to their attempts 'to get a little bread & meat served out to us', but the order of 'Stand to your arms men' in response to the French advance ended all prospect of any sustenance for the day.[58] Shortly after dawn, the 2nd Battalion the Coldstream Guards acquired, with great difficulty, noted Ensign Charles Short, 'some gin and we found an old cask full of wet rye loaves which we breakfasted upon. Everybody was in high spirits. We broke up the cask and got some dry wood and made some fine fires, got some straw and I went to sleep for a couple of hours.'[59]

On the other hand, according to Private George Hemingway, not only had the 33rd Foot not eaten since the 15th, there was no fresh water available on the morning of the battle, notwithstanding the torrential rainfall of the night before.[60] At dawn on the 18th, Lieutenant Colonel Sir George Scovell, Assistant Quartermaster General, inspected the road between Waterloo and Brussels and discovered it 'completely closed up by carriages, many of them laden with corn and stores, whose drivers had abandoned them, and taken away the horses'. The Duke ordered him to take a squadron of dragoons and clear the road. On encountering Sir John Lambert's division halted and preparing to cook a meal, Scovell offered the wagons as firewood, an inducement which immediately began the process of clearing the congestion.[61] Still, no supplies reached the troops on the morning of the 18th.

As Anglo-Allied troops did their best to warm and feed themselves, the French did the same. Lieutenant George Blathwayt, 23rd Light Dragoons, sent on picket duty in front of La Haye Sainte and looking towards La Belle Alliance, watched Napoleon passing along the front of his troops. Lord Uxbridge and several staff officers did the same, borrowing the young officer's 'glass' or telescope for the purpose.[62] According to Lieutenant Colonel Frederick Ponsonby, stationed with his regiment on the extreme left wing, the rival armies stood 800 yards part, with opposing vedettes stationed so close as to be capable of speaking to each other. He, like so many of his other comrades, observed Napoleon and his staff riding along the front opposite.[63]

Around 9.30 a.m., Wellington rode along his own front line to the cheers of his troops, giving encouragement to individual units as he went. The 10-year-old triangle player John Scott, attached to his father's regiment, the Black Watch, recalled: 'the Duke of Wellington came riding up to us and cried, "Now, I hope you are well and ready." One of our soldiers saluted him and replied, "Yes, we know our duty". Wellington smiled and rode off.'[64]

The Ground

Having established himself along the Mont St Jean ridge on the evening of the 17th, Wellington planned to establish a defensive position and fight Napoleon, although he had yet to learn that Blücher would support him there. He did not intend to remain in that position without aid from at least one Prussian corps – and with good reason. The Dutch-Belgians had performed poorly the previous day at Quatre Bras and the other Allied troops under his command did not match the standard of his own British forces. On the 17th he had fewer than 68,000 troops – rising to 73,200 by the time action commenced the following day – whereas he understood Napoleon to command over 100,000 men – correct before the detachment of Grouchy – of fine quality, with the components which fought at Quatre Bras and Ligny perhaps now consolidated to fight either the Prussians separately, or to concentrate entirely on the Anglo-Allied position at Mont St Jean. He knew it was foolhardy to fight the French without Prussian support; but despite Blücher's promise of aid, the Duke obviously could not be certain that the Prussians would materialise on the day. Nor did he wish to contemplate retreat, for if he abandoned his present position and moved north, he would forfeit the best possible defence between Waterloo and Brussels, thus imperilling the capital and possibly Ghent, as well. In short, without resisting now, Wellington risked losing the campaign altogether. The matter was settled before 3 a.m. on the 18th when he received a dispatch from Blücher reporting that two Prussian corps would proceed at first light to support Wellington's army. The die was cast: the Duke would stand and fight. Nonetheless, intelligence received the night of the 17th indicated that Napoleon had detached a force of indeterminate strength to pursue the Prussians, who had halted at Wavre, about 11 miles east of the Anglo-Allied left flank. Wellington correctly assumed this force – in fact Grouchy's – was meant to block the Prussians from assisting Wellington on the 18th. But he could not know the size of that formation and had to assume that it might succeed in its object. In this respect the Duke's decision to stand and fight at Waterloo carried with it considerable risk.

Wellington had first inspected the field that was to become the Waterloo battlefield during an excursion to the area in August 1814,[65] when he had written to Lord Bathurst, Secretary of State for War and the Colonies, enclosing a memorandum on the defence of the Netherlands which included some important observations: 'About Nivelles, and between that and Binche,' the Duke observed, 'there are many advantageous positions; and the entrance of the forêt de Soigne, by the highroad which leads to Brussels from Binche, Charleroi and Namur, would, if worked upon, afford others.'[66] The 'advantageous' position he decided to defend stretched from a ravine near Merbe-Braine on his right, extending just beyond the hamlet of La Haye, which would serve as his extreme left.[67] Lieutenant Colonel Sir Robert Gardiner, Royal Artillery, briefly described the area thus:

> The ground selected by the Duke for the position of his army, ran on a ridge
> of heights in front of the Bois de Soignies, crossing the high roads from
> Charleroi and Nivelles to Brussels and distant about two miles in front of
> Waterloo. The course of these hills kept generally, a straight line, rising in an
> open and gradual ascent from all sides, without having any particular feature

which could be considered as securing our flanks, and perfectly open to our front, admitting with equal and perfect facility, the operations and manoeuvres of the two armies.[68]

Sergeant Major Cotton provides a somewhat more detailed survey:

> The field of Waterloo is an open undulating plain; and, on the day of the battle, was covered with splendid crops of rye, wheat, barley, oats, beans, peas, potatoes, tares and clover; some were of great height. There were a few patches of ploughed ground. The field is intersected by two high-roads which branch off at Mont-Saint-Jean; these are very wide: the one on the right, leading to Nivelles and Binche … is straight as an arrow for miles; that on the left, lying in the centre of both armies leading south to Genappe, Charleroi and Namur, is not so straight as the former; about eleven hundred yards in advance of the junction, is a gently elevated ridge which formed a good natural military position …
>
> Upon the crest is a cross-road running east and west, intersecting the Genappe road at right angles, about two hundred and fifty yards on this side of the farm of La Haye-Sainte. The cross-road marks the front of the allied position … [and] runs curving forward a little for about six hundred yards, when it first gently and then abruptly falls back into the Nivelles road, near the termination of the ridge, where it takes a sweep to the rear.[69]

The main feature consisted of the Mont St Jean ridge, upon which the bulk of the Anglo-Allies would be deployed and which Lieutenant Colonel Frederick Ponsonby described as 'a gentle declivity', with 'a small valley' separating the rival armies.[70] Much of the area was covered in grain, mostly rye, which Captain William Burney, 44th Foot, described as standing about 5ft high,[71] Ensign Charles Dallas of the 32nd observed as 'chest high',[72] and Ensign Edward Macready recorded as 'higher than our heads',[73] while Lieutenant Colonel Henry Murray wrote of 'luxuriant crops'.[74] In the centre, immediately to the west of the Genappe road, stood the farm of La Haye Sainte, a small complex which Cotton described as:

> A post far from being so commodious as Hougoumont, but considerably nearer our position, consequently easier of access, although more exposed to the enemy's attacks and cannonade. It was a strong stone and brick building, with a narrow orchard in front, and a small garden in the rear, both of which were hedged round, except the east side of the garden, on which there was a strong wall running along the high-road side, then taking a western direction terminated upon the east end of the barn; a large and

small gate opened on the road; on the western side, a door in the yard, and another at the end of the barn, led into the fields and afforded the means of communicating with the orchard. At this point was the chief tug of war. A passage led through the house from the farm yard into the garden, which lies on the north or allied side or the buildings, the door of which was four feet wide ...[75]

Further west, the farm complex of Hougoumont stood 500 yards ahead of the centre-right of the Allied line, with the end of the ridge behind it inclining slightly to the south. Hougoumont formed a natural obstacle to a French advance, composed as it was of an enclosure containing stout buildings as well as an attached walled garden, orchards and woods. Trees to the south and east of the woods provided protection from distant observation and virtually all line-of-sight artillery fire – though not from high-angle, indirect fire. Cotton described Hougoumont as:

A gentleman's seat, with château, farm house and gardener's house, outbuildings, garden (walled on the south, east, and west sides), orchard and wood ... The buildings are more than two hundred years old, and were erected for defence ... A ravine or hollow-way ... bounds the whole of the northern side of the smaller orchard ...

The ... Eastern portion of the north side of the large orchard was bounded by a thick banked up hedge ...

This post is situated about midway between the positions of the two hostile armies. The château, farm, walls, etc., were at the time of the battle of a substantial nature. The garden, or park, was enclosed, on the east and south sides, by a wall ...[76]

The area west of Hougoumont stood entirely open, with no villages or natural obstacles for miles, apart from a defile west of the Nivelles road.

East of the Anglo-Allied centre stood the farms of Papelotte and La Haye, as well as the hamlet of Smohain. Each of these positions could be garrisoned and strengthened by even the most rudimentary forms of fortification. Cotton described this general area thus:

On the east side of the Genappe road, the cross-road was lined by two broken banked-up hedges, extending about half a mile; near the termination of which is a knoll, with a bit of copse or brushwood on the rear slope: this mound, or knoll, overlooks the farms of Papelotte, la Haye, Frischermont and the hamlet of Smohain in the valley.[77]

The whole area over which fighting would take place was small by the standards of most battlefields – especially those involving such large numbers of
troops. The distance from the area of Papelotte and La Haye in the east to the
Nivelles road to the west measured about 3,500 yards, with the Genappe road
running down its middle almost precisely. Papelotte and La Haye stood about
500 yards in front of the eastern flank of the main ridge. La Haye Sainte stood
approximately 250 yards in front of the Ohain–Wavre road, which bisected
the Waterloo–Genappe road. Part of the Ohain–Wavre road was 'hollow' – a
sunken lane – as described by a senior officer thus:

> For about 100 yards, more or less, it was very hollow. At the end going down
> into the high road it might have been 10 or even 15 feet deep. I have reason
> to know it, for there was but one way of going down into it from the field at
> the back of La Haye Sainte, which was very slippery, would admit not more
> than two horses at a time, and might have been at an angle of 45 [degrees].[78]

Napoleon's forces stood on another ridge, about 1,200 yards to the south,
with the intermediate ground forming a shallow valley 'richly covered,' as
Henegan described it, 'with luxuriant corn'.[79]

Wellington's position was not ideal; indeed Picton considered it poor –
certainly when compared to many of those established in the Peninsula, and
Major General Sir Hussey Vivian, commander of the 6th Cavalry Brigade,
described it five days after the battle as 'no very strong one …'[80] and in even
less favourable terms in 1839: 'That the position of Waterloo is by no means a
strong one cannot for a moment be disputed,' he concluded.[81] To be sure, the
ridge was not a continuous one, but rather a series of ridges, thus leaving small
gaps along its front, most notably just east of the Genappe road. Moreover,
like the Anglo-Allies, the French occupied a series of small ridges of their
own parallel to those on which most of Wellington's forces stood – and thus
offered Napoleon the opportunity to fire on any troops standing exposed;
that is, in advance or on the front face or top of, the Mont St Jean ridge.
Indeed, Lieutenant Colonel Francis Home, 3rd Foot Guards, noted that his
men stood on a height no greater than 20ft, sufficiently low, he reckoned, to
enable a carriage to be driven up at full gallop.[82]

The chief weakness of the position lay in Wellington's exposed right.
Captain Alexander Mercer, looking down from his battery atop the ridge,
described ground well suited to any attacker inclined to exploit this vulnerability: 'To the right,' he wrote in his journal – a classic of its type – 'we looked
over a fine open country, covered with crops and interspersed with thickets
or small woods.'[83] In light of Napoleon's long record of out-flanking manoeuvres over the course of his military career, this defect loomed large amongst

the Duke's concerns. But failure to hold Hougoumont could also spell disaster. As Tomkinson observed: 'The house, garden and wood in possession of the enemy would enable them to form any number of men unmolested immediately below the [Anglo-Allied] position, and admit of their making an instantaneous attack [on its centre].'[84] The weakest point, in Tomkinson's view, lay in the position between the Nivelles and Charleroi roads, for 'here the hill was of a gentle declivity, and [with] Hougoumont and La Haye Sainte in the enemy's possession, an attack on that point would be made to advantage'[85] He was quite right: seizure of both positions was tantamount to splitting the Anglo-Allied centre.

Yet notwithstanding these disadvantages, for a country like Belgium, well known for its flat terrain, the position at Mont St Jean had much to recommend it. Wellington was accustomed to positioning his troops on an elevated position, and the ridge at Mont St Jean offered a number of advantages. It was not so steep as to prevent his artillery from firing on the attacker; he could deploy skirmishers to his front; and he could conceal most of his infantry on the reverse slope, not only denying the French intelligence on the strength of Allied forces, but protecting them from superior numbers of guns. To the rear Wellington benefited from a road system capable of conveying troops and guns to different points along the front – and, critically, to do so without French detection. On his flanks he could find protection from Hougoumont to the west and from Papelotte and La Haye to the east. Compared to some notable Peninsular battles, such as Busaco, the topography of the Waterloo battlefield offered relatively little protection; yet considering the paucity of good ground on which to establish a defence, this constituted the best option for blocking the French advance on Brussels via Charleroi, Quatre Bras and Genappe.

Most contemporaries agreed that Wellington's position, though not formidable, offered a number of advantages. Lieutenant General Sir Henry Clinton, commander of 2nd Division, dubbed the position 'a good one',[86] while Captain Digby Mackworth, 7th Foot, aide-de-camp to Lieutenant General Hill considered it 'a moderately strong position'.[87] Lieutenant Colonel James Stanhope, 3/1st Foot Guards, believed 'it did not appear so strong as more accurate observation proved it to be. It was the best sort for English troops, a steep glacis on the French side and a moderate slope on ours, so that all movements might take place without being exposed to the observation or fire of the enemy.'[88] Captain George Bowles, Coldstream Guards, offered an somewhat blander conclusion, observing that 'the position we occupied was a good one but not by any means a particularly strong one; indeed, the nature of the country is such as to preclude the possibility of it.'[89] A few observers, like Captain Rees Gronow, 1st Foot Guards, assessed the ground as very strong:

The position taken up by the British army was an excellent one: it was a sort of ridge, very favourable for artillery, and from which all the movements of the French could be discerned. In case of any disaster, Wellington had several roads in his rear by which a masterly retreat could have been effected through the forest on Brussels.[90]

Tomkinson also regarded this position as favourable ground for the defender: 'From La Haye Sainte to the left was … strong, and any force attacking at that point had a very considerable length of plain to cross, exposed to our artillery, and also a height to ascend on coming in contact with our line.' Wellington's right, he added, was not especially vulnerable, for an attacker either must seize a formidable obstacle to his front or execute a wide flanking manoeuvre. A thrust against the Anglo-Allied left similarly posed its own problems:

> With regard to the position we held, on our right, it is evident, for any enemy to attack, they must either possess themselves of Hougoumont, or make a detour round it. In doing this they must show the force they moved to that point, and enable a general holding the position of Waterloo to reinforce his right. They could not make a feint with a small body on that point, as their object would be defeated by our seeing the strength they brought, and nothing but a very large body would cause any fears; and if a large one, we could spare men from other parts of our line.
>
> A successful attack on our right would open Brussels to the enemy, but would drive us back on the Prussians at Wavre, and so unite the two armies. An attack on our left had the strong ground on that point to contend with, and also some fear of interruption from the Prussians, whose situation Napoleon, from his patrols and information, ought to be aware of.[91]

Wellington's position offered a degree of elevation to his front sufficient to provide concealment from observation and moderate protection from artillery fire for much of his army. The marshy valleys of the rivers Dyle and Lasne, moreover, offered protection to the Allied left flank, especially after the recent heavy rainfall. And of course the two enclosed farms – Hougoumont and La Haye Sainte – added further protection and points of defence. Finally, if *in extremis*, notwithstanding these advantages, the Duke nevertheless failed to retain his ground, he would still retain communications with Brussels to the north and thence to Ghent and Antwerp. On balance, therefore, Wellington's position, if not formidable, certainly satisfied his basic defensive needs.

Allied Dispositions

As discussed earlier, the great majority of the troops that had left Quatre Bras on the 17th were by that evening settled in the general area Wellington intended for the confrontation of the following day – provided, of course, that Blücher still intended to offer his intervention. However, since most of the troops arrived on the 17th amidst heavy rain and in an exhausted and hungry state, they naturally did not assume the precise positions the Duke had in mind for their deployment which, according to Major John Oldfield, Royal Engineers, were indeed those chosen by Wellington – not Sir William De Lancey, as Somerset claimed – based on a map prepared by various officers, as Oldfield recorded in his journal:

> Shortly after my chief had joined headquarters, he sent into me for the plan of the position of Waterloo, which had been previously reconnoitred. The several sketches of the officers had been put together & one fair copy made for the Prince of Orange. A second had been commenced in the drawing room for the Duke, but was not in a state to send, I therefore forwarded the original sketches of the officers.[92]

It is also important to note that the Duke employed a host of officers to reconnoitre the area and report back to him.[93] Thus, his deployments were based on a range of information: his own observations in the 1790s, again in 1814 and on the evening of 17–18 June, various contemporary maps, and the advice of De Lancey and other officers. These arrangements Wellington began at daybreak, though Hill, with the efficiency characteristic of his service in the Peninsula, had already organised 2nd Corps by the time the commander-in-chief came to see to its deployment.[94]

Let us examine the Anglo-Allied position from west to east.[95] Well beyond the end of the Anglo-Allied right flank stretched the open fields described earlier; this constituted a vacuum Wellington did not intend to fill, notwithstanding the considerable risks this entailed. Having said this, he did not leave his right entirely vulnerable to a flanking manoeuvre, for a detached force from Sir Charles Colville's 4th Division, consisting of two infantry brigades, one each of British and Hanoverians, supported by two batteries from the Royal Artillery – in all approximately 15,500 men – held the tiny villages of Hal and Tubize, situated approximately 8 miles west of Hougoumont, and thus stood ready to resist any especially wide flanking movement.

At the western end of the Anglo-Allied main line, approximately 1,200 yards west of Hougoumont, Wellington deployed the 3rd Dutch–Belgian Division

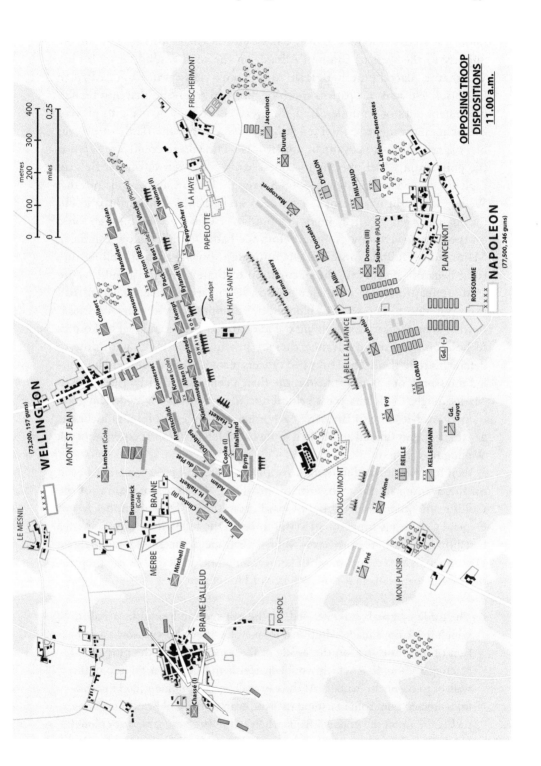

OPPOSING TROOP DISPOSITIONS 11.00 a.m.

under Lieutenant General Baron Chassé in the village of Braine l'Alleud. Slightly to the west of Braine l'Alleud, on the road extending to Tubize, Wellington placed Dutch-Belgian and Hanoverian cavalry under Prince Frederick. He sent out patrols south of this road to ensure that any French movement did not go undetected, for every effort must be made to prevent a flanking movement, as the French had executed after the Battle of Fleurus in 1794 as a means of advancing on Brussels. The village could also serve as the point from which the Anglo-Allied Army could retreat on the Belgian capital if necessary.[96] Lieutenant John Sperling, a Royal Engineer, records that Wellington's right was meant to have been strengthened with earthworks but the engineers sent to fortify it got lost amidst rural lanes passing through forest on the excessively rainy evening before the battle,[97] while fellow Engineer, Major John Oldfield, noted in his campaign journal that if Wellington's right began to be turned, the occupation of Braine l'Alleud would secure a safe retreat for at least a major portion of the army, since the main road from Waterloo to Brussels was blocked by commissariat and other vehicles.[98] Further west, the garrison holding the area around Tubize and Hal had orders to hold up any French advance, thereby providing the Duke with time to defend his right flank. The Duke had officers reconnoitre the area, and he studied the sketch of a position held more than a century earlier by the Duke of Marlborough.[99] This area was a critical one, for it contained a 'wide and good military road' leading to Brussels,[100] according to Lieutenant John Hildebrand, 2/35th, and thus offered a potential route by which the French could outflank Wellington's right.

Wellington's initial deployment of the area around Hougoumont began on the evening of the 17th, initially involving the light companies of the Coldstream Guards and 3rd Foot Guards from the 1st Division under Major General Cooke. He supplemented this force on the following morning with a battalion of Nassauers from Saxe-Weimar's brigade of the 2nd Dutch-Belgian Division, plus two companies of Hanoverians. Cotton describes the preparations these troops made for the defence of Hougoumont:

> The garden, or park, was enclosed, on the east and south sides, by a wall, in which our troops made additional loop-holes; they also cut down a portion of the buttresses, on the inside of the south wall, for the purpose of erecting a scaffolding, which would enable them to fire over the top of the wall, or to bayonet intruders. At the east wall, an embankment, and the scaffolds erected with some farming utensils, enabled the Coldstream to throw such a fire upon the enemy's flank when in the large orchard, that colonel Hepburn, who commanded there from about two o'clock, considered it (the east wall) as the strength of his position. Loop-holes were also made in

the stable joining the south gate, and a scaffold was erected against the wall on the west, that ran from the south-stables to the barn. The flooring over the south gateway was partly torn up, to enable our men to fire down upon the enemy, should they force the gate which had been blocked up, and was not opened during the action.[101]

The rest of Cooke's (Guards) Division the Duke positioned east, and immediately to the rear of, Hougoumont.

Colonel Mitchell's brigade from Colville's 4th Division stood, at least initially, west of the Nivelles road roughly aligned with Hougoumont. Further to the rear, in the area around the village of Merbe-Braine, Wellington placed the whole of the Brunswick contingent and Clinton's 2nd Division, consisting of three brigades: one British, under Major General Adam, one King's German Legion under Colonel du Plat, and one Hanoverian, under Colonel Hew Halkett. These collectively formed the Anglo-Allied tactical reserve, initially positioned west of Hougoumont on the basis that they might be required there rather than further east.

Looking at dispositions east of Hougoumont, Alten's division, consisting of Major General Sir Colin Halkett's British units, Hanoverians under Major General Count Kielmannsegge, and Colonel von Ompteda's King's German Legion troops, the former two had fought at Quatre Bras, whereas the King's German Legion had yet to see action. All three brigades stood in the front line stretched as far as the Genappe road. Attached to them were Nassauers under General von Kruse. In the Anglo-Allied centre stood the farm of La Haye Sainte, held by the 2nd Battalion of the King's German Legion Light Infantry from Ompteda's brigade. Lack of foresight, simple incompetence and the absence of engineer support left La Haye Sainte largely unfortified, with some exceptions, rendering it far less formidable than circumstances required. Cotton described the position thus:

> A passage led through the house from the farm yard into the garden, which lies on the north or allied side of the buildings, the door of which was four feet wide … there were also on the same side four windows and ten loop or airholes, by which any quantity of ammunition might have been thrown in … Loop-holes were made in the south and east walls as well as in the roofs, and the post strengthened on being occupied by our troops.
>
> A barricade was thrown across the high-road, near the south-east angle of the wall; but there were several drawbacks to the strengthening of this post. The [en]trenching tools had been lost, the carpenters had been sent to assist at Hougoumont; half of the large west barn door was wanting, and in addition, the post was exposed to a line of batteries, that had been pushed

forward upon the inner ridge of the French right wing, at a range of from six to eight hundred yards.[102]

In the sandpit just north of the complex, as well as on the east side of the Genappe road and in front of La Haye Sainte, stood the riflemen of the 1st Battalion 95th Foot, part of Kempt's 8th Brigade. Kincaid described the position thus:

> Our battalion stood on what was considered the left centre of the position. We had our right resting on the Namur Road, about a hundred yards in rear of the farm-house of La Haye Sainte, and our left extending behind a broken hedge, which ran along the ridge to the left. Immediately in our front, and divided from La Haye Sainte only by the great road, stood a small knoll, with a sand-hole in its farthest side, which we occupied, as an advanced post, with three companies. The remainder of the division was formed in two lines; the first, consisting chiefly of light troops, behind the hedge, in continuation from the left of our battalion reserve; and the second, about a hundred yards in its rear. The guns were placed in the intervals between the brigades, two pieces were in the roadway on our right, and a rocket-brigade in the centre.
>
>   The road had been cut through the rising ground, and was about twenty or thirty feet deep where our right rested, and which, in a manner, separated us from all the troops beyond ... The whole position seemed to be a gently rising ground, presenting no obstacle at any point, excepting the broken hedge in front of our division, and it was only one in appearance, as it could be passed in every part.[103]

The 95th did what they could to put their position in a state of defence. Lieutenant George Simmons formed one of a party of riflemen sent out to establish an abatis – an obstacle consisting of felled trees and sharpened branches – on the Charleroi road near the gravel pit where his battalion was posted.[104] 'From the moment we took possession of the knoll,' Kincaid, recorded, 'we had busied ourselves in collecting branches of trees and other things, for the purpose of making an abatis to block up the road between that and the farmhouse, and soon completed one, which we thought looked sufficiently formidable to keep out the whole of the French cavalry ...'[105] On the opposite side of the Genappe road stood a Dutch-Belgian brigade under Major General Count Bylandt, from the 2nd Netherlands Division under Lieutenant General Baron de Perponcher. These occupied the front face of the crest of the ridge. Just behind Bylandt's troops stood Picton's 5th Division, formed up in line from west to east – Major General Sir Denis Pack's 9th British Brigade, Kempt's 8th British Brigade, and Colonel von Vincke's Hanoverians.

Apart from the battalion of Nassauers at Hougoumont, the area east of Picton's division, around Papelotte and La Haye, was held by the 2nd Nassau Brigade under Prince Bernhard of Saxe-Weimar, part of Perponcher's division. The outlying village of Frischermont would remain unoccupied on the basis that it could not be supported by troops positioned along the main line, thus leaving the troops in La Haye and Papelotte to look to their own defence. These villages therefore marked the easternmost dispositions of Wellington's infantry. Since the Duke depended on Prussian assistance coming from the east, that is, from the direction of Wavre, he depended for the defence of his left flank on these reinforcements and, pending their arrival, the difficulties the French stood to face should they attempt a wide cavalry sweep over the marshy ground east of La Haye and Papelotte. But Wellington also depended on his light cavalry for the protection of his left; accordingly, the British cavalry brigades under Major General Sir Hussey Vivian and Major General Sir John Vandeleur stood behind Vincke's Hanoverians for an extended length to the rear of Papelotte and La Haye. From there troopers went out on patrol to the south and east. Vivian was specifically ordered by De Lancey, via Wellington, to remain in the position assigned to him until such time as the Prussians arrived on the Anglo-Allied left.[106]

The remainder of the cavalry lay behind Wellington's centre. These consisted of the Household Brigade under Major General Lord Edward Somerset to the west of the Genappe road, the Union Brigade under Major General Sir William Ponsonby to the east of the road, and three brigades of mixed British and King's German Legion light cavalry (Major General Sir Colquhoun Grant, Colonel Sir Frederick von Arentschildt and Major General Sir William Dörnberg) behind the 1st Division. Three brigades of Dutch-Belgian cavalry, revealed to have been of negligible value at Quatre Bras, were arrayed behind the centre and right. Finally, the two regiments of Brunswick cavalry remained with their infantry counterparts near Merbe-Braine.

With respect to the deployment of Anglo-Allied artillery, Cotton noted that, 'According to the nature of the ground, the guns were skilfully ranged at points whence the melancholy work of destruction could be best effected; yet, from its undulating form, it concealed from the enemy's view a great portion of our force.'[107] Ensign Edward Macready noted: 'Our artillery arrived at full gallop, and the guns were disposed on the most favourable ground in front of their respective divisions…The men were in great measure covered by the crest of the hill, but the whole French army, with the exception of its reserve, was exposed to our artillery.'[108] In front of the guns, a skirmish line extended all along the front, initially as far east as Frischermont but later contracted to La Haye and Papelotte, and in the west to the southern edge of the woods at Hougoumont.

Wellington had ordered no fieldworks anywhere on the battlefield, as he believed this sapped the troops of their initiative and fighting spirit. By declining to build field fortifications, moreover, he could more realistically encourage Napoleon to launch a frontal assault rather than execute an enveloping manoeuvre. Based on his previous conduct in the Peninsula, it is safe to assume that while the Duke intended to remain on the defensive, he wished to retain a strong degree of mobility, allowing him to react to French moves as he saw fit. Digging in would consequently not facilitate this objective.

Wellington could not know where Napoleon would strike, but he almost certainly hoped he would strike Hougoumont, the strongest position in the Anglo-Allied line. He had fought brilliant defensive battles in the Peninsula and hoped to repeat such successes here. He could not hope, especially with a force of mixed nationalities, to manoeuvre with the same ease as the French, so he must depend on the inherent defensive nature of the ground he had chosen, calculate that any French manoeuvre on his far right would find itself stalled by the force left at Hal and Tubize, that his dispositions between Hougoumont and Frischermont would hold, and that sufficient numbers of Prussians would reach him from Wavre in the event that the French could bring greater pressure than Wellington's line could bear.

If, as discussed earlier, Wellington's position could not be considered an unassailable one, the manner in which he deployed his forces prior to battle made about the best possible use of the ground available to him. The 2-mile crescent-shaped ridge of Mont St Jean had much to commend it, with the Duke's left anchored on the villages of Papelotte and La Haye and his centre strongly bolstered by the farm of La Haye Sainte, which stood near the crossroads formed by the thoroughfares leading from Ohain and Charleroi to Brussels. The formidable château of Hougoumont, ideal for improvised fortification, anchored the Duke's centre-right, albeit lying slightly forward of his main line. Appreciating the defensive capabilities of La Haye Sainte and Hougoumont, Wellington had garrisoned them with some of his best infantry, thereby confronting the French with obstacles which they could not ignore, for any attack which sought to press past these positions would receive flanking fire from the defenders. Hougoumont in particular posed such a large impediment to a French attack, moreover, that its fall effectively stood as a prerequisite to any serious attempt by Napoleon to outflank the Anglo-Allied right.

Having chosen this ground in advance, Wellington had carefully studied its topography and considered its defence in the context of his years of experience in the Peninsula. The folds, dips and slopes around Mont St Jean stood to offer at least limited protection from French artillery, which invariably appeared in far greater numbers than his own. Thus, as one of

General Hill's aides-de-camp noted: 'Our infantry was concealed from the view of the enemy, being posted a little behind the summit of the ridge, and was formed in small squares of battalions, having only the artillery and a few small parties of cavalry visible.'[109] Cotton, too, identified a number of very positive features:

> The great advantage was that the troops could rest in rear of the crest of the ridge, screened in a great measure from the enemy's artillery and observation, whilst our guns were placed at points, which whence they could sweep … the slope that descends to the valley in front … The undulation in rear of the ridge afforded excellent protection to the second line, cavalry and reserves, which were quite concealed from the enemy's view …[110]

Lieutenant John Sperling also observed obvious advantages:

> The superiority which our position gave us for defence was very manifest. Along the ridge of the hill there was a raised field road, which gave us the advantage of a sort of parapet, and served to screen our infantry from the sight of the French artillery and army drawn up on the opposite hill. Our artillery were arranged in advance upon the summit of the ridge. It was a position in which they themselves were very much exposed, yet most important as it respected the issue of the battle. All the attacking columns, descending from their own position and in the ascent to ours, were exposed to its fire.
>
> The infantry were drawn up in two lines of squares, flanking each other, on the slope of the hill, a little retired from the summit, so as to be completely under cover, yet able to act as occasion might require, and capable of resisting any attack of cavalry. Skirmishing parties were in advance and on both flanks. Cavalry were also on the flanks, and some in rear of the infantry, to be ready for action as might be required. Some reserves of infantry occupied a rise a little in the rear. Our position was thus admirable for defence, but not at all adapted for attack, as we should have been subjected to all the disadvantages of our opponents, had any advance been attempted towards them …[111]

Wellington could also confidently expect to benefit from the previous night's downpour, for the sodden ground meant that round shot would simply plunge into the earth on first graze rather than bound along the field, causing havoc in the tightly packed ranks of Anglo-Allied infantry and cavalry. Cotton summed up well the manifold advantages to the Duke's position:

1. The junction of the two high-roads immediately in rear of our centre, from which branched off the paved broad road to Brussels, our main line of operation, and the paved road to the capital by Braine-l'Alleud and Alsemberg. This added to the facility of communication, and enabled us to move ammunition, guns, troops, the wounded, etc., to or from any part of our main front line, as circumstances demanded.

2. The advanced posts of Hougoumont, La Haye-Sainte, Papelotte, and La Haye farms, near which no enemy could pass without being assailed in flank by musketry.

3. The continuous ridge from flank to flank towards which no hostile force could advance undiscovered, within range of our artillery upon the crest. Behind this ridge our troops could manoeuvre, or lie concealed from the enemy's view, while they were in great measure protected from the fire of the hostile batteries.

4. Our extreme left was strong by nature. The buildings, hollow-ways, enclosures, trees and brushwood, along the valley from Papelotte to Ohain, tightly peopled with light infantry, would have kept a strong force long at bay. Our batteries on the left on the knoll commanded the valley and the slopes. The ground from those batteries to Ohain ... was admirably adapted for cavalry.

5. Our extreme right was secured by numerous patches of brushwood, trees and ravines, and further protected by hamlets, and by lord Hill's troops *en potence*, part of which occupied Braine-l'Alleud and the farm of Vieux-Forrier, on the height above that town.[112]

On the French side, in his front line Napoleon positioned Lieutenant General Comte Reille's II Corps (minus Girard's division) on his left and Comte d'Erlon's I Corps on his right. Lieutenant General Comte Lobau's VI Corps (minus Teste's division, detached to Grouchy's command) and the reserve cavalry stood behind these formations, with the Imperial Guard under Lieutenant General Comte Drouot behind Lobau. Napoleon boasted four cavalry corps, of which III Cavalry Corps under Kellermann stood behind Reille, and Milhaud's IV behind d'Erlon. Napoleon's impressive Armée du Nord numbered 77,500 troops and 246 guns, opposing Wellington's 73,200 men and 157 guns.

5

THE
DEFENCE OF
HOUGOUMONT

Despite its substantial value, Napoleon did not regard the capture of Hougoumont as vital, notwithstanding the fact that its fall would fatally imperil the Anglo-Allied right and centre-right. True, seizing Hougoumont would secure his left flank in the event that Napoleon wished to prosecute further attacks on the Anglo-Allied centre-right; but apart from a direct assault, the French possessed three remaining options respecting this formidable farm complex: outflank it with a wide enveloping movement to the west; launch a feint attack in an attempt to induce Wellington to reinforce the position with infantry reinforcements drawn from his reserve; or ignore it altogether and launch an assault in the gap between it and La Haye Sainte, as well as to the east of the Waterloo–Genappe road, accepting whatever losses they sustained by relatively insubstantial flanking fire certain to be offered by whatever infantry occupied the eastern portion of the complex. According to the orders issued on the morning of battle, Napoleon wished to thrust through Wellington's centre and capture the tiny village of Mont St Jean behind it, and in pursuit of that objective chose a feint against Hougoumont – not the series of direct assaults that would actually develop and gradually escalate from the outset of the fighting.

Wellington, for his part, had only to hold the position. Still, that constituted no mean feat, and its fall would render considerably more vulnerable the Mont St Jean ridge. Supported by lesser though easily defensible positions at La Haye Sainte and the area containing Papelotte, La Haye and Smohain, Hougoumont constituted a superb forward defensive position, whose defenders – of whom comparatively few were required to hold it – could divide and weaken the strength of French thrusts, and indeed channel their direction, for so long as it remained in Anglo-Allied hands any attack of scale on Wellington's centre was obliged to advance to the east of Hougoumont, thus traversing the 1,000-yard gap between the easternmost hedge of the Great Orchard and the western wall of La Haye Sainte. Any attacker wishing to reduce enfilading fire from these positions would find his frontage still further reduced to about 700 yards – but in so contracting his forces woud render them more concentrated and therefore more vulnerable to artillery fire. This was readily to hand, for Wellington's guns could fire from the ridge in support of the strongpoint of Hougoumont. Even without seizing Hougoumont outright, by contesting its possession Napoleon intended to draw off Wellington's troops from other sectors of the Anglo-Allied line, so depleting the Duke's strength elsewhere. Thus, initially, elements of Comte Reille's II Corps attack functioned as a diversion, for the French at the outset never intended an attack against it to constitute a major effort.

Yet it was destined to become so, for Hougoumont constituted more than an ordinary farm complex: it was an impressive obstacle which its occupants would render even more formidable during the night of the 17th. The enclosure was only accessible via several heavy doors, with the South Gate – or rather, gates, since it comprised two sets of doors at either end of a stone carriage passage – barricaded shut but the North Gate left open or in any event readily accessible in order to facilitate the movement of ammunition and reinforcements. On the west side of the complex stood a large structure, the 'Great Barn'. The château, or main building, stood on the east side, with a farmer's house on the north side and the North Gate beside it. Various other buildings also composed this structure. Some of the interior features were vulnerable to fire, such as the floors, roofs, ceilings and doors, but the structures themselves were fashioned from brick and stone. All told, the complex and adjoining features measured about 600 yards square. Most of the area to the south of the buildings constituted an extensive wood, about 30 yards from the garden wall, and measuring about 300 yards long and 250 yards wide, enclosed by thick, high hedges and ditches. Tall trees in the wood not only obscured vision from the south (i.e. the French direction of approach) but, crucially, blocked artillery fire from that direction against the buildings and garden walls. The wood also allowed the free movement of infantry, since no undergrowth restricted their movement.[1] Immediately to the east of the complex stood a formal garden with a 7ft brick-and-stone wall enclosing it – too high for soldiers to clamber over it unless hoisted up by their comrades, since the French possessed no scaling ladders. The wall extended away from the farmhouse section of the complex, then east along the southern side before turning north along the east side of the complex to meet the northern end of the surrounding wall. East of the formal garden stood an apple orchard about 200 yards square, bordered to the south, east and north by hedges with high earthen banks and ditches on the inside. A sunken road, known as the covered or sunken way, lay on the northern edge of the farm, with a hedge on the near side. Further north, open fields stretched as far as

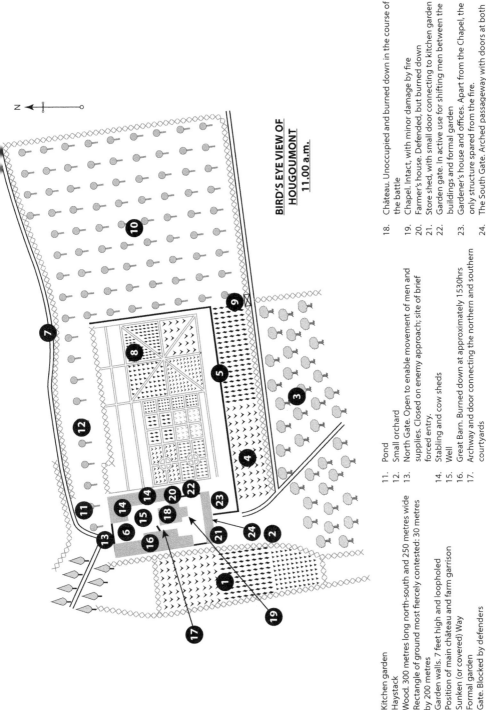

BIRD'S EYE VIEW OF HOUGOUMONT
11.00 a.m.

1. Kitchen garden
2. Haystack
3. Wood. 300 metres long north-south and 250 metres wide by 200 metres
4. Rectangle of ground most fiercely contested: 30 metres by 200 metres
5. Garden walls. 7 feet high and loopholed
6. Position of main château and farm garrison
7. Sunken (or covered) Way
8. Formal garden
9. Gate. Blocked by defenders
10. Great Orchard
11. Pond
12. Small orchard
13. North Gate. Open to enable movement of men and supplies. Closed on enemy approach; site of brief forced entry.
14. Stabling and cow sheds
15. Well
16. Great Barn. Burned down at approximately 1530hrs
17. Archway and door connecting the northern and southern courtyards
18. Château. Unoccupied and burned down in the course of the battle
19. Chapel. Intact, with minor damage by fire
20. Farmer's house. Defended, but burned down
21. Store shed, with small door connecting to kitchen garden
22. Garden gate. In active use for shifting men between the buildings and formal garden
23. Gardener's house and offices. Apart from the Chapel, the only structure spared from the fire.
24. The South Gate. Arched passageway with doors at both ends

the Ohain road and the main Anglo-Allied ridge beyond. To the west stood a narrow kitchen garden surrounded by a hedge, which provided some cover from small-arms fire to defenders, but not from artillery. Crucially, no trees screened the western approach to the farm. It is not surprising that the commanding officer of the Coldstream Guards should describe the place as 'well calculated for defence':

> The dwelling-house in the Centre was a strong square building, with small doors and windows. The barns and granaries formed nearly a square, with one door of communication with the small yard to the South; and from that yard was a door into the garden, a double gate into the wood, under or near the small house … call[ed] the Gardener's house; and another door opening into the lane on the West. There was also another carriage gate at the North-West angle of the great yard, leading into the barn, which conducted to the road to Braine-la-Leud [*sic*].[2]

The first elements to comprise the garrison began to leave the ridge around 6 p.m. on the 17th and marched the short distance to Hougoumont. Captain Robert Ellison, 1st Foot Guards, recorded this force as:

> … four Light Companies of the Guards, one of which I commanded, [and which] were suddenly ordered from our bivouac to take possession of the farmhouse, garden, orchard, and wood of Hougoumont.
>   The two Light Companies of the 1st [Guards] Brigade occupied the orchard, the two Light Companies of the 2nd [Guards] Brigade the farmhouse and garden. During the whole of the night we were occupied in making the position as strong as our means would allow. I was on picket that night. The French brought up their advanced posts close to ours, but gave us no molestation.[3]

By about 7.30 p.m. the garrison therefore consisted of one light company from 2nd Battalion 1st Foot Guards (2/1 Guards) and another from the 3/1 – in total about 200 men under Lieutenant Colonel Lord Saltoun, plus two further light companies, one from 2nd Battalion 2nd Foot Guards (2/2 Guards, referred to hereafter by their more widely known, later designation as the Coldstream Guards) and another from 2nd Battalion 3rd Foot Guards (2/3 Guards, now Scots Guards), both under Lieutenant Colonel James Macdonell. These approximately 200 men assumed positions in the buildings, garden, orchard and wood. In the torrential downpour the guardsmen proceeded to make loopholes – especially in the garden wall facing the wood and along the eastern wall facing the Great Orchard – as well as firing platforms on the inside fashioned out of whatever materials they could find within the complex.[4] According to Lieutenant G.D. Graeme, a British officer serving in the 2nd King's German Legion Light Battalion defending La Haye Sainte, pioneers (engineers) had been supplied to assist with these tasks on the evening of the 17th,[5] though this is not corroborated elsewhere. Platforms would enable infantry to fire over the top, thus covering the 30-yard approach of open ground from the wood. Sometime between 5 and 6 a.m. on the 18th Wellington visited the complex and informed Macdonell that the position was to be defended to the last man. Around 10 a.m. on the 18th the Duke sent additional troops to supplement the four light companies and to redeploy them. Saltoun's two companies were ordered to return to 1st Brigade by one of Maitland's aides-de-camp, while Macdonell's two light companies shifted position to the kitchen garden and elsewhere just west of the buildings. Approximately 200 Hanoverians – *Jäger* and light infantry – arrived and occupied the wood, and the 1st Battalion 2nd Nassau Regiment (1/2 Nassau, about 800 men) from Saxe-Weimar's brigade, established defensive positions, with two companies in the garden, one company in the Great Orchard, two companies in the wood with the Hanoverians, and one company of Nassauers in the château buildings.

When Wellington returned for his second visit to Hougoumont around 10.30 a.m. he encountered Saltoun and countermanded the order for his withdrawal, sending the guardsmen back so his men could deploy in the orchard. Thus, when action began the garrison of Hougoumont numbered about 1,200 men (800 Nassauers, 200 Hanoverians and 200 British guardsmen – not including Saltoun's two companies, which were then en route). By virtue of this deployment, therefore, none of the British guardsmen held any of the buildings, garden, wood or orchard at the outset of the battle. Meanwhile, Reille deployed his corps between the Nivelles and Genappe roads, with Bachelu's brigade on the right, Foy's division in the centre and Jérôme's division on the left.

Action commenced at 11 a.m. when substantial elements of Reille's II Corps[6] advanced on Hougoumont – specifically, three battalions of the 1st Légère and four of the 2nd Légère, both from Baudin's brigade, totalling approximately 4,100 men, supported by at least five batteries of foot and horse artillery. Clouds of French skirmishers drove back their less numerous counterparts,[7] Ross-Lewin noting how 'the enemy sent forward a swarm of tirailleurs to the attack of Hougoumont; they spread over all the ground in front of the house and plantations, and advanced, firing, without any seeming system'.[8] Henegan similarly observed 'a numerous host of tirailleurs advanced close to the wood and orchard of the château, followed by two massive columns of the 2nd corps of the French army ... Pressing rapidly through the waving corn, these columns were next seen as rapidly pressing up the slopes that led to Hougoumont ...'[9]

Shortly thereafter the French opened an artillery bombardment that proceeded to exact a mounting toll on the infantry atop the ridge.[10] In many cases, however, the gentle slopes which separated the two antagonists shielded many of Wellington's troops from the view of French gunners,[11] thereby rendering them considerably less vulnerable than those exposed on the front face and crest of the ridge. Several batteries helped support the defence of Hougoumont, including Bull's,[12] Webber-Smith's,[13] Ramsay's and Lloyd's,[14] situated on the ridge just behind, with at least five others[15] further east, though the number of those in direct support is impossible to establish precisely. Several sources agree, however, that a British battery fired the first shot of the battle against one of the columns advancing against Hougoumont.[16] The identity of the battery concerned is not known, but it is clear that Captain Alexander Mercer's guns engaged their French opposites from the start, in violation of the Duke's ban, issued prior to battle as a measure against excessive expenditure of ammunition, on counter-battery fire. Engaging French 4-pounders along the Nivelles road, Captain Alexander Mercer was confident that his 9-pounders would soon silence them:

> My astonishment was great, however, when our very first gun was responded to by at least half-a-dozen gentlemen of very superior calibre, whose presence I had not even suspected, and whose superiority we immediately recognised by their rushing noise and long reach, for they flew far beyond us. I instantly saw my folly, and ceased firing, and they did the same – the 4-pounders alone continuing the cannonade as before.[17]

All the other Anglo-Allied batteries in the area, however, conformed to their orders, with sufficient success in fact that they checked the progress of the first attack. According to Lieutenant General Sir Henry Clinton, commanding the 2nd Division:

> A very strong column debouched from the enemy's left, from by the Genappe road, towards the post of Hougoumont. As soon as this was within reach of the guns of the 1st Corps the prince [of Orange] ordered 12 pieces to open upon him [i.e. the enemy] & in the course of a few rounds the column staggered & retired out of sight. This occasioned a delay & gave time to strengthen this point, the 2nd Division [i.e. Clinton's formation] was brought nearer up & its right brought considerably forward beyond the line of Braine l'Alleud. The enemy now brought on a very powerful artillery & under the protection of that renewed his attack, though from a greater distance from our guns, on the post of Hougoumont.[18]

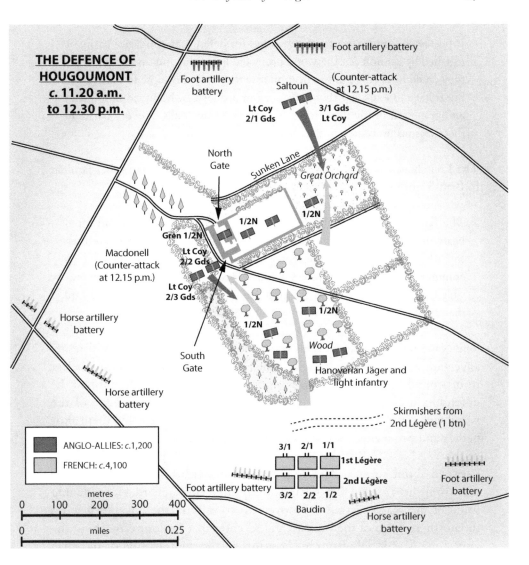

THE DEFENCE OF HOUGOUMONT
c. 11.20 a.m. to 12.30 p.m.

Foot artillery battery

Foot artillery battery

Saltoun

(Counter-attack at 12.15 p.m.)

Lt Coy 2/1 Gds

3/1 Gds Lt Coy

North Gate

Sunken Lane

Great Orchard

1/2N

1/2N

Grén 1/2N

Macdonell (Counter-attack at 12.15 p.m.)

Lt Coy 2/2 Gds

Lt Coy 2/3 Gds

Horse artillery battery

1/2N

South Gate

1/2N

1/2N

Wood

Hanoverian Jäger and light infantry

Horse artillery battery

Skirmishers from 2nd Légère (1 btn)

3/1 2/1 1/1

1st Légère

2nd Légère

Foot artillery battery

Foot artillery battery

3/2 2/2 1/2

Baudin

Horse artillery battery

ANGLO-ALLIES: *c.*1,200

FRENCH: *c.*4,100

metres
0   100   200   300   400

miles
0   0.25

Meanwhile, with the remainder of the Anglo-Allied line waiting quietly for the French to engage them, Wellington stood free to observe the fighting around Hougoumont from open ground to the north-east, a spot of sufficient elevation to provide him a clear view of the French moving towards the woods. Major Robert Bull's battery of horse artillery, at Uxbridge's direction, fired spherical case (shrapnel) rounds from about 1,000 yards into the woods at Hougoumont and round shot at infantry columns approaching from the south, apparently with considerable effect.[19]

As for Hougoumont itself as the target for artillery, the French directed very little fire against it for the first two hours of the assault,[20] for the reasons outlined by Lieutenant Colonel Francis Home, commander of the 3rd Foot Guards:

It possessed some important advantages for defence, it could not easily be touched by cannon &c, the wood protected it in front and on its right flank they could not bring guns to bear on it without coming close to the edge of the ridge and exposing themselves to our artillery ... Many common shot and grape fell in my direction and perforated the walls in every part, but these reasons prevented it from being steady or effective.[21]

The French advanced against Hougoumont in the same style as that familiar to British troops in the Peninsula, as Gronow related:

The rapid beating of the *pas de charge* [rapid charge], which I had often heard in Spain – and which few men, however brave they may be, can listen to without a somewhat unpleasant sensation – announced that the enemy's columns were fast approaching. On our side the most profound silence prevailed, whilst the French, on the contrary, raised loud shouts, and we heard the cry of '*Vive l'Empereur!*' from one end of their line to the other.[22]

The Nassauers and Hanoverians positioned in the wood put up stiff resistance with sustained fire, particularly the rifle-armed Nassauers. Nonetheless, from around 11.30 a.m. the more numerous French gradually pushed the defenders back through the undergrowth to the northern edge of the wood where the latter held on briefly, before the French ejected them altogether and proceeded into the Great Orchard, seizing it from a company of the 1/2 Nassau. But the French did not maintain possession for long; between about 12.15 and 12.30 p.m. Saltoun, with his two light companies from the 2/1 and 3/1 Guards, recaptured the orchard, emboldening some of the Nassauers and Hanoverians to rally in the covered way on the northern edge of the orchard and re-enter that enclosure. At about the same time Macdonell, from his position on the western side of the farm complex, counter-attacked into the wood with his two light companies and halted the further advance of Baudin's high-spirited men.[23] Ensign Standen recalled the unequal fight for possession of the wood thus: 'When we in turn retreated, our attacks became each time more feeble. Although we drove them out, our advances became shorter. They fed [in] an immense force of skirmishers; we had no support.'[24]

The weakened light companies regularly charged the French in the wood, the 3rd Foot Guards employing a haystack, which eventually caught fire, as a rallying point from which to form up before resuming their attacks. Those holding the wood could not resist for long and gradually withdrew into the buildings, the formal garden and the Great Orchard, having contested their ground commendably – the Nassauers, according to Captain George Barlow, 69th Foot, having 'quitted their post after making an admirable defence'.[25] Thus, by 12.30 p.m. the French had cleared the wood but had failed to take the orchard.[26]

Then, emerging from the woods, Jérôme's men discovered a 30-yard gap between them and the southern wall and buildings held by defenders who instantly unleashed a volley and, later, independent fire, against uncoordinated clumps of assailants. Some reached the walls unscathed, only to find that they could not drive off defenders holding an elevated position by virtue of the 'rudely constructed' platforms running much of the length of the garden wall, while at other places the earthen banks proved high enough to furnish the defenders the same facility for firing over the wall.[27] Men also made use of loopholes through which, as Home observed, 'the men fired securely & the slaughter was immense'. Unable to breach the garden wall, the crush of attackers intermingled among the dead and wounded; as French losses continued to mount, some of the grievously injured called out to Home to order his men to shoot them dead that they might end their sufferings.[28] But the French never attempted to scale the walls in a concerted fashion, instead lapping around them, while others maintained a constant fire from the wood against the garden, answered very effectively by the defenders standing on their firing platforms and behind banks of earth, as well as from the upper windows of the buildings.[29]

Most of the attackers were left merely to fire at those defenders who briefly popped their heads over the tops of the walls or aimed at the small loopholes – neither of which presented effective targets. Those Frenchmen audacious enough to attempt to mount the walls briefly crossed bayonets with the defenders, but even the dauntingly superior numbers of attackers could not compensate for the seemingly unassailable face of stone and brick that confronted them, backed by the desperate efforts of guardsmen, Hanoverians and Nassauers. Consequently, after suffering heavy losses, with the most gallant falling wounded or dead into the garden after attempting to clamber over its walls, Jérôme's men retired into the woods to lick their wounds and prepare for a renewed assault. All the while, tirailleurs concealed in the rye continued to issue regular fire, particularly those exploiting the rising ground on the south-west corner of the farm, while on elevated ground along the eastern hedge of the estate at least one sharpshooter, also employing cover, peppered the door which connected the courtyard and garden.[30]

Recognising the stalemate, around 12.30 p.m. Jérôme sent forward Soye's brigade in support of Baudin, while at approximately the same time infantry attacked the west side of the complex, driving back Macdonell's two light companies (2/2 and 2/3 Guards) into the courtyard of the farm via the North Gate. Then, around 1 p.m., frustrated by the continually unsuccessful attempts to batter in the South Gate, which they found barricaded and covered by fire from the large window above and a small section of the garden wall immediately to the attackers' right, French infantry made their way down the lane running along the western side of Hougoumont[31] towards the North Gate. Macdonell's men had been forced back along this wall, and the 2/3 Guards had followed, closing the gates behind them with the French just on their heels.

One of the battle's many iconic episodes now took place as Sous-Lieutenant Legros of the Second Battalion 1er Légère, wielding a pioneer's axe and assisted by the brute force of his comrades forced open the gate, allowing about thirty men to rush into the farmyard, causing a number of defenders to rush for the cover of the buildings from which to fire at the intruders from windows and doors. Others engaged in hand-to-hand combat in the courtyard. It was a desperate time, for the position now stood in peril. Macdonell, seizing the initiative, called out to several Coldstream officers to assist him, together with a handful of soldiers – two Coldstreamers and six men from the 2/3 Guards – in closing the gates. Some fought to prevent more French from gaining access while their comrades, including Macdonell, using main force, forced the gates closed, barricaded them and returned the crossbar to its place. This left about thirty men trapped inside, probably all of whom were killed, except a drummer boy, though Private Matthew Clay's reference to French wounded in the compound suggests some of this party were either spared, or the wounded represented those who had managed to clamber over the walls, only to be shot or bayoneted in the act. Woodford later wrote of the intruders being 'speedily driven out, or despatched'[32] with Ensign Standen providing slightly more detail:

> After a severe struggle the French forced the rear gate [i.e. the North Gate] open and came in with us. We flew to the parlour, opened the windows and drove them out, leaving an Officer and some men dead within the wall.
>
> The ditch at the corner of the wood leading into the orchard ... was full of dead bodies (we had blocked up the gate), as the French strove repeatedly and gallantly to get through in defiance of the fire from the loopholes so close to them.[33]

Aware of the threat to the North Gate, Lieutenant Colonel Mackinnon, with three companies of the 2nd Battalion Coldstream Guards, arrived at about 1.15 p.m. and forced the attackers back around to the west side of the complex, with another four companies from the same unit. Lieutenant Colonel Woodford's men then entered the complex, where they remained to bolster the defence for the rest of the day. Much 'tiraillerie', as Woodford described it, continued thereafter.[34] By this time, around 1.15 p.m., the defenders now numbered about 1,850 men, opposed to about 7,500 French[35] who, undaunted, continued to assail the position, Tissot's brigade assaulting the Great Orchard with the aid of a swarm of tirailleurs operating outside the eastern hedge so as to lay down fire against the occupiers from the flank and rear and forcing Saltoun out of the orchard and into the covered way.

Around 1.30 p.m., several shots penetrated some of the buildings, where wounded men lay on the floors and a shell set the barn on fire. Lieutenant Colonel Francis Home, 2/3 Guards, related how when straw bales caught fire:

> It burst out in an instant in every quarter with an amazing flame and smoke. The confusion at the time was great and many men burned to death or suffocated by the smoke. The Duke of Wellington was at this moment in considerable anxiety. He sent Lieutenant Colonel Hamilton then aide-de-camp to Sir E Barnes to the château with orders to keep it to the last and if that could not be done from the fire as to occupy the strong ground on the right and rear and defend it to extremity. Colonel Hamilton delivered these orders to me and added these words, 'Colonel Home the Duke considers the defence [of] this post of the last consequence to the success of the operations of the day; do you perfectly understand these orders?' I said 'Perfectly, and you may assure the Duke from me that his orders shall be punctually obeyed.'[36]

As the garrison fought the flames with water drawn from a well, Wellington sent a note to Macdonell respecting its defence:

> I see that the fire has communicated from the hay stack to the Roof of the Château. You must however still keep your Men in those parts to which the fire does not reach. Take care that no Men are lost by the falling in of the Roof or floors. After they will have fallen in occupy the Ruined Walls inside of the Garden, particularly if it should be possible for the Enemy to pass through the Embers to the Inside of the House.[37]

Heat and smoke prevented the rescue of an indeterminate number of wounded – Woodford claimed 'several' – men trapped in the barn despite Woodford's and Macdonell's attempts to save them. The flames quickly reached the chapel, but burned out just as the flames reached the foot of the crucifix,[38] a sign to many of the survivors of divine intervention. In the event, fire did not seriously hamper the defenders' ability to resist the continuing onslaught. Thus, despite setting fire to part of the complex, repeated yet unco-ordinated French attacks failed to seize the main components of the farm.

But we must turn to events elsewhere.

PART 3

6

D'ERLON'S
ATTACK

While Reille's II Corps, west of the Brussels–Genappe road,[1] occupied itself around Hougoumont, d'Erlon's I Corps extended itself east of that thorough-fare as far as Papelotte and La Haye, but with the bulk of its forces facing Lieutenant General Sir Thomas Picton's 5th Division, which stood just behind the crest of the Mont St Jean ridge. Napoleon intended to unleash I Corps next, preceded by the massed fire of a grand battery of eighty guns established on rising ground extending east of the Brussels–Genappe road and about 700 yards from the Anglo-Allied ridge – but providing the artillery as little as 500 yards' range against about 900 yards' frontage of Wellington's first line. Shortly before 1 p.m., Ney learned that the grand battery was ready to fire, with 17,000 infantry arrayed in columns behind it under d'Erlon and flanked by a brigade of 800 cuirassiers under Dubois west of the Genappe road. Meanwhile, far on the French right, the first elements of the Prussian vanguard could be seen by telescope from Napoleon's headquarters on a knoll near the road at Rossomme. The Emperor had only just completed a dispatch to Grouchy ordering him to continue pursuing the Prussians in the direction of Wavre, their last reported position. Changing circumstances now required an addendum: that marshal was to detach himself and join the main body facing Wellington. In the event, the courier did not reach Grouchy until about 3.30 p.m., by which time it was impossible for him to disengage and march the 33,000 men of his corps, including guns and wagons, the distance required, over muddy ground, in time to exercise any more than a mini-mal impact on the fighting at Waterloo. In the meantime, Napoleon shifted Lobau's VI corps to his right flank to forestall the Prussians once they reached the battlefield, though the Emperor's plan remained unaltered: a major assault against the Anglo-Allied line.

At 1 p.m. the grand battery commenced firing. There was no precedent for such a bombardment in Wellington's long experience in Iberia. The 6lb and 12lb balls cut swathes through the infantry standing on the ridge before the onslaught; but while the bombardment constituted a dreadful ordeal for the infantry who had no choice but to endure it, it failed to break the men's nerve and drive them off, not least because the Duke had resorted to his old tactic of deploying most of his units on the reverse side of the ridge. Shots striking the top of the ridge continued on over and into the ranks of seemingly sheltered infantry, but many others, with a higher trajectory, passed completely over and more often than not fell harmlessly into the soft earth, incapable of bounding further into units standing in reserve. Thus, part of the Anglo-Allied front line – with one dreadfully exposed Dutch-Belgian and Nassau brigade forming a notable exception – benefited from the comparative protection of the rear slope, where many colonels took the additional precaution of order-ing their battalions to lie prone. This, in turn, left French observers situated beyond the valley which lay between the protagonists wrongly to surmise that the defenders had withdrawn under the heavy weight of fire. The height of the grain may also have helped obscure the Anglo-Allied position. Captain Rudyard, Royal Artillery, noted that in his battery's initial position the grain stood above his head until trampled.[2] Concealed by high-growing crops and the folds of the ground and shrouded in the smoke, Picton's infantry seemed to those peering through their telescopes to have disappeared. Lieutenant Colonel James Stanhope, 3/1st Foot Guards, writing in his campaign journal, described how at the outset of the fighting, 'our army was invisible behind the hill & the enemy could see nothing but a few horsemen & spectators amid untrodden & waving grain.'[3]

After a 'most dismal and dreary'[4] but rainless mid and late morning, the after-noon was fine[5] – reasonably good conditions for an infantry attack. At about 1.30 p.m., after thirty minutes of preparatory artillery fire – what an uniden-tified officer of the 95th described as 'a most tremendous cannonade'[6] – the firing largely ceased,[7] with the roar of the grand battery replaced by the distant sound of beating drums and troops shouting and cheering '*Vive l'Empereur!*'[8]

D'Erlon's attack consisted of six principal components: one brigade under Quiot advancing west of the Brussels–Genappe road towards the Dutch-Belgian, Hanoverian and King's German Legion infantry on the ridge; one brigade under Charlet moving directly against La Haye Sainte from the south; a third brigade, under Bourgeois, proceeding up the ridge with La Haye Sainte on its left; a column of divisional strength under Donzelot on Bourgeois' right; another of divisional strength under Marcognet about 150 yards further east still, and finally a brigade under Pégot well to the east. These formations proceeded across undulating farmland and ascended the slope, flanked by cav-alry and screened by clouds of skirmishers.

Columns on this scale had succeeded regularly on battlefields before, particularly where a preliminary bombardment by massed guns had blown holes in the defender's front line, shattered the cohesion of his formations and crippled the morale of those awaiting the onslaught. But Napoleon's bombardment had not achieved this; d'Erlon's seemingly irresistible columns were gradually approaching steady, disciplined infantry – bloodied, certainly, by the cannonade – but whose ranks remained firm. Moreover, massive French columns composed of several regiments – Donzelot's and Marcognet's of four each – advancing thus were not invulnerable, for apart from being slowed by thick mud and wet, shoulder-high rye, they presented a magnificent target to the batteries of Rogers and Bijileveld on the top of the ridge, and could not form square, if necessary, with anything approaching the same rapidity as individual battalions. Thus, impressive though these columns appeared – marching as if on parade in some cases twenty-four ranks deep and about 150 men wide – thousands could neither see the object of their attack nor make use of their muskets, for only the front three ranks could issue fire. D'Erlon's corps might very well punch a hole through the defender's line, but if it failed, this unwieldy formation could not expect, under fire, to form into line to increase its firepower without suffering heavily in the process, especially if Wellington counter-attacked.

The capture of La Haye Sainte constituted the principal object of d'Erlon's attack. The farm stood immediately to the west of the Brussels–Genappe road and about 250 yards south of Wellington's main line deployed behind the Ohain–Wavre road, which ran roughly east–west along the crest of the ridge, nearly the whole portion in front of Picton's infantry flanked by hedgerows. As noted earlier, La Haye Sainte was smaller than Hougoumont and less defensible, consisting of a compound of masonry-and-brick buildings with connecting walls forming a rectangle including a pasture and orchard, with a strong hedge to the south, and a lower hedge enclosing a kitchen garden to the north. As all available Royal Engineers had been sent to fortify Hougoumont prior to battle, the garrison of La Haye Sainte had done little to prepare their position apart from creating loopholes and erecting some scaffolding to enable the defenders to fire down on their assailants. With a shocking lack of foresight, one of the gates had been taken down and used to provide fuel for a bivouac fire the evening before the battle. Nonetheless, the troops sent to hold this position were of exceptionally high quality, consisting of the 2nd Light Battalion of the King's German Legion under the command of Major George Baring. Armed with the accurate Baker rifle, these men, in their distinctive green uniforms and black leather accoutrements, held the buildings as well as the pasture, orchard, and the kitchen garden.

Tirailleurs and voltigeurs[9] from d'Erlon's corps and others from Bachelu's division of Reille's corps advanced around 1.45 p.m. to engage their Anglo-Allied opposite numbers. The French enjoyed a clear advantage here,

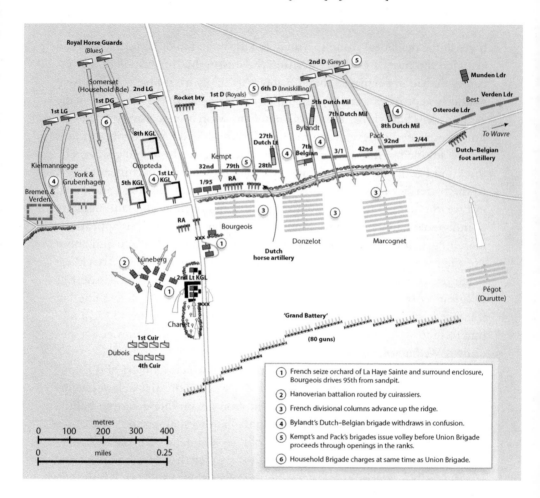

1. French seize orchard of La Haye Sainte and surround enclosure, Bourgeois drives 95th from sandpit.
2. Hanoverian battalion routed by cuirassiers.
3. French divisional columns advance up the ridge.
4. Bylandt's Dutch–Belgian brigade withdraws in confusion.
5. Kempt's and Pack's brigades issue volley before Union Brigade proceeds through openings in the ranks.
6. Household Brigade charges at same time as Union Brigade.

particularly over their Dutch-Belgian counterparts, with those sent forward from British and King's German Legion battalions of at least respectable quality – though still not a match for their opponents. The French skirmishers soon forced back the screen of light infantry confronting them and prepared to make contact with the King's German Legion riflemen in and around La Haye Sainte, together with two companies of the 1/95th in a small gravel quarry known as the sandpit, three companies on a nearby knoll and, to the rear of both, one company in front of a short stretch of a hedgerow which had furnished the materials the night before for constructing an abatis[10] to block the main road just above the sandpit.[11] Lieutenant John Kincaid of the 95th offers this anecdote connected with this sector:

> When we first took possession of the knoll, before the Battle began, there
> was almost a hedge of bushes and underwood, with a tall tree in the centre,
> lining the abrupt face of it on our side. We cut down most of the bushes
> to form an abatis across the road, and our two Medical Officers took post

behind the tree as the most secure place for their operations. The tree was a naked one with a bushy top. One of the first of the Enemy's round shot struck it about two-thirds up, bringing the whole of the bushy part down on their devoted heads and nearly smothering them among the branches.[12]

Meanwhile, west of La Haye Sainte, a brigade of cuirassiers under Dubois advanced on Bourgeois' left flank across undulating ground not visible from the crest of the ridge to their front and charged the western end of Baring's position, catching the Lüneburg battalion, sent forward from Kielmannsegge's Hanoverian brigade, before they could form square. The Lüneburgers promptly broke and fled, with heavy casualties, enabling their attackers to proceed towards the crest of the Anglo-Allied position. Wellington soon appeared in this sector and sought to bring a halt to Quiot's light infantry and Dubois' cuirassiers by ordering the rest of Kielmannsegge's other two battalions and the three in Ompteda's King's German Legion brigade to form square.

Meanwhile, on the opposite side of the Genappe road, having cleared the King's German Legion skirmishers south of La Haye Sainte, Charlet's brigade moved against the orchard, quickly seizing it and driving back its defenders into the buildings, which the attackers soon surrounded.[13] At about the same time, Bourgeois' brigade, passing La Haye Sainte on its left, reached the sandpit, drove out the two companies of riflemen holding it and forced them to withdraw and join the company behind the hedge, where from their new position they held their ground with sufficient tenacity to shift Bourgeois' direction of attack slightly to the right.[14] But this diminutive element of the 95th could not remain there for long against much superior numbers, and soon the three companies joined the other three of the battalion behind the hedge along the Wavre road, with the 32nd Foot close behind.[15] Kincaid described the advance of Bourgeois' brigade and the Rifles' inevitable withdrawal thus:

> That part of our position, in our own immediate front, next claimed our undivided attention. It had hitherto been looking suspiciously innocent, with scarcely a human being upon it; but innumerable black specks were now seen taking post at regular distances in its [the battalion's] front, and recognising them as so many pieces of artillery, I knew, from experience, although nothing else was yet visible, that they were unerring symptoms of our not being destined to be idle spectators …
>
> The scene at that moment was grand and imposing, and we had a few minutes to spare for observation. The column destined as our particular friends, first attracted our notice, and seemed to consist of about ten thousand infantry.[16] A smaller body of infantry and one of cavalry moved on their right; and, on their left, another huge column of infantry, and a formidable body of cuirassiers, while beyond them it seemed one moving mass.

We saw Buonaparte himself take post on the side of the road, immediately in our front, surrounded by a numerous staff; and each regiment, as they passed him, rent the air with shouts of '*Vive l'Empereur,*' nor did they cease after they had passed; but, backed by the thunder of their artillery, and carrying with them the rubidub of drums,[17] and the tantarara of trumpets,[18] in addition to their increasing shouts, it looked, at first, as if they had some hopes of scaring us off the ground; for it was a singular contrast to the stern silence reigning on our side, where nothing, as yet, but the voices of our great guns, told that we had mouths to open when we chose to use them. Our rifles were, however, in a very few seconds, required to play their parts, and opened such a fire on the advancing skirmishers as quickly brought them to a standstill; but their columns advanced steadily through them, although our incessant tiralade was telling in their centre with fearful exactness, and our post was quickly turned in both flanks, which compelled us to fall back and join our comrades, behind the hedge, though not before some of our officers and theirs had been engaged in personal combat.[19]

Captain Leach, also of the 1/95th, corroborates Kincaid's account:

Previous to the attack on the 5th Division, I was sent in command of two Companies of Riflemen to occupy an excavation (from which sand had been dug) close to the [Brussels–]Genappe road and on its left. This was at the base of the hillock, on the summit of which the remainder of the 95th Rifle Corps was posted to support the two advanced Companies.

The fierce onset of the French with overwhelming numbers forced back my two Companies on the main body of the 95th Regiment, and this hillock was also instantly assailed in such a manner as to render it impossible for one weak Battalion, consisting only of six Companies, to stem the torrent for any length of time. We were consequently constrained to fall back on the 32nd Regiment, which was in line near the thorn hedge which runs from the Genappe road to the left [of the crossroads], and along the front of Picton's Division.

We were closely pressed and hotly engaged during the retrograde movement ...[20]

Meanwhile, as fierce fighting continued to rage around La Haye Sainte with the light infantry and Rifles driven into the buildings and behind the main hedge line, respectively, the principal columns of d'Erlon's corps continued their advance against Picton's division deployed in line behind the crest of the ridge, together with Bylandt's Dutch-Belgian and Nassauer brigade which stood on the front face of the ridge – and thus found itself the target of much of the artillery fire preceding d'Erlon's advance. Picton's division consisted of two British infantry brigades: the 8th under Major General Sir James Kempt, situated just east of the main Brussels–Genappe road and slightly behind the Ohain–Wavre road, and the 9th Brigade under Major General Sir Denis Pack, who had deployed his formation further east, slightly beyond Bylandt's. Finally, Picton's Hanoverians – two brigades under Best and Vincke, respectively – stood further east still, in support of Saxe-Weimar's brigade of Nassauers around and behind the villages of Papelotte and La Haye – and as such destined not to bear the brunt of this massive French assault.

Confirming Wellington's worst fears, as Donzelot's divisional column drove in the skirmish line screening Bylandt's brigade, the whole of the latter formation – apart from the 7th Dutch-Belgian Line and thus mostly made up of militia and Jägers – retired and played no further part in the fighting that day.[21] The men withdrew in columns in the direction of Ponsonby's heavy cavalry brigade drawn up behind them. Various eyewitnesses attest to the retreat of Bylandt's troops. According to Sergeant William Dewar, 1/79th, the French 'broke through the foreign troops and put them all in confusion. They began by running away in all directions.'[22] Ensign Edward Macready wrote of the Dutch-Belgians immediately fleeing.[23] Lieutenant George Gunning, 1st Dragoons, described how they 'came through the intervals of our squadrons in great confusion, all order being quite destroyed among them'.[24] Many British accounts were scathing of Dutch-Belgian conduct. 'As for Belgic bravery and a high Dutch heroism,' Ensign Macready recorded vitriolically, 'I recommend people to look for an account of it in books whose authors have heard of these things; unfortunately, nothing of the kind came under my inspection.'[25] Lieutenant James Crummer described their conduct as 'most cowardly & infamous',[26] while Lieutenant James Gairdner of the 95th Rifles condemned these troops who 'in general behaved ill'.[27] This left a dangerous gap in the line, Kincaid noting a 'number of vacant spots that were left nearly along the whole of the line, where a great part of the dark dressed foreign troops[28] had stood, intermixed with the British, when the action began'.[29] Major De Lacy Evans, one of Ponsonby's aides de camp confirms this: 'The Dutch Belgian Infantry yielded with slight or no resistance to the advancing Columns, and got quickly to the rear; and not in the stubborn, reluctant, deliberate way of our Infantry.'[30] Nonetheless, the French were not aware of the gap created in the Anglo-Allied line, for as Jackson observed in his memoirs, 'the French could then see no opponents before them, the British having been kept just under the brow of the rising ground'.[31] On the other hand, this left only Picton's two British brigades – about 1,900 men under Kempt and 1,700 under Pack – to hold back Bourgeois' brigade of about 1,800 men, Donzelot with 5,200 troops and Marcognet with 4,100.

Kempt's brigade consisted of the 28th (North Gloucestershire) Foot occupying the left-hand position, the 79th (Cameron Highlanders) in the centre, and the 32nd (Cornwall) Foot on the right, in front of whom it will be recalled the 1/95th assumed a new position after being driven from the sandpit and forward hedge near La Haye Sainte. Bourgeois' brigade halted at about 50 or 60 yards from the hedge, according to Jackson, and began to deploy into line.[32] The brigade may have reached the hedge itself, for an officer of the 95th recorded an engagement with muskets 'almost muzzle to muzzle'.[33]

Immediately to the left of the 32nd, the Highlanders of the 79th Foot also opposed Bourgeois' column, as described by an enlisted man named Cruickshank:

> When the 79th were deploying into line at the commencement of the Action (they having been previously in column) the Light Company, to which I then belonged, were ordered out and extended. On our reaching the hedge (or nearly so), where the Guns (I think Rogers's Brigade) were stationed, we passed through the [Dutch-]Belgian Infantry, who were retiring, and pushed down the slope in front of the hedge into the valley, where we were for some time engaged with the French skirmishers; but a strong Column of the Enemy appearing on the top of the opposite ridge immediately in our front, and a second Column [Donzelot's] was at that moment seen advancing along the valley to our left, which must have come in contact with the 28th Regiment, we were consequently obliged to retire, and joined the Regiment on its reaching the hedge, when a tremendous conflict ensued between our Line and the opposing Columns, which, it has been said, pushed themselves so far forward as to reach the hedge; but I can positively assert that the French did not reach that point, if I except indeed some few of their sharpshooters which came up the hill with the Light Infantry, but were quickly driven back.
>
> At this time I saw, but certainly very imperfectly, a forward movement of the French Cavalry [Dubois'] on our right, and some of the Cuirassiers had actually reached the point of the hedge on the main road (and the scene was altogether extraordinary) ...[34]

Ensign Mountsteven observed Donzelot's advance:

> The 28th was lying a short distance behind the hedge when the Enemy's Columns were put in motion. When they had advanced pretty near, we were moved up to the hedge, and on our reaching it found a French Column attempting to deploy at probably thirty or forty yards on the other side.[35]

Further east by about 150 yards – with a gap left by Bylandt's absent formation – Pack's brigade consisted of the 1st Foot, also known as the Royal Scots or simply Royals, which stood on the right. The 3rd Battalion 42nd Foot

(Royal Highlanders) occupied the next position to the left, followed by the 92nd Foot (Gordon Highlanders), and finally the Second Battalion 44th Foot (East Essex) on the brigade's left. When d'Erlon had begun his advance Picton ordered Pack's brigade forward from its position 200 yards down the reverse face of the slope to line the hedgerow behind the Wavre road, though in the event part of the 92nd and all of the 44th enjoyed no such protection owing to the termination of the hedgerow along the brigade's eastern end.

While Donzelot's divisional column advanced on the gap left by Bylandt's Dutch-Belgian and Saxe-Weimar's Nassau brigade – that is, the whole of the 2nd Netherlands Division – Marcognet's divisional column proceeded against Pack's position, specifically that held by the 92nd Highlanders. Lieutenant Winchester watched what he estimated to be 3,000–4,000 men (in fact, about 4,100) approaching the position held by his regiment, lying prone for protection against artillery.[36]

British artillery stood ready to play its part in repulsing the attack. Major Whinyates fired his rockets from a position behind the double hedge and amidst high-growing grain. Their effectiveness was dubious, the French cursing them but probably not suffering much materially, although Captain Warde claimed the troop dispersed cavalry and destroyed a French horse artillery battery.[37] Meanwhile, at least two guns from a British horse artillery battery, but perhaps all six, on the ridge were 'driven in': the gunners, sensing their inability to stem the tide of attack, either abandoned the guns temporarily or limbered them up and drove them away. One officer referred to the 'considerable bustle in getting the guns away while the column was approaching, against which they had done heavy execution',[38] while an NCO, clearly anxious of losing his gun to the French, spiked one of the 9-pounders of Major Rogers' battery, the only gun put out of action at Waterloo by this means.[39]

Picton's Counter-attack

With the French now upon the hedge, Picton ordered his regiments to issue a volley and charge. Kincaid reckoned Kempt's brigade fired at about 20 yards from the hedge – and charged in line just as Bourgeois was reaching the hedgerow in front of the Wavre road,[40] while Jackson recalled how the same formation:

> … poured a withering fire upon the enemy, followed by a charge with the bayonet. Having but a moment to glance at the unexpected foe, unable to form any estimate of his strength, while hidden by the smoke, staggered by so sudden and unexpected a fire, confounded, panic-stricken, the French fell into immediate confusion, broke, and fled.

The second column,[41] being treated in a similar manner, followed suit ...[42]

Sergeant William Dewar wrote of Kempt's brigade making 'a most desperate charge with the bayonet after firing a volley ... and met the enemy who had just advanced to the mouth of our guns and after a few minutes of butchery the enemy retired in all directions.'[43]

Ensign Mountsteven of the 28th recalled his regiment's role in repulsing the French:

We then poured in our fire, sprung over the fence [*sic*: hedge], and charged. The Enemy ran before we could close with them, and, of course, in great confusion.

In advancing in pursuit of them the wings of the Regiment separated, and I, carrying the King's Colour, went on with the right wing. When we had proceeded a little way we perceived through the smoke another body of troops in column immediately in our front, which we mistook for some Corps of the Allies, and many of the Officers (I amongst the rest) cried out to the men, 'Don't fire, they are Belgians.'

This caused a momentary check of the wing, when we quickly discovered our mistake by the Enemy making off with all speed in the direction of the French position.

Immediately after this, when all the force that was originally opposed to the 28th had been driven back in confusion, the Regiment was ordered to halt and re-form ...[44]

Kincaid, similarly, provides the perspective of the 1/95th, deployed on the right and in front of the 32nd Foot:

When the heads of their columns showed over the knoll [near La Haye Sainte] which we had just quitted, they received such a fire from our first line, that they wavered, and hung behind it a little; but, cheered and encouraged by the gallantry of their officers, who were dancing and flourishing their swords in front, they at last boldly advanced to the opposite side [that is, in front] of our hedge, and began to deploy.[45]

There, as they attempted to form into line, the 105th Line met with the reception Picton had ordered, for Major Leach, of the same battalion, noted that 'a volley and a charge of bayonets caused the French to recoil in disorder and with a heavy loss ...'[46]

Lieutenant Shelton's account, from the perspective of the position held by the 28th Foot, confirms that Kempt's brigade issued only a single volley before charging and that the French had not crossed the hedge at that point. The brigade, he wrote:

> … gave a very steady volley into the Enemy's Column, and charged (after having crossed the hedge) while the Enemy, who were in great confusion, attempted a deployment to their right, but which they were unable to complete, and got into great irregular bodies.[47]

Pack received the same orders as his fellow brigade commander. Instantly ordering the 92nd to stand to arms, he then called out to them to charge. Forming up four deep the Highlanders issued a volley against their assailants, who, in the process of shouldering arms, clearly were unaware of the presence of the Scots when the volley crashed out.[48]

At this point Picton was shot in the right temple and fell dead from his horse near the sandpit, according to one of Uxbridge's aides-de-camp.[49] Specifically, Picton was killed near Major Rogers' battery,[50] in the act, according to Captain Horace Seymour, of rallying Highlanders 'overpowered by the masses of French Infantry',[51] though there is no evidence the two sides had made contact at this time. Picton's instantaneous death did not halt the pursuit; rather, Kempt assumed command of the 5th Division and sought to check the extent of his troops' pursuit, aware that he possessed no reserve.[52] The French retreat appears to have been precipitous, for Ross-Lewin confirmed that Kempt's troops did not actually make contact with the French:

> Our troops pursued the retiring column down the slope, and would inevitably have closed with them, had they [the pursuers] not begun to [stop and] fire, and thereby retarded their [own] advance.[53]

This version of events is contradicted, however, by an officer of the 95th: 'When the French saw us rushing through the hedge, and heard the tremendous huzza which we gave, they turned; but instead of running, they walked off in close columns with the greatest steadiness, and allowed themselves to be butchered without any material resistance.'[54] Similarly, another account refers to close combat between the 32nd Foot and, in all probability, the 105th Ligne – the leading regiment in Bourgeois' column – during the French retreat:

> Sir Thomas Picton instantly placed himself at the head of his division to meet the attack, crossed the lane, and charged the French, who, firing a volley, faced about and retired … The attack cost a gallant leader, for Sir Thomas Picton received a ball through his right temple, and fell dead from his horse. His body was borne off the ground by two grenadiers of the

32nd regiment ... During the charge a French officer seized a stand of colours belonging to the above-mentioned corps, but he was instantly run through the body by a sergeant's pike, as well as by the sword of the ensign who held the colour.[55]

The recollections of an unidentified officer of the 1/95th confirms this account, maintaining that a mounted French officer attempted to seize the Colours of the 32nd Regiment but was foiled by Sergeant Switzer of the Colour party, who rapidly lunged his pike into him, while Ensign John Birtwhistle simultaneously stabbed him with his sword.[56]

The weight of evidence, however, indicates that no other substantial contact was made between pursuer and pursued, perhaps because the effort involved for battalions to negotiate their way through both hedges lining the road – as well as the time required to reform afterwards – denied them the time in which to reach the retreating French. Having said this, the French withdrawal did not constitute a full-scale rout, for, according to the commanding officer of the 1/95th, 'they began to move off as soon as it was possible for such a mass to effect it ...',[57] which suggests a disorderly retreat but hardly battalions dissolving into a chaotic mass of fugitives. Yet other eyewitnesses suggest a more hurried affair. Leach claimed the volley and bayonet charge of the 1/95th and the 32nd left the attackers 'shattered and broken',[58] while a Highlander of the 79th described the French as 'flying'.[59] Exactly how far Kempt pursued is not known, though Kincaid stated that the riflemen reached as far as the knoll near La Haye Sainte, while the 32nd appears to have halted close to the Wavre road.[60] The 28th, on the other hand, as we shall see shortly, proceeded a considerable distance down the slope.

Kempt returned his battalions to the positions they had occupied before d'Erlon's attack.[61] The 1st Foot – and possibly the other units as well – were ordered to form line and lie down,[62] while Major Leach with two companies of the 1/95th reassumed their post in the sandpit and the other four companies occupied the knoll above it.[63] Nevertheless, the sector never remained quiet, for the French resumed their cannonade, their infantry harassed Picton's division for the remainder of the afternoon, and they redoubled their efforts to capture La Haye Sainte.

7

THE CHARGE OF THE UNION AND HOUSEHOLD BRIGADES

The Union Brigade

We must now turn to examine the role of the cavalry east of the Brussels–Genappe road. Lord Uxbridge, commander of the Anglo-Allied cavalry,[1] was positioned on the right, near Hougoumont, when he saw d'Erlon's infantry advancing to the sound of the *pas de charge*, upon which he ordered both heavy cavalry brigades to attack. The 2nd (Heavy) Cavalry Brigade, popularly known as the 'Union Brigade' as it contained regiments from England, Scotland and Ireland, was commanded by Major General Sir William Ponsonby. The brigade was superbly mounted on large horses with 1,332 strong, experienced troops divided between three understrength regiments: the 1st (Royal) Dragoons, the 2nd (Royal North British) Dragoons, or 'Scots Greys', and the 6th (Inniskilling) Dragoons. No other cavalry was available to support this brigade.[2]

According to Sergeant Archibald Johnston of the Scots Greys, the charge was initiated by the arrival of an aide-de-camp from the Duke of Wellington; but this must be false, as all the evidence indicates that Uxbridge ordered the charge without consulting the Duke.[3] 'I received no order from the Duke of Wellington to make the first charge or any other during the day,' Uxbridge later wrote. 'I felt that he had given me carte blanche, and I never bothered him with a single question respecting the movements it might be necessary [for the cavalry] to make.'[4]

In fact, the Union Brigade was set in motion when Ponsonby, accompanied by De Lacy Evans, one of his aides-de-camp, rode up to the crest of the ridge to observe the French in order to determine the correct timing for the brigade to advance. While dismounted to collect his cloak, which had fallen when his horse was frightened by a round shot, Ponsonby directed De Lacy Evans to make a signal, whereupon the aide-de-camp waved his hat accordingly and set the two brigades in motion.[5]

At the time of the charge, the Royals stood in a hollow about 250 yards to the rear of Kempt's brigade, with the Inniskillings on their left facing the gap left by the absence of Bylandt's brigade, and the Scots Greys slightly to the left rear, behind Pack's brigade. The right of the brigade stood about 250 yards left of the Brussels road.[6] The Scots Greys were in column prior to the charge, but there is no question but that the brigade formed into line in preparation for the attack.[7]

If the formation of the regiments is not in dispute, there is some contention over whether or not they stood contiguous to one another. Lieutenant Colonel Miller of the Inniskillings later claimed that the Greys were in reserve, with the Royals in the front line on the right and the Inniskillings on the left.[8] This confusion may have arisen from the possibility that Uxbridge originally intended this, but the order was not executed, for, according to Captain Phipps of the Royals, Uxbridge directed the Greys to support the Royals and Inniskillings, though in the event they did not.[9] Captain Clark Kennedy of the Royal Dragoons claimed twenty years after the battle that the Greys served in support behind the Inniskillings and Royals, but he freely admitted that 'at this distance of time I may fall into error …' Indeed he did, for the Greys were in fact aligned with the other regiments of the brigade and the first French column did not cross the double hedge running along the Wavre road on the crest of the ridge. Nor, therefore, could the French have passed over several British batteries of guns deployed behind the hedge as he claims.[10] Major De Lacy Evans believed the Inniskillings charged in alignment with the Royals and Greys,[11] which is in fact correct.

Thus, with the Royals on the right, the Inniskillings, led by Ponsonby himself[12] in the centre, and the Greys on the left, the brigade advanced up the rear face of the slope and negotiated its way through the double line of hedges straddling the Wavre road. Then, at a point which Leach called 'this moment of fire, smoke, and excitement'[13] the Royals appeared in the gaps between the infantry companies of the 32nd, 79th and 28th Regiments – and in some places directly through their ranks – before advancing against Bourgeois' fleeing column in what Captain Charles Radclyffe, who commanded the left squadron, described as 'a magnificent sight … Nothing could exceed the enthusiasm of that part that fell under my notice.'[14] According to Captain Phipps, the right squadron of the Royals in fact passed through the ranks of the 32nd Foot, which therefore reveals that most of the regiment, extended in line, advanced through the ranks of the 79th and 28th.[15]

Lieutenant Shelton of the 28th explains how the Royal Dragoons managed its way through the infantry's midst:

It was at this moment that the Heavy Brigade came up, when the 28th wheeled by sub-divisions to its right and made way for the [Royal] Dragoons, who passed through the intervals; but as the latter came up in most regular order, there was in some cases not room for a Troop to pass through, and I perfectly recollect a Squadron of the Royals inclining considerably to its left to clear our left wing, which, after crossing the hedge, became separated from the right, and some way down the slope encountered a Column of the Enemy on its own left …

The Column which was charged by the Royals was broken, and the greater part of both taken prisoners.

I do not recollect that the Dragoons charged the Column (it was a small one, apparently of not more than two Battalions) which the left wing of the 28th encountered after its separation from the right wing, but I distinctly saw them charge the heavy Reserve Column and break it. The greater number of the French threw down their arms when broken by the Cavalry.

The left wing of the 28th followed the Royal Dragoons some distance down the slope of the hill after their successful charge, and assisted in securing about 1,000 prisoners, whom they guarded to the rear of the hedge, and rejoined the right wing, which they found already formed about eighty paces to the rear of the hedge.[16]

At the same time the other two regiments, the Inniskillings and the Greys, emerged from the hedges. Lieutenant Wyndham, Scots Greys described this process:

We … wheeled into line and went, in not the most regular order, over and through the hedge in the best way we could, encountering at the same [time] the French fellows who had formed themselves at the hedge, and gave us their fire as we came up the hill. We had several killed and wounded at this moment from small [i.e. musket] shot, and our remark ever since that memorable day was the extraordinary manner in which bullets struck our swords as we ascended.[17]

As they emerged on the other side of the hedge the Greys, in 'irregular order', encountered the 92nd Highlanders falling back a short distance as the troopers passed through their ranks.[18] The Highlanders were in fact in a state of confusion, according to Captain Horace Seymour, an aide-de-camp to Uxbridge:

At the moment Sir Thomas Picton received the shot in his forehead which killed him, he was calling me to rally the Highlanders, who were for the instant overpowered by the masses of French Infantry, who were moving up to their right of the high road.[19]

Exactly what caused the Highlanders to retire is difficult to establish, since
Seymour appears to refer to a clash of arms which no other account corroborates; however, there is no disputing that the Scots Greys rode through
the Highlanders' ranks, carrying some of them with them, as Lieutenant
Winchester confirms:

> The Scots Greys came up at this moment, and doubling round our flanks
> and through our centre where openings were made for them, both
> Regiments charged together, calling out 'Scotland for ever', and the Scots
> Greys actually walked over this Column, and in less than three minutes it
> was totally destroyed, 2,000, besides killed and wounded, of them having
> been made prisoners, and two of their Eagles captured. The grass field in
> which the Enemy was formed, which was only an instant before as green
> and smooth as the 15 acres in Phoenix Park [in Dublin], was in a few min-
> utes covered with killed and wounded, knapsacks and their contents, arms,
> accoutrements, &c., literally strewed all over, that to avoid stepping on either
> one or the other was quite impossible; in fact one could hardly believe,
> had he not witnessed it, that such complete destruction could have been
> effected in so short a time.[20]

Crawford appears to corroborate Wyndham's recollection that the 92nd were
in the act of withdrawing when the Scots Greys approached, describing how
Highlanders 'turned [around] and ran into the charge with us'. Johnston confirms that the Highlanders accompanied the Greys in their charge:

> Our brave commander [Ponsonby] ... advanced at the head of his brigade
> whose heroic breasts panted to encounter the advancing enemy; we marched
> on, cock sure of victory, cheering and waving our glittering swords to meet
> the chosen troops of France as they rapidly advanced to meet us. We gave
> all speed to the noble animals on which we were seated, each anxious to be
> the first to exchange a blow with the impudent rebels who dared to advance
> upon us; as we advanced we came up with the Highland Brigade whom
> as I have before mentioned, formed the outposts of our brigade and the
> preceding night and who on our advance wheeled into open column right
> in front to enable us to pass through their lines; as soon as our brigade had
> passed through the intervals, they were ordered to wheel into line and wait
> further orders; but all entreaty on this head was in vain for instead of doing
> this they were so overjoyed to see us that they pulled off their bonnets and
> gave us three Scottish cheers, and called out 'Scotland for ever', and instead of
> remaining in the position ordered, these hardy sons of Scotia! mingled them-
> selves amongst us, some holding by our stirrups others ran like bucks down

the hill after us, and in this manner we penetrated and broke the first French line which was composed of veteran troops of France ...[21]

The Greys and 92nd, according to a subaltern of the latter regiment, cheered each other on as the cavalry passed through the infantry, while 'the 92nd seemed half mad, and ... it was with the greatest difficulty the Officers could preserve anything like order in the ranks'.[22]

In all, the Inniskillings and Greys passed through three out of four of Pack's regiments – the 1st Foot, the 42nd Highlanders and the 92nd – with the 2/44th too far east to find themselves in the path of the horsemen. It was not long before Lieutenant Wyndham of the Greys received his first wound a few yards on the other side of the hedge before his regiment ploughed into the infantry and continued down the hill, sabring many as they went. Two 6-pounders from Sir Robert Gardiner's troop advanced to support Ponsonby's charge, but the muddy ground proved so difficult to traverse, with 'the horses sinking up to their girths nearly', that this effort proved ineffectual.[23]

Within a few minutes the cavalry reached a second column, when Wyndham received a second wound – a shot through the foot.[24] Lieutenant Belcher of the 32nd recalled how:

> During this attack I observed one of the Scotch Greys, who either broke or lost his sword in an attack with one of the Cuirassiers, obliged to retreat along the line, pursued by his assailant, and when enabled to gain some distance from him, secure a sword and return to the attack, cutting down his pursuer.[25]

Wyndham, in agreement with other accounts, believed the 92nd Highlanders were withdrawing when the Greys reached the crest of the hill on which the hedge stood. He confirms that the 92nd then passed through the intervals of the cavalry and several accompanied the horsemen as they descended the ridge, shouting 'Scotland forever!', and relates what followed:

> In descending the hill, about three or four hundred yards from the hedge, the Greys came in contact with a 2nd French Column or Square, regularly formed, the fire from which they received [and which] did great execution. The loss at this moment in men and horses was most severe. This column was nearly destroyed, and the remainder of it were taken prisoners.[26]

A sergeant of the Scots Greys described the close-quarter fighting thus:

> When we came up the foot [i.e. infantry] fell back, then we were within 20 yards of them, then with sword in hand every one killing another, so

awful was the sight that it could be compared to nothing but the day of judgement ... I was the orderly sergeant so I was covering my captain and while he was engaged with a lancer a spearman came up to run him through, I struck the man and wounded him and saved my captain's life, he immediately made a push at me but I struck at him again and just as the spear was entering my breast I cut his arm off. When I was galloping off a rifleman shot my poor horse in the head which killed him on the spot, he fell (poor fellow) and me under him, there I was [a] prisoner but the Frenchman thinking it too much trouble to draw me from under the horse or perhaps thought I had no money left me ...[27]

In the course of the fighting, Sergeant Charles Ewart of the Scots Greys seized the eagle and Colours of the 45th Regiment, the formation occupying the leading position in Marcognet's divisional column:

The officer who carried it and I had a short contest for it; he thrust for my groin, I parried it off and cut him through the head; in a short time after whilst contriving how to carry the eagle (by folding the flag round my bridle arm and dragging the pole on the ground) and follow my regiment I heard a lancer coming behind me; I wheeled round to face him and in the act of doing so he threw his lance at me which I threw off to my right with my sword and cut him from the chin upwards through the teeth. His lance merely grazed the skin on my right side which bled a good deal but was well very soon. I was next attacked by a foot soldier who after firing at me, charged me with the bayonet; I parried it and cut him down through the head; this finished the contest for the eagle which I was ordered by General Ponsonby to carry to the rear.[28]

But in carrying on too far, the brigade encountered the grand battery – unable to fire with masses of friendly troops to its front – as well as cavalry further behind. Sergeant Johnston continues with one of the best first-hand descriptions of the fate of the Union Brigade:

We continued to charge until we broke through the 2nd line which we dispersed in the same manner; in this affair we suffered greatly both in men and horses, owing to a battery placed on an eminence to our left as we charged; which battery was silenced and took after totally annihilating the first line. After the above battery was silenced there was nothing to be heard but the clashing of swords and bayonets, and the cries of the dying and wounded. Here the carnage was dreadful beyond human conception. Many of our brigade after dispersing the second line advanced as far as the third, which was chiefly composed of lancers and cuirassiers, whose horses were quite fresh and which our brigade could not penetrate being few in number occasioned by the great loss sustained upon the advance, at this time we were obliged to form our retreat which was soon discovered by the before mentioned columns of lancers &c who made an oblique movement and got round between us and the British lines, by which a severe conflict [ensued and] from which few indeed of the Greys returned to give an account of what happened.[29]

Cornet James Gape of the Greys gives further insight into the failure of the regiment to return to friendly lines:

We were ordered up the hill, and after 3 hours, charged the enemy in the finest style possible. The men were only too impetuous, nothing could stop them, they all separated, each man fought by himself. I received a bullet from a Frenchman not 20 yards from me; it went through my cloak, and lodged in my saddle, which it has completely spoiled. I was the last person with Colonel Hamilton, who was just like a madman. He was crying 'Halt, halt, the Greys', when there was none to be seen. He then galloped completely into the French lines, where I thought it time to leave him; and make the best of my way back, which by the greatest good fortune I effected. If we had been supported by the light dragoons, we should have lost very few, and done three times the execution.[30]

Turning to the Inniskillings, on the Greys' left, Major Miller recorded that they sustained casualties from artillery fire even as they ascended the reverse slope, some troopers moving up on foot and then mounting their horses at the top. There they saw the French approaching the hedge.[31] The engagement then began in earnest and, in Miller's view, not a moment too soon:

On seeing us they hesitated, and were inclined to turn. A person in plain clothes, standing near the hedge close to the left of my Squadron, cried out, 'Now's your time', so over the hedge I went, and waited a moment or two for the men to collect, and then we were into the Column, in a second. There it was I received my bayonet wounds, and lost my horse. From our scattered state in getting over the hedge, I do not conceive we should have made any impression on our opposing Columns had they not been inclined to retire, and had they reached the hedge we could have done nothing with them.[32]

According to Lieutenant Colonel Muter, the Inniskillings engaged French infantry almost immediately after clearing the hedge, with the first of what two fellow officers later recalled as a total of three columns, encountered about 20–30 yards down the front face of the slope. According to Muter:

> The French column did not attempt to form square, nor was it, so far as we could judge, well prepared to repel an attack of cavalry. Our impression is that, from the formation of the ground, the cavalry was not aware what they were to attack, nor the infantry aware of what was coming upon them. Sir William Ponsonby knew, and I knew, he having called me to the front; other individuals may also have known, but not the mass. I have always considered it a splendid illustration of the maxim that the attacks of cavalry against columns of infantry should be unforeseen and unexpected ... The cavalry, on reaching the crest, or a moment before that, saw, from being a little raised on horseback, the solid columns, and increasing their speed, attacked with great impetuosity, cheering by the three countries, England, Scotland, and Ireland. The French Infantry made good use of their musquets [*sic*] and fire, but had not time to throw themselves into square; any attempt to do so would, I think, have been frustrated by the momentum which the Cavalry had [gained] by plunging over the hedges, and their increased ardour [which] by this time [they had] acquired.[33]

Major George De Lacy Evans, as an extra aide-de-camp of Ponsonby's, almost certainly accompanied his superior at the head of the Inniskillings. His description of the state of the French is illuminating:

> The Enemy's Column, near which I was, on arriving at the crest of the position seemed very helpless, had very little fire to give from its front or flanks, was incapable of deploying, must have already lost many of its Officers in coming up, was fired into, close, with impunity, by stragglers of our Infantry who remained behind. As we approached at a moderate pace the front and flanks began to turn their backs inwards; the rear of the Columns had already begun to run away...[34]

As with De Lacy Evans's account, Kempt's description of the charge does not identify a particular regiment; but from the position of the unit to which he refers, it must be the Inniskillings, as well:

> ... and almost at the same instant, as well as I can recollect, I saw a Regiment of Dragoons charge a Column or Square – for which it was I really cannot tell – and instantly break it.
>
> I well remember the intense anxiety we felt when we saw some of the gallant, but over-rash fellows, without stopping to form again, ride on

headlong at what appeared to me an immensely strong Corps of support in perfect order ...

The charge on the Square which was broken took place some distance in our front, but a little to the left, from which it is evident Sir William Ponsonby's Brigade must have passed our flanks ...[35]

Lieutenant Colonel Joseph Muter, of the Inniskillings, explained the means by which the regiment avoided trampling their comrades on foot:

As to passing through the [British] Infantry – part wheeled back to make room for the cavalry – part passed through the intervals of squadrons, and some, I fancy, got through rather irregularly. I recollect most distinctly the attack on a column of infantry by the Inniskillings. One circumstance I cannot forget – an infantry French soldier on his knees, deliberately taking aim at the Adjutant of the Inniskillings, who was close to me, in the midst of one of the French columns, and sending his bullet through his head.[36]

It was more than apparent that d'Erlon's massive columns were much better suited to an attack against other infantry, since they could bring to bear a broad frontage of muskets; but they were ill-suited to receive cavalry, for such a slow-moving mass of men could not readily form square in the narrow space available. Instead the French stumbled in the mud and trampled grain, many cut down by the sabres of pursuing cavalry.

The Royal Dragoons, meanwhile, whom Captain Radclyffe described as 'a magnificent sight',[37] struck Bourgeois' brigade, during which attack Captain Clark Kennedy seized the eagle and Colour of the leading regiment, the 105th:

I did not see the Eagle and Colour (for there were two Colours, but only one with an Eagle) until we had been probably five or six minutes engaged. It must, I should think, have been originally about the centre of the Column, and got uncovered from the change of direction. When I first saw it, it was perhaps about forty yards to my left a little in my front. The Officer who carried it and his companions were moving ... with their backs towards me, and endeavouring to force their way into the crowd.

I gave the order to my Squadron, 'Right shoulders forward, attack the Colour,' leading direct on the point myself. On reaching it, I ran my sword into the Officer's right side a little above the hip joint. He was a little to my left side, and he fell to that side with the Eagle across my horse's head. I tried to catch it with my left hand, but could only touch the fringe of the flag, and it is probable it would have fallen to the ground, had it not been prevented by the neck of Corporal Style's horse, who came up on my left at the instant, and against which it fell. Corporal Styles was Standard Coverer; his post was immediately behind me, and [it was] his duty to follow wherever I led. When I first saw the Eagle I gave the order, 'Right shoulders forward, attack the Colour,' and on running the Officer through the body I called out twice together, 'Secure the Colour, secure the Colour, it belongs to me.' This order was addressed to some men close to me, of whom Corporal Styles was one. On taking up the Eagle, I endeavoured to break the Eagle from off the pole with the intention of putting it into the breast of my coat; but I could not break it. Corporal Styles said, 'Pray, sir, do not break it,' on which I replied, 'Very well, carry it to the rear as fast as you can, it belongs to me.'[38]

According to De Lacy Evans, Ponsonby and many of his officers did their utmost to try to stop his brigade from moving up the opposite ridge, but on accepting failure they felt obliged to carry on with their men to continue their efforts to bring the brigade under control and return it safely to friendly lines.[39] Like the Greys and Royals, the Inniskillings lost all order. 'After charging through the Infantry,' Muter recalled, 'there was no line preserved – imperfect, at any rate.'[40] The attack accordingly pressed on, its momentum and enthusiasm carrying it up the French-held ridge and placing it amongst about twenty guns of the grand battery. The cavalry duly sabred the gunners and drivers with ferocity and cut the traces and harnesses of the gun teams,[41] having no means of limbering up and removing the guns. According to Lieutenant Ingilby, Royal Horse Artillery, watching from the summit of the ridge, Ponsonby's brigade held undisputed possession of the guns at the eastern end of the grand battery for fifteen or twenty minutes – more than adequate time, had it possessed the right tools – to spike the guns and render them useless for the remainder of the day.[42] This success, however, proved shortlived, for the Greys soon faced a spirited counter-charge by Milhaud's cuirassiers to their front and Jacquinot's lancers on their flank.[43] 'The French cavalry, cuirassiers leading,' Ross-Lewin described in his memoirs, 'then fell upon Sir William Ponsonby's brigade in very superior force, and a sharp and well-sustained, though unequal, combat ensued.'[44]

De Lacy Evans described the disaster which confronted the dragoons as a consequence of the sheer over-excitement and ill-discipline which continued to lead them – yet without any fresh supporting cavalry designed to facilitate their safe withdrawal:

The Enemy fled as a flock of sheep across the valley – quite at the mercy of the Dragoons. In fact, our men were out of hand. The General of the Brigade, his Staff, and every Officer within hearing, exerted themselves to the utmost to re-form the men; but the helplessness of the Enemy offered too great a temptation to the Dragoons, and our efforts were abortive.

It was evident that the Enemy's reserves of Cavalry … would soon take advantage of our disorder. Anticipating this, I went back for a moment to where Sir James Kempt was, to ask him to advance to cover our retreat, which appeared inevitable. He told me he would advance a couple of hundred yards, but that he could not quit the position altogether without orders. Besides, it was evident Infantry could not do it.

It was Vandeleur's Light Cavalry Brigade on the [Anglo-Allied] left which perhaps could have been useful at the moment by a more forward movement. But I did not see it. I galloped back to Sir William Ponsonby. The Dragoons were still in the same disorder, cutting up the remnant of the dispersed Infantry. We ascended the first ridge occupied by the Enemy, and passed several French cannon, on our right hand towards the road, abandoned [on] our approach by their gunners, and there were some French Squares of Infantry in rear.

The French Lancers continued to advance on our left in good order. If we could have formed a hundred men we could have made a respectable retreat, and saved many; but we could effect no formation, and were as helpless against their attack as their Infantry had been against ours. Everyone saw what must happen. Those whose horses were best or least blown, got away. Some attempted to escape back to our position by going round the left of the French Lancers. Sir William Ponsonby was of that number. All these fell into the hands of the Enemy. Others went back straight – among whom myself – receiving a little fire from some French Infantry towards the road on our left as we retired.

It was in this part of the transaction that almost the whole of the loss of the Brigade took place.[45]

At some point in this frenzied melee Ponsonby fell, though accounts differ slightly as to the precise circumstances of his death. According to Gronow, while returning to friendly lines Ponsonby, 'riding a very inferior horse, which was completely blown', became mired in boggy ground and fell to the sword of a sergeant of dragoons,[46] while Ross–Lewin attributed his demise to Polish lancers, who, charging from the flank 'came suddenly upon Sir William Ponsonby at a moment when he unfortunately was separated from his men, and, owing to the weakness of his horse, which stuck fast in the mire, he could not effect his escape, and was killed on the spot'.[47] The weakness of Ponsonby's horse is explained by one of his aides-de-camp, who thought the brigade commander:

… might perhaps have been spared to his country had he been better mounted. He rode a small bay hack. He had a handsome chestnut charger, which he meant to mount when real business began, but the groom or Orderly who had charge of the chestnut was not forthcoming or within call at the moment the General wanted his horse.[48]

Captain Charles Methuen, a Royal Dragoon who, it should be noted, was in Brussels at the time, claimed that Ponsonby was killed by a shot through the head while in the act of reforming his men after the first charge.[49] Sergeant Johnston of the Scots Greys offers an alternative version of Ponsonby's death:

I have to observe that on our advance to charge, the brave Sir W. Ponsonby who was charging at the head of his brigade, after he had the satisfaction of seeing his brigade annihilate the first line of Bonaparte's chosen troops, and advancing upon the second, while crying out 'Well done my brigade' was shot through the breast by a musket ball and instantly expired.[50]

Sergeant William Clarke's account substantiates this:

Brave General the Honourable Sir William Ponsonby being at our head the whole time, fought like a lion and when he was just in the act of crying out 'Well done Greys! This will be a glorious day' he received a musket ball through his heroic breast which laid him lifeless on the ground. Colonel Hamilton, our first colonel, was likewise killed on the same spot and 7 more of our officers.[51]

However Ponsonby actually met his end, it is clear he fell a considerable distance from friendly lines on the forward slope of the ridge, where his body was recovered the following day.[52] The commanding officer of the Greys also perished:

Our brave Colonel Hamilton who was a pattern of bravery to his officers and men, and a true honour to his country, was carried by the fleetings of his horse a good way in advance of his regiment, nor was he daunted by this, but advanced upon numerous bodies of the enemy alone; but alas his bravery could not protect him from the murdering shot and shell which swiftly flew as thick as hail amongst us. He also fell at the head of his regiment, a loss to his country not to be sustained without grief and his fate was most deeply deplored by his soldiers.[53]

Wyndham noted that the Greys could penetrate no further once the lancers engaged them. Indeed, without explicitly admitting it, the regiment had lost all cohesion:

The Greys, and I believe the Brigade, were not engaged with the cavalry beyond the lancers cutting up our wounded stragglers, &c, and some who were rallying; but depend upon it there was no order of 'parade', or any dressing of 'lines'. *Pêle-mêle* we went to work, and from the circumstance of our first, second, third, and fourth in command being *hors de combat*, rely upon it there was not the time for meditating who was to halt the Corps or Brigade. It was an affair of, you may almost say, a moment, but had its desired effect, though not according to Cocker or Hoyle.[54]

It appeared that the cavalry had achieved a spectacular success; but, like so often seen in the Peninsula, the cavalry officers, caught up in the exhilaration of the moment and incapable of reigning in the impetus of the attack, led the brigade to effective destruction. It may have been, as Tomkinson described it, 'one of the finest charges ever seen' but it rendered the Union Brigade effectively *hors de combat* for the rest of the day. He described the predicament that befell the three regiments thus:

> After their success they continued to advance, and moved forward in scattered parties up to the reserve of the enemy, and to the top nearly of the heights held by them. In this scattered state they were attacked by a heavy brigade of cavalry belonging to the 1st corps of the enemy and one of Lancers. They were obliged to retreat, and on our moving out in front of the left of the position, were seen riding back to our line in parties of twenty and thirty, followed by the enemy, whose horses were not blown, and suffering greatly from theirs being scarcely able to move.[55]

Still, some help was at hand, chiefly in the form of Major General Sir John Vandeleur's light cavalry brigade, which consisted of the 11th Light Dragoons, the 12th (Prince of Wales's) Light Dragoons, and the 16th Light Dragoons. During the morning, around 9 a.m., Vandeleur's brigade had been deployed on the Anglo-Allied left behind the farms of Papelotte and La Haye, with Major General Sir Hussey Vivian's light cavalry brigade on its left.[56] But in the course of the morning, with artillery taking its toll on Vandeleur's brigade, it had been ordered, together with Vivian's, to retire to the rear side of the slope and dismount for protection.[57] Now, during the Union Brigade's charge, Vandeleur's brigade was ordered to the right to support that effort, but owing to the sodden condition of the ground did not reach the area until after Ponsonby had begun his attack and was retiring to friendly lines in disorder.[58]

While the 11th Light Dragoons remained in reserve on the brow of the hill, the leading regiment, the 12th Light Dragoons, commanded by Lieutenant Colonel Frederick Ponsonby – second cousin to his fellow cavalry commander

– advanced in line into the area between the slopes held by the rival armies and engaged Durutte's column, then in the process of advancing east of the area swept by the Union Brigade. Major Barton described the scene:

> The left of our line being attacked by a strong Column of Infantry, com-
> manded by General Durutte, the Regiment was ordered to advance by its
> [commander] who, I believe, had orders to act discretionally. We advanced
> unperceived by the Enemy, and on passing the hedge-row, occupied by the
> Highlanders, immediately made a flank attack on the French Column. This
> attack was successful, and threw the Enemy into disorder, who retreated in
> the greatest confusion followed by the Regiment till we were stopped by
> their standing Columns of reserve on the opposite side of a ravine.[59]

All the while, the French plied the ranks of Vandeleur's brigade with artillery fire, Barton noting that it was of such an indiscriminate nature as to strike the retreating French infantry as well.[60] The 12th, together with elements of the 16th, both in line and with Vandeleur at the head of the latter, then 'charged and penetrated a mass of unsteady Infantry on the plain below',[61] in the process of which Major Tomkinson, 16th Light Dragoons, encountered two lines of muskets laid neatly on the ground where the Union Brigade had compelled the surrender of large numbers of infantry.[62] The 12th proceeded to engage French lancers in the flank, while the 16th, also in line and with Vandeleur at their head charged the lancers in their front, the two regiments forcing back the lancers to at least the base of the French ridge and possibly beyond, but sustaining heavy casualties in the process, including the severely wounded commander of the 16th, Lieutenant Colonel Hay.[63] Frederick Ponsonby later admitted the folly of engaging the French to such a distance:

> … a good many men fell on the crest of the French position. I know we
> ought not to have been there, and that we fell into the same error which
> we went down to correct, but I believe that this is an error almost inevitable
> after a successful charge, and it must always depend upon the steadiness of a
> good support to prevent serious consequences. In a great battle the support
> is at hand, and I am therefore firmly of opinion that although we sustained
> a greater loss than we should have done if our Squadrons had remained
> compact, the Enemy suffered a greater loss, was thrown into more confu-
> sion, and required more time to re-establish order, than if greater regularity
> had been preserved.[64]

Ponsonby, like Hay, fell severely wounded,[65] but their interventions had not been in vain, for they provided some support to the heavies. The Royal Dragoons, for instance, returned to friendly lines with part of the King's Dragoon Guards[66] from Somerset's brigade, whose charge we will examine shortly, even though these regiments began their respective advances on different sides of the Brussels–Genappe road.[67]

Various participants in Ponsonby's charge agree that his brigade took about 2,000 prisoners.[68] Elements of all three cavalry regiments appear to have escorted the captives to the rear, Major Macdonald of the 1st Foot recalling his men cheering the Royals and Greys as they brought back their quarry, while Muter, De Lacy Evans and Miller, all of the Inniskillings, claim a party of their regiment also formed a prisoner escort.[69] Having said this, many French soldiers ran off when it became apparent that their captors could not manage such an extensive haul. No time was lost in marching the prisoners on to Brussels, which helped stem the tide of unjustified panic spread by deserting Dutch-Belgian troops who claimed, according to Ross-Lewin, that 'the battle was lost, our army nearly cut to pieces, and the speedy entry of the victorious French inevitable'.[70] This is corroborated by Lieutenant Archibald Hamilton, Scots Greys, who noted in his diary that 'the Belgian cavalry ran off to Brussels, saying the army was defeated'.[71] Lieutenant John Sperling wrote similarly of Dutch-Belgian cavalry, stating they 'had taken flight, and spread the report that the battle was lost. Brussels was filled with alarm, and the road to it with confusion.'[72] In addition to prisoners, the brigade had inflicted heavy losses. The number of French killed is not known, but according to Captain Charles Methuen, Royal Dragoons, officers across Ponsonby's command believed that these numbered 2,000. 'There never was such a slaughter,' he wrote shortly after the battle.[73] In addition, the brigade had taken two Eagles.[74] Sometime around 2 or 3 p.m. an officer of the 42nd ordered Sergeant Ewart to leave the ranks and take his prize to Brussels – presumably for safekeeping. While in the process, one of Ponsonby's aides-de-camp overtook Ewart to announce the death of the brigade commander.[75]

A detachment of wounded or otherwise disabled Scots Greys and Inniskillings carried the prizes in triumph into Brussels, as Commissary Tupper recorded: 'One eagle was still on the pole of the standard, and was held up high in the air; the other had been broken off the pole in the scuffle, and was in the possession of two other men, who equally did their utmost to show their trophies to the best advantage.'[76]

Even before the survivors limped back to Allied lines their severely depleted ranks revealed that much of Wellington's cavalry could play no further role in the battle. True, they had blunted the attack of d'Erlon's corps, which represented almost 30 per cent of Napoleon's infantry and artillery on the field, and silenced the eighty guns of the grand battery – a quarter of which were dismantled or spiked according to Gronow.[77] It was also true that only Durutte's division, now facing Papelotte and La Haye – and therefore not in the path of either of the heavy cavalry brigades – remained intact; but even this remarkable achievement came at grievous cost. Captain Charles Methuen, Royal Dragoons, claimed that the Union Brigade charged seven different elements during the course of its attack, 'till there was little of the brigade left'.[78] Lieutenant Wyndham noted that the lancers killed and wounded as many of the Scots Greys as round shot and shell did, not least by striking the regiment in the rear.[79] According to Tomkinson, 'What with men lost and others gone to the rear in care of the wounded, and many absent from not knowing where to assemble, and other causes, there did not remain efficient above a squadron.'[80] In fact the brigade lost 616 killed and wounded, or 46 per cent of its strength, including of course its commander[81] – fully justifying Captain Methuen's description of its loss as 'immense'.[82]

Methuen may have been correct in claiming that his 'regiment behaved in the most gallant way', but his excuse that 'their ardour led them too far' hardly exonerates their officers' mismanagement. His claim, moreover, that 'the French cavalry were so frightened they did not dare take advantage of it'[83] also defied the tragic facts. Wyndham showed greater honesty: the Scots Greys were rendered effectively useless after their charge – so much so that in the evening, while occupying a new position west of the Brussels road and 'very much exposed to fire', they were capable only of facing their opposite numbers and attempting to intimidate them by mere feints, advancing and retiring. Methuen therefore deemed it fortunate that the large body of French cavalry fronting the Greys never actually attacked.[84] Still, a strong case may be made for the effectiveness of the two brigades' efforts. Captain Kennedy, Royal Dragoons, was not alone in praising the results of Uxbridge's cavalry:

> Do not consider it conceit on my part, but I cannot, as an individual concerned, think that justice has been done to that charge, and I ask you as an Officer of experience, how long the British Army could have held its position if the Count d'Erlon's Corps had been able to occupy the ridge that the head of their Columns had gained?
>
> I may be in error, but I cannot help thinking it the most critical moment of the day. But we had lost General [Ponsonby], there was no one to speak for us, and the Duke did not see the charge himself, his hands being at that time quite full enough, I believe, on the right centre.[85]

Sir Hussey Vivian, commander of the 6th (Light) Cavalry Brigade – and thus in a strong position to render a sound judgement upon the matter – unequivocally declared Ponsonby's charge an overwhelming success:

The desperate attack of the Brigade of Heavy Cavalry under the command of Major General Sir William Ponsonby on the Columns of French Infantry advancing against our position on the left of the [Brussels–Genappe] road, and its complete success, had an influence on the Battle infinitely greater than has ever been admitted; indeed, having myself witnessed from my position on the left the complete success of the charge, and the consequences to the French Infantry, I cannot but consider it as one of the most important features of the Battle.[86]

The Household Brigade

The 1st (Heavy) Cavalry, better known as the Household Brigade, was composed of, from right to left, the 1st Life Guards, the 1st (King's) Dragoon Guards, and the 2nd Life Guards, with the Royal Horse Guards (Blues) occupying a second line to the rear.[87] The whole was led by Major General Lord Edward Somerset, with a strength of 1,319 sabres and stood with its left beside the Brussels–Genappe road, about 300 yards south of the crossroads in a large expanse of standing grain.[88] Prior to receiving orders to advance, the Household Brigade was formed in columns of squadrons and dismounted, resting on the reverse side of the ridge with the French hidden from view.[89] They could hear the sound of battle and watched as the walking wounded passed to the rear or dropped dead. Behind the brigade's position artillery pounded the earth. 'Sometimes the turmoil of battle appeared greatest on our right; at other times on our left,' recalled Private Thomas Playford, 2nd Life Guards:

and at length there was a tremendous thunder of cannon which drowned every other sound, immediately in front of us; but the rising ground before us concealed from our view what was taking place; yet we naturally concluded a powerful attempt was being made to force the centre of the British army; and as there were no troops in our rear, we viewed ourselves as a last resource to defeat this project. The conflict was raging violently beyond the rising ground in front of us, and the roar of artillery with the report of small arms was incessant, yet we could not see what was taking place; but the commander of the cavalry, the Earl of Uxbridge, rode forward to gain a full view of the conflict and to watch the progress of events, that he might bring our brigade of a thousand powerful swordsmen into action under the most favourable circumstances and at a moment when a charge of heavy cavalry was particularly wanted.[90]

Uxbridge watched as Dubois's cuirassiers ascended the slope south of the Wavre road and to the right of La Haye Sainte. He thereupon ordered the brigade to mount and immediately form line. Precisely where he placed himself is not known, but he had a reputation for always maintaining a post at the front of a charge.[91]

The brigade was meant to have the support of a Hanoverian regiment known as the Duke of Cumberland's Hussars, under a British officer, Colonel Hake, but as soon as the brigade was set in motion this regiment fled the field, riding as far as Brussels.[92] Lieutenant Waymouth of the 2nd Life Guards remembered their position and conduct thus:

> They were in rear of the 2nd Life Guards, their left not far from the *chaus-sée*, and immediately in front of the hedge or skirt of the forest that was between the field of battle and the village of Waterloo. My thoughts at the time were what could possess them to sit upon their horses to be knocked over by cannon balls when they saw our Brigade [lying] upon the ground. I always have understood that this Regiment was ordered to charge in our support, but that when we attacked they ran away.[93]

Let us examine each regiment's experience in turn.

Lieutenant Colonel William Fuller, commanding the 1st Dragoon Guards no sooner had his regiment in motion than he fell dead at its front.[94] Undaunted, the squadrons carried on. Sergeant Major Page recorded:

> We overturned everything, both infantry and cavalry that came in our way, such cutting and hacking never was before seen. When the French lines broke and turned and ran, our regiment being too eager, followed the French cavalry while the cannon and musketry was sweeping our flank. Many fell and our ranks suffered severely ... We lost but few men by their swords; it was the grapeshot and the musketry that cut us down before we got amongst them. We had to charge to meet them so far over heavy ground that many of our horses were stuck in deep mud. The men were obliged to jump off, leave them and seek their safety away from the cannon fire. My mare carried me in famous style, she got a light wound in her off hind leg by a French lancer. I was after a French officer who was riding away from me, I came up to him and he thrust his lance at me, I turned it with my sword, it glanced down and cut my mare below the hock of the hind leg.[95]

Captain William Elton left a superb account of the Dragoon Guards' charge:

The infantry suddenly broke out of their line into solid squares & we saw the crests of the cuirassiers. The line without waiting for any particular orders, drew swords & set off at full speed. Every squadron took the interval of our infantry which was next to them and there the right squadron & mine paired off & I never saw them more.

What particular resistance they met with at first, I never could ascertain, but every officer belonging to them was killed. Owing perhaps to their going faster than the Life Guards who were, or ought to have been upon their right flank, the enemy flying & drawing them on without order & afterwards surrounding them with their very superior numbers of cuirassiers & lancers. The squadron I had the honour to command fortunately met with resistance early & ground which could not be traversed at that pace. The enemy stood very well till we came within 20 yards. They had every appearance of being picked men, extremely large & well mounted; which I believe was the case, as they were cuirassiers of the Imperial Guard [*sic*]. Our men setting up a general shout, many of them went about immediately. Those who could escape lost no time; the others were blocked up in a corner, a large fence on one side & a broad ravine on the other, these were all killed by our people, but their cuirass secured them to such a degree, that not one blow told out of five.

Here Lord Uxbridge had a round with one of their officers & though two of our men charged him and gave him plenty of cuts & thrusts on both sides, the man escaped into the lane where he was killed by the others. Lord E[dward] Somerset who charged with us, crossed the ravine & was followed by all of us whose horses could leap in such slippery ground. Many dragoons lost their lives by falling in, others went round. The lane leading from the Duke of Wellington's position into the plain was quite choked up with cuirassiers & our men mixed & engaged with each other. At length it was tolerably well cleared & Lord Edward having heard that the greater part of the K[ing's] D[ragoon] G[uards] were broke & gone away without order into the enemy's lines, ordered me to rally & halt as many as possible, which was done, but too late, as no one seemed to know what was become of the right squadron and other broken troops & the ground in the plain where they had so far advanced was covered with immense columns of the enemy. Scarcely a man belonging to the right of the regiment has returned. Colonel Fuller went with them at least a mile in advance of the Duke's position, behind the whole French army. Part of the left squadron did the same, but the resistance there was not so great. The colonel & all the men with him were entirely surrounded & cut to pieces. He was heard calling to his men to advance, without any support & not a squadron of the regiment together. Poor Bringhurst was seen lying dead on the side of the hill between the English & French position. It is reported that he killed four of the enemy's lancers, who seem to have attacked him [from] behind. He had a wound in the side near the loins from a lance or sword, which from the man's report who examined his body, must have been instantly mortal.[96]

Lieutenant John Hibbert's account corroborates Elton's:

Our brigade, never having been on service before, hardly knew how to act. They knew they were to charge, but never thought about stopping at a proper time, so that after entirely cutting to pieces a large body of Cuirassiers double their number, they still continued to gallop on instead of forming up and getting into line; the consequence was that they got among the French infantry and artillery, and were miserably cut up. They saw their mistake too late, and a few (that is about half the regiment) turned and rode back again; no sooner had they got about five hundred yards from the French infantry than they were met by an immense body of lancers who were sent for the purpose of attacking them in the way. Our men rendered desperate by their situation. They were resolved either to get out of the scrape or die rather than be taken prisoners, so they attacked them, and three troops cut their way through them; about a troop were killed or taken prisoners. In this affair poor Fuller lost his life; his horse was killed by a lance, and the last time he was seen he was unhurt but dismounted. Of course the lancers overtook him and killed him, for our men were on the full retreat; he made a sad mistake in pursuing the cuirassiers so far.[97]

At about the same time as Kempt's brigade moved through the hedge on the opposite side of the road, the 2nd Life Guards soon encountered cuirassiers near the Ohain–Wavre road,[98] and engaged them in a melee whose sound some of the wounded likened to 'the ringing of ten thousand blacksmiths' anvils,'[99] and resulted in heavy losses to the French.[100] One eyewitness claims a trooper named Dakin, of the 2nd Life Guards, fought two cuirassiers while dismounted, striking each in the head.[101]

Further evidence that French heavy cavalry reached as far as the Wavre road is provided by Kincaid of the 95th, who saw them at disconcertingly close hand just as Kempt's brigade were moving forward. He remembered Kempt:

… galloping along the line, animating the men to steadiness. He called to me by name, where I happened to be standing on the right of our battalion, and desired 'that I would never quit that spot.' I told him that 'he might depend upon it': and in another instant I found myself in a fair way of keeping my promise more religiously than I intended; for, glancing my eye to the right,

> I saw the next field covered with the cuirassiers, some of whom were making directly for the gap in the hedge, where I was standing. I had not hitherto drawn my sword, as it was generally to be had at a moment's warning; but, from its having been exposed to the last night's rain, it had now got rusted in the scabbard, and refused to come forth! I was in a precarious scrape. Mounted on my strong Flanders mare, and with my good old sword in my hand, I would have braved all the chances without a moment's hesitation; but, I confess, that I felt considerable doubts as to the propriety of standing there to be sacrificed, without the means of making a scramble for it.[102]

In fact he had no need to draw his sword, for Kincaid went on to witness the 2nd Life Guards wreaking havoc among the cavalry and infantry on the east side of the Genappe road:

> … the next moment the cuirassiers were charged by our household brigade; and the infantry in our front giving way at the same time, under our terrific shower of musketry, the flying cuirassiers tumbled in among the routed infantry, followed by the life-guards, who were cutting away in all directions. Hundreds of the infantry threw themselves down, and pretended to be dead, while the cavalry galloped over them, and then got up and ran away. I never saw such a scene in all my life.[103]

The left of the 2nd Life Guards veered onto the Genappe road and proceeded up it to the crossroads and down it in the direction of La Belle Alliance, while the bulk of the regiment proceeded up the rear of the slope, passing to the left of the 8th King's German Legion Line and, nearer the crest, the 1st King's German Legion Light Battalion, both of Ompteda's brigade, the whole of which had formed in square for protection against the cuirassiers. The regiment then crossed the Wavre road and encountered cuirassiers on the other side, which they pushed across the road above La Haye Sainte and down the slope to the right of Kempt's brigade. In this endeavour they were joined by the King's Dragoon Guards, who had also crossed the road to the north of the farm. The two regiments became intermingled with part of the 1st Dragoons from Ponsonby's brigade, in so doing losing much of their cohesion but completely clearing the area of French cavalry. Lieutenant Colonel Sir Andrew Barnard of the 1/95th noted that those cuirassiers finding themselves to the rear of the Rifles' position struggled amidst the abatis and lost a number of men to the 2nd Life Guards in that area.[104]

Lieutenant Waymouth is certain that his regiment – and at least part of the 1st Dragoon Guards – passed east of La Haye Sainte during its charge against d'Erlon's advance, and thus were not as well aligned with the brigade as the

1st Life Guards and the Dragoon Guards;[105] indeed, so little so that the regiment in fact passed well east of the road, there discovering a roofless hovel – probably a farmer's shed of some sort – containing a small group of men from the 2nd Light Battalion of the King's German Legion. This clearly comprised a detachment from La Haye Sainte – including one officer whom Waymouth recognised, sitting on one of the remaining rafters. Waymouth also confirms that troopers from the Royals and the Inniskilling Dragoons from Ponsonby's brigade became intermingled with men from the 2nd Life Guards.[106]

Somewhere on the slope east of La Haye Sainte, Corporal Shaw of the 2nd Life Guards, a man of powerful build and a champion pugilist, is reputed to have fought two cuirassiers simultaneously and taken an eagle, which he subsequently lost.[107] Corporal Webster, contributing further to Shaw's mythical status, claimed he observed Shaw in single combat with a cuirassier who 'gave point' – that is, thrust, rather than slashed with, his sword. Shaw parried it and cut right through his opponent's brass helmet to the chin, whereupon 'his face fell off him like an apple'.[108]

According to Colonel Sir John Elley, Shaw taught his fellow Life Guardsmen 'not to use their swords against the cuirassiers, but to strike them on the side of the head with the basket hilt by which the weight of their armour bore them from their equilibrium, also when they retreated, to cut at the back of the neck, by which so many were decapitated.'[109] The cuirass did protect the abdomen from cuts and thrusts, such that bodies discovered after the battle 'were dreadfully cut to pieces about the arms ...' Some soldiers reported their officers calling out 'cut at the bridle arm'.[110]

Private Thomas Playford, of the same regiment, described Shaw as almost larger than life:

> Shaw was six feet high, and possessed a powerful athletic frame. His features were large and rather course, his countenance indicated a measure of good nature as well as of determined purpose. His broad chest, muscular arms, and large boney hands, denoted a powerful antagonist to be encountered in close combat. He was not only well versed in the use of the broad sword and could use the shining blade with a speed of a flash of light, but he also knew the science of pugilism, and few men could stand before him. A blow from his sword would have been dangerous and disabling if not fatal to an armed man and a stroke from his clenched fist dreadful to a weak man.[111]

Shaw did not survive the day, but the form of his demise is unclear. According to one source, he was wounded by a shell fragment and taken to the yard at La Haye Sainte.[112] Lieutenant Wayworth, on the other hand, recalled that when the 2nd Life Guards proceeded to the east of the *chaussée* and passed the Rifles near La Haye Sainte, they clashed with scattered groups of cuirassiers, whom Shaw fought ferociously before being shot by a trooper with a carbine at some distance to his left.[113] Ensign Marten declared his certainty that Shaw was killed in the first charge. On the other hand, he related the alternative theory:

> It was said he did not die at the moment, but received in that charge several wounds of which he lingered till night. He could not have been alive the next morning, because I was ordered, in company with the Assistant-Surgeon, to collect our wounded, and see them safely conveyed to Brussels, which I did, and Shaw was certainly not one.[114]

Further west, on the brigade's right, the 1st Life Guards 'in perfect line'[115] passed between the squares of Kielmannsegge's Hanoverian infantry and veered obliquely to the right as they passed over the Wavre road in the direction of La Haye Sainte before cutting through the ranks of cuirassiers. According to Assistant Surgeon John Haddy James, 1st Life Guards, Captain Edward Kelly not only killed the colonel of the 1st Cuirassiers and cut off his epaulettes as a trophy, but personally dispatched as many as a dozen adversaries.[116]

Benjamin Haydon, the famous artist, recorded an account of another trooper, Hodgson, in hand-to-hand combat during Somerset's charge:

> The first cut he gave was on the cuirass, which Hodgson thought was silver-lace; the shock nearly broke his arm. Watching the cuirassier, however, he found he could move his own horse quicker; so, dropping the reins, and guiding his horse with his knees, as the cuirassier at last gave point, Hodgson cut his sword-hand off, and then dashing the point of his sword into the main's throat turned it round and round ... As he rode back, a French regiment opened and let him pass at full gallop, then closed and fired a volley, but never hit him or his horse. Then a mounted French officer attacked him; Hodgson cut his horse at the nape and as it fell, the officer's helmet rolled off, and Hodgson saw a bald man and grey hairs; the officer begged for mercy, but at that instant a troop of lancers were coming down full gallop, so Hodgson clove his head in two at a blow and escaped. He said the recollection of the old man's white hairs pained him often. Before he got back to the British lines, a lancer officer charged him and missing his thrust came right on to Hodgson and his horse. Hodgson got clear and cut the man's head off at the neck at one blow. The head bobbed on to his haversack, where he kept the bloody stain.[117]

Corporal Richard Coulter, 1st Life Guards, wrote this account of his regiment's charge a month after the event:

> I found my little knowledge which I had of the Highland sword of great benefit to me. I received a cut on my bridle hand, had a sword run through my jacket in the shoulder but did not touch my skin; my horse had his eye almost cut out. We drove them under their own cannon into their own lines and stay'd there too long, for the infantry began to play upon us. We retired and left but 3 or 4 behind and they were shot. I think more in this charge fell by sword; this was a glorious charge, we retired and was huzza'd by the infantry which they had threatened with destruction and [a] regiment of Belgian cavalry, our swords reeked with French blood.[118]

Somerset also described the 1st Life Guards' charge. Clashing with the cuirassiers, he remembered, was:

> … like two walls, in the most perfect lines he ever saw; and I believe this line was maintained throughout. A short struggle enabled us to break through them, notwithstanding the great disadvantage arising from our swords, which were full six inches shorter than those of the Cuirassiers, besides its being the custom of our Service to carry the swords in a very bad position whilst charging, the French carrying theirs in a manner much less fatiguing, and also much better for either attack or defence. Having once penetrated their line, we rode over everything opposed to us.[119]

The 1st Life Guards then carried on down onto the Genappe road about halfway down the ridge. Here, having already suffered heavy losses from their earlier contact with cuirassiers, they now sustained worse from light infantry who, lining the high banks of the sunken road, shot down many troopers from above.[120] Still, in the course of their charge the Household Brigade 'did great execution' in Somerset's words, and succeeded in driving off the opposing cavalry to the opposite ridge, to which point they continued their pursuit.[121] But in doing so the 1st Life Guards had clearly penetrated too far behind French lines where, as Assistant Surgeon John Haddy recorded, 'they were cut to pieces', effectively condemning themselves to horrific losses, much of them borne by the right squadron of the Dragoon Guards, most of which were killed or wounded.[122]

The Blues rode in the second line of support behind the 2nd Life Guards and the King's Dragoon Guards. The first obstacle encountered by the Blues was the road running along the top of the ridge which the horses found too wide to leap across and the banks too high to negotiate; once across, they next had to skirt round to the left of La Haye Sainte, while the King's Dragoon

Guards went round its right – which meant that the Household Brigade was divided into two by this major obstacle.[123] The Blues appear to have joined the front line of the brigade during the course of the charge and, having maintained their ranks, were able to encourage the other regiments not to proceed any further. Surgeon David Slow of the Horse Guards recalled how:

> The clash of our horse against the picked mounted troops of Bonaparte was something I shall never forget. It made me hold my breath. For some minutes no one could tell how it was going to end. Neither side appeared to give way an inch. At last to our great joy the French right wheeled about and rode off in disorder, our men after them.[124]

The Household Brigade withdrew back up the ridge and, Uxbridge records, resumed its former position on the reverse slope.[125]

Exhausted from their engagement with the cuirassiers and stricken with horrific casualties – 632 killed and wounded, or 48 per cent of their total – it was no wonder Private Joseph Lord described the action as 'terrible beyond description'.[126] Uxbridge may very well have ridden up to the 2nd Life Guards to praise them for 'surpassing all his expectations',[127] but the fact remained that for the remainder of the day – that is to say, before the decisive outcome of the battle became apparent to all and as a result of which all command-ers' tactical blunders could be forgiven – some officers blamed Uxbridge for having 'thrown away' the Household Brigade by sending it forward without adequate support.[128] Still, despite the brigade's severe losses, its sacrifice paid an important dividend for, as Captain William Elton, King's Dragoon Guards, correctly noted, Somerset's regiments prevented the French from occupying a vital part of the Anglo-Allied position:

> The French ... would have had possession of it in a few minutes, had it not been for our brigade making a rapid charge, which took such effect, and repulsed them, and drove them to confusion, which lightened the hearts of our infantry, and encouraged them to rally together, which was of great service at that point.[129]

With d'Erlon's attack now in tatters, apart from the area around Hougoumont, the French paused to consider their next move. Meanwhile, the rumble of the grand battery's cannonade had not gone unheard by Grouchy, 11 miles to the east at Wavre, where some of the marshal's staff urged him to march to the sound of the guns on the grounds that the Emperor had clearly made contact with Wellington and now required reinforcement. Grouchy, not yet having received revised orders, refused on the basis that his orders bade him pursue the Prussians; besides, he was at that time already engaged with Thielemann's III Corps. The Prussians, of course, heard the sound, also, and, determined to fulfil his promise that he march to Wellington's assistance, Blücher was already en route, leading his troops through the morning and offering encourage-ment as his guns and wagons struggled through lanes – much more modest than the proper roads available to the British and French – made sodden by the previous night's torrential rain. The Prussians were unseen by both friend and foe at Waterloo, so when the vanguard came distantly into view around 1.30 p.m. neither side were aware that this constituted only a fraction of the tens of thousands of Prussians on the march, some bound for Wellington's left, and others for the village of Plancenoit, on Napoleon's right flank, to the east of Rossomme. The bulk of Blücher's troops trudged slowly under difficult conditions but, all-importantly, unopposed.

PART 4

8

THE FRENCH ARTILLERY BOMBARDMENT:
'UNCEASING DESTRUCTION'[1]

The intensity of the artillery bombardment unleashed by the 246 French guns at Waterloo had scarcely any parallel in the Napoleonic Wars; certainly the British, with only 157 guns of their own, plus one rocket troop, had never experienced anything like it in the Peninsula. In fact, artillery fire inflicted greater losses on Wellington's forces than any other form of fighting. Hardly surprising, then, that Ensign William Thain, 33rd Foot, one of the regiments most severely affected, should declare: 'We all thought from the strength of the enemy and the manner in which their artillery mowed us down in the evening that we had lost the day ...'[2] Not only did the French enjoy superiority in numbers of artillery pieces, Wellington's decision to ban counter-battery fire[3] meant that only riflemen enjoyed the sort of range necessary to target French gunners. Consequently, apart from those batteries attacked by British cavalry, discussed earlier, Napoleon's artillery crews were generally free to fire without molestation throughout the course of the day. Having said this, various British battery commanders violated Wellington's orders not to engage in counter-battery fire.[4]

No proper study of Waterloo is possible without at least some treatment of the continual French artillery bombardment, whose intensity prompted Lieutenant Colonel Augustus Frazer, commander of Wellington's horse artillery, to identify the significant role played by gunnery at Waterloo: 'The greater part of the action may be called an action of artillery,' he wrote in a letter the day after the battle.[5] Sir Robert Gardiner, another senior officer in the Royal Artillery and thus in a position to render a competent assessment of his opponents' gunnery, judged French batteries 'admirably served throughout the day' and 'causing dreadful havoc'.[6] Captain Arthur Kennedy agreed, observing that 'never was any cannonade known so heavy nor their guns better directed',[7] while Captain Horace Churchill, 1st Foot Guards, described the cannonade as 'butchery'.[8] One can only speculate at the still more horrific effects of such concentrated fire had the ground been dry, for as a result of the previous night's torrential downpour shot tended to bury itself in the sodden ground on first impact rather than bound along the ground, killing and maiming anything in its wake.[9] Lieutenant John Pratt of the 39th Foot noted how 'Several large shells ... fell with precision in the midst of us, but the ground being very soft, generally buried themselves deep, and did not do as much mischief as under other circumstances might have been the case ...'[10] Major John Oldfield recorded in his journal that while the fire was very heavy, 'few of the enemy's shells burst as they fell and several were buried in the soft ground without bursting. Whilst we were on the right a shell burst in the midst of us, it was harmless as we were dispersed and rode off before it burst.'[11] Captain T. W. Taylor, 10th Hussars, echoed this view: 'While on the ridge of the hill there were a good many shells sent over us or pitched near us,' he recorded. '[T]he latter did no harm, as they buried in the mud and burst upwards.'[12]

British officers' and soldiers' accounts of Waterloo refer to almost unabated heavy fire, from 11 a.m. to 8 p.m., with one of the opening shots of French artillery smashing to pieces the head of a rifleman of the 95th[13] and one of the last, as is well known, severely injuring – but not severing, as popular legend would have it – the leg of the Earl of Uxbridge. Major Latour, 23rd Light Dragoons, organised the small party which took Uxbridge from the ground after he fell wounded.[14]

Injury and death could manifest themselves in gruesome form: Captain Norman Ramsay, Royal Artillery, lost his head to a round shot at Waterloo,[15] as did a rifleman of the 95th. In the latter case, according to Kincaid, 'A cannon-ball ... came from the Lord knows where, for it was not fired at us, and took the head off our right-hand man.'[16] Lieutenant Phillips of the Light Dragoons also lost his head to a round shot,[17] while Captain Hay, 33rd Foot was cut in two by a like projectile that spattered the brains of another officer across Lieutenant Pattison's shako and face.[18] A captain in the 40th Foot noted not simply a decapitation, but an extraordinarily high casualty rate inflicted by a single shot:

> Towards the evening, whilst the Regiment was in open column, a round shot from the Enemy took off the head of a Captain (Fisher) near me, and striking his Company on the left flank, put *hors de combat* more than twenty-five men. This was the most destructive shot I ever witnessed during a long period of service.[19]

Of course not all wounds proved fatal – at least not instantly: one of Captain Alexander Mercer's gunners, for instance, was hit by a round shot thus: 'I shall never forget the scream the poor lad gave when struck. It was one of the last they fired, and shattered his left arm to pieces as he stood between the wagons. That scream went to my very soul …' Mercer sought to calm his men by showing no emotion, ordering them to 'Stand to their front' as he paced back and forth, while a medical officer treated the wounded gunner.[20] Lieutenant Cromie of Major Bean's battery of 6-pounders lost both his legs to a round shot,[21] while an aide-de-camp to Lord Uxbridge recorded how he 'was knocked off the perch by a cannon-shot which carried off a portion of my neck, paralysed my right ear and right nostril, and you will say the right side of my memory also'.[22] Ensign George Keppel of the 3/14th, only just 16 at Waterloo, narrowly escaped death at the hands of a round shot, as Lieutenant Colonel Tidy, his battalion commander, recorded: 'He was a boy in every sense of the word. Nay, I have heard he was flogged at Westminster [School] only four months before he was at Waterloo.' While sitting on a drum a round shot struck the horse Keppel was stroking, broke the bridle bit and knocked the young ensign to the ground: 'The animal plunging in her agony,' Tidy continued, 'threw the square into great confusion, and her misery was speedily put an end to by the soldiers' bayonets.'[23] Wheatley provides one of the more moving accounts of wounds caused by artillery fire:

> One could almost feel the undulation of the air from the multitude of cannon shot. The first man who fell was five files on my left. With the utmost distortion of feature he lay on his side and shrivelling up every muscle of the body he twirled his elbow round and round in acute agony, then dropped lifeless, dying as it's called a death of glory, heaving his last breath on the field of fame. *Dieu m'engarde!* [*sic: Dieu m'en garde* – God forbid!][24]

The geographical extent of the French cannonade is also noteworthy, for no sector of the front remained quiet. As Sergeant Archibald Johnston, Scots Greys, recalled, 'a very heavy cannonade was commenced from the French batteries on our right wing …' and within an hour and a half he noted how the firing had extended across the whole front.[25] While French batteries inflicted the majority of casualties on those troops deployed on the Allied centre and right, Napoleon's guns did not entirely spare those positioned on Wellington's left. Major General Sir Hussey Vivian's brigade of light cavalry, stationed in that sector during the morning and for much of the afternoon observed that 'we were exposed to a very severe cannonade which they [the men] stood in a manner the most creditable …'[26] but which required him to shift the brigade to reduce the formation's losses. Thereafter, as Sergeant Matthew Colgan, 18th Hussars, observed, the cannonade had 'no effect further than dashing the earth in our faces, some [shot] falling short and others over-reaching us'.[27]

Contemporary correspondence is rich in descriptions of the sight, sound and effects of French artillery fire. Private Joseph Lord of the 1st Life Guards described a surreal storm of iron spheres which 'flew like hailstones',[28] one of which smashed the head of a horse in Mercer's artillery troop, covering that captain with blood and brains. By the evening of the 19th his saturated trousers had hardened to a point that obliged him to ride side-saddle for the entire advance to Paris.[29] Observers also commented on the distinctive sound of round shot whizzing through the air. A medical officer, having no comprehension of the source of all the noise around him, made frantic enquiries to Mercer. 'He was close to me as we ascended the slope,' Mercer recalled:

> and, hearing this infernal carillon about his ears, began staring round in the wildest and most comic manner imaginable, twisting himself from side to side, exclaiming, 'My God, Mercer, what is that? What is all this noise? How curious! – how very curious!' And then when a cannon-shot rushed hissing past, 'There! – there! What is it all?'[30]

Quite apart from the sensation of hearing a round shot, which weighed between 6lb and 12lb, depending on the type of artillery piece which projected it several hundred yards, the careful observer at Waterloo – like Lieutenant Edward Byam, 15th Hussars, who saw two separate shots emerge from the mouth of a gun and pass near his head[31] – could actually track its flight if he followed its path from the mouth of the gun which fired it. As for the actual killing power of such ordnance, a single round shot proved more than capable of rendering several men *hors de combat*. Lieutenant William Sharpin witnessed his battery commander die at the hands of a round shot:

> Captain Bolton at the time he was killed was on horseback. I was standing on his left side with my hand on his stirrup talking with him. The shot from a French Battery at that time flew very thick amongst us, and one passed between me and Bolton, upon which he coolly remarked that he thought we had passed the greatest danger for that day; but scarcely were the words uttered before another ball, which I saw strike the ground a little in front of us, hit him in his left breast. The shot having first severely wounded the horse in the left shoulder caused the animal to stagger backwards, thereby preventing my catching poor Bolton as he fell from his horse.[32]

Other correspondents noted the horrific phenomenon of round shot striking horses. One of the first shots fired destroyed the limber of a battery, killed the sergeant and passed through the shoulders of Lieutenant William Ingilby's charger just above his knees.[33] While resting his arm between the ears of a fellow officer's mount, the animal itself leaning against Mercer's thigh, a round shot 'smashed the horse's head to atoms. The headless trunk sank to the ground ...'[34] Captain Rudyard, a Royal Artillery officer, lost his horse to a round shot that passed through his mount behind the saddle flap.[35] Lieutenant Samuel Phelps, Royal Artillery, wrote of 'mounting my horse, one foot in the stirrup, when a cannon shot struck him dead having gone through him'.[36] In Mercer's troop one such animal lost the lower part of its head beneath the eyes and yet remained on its feet, pressing itself against the lead horse of one of the ammunition wagons. Mercer ordered the farrier to dispatch the poor animal, which he did with a thrust of his sword to the heart.[37] In another instance, a round shot, bounding along the ground and passing over the top of the ridge, severed the leg of Lieutenant Colonel Dalrymple, commander of the 15th Hussars, before passing through the body of Sir Colquhoun Grant's horse.[38]

Occasionally a round shot would strike an ammunition wagon, with predictable results, as Wheatley described in his diary:

> An ammunition cart blew up near us, smashing men and horses. I took a calm survey of the field around and felt shocked at the sight of broken armour, lifeless bodies, murdered horses, shattered wheels, caps, helmets, swords, muskets, pistols, still and silent. Here and there a frightened horse would rush across the plain trampling on the dying and the dead. Three or four poor wounded animals standing on three legs, the other dangling before [them]. We killed several of these unfortunate beasts and it would have been an equal Charity to have perform'd the same operation on the wriggling, feverish, mortally lacerated soldiers as they rolled on the ground.[39]

The destructive capacity of Napoleon's guns may best be examined from the perspectives of the three major arms of Wellington's forces: infantry, cavalry and artillery – though even formations as small as the Duke's staff headquarters did not escape harm. A round shot unhorsed Lieutenant Colonel Charles Fox Canning, one of Wellington's aides-de-camp, who died a few moments later after enquiring into the Duke's safety,[40] while Colonel Alexander Gordon was also knocked from his horse, living only long enough to be carried to the rear in a blanket,[41] the stretcher not yet a feature of British medical services. Early in the day, near a solitary tree opposite La Haye Sainte,[42] Colonel Sir William De Lancey, Deputy Quartermaster General and as such a member of the headquarters staff, suffered a similar fate: struck by a round shot on the back by his right shoulder, the force of the impact unhorsed and cast him several yards. Soldiers conveyed De Lancey, who perceived the wound as mortal,[43] in a blanket to a barn in the rear of the battlefield where orderlies dressed his wound before sending him on to Brussels, where he subsequently died from internal injuries.[44]

Unquestionably, the greatest proportion of the destructive power of French artillery fell upon the squares of infantry lining the slopes of Mont St Jean: 'In order to destroy our squares,' Wheatley noted in his diary, 'the enemy filled the air with shells, howitzers and bombs, so that every five or six minutes, the whole Battalion lay on its face then sprang up again when [the danger] was over.'[45] Ensign Edward Macready's anecdotes of death in the square of the 30th Foot at the hands of French artillery bears study:

> When [Major Thomas] Chambers fell, his friend [Lieutenant Benjamin] Nicholson threw himself on the body, and sobbed aloud, 'My friend – my friend!' As Harrison was standing near me in our square, a poor fellow, his servant, came up and said, 'My dear master, I am wounded and must go away; but I wished to say goodbye to you, for I know I shall never see you again.' The words were hardly out of his mouth, when a round shot dashed his head to pieces, and covered us with his blood and brains.

The battalion's trials would carry on into the evening, as his journal attests:

> About six o'clock I perceived some artillery trotting up our hill, which I knew by their caps to belong to the Imperial Guard. I had hardly mentioned this to a brother officer when two guns unlimbered within seventy paces of us, and by their first discharge of grape blew seven men into the centre of the square. They immediately reloaded and kept up a constant and destructive fire. It was noble to see our fellows fill up the gaps after every discharge. I was much distressed at this moment. I ordered up three of my light bobs, and they had hardly taken their station when two of them fell horribly lacerated. One of them looked up in my face and uttered a sort of reproachful groan, and I involuntarily exclaimed, 'By God, I couldn't help it'. We would willingly have charged these guns, but had we deployed the cavalry that flanked them would have made an example of us...It was now to be seen which side had most bottom, and could stand killing longest.[46]

The 27th Foot, standing just behind Picton's 5th Division, suffered particularly grievously,[47] while a 95th Rifleman complained how 'we were obliged to stand still in squares and be mowed down like sheep'.[48] Major General Peregrine Maitland, referring to the 3rd Battalion 1st Foot Guards, noted serious losses sustained by artillery during the late afternoon, after the massed cavalry attacks:

The enemy poured on us a heavy fire of his artillery, mowed a passage two or three times through the faces of our square, while the cavalry were prepared on our right to take advantage of the least disorder. The coolness and rapidity with which our ranks were closed [however], left him no opportunity of which he thought proper to avail himself.[49]

Maitland noted his soldiers' ability to stand firm even while deployed in the formation most vulnerable to artillery fire – yet recognised that he could not sustain substantial losses for long: 'The cannonade which began the action was very heavy and we suffered in our squares from this with the greatest steadiness.' Eventually, he added, '[f]inding the fire too deadly to be long [endured] and that I was too far in front of the line, I caused the square to retreat up the hill about forty yards, which it did with the greatest good order.'[50]

When fighting began the 2/95th, like the rest of Adam's brigade, were deployed in battalion columns, in which formation, Captain Joseph Logan recorded, 'we were cruelly mauled with shot & shell'. Within minutes of the commencement of action three field officers fell severely wounded, command of the second battalion thus devolving upon Logan.[51] Private John Lewis, 95th, described the intensity of fire, both musket and round shot:

My front rank man was wounded by a part of a shell through the foot & he dropt as we was advancing [*sic*]. I covered the next man I saw and had not walked twenty steps before musket shot came sidewards and took his nose clean off, & then I covered another man which was the third; just after that the man that stood next to me on my left hand had his left arm shot off by a nine pound shot just above his elbow & he turned round and caught hold of me with his right hand & the blood ran all over my trousers, we was advancing so he dropt directly.[52]

Ensign Charles Fraser, 3/14th, whilst holding the battalion's Colours, was splattered by the blood and brains of a bugler of the 51st who, having just taken refuge in the square of the 14th Foot, was struck in the head by a round shot: 'When the smoke cleared away,' Lieutenant Colonel Tidy recorded, 'the ensign's condition was discovered, his uniform being soiled, and he carefully wiping it. "I should like," said he, very quietly, "to wash my face and hands after this!"'[53] Ensign Leeke, 52nd Foot, vividly described the phenomenon of watching the path of an approaching round shot and the effect of it striking its target:

After we had been stationed for an hour or so far down in front of the British position, a gleam of sunshine, falling on them, particularly attracted my attention to some brass guns in our front which appeared to be placed lower down the French slope, and nearer to us, than the others; I distinctly saw the French artilleryman go through the whole process of sponging out one of the guns and reloading it; I could see that it was pointing at our square, and when it was discharged I caught sight of the ball, which appeared to be in a direct line for me. I thought, shall I move? No! I gathered myself up, and stood firm, with the colour in my right hand. I do not exactly know the rapidity with which cannon-balls fly, but I think that two seconds elapsed from the time I saw this shot leave the gun until it struck the front face of the square. It did not strike the four men in rear of whom I was standing, but the four poor fellows on their right. It was fired at some elevation, and struck the front man about the knees, and coming to the ground under the feet of the rear man of the four, whom it most severely wounded, it rose, and passing within an inch or two of the colour poles, went over the rear face of the square without doing any further injury. The two men in the first and second ranks fell outward, I fear they did not survive long; the two others fell within the square. The rear man made a considerable outcry on being wounded, but on one of the officers saying kindly to him, 'O man, don't make a noise', he instantly recollected himself and was quiet ... I should not omit to mention that it was said, after the action, that a round shot had expended its force on the solid square of the 71st Highland L[ight] I[infantry] on our right front, and only stopped when it had killed or wounded seventeen men; I can easily suppose this to be possible from what I saw of the effects of their shot which passed so close to me.[54]

Sergeant William Lawrence, 40th Foot, also left a graphic record of the havoc wrought by artillery fire – in this case on the colour party of his battalion:

About four o'clock I was ordered to the colours. This, although I was used to warfare as much as any, was a job I did not at all like; but still I went as boldly to work as I could. There had been before me that day fourteen sergeants already killed and wounded while in charge of those colours, with officers in proportion, and the staff and colours were almost cut to pieces. This job will never be blotted from my memory ... I had not been there more than a quarter of an hour when a cannon-shot came and took the captain's head clean off. This was again close to me, for my left side was touching the poor captain's right, and I was splattered all over with his blood.[55]

Options for protection against such carnage proved very limited, for troops standing in the ranks were expected to remain still so as not to disturb their order – nor even to duck their heads. Standing in line certainly offered a less tempting target than a column or square, but nothing more, for if a ball passed over one line it was likely to strike another formation behind it, as Wheatley attested: 'We still stood in line. The carnage was frightful. The balls which missed us mowed down the Dutch behind us, and swept away many of the closely embattled Cavalry behind them.'[56] Some units, however, were at various periods ordered to lie down, like the 3rd Battalion 1st Foot Guards, whom Gronow recorded spending at least part of the battle employing this reasonably effective expedient. 'We could hear the shot and shell whistling around us, killing and wounding great numbers ... The French artillery ... committed terrible havoc ...' he recalled.[57] Ensign Thomas Wedgwood, 3rd Foot Guards, also wrote of his regiment lying prone to minimise their exposure to the whirlwind above them – what he described as the 'shells and shot coming over like hailstones' which despite the men's efforts still managed to inflict losses.[58] The battalion's commanding officer noted that one officer, 'dreadfully lacerated', requested 'to be put out of his pain' – but nevertheless survived until evening.[59] Lieutenant Colonel James Stanhope, commanding the 3/1st Foot Guards, also ordered his to men lie down, his soldiers first forming an echelon of squares with a field officer holding command of each face.[60] Captain Mercer recorded seeing the 14th Foot in the rear of his battery lying down in square,[61] providing some protection while enabling them to face a cavalry onslaught at a moment's notice.

Similarly, Private John Smith of the 71st wrote that while 'Limbs, arms, heads was flying in all directions, nothing ever touched me in the smallest [way].' His battalion halted behind some artillery and, like Wedgwood's unit, was ordered to lie down for the men's protection: 'There was a great many of us killed,' Smith continued, while 'a great deal of them fell asleep with the fatigue for all their neighbours being knocked to pieces beside them, it was a shocking thing to see it.'[62]

Nothing, of course, could stop a round shot hurtling through the air, but some counter-measures could be taken by the quickwitted against howitzer shells before they exploded. Lieutenant Winchester of the 92nd Highlanders observed a novel solution to the problem when a howitzer shell landed amidst men of his regiment: 'The Companies in rear of it [the shell] faced about and doubled to the rear until it had burst, then faced about again, and doubled up to their proper distances from the leading divisions without any word of command having been given.'[63] Those of exceptional bravery stood a very narrow chance of survival against a shell if they could dispose of it before the fuse burned through and detonation occurred, as Gronow related in his memoirs:

We were lying down, when a shell fell between Captain (afterwards Colonel) Colquitt and another officer. In an instant Colquitt jumped up, caught up the shell as if it had been a cricket ball, and flung it over the heads of both officers and men, thus saving the lives of many brave fellows.[64]

Those unfortunate enough not to escape flying fragments tended to suffer multiple injuries or instant death. Wyndham recalled how a shell exploded with deadly effect amidst half a dozen men carrying a wounded Highland officer in a blanket.[65] Wheeler also experienced the peculiar phenomenon of exploding shell:

> On the hill behind us … was posted some 20 or 30 guns blazing away over our heads at the enemy. The enemy on their side with a battery of much the same force were returning the compliment, grape [shot] and shells were dupping about like hail, this was devilish annoying. As we could not see the enemy, although they were giving us a pretty good sprinkling of musketry, our buglers sounded to lie down. At this moment a man near me was struck and as I was rising to render assistance I was struck by a spent ball on the inside of my right knee … it was a glance and did no harm, only for the moment caused a smart pain. A shell now fell into the column of the 15th Huzzars and bursted. I saw a sword and scabbard fly out from the column. It was now time to shift our ground to a place of shelter, the Huzzars moved to the left and we advanced again to the cross road under a sharp shower of shells. One of the shells pitched on the breast of a man some little distance on my right, he was knocked to atoms.[66]

Sergeant Lawrence of the 40th also witnessed the power of shell fire, though he himself miraculously escaped serious harm:

> During this movement a shell from the enemy cut our deputy-sergeant-major in two, and having passed on to take the head off one of my company of grenadiers named William Hooper, exploded in the rear not more than one yard from me, hurling me at least two yards into the air, but fortunately doing me little injury beyond the shaking and carrying a small piece of skin off the side of my face. It was indeed another narrow escape, for it burnt the tail of my sash completely off, and turned the handle of my sword perfectly black.[67]

Cavalry offered an even more tempting target for French gunners than infantry, though not invariably at great cost, Lieutenant Colonel Henry Murray, 18th Hussars noting that Vivian's brigade, though it stood under a cannonade for an extended period, did not suffer heavily.[68]

A cornet in the Scots Greys recalled how 'a most destructive fire was kept up, and from which we suffered most severely, both in officers and men, and also horses'.[69] Similarly, Private Joseph Lord of the 2nd Life Guards noted how 'The shot from the enemy fell like hail.'[70] Horses naturally bore a disproportionate share of the losses and suffering. Sergeant Johnston of the Scots Greys was trapped under his horse when it was killed by a shell splinter:

> Here I was left in an awkward predicament for when the animal received the fatal blow he fell to the right and entangled my right leg under his body, from which position the utmost efforts of which I were capable could not extricate myself and in which position I continued until discovered by some of my comrades by whose ready assistance I soon disengaged myself.[71]

Captain Edward Kelly, 1st Life Guards, observed how the centre of his squadron was 'shelled to pieces with cannon shot', and 'all my fine troopers knocked to pieces...',[72] while Lieutenant William Turner, 13th Light Dragoons, recorded one shot killing two officers' horses, one of whose legs it severed before passing between Turner and another officer.[73]

Apart from opening their ranks in extended order – a formation only ever assumed by light cavalry in any event and one which precluded a speedy return to formed order, column or line – protection from artillery could be sought principally in two ways: shifting the regiment to a less exposed position or ordering the men to dismount. Thus, when early in the action Ponsonby observed the Union Brigade sustaining an unacceptable level of casualties he accordingly ordered his three regiments:

> ... to retire a short distance under cover of a hill, where we had continued but a short time when the shot and shell began to work dreadful havoc amongst us ... With a view to shelter us we were again ordered to break into open columns of half squadrons ... and advanced a short distance up the valley, but all was in vain, we were then halted and ordered to wheel into line. At this time, Lieutenant Colonel Hankins, who commanded our right squadron, received a severe contusion by his horse falling with him, on which he was obliged to quit the field ... During this time the shot and shell were playing very hard upon us.[74]

Somerset's Household Brigade also found itself exposed to a rain of round shot. 'Some passed over our heads and through the ranks,' Private Joseph Lord noted, 'others struck the ground a few yards in front of us, at last one struck a man & horse and killed them both, which obliged us to move as they [the gunners] had got their distance [i.e. perfected the range].'[75] Similarly, as a consequence of losses incurred by artillery fire, the Scots Greys were ordered to shift their position slightly:

I perfectly recollect the hollow from our having had two or three men and horses severely wounded by cannon shot, and in consequence of this, of our having been ordered to advance a short distance so as to place us more under cover, where we were for a short time, and then ordered to charge ...[76]

According to Sergeant Archibald Johnston, some time after their ill-fated charge, the Union Brigade 'received orders to retire a considerable distance under the cover of a small wood, where we remained for a considerable time, in which position the cannon shot played very thick upon us; but providentially for us the elevation was too high, which carried it chiefly over our heads.'[77] Coming under artillery fire while deployed behind friendly batteries, the King's Dragoon Guards did the same, shifting position and, in their case, forming line. Nonetheless, as Captain William Elton observed, the guns 'still did us considerable mischief, the more in horses than men'.[78] Grant's cavalry brigade, though deployed on the far right – a particularly quiet sector – was nevertheless obliged to shift positions several times as a result of artillery fire directed from guns positioned in front of the small village of Mon Plaisir and elsewhere.[79] Captain T. W. Taylor, 10th Hussars, also recorded his regiment shifting position to the best available cover:

We took ground towards the rear of the position by Threes right, so as to get under the shelter of the hill, and passed through a coppice of low brushwood behind the hill, and after halted in close columns just behind, and with our left to the end of a ridge.[80]

Cavalry seldom dismounted prior to Waterloo, and thus its practice confirms the extraordinary lethality of French artillery fire that day. Private Lord wrote of his regiment's position in a depression where most of the shot passed over them, though they still took the extra precaution of dismounting for a few minutes.[81] Similarly, when action began the King's Dragoon Guards were dismounted behind rising ground, thereby concealing them from the view of the French. Yet, notwithstanding these precautions, Private Hasker observed, 'the balls came whistling over the hills, occasionally striking one or other of our men or horses'.[82] Sergeant Major James Page of the same regiment observed how:

During the morning part of the day, the whole of the British cavalry were in columns behind the infantry and artillery. We lost many men and horses by the cannon of the enemy. While covering the infantry we were sometimes dismounted in order to rest our horses and also when we were in low ground so that the shot from the French might fly over our heads. Whilst in this situation I stood leaning with my arm over my mare's neck when a large shot struck a horse by the side of mine, killed him on the spot and knocked me and my mare nearly down, but it did us no injury.[83]

The 1st Life Guards, finding themselves in the same predicament, not only dismounted but also lay prone, as their assistant surgeon recorded:

The whole rear of our position was as completely exposed to cannon shot as any part of it or more so for the army was principally drawn up on the reverse of a hill & the shot which were directed at the ridge came over upon us. The principal battery of the French was opposite to us and as there was not the cover of a tuft of grass to protect us, we medici were obliged to retire to some houses in the rear, at the same time the men were dismounted and lay on the ground by the side of their horses.[84]

The 23rd Dragoons were also dismounted for four hours; that is, until the time of the massed French cavalry attacks – about 4 p.m.[85]

However, most cavalry had little choice but to remain in the saddle, so as to be capable of advancing at a moment's notice. Playford expressed frustration at possessing no option but to sit powerlessly while gunners trained their pieces on his formation:

… again [we] occupied a position under the brow of the hill, but much nearer the combatants; and in this instance many cannon shots took effect, so that officers, soldiers, and horses fell one after another: and I noticed the same taking place in other regiments of our brigade. This is, perhaps, one of the most painful situations a human being can be placed in; to sit still and be shot at, and to see men and horses falling on each side of you, and yet you are not allowed to move. When men are fully engaged in the hot work of war, their animal nature becomes fired, and their blood appears to boil within them; and they are too busy to think or to fear: but when a man has to sit still and be shot at; with nothing to think about but that the next shot will probably deprive him of life or of a limb; and that in a moment or two he shall be weltering in his blood in the agonies of death … At the same time his thoughts are apt to wander home to a father, mother, wife, or child; particularly if the individual is not given to thinking on such subjects. And I felt glad that my mother did not know the danger her son was in.[86]

Similarly, the 13th Light Dragoons, positioned on the Allied right, stood under a bombardment for two or three hours from about noon. At about three o'clock a shell fragment struck Lieutenant George Packe in the left part of his groin, knocking him from the saddle. He was carried to the rear and later to Brussels, where he recovered.[87]

Sometimes poor gunnery could spare men and horses. Lieutenant George Blathwayt, 23rd Light Dragoons, noted how at one stage his regiment stood in close column behind a friendly battery positioned on the crest of the slope near Hougoumont. Although the troopers of his regiment suffered little from the shot and shell which struck the ground to their front, the missiles continued on, bounding over them and doing 'great mischief' to the Household cavalry, who stoically stood their ground and grimly endured the fire.[88] Private Lord of the 2nd Life Guards shared the same experience, writing of 'sitting still in a shower of cannon shot which we did several times till we had an opportunity of charging'.[89]

Anglo-Allied infantry and cavalry were not alone in finding themselves at the sharp end of French fire. British batteries also suffered at the hands of their counterparts and could not return the compliment, due to Wellington's ban on counter-battery fire. Only infantry and cavalry constituted legitimate targets.[90] One Royal Horse Artillery officer referred to the French gunners' 'iron dumplings' and noted how:

> About ten or eleven the next morning we moved to the position assigned us on the right of our line in rear of Hougoumont, inactive spectators of the death struggle going on within its precincts, and passive recipients of the stray shot that knocked into us from the enemy's batteries …[91]

Lieutenant General Sir Henry Clinton, commander of the 2nd Division, claimed that French counter-battery fire became so intense that his artillery crews frequently abandoned their guns,[92] some of which French round shot managed to disable.[93] Yet if flying ordnance naturally caused consternation, generally speaking British artillery crews continued to work their guns and ignored the hazards as best they could. Thus, Captain Mercer recalled a party of three officers who came to observe his battery in action, only themselves to be driven off by intense fire while the crews continued to work the guns as before. One of his visitors threw himself on the ground on all fours on perceiving a shot passing close to him while a second, holding a silk umbrella aloft, ran off: 'away he scrambled like a great baboon,' Mercer wrote contemptuously, 'his head turned fearfully over his shoulder, as if watching the coming shot, whilst our fellows made the field resound with their shouts and laughter.'[94] Mercer described in detail the effectiveness of French fire directed against Wellington's artillery:

Whilst thus occupied with our front, we suddenly became sensible of a most destructive flanking fire from a battery which had come, the Lord knows how, and established itself on a knoll somewhat higher than the ground we stood on, and only about 400 or 500 yards a little in advance of our left flank. The rapidity and precision of this fire were quite appalling. Every shot almost took effect, and I certainly expected we should all be annihilated. Our horses and limbers, being a little retired down the slope, had hitherto been somewhat under cover from the direct fire in front but this plunged right amongst them, knocking them down by pairs, and creating horrible confusion. The drivers could hardly extricate themselves from one dead horse ere another fell, or perhaps themselves. The saddle-bags, in many instances, were torn from the horse's backs, and their contents scattered over the field. One shell I saw explode under the two finest wheel-horses in the troop – down they dropped. In some instances the horses of a gun or ammunition wagon remained, and all their drivers were killed. The whole livelong day had cost us nothing like this. Our gunners too – the few left fit for duty of them – were so exhausted that they were unable to run the guns up after firing, consequently at every round they retreated nearer to the limbers; and as we had pointed our two left guns towards the people who were annoying us so terribly, they soon came altogether in a confused heap, the trails crossing each other, and the whole dangerously near the limbers and ammunition wagons, some of which were totally unhorsed, and others in sad confusion from the loss of their drivers and horses, many of them lying dead in their harness attached to their carriages, I sighed for my poor troop – it was already but a wreck.

I had dismounted, and was assisting at one of the guns to encourage my poor exhausted men, when through the smoke a black speck caught my eye, and I instantly knew what it was. The conviction that one never sees a shot coming towards you unless directly in its line flashed across my mind, together with the certainty that my doom was sealed. I had barely time to exclaim 'Here it is then!' – much in that gasping sort of way one does when going into very cold water takes away the breath – 'whush' it went past my face, striking the point of my pelisse collar, which was lying open, and smashed into a horse close behind me. I breathed freely again.

Under such a fire, one may be said to have had a thousand narrow escapes; and, in good truth, I frequently experienced that displacement of air against my face caused by the passing of shot close to me; but the two above recorded, and a third which I shall mention, were remarkable ones, and made me feel in full force the goodness of Him who protected me among so many dangers. Whilst in position on the right of the second line, I had reproved some of my men for lying down when shells fell near them until they burst. Now my turn came. A shell, with a long fuse, came slop into the mud at my feet, and there lay fizzing and flaring, to my infinite discomfiture. After what I had said on the subject, I felt that I must act up to my own words, and, accordingly, there I stood, endeavouring to look quite composed until the cursed thing burst – and, strange to say, without injuring me, though so near. The effect on my men was good ...[95]

PART 5

9

RESISTING THE MASSED FRENCH CAVALRY ATTACKS:

'WE STOOD LIKE A ROCK'[1]

If the repulse of d'Erlon's corps had seriously blunted the French effort in the centre and protected La Haye Sainte, Wellington's position stood far from secure: Uxbridge's two heavy cavalry brigades had paid a heavy price for their efforts; the grand battery, re-crewed by those who had survived Ponsonby's onslaught and supplemented by gunners and engineers drawn from elsewhere, continued to exact, as we have seen, a heavy toll even on those positioned behind the slope, where hundreds died in the bombardment; Reille's infantry continued its ferocious attempts to breach and scale the walls of the Hougoumont complex; and La Haye Sainte would come under renewed assault around 3 p.m.

As discussed earlier, black smoke swirled above Hougoumont, where it will be recalled the thatched roofs of the barn and outhouses had been set alight by howitzer fire. The flames soon spread to the château, causing dreadful suffering to the helpless wounded, who had crawled there for safety to join others left by their able-bodied comrades. These wretched men could not be evacuated by the few who remained to man the walls and defend the gates, leaving many to burn to death or succumb to billowing smoke. Paradoxically, the fires also contributed to the strength of the defence, for they barred the French from reaching the courtyard. By early afternoon the French had made their way around to the North Gate, but failed to batter this in and, most crucially, neglected to bring up artillery to breach the walls. When these attacks receded, Lieutenant Colonel Macdonell summoned reinforcements and ammunition from the ridge. The defenders plugged or manned every gap and, miraculously, the place continued to hold in what had become a major distraction for the French, who continued to funnel increasing numbers of infantry from other parts of the field into a struggle which, owing to its relative isolation from other events, amounted to a battle within a battle – an almost wholly separate engagement in which by continuing to preserve the integrity of the Anglo-Allied centre-right, the relatively small number of defenders drew in French infantry needed elsewhere.

As the fighting continued to rage into the early afternoon around Hougoumont, much of Wellington's infantry lay prone on the reverse slope of the ridge, affording them some measure of protection from the ravages of French artillery fire described earlier. Wellington, as had been customary in the Peninsula, rode along the ridge, calmly directing the repositioning of units and offering encouraging words to his troops. At the same time, Napoleon remained at Rossomme in an armchair. In his former days he, like Wellington, paid close attention to the conduct of battle, though on this day, suffering from piles, the Emperor preferred to devolve most of his power to his marshals and generals. Indeed, this was taken to an extreme; he remained *in situ* – a mile and a half from the principal points of action – and therefore unable to make the crucial decisions that necessarily devolve upon the senior commander. When he did so, by dint of a galloping messenger, distance, the difficulty of the ground and fatigue necessarily led to delays in transmitting orders and the receiving of reports from subordinate commanders in the front line. As a result, most commanders sent him nothing, and the Emperor himself only issued perhaps half a dozen orders between 11.30 a.m. and 5.30 p.m., a third of these of little significance. Actual command effectively devolved upon Ney who, though utterly brave in battle, would constantly place himself at the head of units in the front line, rending him difficult to contact and detached from the wider perspective of the action – and thus compromising his ability to act in the proper capacity of a commander-in-chief.

Ney watched the ridge line along Wellington's centre with no inkling of what lay beyond it, contemplating his next move. In the meantime, around 3 p.m. his men renewed their assault against La Haye Sainte – a position not ideally situated in Wellington's estimation, for it did not fit neatly into his defensive line – in fact it bisected it – and yet it could not go undefended owing to its proximity (200 yards) to the forward face of the ridge, which meant that its fall would split Wellington's army and enable the French to seize the vital Brussels road. Nor, as discussed before, was it anything like as formidable an obstacle as Hougoumont. On the other hand, recognising this little farm's importance and determined to secure its preservation, it will be recalled that Wellington had left within its walls approximately 400 men of the rifle-armed 2nd King's German Legion Light Battalion under Major Baring, supported outside the perimeter by the 1st Light Battalion, with the rest of the brigade to which his command belonged, under Colonel Christian von Ompteda, occupying the area to the right of the crossroads, behind the farm.

The garrison had managed to hold out during d'Erlon's assault, when a cloud of French skirmishers had approached from the east, obliging Baring to summon all his forces into the buildings and yard, leaving the orchard and garden to the French. The defenders fired from loopholes, windows and rooftops while the French came so close to the walls as to seize some of the rifles through the loopholes. The attackers swarmed around the orchard and approached the wall of the barn, nearly penetrating into the courtyard through the archway between the barn and stable until the defenders' fire shot down so many attackers that access became impossible with the whole area choked with bodies. Henegan described how:

> The walls had been loop-holed for musketry, and from these apertures, as well as from a loft, commanding the road, the marksmen of the Legion committed murderous havoc on the assailants. Officers were the principal objects of their aim, and numbers of these were stretched under the walls by the unerring shots of the Germans.[2]

Nonetheless, soon the barn caught fire, which the defenders managed to extinguish with water in kettles transferred from a small pond inside the compound. At about this time the attack dwindled away and the French beat a retreat. It had been a narrow escape, but in the process the garrison had lost many men to French musket fire and expended more than half its ammunition. Yet again, as with Hougoumont, the French had failed to employ combined arms tactics – bombarding the position with their heavy artillery, followed by a determined infantry assault designed to overwhelm the tiny garrison. Unless the French were prepared to change their tactics, Baring's position appeared unassailable so long as supplies of ammunition continued to reach him. With this in mind, he sent word up the ridge for more. Meanwhile, the Prussians had not yet appeared in substantial numbers on the field and Wellington and his staff were growing increasingly anxious.

And rightly they should; around 4 p.m.[3] the guns of the French centre fell silent, their sound replaced by the distant rumble of horses on the move, advancing in their thousands across the gently rolling fields stretching between La Haye Sainte and Hougoumont, a distance of about 1,000 yards. The phenomenon seemed perplexing to observers on the ridge, for the Anglo-Allied line – admittedly weakened by preparatory artillery fire and its infantry shaken – remained intact and ready to defend its ground, with its supporting guns continuing to fire. Moreover, an attack conducted by cavalry without supporting infantry[4] of its own – and, irrespective of numbers, launched against unbroken infantry – defied conventional wisdom. Nor could the French be aware of exactly what they would be facing on the other side of the ridge, for in most cases the attackers could not see the bulk of the Anglo-Allied infantry until they had breasted the ridge. The 1st Foot

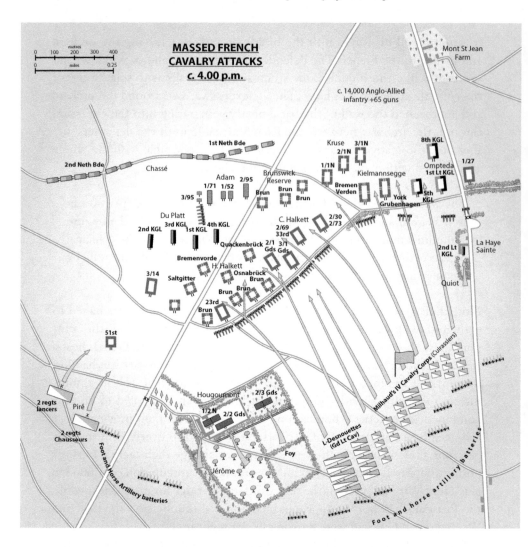

Guards, as simply one example, were deployed on a rear slope and out of the initial sight of the cavalry.[5] For these reasons, Wellington initially believed the approaching wave of horsemen constituted some sort of feint to distract him from Napoleon's true intention: to execute a substantial outflanking manoeuvre well to the west of Hougoumont. He soon discovered the attack to be in earnest, directed against various Anglo-Allied infantry brigades – Kielmannsegge's Hanoverians, Ompteda's King's German Legion infantry, Colin Halkett's 5th British Brigade, Hew Halkett's Hanoverians, the Brunswick Corps, Byng's and Maitland's Foot Guards, Adam's light infantry, Kruse's Dutch-Belgians, and others – the bulk of whom had yet to see any of the fighting, though subjected to galling artillery fire now for several hours.

On the reverse side of the ridge, most of the twenty-five battalions already stood in square or began to form themselves accordingly. Contrary to popular belief some regiments were not in square when the charges began: Captain Ilbert, Royal Artillery, for instance, speaks of regiments 'obliged to form squares'[6] and Sergeant Lawrence, 40th Foot, specifically states that his battalion was not in square at this time: 'Few as we were,' he wrote, 'when we saw it [the cavalry attack] coming we formed squares and awaited it.'[7] Some battalions, like the 2/95th, formed square only very belatedly, leaving themselves practically no time in which to receive their assailants,[8] while others, like the 32nd, had established that formation an hour earlier.[9] According to Colonel Colin Campbell, one of Wellington's staff officers, a few units – none specifically identified and for reasons which he does not elucidate – remained out of square.[10] Lieutenant Colonel Willoughby Rooke noted that some of the infantry – certainly his own unit, the 2nd Battalion 3rd Foot Guards – formed squares of half battalions, supported by cavalry in their rear,[11] but most units deployed as entire battalions.[12] In some cases two battalions formed square together, such as the 1/3rd and the 28th Foot.[13] The 2/30th and the 73rd, both in Halkett's brigade and badly mauled at Quatre Bras, did the same.[14] Lieutenant Colonel William Elphinstone, commanding officer of the 33rd Foot, recorded that his unit was formed in square with the 69th in the rear of La Haye Sainte.[15]

No satisfactory explanation has yet come to light to explain Ney's decision for launching the cavalry in such numbers and without proper support, though many have speculated. He may have believed that Wellington was in the act of retreating: earlier in the day, just prior to d'Erlon's attack, Ney had observed the empty crest of the ridge and reached that conclusion – wrongly in the event. Some of his scouts may have managed to reach a point from which they could observe the other side of the ridge, there mistaking for the Duke's infantry the large body of prisoners being marched off towards the forest behind the Anglo-Allied rear. Whatever the cause, Ney called upon the whole of the heavy cavalry to follow him, including both Kellermann's and Milhaud's Reserve Cavalry Corps (6,700 all ranks and twenty-four guns of horse artillery). Unaccountably – for they answered only to the Emperor's orders – the lancers and chasseurs of the Imperial Guard, posted near La Belle Alliance, the small farm located almost exactly in the centre of the French front line, followed suit, perhaps leading Ney to believe that Napoleon sanctioned the entire enterprise. All told, sometime after 5 p.m. this onslaught amounted to nearly 9,000 magnificently accoutred cavalry: twenty regiments, representing just over 60 per cent of the French mounted arm on the field. Whatever Ney's motive, the Emperor, who continued to brood at Rossomme and had not observed this great spectacle, did not instigate the attack.

Up came the tide of men and horses in their thousands – mostly cuirassiers – but lancers and chasseurs, too, led by the intrepid Marshal Ney. The cavalry cantered up the slope separating Hougoumont from La Haye Sainte – both of which remained under infantry attack – contracting their ranks to lessen the effects of small-arms fire on their flanks, but otherwise mounting the rise in magnificent splendour and incontestable bravery, with a frontage of perhaps 500 abreast and many ranks in depth. The approximately 14,000 defenders watched with awe, incredulity and, to an extent, a measure of relief, for while all agreed the attack offered an imposing sight, the horsemen stood no chance against about twenty-five battalions of steady infantry with more than sufficient time to form mutually supporting squares for, as Uxbridge himself recalled, 'they never charged at speed'.[16] Moreover, the approaching cavalry obliged the harassing guns to cease fire, furnishing the hard-pressed infantry with a much welcomed respite from the steady bombardment to which the far less numerous and smaller-calibre British guns could offer no equivalent reply.

Still, Anglo-Allied gunners continued to fire at the advancing horsemen as quickly as they could before casting away rammers and slow matches and scurrying into the refuge of the nearest square. Anglo-Allied battery commanders had explicit orders passed down from Wellington that if attacked by cavalry, the crews were to seek refuge in infantry squares,[17] although at least for a time – in the case of a gun from Webber-Smith's troop – the captain did not hear the order and remained *in situ*.[18] Ross-Lewin noted in his memoirs:

> Our artillery … made dreadful havoc in the ranks of the enemy in all their advances, yet the cuirassiers would ride up to the very muzzles, and at one time had possession of a great part of our guns, although they could not remove them, the limbers being in the rear. Whenever the cuirassiers found it necessary to retire our artillerymen advanced from the squares in which they had been compelled to take refuge, and renewed their fire.[19]

Other forms of protection existed for gunners, like those of Captain Hew Ross's troop of 9-pounders – reduced to only four guns by the time of the massed cavalry attacks. Situated in front of a sunken section of the Wavre road behind La Haye Sainte, the battery's crew retired into the 'hollow-way' or sheltered under their own guns.[20]

Such a large body of cavalry presented a magnificent target for Allied artillery. Gunner John Edwards watched as the cuirassiers advanced on both sides of the main road: '[We] fired case shot at them and swept them off like a swathe of grass before a scythe. The ground was covered with men and horses in 5 minutes, we limbered up but before we could move one yard the French was all round us.'[21] Wheatley noted how:

All our artillery in front fell into the French power, the bombardiers skulking under the carriages. But five minutes put them again into our hands and the men creeping out applied the match and sent confusion and dismay into the retreating enemy.

Several times were these charges renewed and as often defeated. Charge met charge and all was pell-mell. The rays of the sun glittered on the clashing swords as the two opposing bodies closed in fearful combat and our balls clattered on the shining breastplates like a hail shower.

The field was now thickened with heaps of bodies and shattered instruments. Carcases of men and beasts lay promiscuously entwined.[22]

Lieutenant Samuel Phelps, Royal Artillery, observed cavalry emerging from amidst tall grain in such close proximity that his crews had difficulty reaching the safety of the squares and returning to their guns, with which they 'peppered them finely' as the tide of the attack receded. He counted at least five cavalry charges over the wet ground, which made working his guns problematic,[23] presumably because they got mired in mud and were difficult to manhandle back into the correct firing position after each discharge.

Captain Rudyard offered insight into the manner in which batteries under attack conducted themselves during this phase of the fighting:

My horses, ammunition waggons, were in rear of our Guns under cover of a little hollow between us and our Squares of Infantry. The forge cart, artificers' stores, and such like were in the rear of all out of fire. When ammunition was to be replenished, a Subaltern conducted such waggons as could be spared. They were supplied from the depot in the wood, and returned without delay. The ground we occupied was much furrowed up by the recoil of our Guns and the grazing of the shot, and many holes from the bursting of shells buried in the ground. As horses were killed or rendered unserviceable, the harness was removed and placed on the waggons, or elsewhere. Our men's knapsacks were neatly packed on the front and rear of our limbers and waggons, that they might do their work more easily. Every Gun, every carriage, spokes carried from wheels, all were struck in many places.

The Cuirassiers and Cavalry might have charged through the Battery as often as six or seven times, driving us into the Squares, under our Guns, waggons, some defending themselves. In general, a Squadron or two came up the slope on our immediate front, and on their moving off at the appearance of our Cavalry charging, we took advantage to send destruction after them, and when advancing on our fire I have seen four or five men and horses piled upon each other like cards, the men not having even been displaced from the saddle, the effect of canister.[24]

But it is to Captain Alexander Mercer to whom historians are chiefly indebted for the most vivid account of the attacks and the role of the artillery in opposing them. As French cavalry began to mass for the assault, Sir Augustus Frazer, commander of the horse artillery, galloped up to Mercer and ordered his troop to ascend the slope and unlimber in a position to oppose it. 'As he spoke,' Mercer recorded later:

we were ascending the reverse slope of the main position. We breathed a new atmosphere – the air was suffocatingly hot, resembling that issuing from an oven. We were enveloped in thick smoke, and, *malgré* [despite] the incessant roar of cannon and musketry, could distinctly hear around us a mysterious humming noise, like that which one hears of a summer's evening proceeding from myriads of black beetles; cannon-shot, too, ploughed the ground in all directions, and so thick was the hail of balls and bullets that it seemed dangerous to extend the arm lest it should be torn off.[25]

Mercer took up a position between two wavering squares of Brunswickers and chose to remain at his guns lest his men's fleeing for protection in the face of the cavalry onslaught act as a signal for the visibly unsteady infantry to flee. 'Our first gun had scarcely gained the interval between their squares,' Mercer observed:

when I saw through the smoke the leading squadrons of the advancing column coming on at a brisk trot, and already not more than one hundred yards distant, if so much, for I don't think we could have seen so far. I immediately ordered the line to be formed for action – case shot! and the leading gun was unlimbered and commenced firing almost as soon as the word was given: for activity and intelligence our men were unrivalled. The very first round, I saw, brought down several men and horses. They continued, however, to advance ... [and] the remaining guns ... rapidly succeeded in coming to action, making terrible slaughter, and in an instant covering the ground with men and horses. Still they persevered in approaching us (the first round had brought them to a walk), though slowly, and it did seem they would ride over us. We were a little below the level of the ground on which they moved – having in front of us a bank of about a foot and a half or two feet high, along the top of which ran a narrow road – and this gave more effect to our case-shot, all of which almost must have taken effect, for the carnage was frightful. I suppose this state of things occupied but a few seconds, when I observed symptoms of hesitation, and in a twinkling, at the instant I thought it was all over with us, they turned to either flank and filed away rapidly to the rear. Retreat of the mass, however, was not so easy. Many facing about and trying to force their way through the body of the column, that part next to us became a complete mob, into which we kept a steady fire of case-shot from our six pieces. The effect is hardly conceivable, and to paint this scene of slaughter and confusion impossible. Every discharge was followed by the fall of numbers, whilst the survivors struggled with each other, and I actually saw them using the pommels of their swords to fight their way out of the melee. Some, rendered desperate at finding themselves thus pent up at the muzzles of our guns, as it were, and others carried away by their horses, maddened with wounds, dashed through our intervals – few thinking of using their swords, but pushing furiously onward, intent only on saving themselves. At last the rear of the column, wheeling about, opened a passage, and the whole swept away at a much more rapid pace than they had advanced, nor stopped until the swell of the ground covered them from our fire. We then ceased firing; but as they were still not far off, for we saw the tops of their caps, having reloaded, we stood ready to receive them should they renew the attack … The retreat of the cavalry was succeeded by a shower of shot and shells, which must have annihilated us had not the little bank covered and threw most of them over us. Still some reached us and knocked down men and horses.[26]

Mercer continued:

At the first charge, the French column was composed of grenadiers à cheval and cuirassiers, the former in front. I forget whether they had or had not changed this disposition, but think, from the number of cuirasses we after-wards found, that the cuirassiers led the second attack. Be this as it may, their column reassembled. They prepared for a second attempt, sending up a cloud of skirmishers, who galled us terribly by a fire of carbines and pistols at scarcely forty yards from our front. We were obliged to stand with port-fires lighted, so that it was not without a little difficulty that I succeeded in restraining the people from firing, for they grew impatient under such fatal results. Seeing some exertion beyond words necessary for this purpose, I leaped my horse up the little bank, and began a promenade (by no means agreeable) up and down our front, without even drawing my sword, though these fellows were within speaking distance of me. This quieted my men; but the tall blue gentlemen, seeing me thus dare them, immediately made a target of me, and commenced a very deliberate practice, to show us what very bad shots they were and verify the old artillery proverb, 'The nearer the target, the safer you are.' One fellow certainly made me flinch, but it was a miss; so I shook my finger at him, and called him coquin, etc. The rogue grinned as he reloaded, and again took aim. I certainly felt rather foolish at that moment, but was ashamed, after such bravado, to let him see it, and therefore continued my promenade. As if to prolong my torment, he was a terrible time about it. To me it seemed an age. Whenever I turned, the muzzle of his infernal carbine still followed me. At length bang it went, and whiz [*sic*] came the ball close to the back of my neck, and at the same instant down dropped the leading driver of one of my guns (Miller), into whose forehead the cursed missile had penetrated.[27]

The column now once more mounted the plateau, and these popping gentry wheeled off right and left to clear the ground for their charge. The spectacle was imposing, and if ever the word sublime was appropriately applied, it might surely be to it. On they came in compact squadrons, one behind the other, so numerous that those of the rear were still below the brow when the head of the column was but at some sixty or seventy yards from our guns. Their pace was a slow but steady trot. None of your furious galloping charges was this, but a deliberate advance, at a deliberate pace, as of men resolved to carry their point. They moved in profound silence, and the only sound that could be heard from them amidst the incessant roar of battle was the low thunder-like reverberation of the ground beneath the simultaneous tread of so many horses. On our part was equal deliberation. Every man stood steadily at his post, the guns ready, loaded with a round-shot first and a case over it; the tubes were in the vents; the port-fires glared and sputtered behind the wheels; and my word alone was wanting to hurl destruction on that goodly show of gallant men and noble horses. I delayed this, for experience had given me confidence … It was indeed a grand and imposing spectacle! The column was led on this time by an officer in a rich uniform, his breast covered with decorations, whose earnest gesticulations were strangely contrasted with the solemn demeanour of those to whom they were addressed. I thus allowed them to advance unmolested until the head of the column might have been about fifty or sixty yards from us, and then gave the word, 'Fire!' The effect was terrible. Nearly the whole leading rank fell at once; and the round-shot, penetrating the column carried confusion throughout its extent. The ground, already encumbered with victims of the first struggle, became now almost impassable. Still, however, these devoted warriors struggled on, intent only on reaching us. The thing was impossible. Our guns were served with astonishing activity, whilst the running [musket] fire of the two squares was maintained with spirit. Those who pushed forward over the heaps of carcasses of men and horses gained but a few paces in advance, there to fall in their turn and add to the difficulties of those succeeding them. The discharge of every gun was followed by a fall of men and horses like that of grass before the mower's scythe. When the horse alone was killed, we could see the cuirassiers divesting themselves of the encumbrance [i.e. their breast and back plates] and making their escape on foot. Still, for a moment, the confused mass (for all order was at an end) stood before us, vainly trying to urge their horses over the obstacles presented by their fallen comrades, in obedience to the now loud and rapid vociferations of him who had led them on and remained unhurt. As before, many cleared everything and rode through us; many came plunging forward only to fall, man and horse, close to the muzzles of the guns; but the majority again turned at the very moment when, from having less ground to go over, it were safer to advance than retire, and sought a passage to the rear. Of course the same confusion, struggle amongst themselves, and slaughter prevailed as before, until gradually they disappeared over the brow of the hill. We ceased firing, glad to take a breath. Their retreat exposed us, as before, to a shower of shot and shells: these last, falling amongst us with very long fuses, kept burning and hissing a long time before they burst, and were a considerable annoyance to man and horse. The bank in front, however, again stood our friend, and sent many over us innocuous.[28]

On passing over the abandoned batteries – other than Mercer's – and descending the other side of the slope, Ney and his followers now glimpsed infantry whose presence in such numbers they did not expect to see – and from whose perspective we shall now examine events in some detail. The sight of the sun's glint on the cavalry's helmets and cuirasses and the sound of the pounding of horses' hooves grew more palpable as the cavalry emerged over the lip of the ridge where the infantry lay ready in square, the front rank with one knee and the butt of their muskets resting on the ground, while two or three further ranks stood behind, the whole forming a wedge of impenetrable bayonets – for a horse will not willingly charge headlong into such an obstacle. Wheatley vividly described in his diary the sensation of first seeing the assailants:

A black consolidated body was soon seen approaching and we distinguished by sudden flashes of light from the sun's rays, the iron-cased cavalry of the enemy. Shouts of 'Stand firm!' 'Stand fast!' were heard from the little squares around and very quickly these gigantic fellows were upon us.

No words can convey the sensation we felt on seeing these heavy-armed bodies advancing at full gallop against us, flourishing their sabres in the air, striking their armour with the handles, the sun, gleaming on the steel. The long horse hair, dishevelled by the wind, bore an appearance confounding the senses to an astonishing disorder. But we dashed them back as coolly as the sturdy rock repels the ocean's foam. The sharp-toothed bayonet bit many an adventurous fool, and on all sides we presented our bristly points like the peevish porcupine assailed by clamorous dogs.[29]

On the other hand, the vulnerable corners of a square and any gaps opened by artillery fire offered a narrow opportunity for success to an attacker. Thus, as Captain Gronow, 3/1st Foot Guards, observed:

> The cuirassiers and heavy dragoons approached so close that it was feared they would enter by the gap which had been made in our square. [Captain Robert] Adair rushed forward, placed himself in the open space, and with one blow of his sword killed a French officer who had actually got amongst our men.[30]

With no hope of breaking the squares the flood of horsemen could do little more than lap around their edges, discharging their pistols and carbines – for they could seldom reach the defenders with sword or sabre.

There is no question but that the French ventured as close to the squares as physically possible. Captain George Barlow of the 2/69th, for instance, noted that 'these charges were made in the most daring manner up to the bayonets of the infantry & the muzzles of our cannon, but every attempt was punished with frightful loss,'[31] while Willoughby Rooke wrote how the cavalry 'came up very boldly' to be met by 'the very great steadiness of the infantry' who withheld their fire until the attackers came within 50 yards of the squares.[32] Sometimes small numbers of detached cavalry approached and discharged their pistols, which did not provoke a response from the infantry, whose officers ordered them to withhold their fire for the principal attacks.[33] On the other hand, those troopers armed with a lance possessed a weapon of great facility in such circumstances; not only could their 9ft-long weapons reach the front and second ranks of a square, the lancers made short work of the wounded they encountered on the slopes,[34] probably a combination of infantry felled from artillery fire on the reverse slope and men of Ponsonby's and Picton's brigades from the period of d'Erlon's attack a few hours earlier. Kincaid wrote with disgust of the same practice by the French heavy cavalry:

> It made me mad to see the cuirassiers, in their retreat, stooping and stabbing at our wounded men, as they lay on the ground. How I wished that I had been blessed with Omnipotent power for a moment, that I might have blighted them![35]

Lieutenant Donald Mackenzie, 1/42nd, also noted French cavalry stabbing soldiers lying on the ground – an otherwise deplorable act slightly mitigated by the fact that at least some of the infantry feigned death when caught outside the protection of a square:

On one such occasion, being unable to get into a square in time, and seeing a squadron of cavalry bearing down where I and a few men were, [I] ordered them to fling themselves on the ground and allow the horses to pass over. This we did, but it required some nerve to be perfectly still and be thus ridden over. I escaped unhurt, but, as the troopers passed back, I got a sword thrust as a sort of query whether I was as dead as I looked! However, I lay motionless, and the bullets whizzing about did not allow my inquisitive friend to prolong his enquiries.[36]

Stationary though the infantry in squares remained, the men were not inactive, unleashing a series of volleys on successive waves of attackers whose formations broke up, forcing them to recede like an outgoing tide, leaving riderless horses careering about everywhere as mounds of wounded and dead formed across the field, obstructing the progress of those waiting their own chance to drive from the ridge the stalwart, red-coated infantry. Sergeant Charles Wood, 3/1st Foot Guards, reported his battalion withholding its fire until the cavalry came within about 30 yards,[37] while Ensign Jack Barnett, 1/71st, reported the same:

Our men never fired a single shot, till they were nearly touching our bayonets, front rank kneeling, they then gave a volley. You heard a scream & saw them fall like leaves, horses with legs shot off limping about, the few who were not killed, faced about & our dragoons who were in rear of us, past [*sic*] by us & cut them down in all directions.[38]

According to Captain James Nixon, the 1st Foot Guards' small-arms fire played an important part in their repulse for the horsemen 'were arrested by a continued echelon of squares … whose cross fire cut them absolutely to pieces, our men standing like statues'.[39] Sergeant Lawrence, 40th Foot, wrote how:

We instantly threw ourselves into three squares with our artillery in the centre; and the word having been given not to fire at the men, who wore armour, but at the horses, which was obeyed to the very letter, as soon as they arrived at close quarters we opened a deadly fire, and very few of them wholly escaped. They managed certainly at first to capture our [crewless] guns, but they were again recovered by the fire of our three squares; and it was a most laughable sight to see these Guards [in fact, cuirassiers] in their chimney-armour trying to run away after their horses had been shot from under them, being able to make very little progress, and many of them being taken prisoners by those of our light companies who were out skirmishing … We did not lose a single inch of ground the whole day, though after these successive charges our numbers were fearfully thinned; and even during the short interval between each charge the enemy's cannon [on the opposite ridge] had been doing some mischief among our ranks besides.[40]

Lawrence continues his narrative, describing his battalion's conduct in the face of successive charges:

We poured volley after volley into them, doing fearful execution, and they had to retire at last before the strong dose we administered; not, however, without our losing more men and so becoming weaker than before. We were dreading another charge, but all the help we got was the cry of 'Keep your ground, my men, reinforcements are coming!'[41]

Henegan adds further detail to the reception the infantry offered:

The French cuirassiers advanced in heavy masses, covered by their artillery. As they boldly ascended the slopes, exposed to a murderous fire from the batteries, our gunners were again driven to seek shelter in the squares, or under the limbers of their guns, where many were lanced and sabred. The bold horsemen would then advance, at furious speed, until within a horse's length of our firm and close-knit squares; here they would brandish their long swords in impotent defiance, and often strike the bristling bayonets that stood as barriers to their further advance. Imprecations, screams, and even jests were levelled at the impassable obstruction. Carbines and pistols were discharged in mock revenge; but not a trigger returned the challenge until the word 'fire' ran clearly down the line of the menaced square. Then down went the front men and horses of the leading squadron. A well directed fire from the next square threw the rest into confusion ...[42]

Private John Smith of the 1/71st noted that losses amongst the cavalry were so great that they impeded the movement of infantry attempting to shift their ground:

The cavalry was the boldest we ever seed [*sic*], charged us many times but we stood like a rock, they came close to us when they fell to the ground in fifties and sixties, horses and men tumbling in heaps that we could not get advanced over them.[43]

Lieutenant John Black, 1/3rd Foot, recorded how the assailants attacked the right face of his square, containing men of his battalion as well as of the 28th Foot: 'It was the grandest sight you can imagine,' he wrote:

to see the men coming at full gallop all in shining armour and shouting
'*Vive l'Empereur*' with all their souls and our men shouting too as loud as
they could bawl. We gave them such a volley [that] their two front ranks fell
to a man and away they scampered, our men pricking them down in the
most horrid manner until they rode round the outside of the hill and came
down on the opposite face, here they met the same reception and faced
about again but returned in the most determined way to our rear, where
they made their third charge with their lancers in front. The cuirassiers were
nearly all destroyed, the few remaining were in rear of the lancers, they
pushed the charge within ten yards of us but our fire was so hot they could
not stand it and they broke in the centre and a part ran round one side of
our square and some on the other, so they had the whole fire of these two
sides and also our front and some of the men ran to the top of the hill and
snapped them going down ...[44]

One of Lord Hill's aides-de-camp remarked on the bravery of the French and
the losses they sustained from small arms:

For upwards of an hour our little squares were surrounded by the elite of
the French cavaliers; there they gallantly stood within 40 paces of us, unable
to leap over the bristling line of bayonets, unwilling to retire, and determined never to surrender: hundreds of them were dropping in all directions
from our murderous fire, yet as fast as they dropped others came up to
supply their place; finding at last that it was in vain to attempt to break our
determined ranks, they swept round our rear and, rushing into the Nivelles
road, attempted to cut their way back to their own lines. But the whole
road was lined with our infantry on both sides, and at the advanced part of
it was an almost impassable barricade of felled trees. Here fell the remainder
of these brave cuirassiers, of whom not one was taken without a wound.[45]

Two other sources, both from Colonel Mitchell's brigade, confirm this evidence, Lieutenant R.P. Holmes, 23rd Fusiliers, observing that:

Having suffered much from the Squares they attempted to retreat by the
Nivelles road, which was thickly lined with skirmishers, and the Officer
who commanded the left Company of the Regiment stationed on that road
assured me at the time [that] scarcely a man succeeded in making his escape.[46]

The recollections of Lieutenant Colonel Rice, 51st Foot, also reveal that the
abatis constructed the night before the battle proved effective against cavalry:

... the charge of the French Cuirassiers on the left of Hougoumont farm, on the position. After [being] foiled in this attempt against the Squares, a considerable body passed down the Nivelles road, on which there was an abatis. The [infantry] fire was successful, though some few miraculously cleared the abatis.[47]

Lieutenant Henry Lane, 15th Hussars, recorded the same incident, noting that 'they were annihilated by infantry concealed in that position'[48] – a reference to a body of the 95th Rifles.

Captain George Barlow, 2/69th, noted that some of the artillery crews, on perceiving the approach of the cavalry, galloped off with the limbers and traces to prevent the French from removing the guns, though according to Captain Walcott, Royal Horse Artillery, some French troopers penetrated so far behind Anglo-Allied lines as to enable them to kill and wound men and horses belonging to the limbers and ammunition carriages of the batteries sitting temporarily abandoned on the crest of the ridge.[49] But if the cavalry could not actually drive off or disable the limbers themselves, there was nothing to stop them from spiking the guns while they remained in temporary possession of them. This, however, they comprehensively failed to do, and as each wave receded, the gunners re-emerged from their squares to fire on the attackers' backs with canister and then, as the distance lengthened, round shot. According to Mercer, by the time of the third charge, the momentum of the attack had already petered out. 'This time,' he observed, 'it was child's play. They could not even approach us in any decent order, and we fired most deliberately; it was folly having attempted the thing.'[50] But as the cavalry retreated, a fresh wave approached, repeating the futile process, displaying the utmost boldness in approaching the squares and riding:

up to the very muzzles of our men's firelocks and cut[ting] at them in the squares. But this was of no use, not a single square could they brake [sic], but was always put to the rout, by the steady fire of our troopes [sic]. In one of those charges made by the enemy a great many over charged themselves and could not get back without exposing themselves to the deadly fire of the infantry.[51]

To compound the problems suffered by the French cavalry, Anglo-Allied cavalry, with Uxbridge at the head of many of their charges,[52] intervened regularly to engage their counterparts, retiring through the gaps in the squares and rallying behind them before advancing again. Uxbridge left a superb account from his perspective as commander of the whole of Wellington's mounted arm:

They (the French) very frequently attacked our Squares, but never in over-whelming masses, and with that vigour and speed, which would have given them some chance of penetrating. No heavy mass having a well-formed front actually came collectively against our bayonets. Constantly a few devoted fel-lows did clash with them, and some pierced between the Squares, and when I had not Cavalry at hand I frequently entered the Squares for protection.

In the afternoon a very heavy attack was made upon the whole of our line to the right of the road, and connecting itself with the troops attacking Hougoumont. It was chiefly made and frequently repeated by masses of Cuirassiers, but never in one connected line, and after the first grand attack of the morning they never came on with the degree of vigour which could give them a hope of penetrating into our immovable Squares of Infantry.

The Infantry never fired till the Cavalry were very close, and they (the Cavalry) dispersed, some coming through the intervals where they were either killed by the fire of the Squares, or repulsed by the Cavalry in [the] 2nd line. For several minutes some few Cuirassiers were in possession of several of our Guns about the centre of our line, at the time the British Cavalry was in pursuit elsewhere, and these desperate men remained there to be picked off.[53]

The number of charges instigated by Anglo-Allied cavalry is not known, but eyewitness accounts agree that they were numerous,[54] with Uxbridge him-self frequently in the van, one of his aides-de-camp, Major William Thornhill, observing that he observed Uxbridge 'in the thick of the fight giving orders with his accustomed clearness, and ever after, as it seemed to me, seeking to place himself con amore in the torrent of attack wherever he felt that his encouraging example was most needed'.[55]

According to an unidentified officer of the 11th Hussars, his regiment exe-cuted at least twelve charges during the course of the day, at least some of these during this phase.[56] Lieutenant Standish O'Grady claimed the 7th Hussars charged at least a dozen times, cutting off and annihilating an entire squad-ron of cuirassiers apart from two officers taken prisoner and sent to the rear.[57] Major General William Dörnberg's 3rd Cavalry Brigade, consisting of the 1st and 2nd King's German Legion Light Dragoons and the 23rd Light Dragoons, was posted behind Halkett's brigade in the right centre and therefore ideally placed to repel, insofar as it could, the massed French cavalry, but in particular to bring relief to the guns on the summit of the ridge.[58] On one occasion, the 23rd Light Dragoons drove back a body of cuirassiers and lancers on their own guns and, with Uxbridge at their head, repulsed cavalry menacing the 33rd Foot in a separate charge.[59] The brigade's losses were unsurprisingly high, including the severely wounded Dörnberg himself. Major General

Colquhoun Grant's cavalry brigade, consisting of the 7th and 15th Hussars and the 13th Light Dragoons, also played its part, having been moved from their original position on the extreme right of Wellington's line, in front of the Nivelles road, near its junction with the Wavre road.[60] Somerset's heavy cavalry also joined in what that brigade commander described as 'a severe and bloody conflict' before again returning his formation to its original position, losing in the process Colonel Ferrier, commander of the 1st Life Guards and several other officers and men of both that regiment and of the Horse Guards.[61]

In the final analysis, however determined and persistent, Anglo–Allied cavalry produced a very limited impact on their much more numerous counterparts. 'It invariably advanced,' Uxbridge declared understatedly, 'but the Light Cavalry was not always successful.'[62] To be fair, failure rested not in any absence of spirit, but in simple arithmetic, as Lord Greenock, Assistant Quartermaster General to the cavalry, concluded:

> The different Brigades [of Anglo–Allied cavalry], having been scattered ... along the whole extent of the Line, without any view to such an arrange-ment, their operations were unfortunately never combined during any part of the day, whilst the French Cavalry acted in Corps or Divisions; conse-quently, in these desultory attacks small bodies of the former were constantly opposed to large masses of the latter, and although the first efforts of the British were generally successful, the superiority of the Enemy's numbers in the end always turned the scale in their favour.[63]

Captain Arthur Kennedy, 18th Hussars, described the French attacks as nearly 'an irresistible torrent', which Somerset's heavy cavalry helped repulse,[64] suggesting that the Household Brigade did not constitute an entirely spent force after its earlier charge against Dubois' cuirassiers west of La Haye Sainte. Observations made by Ensign Charles Short, Coldstream Guards, confirm this view, for he watched the Horse Guards take part in engaging the French cavalry on the ridge.[65]

Other units of the Household Brigade sought to drive off the successive waves of cavalry. Private Thomas Hasker, 1st Dragoon Guards, provides an engaging description of his experiences:

> We were ordered to mount and ascend the acclivity, sword in hand. There we found French cuirassiers cutting down our infantry. We charged them; on which they turned about and rode off, we following them, and as many as were overtaken were cut down. I observed, however, that many of them on our right flank got behind us, and thus we were at once pursuing and pursued. The regiment then took a direction to the left, and I found myself

opposed to one man. We made several ineffectual passes at each other, and he then rode off. I turned to follow the regiment, but had not proceeded far when my horse fell. Before I had well recovered my feet, one of the cuirassiers rode up and began cutting and slashing at my head with his sword. I soon fell down with my face to the ground. Presently a man rode by, and stabbed me with a lance. I turned around, and was then stabbed by a sword by a man who walked past me. Very soon another man came up with a firelock and bayonet, and, raising both his arms, thrust his bayonet (as he thought) into my side near my heart. The coat I had on was not buttoned, but fastened with brass hooks and eyes. Into one of these eyes the point of the bayonet entered, and was thus prevented penetrating my body. One of my fingers was cut off before I fell; and there I lay bleeding from at least a dozen places, and was soon covered with blood. I was also at that time plundered by the French soldiers of my watch, money, canteen, haversack, and trousers, notwithstanding the balls from the British army were dropping on all sides as I lay there.[66]

The timings of such engagements are impossible to confirm, but the evidence suggests that at least some were executed against French cavalry as it withdrew back over the ridge, for Captain Ilbert, Royal Artillery, noted British cavalry advancing 'when they [the infantry] had done their duty', which suggests the cavalry struck when the cuirassiers and others were returning to friendly lines.[67] This seems plausible, for Sir John May, Royal Artillery, wrote of pursuit, not merely a clash of arms: 'a reciprocal charge on the part of our cavalry, when the enemy without making any impression retreated with precipitation, pursued close to their infantry'.[68] This is confirmed by Lieutenant William Turner, 13th Light Dragoons, whose regiment 'charged them again in the grandest style between our masses of infantry; they retreated and we charged them close to their infantry, who were formed in squares the same as ours'.[69] In the course of this action Turner shot an opponent with his pistol and noticed Wellington pass his regiment several times – more confirmation that the Duke took an active part in directing the defence in close proximity to the French.

The extent to which Uxbridge's cavalry contributed to the defeat of their opposite numbers during this phase of the battle is debatable, for the cuirassiers seemed always to return, first thundering up and, later, as the horses grew increasingly fatigued, slowing to little more than a walk, while in the intervals the French guns resumed their bombardment, inflicting grievous losses on infantry obliged to remain in their tightly packed, extremely vulnerable formations. Mercer, for one, suggests his mounted comrades had little impact on the course of events:

Amongst the multitudes of French cavalry continually pouring over the front ridge, one corps came sweeping down the slope entire, and was directing its course straight for us, when suddenly a regiment of light dragoons (I believe of the [King's] German Legion) came up from the ravine at a brisk trot on their flank. The French had barely time to wheel up to the left and push their horses into a gallop, when the two bodies came in collision [*sic*]. They were at a very short distance from us, so that we saw the charge perfectly. There was no check, no hesitation, on either side; both parties seemed to dash on in a most reckless manner, and we fully expected to have seen a horrid crash – no such thing! Each, as if by mutual consent, opened their files on coming near, and passed rapidly through each other, cutting and pointing, much in the same manner one might pass the fingers of the right hand through those of the left. We saw but few fall. The two corps reformed afterwards, and in a twinkling both disappeared, I know not how or where.[70]

Lieutenant Edward Byam, 15th Hussars, noted how his regiment and that of the 13th Light Dragoons engaged and even drove back some elements of cuirassiers and lancers, but with their own flanks exposed they were obliged to retire. The 15th Hussars charged several times further, but Byam admitted this resulted in considerable cost to his regiment.[71] The account left by Lieutenant George Blathwayt, 23rd Light Dragoons, suggests a see-saw action with no decisive impression made by Anglo-Allied cavalry, disadvantaged by woeful numerical inferiority and the superior weight of their French opponents. Thus, with orders to recapture some guns, Blathwayt's regiment charged numerous times during this phase of the action but his account does not report any meaningful result:

The excitement became very great, we drove back the cuirassiers and were ourselves driven back in turn when we passed between the two squares of infantry who fired upon the cuirassiers as they advanced upon us and as they broke we attacked them when the infantry cheered us and we them in return. This sort of thing lasted for some time.[72]

Yet if Ney's cavalry appeared to make no impression on the infantry, what little horse artillery accompanying these determined horsemen, together with the renewed bombardment between charges, clearly did, for many squares suffered losses as opportunities presented themselves to French gunners, inspiring Private Wheeler of the 51st to admire 'the cool intrepid courage of our squares' under their fire.[73] The 2/95th constituted one such unit; not only did they barely form square in time, but they lost their senior commander, probably to horse artillery. The attackers also discharged their carbines at point-blank range, Private John Lewis recalled, leaving a soldier near him shot through the body:

> [bleeding] out of his belly & back like a pig stuck in the throat … All this time we kept up a constant fire … they retreated but they often came to the right about & fired and as I was loading my rifle one of their shots came & struck my rifle not two inches above my left hand as I was ramming down the ball with my right hand & broke the stock & bent the barrel in such a manner that I could not get the ball down. Just at this time we extended again & my rifle was of no good to me, a nine pound shot came and cut the sergeant of our company right in two, he was not above three file from me so I threw down my rifle and went and took his rifle as it was not hurt.
>
> At this time we had lost both our colonels, [a] major, and the two oldest captains & only a young captain [Joseph Logan] to take command of us, as for [Lieutenant] Colonel [Hamlet] Wade he was sent to England about three weeks before the battle. Seeing we had lost so many men & all our commanding officers my heart began to fail, & Boney's Guards [*sic*: cuirassiers] then made another charge on us, but we made them retreat as before & while we was in square the second time the Duke of Wellington and all his Staff came up to us in the midst of all the fire & saw we had lost all our commanding officers. He himself gave the word of command, the words he said to our regiment was this, '95th unfix your swords, left face & extend yourselves once more, we shall soon have them over the other hill' & then he rode away on our right & how he escaped being shot God only knows, for all this time the shots were flying like hail stones.[74]

Ensign Edward Macready, 2/30th, also sheds some interesting light on the French use of artillery, observing that skirmishers thrown out by his battalion took advantage of the ramparts of corpses to shield themselves from close-range artillery fire:

> A most murderous conflict took place, their cuirassiers charged us every second, were every time repulsed, and such numbers left dead, that latterly when we went out skirmishing, we covered ourselves with dead men and horses; they then brought a piece of artillery within 50 yards of our square and threw grape into us like smoke, opened the flanks of the square, which were immediately replaced by other men stepping up. The enemy then sent a strong column of the Grenadiers of the Guard[75] to drive us, but when they came within twenty paces, we gave them a volley and a huzza; and prepared for a charge, but they spared us the trouble, [for] away they went, our cavalry got among them, and I pitied the '*pauvres diables*' [poor devils].[76]

The 2/95th found itself greatly tried by cuirassiers and lancers supported by eighteen guns of horse artillery in support at 100 yards' distance. 'We repulsed this attack but suffered cruelly,' Captain Logan recorded. '[O]ne shot knocked down nine men. We were attacked again four different times but my little battalion maintained their ground. The general finding we were so terribly exposed, sent me an order to fall back upon our guns.'[77] Other evidence confirms the presence of French horse artillery in support of their cavalry. Lieutenant Colonel Alexander Hamilton, 2/30th, referred in his correspondence to 'two field pieces brought against it [their square] without effect'.[78] Still, most of the infantry did not suffer from supporting horse artillery fire. Indeed, in his autobiography, Sergeant William Lawrence, 40th Foot, rightly identified its absence as a grave tactical error:

> I must here say that I cannot think why those charges of cavalry were kept up against our unbroken squares, in spite of their being so constantly sent back. It is murder to send cavalry against disciplined infantry unless they have artillery to act in conjunction with them, in which case they might possibly succeed in routing them if they could take advantage of their falling into confusion, but not otherwise.[79]

The daughter of Lieutenant Colonel Tidy, 14th Foot, recorded his description of the cavalry attacks:

> A large body of French cuirassiers appeared in sight. It seemed doubtful which of the squares that were dotted about, they would honour with a visit. In the mean time, my father's anxiety for his 'boys' induced him to address them in the following style … 'Now my young tinkers' said he, 'stand firm! While you remain in your present position, old Harry himself can't touch you; but if one of you give[s] way, he will have every mother's son of you, as sure as you are born!' After a slight pause, the cuirassiers made a sudden charge upon the regiment to the left of [the 14th]; and after several attempts to break the square, they sounded a retreat, and retired in the utmost confusion. The attacked regiment waited only till the enemy was entirely clear of the 14th, when they opened upon them with a murderous fire, while at the same moment several guns on the other side of [the 14th] played upon them. For a minute or two, the smoke was so dense, that it was impossible to see a yard in advance; but when it cleared away, a scene of the greatest disorder presented itself. Numbers lay strewed about in all directions, dead, dying and wounded. Horses running here and there without their riders; and the riders, encumbered with their heavy armour, scampered away as they best could, without their horses.[80]

Mercer described the massed attacks with wonderful metaphors:

> I can compare it to nothing better than a heavy surf breaking on a coast
> beset with isolated rocks, against which the mountainous wave dashes with
> furious uproar, breaks, divides, and runs, hissing and boiling, far beyond up
> the adjacent beach. In a moment such shoals of Lancers and others came
> sweeping down the slope that the whole interval between the lines was
> covered with them, a mixed and various multitude, all scattered and riding
> in different directions.[81]

Yet the French, undaunted, continued to return, as Gronow recorded in his
memoirs:

> We saw large masses of cavalry advance: not a man present who survived
> could have forgotten in after life the awful grandeur of that charge. You
> perceived at a distance what appeared to be an overwhelming, long moving
> line, which, ever advancing, glittered like a stormy wave of the sea when
> it catches the sunlight. On came the mounted host until they got near
> enough, whilst the very earth seemed to vibrate beneath their thundering
> tramp. One might suppose that nothing could have resisted the shock of
> this terrible moving mass. They were the famous cuirassiers, almost all old
> soldiers, who had distinguished themselves on most of the battle-fields of
> Europe. In an almost incredibly short period they were within twenty yards
> of us, shouting '*Vive l'Empereur!*' The word of command, 'Prepare to receive
> cavalry', had been given, every man in the front ranks knelt, and a wall of
> bristling steel presented itself to the infuriated cuirassiers …
>
>   The charge of the French cavalry was gallantly executed; but our well-
> directed fire brought men and horses down, and ere long the utmost
> confusion arose in their ranks. The officers were exceedingly brave, and by
> their gestures and fearless bearing did all in their power to encourage their
> men to form again and renew the attack …
>
>   Again and again various cavalry regiments, heavy dragoons, lancers, hus-
> sars, carabineers of the Guard, endeavoured to break our walls of steel. The
> enemy's cavalry had to advance over ground which was so heavy that they
> could not reach us except at a trot; they therefore came upon us in a much
> more compact mass than they probably would have done if the ground had
> been more favourable. When they got within ten or fifteen yards they dis-
> charged their carbines, to the cry of '*Vive l'Empereur!*' but their fire produced
> little effect, as is generally the case with the fire of cavalry. Our men had
> orders not to fire unless they could do so on a near mass; the object being
> to economise our ammunition, and not to waste it on scattered soldiers.
> The result was, that when the cavalry had discharged their carbines, and

were still far off, we occasionally stood face to face, looking at each other inactively, not knowing what the next move might be.

The lancers were particularly troublesome, and approached us with the utmost daring. On one occasion I remember, the enemy's artillery having made a gap in the square, the lancers were evidently waiting to avail themselves of it, to rush among us, when Colonel Staples, at once observing their intention, with the utmost promptness filled up the gap, and thus again completed our impregnable steel wall; but in this act he fell mortally wounded ...

When we received cavalry, the order was to fire low; so that on the first discharge of musketry, the ground was strewed with the fallen horses and their riders, which impeded the advance of those behind them, and broke the shock of the charge. It was pitiable to witness the agony of the poor horses, which really seemed conscious of the dangers that surrounded them: we often saw a poor wounded animal raise its head, as if looking for its rider to afford him aid. There is nothing perhaps amongst the episodes of a great battle more striking than the débris of a cavalry charge, where men and horses are seen scattered and wounded on the ground in every variety of painful attitude. Many a time the heart sickened at the moaning tones of agony which came from man, and scarcely less intelligent horse, as they lay in fearful agony upon the field of battle.[82]

All through the carnage the infantry regularly dragged their wounded inside, unceremoniously cast the dead outside and closed the ranks before the cavalry could detect gaps in which to ride through. Gronow vividly described the experience thus:

our square was a perfect hospital, being full of dead, dying, and mutilated soldiers. The charges of cavalry were in appearance very formidable, but in reality a great relief, as the artillery could no longer fire on us: the very earth shook under the enormous mass of men and horses. I never shall forget the strange noise our bullets made against the breastplates of Kellermann's and Milhaud's cuirassiers ... who attacked us with great fury. I can only compare it, with a somewhat homely simile, to the noise of a violent hail-storm beating upon panes of glass.

The artillery did great execution, but our musketry did not at first seem to kill many men; though it brought down a large number of horses, and created indescribable confusion. The horses of the first rank of cuirassiers, in spite of all the efforts of their riders, came to a stand-still, shaking and covered with foam, at about twenty yards' distance from our squares, and generally resisted all attempts to force them to charge the line of serried steel. On one occasion, two gallant French officers forced their way into a gap momentarily created by the discharge of artillery: one was killed by Staples, the other by Adair. Nothing could be more gallant than the behaviour of those veterans, many of whom had distinguished themselves on half the battle-fields of Europe.

In the midst of our terrible fire, their officers were seen as if on parade, keeping order in their ranks, and encouraging them. Unable to renew the charge, but unwilling to retreat, they brandished their swords with loud cries of '*Vive l'Empereur!*' and allowed themselves to be mowed down by hundreds rather than yield. Our men, who shot them down, could not help admiring the gallant bearing and heroic resignation of their enemies.[83]

All the while, senior officers stood in the centre of the squares, issuing encouragement to their men to keep steady and to maintain regular fire. Major General Frederick Adam numbered amongst these,[84] as well as the Duke of Wellington himself, who sought protection as the tide of horsemen ebbed and flowed. Captain Gronow recalled the Duke, accompanied by a single aide-de-camp, entering the square of his own unit, the 3rd Battalion 1st Foot Guards:

> As far as I could judge, [Wellington] appeared perfectly composed; but looked very thoughtful and pale. He was dressed in a gray great-coat with a cape, white cravat, leather pantaloons, Hessian boots, and a large cocked hat à la Russe ... The duke sat unmoved, mounted on his favourite charger ...[85]

Clearly, the Duke spent a considerable time on the ridge during this critical phase of the action for, quite apart from an indeterminate time with the Foot Guards, Major Dawson Kelly, the Assistant Quartermaster General, recalled how Wellington and his staff were obliged to take shelter in the combined square formed by the 73rd and the 30th Regiments.[86] But if the interior of a square offered protection, it nevertheless 'presented a shocking sight', Gronow recalled:

> Inside we were nearly suffocated by the smoke and smell from burnt cartridges. It was impossible to move a yard without treading upon a wounded comrade, or upon the bodies of the dead; and the loud groans of the wounded and dying were most appalling.[87]

Still, the Duke was regularly on the move, as Sergeant Major Cotton attested:

> The Duke generally rode alone, or rather without having any one by his side, and rarely spoke, unless to send a message or to give orders; sometimes he would suddenly turn round and glide past his followers; halting occasionally, and apparently paying no attention to his own troops, his Grace would observe through his telescope those of the enemy, which the docile

Copenhagen [his horse] appeared perfectly to understand, from his showing
no impatience nor getting restive.[88]

At about 6 p.m., after nearly two hours[89] of valiant though fruitless, wasteful
sacrifice, the attacks subsided. The Anglo-Allied centre, though badly mauled,
stood weakened but not crippled, whereas the French had thrown away more
than the flower of their mounted arm: they had squandered precious time –
time during which the Prussians continued to filter gradually onto the field
far on Wellington's left.

Therein lay, as revealed elsewhere on the battlefield, Napoleon's fundamental tactical error: his failure to launch coordinated, all-arms attacks.
Had sufficient horse artillery accompanied the cavalry, not only might their
gunners have spiked the Anglo-Allied guns, they could have pounded their
squares into oblivion, with the cavalry needed merely to complete their
destruction by sabring those remnants still in a semblance of formation or,
still more effective, to pursue the fugitives. Instead, after two hours' self-
destructive carnage, the onslaught subsided, leaving the field strewn with
weapons, equipment and ghastly ramparts of men and horses. Thousands
writhed in agony on the ground while the infantry – exhausted and blackened with burnt powder – remained unmoved. When Wheeler later went to
examine the effect of firepower he was astonished by what he found:

> [I] never before beheld such a sight in as short a space, as about an hun-
> dred men and horses could be huddled together, there they lay. Those who
> were shot dead were fortunate for the wounded horses in their struggles by
> plunging and kicking soon finished what we had began.[90]

The frequency with which the French assaulted the Anglo-Allied line is
not known, but Colonel Colin Campbell reckoned it to have been as many
as ten times.[91] Private Henry Swan, 3rd Battalion 1st Foot Guards, claimed
that the cavalry 'charged us ten times in succession and they could not break
us'.[92] Ensign Charles Short does not in his correspondence state the number
of charges his battalion received, describing them only as 'several',[93] Ensign
William Thain, 33rd Foot, stating eight,[94] but whatever their number there is
no questioning their magnificent determination, which won the admiration
and respect of their foes. Stanhope rightly observed how the French cavalry
attacked 'with the most persevering gallantry',[95] while Lieutenant Colonel
Augustus Frazer, Royal Horse Artillery, thought they 'behaved nobly'.[96]

Two principal factors contributed to the preservation of the Anglo-Allied
centre and the destruction of much of Napoleon's mounted arm. First, the
superb discipline and steadfastness of the infantry – what Maitland, commander

of a brigade of Foot Guards, called 'unshakable perseverance'.[97] The Guards, Lieutenant Colonel Stanhope declared, 'behaved as if they were at a field day, firing by the ranks & with the best possible aim. Under a most destructive cannonade & having several shells burst in the middle of us, not a man moved from his place.'[98] Captain James Nixon, 1st Foot Guards, echoed these sentiments:

> not one man fell back, the whole stood firm. The French cavalry repeatedly attacked echelon of squares after echelon and were ten or eleven times cut to pieces. Our squares stood in the face of grape, shell and everything else …[99]

Second, there appeared to be no thought to French tactics – merely a repetition of the same, pointless attempts to locate weaknesses in what proved impenetrable obstacles.

With the flower of Napoleon's cavalry squandered, Wellington's centre remained intact – but not yet out of the storm.

PART 6

10

THE FALL OF LA HAYE SAINTE AND THE STRUGGLE FOR PLANCENOIT

By 5 p.m., despite dispatching four messengers up to the ridge to request ammunition, Major Baring had received none for his small garrison at La Haye Sainte. He did receive reinforcements (two companies of the 1st Light Battalion, King's German Legion, one company of the 5th King's German Legion Line and one or two companies of Nassauers), so bringing his force up to about 550 strong by late afternoon, but powder and rifle ammunition remained the priority. Around 6 p.m. he sent desperate word that his position was untenable without further supplies. Unbeknownst to Baring, his battalion's ammunition wagon – containing, of course, the specialised requirements for rifle-armed troops – had overturned on a road that morning and no one had bothered to recover its contents. Thus, the key position in Wellington's centre remained unsupplied throughout the whole day, its garrison having expended most of their ammunition not only by tending to their own defence but also in firing at the infantry and cavalry columns which had passed their position to engage the main line. The men were confident of holding the place so long as their ammunition held out, notwithstanding the fact that their casualty rate now exceeded 40 per cent.

Shortly after the cavalry attacks subsided, the Germans perceived the approach of a fresh advance against their position, both from the fields and along the road. Ney now renewed his previous attempt to seize the farm, according to Napoleon's orders of earlier that afternoon. The French again swarmed along the walls, some penetrating the barn, where another fire broke out. Others forced their way through a door to the yard, only to be killed by thrusts of the bayonet. Still others tried to smash down the main gate with an axe, each successive attempt thwarted by men firing from atop the pigsty with what little ammunition they could still muster, much of it recovered from their dead and wounded comrades. But the attackers continued to come and when some climbed up on to the roof of the stables and began to fire into the yard against men now out of ammunition, Baring ordered the small remaining knot of defenders – wearied by hours of resistance and their faces blackened by burnt powder – to abandon the place, now a veritable charnel house. By this time, around 6.30 p.m., only one route of escape remained: through the house and out the door to the garden. As the survivors made their way out, the French finally managed to batter in the gate and poured into the yard in over-whelming numbers. In the event, of the approximately 800 defenders who had filtered in and out of La Haye Sainte during the course of the day, an estimated half had fallen in its defence.

The fall of La Haye Sainte marked a critical stage in the battle, for it offered Napoleon the opportunity to split the Anglo-Allied centre and open the road to Brussels. Kincaid, summing up the seriousness of the situation, regarded the loss as 'of the most serious consequence, as it afforded the enemy an establish-ment within our position'.[1] Leach explains some of the dire consequences connected with the loss of La Haye Sainte which:

> … however unavoidable, was highly disastrous to the troops of Picton and Lambert, for the French instantly filled the house with swarms of sharp-shooters, whose deadly fire precluded the possibility of our holding the knoll and the ground immediately about it, and they established also a strong and numerous line of Infantry, extending along the front of Kempt's Brigade.
>
> Those Frenchmen, however, *knelt down*, and exposed only their heads and shoulders to our fire, and in this manner the contest was carried on … [until the end of the battle].
>
> From the time that La Haye Sainte fell into the hands of the French until the moment of the General Advance of our Army, the mode of attack and defence was remarkable for its *sameness*. But I speak merely of what took place immediately about *our* part of the position.
>
> It consisted of one uninterrupted fire of musketry (the distance between the hostile lines I imagine to have been rather more than one hundred yards) between Kempt's and some of Lambert's Regiments posted along the thorn hedge, and the French Infantry lining the knoll and the crest of the hill near it. Several times the French Officers made desperate attempts to induce their men to charge Kempt's line, and I saw more than once parties of the French in our front spring up from their *kneeling position* and advance some yards towards the thorn hedge, headed by their Officers with vehement gestures, but our fire was so very hot and deadly that they almost instantly ran back behind the crest of the hill, always leaving a great many killed or disabled behind them.
>
> During this musketry contest, which I firmly believe was the closest and most protracted almost ever witnessed, some apprehension was entertained that the French would endeavour to force their way along the *chaussée*

[Waterloo-Genappe road], and attack the *rear* of the troops lining the thorn hedge, and on a report of the kind being made to me by one of our Officers, coupled with a suggestion that a part of the 95th Riflemen should be *concentrated* on the *extreme right*, so as to fire into the road, my reply was, 'The 27th Regiment is in square in our rear, having one of its faces looking directly into the road, and that Regiment must protect our rear, for the French are gathering so fast and thick in our *front* that we cannot spare a single man to detach to the right.'

I merely mention this to show in what manner we were employed at this period of the day. I concluded also that the Regiments of Infantry, which were in reserve behind us, and (I believe) some Cavalry not far off, would have instantly attacked any French force which might have menaced the rear of Kempt's Brigade by the *chaussée*.[2]

Colonel Ompteda's brigade of King's German Legion infantry, situated 200 yards behind, and from which Baring's men had been detached, soon became seriously engaged. Fresh from their success in seizing the farmyard, the French proceeded to bring up all arms; skirmishers began to harass the main line from 80 yards' distance; artillery unlimbered within case shot range; and cuirassiers appeared in a dip to the French right of the farm. The Anglo-Allies' vulnerability in this sector was now obvious, for Colonel Ompteda's Hanoverians, though sheltering in the protection of a sunken lane, had incurred heavy losses, with their ranks so thinned as to be unable to fill the wide gaps now plain for all to see. To the colonel's right stood a British brigade, but it too had suffered heavy losses and no reserves lay behind this inadequate front line. The 95th Rifles, to Ompteda's left and across the main road, also stood behind the scarce protection offered by the broken hedges along the lane.

Seeking to maintain the momentum of the attack, the French drove forward towards Ompteda's formation, when the Prince of Orange dispatched one of his aides-de-camp to the Hanoverian commander, ordering him to deploy one of his battalions in line and move against a line of skirmishers. Ompteda deemed this suicidal and, arguing that he held a sound, well-defended position, requested the order be rescinded on grounds that French cavalry, situated only 200 or 300 yards away, would simply run his infantry down before they could form square. Perceiving insolence, the Prince appeared on the scene, accompanied by General Alten, Ompteda's corps commander. Alten repeated the order, only to be queried by Ompteda, who asked for cavalry support and recommended an advance in square. The Prince peremptorily identified the cavalry under cover as Dutch — clearly a mistake given their position behind the enemy front line. While the two Hanoverians persuaded the Prince that the horsemen were clearly French, Orange nevertheless insisted that Ompteda obey his order. Accordingly, the battalion emerged from the sunken lane, bay-onets at the ready, and descended the slope in line formation, two ranks deep. The skirmishers duly withdrew into the cover of the hedges surrounding the garden of La Haye Sainte, and the cavalry – cuirassiers – charged the advanc-ing infantry in the flank, inflicting dreadful losses on Ompteda's men, their commander dying from a shot fired from the garden.

With the loss of an entire battalion the crisis in the Allied centre only deepened. A serious thrust by the French could now easily split Wellington's forces and oblige wholesale retreat. The Duke, informed of the situation while riding on the extreme right, beyond the Nivelles road, ordered all the German troops and the guns that could be mustered to converge on the centre and close the gap, from which some batteries had already shifted to a safe distance, for the fall of La Haye Sainte threatened several troops of Anglo-Allied artillery, obliging them to shift position. Whinyates's battery of 6-pounders and rockets, for instance, fell back to the abatis when La Haye Sainte changed hands[3] and Captain Hew Ross's battery was forced to move further west.[4] Other units, on the other hand, converged on the threatened sector. Infantry, backed by the pitiful remnants of the Union and Household Brigades, for instance, were moved near the main road and formed into square to block a possible breakthrough by French cavalry along that route. Elements of Halkett's brigade had attempted to advance against La Haye Sainte when that position fell to the French, but unsuccessfully and with heavy casualties.[5] Other minor attempts to keep the French at bay occurred; at about 7 p.m., the 92nd numbered amongst several units which Wellington ordered from his left to the centre to plug the gap left by the fall of La Haye Sainte. The 92nd Highlanders, from Pack's brigade, reached the centre from considerably left of the Waterloo–Genappe road and charged French infantry, driving them 'in great confusion' into the sandpit and then beyond it to a hedge beside La Haye Sainte.[6] Other units simply carried on the firefight, like the 1/95th.[7] Grant's light cavalry brigade, bruised but recovered from its fight with the cuirassiers a short time earlier, stood ready to hold at bay any advance against the main ridge, now perilously close to the new French front line. In addition, the Duke soon appeared with Brunswickers to help fill the gap, all the while demanding that regimental officers hold their positions, for there were no reinforcements to hand and retreat was out of the question. The greatest crisis of the day was now upon him, for any substantial French attack could not be resisted. Salvation could come in one of two forms: dark-ness or the Prussians.

Ensign James Howard, 33rd Foot, gave this vivid account of the tenuous nature of Wellington's centre after the fall of La Haye Sainte:

Towards the latter part of the day the enemy made a most desperate and furious attack on our centre, here we had our share of bloody work. I never shall forget the scene and the carnage. Really the French cavalry, who behaved admirably, charged so repeatedly and so many wounded officers went to the rear and much less men. Just at this moment was pointed out to me the meaning of being warmly engaged. Our brigade and a brigade of guards were the only soldiers that we could see, and we were so that I thought that things were going badly, and we made up our minds to send all our colours to the rear, still determined to stay while we had a man left. There we were, we could just maintain our ground, when to our delight came up lots of reinforcements. Indeed Lord Wellington had been with us in very hot fire. I said that we should be immediately supported.[8]

Quite apart from their probes with infantry and cavalry, the French redoubled their artillery bombardment against the now exposed Anglo-Allied centre. Lieutenant George Simmons of the 1/95th explained how by threatening Wellington's centre with cavalry, the infantry deployed there had little choice but to remain in square, so rendering them particularly vulnerable to artillery fire. Still, no matter how intense the cannonade, Wellington's infantry simply stood and took it. There was never any question that fire alone would drive them from the ridge – only infantry or cavalry could actually achieve that. As Tomkinson rightly put it: 'We might run a chance of losing the position from a severe attack of one of their columns, but could not by their cannonade.'[9]

Still, Ross-Lewin explained the serious situation faced by his regiment, the 32nd, part of Kempt's brigade, and that faced by Major General Sir John Lambert's 10th Brigade, which had thus far seen little of the fighting, having stood in reserve behind the village of Mont St Jean for most of the day. Indeed, it had only arrived in the front line about 3 p.m., positioned beside Kempt's brigade behind the Wavre road and east of the Brussels–Genappe road. With the fall of La Haye Sainte, and the French occupation of the knoll and high ground in front of the Wavre road, now Lambert's, as well as Kempt's, brigades came under intense artillery and small-arms fire. The 27th Foot, in particular, standing in square at the angle of the two roads, suffered horrific casualties, as Ross-Lewin explained:

After the enemy's success at la Haye Sainte ... their fire from it was very annoying, and my regiment suffered a good deal. At length the 27th (the Enniskillen foot), which had not been previously engaged, was led up by General Lambert, and occupied the ground on which we had hitherto stood. My regiment retired a few yards, formed square, and lay down; but even in this situation some of our officers were wounded and we lost several men. The 27th had not been long in their new position before they lost 400 men without firing a shot, thus affording a fine example of steadiness, discipline, and passive courage. The possession of that farm-house was a great advantage to the enemy. It not only exposed a portion of our troops to a very destructive fire, but it also afforded a convenient and sheltered point where masses of theirs, both cavalry and infantry, might be collected, preparatory to fresh attacks. In the hope of victory, Napoleon now made the most strenuous efforts, and employed every kind of force, artillery, cavalry, and infantry, to overwhelm the brave but weakened battalions of the centre. Their ranks were thinning fast; the partial charges of our cavalry, however gallant, afforded them little respite from the repeated assaults of cuirassiers and lancers, as well as of infantry; and the fire of the British artillery could not reply sufficiently to that of the French; yet all the energy and pertinacity of Napoleon, the fury and enthusiasm of his troops, and the superiority of his numbers, cavalry, and artillery, prevailed not over the firmness and discipline of those exposed and ill-supported squares. This furious and sanguinary conflict was long maintained; but about five in the evening it suddenly slackened.

At this time two of Lord Hill's brigades were brought up and placed in the first line of the centre, and dispositions were made to meet an expected attack on the part of the position above [i.e. north of] la Haye Sainte. The cannonade still continued without intermission, and there was every indication that the pause on the close fighting would not last long. It was then that the Prussians first appeared. Bulow had come up with a small body of infantry and cavalry, rather to the rear of the enemy's right [at Plancenoit].[10]

The cavalry also faced the renewed efforts of French artillery. After the repulse of Ney's massed cavalry charges, for instance, the Household Brigade held a position on the right of La Haye Sainte which contained no British infantry but was threatened by French infantry and well within range of their guns. There, Somerset recalled, the two brigades were 'exposed to a destructive fire both of musketry and artillery, from which they sustained such severe loss … as to reduce them to a single squadron'.[11]

Advances by French infantry continued, though none could make headway, as Captain George Barlow, 2/69th, explained:

Between six & seven o'clock Bonaparte ordered forward his infantry; several large masses were put in motion and began to ascend the British position in various directions covered by the fire of their batteries and cannon were then ordered to be poured against them to retard their advance. As soon as they had arrived at the proper distance the infantry commenced [firing] and after a very heavy fire on both sides succeeded in making them retire.[12]

Fortunately for Wellington at this critical time, Blücher's troops were arriving, but not where the Duke desperately needed them, for the Prussian commander had directed them against Napoleon's right at the village of Plancenoit, a place not even visible from the Anglo-Allied centre, with events there consequently unknown to the Duke. What Wellington needed from Blücher was several thousand fresh men to plug the gap in his centre created by the loss of La Haye Sainte or to strengthen his left, freeing up troops there for deployment in the centre.

Accordingly, one of the Duke's aides-de-camp galloped off and upon encountering the commander of the leading Prussian corps, Ziethen's, implored his assistance. Ziethen agreed, but would not engage the French without first assembling his whole corps, which still lay strung out along the line of march from Wavre. Meanwhile, one of Ziethen's staff officers went ahead to reconnoitre. Mistaking the large numbers of walking wounded, wagons, prisoners and deserters moving for the forest north of Wellington's line, he returned to this superior's side to announce the retreat of the Anglo-Allied Army, whereupon Ziethen declined to bolster Wellington's left and instead directed his troops south with the intention of linking up with the rest of Blücher's troops fighting at Plancenoit.

Plancenoit consisted of a small village of cobbled streets, walled gardens and stoutly built houses. With the arrival from the east between 4.30 and 5.30 p.m. of Bülow's IV Corps, most of which fought savagely for possession of the place – and bolstered after dark by elements of Pirch's II Corps which in all committed 30,000 Prussians to its capture – the village became a cauldron of bitter, close-quarter fighting with bayonet, sword and clubbed musket. While the carnage initially involved Lobau's French VI Corps, as the weight of Prussian numbers began to tell Napoleon committed the whole of the Young Guard (eight battalions totalling 4,750 men) around 6.45 p.m., supplemented half an hour later by two battalions (1,163 men) of the Old Guard. Over the course of three hours the village changed hands several times, with mounds of bodies choking thoroughfares and, most grimly of all, the churchyard – leaving in the wake of this ghastly affair 6,350 Prussian and 4,500 French dead and dying amongst the ruins of this hitherto sleepy village.

11

THE CONTINUING DEFENCE OF HOUGOUMONT

At about 2 p.m. two companies of the 2/3 Guards arrived to support Saltoun, whose two light companies had been forced out of the Great Orchard and into the sunken road on its northern edge. Saltoun sought unsuccessfully to attack and drive off a howitzer established just outside the Great Orchard near the corner of the wood:

> ... [it was] in one of these attacks when I had been driven from the front hedge of the orchard to the hollow way in the rear of it, that they [the French] occupying the outward side of the front hedge with Infantry, brought a Gun [which] I endeavoured to take, but failed. I, however, regained the front hedge of the orchard, and from which I never was again driven ... We suffered very little from Artillery on the post, but it is quite clear that the house and farmyard of Hougoumont was set on fire by that arm.[1]

Captain Robert Ellison, commanding a company of the 1st Foot Guards, recorded fighting at this time which not only confirms the recapture of the orchard, but alludes to an impressive, yet only very briefly successful, effort to recapture the wood:

> I was sent at one time of the day (I believe about two o'clock) from the orchard with some Light Troops to drive the French Tirailleurs back, who had become very annoying to the farm, and were gradually gaining ground, particularly on the right flank of our position.
>
> We drove them quite out of the wood upon three French columns, which were posted at the bottom of the hill outside the wood, ready to move up and renew their attack upon the farmhouse, two of these Columns just beginning to move, the third unpiling arms and falling in to the support. We, of course, were driven back immediately.[2]

At 2.15 p.m. Foy sent forward Jamin's brigade into the Great Orchard from the south, with Byng, commander of the 2nd (Guards) Brigade, sending another company under Lieutenant Colonel Francis Hepburn from the 2/3 Guards which reached the sunken road at about 2.30 p.m.[3] Home described this development thus:

> … about half past two Colonel Hepburn arriving with some fresh troops, things got again into good order, and after that no very violent attack was made upon this post but only a sharp firing kept upon it by light troops until about 6 in the evening when an attack being made along our whole line the enemy turned the left of the orchard and [pushed?] the troops there back upon our right.[4]

Shortly thereafter, his men now greatly diminished in strength and exhausted from their continuous struggle, Saltoun's two companies were ordered to withdraw back to their parent regiments in Maitland's brigade on the ridge. Thus, by this time the French held the wood and orchard, having committed thus far an impressive twenty-four battalions, or about 12,500 men, the Anglo-Allies were clinging on with a mere 2,600 men, divided between about 900 Coldstreamers holding the château and other buildings, 900 men of the 3rd Foot Guards and 800 Nassauers holding what remained of the château and other buildings. These respective strengths were to remain more or less static for the remainder of the battle, but it is important to note that the French now outnumbered their opponents by a factor of five to one; in other words, almost a quarter of Napoleon's infantry had been committed to the struggle for Hougoumont, as opposed to the 5 per cent invested by Wellington.[5]

Events turned more favourably for the defenders at about 2.45 p.m., when Hepburn's men recaptured the Great Orchard and, shortly thereafter, Campi's brigade from Bachelu's division, sent to reinforce Foy, was driven off by artillery fire from the ridge. Hepburn related the see-saw course of the fighting around Hougoumont in the afternoon thus:

> After some time we advanced, crossed the orchard, and occupied the front hedge, which I considered my post, driving the Enemy through a gate at the corner of the garden wall into the wood. Soon after this the Enemy's Cavalry passed close to our left, and ascended the position, at the same time we were warmly attacked, our left turned, and we were driven back to the hollow way, where we rallied; but when the attacking troops attempted to pass the orchard they received so destructive a fire from the Coldstream Guards, posted inside the garden wall, that they were completely staggered, and we meanwhile advanced and regained our post.

After some considerable time had elapsed, during which I presume the Enemy's Cavalry had been driven back, Columns of Infantry passed over the same ground on our left. We were again outflanked and driven back to our friendly hollow way, and again the fire of the Coldstreams did us good service, in fact, it was this fire that constituted the strength of the post.

We once more advanced, and resumed our station along the front hedge, from whence there was no further effort to dislodge us. But soon after Sir Henry Clinton having sent down some Landwehr (with offers of further reinforcements, if necessary), I sent them with two of my own Companies into the wood, where they kept up a heavy fire. I may remark here that the attacks made upon us were in general upon our flanks, and not in our front.[6]

Still, even after the orchard and wood fell the buildings and walled garden continued to remain in Anglo-Allied hands, even as masses of French infantry continued to swirl round the walls, at times scaling them, only as before to be shot down or bayoneted in the act. At the same time, French artillery continued to fire at the ridge behind Hougoumont,[7] obliging many British units on the reverse slope to lie down to reduce the toll reaped by the storm of shot and shell. In short, throughout the course of the day Hougoumont would absorb increasing numbers of French infantry, siphoning off men better deployed elsewhere, and rendering this sector effectively a battle within a battle – and an exceedingly ferocious one at that – with Saltoun characterising the defence as 'touch and go – a matter of life and death – for all within the walls had sworn that they would never surrender'. Gurthorpe, his adjutant, added: 'Our officers were determined never to yield, and the men were resolved to stand by them to the last.'[8]

In the course of the late afternoon and early evening French infantry continued in their efforts to seize Hougoumont, with Byng bearing responsibility for the defence of the buildings, orchard and garden, for which he bore orders from Wellington 'to keep the house to the last moment, relieving the troops as they required it …'[9] This task, despite his staggering numerical inferiority, he faced with increasing confidence, for French attacks no longer assumed the ferocity of those of the morning.

Ensign Thomas Wedgwood, 2/3 Guards, also observed that the garrison had 'orders to defend it to the last', and described the general course of events in the afternoon, when the French:

… sent fire balls upon the house and set a barn and all the out houses on fire. After being exposed to a heavy fire of shot and grape and shells for two hours and a half, in which we had 3 officers wounded besides a number of men, the right wing of our regiment and my company went to the assistance of the Coldstreams in the wood, in which there was a very heavy fire of musquetry [*sic*]. The French were during the whole of this [time, firing] at the house into which my company and another entered, nearly one hundred men having now been consumed in the flames. The French forced the gates 3 times,[10] and 3 times were driven back with immense loss, for we were firing at one another at about 5 yards distance. There was a large garden to the house which was surrounded by a wall on 2 sides, the house on the 3rd, and on the remaining side a hedge. We had another company brought into it, and a few Dutch [in fact Nassauers] who lined the garden wall, in which they made port holes and annoyed the French very much.

About five o'clock the French gained ground very much and made the English retire from the position on the heights, but were again driven back by a strong column consisting of cavalry and the 2nd and 3rd Battalions of the 1st Guards, and the remaining parts of ours, and after a hard struggle were obliged to give ground and retreat through the wood. They attacked the house again with renewed force and vigour, but could not force it.

'We afterwards,' Wedgwood continued, 'received a fresh reinforcement of Guards into the house, and my company was sent out to skirmish.'[11]

Meanwhile, not only had Jérôme's and Foy's divisions, unable to move in formation through the wood, lost heavily in the course of their piecemeal attacks, they had squandered thousands beneath the walls, where the dead lay in heaps with their stricken comrades. At the same time, Wellington repositioned a number of formations: Colonel Hew Halkett's Hanoverian brigade, consisting of four battalions of infantry from Clinton's division, marched from the other side of the Nivelles road and joined du Plat's four King's German Legion battalions slightly north of the covered way. The Duke also moved part of Mitchell's brigade – the 3/14th, the 1/23rd and the 51st – from west of the Nivelles road to the east.

As had characterised the fighting in the morning, Hougoumont continued to draw off men which the French might have deployed with greater effect further east, and those which they did deploy west of the Brussels–Genappe road found themselves in such a confined space as a consequence of the Anglo-Allied possession of Hougoumont that they could not manoeuvre with ease and found their flank exposed to musket fire from the orchard.

Quite apart from the extraordinary discipline and determination required of the defenders, much depended on a continuous supply of ammunition – for we have seen that the fate of La Haye Sainte had substantially rested on this point. Indeed, one of Uxbridge's aides-de-camp noted that the successful defence of the position may very well have depended on a single supply of powder and ball which he saw arrive sometime between 3 and 4 p.m.:

Late in the day of the 18th, I was called to by some Officers of the 3rd Guards defending Hougoumont, to use my best endeavours to send them musket ammunition. Soon afterwards I fell in with a private of the Waggon Train in charge of a tumbril on the crest of the position. I merely pointed out to him where he was wanted, when he gallantly started his horses, and drove straight down the hill to the Farm, to the gate of which I saw him arrive. He must have lost his horses, as there was a severe fire kept on him. I feel convinced to that man's service the Guards owe their ammunition.[12]

Thereafter, as the French began to grow weary from about 3.30 p.m. until about 7 p.m., the determination and frequency of French attacks diminished both against the southern and western approaches to the farm and against the orchard, and with the repulse of the Imperial Guard – described in the next chapter – Hanoverian, Brunswick and King's German Legion infantry arrived and engaged the French in the orchard and wood.

When the defenders finally opened the South Gate at the end of the battle, after nearly nine hours of fighting, they discovered their position utterly choked with the dead and dying of both sides. Hougoumont had become a true killing ground for thousands of men, the French having failed to provide any meaningful artillery support to their gallant infantry. Practically all the buildings had been destroyed by fire; the chapel survived – only the legs of the figure of Christ on a wooden cross being charred – together with the buildings on the southern side to which the flames could not easily spread: a shed, the gardener's house, offices and a stable. The château, farmer's house, cowshed, barn and other buildings now stood as burnt-out, smoking ruins. Despite the fact that Napoleon's orders that morning had never directed the actual seizure of Hougoumont, Reille had allowed Jérôme unfettered initiative and compounded the problem by ordering Foy to join him, eventually committing twenty-four battalions of infantry into a desperate and futile endeavour which failed both to seize the position and to divert Wellington's reserve infantry to its defence.

The extent to which each side supported their attacks with artillery is not clear, but the French appear to have directed the overwhelming weight of fire on Anglo-Allied formations and batteries elsewhere, especially once their infantry had secured the wood. As for the Anglo-Allies, several batteries are known to have aided in the defence of Hougoumont, but it is impossible to determine their exact number, the period over which that support continued, or the proportion of casualties inflicted on the French as compared with small-arms fire. The French, for their part, squandered the opportunity to deploy even a single battery of guns on the west or, less helpfully, the east side of the complex. In short order, round shot directed at the gates or walls

would have provided the breaches necessary to render the strongpoint indefensible against the overwhelmingly numerically superior infantry desperate
for a chance to gain access to the complex.

Sixteen years after Waterloo an unidentified British officer who had served
at Hougoumont acknowledged the good fortune the garrison experienced
by the failure of the French to bring guns to bear against the western side of
the farm, where the absence of woods offered no protection to the defenders:

> On the French side of the house and garden, coming down close to both,
> was an open but thickly planted wood of about five acres. Upon this wood
> did the successful issue of the defence and real strength of the post entirely
> depend; for the house and garden, although proof against musketry, could
> not have stood for ten minutes against the fire of a few pieces of field-
> artillery, but, ill-built, must have tumbled down and buried its defenders in
> the ruins. Neither could the orchard have been kept for one moment after
> the fall and occupation of the house and garden … But the wood entirely
> screened the house, garden and offices from the sight and operation of the
> enemy's artillery: rendering mud-cemented walls [in fact proper cement]
> – through which their shots would have passed like brown paper – thus
> equal for the purposes of the defence, to the strongest fortification. Owing
> to the existence of this wood, the troops occupying the house and garden
> enjoyed a complete exemption from the storm of shot and shells which
> fell with such fury on the other parts of the [main] position. Except an ill-
> directed shell, which occasionally passed over, and now and then a discharge
> of grape, which was lost among the branches of the trees, the attack and
> defence consisted entirely of musketry.[13]

Having said all this, one source suggests that at some point in the afternoon
the French attempted to force the gates with artillery, with an explicit reference to the alleged incident from Private Matthew Clay, 2/3 Guards, who
also indicated – by reference to French wounded – that at least some of the
attackers who had penetrated the courtyard in the morning were not killed
after Macdonell and his small party of Guardsmen closed the North Gate.
Clay's reminiscences are revealing and deserving of attention, as they provide
a new perspective on the defence of a key point in the Anglo–Allied line:

> The enemy's artillery having forced the upper gates, a party of them rushed
> in who were as quickly driven back, no one being left inside but a drum-
> mer boy without his drum, whom I lodged in a stable or outhouse; many
> of the wounded of both armies were arranged side by side, having no
> means of carrying them to a place of greater safety. The upper gates being

again made secure, a man (killed in this action of the name of Philpot) and myself were posted under the archway for its defence, the enemy's artillery still continuing their fire, at length a round shot burst them open; stumps intended for firewood, laying within, were speedily scattered in all directions, the enemy not having succeeded in gaining an entry, the gates were again secure although much shattered. After this we were posted to defend a breach made in the wall of the building, it being up stairs and above the gateway …[14]

It is clear that by the 'upper gates' Clay meant the South Gate, that is, that facing the French position, for Clay's employment of the plural undoubtedly refers to the two doors of a single gate. Moreover, only the South Gate had an archway, with rooms and windows above it. The North Gate, or what Clay calls the 'lower gates', consisted simply of two wooden doors. His reference to the breach in the wall 'up stairs and above the gateway' also strongly suggests the employment of at least one piece of artillery, possibly a howitzer.

But if the failure to employ artillery and poor strategy in general played a significant role in the failure of the French to seize Hougoumont, other factors bore heavily on the outcome of the day. Wellington invested considerable time and attention into this sector of the battlefield. He visited the farm twice during the action, remained on the ridge and observed the attack from there for at least ninety minutes, ordered its reinforcement of Nassauers, issued instructions to Macdonell personally, spoke directly to one of the battery commanders when calling for indirect fire against the wood, issued orders for the buildings to be defended to the last extremity, and even advised specific action once the buildings caught fire. Wellington may also have taken it upon himself personally to order some of the British reinforcements who arrived in the course of the day. In the end, of course, the successful defence must be attributed to the determination and fortitude of its garrison, which never numbered more than about 2,600 men at any one time.[15]

Casualty rates amongst the units defending Hougoumont testify to the intensity of the fighting there, with an overall loss of one third – or 847 officers and men – divided between the Coldstream Guards (308, or 29 per cent), the 2/3rd Guards (239, or 23 per cent), the Light Company of the 2/1st Guards (30, or 23 per cent), the Light Company of the 3/1st Guards (c. 30, about 25 per cent), the 1/2nd Nassau (c. 200 or about 25 per cent), and about 40 killed and wounded from among the Hanoverians and *Jägers*, representing about a quarter of their casualties.

12

REPULSE OF THE IMPERIAL GUARD AND THE ANGLO-ALLIED ADVANCE:

'THE CRISIS OF THIS EVENTFUL DAY'[1]

By 7 p.m., despite their determined efforts, the French had failed to break the Anglo-Allied centre. Picton and Uxbridge had repulsed d'Erlon's attack spectacularly, Hougoumont continued to hold out, and even the fall of La Haye Sainte had failed fatally to compromise Wellington's position. With darkness approaching and the Prussians gradually appearing on Wellington's left and of course now fully engaged in Plancenoit, Napoleon had been forced to commit the whole of Lobau's VI Corps, two battalions of the Old Guard and eight of the Young Guard, drawing away 10,000 men from the fight elsewhere. With time against the Emperor and increasing pressure on his right, he possessed only one final chance to grasp victory, end the campaign, and thus secure his political future: 'If at any part of the day victory was at all doubtful,' a senior Royal Artillery officer observed, 'I should say it was at this moment.'[2]

Ney wished desperately to deliver the decisive blow that circumstances now demanded, but he simply had nothing left to commit. True, he held La Haye Sainte, but the garrison was not sufficiently strong – or fresh – to emerge from its position and drive off the thin screen of Allied troops near the crossroads. His cavalry, weary and crestfallen at the horrendous losses suffered in the afternoon, amounted to a mere shadow of its former self, for the continuous, futile charges earlier in the day had left nothing but an ad hoc force composed of the remnants of the magnificent regiments squandered in the narrow gap between Hougoumont and La Haye Sainte.

But if Ney possessed no troops for a last, decisive thrust, Napoleon did. Since morning, eleven battalions of the Imperial Guard stood perfectly fresh and untouched at Rossomme. Sensing an opportunity, Ney therefore dispatched an officer requesting permission to deploy part of the Guard. There was no time to waste, for only ninety minutes of sunlight remained. A breakthrough would spell incontestable defeat and clear the way to Brussels. The Emperor returned a refusal. From his position, now at La Belle Alliance – too far back from the main line and with the valley and ridge beyond it filled with the smoke of battle – Napoleon could neither appreciate nor see the state of affairs, nor properly judge the soundness of Ney's request. By neglecting either personally to stay abreast of the day's events or to trust those closer to the action, Napoleon failed to appreciate the pivotal importance of the opportunity before him – and thus squandered the chance to achieve a decisive result while time still remained. On the other hand, while Napoleon failed to understand that Ney held victory in his hands, the marshal, in turn, could not appreciate why the Emperor should refuse to release the Guard; that is, that the outcome of the bitter struggle for possession of Plancenoit remained in the balance – and that its fall would enable the Prussians to sever the main road of retreat back to France. Their artillery was already almost within range of this route, a painful fact which opened the possibility of Blücher cutting the only line of communication and trapping the army on three sides, leaving it with no obvious route of retreat to the west. Of this potential catastrophe Ney stood totally ignorant. For this reason, Napoleon may perhaps be forgiven for retaining much of the Imperial Guard as the only remaining force capable of averting disaster. Perhaps an element of mistrust influenced his mind, as well, for if the marshal could send the cavalry to its destruction there was no accounting for what might befall his precious Guard in Ney's hands.

Napoleon did not remain idle. Observing the weakening resolve of his troops near the crossroads and aware that they could now see the Prussians approaching, the Emperor employed a cynical ruse, spreading false reports that the approaching blue-coated infantry – difficult to distinguish at a distance from the similarly dressed French – were in fact Grouchy's. For a while his troops believed it – and word rapidly spread along the front all the way to Hougoumont, where it emboldened men still fighting to redouble their efforts against its stalwart defenders. With their energy and resolve flagging this news was precisely the boost the Emperor's troops required.

General Müffling, Blücher's liaison officer at Wellington's headquarters, galloped after Ziethen and persuaded him to turn around his I Corps and reinforce the Duke's left. The Anglo-Allies, he insisted, were not leaving the field – but desperately required assistance. Ziethen agreed, and when his vanguard reached the Anglo-Allied left around 6 p.m.[3] word spread along Wellington's line: the Prussians were at last arriving in force.

Wellington, meanwhile, had ordered various as yet largely or wholly uncommitted formations to take up positions west of the Genappe road behind the brigades of Adam, Maitland and Colin Halkett. Vivian and Vandeleur's light cavalry brigades began to move from their position well east of the Brussels road into the area immediately behind the crest of the ridge between Hougoumont and La Haye Sainte. Lieutenant General Sir Henry Clinton, commander of the 2nd Division, was also called forward into the line:

The Duke of Wellington came to the right & though appearances were very favourable, he desired me to strengthen the right as he expected to be attacked by the infantry & cavalry (a French officer had just passed over [i.e. defected] & had brought the intelligence). The greater part of the division had been engaged excepting two battalions of Hanoverians which were still in reserve & upon the other side of the Nivelles road.[4]

Wellington also called up a 7,000-strong Dutch-Belgian division, half of it militia, under Chassé and consolidated his batteries along the top of the ridge. Hours of continuous fire had exhausted the crews, many of whom, along with horses, had fallen to counter-battery fire, with many guns disabled. The loss of La Haye Sainte had enabled the French to shift many of their guns forward, with dire results for some Anglo-Allied batteries, including Mercer's, whose position came under French fire from 400 yards:

The rapidity and precision of this fire were quite appalling. Every shot almost took effect and I certainly expected we should all be annihilated. Our horses and limbers, being a little retired down the [reverse] slope, had hitherto been somewhat under cover from the direct fire in front; but this plunged right amongst them, knocking them down by pairs, and creating horrible confusion … The whole livelong day had cost us nothing like this. Our gunners too … were so exhausted that they were unable to run the guns up after firing … they [the guns] soon came together in a confused heap, the trails crossing each other … I sighed for my poor troop – it was already but a wreck.[5]

Shortly before 7 p.m. Napoleon relented and decided to commit a strong element of his Imperial Guard infantry. Ross-Lewin surmised the considerations that must have been on the Emperor's mind:

It was now evident that the arrival of the Prussians in force could not be delayed for any considerable time. The loss of the French, especially in cavalry, was already very severe, to say nothing of the discouraging effects of their repeated repulses; and neither Hougoumont, nor any point in the main position of the British [apart, of course, from La Haye Sainte], had been carried. Napoleon, therefore, must have felt from this moment, if he did not think so before, that a complete victory was no longer within his grasp, and that all he could hope for was such a success as might enable him to avert the calamity of a total defeat. He had yet a strong reserve, composed of the infantry of the Imperial Guard, the flower of his troops, and with these he determined to make a desperate effort.[6]

Captain H.W. Powell, 1st Foot Guards, wrote that Napoleon's 'Artillery were ordered to concentrate their whole fire on the intended point of attack. That point was the rise of the position about half-way between Hougoumont and La Haye Sainte.'[7]

Wellington enjoyed the great fortune of learning of Napoleon's intentions in advance, for just before 7 p.m. a colonel of cuirassiers galloped out of the French ranks and approached Adam's brigade, which stood behind the slope, repeatedly shouting '*vive le roi*!' and announced to Lieutenant Colonel Sir John Colbourne, commander of the 52nd, that Napoleon was with his Guard and would advance within half and hour on that sector. This prompted Sir Augustus Frazer, commander of the Horse Artillery, to ride off to inform Wellington,[8] who in turn rode over to Maitland's position and personally ordered him to form his brigade into line four ranks deep, partly out of concern that French cavalry would accompany the infantry attack.[9] Halkett's and Adam's infantry formed up likewise.[10]

In all, Napoleon sent forward eight battalions, five from the Middle Guard in the first line, accompanied by a battery of horse artillery, which would separate into sections and operate between the advancing squares, and three from the Old Guard in the second. Remnants of the grand battery were also in a position to support the attack. It is important to note that from the British perspective these five battalions appeared as two or even three columns,[11] though they actually advanced as individual battalions – albeit close enough to one another to give the impression of large columns of attack. A ninth battalion, 2nd Battalion 3rd Grenadiers, remained behind in reserve about halfway between Hougoumont and La Haye Sainte on elevated ground. The 1st and 2nd battalions of the Old Guard, under Maréchal de Camp Petit, remained behind in square straddling the road south of La Belle Alliance, together with artillery, engineers and marines. The last of the Imperial Guard infantry, the first battalion of the 1st Chasseurs, stood at Le Caillou protecting the Emperor's baggage and treasury. The remainder of the Guard infantry – two of the Old Guard and eight of the Young, were already fully engaged at Plancenoit. It is important to note that, contrary to popular belief, the attack of the Imperial Guard did not operate in isolation, but rather as part of a larger, general French advance, with the Guard's advance but the principal part of the whole. Troops fighting in Plancenoit naturally carried on as before, but other formations, such as d'Erlon's I Corps and Reille's II Corps received orders to assist. Thus, Donzelot and Marcognet's divisions began moving over old ground east of the Genappe road while further east Durutte's 4th Division proceeded up the ridge just west of Papelotte. West of the Genappe road, from Reille's II Corps, Jérôme's 6th Division and Foy's 9th continued with their assaults against Hougoumont while Bachelu's 5th Division advanced on the left flank of the Guard, which now must be the focus of our attention.

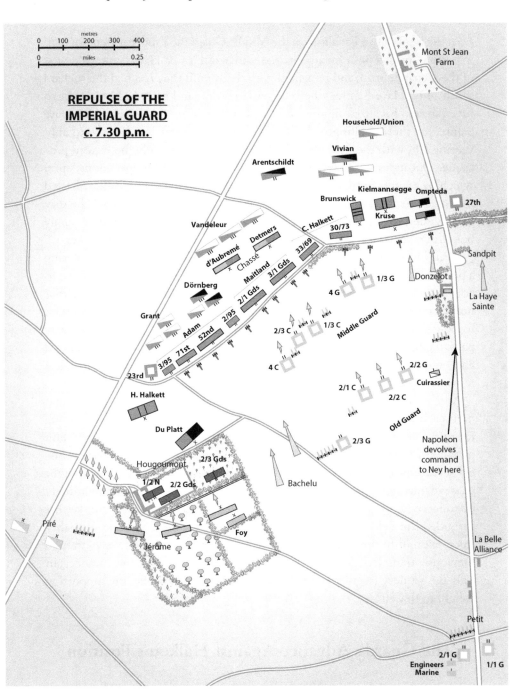

REPULSE OF THE IMPERIAL GUARD
c. 7.30 p.m.

metres
0 100 200 300 400

0 miles 0.25

Mont St Jean Farm

Household/Union

Vivian

Arentschildt

Kielmannsegge Ompteda

Brunswick

27th

C. Halkett Kruse

Vandeleur

Detmers 30/73

Sandpit

d'Aubremé

33/69

Chassé

Maitland

3/1 Gds Donzelot

Dörnberg 2/1 Gds 1/3 G

La Haye Sainte

Grant 4 G

2/95

Adam 2/3 C 1/3 C Middle Guard

52nd

71st 4 C 2/2 G

3/95

23rd 2/1 C Cuirassier

H. Halkett 2/2 C

Du Platt Old Guard

2/3 G Napoleon devolves command to Ney here

Hougoumont 2/3 Gds

1/2 N 2/2 Gds Bachelu

Piré

Foy La Haye Alliance... La Belle Alliance

Jérôme

Petit

2/1 G 1/1 G

Engineers Marine

At the head of five battalions of the Middle Guard the Emperor went forward in person[12] from a position around 500 yards south of La Haye Sainte and west of the Genappe road, and remained with them until they reached the orchard south of La Haye Sainte, where he passed command to Ney. Ney ought to have directed his attack up the road that led straight up the ridge past La Haye Sainte, for there Wellington's line stood at its weakest. Yet, unaccountably, veering left, with the orchard of La Haye Sainte on his right, he instead proceeded through the fields between La Haye Sainte and Hougoumont, upon which lay the thousands of dead and dying horses and men of his earlier ill-fated mounted offensive. While it is unclear why he chose this line of attack, he may have wished to avoid contact with the newly arriving Prussians increasingly bolstering Wellington's left, and judged the Anglo-Allied right to be weaker.

In any event, the area traversed measured 1,000 yards of open fields, offering a perfect killing ground to the batteries of artillery Wellington had ordered to concentrate on the top of the ridge. Ground already sodden from the earlier heavy rains, churned up by the great cavalry action, was now a morass certain to slow the attackers' advance. Moreover, the defending formations – principally the brigades under Adam, Maitland and Halkett – although exhausted and badly mauled from the day's fighting and bombardment, nevertheless remained intact and determined to hold their ground.

At 7.30 p.m. the five French battalions, containing about 600 officers and men each and all deployed in square – but with all ranks of course facing forward – advanced in echelon, the 1/3rd Grenadiers and the single battalion of the 4th Grenadiers of the Middle Guard in the lead, with no skirmishers screening their front. Although their ranks suffered under the weight of steady artillery fire[13] they calmly closed them and continued seemingly unconcerned, sometimes momentarily disappearing in the thick smoke that shrouded the field or in the gently undulating ground. The slope was fairly steep, enough to slow the march of the French, who traversed wet, although previously trampled, grain. Small bodies of cavalry supported the advance, but only the artillery (regular and Imperial Guard) genuinely lent any supporting weight to this effort.

The Guard's Advance Against Halkett's Position

Some batteries of French artillery, operating in the gaps between the infantry battalions,[14] ventured to within 100 yards of the main Anglo-Allied line, and upon unlimbering proceeded to inflict severe losses on Halkett's brigade, consisting of the 33rd, 69th, 30th and 73rd Regiments. Captain George Barlow, 2nd Battalion 69th Foot, described the scene thus:

... the Imperial Guard infantry advanced and made a most formidable attack. These fellows came up with carried arms and in the most determined manner to within seventy or eighty yards of the heights along which our infantry were placed and poured a terrible fire, two pieces of cannon accompanied them and being placed affront our brigade, which was formed en masses [*sic*], raked it most severely with grapeshot as did shells from some more distant howitzers. This was indeed the crisis of this eventful day, both armies were in close contact and hot action and the cannonade really tremendous along the whole line as the entire artillery of either army were in full play to support their respective parties in an effort which was to decide the fortune of the battle, an effort worthy of the great stake for which each contested.[15]

Ten minutes from their start line the two foremost Guard battalions – the 4th Grenadiers and the 1/3rd Grenadiers came within small-arms range of Halkett's brigade, formed up in line, four ranks deep. On his left stood Brunswickers and Nassauers, with Wellington present for some time to ensure they remained firm in the face of Donzelot's brigade approaching just west of La Haye Sainte. One battalion of Nassauers fell back, but another kept the French at bay. To their right, meanwhile, the 1/3 and 4th Grenadiers of the Imperial Guard came within musket range of Halkett's brigade, all of whose four severely depleted battalions had suffered from the fighting at Quatre Bras, where the 69th had lost their regimental colours and the 33rd nearly so – not to mention losses sustained from intense artillery fire over the course of the day's action at Waterloo. Their reduced numbers had required them to form two combined battalions (the 33rd and 69th and the 30th and 73rd Foot) earlier in the day to resist the cavalry attacks. Ensign Edward Macready of the 30th described the scene thus:

It was near seven o'clock, and our front had sustained three attacks from fresh troops, when the Imperial Guard were seen ascending our position, in as correct order as at a review. As they rose step by step before us, and crossed the ridge, their red epaulettes and cross belts, put on over their blue greatcoats, gave them a gigantic appearance, which was increased by their high hairy caps and long red feathers, which waved with the nod of their heads as they kept time to a drum in the centre of their column. 'Now for a clawing', I muttered; and I confess, when I saw the imposing advance of these men, and thought of the character they had gained, I looked for nothing but a bayonet in my body, and I half breathed a confident sort of wish that it might not touch my vitals.

While they [the Guard] were moving up the slope, Halkett, as well as the noise permitted us to hear him, addressed us, and said, 'My boys, you have done everything I could have wished, and more than I could expect, but much remains to be done; at this moment we have nothing for it but a charge.' Our brave fellows replied by three cheers. The enemy halted, carried arms about forty paces from us, and fired a volley. We returned it, and giving out 'Hurra!' brought down the bayonets. Our surprise was inexpressible when, pushing through the clearing smoke, we saw the backs of the Imperial Grenadiers. We halted, and stared at each other as if mistrusting our eyesight. Some nine pounders from the rear of our right poured in the grape amongst them, and the slaughter was dreadful. In no part of the field did I see carcases so heaped upon each other. I could not account for their flight ...[16]

The perspective of Lieutenant William Sharpin, of Bolton's battery, provides further details of the Guard's approach:

We saw the French bonnets just above the high corn, and within forty or fifty yards of our Guns. I believe they were in close Columns of Grand Divisions, and upon reaching the crest of our position they attempted to deploy into line, but the destructive fire of our Guns loaded with canister shot, and the well-directed volleys from the Infantry, prevented their regular formation.[17]

The guns to which Sharpin refers – four 9-pounders and two howitzers – fired case shot as soon as the Middle Guard approached within 200 yards, inflicting heavy losses, a fellow officer noting 'the Column waving, at each successive discharge, like standing corn blown by the wind'.[18] The efficacy of the artillery can only be surmised; but it is clear that only a single volley from the infantry was required to drive off the attackers, as Macready confirms:

That column which advanced on us (30th and 73rd), and which, though it came over the hill in beautiful order, was an inconceivable short time before us, turning and flying to a man at the single volley we fired, and the hurrah that followed it. Having expected great things from them, we were astonished at their conduct, and we young soldiers almost fancied there was some 'ruse' in it.[19]

Major Dawson Kelly, 73rd Foot, concurred, recording his belief that the attacking troops, since they 'retreated without any very apparent cause' might have belonged to d'Erlon's corps rather than the Imperial Guard, or simply had been attacked in the flank.[20] He left a thorough account of the encounter:

Having observed that the different Battalions of the Brigade had got inter-mixed from the frequent formation of squares, I advised Colonel Elphinstone to order both Officers and men to resume their respective stations, to form as extended a front as possible, directing them to cover themselves as well as they could by lying down, to renew, or check their flints, and to fresh prime, so as to meet the next attack with the best means left us. This he instantly directed, and I should mention here that while in conversation with Colonel Elphinstone, one or two sergeants of the 73rd came up and told me they had no one to command them, the Officers all being killed or wounded.

I therefore considered it my duty to remain with them, and upon my saying so, they cheered and instantly returned to their several posts. Thus situated we remained for a short time inactive, when the last attacking Column made its appearance through the fog and smoke, which through-out the day lay thick on the ground. Their advance was as usual with the French, very noisy and evidently reluctant, the Officers being in advance some yards cheering their men on. They however kept up a confused and running fire, which we did not reply to until they reached nearly on a level with us, when a well-directed volley put them into confusion [from] which they did not appear to recover, but after a short interval of musketry on both sides, they turned about to a man and fled.[21]

As for his other combined battalion, Halkett moved the 33rd/69th slightly forward, but at considerable loss to this unit[22] when the French returned fire, wounding Halkett himself, who, struck in the mouth, passed command of his brigade to the commander of the 33rd Foot, Lieutenant Colonel William Elphinstone,[23] whose own account agrees that the French 'when within a short distance of our position, halted and soon after gave way'.[24] The column of Imperial Guard that advanced opposite Major Lloyd's battery must have been a very 'short distance' indeed, for a lieutenant in that unit recalled Lloyd's receiving a mortal wound from a French officer – doubtless a pistol shot, since officers did not carry muskets and the attackers' failure to make physical contact with the British line discounts the possibility of a sword wound.[25]

Nevertheless, through a confusion of orders, Halkett's formation now fell into disorder. In the midst of complying with instructions to face about and return to the cover of the hedge behind the crest of the ridge, the ranks pan-icked as artillery fire drove lanes through the retiring units. All four battalions – or rather the two combined battalions – intermingled before running for cover. Macready described the confusion thus:

Late in the day the French had brought up two guns on the crest of our posi-tion, which fired grape into our square (30th and 73rd) with very deadly effect.

Some one in authority must have thought that the bank of a hedge which ran a very short distance in our rear would afford us some cover, and in an evil moment we received the commands to face about and march down [to] it.

You may readily conceive that fire would not slacken on a body effecting such a movement; but though suffering sadly, and disordered by our poor wounded fellows clinging to their comrades thinking they were being abandoned, our little Square retained its formation, and we had all but reached the hedge, when a body of men (British) rushed in amongst us, turned us altogether into a mere mob, and created a scene of frightful confusion. Fortunately the Enemy took no advantage of it.

Nothing could be more gratifying than the conduct of our people at this disastrous period. While men and Officers were jammed together and carried along by the pressure from without, many of the latter, some cursing, others literally crying with rage and shame, were seizing the soldiers and calling on them to halt, while these admirable fellows, good-humouredly laughing at their excitement, were struggling to get out of the melee …

I know nothing that remedied this terrible disorder but a shout which some one raised, and in which all joining the mass halted as if by word of command.

Macready described the retrograde movement as 'unaccountable' and 'as near as possible being fatal to the remains of Halkett's Brigade at a most eventful period of the day'.[26]

Lacking cavalry support, the French had missed an invaluable opportunity to exploit this temporary crisis in Wellington's line, though this crisis may not have affected Halkett's entire brigade, for an officer belonging to the 33rd/69th asserted that his battalion remained steady throughout:

I never was aware … that there was any published account of our Line having been forced at any period of the Battle, and though I have often fought the Battle o'er again with my old companions in arms, I never heard the circumstance alluded to, nor do I believe it ever occurred. If it had, I must have heard it from my brother Officers who had the good fortune to see the Enemy retreat. I believe I may say run.[27]

Whatever the extent of the temporary crisis within the brigade, within a few minutes, with Halkett's men returned to their former position behind the hedge officers restored the ranks to order. Within minutes Detmer's Dutch-Belgian brigade from Chassé's division swung round Halkett's left and charged down the slope, almost certainly after the two battalions of the Guard had fled – a circumstance more than apparent by the fact that as far as the

30th/73rd was concerned the danger had passed, as Macready's account of their conduct confirms:

> A heavy column of Dutch[-Belgian] infantry (the first we had seen) passed, drumming and shouting like mad, with their shakos on the top of their bayonets, near enough to our right for us to see and laugh at them, and after this the noise went rapidly away from us. Soon after we piled arms, chatted, and lay down to rest.[28]

The Advance Against Maitland's Position

Further to the west, the 1/3 Chasseurs and 2/3 Chasseurs à Pied, also of the Middle Guard, having traversed about 800 yards, all the while under artillery fire, reached the top of the ridge, still in square. Before them lay a seemingly unoccupied position; in fact, it was held by Major General Peregrine Maitland's brigade, composed of the 2nd and 3rd Battalions of the 1st Foot Guards. It will be recalled that Wellington had posted it behind the ridge in a position between the brigades under Halkett and Byng, with its light companies detached to defend the woods and orchard of Hougoumont farm – though after such prolonged and severe fighting these last had largely disappeared by 2 p.m. The two battalions had stood under a heavy cannonade the whole day and received numerous charges by French cavalry.

The advancing French did not perceive the presence of Maitland's brigade, as Wellington had ordered them to lie down for protection from artillery fire. Gronow revealed the timing and reasoning behind his unit's unusual deployment:

> It was about five o'clock on that memorable day, that we suddenly received orders to retire behind an elevation in our rear. The enemy's artillery had come up en masse within a hundred yards of us. By the time they began to discharge their guns, however, we were lying down behind the rising ground, and protected by the ridge referred to. The enemy's cavalry was in the rear of their artillery, in order to be ready to protect it if attacked; but no attempt was made on our part to do so.[29]

Captain Powell, also of the 1st Foot Guards, explains terrain features which not only concealed his unit from the view of the attackers but offered protection from the continuing bombardment:

> There ran along [our] part of the position a cart road, on one side of which was a ditch and bank, in and under which the Brigade sheltered themselves

during the cannonade, which might have lasted three-quarters of an hour. Without the protection of this bank every creature must have perished.[30]

When the French neared to about 30 yards, Wellington shouted for the brigade to stand and fire – according to Henegan, 'Up, Guards, and at them.'[31] With a frontage of about 250 yards, the 1,400 guardsmen, deployed in four ranks instead of two, issued a devastating volley, killing and wounding perhaps 200 of their opponents – or a fifth of the attacking force. The remainder halted, some answering with uncoordinated fire, while others, shaken by the sudden appearance of an enemy seemingly out of thin air, began to waver in the ranks, thus evaporating the impetus of the attack. According to Ensign Joseph St John, 2/1st Foot Guards, 'When we laid down the Imperial Guards thought we were gone and they came up very fast, the moment they came near we jumped up and poured in such a volley upon them that they could not stand it ...'[32] Powell again offers an excellent perspective on events at this critical time, describing the Guard's progress from the outset of its attack:

Suddenly the firing ceased, and as the smoke cleared away a most superb sight opened on us. A close Column of Grenadiers ... of La Moyenne Garde, about 6,000 strong, led, as we have since heard, by Marshal Ney, were seen ascending the rise *au pas de charge* [at high speed] shouting '*Vive l'Empereur.*' They continued to advance till within fifty or sixty paces of our front, when the Brigade were ordered to stand up. Whether it was from the sudden and unexpected appearance of a Corps so near them, which must have seemed as starting out of the ground, or the tremendously heavy fire we threw into them, La Garde, who had never before failed in an attack suddenly stopped. Those who from a distance and more on the flank could see the affair, tell us that the effect of our fire seemed to force the head of the Column bodily back.

In less than a minute above 300 were down. They now wavered, and several of the rear divisions began to draw out as if to deploy, whilst some of the men in their rear beginning to fire over the heads of those in front was so evident a proof of their confusion, that Lord Saltoun (who had joined the Brigade, having had the whole of his Light Infantry Battalion dispersed at Hougoumont) holloaed out, 'Now's the time, my boys.' Immediately the Brigade sprang forward. La Garde turned and gave us little opportunity of trying the steel. We charged down the hill till we had passed the end of the orchard of Hougoumont, when our right flank became exposed to another heavy Column (as we afterwards understood of the Chasseurs of the Garde) who were advancing in support of the former Column. This circumstance, besides that our charge was isolated, obliged the Brigade to retire towards their original position.[33]

Right: Wellington writing the Waterloo Dispatch. The Duke's description of the battle lacked detail and apportioned praise controversially, failing to mention commanders and formations more deserving of recognition than some of those whose names actually appear. Compared to Vice Admiral Collingwood's report on the Battle of Trafalgar almost a decade earlier, Wellington's effort compares very unfavourably. (Author's collection)

Below: Cuirassiers about to charge. Ney's massed attacks squandered these fine regiments in a fruitless attempt to penetrate the Anglo-Allied centre. His inability to see infantry squares sheltered on the reverse slope may excuse his initial error in launching cavalry against defenders fully prepared to receive even the much-vaunted cuirassiers, but his insistence of continuing the attacks over two hours with no result beyond destroying the French cavalry reserve is less easily explained.

Above left: Major General George Cooke (1768–1837), commander of the 1st British (Guards) Division, which played a prominent role in the struggle at Hougoumont, holding the line above that position against French cavalry and in the repulse of the Imperial Guard. Cooke lost his right arm after the fall of La Haye Sainte. He had served in Flanders in 1794, in Holland in the abortive expedition of 1799, and two years in Cadiz in southern Spain. He commanded a brigade during the failed assault on Bergen-op-Zoom in 1814. (Mary Evans Picture Library)

Above right: Major General Lord Edward Somerset (1776–1842). The elder brother of Wellington's military secretary, he commanded a heavy cavalry formation at Waterloo known as the Household Brigade, consisting of two regiments of Life Guards and the Royal Horse Guards. Somerset had joined the army in 1793, the first year of the war with France, and served in the Flanders campaign of 1799 and during the whole course of the Peninsular War. At the Battle of Salamanca, while leading a squadron of light dragoons, he captured five French guns. He served at numerous other major actions including Vitoria and Toulouse. (Mary Evans Picture Library)

British infantry in square (Wollen). Although highly vulnerable to infantry and, above all, artillery fire, the square stood virtually proof against cavalry attack so long as the troops held their nerve, maintained close ranks and continued to issue coordinated fire. (Getty Images/Hulton Picture Library)

Above: Highlanders deployed in square facing the onslaught of cuirassiers. (Philippoteaux). The only realistic likelihood of breaking Anglo–Allied resistance rested with the artillery support that never materialised in sufficient numbers. (Getty Images/Hulton Picture Library)

Left: Scotland Forever! (Butler). Lady Butler's stirring, late Victorian depiction of one of the epic events of the battle – the charge of the Scots Greys. (Getty Images/Hulton Picture Library)

Above left: Field Marshal the Duke of Wellington, by Sir Thomas Lawrence, 1814. His series of virtually unbroken victories marks him out as probably Britain's greatest military commander, though some argue the Duke of Marlborough or Lord Nelson exceeded his achievements in the Peninsula and at Waterloo. (Apsley House Collection)

Above right: Lieutenant General Henry William Paget, Earl of Uxbridge (1768–1854), who commanded all Anglo-Allied cavalry at Waterloo. He fought in Flanders in 1794 and again in 1799. In Iberia he earned a strong reputation for successful cavalry actions at Sahagun and Benevente. During the retreat to Corunna he served with distinction by holding the pursuing French at bay. When Paget deserted his wife and eloped with Wellesley's sister-in-law, the two men fell out for several years. Uxbridge was badly wounded at Waterloo but bore the amputation of his leg with extraordinary stoicism. (Apsley House Collection)

Right: The 42nd and 92nd Highlanders, some of the infantry composing Pack's brigade, which played an important role in repulsing Comte d'Erlon's attack in the early afternoon at Waterloo. (National Army Museum)

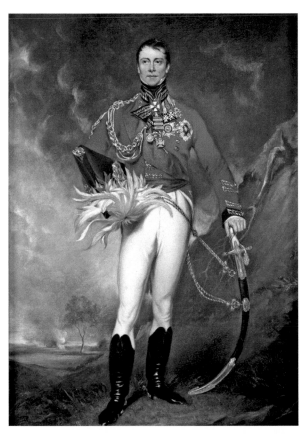

Major General Sir James Kempt (1764–1854), who commanded the 8th British Brigade at Waterloo, which helped repulse d'Erlon's attack and succeeded Picton, upon that general's death, as commander of the 5th Division. An ADC of General Abercromby in Holland in 1799, he became his military secretary in Egypt in 1800. He commanded the 81st Foot at Maida in 1806 and six years later led a brigade in the Peninsula, where he was severely wounded at Badajoz. On recovering, Kempt served at Vitoria, the Nivelle, the Nive, Orthez and Toulouse. His brigade played a prominent part both at Quatre Bras and at Waterloo. (National Army Museum)

Major General Sir William Ponsonby (1772–1815), commander of the 2nd British Cavalry Brigade at Waterloo, where his formation was better known as the Union Brigade, owing to its composition of regiments from England, Scotland and Ireland. Ponsonby served as a cavalry brigade commander in the Peninsula from 1813. At Waterloo his brigade smashed into two of d'Erlon's divisions and rode over the grand battery, only to be severely mauled by lancers, who inflicted heavy casualties, including Ponsonby himself, who died at their hands. (National Army Museum)

The field of battle on the morning of 19 June. Numerous contemporaries remarked in their correspondence on the staggering magnitude of the losses suffered. While the French had witnessed colossal bloodlettings at Wagram, Borodino, Leipzig and elsewhere, British soldiers had experienced nothing of comparable scale in Iberia. (National Army Museum)

The defence of Hougoumont, showing the South Gate and Guardsmen emerging from the wood to engage in close combat. Although the capture of this position did not figure in Napoleon's original plan of battle, it soon absorbed the attention of thousands of French infantry which would eventually outnumber the defenders by a factor of five to one. (National Army Museum)

Cavalry assail British squares. French cavalry displayed the utmost bravery in their repeated attempts to drive Wellington's infantry off the ridge. (National Army Museum)

The advance of the Anglo-Allied army at Waterloo, the first and only battle in which Wellington confronted Napoleon on the battlefield. By the superb use of favourable ground – anchoring his position on Hougoumont, La Haye Sainte and Papelotte/La Haye, and shielding his forces behind the Mont St Jean ridge – Wellington compensated for the qualitative advantages of an army enjoying high morale and composed of a single nationality. Few battles end so conclusively as Waterloo. (National Army Museum)

Charge of the 1st Life Guards, part of Somerset's brigade of heavy cavalry, which achieved results out of all proportion to their numbers. (National Army Museum)

Lieutenant General Lord Hill (1772–1842). Commissioned into the 38th Foot in 1790, he served in Egypt in 1801 and in the Peninsula from 1808 to 1814, participating as a brigade and, later, divisional commander, at major engagements, including Corunna, Talavera, Vitoria, the Nivelle, the Nive, Bayonne and Toulouse. His troops referred to him affectionately as 'Daddy Hill' owing to the strong sense of commitment he displayed for his soldiers' welfare. After Waterloo he served as second-in-command of the Army of Occupation. (National Army Museum)

Evidence suggests that the remark supposedly made by Wellington, 'Up Guards, and at them!' is apocryphal. According to Saltoun, commander of the 3rd Battalion:

> I did not hear him, nor do I know any person, or ever heard of any person that did. It is a matter of no sort of importance, has become current with the world as the cheering speech of a great man to his troops, and is certainly not worth a controversy about. If you have got it I should let it stand.[34]

A rare account by an enlisted soldier, Private Henry Swan, repeats the anecdote, though his undated account may reflect the popular acceptance of the phrase – perhaps adopted some time later – rather than actual fact:

> The Duke of Wellington come to us and told us that we was agoing [*sic*] to be exposed against Guards, the first time that ever we was in our lives. When he said 'Now Guards, for your honour you must stand, form four deep and every man to load and lay down, and when I orders you up, you will fire a volley into them, come to the port and charge.' When he ordered us up with 'Up Guards and at them', which we did with a Huzza and the French turned round and run for a little way, that being the close of the battle.[35]

The truth may never be known, but the story is firmly entrenched in the popular lore associated with the battle. Captain James Nixon, 1st Foot Guards, related the circumstances that led to the French repulse:

> To our great surprise, the head of an immense column appeared trampling down the cornfields in our front, advancing to within a hundred and fifty yards of us, without deploying or firing a shot. Our wings [i.e. flank companies] immediately threw themselves forward and kept up such a murderous fire, that the Imperial Guard retired losing half their numbers, who without exaggeration absolutely lay in sections.[36]

He added that 'they took to their heels'.[37] An unknown officer of the 1st Foot Guards supports the other accounts, though indicates the presence of skirmishers, which is not mentioned elsewhere:

> They brought up large columns of infantry, the line [of British Guardsmen] lay down, and put one regiment to skirmish in front. They, seeing so few men, thought they had beat us and advanced very rapidly, when all of a sudden we stood up, and poured in such a volley they could not stand and they retired in great disorder, leaving the field covered with dead.[38]

Byng confirmed the high casualties inflicted on the attackers, writing of the 'destructive fire' issued by his men and describing French losses as 'immense', as did another officer independently.[39] Captain William Walton, a Coldstreamer, wrote of them being 'almost entirely cut to pieces, not many remain',[40] but of course the Imperial Guard lost many men after their repulse. Captain George Bowles, also a Coldstreamer and therefore not directly involved in the affair, nevertheless adds weight to the notion that the attackers suffered heavily from musketry. 'The first brigade of Guards advanced to meet the leading division,' he wrote on the 19th, 'and poured in so well-directed a fire as literally to make a chasm in it. For a short time the fire of musketry was really awful, and proved too much for even these hitherto deemed invincible; they gave way in every direction …'[41] Major John Oldfield, a Royal Engineer positioned on the ridge at the time of the Imperial Guard attack, watched as 'they advanced with great gallantry to nearly the brow of the hill, not however without having suffered severely from the fire of our artillery, being received by a tremendous volley, they turned about, this was their final effort.'[42] The weight of fire appears to have been decisive. Lieutenant Colonel James Stanhope, 3/1st Foot Guards, acknowledged the contribution of Adam's brigade, to which we shall turned shortly, but remarked in a letter the day after the battle how 'we poured in a volley close which mowed down the front ranks, cheered & charged, they wavered, opened & turned round'.[43]

In a similar vein, Captain Davis wrote of the Imperial Guard being 'broken and driven back with great slaughter, the field being literally covered with their dead',[44] while one young officer described the number of killed and wounded as 'extraordinary, they lie as thick as possible one on top of the other'.[45]

Both battalions of the 1st Foot Guards now charged to seal their success. Crippled by heavy casualties, compounded by the loss of both battalion commanders and many other officers besides, the two battalions of elite chasseurs could not bear it and rapidly withdrew.[46] Maitland's simple account of the affair is almost matter of fact:

> It was at this period that Napoleon made his last effort against our centre and advanced with masses of infantry supported by cavalry and a blaze of artillery. At the command of the Duke of Wellington our two squares formed into a line four deep. Napoleon himself led his Imperial Guards against us, to the bottom of the hill (or rather the small acclivity). The moment they appeared and began to form about twenty yards in our front, we poured in the most deadly fire that perhaps ever was witnessed, as the field of battle abundantly testified the following day. The Imperial Guard retreated; the whole of our line advanced and the rest on the part of the enemy was all flight.[47]

Gronow described the flight of the Imperial Guard thus:

> The French veterans, conspicuous by their high bearskin caps and lofty stature, on breasting the ridge behind which we were at that time, were met by a fearful fire of artillery and musketry, which swept away whole masses of those valiant soldiers; and, while in disorder, they were charged by us with complete success, and driven in utter rout and discomfiture down the ravine.[48]

Lord Saltoun adds further detail to the flight of the Imperial Guard in a letter he wrote only four days after the event. The French attack, he wrote:

> was a thing I always wished for and the result was exactly what I have often said it would be. To do them justice they came on like men but our boys went at them like Britons and drove them off the field in less than ten minutes. From that moment the day was our own and the French were completely routed...[49]

Sergeant Charles Wood, also of the 3rd Battalion 1st Foot Guards, corroborates the accounts given of the attack on Maitland's position:

> ... they came within 100 yards of us and ported arms to charge; but we advanced upon them in quick time, and opened a brisk file fire by two ranks, they allowed us to come within about 30 yards of them, they stood till then, looking at us, as if panic struck, and did not fire, they then, as we approached, faced about and fled for their lives, in all directions.[50]

Henegan and Byng both confirm other accounts which assert that the Imperial Guard ran off in a panic or rout,[51] yet Gronow, in emphatic contradiction to all his contemporaries, claims that his battalion at the very least not only made physical contact with the Middle Guard, but that the French barely resisted:

> It was at this moment that the Duke of Wellington gave his famous order for our bayonet charge, as he rode along the line: these are the precise words he made use of – 'Guards, get up and charge!' We were instantly on our legs, and after so many hours of inaction and irritation at maintaining a purely defensive attitude – all the time suffering the loss of comrades and friends – the spirit which animated officers and men may easily be imagined. After firing a volley as soon as the enemy were within shot, we rushed on with fixed bayonets, and that hearty hurrah peculiar to British soldiers.

It appeared that our men, deliberately and with calculation, singled out their victims; for as they came upon the Imperial Guard our line broke, and the fighting became irregular. The impetuosity of our men seemed almost to paralyse their enemies: I witnessed several of the Imperial Guard who were run through the body apparently without any resistance on their parts. I observed a big Welshman of the name of Hughes, who was six feet seven inches in height, run through with his bayonet, and knock down with the butt-end of his firelock, I should think a dozen at least of his opponents. This terrible contest did not last more than ten minutes, for the Imperial Guard was soon in full retreat, leaving all their guns [i.e. supporting artillery] and many prisoners in our hands.[52]

Ensign J.P. Dirom, 1st Foot Guards, recalled the attack clearly, but makes no mention of physical contact with the chasseurs:

The Brigade had been formed in line four deep, and ordered to lie down. When the Imperial Guard came in sight, the men were desired to stand up and cautioned at the same time not to fire without orders. The Imperial Guard advanced in close Column with ported arms, the Officers of the leading Divisions in front waving their swords. The French Columns showed no appearance of having suffered on their advance, but seemed as regularly formed as if at a field day.

When they got within a short distance we were ordered to make ready, present, and fire. The effect of our volley was evidently most deadly. The French Columns appeared staggered, and, if I may use the expression, convulsed. Part seemed inclined to advance, part halted and fired, and others, more particularly towards the centre and rear of the Columns, seemed to be turning round.

At this moment our line was ordered to charge, as I always supposed, by the Duke of Wellington himself, who was then immediately in our rear. On our advance the whole of the French Columns turned round and made off.[53]

Yet as the Foot Guards advanced they approached the 4th Chasseurs, also marching up the ridge in square, on the right flank of Maitland's brigade. Maitland ordered his men to halt and reform. The second battalion executed it, but the third, to its left, misunderstood the order as calling for square formation. The battalion's exposure to fire and the possible presence of French cavalry, combined with the noise and smoke attending the action, may explain the confusion; in any event, it resulted in the brigade retreating to its former position, where officers rapidly restored order. For a second time during this phase of the battle the absence of French cavalry robbed Napoleon of exploiting a narrow window of opportunity in which to deliver a potentially mortal blow to Wellington's line.

Lord Saltoun is explicit in stating that no order to form square was issued at that time, nor any order to retire. The order passed down the ranks was 'Halt, front, form up' – the only appropriate order under the circumstances. 'Any other formation was impossible,' he wrote, 'and as soon as this order was understood by the men it was obeyed and everything was right again.' He elaborated further on circumstances thus:

> The left shoulders were then brought forward, and we advanced against the second Column of the Imperial Guards, but which body was defeated by General Adam's Brigade before we reached it, although we got near enough to fire if we had been ordered so to do; and as far as I can recollect at this distance of time we did fire into that Column.[54]

Maitland's account of his brigade's charge corroborates the accounts of others:

> As the attacking force moved forward it separated, the Chasseurs inclined to their left. The Grenadiers ascended the acclivity towards our position in a more direct course, having La Haye Sainte on their right, and moving towards that part of the eminence occupied by the 1st Brigade of Guards. Numerous pieces of ordnance were distributed on the flanks of this Column.
>
> The Brigade suffered by the Enemy's Artillery, but it withheld its fire for the nearer approach of the Column. The latter, after advancing steadily up the slope, halted about twenty paces from the front rank of the Brigade.
>
> The diminished range of the Enemy's Artillery was now felt most severely in our ranks; the men fell in great numbers before the discharges of grape shot, and the fire of the musketry distributed among the Guns.
>
> The smoke of the Artillery happily did not envelop the hostile Column, or serve to conceal it from our aim.
>
> With what view the Enemy halted in a situation so perilous, and in a position so comparatively helpless, he was not given time to evince.
>
> The fire of the Brigade opened with terrible effect.
>
> The Enemy's Column, crippled and broken, retreated with the utmost rapidity, leaving only a heap of dead and dying men to mark the ground which it had occupied.
>
> The Brigade pressed on the retreating Column, and was in some measure separated from the general line of our position.[55]

The 4th Chasseurs, the final element of the Middle Guard, aware of the repulse of the other four battalions of the Guard, nonetheless carried on up the slope, possibly encouraged by the confusion within Maitland's ranks. But by the time the 4th Chasseurs reached their immediate opponents, 2nd Battalion 1st Foot Guards, with a strength of about 1,000 all ranks, were ready to receive them, which they did in line, delivering a devastating volley which stopped the battalion in its tracks.

Adam's Flanking Manoeuvre

Major General Frederick Adam's 3rd Brigade consisted of the 52nd (Oxfordshire) Light Infantry, the 71st Light Infantry (Glasgow Highlanders), the 2nd Battalion 95th Rifles, and two companies of the 3rd Battalion of the 95th Rifles. In the morning it was posted near Merbe-Braine on the extreme right, but in the afternoon shifted to near the Nivelle road, where around 4 p.m. Wellington deployed it to drive off swarms of French skirmishers busy harassing the gun crews along the crest of the ridge.

Having achieved this, the brigade advanced and established itself diagonally in the hollow to the rear of Hougoumont, where it formed into squares and stood against the waves of French cavalry that afternoon, all the while however sustaining heavy casualties at the hands of French guns. Around 6 p.m., with the brigade's right vulnerable to an attack against its flank from the area around Hougoumont, Adam was ordered to redeploy behind the crest of the main ridge line to protect itself from artillery fire. By the time of the attack of the Imperial Guard around 7.30 p.m., Adam's brigade stood in line four deep with, from right to left, the 71st, 52nd, 2/95th and the two companies of the 3/95th in reserve immediately behind the right of the 71st.[56]

The advancing 4th Chasseurs, meanwhile, took fire from, at the very least, Webber-Smith's battery of horse artillery, which discharged its last rounds into the head of this, the last attacking column of the Imperial Guard.[57] Worse still for the chasseurs, they exposed their left flank to Adam's brigade. The commanding officer of the 52nd Foot, Lieutenant Colonel Sir John Colborne, wheeled the companies of his battalion in a manner that brought his front practically parallel with the left flank of the 4th Chasseurs, who halted, wheeled in order to face the 52nd, and began to fire. Wellington rode along the line of the 95th Rifles about the time that Adam's brigade was in the midst of this manoeuvre,[58] which indicates that the Duke left Maitland's brigade immediately after the repulse of the first line of the Imperial Guard and rode over to Adam's position. According to Adam himself, 'It was not judged expedient to receive this attack, but to move forward the Brigade and assail the Enemy instead of waiting to be assailed, and orders to that effect were given.'[59] This flanking fire, combined with that from its front, led the 4th Chasseurs to turn and retreat, though not – like their compatriots in the other four battalions – without first opening a respectable fusillade with the 52nd. Specifically, the 52nd fired at least one volley, followed by a charge by themselves and the 2/95th.[60] Lieutenant Colonel James Stanhope, 3/1st Guards, witnessed the scene:

> A shout burst from the English line and such a shout of victory never can be forgotten when the fire poured in on them on all sides, stopped them as if turned into stone. The front sections fell like cards; they began to show timidity toward the rear & the English line shouted & moved on.[61]

As with the other battalions of the Imperial Guard, no contact was made with their assailants.

Sir John Colbourne related how he deployed his regiment so as to face the left flank of the Imperial Guard:

> My anxious attention had been attracted to the dense Columns moving on the Genappe road towards the centre of our position, and observing their rapid advance I ordered our left hand Company to wheel to the left, and formed the remaining Companies on that Company. Colonel Charles Rowan assisted in completing this formation, with whom I had had some conversation on the intended movement, and on the necessity of menacing the flank of the French columns.
>
> This movement placed us nearly parallel with the moving columns of the French Imperial Guards. I ordered a strong Company to extend in our front, and at this moment Sir F. Adam rode up, and asked me what I was going to do. I think I said, 'to make that Column feel our fire'. Sir F. Adam then ordered me to move on, and that the 71st should follow, and rode away towards the 71st.
>
> I instantly ordered the extended Company of the 52nd, about 100 men, under the command of Lieutenant Anderson, to advance as quickly as possible without any support except from the Battalion, and to fire into the French column at any distance. Thus the 52nd formed in two lines of half Companies, the rear line at ten paces distance from the front – after giving three cheers, followed the extended Company, passed along the front of the Brigade of Guards in line, commanded by Sir John Byng, and about 500[?] yards in front of them. If our line had been produced it would have formed an obtuse angle with this Brigade of Guards.
>
> I observed that as soon as the French Columns were sharply attacked by our skirmishers, a considerable part of the Column halted and formed a line

facing towards the 52nd, and opened a *very* sharp fire on the skirmishers and on the Battalion. The only skirmishers, I think, that were out on that day from *our* Brigade were those of the 52nd which I have mentioned, but I am certain that none fired but those of the 52nd. Three or four Companies of the 95th were formed on our left rather to the rear of our line; the remainder of the Brigade, the 71st, must have been at least six hundred yards to the rear when the 52nd commenced its movement towards the Imperial Guards; but I think I observed the 71st moving on, as well as the whole of Sir H. Clinton's Division, when we had advanced a few hundred paces.

I have no doubt that the fire on the flank of the French Column from the 52nd skirmishers, and the appearance of a general attack on its flank from Sir F. Adam's Brigade and Sir H. Clinton's Division generally, was the cause of the first check received, or halt made by the Imperial Guards. The 52nd suffered severely from the fire of the Enemy; the loss of skirmishers was severe, and the two Officers of the Company were wounded. The right wing of the 52nd lost nearly one hundred and fifty men during the advance; the Officer carrying the Regimental Colour was killed.[62]

Adam describes the role of his brigade in repulsing the 4th Chasseurs:

The first encounter with the Imperial Guard was a very sharp tussle with its Tirailleurs [*sic*], but this did not extend to our right further than the right of [the] 52nd, and hardly to [the] left of [the] 71st.

When their Tirailleurs were disposed of, the 52nd were right shouldered forward by Sir J. Colborne, and the 71st conformed; but it being considered that the interval between the right of [the] 71st and the enclosures of Hougoumont left the right of the Brigade exposed, request was more than once made for troops from the other part of the Division to occupy this space and cover the flank of the 3rd Brigade [Adam], and at length Lieutenant Colonel Halkett, with a part of his Hanoverian Militia Brigade was sent for this purpose, and as it came forward the 3rd Brigade advanced, the Imperial Guard was driven back, and the Brigade, continuing to advance, crossed the Genappe *chaussée*, and continued advancing in a direction nearly parallel to that *chaussée*, which was at some little distance on the right.[63]

The 71st apparently became involved, albeit belatedly, as Tomkinson records:

The Duke himself gave the orders to the 52nd and 95th to charge, and the 71st being in the same brigade, and not hearing the order, were retiring. Colonel Egerton rode up to Colonel Reynell, telling him the 52nd and 95th were charging, and begged him to put his men about and join them.

The 71st were halted, fronted, and joined the charge; and this was done in a very important moment – it was a service of consequence.[64]

The various roles of British units in the repulse of the Imperial Guard has given rise to a competitive atmosphere, in which various participants claim the greatest share in the success. Thus, in 1833, infuriated at the credit claimed by Foot Guards officers for single-handedly driving off the Imperial Guard, Major George Gawler, 52nd Foot, published a work entitled *The Crisis and Close of the Action at Waterloo*, in which he argued that his regiment played the decisive role by virtue of its flanking fire and subsequent charge. In this he received the support, thirty-three years later, of Reverend William Leeke, whose book, *Lord Seaton's Regiment at Waterloo*, made the same contention. The colonel of the 52nd certainly concurred, being convinced that 'the movement of the 52nd took place some time before any forward movement was made by the Guards'.[65] Another officer of the 52nd claimed that while the 71st supported the 52nd, it did not complete its wheeling movement in time to take part in the attack on the Imperial Guard.[66] Captain Joseph Logan of the 2/95th, also under Adam's command, related the part played by his battalion:

Lord Wellington rode up to me & ordered I should attack them immediately. I marched with the 52nd & 71st Regiments on my right & such a carnage I never before beheld. The firing of guns &c was so great that the man next to me could not hear my orders. After some desperate fighting the French began to retire & you may be certain we stuck to their breasts.[67]

Yet other accounts do not single out any particular regiment for special credit. Sir Henry Clinton, commander of the 2nd Division, stated plainly: 'Our Guards advanced to meet it [the attack], Adam's Brigade also advanced & brought up their right',[68] while Saltoun referred to 'their [the 52nd Foot's] attack with the rest of General Adam's Brigade on the 2nd Column of the Imperial Guards',[69] indicating that the entire brigade was involved.

Captain Budgen, 2/95th Rifles, reckoned his battalion, or in any event Adam's brigade, stopped the advance:

I think the French columns halted in consequence of our movement taking them in flank, and that the most effective fire of the Brigade was delivered at a less distance than fifty yards. After receiving it the French column appeared to be in great confusion, and the Brigade rushing forward, they immediately gave way without retaining any order or discipline.

In this charge I am bound to say that the services of the 2nd Battalion Rifle Brigade, then [the] 95th, were as conducive to the result as those of any other part of the Brigade, nor could it be otherwise, for from the moment of the charge no check took place, and the advance was at a most rapid pace.[70]

According to Captain H.W. Powell, 1st Foot Guards, Maitland's brigade was ordered by Wellington to form line four deep and that, rising from the ground, their fire stopped the Imperial Guard in its tracks. He also confirms that the Foot Guards themselves retired owing to the threat to their right flank. But his account indicates that their counter–attack was virtually simultaneous with that of Adam's brigade, which adds further evidence to demonstrate that both Maitland's and Adam's brigades contributed jointly to the repulse of the Imperial Guard.[71]

Whatever the relative contributions of the various units involved, the controversy is never likely entirely to subside, as the successors to the Foot Guards and the 52nd Regiment still dispute this point today. In his autobiography, Sir Harry Smith probably strikes the right tone on this question:

> The Battle of Waterloo has been too often described, and nonsense enough written about the Crisis, for me to add to it. Every moment was a crisis, and the controversialists had better have left the discussion on the battle-field.[72]

Whatever the relative merits of the various sides of the debate, the fact that this phase of the battle was most critical and deserving of subsequent descriptions of it as 'the Crisis', is fully justified, as one unknown officer of the 1/95th explained:

> Until eight o'clock, the contest raged without intermission, and a feather seemed only wanting in either scale to turn the balance. At this hour, our situation on the left was desperate. The 5th Division, having borne the brunt of the battle, was reduced from 6,000 to 1,800. The 6th Division, at least the British part of it, consisting of four regiments, formed in our rear as a reserve, was almost destroyed, without having fired a shot, by the terrible play of artillery, and the fire of the light troops. The 27th had four hundred men, and every officer but one subaltern, knocked down in square, without moving an inch, or discharging one musket; and at that time I mention, both divisions could not oppose a sufficient front to the enemy, who was rapidly advancing with crowds of fresh troops. We had not a single company for support, and the men were so completely worn out, that it required the greatest exertion on the part of the officers to keep up their spirits. Not a soldier thought of giving ground; but victory seemed hopeless, and they gave themselves up to death with perfect indifference. A last effort was

our only chance. The remains of the regiments were formed as well as the circumstances allowed, and when the French came within forty paces, we set up a death-howl, and dashed at them. They fled immediately, not in a regular manner as before, but in the greatest confusion.

Their animal spirits were exhausted, the panic spread, and in five minutes the army was in complete disorder: at this critical moment firing was heard on our left, the Prussians were now coming down on the right flank of the French, which increased their flight to such a degree, that no mob was ever a greater scene of confusion; the road was blocked up by artillery; the dragoons rode over the infantry; arms, knapsacks, everything was thrown away, and '*sauve qui peut*' seemed indeed to be the universal feeling.[73]

Thus, in only twenty minutes Wellington's forces, including Colonel Detmers's Dutch-Belgian brigade and a battery of artillery, had repulsed five battalions of the Imperial Guard.

The General Advance

If French cavalry had been available to exploit any of several opportunities which arose during the attack of the Imperial Guard the battle might have ended very differently. These opportunities involved the unsteady Brunswickers, probably only held in place by Wellington's encouragement; the retirement of the Nassauers in the wake of their success against Donzelot's division; the moment when Halkett's brigade momentarily retreated, its regiments entangled with one another, after suffering heavy losses from artillery fire; and the short period of confusion experienced by the 3rd Battalion 1st Foot Guards, who withdrew when they misunderstood their orders. But having remained firm, the defenders managed to hold the line, with the resulting repulse of the Imperial Guard sending shockwaves down the line of l'Armée du Nord all the way from Hougoumont to Plancenoit. The words '*La Garde recule!*' [Guard retreat] came as a thunderbolt: morale crumbled and panic ensued. Whether the sudden realisation that Grouchy's troops had not in fact appeared on the field contributed to this frenetic atmosphere is unclear, but various observers, including Ensign Thomas Wedgwood, 2nd Battalion 3rd Foot Guards, observed that quite apart from the fact that the Allied advance involved large numbers of troops, it also coincided with the arrival of the Prussians within sight of the Anglo-Allied centre.[74]

The extent to which the arrival of the Prussians contributed to French retreat is not clear, but the repulse of the much-vaunted Imperial Guard symbolised nothing short of disaster, and to cries of '*sauve qui peut!*' the army dissolved into a fleeing mass, with most soldiers crowding the road heading south past La Belle Alliance, while many others – infantry casting away their arms and the gunners cutting the traces of their pieces – endeavoured to make the best retreat they could across the open fields. Those units already in pursuit of the Imperial Guard carried on as before, but ten minutes later the Duke removed his hat and waved it, signalling a general advance intended to ensure that the torrent of French troops did not somehow reform and establish a makeshift defence. As one young officer put it, 'The fate of the day was at length decided by a charge of our whole army in line four deep.'[75]

Contemporary correspondence tells us much about the mayhem resulting from the stampeding fugitives. Captain James Nixon, 1st Foot Guards, observed:

> Their whole army fled in the greatest disorder and ours followed in sweeping lines, as fast as the lines could move. Our cavalry cut them to pieces, they abandoned guns, cuirasses, knapsacks and muskets, with which the ground is choked up and for five miles, which we followed them last night, the field was covered with bodies of Frenchmen only.[76]

Ensign Thomas Wedgwood noted that elements of Maitland's and Byng's brigades charged the French and evicted them from the area around Hougoumont at the point of the bayonet.[77] Maitland's troops, however, did not proceed far during the general advance. They passed several abandoned French guns before receiving the order to halt. Meanwhile, Prussian cavalry proceeded along the Brussels road in pursuit of the French, saluting the Foot Guards as they went, their bands playing 'God save the King'.[78]

As Picton's division and Lambert's 10th Brigade descended the ridge the French rapidly abandoned La Haye Sainte and fled south. Lambert's formation halted at La Belle Alliance, where it bivouacked for the night.[79] Most of the rest of Wellington's army descended the slope, including the artillery, apart from Mercer's and Bull's batteries, and insofar as the state of horses and serviceable guns permitted.[80] In Mercer's case, an aide-de-camp galloped up, shouting 'Forward, Sir! Forward! It is of the utmost importance that this movement should be supported by Artillery!' But the utter wreck of the battery and the exhaustion of its crew spoke for itself.[81] Lieutenant Ingilby, on the other hand, observed that in the case of his own troop, his commanding officer, Robert Gardiner:

> … brought his Guns to fire upon the fugitive crowd instantly, and from that period acted independently from the Brigade of Cavalry, alternately advancing rapidly and halting to fire, whenever we found we had a clear

front from our Cavalry ... and the beginning (more than dusk) of the evening permitted.[82]

Rifleman Kincaid described the scene from his position north of the farm:

> Presently a cheer, which we knew to be British, commenced far to the right, and made every one prick up his ears; – it was Lord Wellington's long-wished-for orders to advance; it gradually approached, growing louder as it grew near; – we took it by instinct, charged through the hedge down upon the old knoll, sending our adversaries flying at the point of the bayonet. Lord Wellington galloped up to us at the instant, and our men began to cheer him; but he called out, 'No cheering, my lads, but forward, and complete your victory!'
>
> This movement had carried us clear of the smoke; and, to people who had been for so many hours enveloped in darkness, in the midst of destruction, and naturally anxious about the result of the day, the scene which now met the eye conveyed a feeling of more exquisite gratification than can be conceived. It was a fine summer's evening, just before sunset. The French were flying in one confused mass. British lines were seen in close pursuit, and in admirable order, as far as the eye could reach to the right, while the plain to the left was filled with Prussians.[83]

Ross-Lewin gives this account of the Allied advance:

> During this part of the day, between seven and eight o'clock, Sir James Kempt was on the right of his division, watching with perfect coolness the progress of the attack; and soon, taking off his hat, he cheered us on towards the enemy. The British commander [Wellington], now seeing that Bulow was again engaged on the enemy's right flank, and that Ziethen's corps was issuing from the woods on the [British] left, ordered his whole line to advance. This inspiring order was received with a general shout, and the movement was made with all the alacrity of which troops so long and so harassingly engaged were capable.[84]

Lieutenant General Sir Henry Clinton, commander of the 2nd Division, also described the pandemonium of the French rout:

> The enemy gave way & was followed across the plain, our cavalry came forward & from this moment there was no check. We drove them across the road to Genappe in which direction the Prussians were pursuing & we pushed them as long as we could see. The road was absolutely choked

with his artillery, many of the guns & tumbrils horsed. I never saw a more complete rout.[85]

Captain Mercer remembered this period in only general terms, that of 'our Infantry appearing in the plain, all firing from the Batteries ceased, and about the same time we saw the Enemy's masses dissolving and streaming from the field in confused multitudes',[86] while Lieutenant Ingilby, a colleague of Mercer's in the Royal Horse Artillery, described the French during the general advance as 'completely routed and flying, in the greatest confusion',[87] while Captain Barton of the 12th Light Dragoons asserted that 'such a scene of devastation and rout had never before been witnessed by any of us ...'[88]

Some formations took a relatively minor part in the advance, such as Halkett's 5th Brigade, which had suffered such heavy casualties at Quatre Bras and Waterloo that it did not advance far at this stage, halting at La Belle Alliance. During the course of the brigade's progress the 71st found large quantities of muskets near Rossomme, evidently cast away by the fleeing French.[89] Various observers in fact noted how many of the fugitives flung away their muskets and knapsacks[90] as a means of speeding their retreat. Captain T.R. Budgen, 2/95th, also found resistance either light or altogether non-existent:

> I have a full recollection that after the Enemy were broken and running away, the word was given to let the Cavalry through, and they passed through our line causing some confusion and breaks in it. After the Cavalry passed to the front the 2nd 95th continued to advance rapidly until it came on some bodies of the Enemy posted on some rising ground. A rush was made at them notwithstanding the disordered state of our line from the interruption of the Cavalry, and the dreadful miry state of the ground ... The opposition they made was very ineffectual and slight. They were immediately driven off. The 2nd 95th certainly participated in this attack with the rest of the Brigade.[91]

Adam's brigade, with the 52nd Foot leading, played the most prominent part of the infantry component in the general advance, with their specific concentration on the pursuit of the broken Imperial Guard, as Adam himself related:

> While advancing, the Duke of Wellington being with the Brigade, some Battalions of the Enemy were re-formed, and appeared inclined to stand. The Duke ordered them to be attacked, but it was suggested to his Grace that the brigade, which from its rapid advance was somewhat loose in its formation, had better be halted and the files closed in. The halt was ordered accordingly, but after a few moments the Duke said, 'They won't stand, better attack them,' and the 3rd Brigade was accordingly again put in

motion, and the Battalions of the Enemy withdrew, and fell into the mass of confusion which existed in our front.[92]

In that confusion the 52nd fired on friendly cavalry, but Wellington called on the light infantry to continue their pursuit, which brought them to elevated ground up which the 52nd and 71st advanced. But it was hardly necessary; as Colborne, commander of the 52nd, later wrote: 'We observed the Enemy in great confusion, some firing, others throwing away their packs and running to the rear.'[93]

Still, a few stalwart battalions of the Imperial Guard refused to give way. Specifically, the three battalions of the second line of the Imperial Guard – 2nd Battalion 1st Chasseurs, 2nd Battalion 2nd Chasseurs and 2nd Battalion 2nd Grenadiers, all of the Old Guard – had halted south-west of La Haye Sainte, untouched and still in square. A junior officer of the 52nd recorded seeing them while forward of his battalion with a detachment ordered to drive off some French artillery:

I was clear of the Imperial Guards smoke, and saw three squares of the Old Guard within four hundred yards farther on. They were standing in a line of contiguous squares with very short intervals, a small body of cuirassiers on their right, while the guns took post on their left … They were standing in perfect order and steadiness … The section advanced to within 200 yards of the squares and halted until joined by the main body of the 52nd …

Up to this moment neither the guns, the Imperial Guard, nor the 52nd had fired a shot. I then saw one or two guns slewed round to the direction of my company and fired, but their grape [in fact canister] went over our heads. We opened our fire and advanced; the squares replied to it, and then steadily faced about, [and] retired … the cuirassiers declined the contest and turned. The French proper right square brought up its right shoulders [inclined to the left] and crossed the *chaussée*, and we crossed it after them.[94]

Captain Reed, 71st Foot, recorded his own regiment, formed four deep, supporting the 52nd in their charge, and encountering the Old Guard. The fact that he mentions the 71st afterwards camping near Plancenoit indicates that it pursued the French for some distance:

We here charged three squares of the Guard, whom we broke and pursued, crossing the road leading to Genappe, when we brought left shoulders forward, the right of the 71st resting on La Belle Alliance … The French squares having separated, the 52nd pursued what had been their right square; the other two fell to our lot. They retreated by the right of Planchenoit [sic], in front of which village we bivouacked for the night.[95]

The 2/3rd Grenadiers were soon surrounded and attacked by infantry, cavalry and artillery firing canister at point-blank range near La Belle Alliance. With its numbers severely dwindled, its commanding officer ordered the men to fire a final volley and disperse to the rear to avert total destruction. The 2/1st Chasseurs and 2/2nd Chasseurs eventually also dispersed, while the 4th Grenadiers practically disappeared under the weight of extreme losses. At the same time the squares of the 1/1st Grenadiers and 2/1st Grenadiers of the Old Guard, together numbering about 1,200 officers and men, stood against the tide of fleeing masses south of La Belle Alliance on either side of the Waterloo–Genappe road, where they refused to be moved, eventually withdrawing towards Rossomme, with Napoleon himself sheltering in the square of the 1st Battalion for a time.

The famous incident in which General Cambronne, commander of the Chasseurs, declared his defiance to calls for the 2/1st Chasseurs to surrender – '*La Garde meurt, mais ne se rend pas!*' ['The Guard dies but does not surrender!']⁹⁶ – occurred during this final phase of the battle. Whether or not Cambronne actually shouted out this phrase remains a matter of some debate – as does the question as to whether or not he was wounded at this time. Notwithstanding his refusal to submit and whatever reply he actually offered to the demand, it is noteworthy that he did become a prisoner. Lieutenant Colonel William Halkett, commander of the 3rd Hanoverian brigade, personally seized the general, as he later described:

> During our advance we were in constant contact with the French Guards, and I often called to them to surrender. For some time I had my eye upon, as I supposed, the General Officer in command of the Guards (being in full uniform) trying to animate his men to stand.
>
> After having received our fire with much effect, the Column left their General with two Officers behind, when I ordered the sharpshooters to dash on, and I made a gallop for the General. When about cutting him down he called out he would surrender, upon which he preceded me [to the rear], but I had not gone many paces before my horse got a shot through his body and fell to the ground. In a few seconds I got him on his legs again, and found my friend, Cambronne, had taken French leave in the direction from where he came. I instantly overtook him, laid hold of him by the aiguillette [ornamental braided cord], and brought him in safety and gave him in charge of a sergeant of the Osnabruckers to deliver to the Duke; I could not spare an Officer for the purpose, many being wounded.⁹⁷

The general may have been wounded and thus incapable of rendering much resistance to Halkett, but the fact of his capture must call into question the likelihood of his having issued the defiant words attributed to him, a case made by some contemporaries even before Victorians properly lent it to posterity.[98] As Gronow asserted some decades after Waterloo, 'Cambronne's supposed answer of "*La Garde ne se rend pas*" was an invention of aftertimes, and he himself always denied having used such an expression.'[99]

While Wellington left the bulk of the pursuit of the French to the Prussian cavalry, the light cavalry brigades of Major Generals Vivian and Vandeleur became engaged from the outset of the general advance. These formations had been deployed on the Anglo-Allied left for most of the day, but when the Prussians had arrived in substantial numbers in that sector, Uxbridge had ordered his cavalry to concentrate to the west of the Waterloo–Genappe road. Accordingly, he sent the Assistant Quartermaster General of the Cavalry and Captain Horace Seymour, an aide-de-camp, to order Vivian's brigade, consisting of the 10th and 18th Hussars, together with the 1st King's German Legion Hussars, over to the right rear of the Anglo-Allied position.[100] It will be recalled that Vandeleur's brigade, consisting of the 11th, 12th and 16th Light Dragoons, had taken part in repelling the massed French cavalry attacks earlier in the day. These regiments now stood in a position to fight again since, on the approach of the Prussians, around 5.30 p.m., the brigade had been moved to the right of the Brussels–Genappe road, together with Vivian's brigade.

At the same time, the remains of the two heavy cavalry brigades, plus a squadron of the 23rd Light Dragoons (from Sir William Dornberg's 3rd Cavalry Brigade) which had somehow become separated from the rest of the regiment, also moved to the right. Uxbridge was struck in the knee by a round shot or shell fragment around 7.30 p.m., just as word arrived back that Vivian's brigade was en route to reinforce the right.[101]

Let us first examine the role of Vandeleur's brigade in the general advance. At this point the 12th Light Dragoons, now only composing two squadrons owing to the considerable losses sustained earlier in attacking Durutte's column,[102] proceeded east of Hougoumont around 5.30 p.m. to a position in a field of trampled crops to the right rear of the Foot Guards. There, in support of and on Vivian's right, Vandeleur's formation itself, supported by the 23rd Light Dragoons from Dörnberg's brigade,[103] engaged and broke a large French square of unidentified infantry near La Belle Alliance,[104] while the 11th Light Dragoons captured the last French battery still in operation in that sector of the battlefield.[105] The 12th engaged the Grenadiers à Cheval of the Imperial Guard – elite heavy cavalry – which, unsurprisingly, the Light Dragoons failed to drive off. Captain Barton described his regiment's part:

> On the failure of the Enemy's last attack the Brigade advanced, passing over the ground on which the struggle had taken place between the French and

English Guards. The scene here was terrific from the great number of killed and wounded. Bodies were lying so close to each other that our horses could scarcely advance without trampling on them, and a great many were wounded in the fetlocks from the bayonets and other weapons that were scattered about on the field.[106]

The 16th Light Dragoons, meanwhile, advanced in line to the crest of the ridge, formed into a column of half-squadrons in order to pass through the intervals between the infantry, proceeded rapidly down the forward slope in pursuit of broken infantry and cavalry of various types intermixed in the confusion, and rode over ground strewn with cuirasses cast away by troopers seeking to lighten themselves in order to speed their retreat. Finally, about a mile and a half from their original position behind the ridge, the Light Dragoons charged and broke a French square,[107] almost certainly one hastily formed.

Numerous contemporary accounts of the conduct of Vivian's light cavalry brigade at this stage of the fighting reveal the decisive role played by that formation – consisting of the 10th and 18th Hussars, and the 1st King's German Legion Hussars – in maintaining the pressure on the retreating French; indeed Vivian emphatically maintained that his brigade – with virtually no immediate support from Vandeleur – must enjoy the credit for maintaining the impetus of the attack and denying the French the opportunity to rally and offer organised resistance.[108] That process began when the brigade shifted, upon the arrival of the Prussians on Wellington's left around 5.30 p.m., to the immediate right of the Brussels–Genappe road. Lieutenant Colonel Henry Murray, 18th Hussars, described his regiment's move west from its position near the hamlet of Smohain:

> The roar was now so great that though close together we could not make ourselves understood except by hollering. The smoke was very thick, and only allowed the enemy's heads to be seen; all at once we burst from the darkness of a London fog into a bright sunshine ... The air of ruin and destruction that met our view in the centre of the line was calculated to inspire us with thoughts by no means akin to anticipations of victory, and many thought that they had been brought from the left to cover another retreat, yet no despondency was visible, and the feeling of reliance on the oft proved skill of our chief cherished the hope that by persevering a little longer our repeated heroic exertions would yet be crowned with success.[109]

Vivian's descriptions of his brigade's predicament once shifted west of the Brussels road reveals how finely balanced the fortunes of the battle still stood prior to the repulse of the Imperial Guard. After reaching a position on the immediate right of the Brussels–Genappe road, drawn up behind Hanoverian infantry to provide moral support, his brigade came under furious fire:

[We] remained for about half an hour exposed to the most dreadful fire of shot, shell, and musketry that it is possible to imagine. No words can give any idea of it (how a man escaped is to me a miracle), we every instant expecting through the smoke to see the Enemy appearing under our noses, for the smoke was literally so thick that we could not see ten yards off.[110]

Once the French retreat began, the brigade advanced, but only at a trot, as Vivian strongly insisted in his recollections many years later.[111] The 18th Hussars, then began the work of destruction, as Lieutenant Colonel Murray related:

Soon we came into ground entirely covered with French Infantry retreating, not in a body, but individually, yet with none of that hurry and confusion that might be imagined when thus suddenly ridden in upon, and especially some of the Ancienne Garde [Old Guard] might be remarked for their cool-ness and bold countenance (one nearly bayonetted me as I passed). Numbers of these were cut down and my Orderly (a man named Dwyer) cut down five or six in rapid succession, the pursuit of the Cavalry continuing.[112]

Captain T. W. Taylor, 10th Hussars, described the scene as the brigade began to come into action. 'As we advanced at a gallop,' he recalled, 'we saw the French Army retiring in confusion up the hill, presenting a most picturesque sight of a mixture of all arms and uniforms. Some Guns in their rear were firing, and there was also some musketry.' They soon passed Foot Guards and line infantry in close columns, cheering them. One squadron managed to break a square, though Major Howard died when, apparently already falling wounded from the saddle, he was struck by an infantryman with the butt end of his musket. Vivian soon approached the regiment and ordered them to halt for the night, being content with their efforts for the day. They accordingly halted on rising ground in fine moonlight. It was just as well, for Taylor's horse was 'so knocked up he could hardly go …'[113]

Vivian's own explanation of the role his brigade played in the closing phase of the battle sheds perhaps the clearest light on affairs:

With respect to the particular situation in which my brigade was placed, it did not suffer much until the last attack. The ground on the left did not admit of the cavalry advancing, and I being on the left of all, consequently suffered only from the cannonade; about 6 o'clock, however, I learnt that the cavalry in the centre had suffered dreadfully and the Prussians about that time having formed to my left, I took [it] upon myself to move off from our left, and halted directly to the centre of our line, where I arrived most opportunely at the instant that Bonaparte was making his last and most desperate effort, and never did I witness anything so terrific, the ground actually covered with dead and dying, cannon shot and shells flying thicker than I ever heard even musketry before and our troops, some of them giving way. In this state of affairs I wheeled my brigade into line, close within 10 yards in rear of our infantry, and prepared to charge the instant they had retreated through my intervals. The three squadron officers of the 10th [Hussars] were wounded at this instant this, however, gave them confidence, and the brigades that were literally running away, halted, on our cheering them, and again began firing. The enemy on their part began to waver, the Duke observed it, and ordered the infantry to advance. I immediately wheeled the brigade by half squadrons to the right, and in column over the dead and dying, trotted round the right of our infantry, passed the French infantry and formed lines of regiments on the first half squadrons. With the 10th I charged a body of French cuirassiers and lancers ... and completely routed them. I then went to the 18th [Hussars] and charged a second body that was supporting a square of the Imperial Guards, and the 18th not only defeated them, but took 14 pieces of cannon that had been firing grape at us during our movement.

I then with the 10th, having reformed them, charged a square of infantry, Imperial Guards, the men of which we cut down in the ranks, and here the last shot was fired. From this moment all was derout.'[14]

He continues:

Towards the end of the battle, the whole of the cavalry on the right being almost annihilated I heard they were in want of us & the Prussians arriving on my left, I trotted along the rear of our line to the right & formed in the rear of our infantry where there was the most tremendous fire of round, grape & musketry I ever experienced; the 10th led the column beautifully. The enemy began to give way, I trotted in column of ½ squadrons from the right, round the flank of the infantry in my front & in this manner the brigade proceeded led by the 10th under the heaviest fire of grape & musketry you can possibly imagine, in as good order, intervals as well preserved & as steady, as if at a field day in England. We led for the left of the French where there were two strong bodies of French cavalry (cuirassiers & lancers in each) with a square of infantry in the centre. I directed the brigade to front lines of regiments on their front ½ squadrons, they did it to perfection;

this done, with the 10th I charged the left body of cavalry; they went in in the best possible line & at full speed & entered the enemy's line which outflanked & wheeled up to receive them, but was in an instant overthrown & great numbers cut down.

I then ordered the 18th to attack the cavalry on the right of the square & the 10th to rally, which they did to perfection, when I directed Major Howard's squadron, supported by the other two, to charge the square; the gallantry with which they did this is not to be expressed; they were received by a most tremendous fire, but they persisted & cut down the French in their ranks. From this moment, not a shot was fired, every man of the French infantry was either sabred by the 10th or made prisoners by General Vandeleur's Brigade which came up shortly after.[115]

The commander of the 18th Hussars explained that Vivian's brigade in fact swept all before it:

It was immediately evident to Vivian that the attack must in the first instance be directed against the advanced artillery and cavalry, and having put the regiment in motion, he placed himself in front of the centre, beside Colonel Murray, for the purpose of putting us into the required direction. He on this said to the regiment, '18th, you will follow me' … He then ordered the charge to sound, when the regiment dashed forward with the greatest impetuosity, and at the same time with as much steadiness and regularity as if they had been at field day exercise on Hounslow Heath. Thus the direction of the charge by the regiment diverged as much to the left as that of the 10th had inclined to the right. Just as our charge commenced, some French artillery coming from their right, and slanting towards the regiment, made a bold push to cross our front at a gallop, but the attempt failed, and we were in an instant among them, cutting down the artillerymen and the drivers and securing the guns. In the next moment we fell upon the advanced cavalry … in another moment the regiment was fiercely and dexterously plying their sabres amongst them, and we next charged the Imperial Guard, their cuirassiers and lancers, a regular medley of them all, including infantry and guns, etc., such a scene! The infantry threw themselves down except two squares, which stood firm, but did no good.[116]

Lieutenant Henry Duperier, also of the 18th Hussars, observed that:

We charged, and of course overtook them, in an instant we fell on the cavalry who resisted but feebly; and in running, tumbled over their own infantry. From that we came on the artillery who was not better treated by the Irish lads in attentions. There were perhaps three 18th Hussars on a regiment of infantry of the French nothing but '*Vive le Roi*' [i.e. claims of loyalty to Louis XVIII, not Napoleon], but it was too late; besides our men do not understand French, so they cut away all through till we came to the body of reserve, when we was saluted with a volley at the length of two swords.[117]

Captain Arthur Kennedy, of the same regiment provided a similar account:

On seeing them [the Imperial Guard] run off a general panic seems to have overtaken the command and pervaded the whole of the enemy's line and '*Sauve qui peut*' was the universal shout, infantry, cavalry and artillery now mixed through each other in the utmost confusion and this fine army became in a moment a confused mob scampering in every direction over a most open country and the remains of them saved only by the night. The ground was so wet owing to the almost incessant rain for two days that almost all their cannon fell into our hands before they had retreated half a league: ammunition wagons, tumbrels [*sic*], coaches, and carriages all stuck fast in the mud before they reached the village of Genappe which was only a league from the field …[118]

Lieutenant T. W. Taylor wrote of a troop from the 18th 'gallantly, though uselessly' charging a square on the French ridge.[119]

Other light cavalry brigades played a part in the pursuit, such as Major General Sir Colquhoun Grant's, composed of the 7th and 15th Hussars, plus the 2nd King's German Legion Hussars. According to Lieutenant Standish O'Grady, 7th Hussars:

After having charged every species of troops, infantry, artillery and cavalry, we halted about ½ a mile in rear of the French position, and there found, though of the 7th and 15th there remained only 35 men, Colonel Kerrison and four officers. We were too weak to act any longer as a brigade, so we joined Vivian's Brigade and acted with the 18th and 1st German Hussars for the rest of the night.[120]

As a result of losses sustained throughout the day, however, the 7th Hussars and the 13th Light Dragoons mustered only a single squadron each.[121] The 15th Hussars, reduced by this time to two squadrons, also saw action, but suffered further heavy casualties in failing to break a French square. By the end of the fighting, like most of Wellington's cavalry, the Hussars were, as Lieutenant Henry Lane put it, 'dreadfully cut up'.[122]

Exhaustion and reduced numbers were circumstances of course not unique to the cavalry. At least some of the artillery simply found themselves unable to move, as Mercer relates:

> Captain Walcot of the horse-artillery had come to us, and we were all look-ing out anxiously at the movements below and on the opposite ridge, when he suddenly shouted out, 'Victory! – victory! They fly! – they fly!' and sure enough we saw some of the masses dissolving, as it were, and those com-posing them streaming away in confused crowds over the field, whilst the already desultory fire of their artillery ceased altogether. I shall never forget this joyful moment! – this moment of exultation! On looking round I found we were left almost alone. Cavalry and infantry had all moved forward, and only a few guns here and there were to be seen on the position. A little to our right were the remains of Major M'Donald's troop under Lieutenant Sandilands, which had suffered much, but nothing like us. We were con-gratulating ourselves on the happy results of the day, when an aide-de-camp rode up, crying 'Forward, sir! – forward! It is of the utmost importance that this movement should be supported by artillery!' at the same time waving his hat much in the manner of a huntsman laying on his dogs. I smiled at his energy, and, pointing to the remains of my poor troop, quietly asked, 'How, sir?' A glance was sufficient to show him the impossibility, and away he went.[123]

Lieutenant General Lord Hill, commander of II Corps, approached the 13th Light Dragoons, part of Colonel Sir F. von Arentschildt's brigade, whose troopers, together with the infantry around them shouted 'huzzah!' and joined the fray, Lieutenant William Turner observing how 'the French retired in the greatest confusion, our infantry advancing kept us at a trot for three miles when we with the whole of the cavalry pursued them about three miles further when darkness, at 9 p.m. put an end to the slaughter, the last charge was literally riding over men and horses, who lay in heaps'.[124] An unknown officer of the same regiment offered his own account:

> Our last and most brilliant charge, was at the moment that Lord Hill, perceiving the movement of the Prussian army, and finding the French Imperial Guard on the point of forcing a part of the British position, cried out 'Drive them back, 13th!' such an order from such a man, could not be misconstrued, and it was punctually obeyed.[125]

Tomkinson, 16th Light Dragoons, part of Vandeleur's brigade, described the part his brigade took in the pursuit, revealing from his perspective greater resistance by the French than those contained in many other accounts of the general advance:

> We were ordered to form line, descend into the plain and pursue the enemy … We were led … by our general betwixt the road to Charleroi … and had to open out and pass over many killed and wounded. In retiring from the last attack the enemy had made considerable haste to the rear, and not until we were lineable with the Observatory did we receive any fire or perceive any intention of stopping us. They were in complete deroute [sic] and confusion. On the top of a small hill they at length opened a couple of guns and fired a few round shot. We continued to advance at a trot, and on coming closer to these guns, they fired once with grape, which fell about fifty yards short of the brigade, and did not the least damage … I rode on before the brigade to an eminence (which we were ascending) to see what force the enemy had in our front. From this point I saw a body of infantry with a squadron of cuirassiers formed in the valley, close to a by-road which ran at right angles to the point we were moving on. The infantry were about 1,000 in column with about three companies formed behind a hedge, which ran alongside of the road in question … in a minute the brigade was on the top of the rising ground, in a gallop the instant they saw the enemy, and proceeded to the charge. The enemy's infantry behind the hedge gave us a volley, and being close at them, and the hedge nothing more than some scattered bushes without a ditch, we made a rush and went into their column with the companies which were stationed in their front, they running away to the square for shelter. We completely succeeded, many of their infantry immediately throwing down their arms and crowding together for safety. We were riding in all directions at parties attempting to make their escape, and in many instances had to cut down men who had taken up their arms after having in the first instance laid them down. From the appearance of the enemy lying together for safety, they were some yards in height, calling out, from the injury of one pressing upon another, and from the horses stamping upon them (on their legs) … After some little delay in seeing they all surrendered; we proceeded in pursuit of the enemy's other scattered troops. It was nearly dark at the time we made the change, and when we moved from the spot it was quite so …
>
> We went up the next brow of a hill, following the enemy, who were scattered in all directions … The men were ordered to stop, not knowing in that light what force the enemy might have, and the brigade being scattered we halted and formed …
>
> Here the pursuit ended, it being ten o'clock, and the brigade was ordered to retire. The ground was covered with muskets, thrown-away guns, ammunition wagons, tumbrils, brandy, etc. We came across some of the latter, and

got as much as the men required. We retired to the edge of the wood near the Observatory, and not half a mile from the point where we charged the infantry, and there bivouacked for the night.[126]

Wellington's heavy cavalry also took part in the general advance, though only to a limited extent, for they were largely incapable of pursuit. By 4 p.m. the Household Brigade had become so weakened by losses of men and horses that it numbered only a single squadron. When the Imperial Guard reached the crest of the ridge, Somerset's brigade stood in line about 300 yards behind and about the same distance to the right of the main road running between La Haye Sainte and the village of Mont St Jean. Upon the repulse of the Imperial Guard, they moved to the front and, accompanied by a small detachment of the 23rd Light Dragoons, joined in the pursuit until darkness set in, though they do not appear to have reached much beyond La Belle Alliance.[127]

The Union Brigade also played a small role in this phase of the battle. Captain George Damer, on the Duke's staff, rode over to deliver an order for the brigade to advance with the remainder of the army, but after a long search he encountered a shattered and critically understrength formation:

> They were reduced to about two hundred and fifty men; many of them wounded, with heads and hands bandaged, were standing by their horses, who were panting and blowing, and looked completely done up. At their head stood the gallant Colonel Muter of the Inniskillings, upon whom the command of the brigade had fallen after Ponsonby's death. This grim veteran had his helmet beaten in, and his arm, which had been badly wounded, was in a sling.
>
> Muter obeyed the order, and his men cantered off.[128]

Sergeant Archibald Johnston, Scots Greys, also noted the perspective of part of the Union Brigade:

> As soon as the French commander saw the British troops put in motion to form line they instantly began to form their retreat, no sooner were our line formed than we received orders to make a general advance which was instantly complied with, giving them as usual three British cheers, which so panic struck the tyrant's troops that thousands of them threw away their arms, knapsacks &c and fled in all directions, and with all speed to save themselves from the murdering shot. Meanwhile those who attempted to retire in an orderly manner were cut to pieces by hundreds by our British guns; by this time the brave old veteran Blucher was so far advanced with his hardy troops as to enable his artillery to open a fire upon the flying enemy

also, whose retreat by this time became an absolute flight which they did in an awful and very rapid manner. Every shot that was fired by the Prussians as well as by us made avenues through their flying columns horrible to behold, in fact in a manner quite inconceivable; here was the awfullest scene ever yet seen. As we advanced in pursuit of the flying enemy the ground over which we marched were strewed with the killed and wounded similar to sheaves of corn behind the reapers on a harvest day. In fact, in some particular places the dead were lying in heaps.[129]

The Anglo-Allied portion of the pursuit continued for a relatively short period; Captain Orlando Bridgeman recorded the action finishing around 9.30 p.m.[130] – but the Prussians, though fatigued from their march from Wavre, showed themselves eager to seal the fate of the French, and relentlessly pursued their opponents through the night and over the following days. In contrast, severely mauled and exhausted by the day's fighting, the Anglo-Allies stood in no meaningful condition to continue. As the remnants of Napoleon's army crowded through Genappe, a few miles south of La Belle Alliance – Prussian cavalry at their heels – the Emperor abandoned his carriage, mounted his horse, and made his way to Paris with a small group of staff officers and an escort of lancers, crossing the Sambre at Charleroi around 2 a.m. on 19 June.

PART 7

13

AFTERMATH
AND BUTCHER'S BILL:
'A FRIGHTFUL SCENE OF CARNAGE'[1]

Whether or not Wellington actually described Waterloo as 'A close-run thing' is not known, but he did express deep regret at the horrendous losses suffered that day – confirming the probably apocryphal quotation attributed to him that 'nothing except a battle lost can be half so melancholy as a battle won' – and acknowledged the very narrow margin by which he achieved victory. According to Captain William Bowles, a Royal Navy officer in Brussels, the Duke stated in a private letter that 'he never knew what fighting was before, and that he was obliged to exert himself to the very utmost to save the day'.[2] According to Assistant Surgeon Donald Finlayson, 33rd Foot, 'The Duke on returning to Brussels next morning is said to have wept in his chamber a long time & to have expressed that he would not gain such another victory for his life.'[3] Lady De Lancey, wife of Sir William De Lancey, an officer on the Duke's staff, provides still further evidence of the Duke's thoughts on the horrendous price in blood paid for victory. During his visit to her mortally wounded husband, the Duke told him that 'he never wished to see another battle; this had been so shocking. It had been too much to see such brave men, so equally matched, cutting each other to pieces as they did.' Sir William himself expressed the view that 'there never [before] had been such fighting; that the Duke far surpassed anything he had ever done before. The general opinion seemed to be that it had been a peculiarly shocking battle.'[4] No wonder that various correspondents employed the word 'slaughter' to describe the action, a term very seldom used by participants in the battles of the Peninsula.[5]

No wonder, further, for after more than nine hours of continuous, ferocious fighting had cost both sides dearly – above all the French. Tabulating their casualties poses particular difficulties for historians since it is impossible to distinguish between losses incurred on the battlefield and those suffered during the retreat following the action, some of which represent deserters rather than losses in killed, wounded and prisoners. At Waterloo Napoleon mustered 77,500 troops; rolls taken eight days after the battle reveal unit returns totalling 30,844 men, which represents an overall loss of 46,656, or 60 per cent of the army. The Prussians had already suffered heavy losses even before Waterloo, with over 31,000 men, a third of these through desertion, in the three days prior to 18 June – mostly at Ligny. On the 18th itself, accounting for fighting at both Wavre and Waterloo, the Prussians suffered approximately 7,000 casualties, nearly 90 per cent of these from IV Corps during the carnage around Plancenoit. The Anglo-Allies suffered casualties of 17,000 at Waterloo,[6] or nearly a quarter of those engaged – losses which prompted Wellington to declare to Thomas Creevey in Brussels the following day: 'Well, we have done the business, but we have paid dearly for it.'[7]

The full extent of the battlefield – the area in which troops were actually *deployed* though not necessarily *engaged* – measured only 5,500 yards (3.1 miles) wide from the western fringe of Merbe-Braine to the eastern fringe of Frischermont, and only 4,400 yards (2.5 miles) deep from Rossomme in the south to Mont St Jean farm in the north. When, however, measuring the ground in which the actual fighting took place, the area forms an irregular rectangle which extends eastwards from Hougoumont, inclusive, a distance of approximately 3,800 yards (2.1 miles). At the opening of the battle, 150,000 men stood within these narrow confines, increasing by a third by the time all the Prussians who were to take part in the fighting had arrived. All told, 200,000 men, 60,000 horses and over 500 guns were deployed in an area of a near-perfect square extending no more than 2.5 x 2.5 miles. In the ten and a half hours between 11 a.m. and 9.30 p.m., 54,000 men fell as casualties – a rate of over 5,000 per hour – rendering the Waterloo battlefield more congested with fallen soldiers than any other patch of ground since, including the Somme in 1916. Around Hougoumont alone, an estimated 5,500 men became casualties in an area measuring 220 x 440 yards. The horrific bloodletting at Plancenoit exceeded this, with 11,000 killed and wounded choking the tiny village's houses, streets and churchyard.

Eyewitness accounts from the day after the battle provide a sobering and graphic record of what such cold statistics represented in reality. Surveying the battlefield at 4 a.m. on the 19th, his horse's legs damp with the blood of the dead and dying, Colonel Felton Hervey, 14th Light Dragoons, expressed horror at the scale of the carnage: 'I have but ten minutes to spare to inform you that we are in a slaughter house,' he wrote in a letter home. 'Never in my life, or in the life of a man, was such scenes seen …'[8] His sentiments were echoed across the correspondence of many other survivors. 'It is quite impossible to describe in a letter the battle of the 18th,' Lieutenant Henry MacMillan wrote. 'The carnage is beyond belief.'[9] Sergeant William Clarke of the Scots Greys found himself at a loss to describe the enormity of the spectacle before him: 'to give a description of the field is far beyond my power',[10] while Private John Abbott adopted a philosophical approach: 'it is dreadful that mankind should make destruction for one another's end, but it fulfils the scripture.' Sergeant Archibald Johnston of the same regiment wrote of 'many a mangled body, whose pitiful cries would have caused the hardest heart to bleed',[11] while a sergeant of the Scots Greys, wrote of 'thousands ... lying weltering in their blood'.[12] Lieutenant Colonel Henry Murray, 18th Hussars, wrote of 'the most terrible bloodshed' and 'the ground of devastation' as his regiment passed through Genappe.[13] Ensign Charles Short, 2nd Battalion Coldstream Guards, expressed a sentiment which ran through much of the correspondence of the day: 'It was very beautiful to see the engagement though horrid afterwards.'[14] Kincaid, too, was appalled. 'The field of battle, next morning, presented a frightful scene of carnage,' he recalled in his diary:

> It seemed as if the world had tumbled to pieces, and three-fourths of every-thing destroyed in the wreck. The ground running parallel to the front of where we had stood was so thickly strewed with fallen men and horses, that it was difficult to step clear of their bodies; many of the former still alive, and imploring assistance, which it was not in our power to bestow.[15]

Captain James Nixon, 10th Hussars, marched with his regiment over the field in the direction of Nivelles, observing as he went 'so horrible a scene scarcely ever any man witnessed. The ground for the space of a league was covered with bodies absolutely lying in ranks, horses wandering about most terri-bly wounded and grouped in heaps with their riders.'[16] Indeed, the wounded were so ubiquitous that moving artillery proved problematic, as Lieutenant Ingilby recalled:

> In traversing the field, following the flight of the French, it was hardly pos-sible to clear with the Guns the bodies of both Armies which strewed the ground, and afterwards late at night ... when despatched to bring up some ammunition waggons, it was with difficulty we could avoid crushing many of the wounded on the road near La Haye Sainte, that had crawled there in hopes of more ready assistance. There were some in whom life was not yet extinct that we supposed the French Artillery had crushed by passing over in their retreat.[17]

Corporal John Stubbings, 1st Dragoon Guards, found the field and miles beyond it so 'covered with wounded and slain [that] in some places my horse could not pass without trampling on them ...'[18] Captain Arthur Kennedy, 18th Hussars, remarked specifically on the French dead, 'strewed in thousands over the field', not least the magnificent cuirassiers 'literally cut to pieces by our cavalry', the Waterloo–Genappe road littered with their armour.[19] Wheatley remarked on the sight of one particular dead cuirassier thus:

> On walking across the field from this house toward the high road, I saw a Cuirassier on his face with outstretched arms soaking in his blood. I never saw so gigantic a figure. I'm confident his height was 6'9". He reminded me as I passed of Goliath in ye Scriptures.[20]

Similarly, Captain George Barlow, 2/69th, described the ground in his sector of the field strewn with helmets, cuirasses and horse carcasses, as well as the bodies of Imperial Guardsmen.[21] Some positions were clearly recognisable because of their distinctive features. Tomkinson, for instance, could identify where French infantry had surrendered to the Union Brigade: 'On going over the ground the following morning, I saw where two lines of infantry had laid down their arms; their position was accurately marked, from the regularity the muskets were placed in.'[22] The position of Mercer's battery, too, was noteworthy by 'the immense heap of bodies of men and horses which distinguished it even at a distance'. Indeed, by virtue of the mounds of bodies – 'dark masses' he called them – which lay in its vicinity, Sir Augustus Frazer could plainly make out the position of G Troop from the ridge originally occupied by the French,[23] while the extent of the damage inflicted by Mercer's battery warrants his own description:

> The heap of slaughter was far greater in front of our Battery than on any other part of the Field, so much so that Colonel Sir Augustus Frazer told me two days afterwards at Nivelles that in riding over the French Position he could distinctly see where G (our Letter) Troop had stood from the dark pile of bodies in front of it, which was such as even to form a remarkable feature in the Field.[24]

Captain Arthur Kennedy, 18th Hussars, offers one of the best descriptions of the battlefield in the wake of the fighting:

> Such a scene of carnage I could have no idea of on so small a space of ground and the work of destruction seems to have made such rapid strides in so short a space of time as to nearly exceed belief. The dead and wounded of every nation were lying indiscriminately as they fell absolutely in heaps all over the field. Horses by half squadrons laying on each other as if the whole squadron had fallen by one discharge of grape shot so exactly did they lie in rows, the ground literally strewed with arms and armour of every description, in short never was there seen such a field of battle

before. No description can give you any idea of the scene. Never was there a butcher's stall more completely drenched with blood than the whole of the field and the wounded French were so numerous that it must have been totally impossible to have carried them all off the ground for several days.[25]

An unidentified officer of the 1/95th wrote of the plight of the wounded thus:

I will not attempt to describe the scene of slaughter which the fields presented, or what any person possessed of the least spark of humanity must have felt, while we viewed the dreadful situation of some thousands of wounded wretches who remained without assistance through a bitter cold night, succeeded by a day of most scorching heat; English and French were dying by the side of each other; and I have no doubt, hundreds who were not discovered when the dead were buried, and who were unable to crawl to any habitation, must have perished by famine.[26]

Consistent with his detailed description of the massed cavalry attacks on the Anglo-Allied centre earlier in the day, Mercer took pains to note the features of the battlefield in the wake of the fighting, including the presence of notebooks and papers strewn on the ground – account-books listing pay, clothing issued and other details, carried by French soldiers. Like many other observers, he watched as droves of peasants stripped the dead and suspected them of quietly murdering those still living to facilitate the process of looting. 'Some of these men I met fairly staggering under the enormous load of clothes, etc., they had collected,' Mercer recorded. 'Some had firearms, swords, etc., and many had large bunches of crosses and decorations; all seemed in high glee, and professed unbounded hatred of the French.' In moving towards the Charleroi road he encountered an entire British battalion asleep, wrapped in blankets and employing their knapsacks as pillows, the men lying in neat ranks, with officers and NCOs apparently occupying the precise positions held hours earlier when the formation had stood to receive the French. Nearby lay two Irish light infantrymen issuing 'such howlings and wailings, and oaths and execrations, as were shocking to hear'. One had lost a leg to a round shot and the other a thigh smashed by the same type of ordnance. Everywhere men begged for help, especially for water, which Mercer instructed his men to provide from their canteens. 'Nothing could exceed their gratitude, or the fervent blessings they implored on us for this momentary relief.' He found the French also grateful, and some conversed with him about the previous day's events. Many begged Mercer to kill them immediately, claiming a desire to be spared an ignoble death at the hands of the 'villainous' Belgian peasants, crying out, '"*Ah, Monsieur, tuez moi donc!*

Tuez moi, pour l'amour de Dieu!" [Ah, Sir, kill me then! Kill me, for the love of God!'] etc. etc. It was in vain I assured them carts would be sent to pick them all up. Nothing could reconcile them to the idea of being left.'[27]

Such observations betrayed the horrendous numbers of casualties sustained, the true extent of which could not be appreciated until daylight on the 19th enabled units to begin the work of mustering the ranks, tending the wounded, and burying the dead. In the meantime, some officers, as yet unacquainted with any accurate figures to impart to their correspondents, offered general observations about the extent of the losses. 'The destruction of men … has been immense',[28] wrote Lieutenant Colonel Sir Alexander Dickson two days after the battle, while Lieutenant Colonel Colin Campbell, on Wellington's staff, expressed astonishment at the magnitude of the losses: 'I never have seen or heard of a field of battle so covered with dead and wounded,' he continued. 'Our loss is alas most severe, and it grieves me beyond measure to enumerate the names of those heroes who have fallen … I have never seen so many British killed and wounded.'[29] 'Lord Wellington calls it the battle of the giants,' Captain Horace Churchill, 1st Foot Guards, observed in a letter six days after the battle, 'and says that there is no hell for any fellow that escaped that cannonade.'[30] The Assistant Adjutant General, Lieutenant Colonel Sir Henry Willoughby Rooke, also wrote in general terms: 'The victory like most others has its drawback in the immense list of killed and wounded.'[31] One wounded officer declared to a group of British civilians in Brussels that 'never had there been such a battle fought before or such things done by officers and men, that the French might be beat by such determined skill & courage, but that the loss was so immense …'[32] Major General John Byng, commander of the 2nd Brigade, echoed this view: 'Sincerely do I regret the loss of so many valuable officers, [and] such excellent men.'[33] Indeed, the high casualty rate features in many letters, like that a week after the fighting by Captain Edward Kelly, 1st Life Guards, who suggested that 'half the families of distinction in England will be in mourning'.[34] Lieutenant John Hibbert's list of the officers' toll for the King's Dragoon Guards is telling. Their colonel, his adjutant, two majors, a captain, and a lieutenant killed, with a cornet missing and presumed dead. Two captains had been severely wounded. This represented 'all our best and worthiest officers killed. It is very singular but really those officers who were the most respected and liked in the regimnent are killed; in fact, the regiment will never be what it was.'[35]

Tellingly, Henry Paget, Uxbridge's son residing in Brussels, discovered that with losses so heavy those making enquiries into the status of their friends sometimes asked the names of survivors rather than those of the killed and wounded.[36]

In recording their thoughts in the immediate aftermath of the fighting, officers and men quite naturally tended to focus their attention on their own unit's losses. Thus, Sergeant Johnston of the Scots Greys recorded that when his regiment established its bivouac for the night and called roll, nothing more of his unit could be mustered beyond three officers, two sergeants, and sixteen privates, with the remainder either killed, wounded, captured, or escorting prisoners to Brussels.[37] Private John Marshall, 10th Hussars, reported that out of the sixty men of his troop he could muster only thirty-five,[38] while in a similar vein Lieutenant William Turner, 13th Light Dragoons, observed that they could muster only sixty-five men of the 260 in the ranks prior to battle.[39] The heavy cavalry were particularly badly affected. Lieutenant John Luard, 16th Light Dragoons, wrote of the Household and Union Brigades as 'completely annihilated'[40] – an exaggeration certainly, yet nevertheless reflecting those formations' excessive losses. Assistant Surgeon John Haddy James, 1st Life Guards, rightly declared that of the cavalry the heavy regiments bore the brunt of the losses, with about half of both brigades *hors de combat* – though he wrongly attributed most of their casualties to artillery, whereas in fact the majority must have fallen during their charge against d'Erlon's infantry and at the hands of counter-attacking cavalry.[41] Captain Arthur Kennedy, also describing Somerset's and Ponsonby's brigades of heavy cavalry, noted: 'Several regiments have been nearly destroyed ... The Scots Greys have buried 8 officers in the field and of the King's Dragoon Guards three squadrons out of four have been totally annihilated. The Life Guards and Blues have lost many likewise.'[42] According to Lieutenant Colonel Henry Murray, 18th Hussars, Somerset's brigade, amalgamated with the wreckage of Ponsonby's, consisted of a mere two squadrons. Murray wrote of Vivian enquiring of Somerset as to the whereabouts of his brigade:

> 'Here', said Lord Edward. The ground was strewn with wounded, over whom it was hardly possible sometimes to avoid moving. Wounded or mutilated horses wandered or turned in circles. The noise was deafening, and the air of ruin and desolation that prevailed wherever the eye could reach gave no inspiration of victory.[43]

Captain Robert Wallace recalled that at 7 p.m. the Household Brigade was 'so much cut up, both as to officers and men, as to form but a small portion of a regiment ...'[44] Sergeant Thomas Critchley, Royal Dragoons, noted how:

> the loss of the [Household] brigade was severe; yet it surprised me that so many escaped as did, for their guns and small arms were playing upon us on every side, pouring like hail, and men falling, and horses, as thick as possible. ... I came off pretty safe, my horse shot through the leg, and myself slightly wounded with a bayonet, but nothing to signify of any consequence; in short, there were but few who escaped wounds or scars.[45]

According to Captain Clark Kennedy, Royal Dragoons, his regiment had been reduced to only one squadron by the evening, with the remains of the Inniskillings and Greys on their left. Following their charge in the early afternoon they stood in an exposed position in line in front of the crest, apparently to lend moral support to nearby squares of Nassau and Brunswick infantry suffering from artillery fire. There a large body of French infantry, supported in front by skirmishers, together with a small force of cavalry, stood opposite them, with artillery at close range firing canister and causing severe casualties. By the time of the general Anglo-Allied advance, Clark Kennedy reckoned the entire Union Brigade, having remained in the same position since about 4 p.m., had been reduced to but a single squadron.[46]

References to regimental and brigade losses also appeared frequently in the correspondence of infantry officers. Ensign James Howard, 33rd Foot, noted that:

> the general and every field officer, but two, of the [5th British] brigade, were either killed or wounded, and the whole strength reduced to about 300 out of 1,500. The 73rd regiment was commanded by a young lieutenant. Things were so bad that I was acting brigade major for some time …[47]

Another ensign, Thomas Wedgwood, 3rd Foot Guards, noted how 'It was a very mournful sight next morning when I was on parade to see but little more than one half the number of men that there were the morning before, and not quite one half the officers.'[48] The 73rd Regiment also suffered staggering losses: twenty-one officers killed and wounded out of twenty-five.[49]

Captain James Nixon found his battalion of the 1st Foot Guards mustering only 340 men on the evening of the 18th, with thirty-two officer casualties amongst the regiment, resulting in senior command changing hands for both the second and third battalions of the regiment: 'Those who have seen Vitoria, Albuera and Leipzig say that their fire was not to be mentioned or their slaughter compared to ours,' he added.[50] No infantry formation fared worse, however, than the 1st Battalion 27th Foot, which numbered about 700 all ranks.

Captain Jonathan Leach, 95th Rifles recorded the dreadful punishment meted out to them:

> The 27th regiment had its good qualities of steadiness, patience under fire, and valour, put more severely to the test than, perhaps, any corps in the field. It was formed in a hollow square, a short distance in rear of the right of our division, with one of its faces looking into the road, as a protection to it against any attempt which the enemy's cavalry might make by charging up

that road. This brave old regiment was almost annihilated in square, by the terrible fire of musketry kept up on it from the knoll, whilst it was impossible for them to pull a trigger during the whole time, as they would thereby have been as likely to kill friends as foes. Those who may chance to visit the field of Waterloo, cannot fail to find on the spot which I have mentioned, near the road, and at a short distance from the thorn hedge, a small square of a darker colour than the ground immediately about it, marking the grave of this gallant Irish regiment.[51]

In its highly exposed position the 1/27th lost more men – almost exclusively to French artillery fire – than any other British unit: two officers killed and fourteen wounded out of nineteen, plus 463 other ranks as casualties, of whom 103 were killed and 360 wounded. Total losses to the battalion amounted to a staggering 68 per cent of its strength – all suffered in the four hours after the unit arrived late on the battlefield around 3.30 p.m.[52]

Turning finally to the artillery, officers highlighted the heavy casualty rates suffered by their respective batteries. 'Our losses were considerable,' Major Lloyd remarked of his battery, 'two officers out of five are severely wounded [and] a great number of our men and horses killed.'[53] Captain Courtenay Ilbert wrote of the army in general, but also of his arm of service in particular: 'The day has been very bloody as you may suppose and we have lost an immense number of men ... Our artillery have suffered greatly, especially in officers.'[54] Lieutenant William Ingilby noted that losses were so high that surviving ensigns stood a good chance of promotion to lieutenant.[55] Lieutenant Colonel Sir Robert Gardiner, Royal Artillery, wrote of the 'lasting loss of numberless friends. Among ourselves particularly, the sacrifice has fallen on our first and most boasted officers'.[56] These were no exaggerations: Sir John May reported the highest rate of officer casualties the Royal Artillery had ever seen.[57]

In fact, losses – both killed and wounded – amongst officers across British units proved so high that command regularly passed down the ranks, with the following constituting but a few examples: Major Arthur Heyland, commander of the 40th Foot, fell dead when in the act of leading his regiment in a bayonet charge, a musket shot striking him in the throat.[58] The Scots Greys lost their commanding officer, Lieutenant Colonel Hamilton,[59] the 73rd Foot suffered such grievous losses as to be commanded by a young lieutenant, Richard Leyne, and the 1st King's German Legion Light Battalion had only one captain left.[60] The 2/95th fared much worse, losing three successive commanding officers, including two colonels and a major.[61] Lieutenant Colonel Campbell commanded the 1st Foot (Royals), but upon being wounded some time between noon and 2 p.m. was succeeded by Captain Macdonald, who himself fell wounded at about 8 p.m.[62] The 1st Battalion 23rd Foot, like so many other units, lost its commanding officer,[63] while General Sir George Cooke, commander of the 1st (Guards) Division, lost an arm.[64] The 27th Foot suffered exceptionally high losses, as mentioned earlier, with only three lieutenants surviving uninjured.[65] Lieutenant Colonel Frederick Ponsonby, commander of the 12th Light Dragoons, received multiple wounds but survived.[66] Colonel Fuller of the King's Dragoon Guards was killed.[67] Lieutenant Colonel Harris, commanding the 73rd Foot,[68] and General Dörnberg, commander of the 3rd Cavalry Brigade, were severely wounded, as was Lieutenant Colonel Cutliffe, commander of the 23rd Light Dragoons.[69]

Nor did general officers and those on the Duke of Wellington's staff escape death or serious injury – a testament to the fact that senior officers regularly stood in the thick of the fighting. A round shot flew within a foot of Captain Nixon's head and struck Major General George Cooke, commander of the 1st Division, in the shoulder, thereby requiring amputation of his right arm.[70] Lieutenant General Sir Thomas Picton, commander of the 5th Division, was killed by a musket shot to the temple during the counter-attack against d'Erlon, while the Earl of Uxbridge, commander of Anglo-Allied cavalry, had his leg amputated after being struck by a round shot toward the close of the fighting. Both the Prince of Orange, commander of I Corps, and Lieutenant General Sir Charles Alten, commander of 3rd Division, were wounded. Major General Sir Colin Halkett, 5th Brigade commander, in the midst of exhorting his troops forward with 'an elegant speech' was shot through the shoulder and jaw by a musket or canister shot that rendered him *hors de combat* but did not prove fatal.[71] Staff officers also suffered heavy losses. Almost all of Uxbridge's aides-de-camp were wounded, Ellery suffering three sabre wounds, and Thornhill, Fraser, Seymour and Dawson all hit by small-arms fire.[72] On the Duke's staff, Lieutenant Colonel Charles Fox Canning, 3rd Foot Guards, and aide-de-camp to Wellington, was mortally wounded by a grape shot to the stomach. He lay on the ground for some time, directed cavalry to move around him after the battle, and refused medical attention, correctly believing his wounds to be mortal. Not content to die with a debt outstanding, Canning is said to have asked a fellow officer to settle his affairs with Sir Colin Campbell.[73] Handing over his sword and watch to a cavalry officer and directing him to deliver the items to his family, Canning died two hours later.[74] Other aides-de-camp on the Duke's staff came to grief. Lieutenant Colonel Alexander Gordon, 2/3rd Foot Guards, died in Wellington's headquarters in the village of Waterloo following an operation to amputate his leg. Lord Fitzroy Somerset, the Duke's military secretary, had his right arm amputated[75] and De Lancey fell mortally wounded. Major the Hon. Henry Percy, one of the Duke's aides-de-camp, sustained three wounds.[76]

Wellington himself was extremely fortunate to survive the battle unscathed, for he had placed himself close to the action – when and where he deemed his presence most needed – a circumstance confirmed by numerous eyewitnesses, including Lieutenant Colonel Stanhope, 1st Foot Guards, who noted how the Duke 'exposed himself in the hottest fire the whole day ...'[77] Lieutenant Colonel Sir John May, Royal Artillery, Assistant Adjutant General, and as such on the Duke's staff, was amazed how Wellington should survive unscathed, having lost two aides-de-camp and his private secretary. 'The Duke indeed was too much exposed and it is difficult to understand how he escaped unhurt.'[78] Similarly, one of Lord Hill's aides-de-camp, noting the very high casualty rate amongst Wellington's headquarters staff, observed that 'it is a miracle how he escaped, for he was in the hottest of the fire the whole day'.[79] Later he wrote:

> Lord Wellington was exposed as much as any soldier in the field, & his escape as well as that of my dear general's [Lord Hill] is a miracle, I was with them both the whole day, I never saw either of them in action before, & it is impossible to say which is the coolest, the greater the danger the more they rise.[80]

Numerous other eyewitnesses attest to seeing Wellington very much in the thick of the action. 'There he was the whole day in a dreadful fire superintending every movement,' Kempt wrote,[81] while Ross-Lewin remarked that:

> I am confident that there was not a man in the army who did not feel elated at the sight of their victorious chief, safe and unhurt after this perilous and bloody day. Never did any general share the dangers of a battle in a greater degree than did the Duke of Wellington on the field of Waterloo. He was frequently in the hottest of the fire ...[82]

Lieutenant Dixon Denham, 54th Foot, commented:

> It is dreadful to reflect on the risks to which his venerable life was exposed. In fact, such was his dauntless activity that he was much more exposed than any private soldier who would only bear the hazard of a single spot, but the Duke was everywhere, at least wherever danger was ...[83]

Lieutenant Colonel Fremantle, on the Duke's staff, wondered the same: 'how the Duke escaped we are at a loss to know, for he was in the thick of it from morning till night.'[84]

Lieutenant James Crummer also noted Wellington's exposure to fire.[85] 'How the Duke of Wellington escaped Heaven only knows,' Captain George Bowles, a Coldstreamer, wrote the day after the battle. 'He was constantly in the heat of the engagement.'[86] And, of course, as discussed earlier, the Duke narrowly escaped injury or death when seated beside Uxbridge when the latter fell severely wounded near the end of the battle.

Horses suffered a terrible toll, as well, though some survived multiple wounds. Kincaid recalled that:

> Some one asking me what had become of my horse's ear, was the first intimation I had of his being wounded; and I now found that, independent of one ear having been shaved close to his head (I suppose by a cannon-shot), a musket-ball had grazed across his forehead, and another gone through one of his legs, but he did not seem much the worse for either of them.[87]

By the conclusion of the fighting, his horse had suffered further injuries: 'My horse had received another shot through the leg, and one through the flap of the saddle, which lodged in his body, sending him a step beyond the pension-list.'[88] Major John Oldfield, Royal Engineers, observed a horse belonging to one of Wellington's aides-de-camp limping on three legs at Quatre Bras,[89] while Cornet James Gape of the Scots Greys observed another, stationary, but upright, on three legs.[90] A British civilian resident in Brussels who visited the field witnessed a horse of the Scots Greys, with a broken lance protruding from one of its wounds, emitting a 'piercing cry' as it snorted and plunged about.[91] On the road to Brussels, Commissary Tupper Carey observed horses bearing wounds caused by sabre cuts, with one, still on its feet and on the move, with 'a large portion of flesh torn off his rump by the splinter of a shell.'[92] Edward Heeley, the servant of a senior officer, rode a wounded horse from the battlefield, the animal leaping over a dead soldier's hand sticking up from the mud.'[93] Artillery horses also suffered particularly heavy losses since in many cases limbers and ammunition wagons stood on elevated ground behind the guns themselves and thus lay in more exposed positions to French artillery fire.[94] Yet quite apart from formations in which horses could be found in concentrated numbers – in the cavalry and the artillery – many individual officers of all arms lost their mounts, sometimes several over the course of the day. According to Harry Smith, 'Every Staff officer had two or three (and one four) horses shot under him. I had one wounded in six, another in seven places, but not seriously injured.'[95] Two Guards officers posted in the area near Hougoumont lost six horses between them.[96] Amongst Uxbridge's aides-de-camp, one had three horses killed under him, another lost two and a third lost one.[97] Uxbridge himself had four horses shot under him,[98] while Major General Sir Colquhoun had five horses killed under him.[99] Captain John Whale of the 1st Life Guards had two horses shot under him.[100] Cornet James Gape and Lieutenant Henry McMillan, both of the Scots Greys, noted that Captain Edward Cheney lost five horses, though, as Gape described, he 'kept mounting the fresh ones with the same coolness that he would had they been at his own stable door. My old mare received three slight wounds. One was a bullet through her ear.' McMillan also recorded Captain Robert Vernor being wounded through the shoulder, apparently by the same musket shot which fatally struck his horse in the head. McMillan's own horse became a casualty from a shot to the shoulder, while he described his cloak as being 'like a riddle from musket balls.'[101] Captain A.K. Kennedy of the Royal Dragoons was wounded twice and had two horses killed as he rode them.[102] Major Percy, sent to London to present the famous Waterloo Dispatch and the two captured eagles to the Prince Regent, had his horse killed under him,[103] while Brevet Major Lawrence, 13th Light Dragoons, lost three.[104]

The loss of a horse could affect some profoundly, for in their beasts men lost much more than their mode of travel, but a trusted companion which had shared all the trials and tribulations of its master. Captain Thomas Fenton felt relief at the slight wound sustained by his 'little mare', whom he described as 'everything I could wish'.[105] 'My favourite mare was badly wounded under me and I fear I shall lose the use of her forever', lamented Colonel Hugh Mitchell of the 51st Foot,[106] while Lord Saltoun also wrote of the loss of his 'favourite little horse'.[107] Captain Edward Kelly, 1st Life Guards, who had three horses wounded under him, wrote mournfully in the postscript of a letter home the day after battle: 'My beautiful bay mare was wounded in the head by a lancer and I fear she is lost, she carried me beautifully in action and I would almost prefer being wounded myself to having lost her.'[108] Expressing a smiliar sentiment, while Lieutenant Colonel Sir William Gomm, Coldstream Guards, regarded his two minor wounds as 'of no consequence', his two wounded horses represented 'great consequence'.[109] Major General Lord Edward Somerset lost his favourite mare to a round shot that penetrated her flank and torn away part of his great coat. 'She is a very great loss to me,' he recorded, 'as being so much the best as well as pleasantest horse that I possess.'[110] Private Thomas Playford encountered one such fellow trooper in mourning:

At the close of another day's march I was affected by noticing a soldier grieving over his dead horse. The faithful animal had been wounded on the 18th of June, but had travelled several days without appearing to be seriously injured. The horse, however, died suddenly at the end of the fourth day, and the soldier shed tears: I listened with deep attention to the afflicted soldier as he spoke of the excellent qualities of his steed, and told how that faithful beast had carried him through [the campaigns in] Spain and France; and had borne him triumphant through the dreadful scenes at Waterloo. The soldier told how the horse would eat out of his hand, lick his face and hands, and give evident signs of attachment to his master. And I felt gratified at these signs of sympathy and tenderness in one of my companions in arms.[111]

Major John Hill, 23rd Foot, also lamented 'Honesty', his faithful mount, whom Hill's servant buried. According to Hill, his horse:

… got three shot, two [from] cannon, one round carried off a fore leg, a shot destroyed the saddle but did not kill, he got also a musket shot in the chest & poor fellow he bled to death, he carried me beautifully…he was in the most beautiful condition you can imagine…You cannot imagine how much I regret [the loss of] Honesty. When I was wounded, I was not on him, but had gone up to him in the middle of the square & took something I wanted out of the holsters. While I was doing this a musket ball struck in the boat cloak strapped in [his front]. I know not exactly if this ball went into him, I almost think not, however I slept [*sic*] a few paces aside & said, 'If you are hit old fellow do not think I did it…'[112]

Those who lost horses were expected to replace them as quickly as possible in order to remain in action. Many officers maintained a second mount in the rear, but of course riderless horses strayed across the field, while troopers who lost their mounts wandered about in search of a replacement.[113] Lieutenant Edward Bowlby, 4th Foot, acquired the horse of a cuirassier, for instance,[114] Major Dawson Kelly, attached to headquarters, replaced his dead horse with that of a dragoon,[115] and Ensign Jack Barnett took possession of a French dragoon's horse after the battle.[116] Lieutenant Colonel F.S. Miller of the Inniskillings received two minor bayonet wounds and lost his horse, probably to musket fire, but he acquired that of a fallen French officer of lancers and rode his new mount for the remainder of the day,[117] while Lieutenant John Sperling, Royal Engineers, managed to end up with four horses and engaged a second servant.[118] Captain Alexander Clark Kennedy, 1st Dragoons, on the other hand, lost contact with his servant on the 17th.[119] De Lacy Evans, one of Ponsonby's aides-de-camp, simply exchanged his wounded animal for a fresh mount:

As to myself, I was well mounted on a powerful, nearly thoroughbred bay gelding. He received a considerable sabre wound from near the eye to the mouth, but his action was not impaired by it. I, however, changed him on getting back to the position for a brown mare, which, however, was very soon after shot by a musket ball, and I lost her. The bay soon recovered …[120]

In the fighting at Quatre Bras and Waterloo, Lieutenant Colonel David Mackinnon, 2nd Battalion Coldstream Guards, lost three horses, the last of which was nearly burnt to death at Hougoumont, where the poor beast also lost an eye. Mackinnon's servant recommended that the animal be shot,[121] but the officer's correspondence does not reveal the horse's ultimate fate. Mercer's account of the sufferings of some of his gun teams is particularly graphic and moving:

> Horses, too, there were to claim our pity – mild, patient, enduring. Some lay on the ground with their entrails hanging out, and yet they lived. These would occasionally attempt to rise, but, like their human bed-fellows, quickly falling back again, would lift their poor head, and, turning a wistful gaze at their side, lie quietly down again, to repeat the same until strength no longer remained, and then, their eyes gently closing, one short convulsive struggle closed their sufferings. One poor animal excited painful interest – he had lost, I believe, both his hind legs; and there he sat the long night through on his tail, looking about, as if in expectation of coming aid, sending forth, from time to time, long and protracted melancholy neighing. Although I knew that killing him at once would be [a] mercy, I could not muster courage even to give the order. Blood enough I had seen shed during the last six-and-thirty hours, and sickened at the thought of shedding more. There, then, he still sat when we left the ground, neighing after us, as if reproaching our desertion of him in the hour of need.[122]

Wounded horses were not dispatched by farriers or kind-hearted soldiers as a matter of course, for animals trained to carry a soldier on campaign and to cope with the noise and fury of battle constituted a valuable commodity not easily replaced. Thus, if they could be rehabilitated, they were spared a shot to the head or a sword thrust to the heart.[123] One such candidate is probably a case in point: an animal from a Royal Horse Artillery gun team with, according to one of the officers of that troop, 'a shot-hole clean through his ear'.[124] Captain Edward Kelly rejoiced at the recovery of his wounded horse, together with the good prospects of two other troop horses he rode in battle, both of which he described as 'much cut about the head'.[125] Even when a horse managed to survive the bloodletting of Waterloo unscathed, it doubtless shared the exhaustion of the troops it meant to serve. Lieutenant Colonel Edward Bowater, 2nd Battalion 3rd Foot Guards noted how his 'very steady' beast, a bay, endured its master in the saddle from 3 a.m. until 8 p.m. with only a handful of unripe clover as fodder. Even then, the musket ball which wounded Bowater managed to graze his horse's belly, though it did no permanent harm.[126] Captain Orlando Bridgeman wrote in a similar vein: 'I rode the same horse all day & had the enemy beat us I must have been taken for my horse was quite smashed up.'[127]

14

THE WOUNDED
AND THE DEAD

On the morning of 19 June 1815 the sun rose over a truly horrific scene. Lieutenant James Gardiner confessed to his astonishment. 'I never saw anything to equal the carnage on this field of battle,' he penned in his journal. 'I have seen many sights of the kind but this out-beggars everything.'[1] Some of Mercer's men confessed to having had virtually no sleep on account of the hideous presence of the body of a driver from their troop who lost most of his head but whose face remained, staring at the living. Mercer ordered him immediately buried and proceeded to take stock of his men, horses and equipment. He mustered the survivors, disentangled horses from equipment, and rounded up 'sound' and lightly wounded horses, whatever their previous affiliation or function, that could be found wandering about the field – enough to convey four guns, three ammunition wagons, and the troop's forge. For this small complement he could barely supply sufficient men; the same applied to his stock of ammunition, whose expenditure proved 'enormous' – an estimated 700 rounds per gun.[2] The field all around Mercer's battery – and indeed the whole area stretching between Hougoumont and Frischermont – was thick with dead and wounded. Private George Hemingway, 33rd Foot, wounded while his battalion stood in square, recalled how he had no choice but to make his own way to Brussels for medical attention – in an era, it must be emphasised, prior to the development of anaesthetics. He spent the night of the 18th in a house with a missing door – doubtless removed for firewood – and reached the city, a journey of 12 miles, the following day. On recovering, he rejoined his regiment.[3]

Two days earlier, at Quatre Bras, Lieutenant Colonel James Stanhope, 1st Foot Guards, had watched the ghoulish sight of a wounded soldier almost certainly in search of medical aid: 'As I passed the spot where a heap of the French cuirassiers were laying,' he recorded in his journal, 'a figure covered & clotted with blood so that his face was indistinguishable rose up from the heap & with a swift but staggering pace went across the country.' By the time the two drummers sent by Stanhope reached the spot in order to lend assistance, the man was gone. 'I never knew who he was or heard of him more, but it was like an apparition, so rising from the mound of dead.'[4]

Such anecdotes reveal the harsh reality of war for the wounded: the complete absence of any systematic method of casualty evacuation, which meant that virtually everyone except senior officers remained where they fell until fighting ceased – and in the case of Waterloo at least until the following morning – unless they could somehow muster the power to make their own way to the rear and seek out medical care. Lieutenant Edward Stephens, 1/32nd, was struck by a musket ball that penetrated the soft tissue of his arm without breaking a bone.[5] As such, he probably left the field on his own accord; thousands were not so fortunate. A gunner named Butterworth from Mercer's battery is a case in point. He lost both his forearms and hands when he slipped in front of the muzzle of a gun precisely at the moment of discharge; but with no one available to attend him while the crew fought furiously to stave off cavalry attacks, he had no choice but to make his own way to the rear, succumbing to blood loss on the way.[6] Indeed, the majority of the lightly or otherwise walking wounded made their way to the rear as best they could. Sergeant William Clarke, Scots Greys, encountered his wounded brother after the battle walking to Brussels. Like so many of the walking wounded, he appeared to be recovering amidst 'so deplorable a massacre'.[7] But in an era before the advent of proper stretchers in British service, those who could not fend for themselves had to await comrades prepared to carry them away in blankets to nearby farmhouses and barns,[8] though makeshift litters were also employed, sometimes with unsatisfactory results. One junior officer in a litter along the road in the village of Waterloo asked the men carrying him to stop for the sake of the pain induced by the movement.[9]

It is important to observe that in contrast to soldiers of today, those at Waterloo possessed no knowledge or training in even rudimentary forms of medical care. Apart from moving the stricken to places where their wounds could be tended, troops could do little more than simply provide water to suppress the raging thirsts of their fallen comrades. In this context the experience of those who remained on the field on the night of 18–19 June – and in many cases for another or even successive days and nights – and the nature of the wounds they had sustained, bears some examination. Private Thomas Hasker, King's Dragoon Guards, numbered among the many tens of thousands sprawled across the battlefield:

> In crossing a bad hollow piece of ground, my horse fell, and before I had well got upon my feet, another of the French dragoons came up, and (*sans cérémonie* [without ceremony]) began to cut at my head, knocked off my

helmet, and inflicted several wounds on my head and face. Looking up at him, I saw him in the act of striking another blow at my head, and instantly held up my right hand to protect it, when he cut off my little finger and half way through the rest. I then threw myself on the ground, with my face downward. One of the lancers rode by, and stabbed me in the back with his lance. I then turned, and lay with my face upward, and a foot soldier stabbed me with his sword as he walked by. Immediately after, another, with his firelock and bayonet, gave me a terrible plunge, and while doing it with all his might, exclaimed '*Sacré nom de Dieu!*' [Holy name of God!] No doubt that would have been the finishing stroke, had not the point of the bayonet caught one of the brass eyes of my coat; the coat being fastened with hooks and eyes, and prevented its entrance. There I lay, as comfortably as circumstances would allow, the [cannon] balls of the British army falling around me, one of which dropped at my feet, and covered me with dirt; so that, what with blood, dirt, and one thing and another, I passed very well for a dead man. I was next plundered of my watch, money, canteen and haversack. I lay till night, the British army marching, some near me, and some over me, in pursuit of the French. At length I was picked up by two Prussian soldiers, and laid beside a fire, when one of their surgeons dressed some of my wounds, and left me for the remainder of the night. Next day I received great kindness from an English regiment, just then arrived. An officer gave me a little rum, and one of the privates carried me in a blanket ...[10]

Sergeant Johnston, Scots Greys, observed that tending the wounded competed with his regiment's ability to locate and bury its own:

We continued in the field until near the evening, but were not able to bury a fourth part of our men, a great deal of time being taken up in giving drink to the wounded, who were in great numbers in all parts of the field, some English and some French; whose pitiful cries demanded assistance from their greatest enemy. We distributed among them all the water, gin and brandy we had in our canteens, and likewise some bread. We bound up their wounds and rendered them every assistance in our power; but the vehement heat of the sun was much against them, and many to whom we rendered assistance must perish soon after in this dismal situation; their cries would have brought tears from the stoutest heart when they saw that [we] were leaving them, however, we had rendered them all the assistance which time and convenience would admit of.[11]

Private Thomas Playford, 2nd Life Guards, reveals that his task in fact involved mustering members of his regiment rather than tending to the stricken:

On the following morning we went in search of the surviving fragments of our regiment, and found a few officers and men; perhaps twenty in all including ourselves. In this search I rode across one part of the field of battle, and Corporal Webster pointed out to me the dead body of Shaw, [and] pointing to a spot where several dead French soldiers lay, said 'There lies Shaw'. I replied 'I rode over that ground this morning, and noticed that one of our regiment was among the slain, but his face was concealed'. Webster said 'I examined the countenance and recognised Shaw. He appears to have received a fatal injury in his body, for there is a deep wound in his side, near the heart, which appears to have been inflicted with either a bayonet or a lance.' This Shaw was only two file from me in the ranks; he was a powerful brave man and fell early. I think I saw him fall but it is possible he revived again. As I did not witness the exploits of Shaw in close combat, nor yet inquire of the wounded French soldiers near his corpse. By whose hand the dead lying roundabout had fallen, I can neither add to, nor take away from the published accounts; but from the position in which Shaw's remains were found among dead adversaries, with only one or two killed Englishmen near, this seems to favour what has been said concerning the havoc he produced among the French troopers before he fell. What I knew of him would favour this: for he was the strongest and most resolute man I ever knew, and had such great confidence in his own prowess that he would not hesitate to attack as many foes as could stand opposed to him.[12]

Private Thomas Hasker, King's Dragoon Guards described his predicament on the morning of the 19th:

I was kindly treated by some English soldiers, come to reinforce the army, and was laid, with many more, on some straw near the road side. The following morning several of my comrades were dead, and I prevailed on some one to take the trousers off one of these, which I managed to put on. There was much crying out for water, and some was brought. I requested to be allowed to taste, but finding there was blood in it, I could not drink. In the course of the day I saw two or three wagons standing, and the wounded men getting upon them, I made an effort, and succeeded in mounting one of these, and we rode on towards Brussels. The stench from the bodies of men and horses was horrible. We stopped more than once when some that had died from the shaking of the wagon were pulled off, and others who had travelled as far as they could on foot were taken up.[15]

Some time after dark, Hasker saw campfires in the distance and attempted to stand:

… but staggered like a drunken man, and soon fell, the dead and dying lay thick about me. Hearing two men talking very near, I called to them as well as I could to come and help me. They said they could not for a while. Soon after this two foreigners passed by, to whom I made signs; they came, and raising me up between them, took me to one of the fires, and brought me a surgeon; they afterwards wrapped a cloak about me, and left me there for the night.[16]

Lieutenant Colonel Frederick Ponsonby, 12th Light Dragoons, left a superb account of his multiple injuries:

At one o'clock observing, as I thought, unsteadiness in a column of French infantry … which were advancing with an irregular fire, I resolved to charge them. As we were descending in a gallop, we received from our own troops on the right, a fire much more destructive than theirs, they having began long before it could take effect, and slackening as we drew nearer; when we were within fifty paces of them they turned and much execution was done among them …

But we no sooner passed through them than we were attacked in our turn, before we could form, by about three hundred Polish lancers, who had come down to their relief. The French artillery pouring in among us, a heavy fire of grape shot, which however for one of our men, killed three of their own. In the melee I was disabled almost instantly in both of my arms and followed by a few of my men who were presently cut down (no quarter being asked or given). I was carried on by my horse, till receiving a blow on my head from a sabre, I was thrown senseless on my face to the ground. Recovering, I raised myself a little to look around (being I believe at that time in a condition to get up, and run away) when a lancer passing by exclaimed '*Tu n'est pas mort, coquin*' ['You're not dead, blackguard'] and struck his lance through my back, my head dropped, the blood gushed into my mouth, a difficulty of breathing came on and I thought all was over.

Not long afterwards (it was then impossible to measure time, but I must have fallen in less than ten minutes after the charge) a tirailleur came up to plunder me; threatening to take my life. I told him that he might search me, directing him to a small side pocket in which he found three dollars, being all I had. He unloosed my stock and tore open my waistcoat, then leaving me in a very uneasy posture, and was no sooner gone, than another came up for the same purpose, but assuring him I had been plundered already he left me, when an officer bringing on some troops (to which probably the tirailleurs belonged) and halting where I lay, stooped down and addressed me saying, he feared I was badly wounded. I replied that I was and expressed a wish to be removed into the rear; he said it was against the order to remove even their own men; but that if they gained the day, as they probably would (for he understood the Duke of Wellington was killed and that six of our battalions had surrendered) every attention in his power should be shown me. I complained of thirst and he held his brandy bottle to my lips, directing one of his men to lay me straight on my side, and place a knapsack under my head. He then passed on into the action and I shall never know to whose generosity I was indebted, as I conceive for my life; of what rank I cannot say, he wore a blue greatcoat. By and by another tirailleur came and knelt and fired over me, loading & firing many times and conversing with great gaiety all the while, at last he ran off ...[13]

To a second correspondent Ponsonby, provided a slightly different but equally extensive account of his experiences:

While the battle continued ... several of the wounded men and dead bodies near me were hit with the balls which came very thick in that place. Towards evening when the Prussians came, the continued roar of the cannon along theirs and the British line, growing louder and louder as they drew near, was the finest thing I ever heard. It was dusk when two squadrons of Prussian cavalry, both of them two deep, passed over me in full trot; lifting me from the ground, and tumbling me about cruelly. The clatter of their approach, and the apprehensions it excited, may be easily conceived. Had a gun come that way, it would have done for me. The battle was then nearly over, or removed to a distance, the cries and groans of the wounded all around me, became every instant more and more audible, succeeding to the shouts, imprecations, outcries of '*Vive l'Empereur*', the discharges of musketry and cannon, now and then intervals of perfect silence which were worse than the noise. I thought the night would never end; much about this time I found a soldier of the Royals lying across my legs, who had probably crawled thither in his agony; his weight, convulsive motions, his noises, and the air issuing through a wound in his side, distressed me greatly, the latter circumstance most of all, as the case was my own. It was not a dark night and the Prussians were wandering about to plunder ... several of them came and looked at me, and passed on; at length one stopped to examine me, I told him as well as I could (for I could say but little German) that I was a British officer and had been plundered already, he did not desist, however, and pulled me about roughly before he left me. About an hour before midnight, I saw a soldier in an English uniform coming towards me, he was I suspect on the same errand, he came and looked in my face, I spoke instantly telling him who I was, and assuring himself of a reward, if he would remain by me; he said that he belonged to the 40th Regiment but had missed it. He released me from the dying man, being unarmed, he took up a sword from the ground and stood over me, pacing backwards and forwards. At eight o'clock in the morning, some English were seen at a distance, he ran to them and a messenger was sent off to Hervey [Colonel Felton Hervey, 14th Light Dragoons]; a cart came for me, I was placed in it and carried to a farm house, above a mile and a half distant, and laid in the bed from which poor Gordon[14] (as I understood afterwards) had been just carried out, the jolting of the cart, and the difficulty of breathing were very painful. I had received seven wounds; a surgeon slept in my room and I was saved by continual bleeding (120 ounces in two days, besides the great loss of blood on the field).[15]

Miraculously, Ponsonby lived another twenty-two years, while others, albeit with a few years ahead of them, eventually succumbed to their injuries, such as Captain Robert Hesketh, 3rd Foot Guards, who struggled on for another five years after Waterloo, or the clearly long-suffering Captain Percival of the 1st Foot Guards, whose wound, Gronow asserted:

… was one of the most painful it ever fell to a soldier's lot to bear. He received a ball which carried away all his teeth and both his jaws, and left nothing on the mouth but the skin of the cheeks. Percival recovered sufficiently to join our regiment in the Tower, three years subsequent to the battle of Waterloo. He had to be fed with porridge and a few spoonfuls of broth; but notwith-standing all the care to preserve his life, he sunk from inanition, and died very shortly after, his body presenting the appearance of a skeleton.[16]

Lieutenant George Simmons, 1st Battalion 95th Rifles, left this engaging account of how he was wounded near La Haye Sainte:

We were soon after fiercely attacked, a musket ball grazed my arm, entered my side, broke two ribs, went through my liver & lodged in my breast. Felix said I jumped as high as myself and fell near the hedge of La Haye Sainte on the left side of the road. On came the French & were soon travelling over me, however, they were unceremoniously handed back again, followed by our Life Guardsmen who galloped [to] the very place where I was depos-ited & gave a good account of a number of the unfortunate infantry who had the ill luck to taste their sabres. The shock I received brought my watch to a full stop at 4 o'clock, the works were broken.

Felix told Sir Andrew my deplorable situation, 'Where is he? Let me see him instantly, poor, poor George Simmons.' He ordered a corporal & 4 men to take me with the greatest care to the farm house of Mont St Jean, to return & report to him when he had done so. I was carried to the place & through the straw yard into a large cow house or stable, the premises were covered with great numbers of dying & wounded soldiers. Doctors were performing their evolutions with knife and saw in hand, most vigorously. Several of my brother officers were congregated together, laid upon straw in the right corner of the building. Poor Stilwell exclaimed 'Dear George, how white you look, lie down by me', which I did. My body soon became so swollen that I had great difficulty in breathing, the warm blood was still oozing from my side into my trousers, the ends of the broken ribs gave me excruciating pain.

At this moment Fairfoot, that glorious fellow, had found me out, he was so shocked that the big tears ran down his manly countenance. 'Oh lift me up, I am suffocating,' he had poor fellow, only one arm at my service, I managed to get upon my knees & clutched a low crib with one hand & a sack with the other, I soon slided [*sic*] down. Our Assistant Surgeon Heyt came & tried to bleed me in the arm.

I now espied my dear old friend [Assistant Surgeon James] Robson, a capital operator & a peninsular surgeon; he saw me & came instantly. 'Old fellow I am hard hit at last, cut the ball out of my breast directly as my game will soon be up.' I could bear nothing on but my shirt, so I had no difficulty in placing my finger over the very spot where the ball was lodged, he made a wide & deep incision into my breast, & with a pair of forceps pulling out a musket ball which was nearly flattened against my broken ribs, he put it into my trouser pocket. A quantity of clotted blood followed the ball, which relieved my breathing. Fairfoot sat upon the straw supporting me during the operation, he appeared as happy at the result, as if one has been extracted from his own carcase.[17]

Lieutenant Richard Cocks Eyre, 2/95th, also fell wounded:

A musket ball entered just below the wrist in my left hand, the bones leading to my thumb and forefinger are a good deal smashed, [and] the ball is still in my hand. Some leather and velvet which was driven in from my sleeve and glove have been already extracted but there is too much inflammation to allow them to cut out the ball. I am however assured that there is no danger of losing the hand and that I shall in great measure recover the use of it. I have now given you a [full?] description of the fight and shall conclude by saying a little more of myself. When I was wounded it was dark, my friend Drummond … got a man of the band to assist me to the rear in quest of a surgeon but after wandering as far as my strength would allow me

I found the attempt to find one useless and therefore got the man who was with me to search for some blankets among the packs of the unfortunate fellows who were pretty thickly scattered about us and after getting well wrapped up laid down for the remainder of the night. In this situation I suffered the most excruciating pains. In the early part of the fight I was struck in the left knee by a piece of shell; whilst I kept myself in motion I felt very little from the blow which did not penetrate but after I had lain some time on the ground it gave me an immensity of pain as it was much swollen and perfectly stiff. At day break on [the] 19th Drummond found me out and to my unspeakable joy procured a dragoon horse that was slightly wounded to take me to Brussels.[18]

Yet many of the wounded perished without ever leaving the field, succumbing to pain, shock or blood loss. Surgeon David Slow, Royal Horse Guards, observed 'many in such pain that they only wish they were dead'.[19] A lieutenant in the Scots Greys recorded how he and a party of troopers:

… traversed this dismal field finding here and there one of our dear departed comrades; when we saw a man moving whom we soon recognised and found to be Lieutenant [James] Caruthers [sic] of our regiment who was stripped of all but his shirt, and resting his head upon the body of a dead man who lay along side him; we helped him up and placed him in a sitting position, when he made signs for something to drink, which we helped him to from the water which we had brought with us in our canteens for such like purposes, after which we administered a little brandy to his lips, which refreshed him a little, and brought him to his speech. When we enquired how he came to be left in so miserable a situation; he said that his horse was shot, and in falling entangled him under him, from which situation he could not disengage himself; a French soldier seeing him thus fixed made at him and plundered him to a considerable amount and in a little time after another came with the same intention, but finding him to be already plundered, inhumanly plunged a spear into his left side and left him; how he got disengaged from his horse he did not inform us. We were in the act of carrying him to a farmhouse, but we had not proceeded far, when he faintly uttered 'My comrades be sure you write to my father' and immediately expired in our arms. We made a hole in the ditch by the wayside and laid him like many other brave men in his peaceful sepulchre.[20]

Captain Curzon, a member of Wellington's staff, was mortally wounded near the end of the fighting and was found bleeding beside his favourite charger, itself suffering badly from a leg shattered by a round shot. A fellow officer went in search of a doctor, but by the time the latter arrived he found Curzon dead, leaning his head against his horse's neck. 'As I approached,' the doctor related to Gronow later with tears in his eyes:

> it neighed feebly, and looked at me as if it wanted relief from the pain of its shattered limb, so I told a soldier to shoot it through the head and put it out of its pain. The horse as well as its master were both old acquaintances of mine, and I was quite upset by the sight of them lying dead together.[21]

Others may have fallen victim to looters, who descended on the battlefield at night. The habit of local peasants stripping the dead was certainly not confined to Belgium, for Gleig observed the practice in Iberia and southern France during his campaigning there.[22] There appear to be no accounts of British soldiers murdering the wounded,[23] but they were not averse to trophy-hunting. Some officers recovered mementoes from the field, as in the case of a colonel of the Royal Engineers, whom Lieutenant John Sperling saw dismount and claim an officer's sword,[24] Sergeant Charles Wood, 3/1st Guards, who brought away the sword of a colonel of the Imperial Guard,[25] and Captain Horace Churchill, also of the 1st Foot Guards and Hill's aide-de-camp, who expressed the intention of sending home a cuirass of 'one of those noble fellows'.[26] Captain Alexander Mercer, who encountered a severely wounded lancer of the Imperial Guard, also took away a keepsake:

> The poor fellow, a fine old warrior, one hand severed at the wrist, lying beside him, and several bullets through his thighs and body, was exhorting his countrymen to bear their sufferings with more fortitude … We had a long conference, and he begged me to take his lance (stuck up by his side) to save it from falling into the hands of the vile Belges, expressing the pleasure it would give him to know that it was with a brave soldier.[27]

Lieutenant Donald Mackenzie, 1/42nd, acquired a souvenir under very different circumstances: unhorsing a French officer, he took his mount, which he sent to the rear with a wounded soldier. He named his prize 'Waterloo' and rode him for many years thereafter.[28]

Some soldiers, like Private John Marshall, 10th Hussars, thought themselves fortunate to have survived the carnage: 'How I escaped the different pokes the fellows [cuirassiers] made at me and the destructive fire of a solid block of infantry, God only knows.'[29] Many other survivors of the fighting left anecdotes of their narrow escape from injury or death under the most peculiar of circumstances. Lieutenant Colonel Henry Murray, 18th Hussars, wrote of a near miss by a round shot which struck the ground under his horse, violently casting up earth into his face and chest.[30] Lieutenant John Pringle, Royal Engineers, struck by either a carbine or musket shot while standing at the angle of a square, nevertheless survived largely unhurt, thanks to the elasticity of the strap of his telescope, which repelled the missile.[31] Lord Hill's cloak was perforated by more than one musket ball,[32] while Lieutenant Colonel Sir George Scovell narrowly escaped death when a round shot tore his cloak as it passed between his arm and abdomen.[33] Sir Hussey Vivian narrowly escaped death in single combat with a cuirassier when he struggled to hold his reins with his right hand, then suspended in a sling, while employing his left hand to thrust his sword into the neck of his opponent. The timely intervention of Sir Hussey's orderly, who cut down the Frenchman probably ensured the brigade commander's survival.[34] Captain Horace Churchill, 1st Foot Guards, related a series of incidents occurring around 6 p.m., any one of which could have cost him his life:

> The French cuirassiers came clean into us. I was on my old brown horse, a grape shot went through his body & a roundshot struck my hat at the same moment. He fell dead. I was a good deal stunned & could not get from under my horse. The French cuirassiers rode over me, without my hat off, [but] did not wound me. I lay there till the French were licked back. They again rode by me, one of their cuirassiers was killed passing me, I seized his immense horse & with some difficulty got upon him. I rode off & hardly was I clear of them before a round shot struck my horse on the head & killed him on the spot. An officer of the 13th [Light] Dragoons dismounted a man of his regiment & gave me his horse. This was shot in the leg about half an hour after.[35]

Tomkinson recalled how a sergeant in the 16th Light Dragoons was struck in the chest by a spent musket ball:

> I fancied the ball had gone through. In a few minutes I saw the ball drop from his overalls at his feet on to the ground, and on desiring him to go to the rear he said he should see it [the battle] out, and fell in again. He had not been five minutes in the ranks before another spent ball struck him, but not with such violence as the first; he continued with us.[36]

Lieutenant Wright from Major Whinyates's troop of rockets and 6-pound guns lost some of the buttons off his jacket to French fire.[37] Colonel Colin Campbell, attached to the Duke's headquarters, had his horse shot under him and received several shots through his uniform but which otherwise did him no harm.[38] Captain Gronow witnessed:

… musket shots flying over us like peas. An officer next to me was hit on the cap but not hurt as it went through, and another next to him was also hit on the plate of the cap, but it went through also without hurting him. Two sergeants that lay near me were hit in the knapsacks, and were not hurt, besides several other shots passing as near us as possible. I never saw such luck as we had.[39]

Henry Paget, a son of Lord Uxbridge and resident in Brussels, wrote of an officer struck by a spent musket ball which, despite creating a hollow place in his chest, did not enter his body.[40] Lieutenant William Chapman received a musket shot which cut his head when it pierced his cap but did him no further harm.[41] Captain Robert Howard and Lieutenants Robert Rogers and John Gowan, 2/30th, each had a musket ball pass through their caps, but otherwise remained unscathed.[42] Similarly, a musket ball passed through the elbow of Lieutenant John Sperling's coat and another struck his saddle without causing him harm.[43] A rifleman of the 95th had two musket balls pass through the legs of his trousers, also without incident.[44] Lieutenant Colonel Sir George Scovell, Assistant Quartermaster General, must have been possessed of the proverbial feline 'nine lives', for according to his servant:

A cannon shot came under his arm. He most fortunately had his hand up to his hat [at] the moment, to save it falling off. It came through his cloak and carried away a great piece of his coat under his shoulder and under his arm, without in the least injuring him. It likewise shaved the hair off the horse's rump, about the size of the palm of your hand, as if done with a razor, leaving it quite white. Shortly after this a shell burst near Sir George and wounded his horse in five places, leaving him [Sir George] still unhurt.[45]

Some soldiers, while injured, were lucky to escape with their lives, like Corporal Richard Coulter, 1st Life Guards, who related a catalogue of near misses:

We charged them several times, but towards night I had my horse shot in a charge against a solid column of infantry. I found he was shot, I endeavoured to get to the rear, but before I had got him twenty yards, he received another ball, [and] he tumbled over another horse which drop't before me. I had my legs out of the stirrups to quit, but another horse came upon me and drop't dead upon my legs, this was about 20 yards from the face of the column of 1,500 or 2,000 men, I struggled to get clear. They saw me and sent some musket shot at me, but they struck in the horses. I squatted down with my head, but I was almost breathless, my poor horse had a great many balls in him but struggled to extricate himself, by this means I got my legs clear, looked over his neck and saw more approaching to bayonet me. I mustered all my strength and run off faster than I ever [did] to school in my life, their flankers fired after me, I tumbled down, but now [that] their shot was spent, I [got] up again and got clear off to Waterloo … During the time I lay amongst the horses I received a dead [spent] ball against my left arm, which made me believe it was broke, but it only turned the arm black.[46]

Lieutenant Archibald Hamilton, Scots Greys, witnessed a musket ball pass through the cheek of a soldier of the 15th Light Dragoons, carrying away all the teeth on both sides of his mouth but miraculously with no injury sustained by the man's upper or lower jaws.[47] Captain Edward Kelly, 1st Life Guards, not only lost part of the flesh of his right leg to a passing round shot, which drove the buttons of his overalls into his body, but did not subsequently succumb to the sort of fatal infection which accounted for so many deaths in the days and weeks after the battle.[48]

Captain Orlando Bridgeman, an aide-de-camp to Lieutenant General Hill, was wounded very late in the action. While sitting on his horse beside Lord Hill, he was 'smacked off my horse by a grape shot that struck me directly on my back; it did not enter, if it had, of course it must have killed me … what a way to pass the Sabbath!'[49] Various officers barely escaped harm. Bridgeman, noted how 'Lord Hill had one [horse] killed under him, & had several shots through his cloak'.[50] Sergeant Major James Page also narrowly escaped injury thus:

> I was struck by a musket shot on the left thigh, but it was prevented from doing me harm in a singular manner, which was as follows. The day before, my sabretache, which is a kind of pocket made of leather, had one of the carriages broken and in order to keep it safe it was taken up very short and lodged on my left thigh. The pocket being very full of books and other things prevented the shot from going right through when it struck me. This shot would have fractured my thigh bone had not the sabretache prevented it.[51]

Lieutenant Colonel James Stanhope, 1st Foot Guards, narrowly escaped harm from French artillery fire when at Quatre Bras a round shot struck a tree and knocked him off his horse; two days later, at Waterloo, another shot struck his sword – whether sheathed or unsheathed he does not specify.[52] Private Joseph Lord, 2nd Life Guards, also had a lucky escape:

> I had a musket ball [clean?] through my coat, waistcoat and shirt just above my right hip which came out on the buttonhole side of my coat without

doing me any injury, only grazing the skin the size of a shilling; a sword passed through my right coat sleeve between the elbow and shoulder and a lance under the left armpit and a cut through the helmet, all without doing me any injury at all.[53]

Lieutenant Edward Stephens, 1st Battalion 32nd Foot, had two narrow escapes – a grape shot which clipped his left shoulder, leaving only a bruise, as well as a slight contusion to his left thigh; but no sooner was he breathing a sigh of relief at his good fortune than a musket ball or grape shot passed through his left arm between his elbow and wrist.[54]

Recovery and Treatment of the Wounded

The task of removing the wounded began in earnest at first light on the morning of the 19th and would carry on for several days. As late as six days after the action, Lieutenant Richard Cocks Eyre of the 2/95th reported that some French wounded still remained on the field.[55] The sheer number of wounded militated against their receiving timely medical attention. Some were carried to farmhouses and cottages nearby to provide them with cover from the elements, there to await transport to Brussels. The task of surgeons and medical orderlies, both in the field and in various makeshift hospitals in villages stretching from Mont St Jean to Brussels, was daunting. Brussels rapidly became the principal concentration point for medical care, but just the sheer effort of transporting the wounded the approximately 12 miles proved difficult owing to congestion on the road. According to Henegan:

> The road that led from the field of battle was so densely thronged, that it was a matter of difficulty to thread a narrow pass through the moving crowd. In some places, carts and wagons, filled with dead and dying, stood wedged so tightly together, that many minutes would elapse before they could be disengaged, while the groans of the sufferers within them, the oaths of the drivers, and the entreaties for help from those wounded soldiers who had managed to crawl into ditches for temporary shelter amidst the confusion, combined to create a scene that can never be forgotten by those who witnessed it.
>
> A little further on, continuing [on] my road, I came up with an artillery cart, in which lay, an officer, stretched upon a blanket. My anxiety for many in that gallant corps, caused me to inquire his name, and I learnt with sorrow, deep and true, that young Robert Manners – the gay, the handsome, the brave – was lying a corpse in that wretched conveyance. I knew that

he had lost his leg in the early part of the day; but I little expected to meet him on that dark road, his eye as dark, his joyous voice silenced for ever. I laid my hand upon his breast – it was cold as marble. I pressed his hand, which for the first time, gave to pressure in return, and turned away more sick at heart than words can well express. It was doubly mournful to reflect that this fine fellow might have been saved by remaining where his leg was amputated; but, removed at his own request, too soon after the operation, hemorrage [*sic*] came on, and his young life ebbed away in that dark, cheerless vehicle, as it jolted over the rough *chaussée* that traverses the gloomy Forest of Soignies.[56]

As the bells rang out across Brussels to celebrate victory, the wounded began to arrive in large numbers. Tents sprang up in some of the streets and the larger squares, as medical officers strained to cope with far greater numbers of wounded than it was possible to treat. Hospitals soon became overcrowded and wounded officers became billeted across the city in private houses, with numbers chalked on the doors to indicate the number of wounded inside.[57] The city's inhabitants took officers into their houses and provided convents and other large buildings as makeshift hospitals for other ranks.[58] Meanwhile, the medical services strained to cope with the throng of sufferers – working three days in succession in the case of Hospital Assistant George Finlayson and his colleagues:

During that time, no medical officer shut an eye; at least I can say this much for myself. Hundreds of wagons, carts, &c., crowded the streets leading to the hospitals. We have had numerous operations, though many of the cases requiring it did not come into our hands [until] four or five days after they had been wounded. Those operated on in the field are doing well.[59]

As early as the 19th, at least 200 lightly wounded British were transferred by canal barge to Antwerp to make space for the more severe cases to be handled in the hospitals in Brussels. There, on the quay, local people awaited their arrival with bread and wine.[60] Officers wounded at Waterloo tended to receive a good standard of care from the residents of Brussels, as Elizabeth Ord noted: 'The way in which they show their personal affection for the English wounded is quite affecting. There seems to be nothing from the highest to the lowest that they could not do for them; they treat them as if they were their own children.'[61] 'We have had lots of legs and arms to lop off,' wrote Isaac James, a hospital assistant wearied by the number of patients to treat. Still, he reported the residents of Brussels 'most particularly kind to the wounded; their attention to them is unremitting'.[62] An unknown private of the Black Watch noted:

Nothing can exceed the kindness and attention of the inhabitants of this city to our wounded men; the hospital is constantly filled with ladies and gentlemen, who, although speaking a different language, personally administer to our wants, with the kindest attention, distributing clean shirts, bread, wine, coffee, tea, milk and fruits of all sorts, with every requisite for our comfort and accommodation.[63]

Ensign William Thain, 33rd Foot, found the residents of Brussels showing 'the greatest kindness and attention to the wounded; they bring them in from the field and take them into their houses voluntarily, and inhabitants of all ranks are employed dressing them and giving them refreshments during the whole day and in every part of the town'.[64] Captain Orlando Bridgeman, 1st Foot Guards, also noted the extraordinary care and attention provided by the citizenry of Brussels,[65] as did Henegan:

[never] in the annals of war were the inhabitants of Brussels ever surpassed in the humanity and tenderness they exhibited towards the distressed wounded of all nations that assisted in the glorious result [at Waterloo].

At that late hour, women of the highest rank were hastening to the hospitals, with lint and necessaries for the sufferers. Some even took upon themselves to assist the surgeons in their painful duties, and watched with gentle assiduity by the pallets of the wounded soldiers, throughout that long night of agony to so many.[66]

In rare instances, wives who had accompanied the army nursed their own husbands. Surgeons later bled the grievously wounded Colonel De Lancey with leeches, and in spite of the devoted care bestowed upon him by his wife, he died on the 26th as a consequence of water gradually filling his lungs.[67]

Even weeks after the fighting had ended, Brussels presented a ghastly spectacle. The city was awash with the wounded. 'You can have no idea of the melancholy of this place,' wrote Charles Grenfell, a British civilian in Brussels, 'so full of wounded mutilated beings that one cannot turn one's eyes without meeting some miserable object; it is quite painful to walk about,'[68] adding a few days later how the wounded comprised 'spectacles of horror and distress'.[69] The range of injuries naturally varied enormously. Sergeant Thomas Stoddart of the Scots Greys lost an arm, while Sergeant Richard Hayward of the same regiment lost both hands.[70] Elizabeth Ord described a captain with an arm shot off and the other badly wounded.[71]

The multiple wounds sustained by Lieutenant Colonel Frederick Ponsonby, 12th Light Dragoons, attest to the multifarious ways in which the weapons at Waterloo could inflict horrendous damage on the human body. Robert Hume, a senior surgeon, described Ponsonby's injuries thus:

... a cut from a sabre on the outside of the fore right arm opposite the edge of the ulna which divided the integuments and muscles longitudinally down to the bones extending from near the elbow to the wrist. He was also struck behind on the left side by a lance, which fracturing the sixth rib entered the chest and wounded the lungs. Besides these two severe wounds, he received several smaller cuts on his head, shoulder and left arm (which was also disabled) and different parts of his body; and was bruised all over in such a manner as to render his recovery very doubtful; his recovery towards convalescence has been very slow; he has still little or no use of his right arm and hand; his breathing is much affected, by the wound in his chest, which is still open, and his strength is so much impaired that it is more than probable his constitution will never recover the shock which it has received.[72]

Assistant Surgeon Donald Finlayson, 33rd Foot, noted how very large numbers of wounds were caused by round shot, so much so that some officers made comparisons between the discharges of artillery and that of muskets. The majority of wounds, he noted, affected the lower extremities, with perhaps fifteen or sixteen legs amputated for every arm, and few bayonet wounds.[73] The number of amputated limbs must have been in the thousands, since doctors had no understanding of treating infection. Thus, a severely injured appendage was better removed to avoid the onset of gangrene and the certain death which followed it. The rate of recovery from this drastic form of crude surgery is not known, but if the patient managed to survive the agonising trauma of the operation and mercifully avoided infection to his severed limb, he faced a reasonable chance of recovery. Thus, three days after surgeons amputated his shattered leg, Uxbridge wrote how he was 'going on extremely well & have just taken some chicken broth & toast'.[74] Still, other life-threatening complications could arise. Lord Fitzroy Somerset, from Wellington's staff, had his right arm amputated above the elbow by a surgeon who fortunately was present in the carriage which took his patient to Brussels, for Somerset's ligature broke and without the doctor's intervention he probably would have bled to death.[75]

Somerset appears to have borne the surgery with great stoicism, with the wounded Prince of Orange lying in the same room yet unaware that an amputation was under way.[76]

In many cases, however, patients who underwent the ordeal of amputation succumbed to shock or blood loss, like Captain Robert Adair:

... who was struck towards the end of the day by a cannon ball, which shattered his thigh near the hip. His sufferings during the amputation were dreadful; the shot had torn away the flesh of the thigh, and the bones were sticking up near the hip splinters. The surgeon, Mr Gilder, had much difficulty in using his knife, having blunted it, and all his other instruments, by amputations in the earlier part of the battle. Poor Adair during the operation had sufficient pluck to make one last ghastly joke, saying, 'Take your time, Mr Carver.' He soon afterwards died from loss of blood.[77]

John Davy worked in a small hospital in charge of a staff surgeon but with no experience of surgery himself. Most of the more serious operations, he noted, such as amputations above the knee, proved fatal.[78] Thus, when Sir Alexander Gordon reached a surgeon around 7 p.m., his prognosis was not encouraging:

A musket ball had entered on the inside of the left thigh [and] had wounded the femoral artery a little above where it pierces the biceps muscle & going downwards had shattered the femur in several pieces lodging in [the] knee near the surface of the integument. The wound was of such a nature that there was no hope of preserving the limb. He had lost a considerable quantity of blood & complained of excessive pain & as the road was crowded with horses and men in great confusion I thought it was better to amputate immediately than to wait till he should reach the Duke's quarters at Waterloo since besides the torture which he was then suffering and which he must necessarily suffer from a broken limb during his removal to a distance of upwards of two miles he would run great risk of sinking should haemorrhage come on in consequence of the wound in the artery. I was assisted in the operation by Dr Kenny of the artillery which I performed entirely to my own satisfaction and notwithstanding that it was necessary to take off the thigh very high up he bore the operation well & though weak was in tolerable spirits asking me several questions about different officers whom he had seen carried from the field wounded and requesting me to tell him how soon I thought he would get well, whether he should not be able to ride.

He said he felt easy and at his own request was removed slowly by the same soldiers who had carried him from the field to the Duke's house in Waterloo which he unfortunately entered at the moment when Mr Gunning was in the act of amputating Lord Fitzroy Somerset's arm. From that instant he became very restless and uneasy, sighing frequently and begging for a little wine. I gave him a small quantity with water & as soon as Lord Fitzroy and the Prince of Orange set out for Brussels I had him put to bed & gave him a few drops of laudanum with a little wine. I was sent for about ten o'clock to see Lord Uxbridge whose leg I found necessary to amputate and whilst I was in the middle of the operation I had a message from Sir Alexander to say that his stump was bleeding & [he was] very uneasy but as I could not go to him myself at the moment, I sent Mr Cartan surgeon to the 15th Hussars who brought me back word that he was very restless but that nothing appeared amiss with the stump. As soon as I had finished with Lord Uxbridge I went over to him & as he complained very much of uneasiness & the bandages appeared a good deal tinged with blood I removed the dressing & examined the face of the wound in the presence found the ligatures on the arteries all perfectly secure … he became perfectly exhausted and expired soon after daylight I should think about half past 3 o'clock of the morning.[79]

Some men, in the face of very poor odds, made quite miraculous recoveries, like a 27-year-old French soldier who had spent three days on the field without food before reaching Brussels. Henry Blackadder, a hospital assistant, described his wound and treatment thus:

A musket ball had entered at the anterior part of the squamous suture of the temporal bone on the right side and passing backwards and downwards fractured the parietal bone and lodged in the brain … the wound was laid open by Mr Charles Bell; three portions of bone were removed and the ball extracted from the posterior lobe of the right hemisphere of the brain immediately over the anterior cerebral … The ball when extracted was covered with the substance of the brain.

Notwithstanding this extensive injury to the head, his constitution could scarcely be said to be at all affected …[80]

Burial

In the wake of the action disposal of the dead became a matter of urgent necessity, though the number of slain was so numerous as to foil attempts to inter them all. Captain Blackman, 2nd Foot Guards, was buried on the spot where he was killed in the garden at Hougoumont, though his and others' remains were disinterred and transferred to Evère Cemetery in Brussels in the 1880s.[81] Officers were sometimes buried in the same graves as their fellows from the same regiment, as in the case of three members of the King's Dragoon Guards.[82] In rare instances some officers were buried even as the battle still raged. When, for instance, Sir Thomas Picton was killed, a staff officer approached the 23rd Light Dragoons and ordered a detachment to bury him pro tem.[83] Lieutenant Colonel Sir Augustus Frazer, commanding the Horse Artillery, recorded burying Captain Norman Ramsay, with that officer's troop present, in the midst of the action.[84] In many cases regimental detachments went in search of specific men known to be among the fallen. Lieutenant Smith of the 10th Hussars took a burying party with him and discovered the body of Major Howard, whom a sergeant proceeded to bury, but which was later, unusually, disinterred and brought back across the Channel.[85] Lieutenant Andrew Hay, 16th Light Dragoons, was killed during the pursuit of the French, but despite a search his body could not be located. He is likely to have been killed amidst the high corn, his body stripped the following morning by local peasants in search of loot, thus making identification all the more difficult amongst a field strewn with tens of thousands of often naked or partially clothed corpses.[86] Private Thomas Bingham, Royal Horse Guards, buried his own brother 3ft under the surface.[87] Several officers of the King's Dragoon Guards – the colonel, the adjutant, a captain, two majors and a lieutenant – were all buried together in a single grave by men of the 32nd Foot.[88] Owing to her husband's death in Brussels, Lady De Lancey arranged for her husband's burial in 'a sweet, quiet, retired spot' in the cemetery of the Reformed Church outside the city, where a stone was laid.[89]

Yet these constituted exceptional circumstances; most corpses were collected in large heaps and buried in mass graves, the sheer scale of the enterprise requiring several days' work. Hospital Assistant George Finlayson's account reveals that as late as eight days after the fighting corpses still lay on the field: 'It has been found impossible to bury the killed, they are thrown with [the] horses on one heap & burnt. A hundred men from all the neighbouring parishes are employed for this purpose & the field of battle will be clean of the dead by today.'[90] Sergeant Johnston of the Scots Greys observed the difficulties of identifying and disposing of the dead:

> At daylight the next morning a detachment of officers and men were sent to the field in search of such of our regiment as might be yet alive in the field, and also to bury the dead of our own regiment. As we approached this solemn scene we saw the Highland Brigade busily employed burying our dead along with their own, which was considered by us an act of very great kindness, notwithstanding it did great harm, for it prevented us from ascertaining correctly the number we had killed in the field. I have to remark that most of our men who were left in the field were either totally or in part stripped of their clothing; and many of our dead were so horribly mangled that we could not distinguish who they were nor that they had belonged to the regiment had it not been for their clothing.[91]

Notification of an officer's death was sent to the deceased's next of kin, together with an offer either to have the personal effects sent home or the money raised by their being auctioned off within the regiment.[92] Captain

Orlando Bridgeman, 1st Foot Guards, collected the possessions of Lieutenant George Gunning, 10th Hussars, lamenting that:

> It is melancholy, very, very melancholy, the number of friends we have lost; in my regiment alone there are thirty-four officers killed & wounded; the French fought with the greatest possible courage, no troops could behave better, ours it is needless to speak of, the event speaks for that, but I assure you, my dear mother, I do not forget that it was the lord of providence that gave us the victory: it is you, my kind parent who has taught me to look there for everything.[93]

In the immediate wake of battle survivors penned letters of condolence, like Private Joseph Lord, 2nd Life Guards, who wrote to his family announcing the death of his own brother:

> At last at the commencement of a charge the French cannon began to play on our left and the balls flew like hailstones, we had gone half way through the charge when the ball destined to put an end to his [his brother's] worldly trouble was discharged from the enemy. Thus did I lose the dearest brother and he did not survive two minutes after he received the ball. Weep not dear mother, weep not dear sister, he is gone I have not doubt to a better world where we shall soon follow. I shall take care that his accounts are closed properly ...[94]

Lord's letter to his own wife goes further in revealing his sense of personal loss:

> I must acknowledge myself though I feel very poignantly the loss of my dear brother, perhaps in a greater degree than you imagine; he was I may express it, a part of myself, brought up from infancy together, the companion of my riper years, my comrade as a soldier, my friend in misfortune, my consoler in distress; he doubled my pleasure and spared my grief. He was a very affectionate brother, respected by all who knew him in the regiment, there is not one but what laments his loss. During the 7 years and a half that he has been in the regiment, he never was confined [by illness]. I could enumerate as many instances of his good qualities but what I have said is enough for all is comprised in the sentence. He was beloved by everyone, [his loss] regretted by every one, his life was sacrificed for his country, his death was glorious.[95]

In the days and weeks that followed the fighting, the Waterloo battlefield became a point of curiosity. Four days after the fighting, bodies still remained in considerable number. 'Nearing the battlefield,' one officer of engineers wrote:

we were sensible of a contagious smell, which increased as we approached the scene of action. Here we were presented with a melancholy sight, for though people had been employed burying the slain, yet the ground was still thickly strewed with dead bodies of horses and men. Peasants were seeking what they might pick up, and taking the little covering that had been left upon the dead. It was a horrid sight, the distortion of some and the immense enlargement of others.[96]

Even as late as a fortnight after the battle, when Lady Uxbridge and a small party toured the field, extensive evidence of the battle still remained. With a degree of morbid curiosity, she visited the sites where her husband and Lord Fitzroy Somerset were wounded before proceeding to the two houses where the respective amputations took place. A farmer's wife then showed her the place where her husband's leg was buried and promised to plant a tree over the spot.[97] The sights and smells appalled her:

The road all the way to the field of battle is dreadfully disgusting, the smell from the dead horses is so horrid, but the field itself is perfectly sweet. The whole ground there is covered with caps, helmets & different bits & scraps that nothing remains, but what I have stated. The whole of the field of battle is now composed of heaps of earth thrown up where the poor dead bodies have been buried, they are as thick as mole hills, & in one part there was still a pile burning of dead bodies which were consuming by fire. There was nothing to be seen but straw & smoke! There is a farm house [Hougoumont] which was filled with wounded in the middle of the action, the walls of which are battered to pieces & the inside entirely consumed by fire; a shell went into the building & set it on fire & all the poor wounded perished in the flames. In the little flower garden belonging to it, showed all the marks of having been filled with troops & trampling of horse.[98]

Visiting the site on 13 July, Charles Grenfell also strolled amongst the remains of Hougoumont, leaving an account which provides more evidence that the French employed artillery against that position:

It is impossible to conceive anything more horrible than must have been the contest, from the effects that still remain of it. The wood leading to the house may be about four or five acres, and there is scarcely a single tree standing in which the marks of bullets are not visible, and all the smaller trees are actually shot in two, in one trunk I counted eighty gun marks. The houses & buildings of every description are wholly destroyed, a few of the walls are standing, but so perforated with cannon balls that it is almost hazardous to approach too near. The gate at the entrance has not a square inch in it through which the shot has not passed and the whole presents a scene of desolation & ruin I never saw before. The remnants of many a poor fellow be scattered about in all directions; and I saw several skulls & bones which had escaped the notice of those employed to bury to dead. The garden walls were in many places covered with blood and even now [more than three weeks after the fighting] the whole field of battle is showered with caps, scabbards, and a variety of things which the peasantry have not thought worth carrying away.[99]

15

VICTORY
AND DEFEAT

However comprehensive the Allied victory, there is no question but that the issue hung in the balance for several hours. Wellington is supposed to have – quite rightly – pronounced the battle 'a close-run thing', a conclusion numerous officers shared. 'The defeat of the enemy was ultimately most complete, but never was action more desperate or longer in doubt,' wrote one officer of the Royal Dragoons. 'For three hours it hung on a thread, and nothing but the most determined bravery on the part of the British (on whom the whole weight of Napoleon's army was thrown) could have sustained the battle till the advance of the Prussians between five and six in the afternoon.'[1] Captain Thomas Wildman, 7th Hussars, expressed a similar view: 'The field was literally lost & won 3 times,' he wrote the day after the fighting. 'The fate of the battle seemed to hang upon a thread, both parties being well aware that defeat & destruction were almost synonymous, there being one road to retreat by & that of course choked up with baggage, ammunition & wounded &c.'[2] Captain Mercer admitted in his journal that even before the great wave of French cavalry attacks he feared the worst, putting faith in the Duke to see the army through:

> Meantime gloomy reflections arose in my mind, for though I did not choose to betray myself … yet I could not help thinking that our affairs were rather desperate, and that some unfortunate catastrophe was at hand. In this case [were it to happen] I made up my mind to spike my guns and retreat over the fields, draught-horses and all, in the best manner I could, steering well from the highroad and general line of retreat.[3]

Lieutenant Colonel Francis Home, 2nd Battalion 3rd Foot Guards, clearly believed possession of Hougoumont to be tenuous, for in his view only the final Allied advance saved the garrison 'from the fate which they would have met with from the enemy'.[4]

Many British officers, like Ross-Lewin, magnanimously hailed the staggering determination of French fighting spirit and doggedness – more generous than the ordinary victor's magnanimity:

> The French never fought with greater *acharnement* [fierceness], as they express it ... Their artillery was admirably served and the gallantry of their cuirassiers, though baffled by the intrepidity of our troops, was most conspicuous, and merited the highest enconiums. They were chosen men, of tried courage and experience, and formed really splendid cavalry; all behaved well, but several acts of chivalric daring performed by individuals of their number, on both these memorable days, were worthy of the olden times of a Dubois and a Bayard. Victories gained over such troops are indeed glorious. The conduct of the infantry of the Guard at Waterloo, at the end of the day, was also most heroic and devoted, although their efforts were also unavailing.[5]

The epic struggle for Hougoumont, in particular, attracted the admiration of many – who rightly regarded its preservation as pivotal to the outcome of the battle. Lieutenant Colonel James Stanhope, 3/1st Foot Guards, generously referring not to his own but to the other brigade of Guards, acknowledged Hougoumont as 'the key of our position' and that its defence 'was most brilliant & saved us'.[6] Tomkinson described both the defence and the attack as 'gallant',[7] while Gronow declared that both sides had performed 'prodigies of valour'.[8] Private Wheeler of the 51st claimed:

> Never was a place more fiercely assaulted, nor better defended, it will be a lasting honor and glory to the troops who defended it. So fierce was the combat that a spectator would imagine a mouse could not live near the spot, but the Guards, who had the honor to be posted there not only kept possession but repulsed the enemy in every attack. The slaughter was dreadful ...[9]

But such sentiments were not confined to Hougoumont, for others heaped praise on the French in general terms. 'We knew we had beaten the French, and that too, completely,' Cotton recorded:

> but they were not defeated because they were deficient either in bravery or discipline. Their bearing throughout the day was that of gallant soldiers: their attacks were conducted with a chivalric impetuosity and admirably sustained vigour, which left no shadow of doubt upon our minds of their entire devotedness to the cause of Napoleon, of their expectation of victory, and the determination of many of them not to survive defeat. The best and bravest of

them fell: but not till they had inflicted almost equal loss upon their conquer-
ors. To deny them the tribute of respect and admiration which their bravery
and misfortunes claim, would tarnish the lustre of our martial glory.[10]

So impressed was he by the fighting spirit of the French, that in the midst of
the struggle Captain Horace Churchill, 1st Foot Guards and aide-de-camp to
Lord Hill, exclaimed to his general, 'By God, these fellows deserve Bonaparte,
they fight so nobly for him.' Everyone around him agreed. 'I had rather fallen
that day as a British infantryman or as a French cuirassier than die ten years
hence in my bed,' he concluded.[11] The French may have been the enemy, but
Ensign Edward Macready, 2/30th, was at least willing to concede them as
'gallant foemen'.[12]

An analysis of both sides' conduct is instructive. French errors connected
with the Waterloo campaign in general, as well as with the battle in particular,
abound; thus, the Allies' success must not be attributed solely to decisions of
their own making, but rather in combination with an examination of French
actions – and Allied errors.

Napoleon committed a fundamental error in failing to initiate his attack
until 11 a.m. He overconfidently assumed that Grouchy possessed the manpower and skill to occupy the whole of the Prussian Army at Wavre, keeping
the Allies apart long enough to inflict a crippling blow on Wellington before
reinforcements could arrive from the east. Time was of the essence: by attacking at first light Napoleon would have gained for himself several more hours
in which to confront the Anglo-Allies without Prussian assistance. Instead,
by waiting until nearly midday in the hopeless expectation that the ground
would harden sufficiently to increase the efficiency of his artillery, the
Emperor cast aside the chance to fight Wellington on his own, with virtual
parity in numbers – albeit the French still facing a well-positioned defender.

Indeed, in light of the strong position he encountered at Waterloo,
Napoleon might have pursued an altogether different course of action, such
as withdrawing and fighting another day, possibly on a field of Napoleon's
choosing or in any event one not of Wellington's. Alternatively, the Emperor
might have executed a wide outflanking manoeuvre, thereby denying
the Anglo-Allies the advantages accruing to them from the possession of
Hougoumont and La Haye Sainte. As Assistant Surgeon John James rightly
put it: 'The strength of the position which the Duke had chosen & his own
increasing exertions & great judgement must certainly be considered as a
principal cause of the victory.'[13]

According to Lieutenant Colonel James Stanhope, when asked at a private dinner in Paris in July what he would have done in Napoleon's shoes
the Duke replied that apart from underestimating the fighting capability of

British infantry as established in Iberia, he would not have launched a frontal assault; specifically:

> ...that I should not have taken the bull by the horns; I should have turned a flank, the right flank. I should have kept the English army occupied by a demonstration to attack or perhaps by slight attacks, whilst I was in fact moving the main body by Hal on Brussels; but if I had determined on attacking as Bonaparte did, *nobody could do more.*[14]

To his cost, Napoleon chose an unimaginative frontal assault against Wellington's main line in a desperate bid to split his army in two, seize control of the critical Brussels road and march on the capital and Antwerp, thereby severing Wellington's lines of supply and communication across the Channel. Thus, while Napoleon chose the correct strategic objective, the tactics he employed to achieve it were fatally flawed.

Some have criticised the Duke for detaching such a large formation, 17,000 men, to the area around Tubize and Hal – from where, incidentally, the troops were not aware of the fighting at Waterloo[15] – for the sake of protecting his extreme right from, as it happened, an attack which never transpired. Once Wellington became aware that Napoleon did not intend to undertake a wide encircling movement no time remained to recall the detachment to participate at Waterloo. Yet Wellington could not have known that in fact the French would execute a full frontal attack rather than attempt to proceed on Brussels via Mons over what amounted to a more circuitous yet much less encumbered route. As Napoleon was known for his great flanking manoeuvres and Wellington had not fought him personally before, detaching men from Lord Hill's division appears to have been a sensible decision under the circumstances.

One may argue with considerable merit that Napoleon should never have attempted to eject the Anglo-Allies from the Mont St Jean ridge – at least not by the methods he employed. Both Hougoumont and La Haye Sainte sat forward of Wellington's main position, offering excellent anchoring for his line; folds in the ground also concealed much of the Duke's position from French view, including the important laterally positioned Ohain road, which stretched east–west, thereby allowing easy communication and supply to units along most of the front line. The topography and the physical obstacles which accentuated these advantages entirely suited the temperament and experience of British troops, who had fought numerous actions in the Peninsula on the basis of Wellington's carefully considered choice of ground, particularly where troops could shelter on the reverse side of a slope, thereby enjoying some protection from enemy artillery fire while simultaneously denying the French information on Anglo-Allied strength and dispositions. Moreover, the state of the ground badly inhibited whichever side operated on the offensive, in this case, the French. Heavy rainfall rendered it particularly boggy, with implications for the movement of both cavalry and artillery, as Tomkinson observed:

> The whole field was covered with the finest wheat, the soil was strong and luxuriant; consequently, from the rain that had fallen, was deep, heavy for the transport and moving of artillery, and difficult for the quick operation of cavalry. The heavy ground was in favour of our cavalry from the superiority of horse, and likewise, in any charge down the face of the position, we had the advantage of moving downhill, and yet we felt the inconvenience in returning uphill which distressed horses after a charge. The difficulty of returning up the hill with distressed horses occasioned so great a loss in the charges made by the heavy brigades.
>
> The ground was so deep that numberless shells burst where they fell, and did little or no injury from being buried in the ground, and many round shot never rose from the place they first struck the ground, instead of hopping for half a mile and doing considerable injury. Many lives on both sides were saved from this circumstance. The corn was laid quite flat, both on the ground held by our troops and before and in the rear of the position.[16]

Yet other factors played a far more critical part in explaining Anglo-Allied success than topography and the state of the soil. British infantry enjoyed a well-deserved reputation for standing their ground irrespective of the weight of fire brought against them. 'Nothing could exceed the good conduct of the troops', declared Captain William Bowles five days after the carnage.[17] As Kincaid wrote in his memoirs:

> The British infantry and the King's German legion continued the inflexible supporters of their country's honour throughout, and their unshaken constancy under the most desperate circumstances showed that, though they might be destroyed, they were not to be beaten.[18]

This conclusion is echoed by Ross-Lewin in his memoirs:

> It is needless to say with what determined valour the greater portion of the different troops, composing the Duke of Wellington's army, resisted and repelled the enemy's most formidable attacks, and endured on exposed positions a terrible and incessant artillery fire; the result speaks sufficiently to that point.[19]

Officers in particular deserve praise for maintaining discipline amongst their men, many of whom had not seen service in the Peninsula. As one officer of the 14th Foot asserted, 'the battle could hardly have been won if commanding officers had not talked cheerily. A sombre remark in the midst of an action is not the way to keep men's courage up.'[20]

Non-commissioned officers also performed superbly. Sergeant Wood, 3/1st Foot Guards, gives us an instructive window into his conduct in action:

> I addressed my company in a few words, to 'be steady and attentive to orders – keep perfect silence – and put your whole trust in God's help, for he is with us; be strong and determined; use all your skill in levelling [your musket]; make sure your mark, and in the charge, use all your strength; and you shall see, by the close of this day's sun, your enemies fly, and the shout of victory shall be yours.'[21]

The unshakeable nature of British troops is borne out by the notably sparse evidence of desertion from the ranks, although Lieutenant Colonel Sir Andrew Barnard, commander of the 1/95th, admitted that at least a hundred of his men, when caught unprepared near La Haye Sainte by cuirassiers, dispersed to the rear and did not return to the front line.[22] Tomkinson found only one deserter from the 16th Light Dragoons to have missed the fighting at Waterloo, having run off in search of plunder the night before. He returned to camp on the morning of the 19th, to be 'booted' by the men.[23] Tomkinson recalled another such case:

> A corporal of the Guards stationed in Hougoumont having left his regiment, passed through the 95th on his way to the rear. He was not wounded, and assigned no reason for leaving his corps. He told the 95th that the enemy had possession of the château, and that all there was lost. From the point the 95th occupied in the line, they saw our fire proceeding out of Hougoumont against the enemy, and therefore knowing his report to be false, they caught him, and gave the corporal a good booting, telling him in future to beware how he spread such incorrect, dispiriting reports.[24]

On the other hand, the Duke may be said to have been ill-advised to allow his headquarters staff and numerous other officers to attend the Duchess of Richmond's ball on the evening of the 15th. Even junior officers could appreciate the degree of irresponsiblilty displayed by the commander-in-chief. Captain Arthur Kennedy, 18th Hussars wrote of the Duke's being 'not a little accused for his want of information of the enemy's movements previous to the attack; from the scattered manner in which our troops were dispersed over the country we did not seem the least aware of the intended attack.'[25] Similarly, Lieutenant Colonel James Stanhope asserted that whether the Duke thought the movement of the French merely a feint or that he reckoned the French insufficiently prepared to be able to open a campaign so soon after taking command of his country's forces, 'it is certain the Duke never had the army so little in hand as on the 16th [of June]'.[26] Tomkinson's defence is hollow indeed:

> Something has been said of the headquarters at Brussels thinking so little of the enemy's advance that they were at a ball, and considerable delay occasioned in consequence. If any army receives information at night which requires an immediate move of troops, it is of great consequence to have the Quarter-Master General and other staff officers collected, in the place of having to seek and assemble them over a large town. There was considerable time saved by this, and no objection to attending a ball twenty miles from an enemy.[27]

On a strategic level, although Napoleon's rapid advance into Belgium on 15 June caught the Allies by surprise, he might well have succeeded in maintaining himself in power simply by consolidating his defensive position within France, depending on the frontier forts to slow his enemies' advance before engaging them on home soil, by which time the combined numbers of French forces would have reached several hundred thousand. After all, with far fewer numbers available to him in 1814, Napoleon had performed a series of miracles until finally overwhelmed.

Still, having rejected that option and proceeded with his campaign in Belgium, the Emperor failed to order Ney to take the crossroads at Quatre Bras until too late in the day, rendering it impossible for him – especially without d'Erlon's assistance – to inflict a properly decisive blow upon Wellington. D'Erlon himself cannot be blamed for marching his corps for six hours on the 16th – in the course of which he failed to arrive at either battlefield – for he possessed contradictory and confusing orders from Ney, Napoleon and Marshal Soult, the Chief of Staff. One might well argue that, appreciating that he could not fight at both Quatre Bras and Ligny, and that time would be uselessly spent on the march given the distances to cover, d'Erlon ought to have made an independent decision, i.e. to obey one order at the expense of another, and simply intervene where he reckoned he could achieve the most good. But that is to assign to a commander rather more initiative than that to which he was entitled. The same principle may be applied to Grouchy, some of whose staff begged him to march west to what appeared to be a much larger engagement than that into which he became simultaneously embroiled at Wavre.

Much might also have been accomplished on the 17th, for with both Wellington and Blücher forced to retreat – the Prussians in particular –

Napoleon failed to grasp the opportunity to pursue them with greater vigour, so placing himself in a position to engage them once again and inflict upon them a mortal blow – or at least channel the direction of their retreat so as to eliminate the opportunity of their co-operating further. By permitting Wellington to withdraw from Quatre Bras, the French enabled the Duke to establish himself in a pre-arranged position of considerable strength – so much so that some, like Sir Vivian Hussey, argued that Napoleon should never have attacked Wellington at Waterloo at all – or at the very least have adopted a radically different plan of attack:

> The French made a great mistake in attacking the position of Waterloo. They should have masked Hougoumont and penetrated with all their force between us and the Prussians by attacking our left, or else they should have attacked Hougoumont in a different manner than that in which they did attack it, not advancing against the garden and wood, but occupying in force the height above it and driving our troops out with their Artillery, and then turning our right altogether, advancing, getting possession of the road to Brussels at the point of junction with that from Nivelles and that from Genappe. They might thus have bothered us terribly.[28]

Napoleon also misjudged the resilience of the Prussians who, although badly mauled, extricated themselves entirely from Ligny, moving northwards to Wavre, unmolested, and requiring the Emperor to observe them with Grouchy's corps. Whether Napoleon ought to have detached Grouchy is debatable. On balance, a covering force of some kind appears sensible, even if only to delay any Prussian attempt to link up with Wellington at some subsequent engagement. But having made the decision to send Grouchy, the marshal required timely orders – which Napoleon ought to have issued early on the 17th and not in the afternoon – for after midday Blücher's exact whereabouts were unknown. In the event, Grouchy of course did engage the Prussians; specifically, III Corps and elements of the other three; but the distribution of Prussian forces permitted Blücher's entire force to avoid being pinned – and the rest is history. Retaining Grouchy with the main body might have offered some advantages, of course, such as an adherence to the fundamental precept of maintaining concentration of force; yet retaining Grouchy with the main body would simply have enabled all four of Blücher's corps to arrive at Waterloo all the more rapidly.

In judging Grouchy's decision not to march to the sound of the guns immediately upon hearing the roar of the grand battery, one must not fall foul of the benefit of hindsight. To have left his position at Wavre would have been to fly in the face of orders received as recently as 10 a.m. that day. Even had

he marched for Plancenoit, where in the event the impact of Prussian intervention at Waterloo was greatest, he is unlikely to have reached the village in
time to offer support to its beleaguered defenders, for the corps of Pirch and
Thielemann probably would have interposed themselves between his line of
march and the village, thus enabling Ziethen and Bülow to proceed towards
Wellington's left and down to Plancenoit unmolested. Over this whole debate
Grouchy is far less to blame than his emperor, for the stark fact remains that –
in light of the serious defeat he had inflicted on the Prussians two days earlier
– Napoleon simply did not believe the Prussians capable of so rapid a recovery – and therefore failed to anticipate any meaningful Prussian intervention
on the 18th.

Once deployed on the 18th, Napoleon ought to have appreciated that
time stood clearly against him. With the protection of his right flank uncer-
tain owing to ignorance of Blücher's dispositions and intentions, Napoleon
ought to have understood the vital importance of launching his attack against
Wellington as soon as the preliminary bombardment of Allied lines could
be construed as sufficient to support d'Erlon's offensive. Any sensible commander could appreciate the benefits to be accrued to the deployment of
artillery on dry ground; but to wait until 11.30 a.m. – well after sunrise – to
fire his guns proved utter folly. No prospect of serious sunshine existed for
the 18th, and in light of the torrential downpour of the previous evening, the
Emperor could not realistically hope for much firmer ground by midday.

Napoleon badly fixed his own headquarters. He had briefly moved his post
from Rossomme to another mound, close to La Belle Alliance, but not for any
substantial period. The latter position would have furnished him with a commanding view of the valley separating the two armies akin to Wellington's
on the slope opposite. The Emperor did not need to be in the thick of things
at the front line; rather, circumstances demanded he place himself in a position personally to observe the progress of the fighting and to maintain direct
control of affairs. By remaining aloof he left matters entirely in the hands
of Ney, who in turn failed to step back from the action and view it with
the wide perspective required of a senior commander. Conversely, Wellington
continuously rode along the front, monitoring events, offering words of
encouragement, ordering up reinforcements or deploying troops as needed.

Napoleon's position on the battlefield may appear less relevant in light of
the fact that he served merely as the *de jure* commander, with Ney actually in
charge. Ill from piles and physically and psychologically disengaged from the
battle until late in the afternoon, the Emperor was unable to see and relied on
messengers to apprise him of events. Thus, one sees the paradox of Ney positioning himself too close to the action – sometimes personally leading attacks
– while, conversely, Napoleon stood too far from it. The two commanders

were not in contact between 9 a.m. and 7 p.m., thus producing a vacuum in command, whereas Wellington, as discussed, adopted the correct procedure – riding across the slopes of Mont St Jean surveying the action and making decisions based on personal observation. Neither Ney nor Napoleon occupied the equally advantageous positions on the opposite ridge, from which they ought to have issued orders, received reports and generally made themselves regularly accessible to subordinates.

One may argue with some justice that, since commonly held doctrine advises a three-to-one numerical superiority to the attacker in order to compensate for the innate advantages accruing to a defender, Napoleon ought to have declined battle at Waterloo in the first place. The French barely outnumbered their opponents – by a few thousand, not enough to offer any genuine benefit, particularly in light of Wellington's strong position. The French held the advantage in cavalry – about 3,000 more than Wellington – and, above all, in artillery, with 246 to 157 guns, a difference of eighty-nine. A detailed comparison of the numbers deployed reveals remarkable parallels:

	Wellington	**Napoleon**
Infantry	53,850	53,400
Cavalry	13,350	15,600
Artillery	157 guns + rockets	246 guns

Such figures highlight the relative importance of the Prussian presence on the field towards the end of the day's fighting, even though the Anglo-Allies had done practically all of the work by the time Bülow's and Ziethen's troops had begun to make a genuine impact around 4.30 p.m. Various eyewitnesses attest to Wellington's anxiety for the arrival of the Prussians – although he never claimed that he could not secure victory unilaterally. According to Lieutenant Colonel James Stanhope, 3/1st Foot Guards, Wellington regarded the battle as 'nearly desperate', but said, 'If the whole artillery can be brought up & the infantry is firm it will all do, for Blucher is coming up'.[29] Some British observers – though not many – openly acknowledged the vital role played by the Prussians. Captain Henry Grove, 23rd Light Dragoons, writing in his campaign journal, noted: 'At one time the action was appearing to be much against us, and but for the Prussians coming up, many thought that we should be obliged to retreat.'[30] Lord Edward Somerset went much further: 'At length about 7 o'clock in the evening the Prussians whom we had been expecting the whole day appeared close upon our left, and decided the fate of the day.'[31] Indeed, in his dispatch, Wellington himself gratefully acknowledged Blücher's support (see Appendix XI). On the other hand, several first-hand British accounts dismiss the impact of the Prussians altogether – a wholly unfair assertion. Kincaid, for instance, noted that 'an occasional gun, beyond the plain, far to our left, marked the approach of the Prussians; but their progress was too slow to afford a hope of their arriving in time to take any share in the battle'. He went further:

> It will ever be a matter of dispute what the result of that day would have been without the arrival of the Prussians: but it is clear to me that Lord Wellington would not have fought at Waterloo unless Blücher had promised to aid him with 30,000 men, as he required that number to put him on a numerical footing with his adversary. It is certain that the promised aid did not come in time to take any share whatever in the battle. It is equally certain that the enemy had, long before, been beaten into a mass of ruin, in condition for nothing but running, and wanting but an apology to do it; and I will ever maintain that Lord Wellington's last advance would have made it the same victory had a Prussian never been seen there.[32]

In fact, by as early as 1.30 p.m., aware of the Prussians' approach and concerned by the threat they posed to his right, Napoleon ordered Lobau's VI Corps, consisting of 10,600 men, to defend his right flank. By doing so, the Emperor denied himself their use against Wellington. Therefore, in re-tabulating the numbers available to prosecute an attack, the French actually deployed fewer troops than the Anglo-Allies, with 66,900 against 73,200. Bare numbers alone do not, of course account for success or failure, since myriad other factors inevitably influence conditions, such as training, tactics, leadership, morale and other considerations. Yet given the British soldier's reputation for doggedness and his remarkable ability to defend from cover, the French might have been well-advised to seek an alternative to a simple frontal attack. In the event, of course, the Prussians did intervene – but to exactly what effect will forever form the basis for energetic debate. British officers in general dismissed the Prussian intervention as too little, too late, though in fairness a minority of officers did seek to do their allies justice, Sir Hussey Vivian not least amongst them:

> In truth, I care not what others may say, we were greatly indebted to the Prussians, and it was their coming on the right and rear of Napoleon that gave us the Victory of Waterloo. We might have held our ground, but we never could have advanced but for the Prussian movement.
>
> … there is not the slightest ground for jealousy, and I must say those are most unjust to the Prussians who refuse them their full share of credit for their most effective aid at the end of the day.[33]

Napoleon's failure to establish the grand battery earlier represented one of at least two errors connected with the French deployment of artillery at Waterloo. Formidable though it was and almost impervious to unsupported infantry, neither Hougoumont's gates nor walls could have withstood artillery fire deliberately sighted to batter them down. Even failing this, the French waited hours before setting fire to the complex – particularly the vulnerable roofs – by employing howitzer fire. Even then, they failed, for they neglected to batter down or blow in the gates, or create a breach in the walls – failures which, arguably, were to deny the French victory. As Ross-Lewin rightly noted in his memoirs: 'Our troops maintained this post during the rest of the day with perfect success, displaying a degree of spirit and intrepidity commensurate with its value, for it certainly was the key of the position.'[34] By failing to employ artillery correctly, the fight for Hougoumont continued for eight hours, draining away brigade after brigade from other sectors of the battlefield to no purpose – unless such attacks went properly supported.

The French also failed to use artillery fire to batter down the walls of La Haye Sainte; and yet the grand battery stood only 300 yards away. Once a breach was made, Napoleon had plenty of infantry to overwhelm the garrison, whereas the position did not fall until evening – and only as a consequence of poor supply.

At La Haye Sainte judicious deployment of artillery would have reduced the place to a shambles. In truth, it was a miracle the farm did not fall sooner, for no one answered Baring's repeated pleas for ammunition, either the result of incompetence or the fact that no one bothered to rescue the overturned wagon which contained the ammunition and powder peculiar to the Baker rifles carried by his men. If Wellington surely cannot be blamed for this, he must answer for his failure to dispatch engineers to fortify the place the night before the battle.

Again, as with Ney's uncoordinated cavalry charges, the failure to employ combined arms proved a fundamentally important contributing factor to French defeat at Waterloo. There is no question but that Ney sacrificed the reserve cavalry to no purpose, squandering some of the best horsemen in Europe in a series of futile attacks. Not only did the assault proceed largely unaccompanied by horse artillery, the presence of so many horsemen confined into a relatively small area not only offered a splendid target to Allied artillery, but actually offered a respite from French artillery fire to the defenders. Nor, extraordinarily, despite the fact that the French held temporary control over numerous British batteries in the course of the series of cavalry attacks, did they spike them, cripple their wheels or carriages, or limber them up and drive them back to friendly lines. Tomkinson observed that:

During the time the enemy were employed in this attack our guns were in their hands, but without any means on their part of either injuring them or carrying them away. It was the most singular, hardy conduct ever heard of, and had such gallantry been properly directed, it must have been turned to some account. Had it happened immediately after an attack, or been once adopted in the zeal of the moment by any officer foiled in his object, there might be some excuse; but for such a thing to be continued for any length of time, and under officers who had been serving all their lives, is a proceeding quite unaccountable.[35]

Ney also ill-timed his assault, for by 4 p.m., in the absence of sufficient firepower deployed against them over the course of the previous four and a half hours, Wellington's infantry remained fully capable of repelling cavalry, irrespective of their number; indeed, all the more so, for as Ney's cavalry mounted the ridge unsupported by infantry and artillery, Wellington's guns continued to fire to the very last moment, bolstering his infantry's confidence. In short, if the cavalry was to be unleashed against the Anglo-Allied line, Ney executed his attack too early – and then waited too long to disengage – a classic case of 'reinforcing failure'. Worse still, when the French Army began to rout in the wake of the repulse of the Imperial Guard, the cavalry was in no position to stem to tide of the Anglo-Allied/Prussian pursuit, as Ross-Lewin noted in his memoirs:

One of the consequences of the irrepressible ardour of the cuirassiers and other French cavalry was that their numbers were so diminished, and their horses so jaded, toward the close of the day, that they became ineffective when their army began to retire, and when their services were much wanted.[36]

But this is not to ignore the misuse of Anglo-Allied cavalry, notwithstanding several officers' attempts to maintain that Uxbridge deployed the heavy cavalry properly. It is not clear if they are alluding the cavalry in general or the heavy or light brigades specifically, but Lieutenant Colonel James Stanhope, 3/1st Foot Guards believed 'the cavalry behaved infamously …',[37] while Lieutenant Colonel Lord Saltoun went so far as to declare that owing to what he described as 'the misconduct of most of your cavalry', the outcome of the battle was 'very doubtful'.[38] According to Ensign William Thain, who interviewed several prisoners, French officers took a dim view of the abilities of British cavalry. As for himself, Thain, though only a junior infantry officer and probably basing his assessment from the narrow confines of his own position on the battlefield, came to a scathing conclusion about the efficacy of what he observed of the light cavalry at the hands of the cuirassiers. 'The fact is,' he penned in his campaign journal, 'that our cavalry were chased about the field terribly and but for our squares and artillery they would have every man been cut to pieces, the French cavalry is so much superior.'[39] With respect to the heavy cavalry in particular, Ross-Lewin argued that:

> Our heavy cavalry maintained a decided superiority over the French force of the same kind in every charge that was made. The household brigade, in particular, rendered themselves formidable to the enemy's dragoons; they were a very fine body of men, and their superb horses were in the best condition.[40]

In truth, Uxbridge overextended himself once both brigades had overrun the French guns and himself felt unease about their conduct, Colonel Colin Campbell, commandant at headquarters, asserting that 'our cavalry made several brilliant charges; the Household Brigade has particularly distinguished themselves and also General Vivian's; but Lord Uxbridge is by no means satisfied with them'.[41]

Still, at the time, Uxbridge did appear to congratulate in person at least Somerset's brigade, if that commander's testimony is to be accepted. 'Lord Uxbridge made us a speech,' Somerset reported on 23 June, 'and declared that the heavy cavalry had took his heart.'[42]

Kincaid, from his perspective as an infantry officer, rightly concluded that 'Our heavy cavalry made some brilliant charges in the early part of the day; but they never knew when to stop, their ardour in following their advantages carrying them headlong on, until many of them "burnt their fingers," and got dispersed or destroyed.'[43] The Union Brigade in particular had rendered itself useless for the rest of the day by the failure of its officers to rally the survivors of its single charge and to maintain regimental cohesion. According to Tomkinson:

> Towards the close of the evening the whole brigade did not form above one squadron. It could not be supposed so few remained over the killed and wounded. The fact was that the men did not know where to assemble after the charge, and this being the first action they had ever been in, they, I suppose, fancied that nothing remained for them to attend to after this one attack, and many went in consequence to the rear.[44]

Wellington complained after Waterloo, with specific reference to the charge of the Household Brigade, that his cavalry 'invariably got me into scrapes. It is true that they have always fought gallantly and bravely, and have generally got themselves out of their difficulties by sheer pluck.'[45] In his memoirs, Gronow described in some detail the Duke's view of the heavy cavalry's mishandling and the infantry's frustration at their virtual absence on the field later in the day:

The Duke of Wellington was perfectly furious that this arm had been engaged without his orders, and lost not a moment in sending them to the rear, where they remained during the rest of the day. This disaster gave the French cavalry an opportunity of annoying and insulting us, and compelled the artillerymen to seek shelter in our squares; and if the French had been provided with tackle, or harness of any description, our guns would have been taken. It is, therefore, not to be wondered at that the Duke should have expressed himself in no measured terms about the cavalry movements referred to. I recollect that, when his grace was in our square, our soldiers were so mortified at seeing the French deliberately walking their horses between our regiment and those regiments to our right and left, that they shouted, 'Where are our cavalry? Why don't they come and pitch into those French fellows?'[46]

Gronow's later observations added further weight to the notion that the sacrifice of the heavy cavalry might have had disastrous consequences had circumstances later in the day absolutely demanded it:

Sir George observed to us that it was lucky for Lord Uxbridge that the field had been won by us; for had this not been the case, he would have got into an awkward scrape for having engaged the cavalry without orders from the Duke. From what Sir George seemed to think, it was evidently the Duke's intention to keep the cavalry in hand, and perfectly fresh, so that they might have charged the French squadrons when the latter had exhausted themselves in their attacks on our squares.

To corroborate this opinion, he told us an anecdote of the war in Spain, which may be interesting, as shewing [*sic*] how opposed the Duke was to the harum-scarum custom of our cavalry officers, who hurled their men at full gallop on the enemy, without supports, and without any actual plan or intimidation beyond the ardour of a sportsman going at a five-barred gate.[47]

Having said all this, given Wellington's defensive position and his determination to hold his ground rather than counter-attack, he could afford substantial losses to his mounted arm more readily than his opponent. He still retained Vivian's, Vandeleur's, Grant's and Dörnberg's brigades after the disaster befalling the heavies, and notwithstanding its own horrific losses, the brigades under Ponsonby and Uxbridge blunted the attack on an entire French corps. Yet, like his criticism of the heavies, Uxbridge apparently expressed anger at the gross shortcomings of the light cavalry. The story may be apocraphyl – and is at minimal an exaggeration, since the light cavalry, to which he obliquely alludes, never declined to charge – but Captain Horace Churchill's anecdote, in his capacity as aide-de-camp to Lord Hill, sheds considerable light on the question of Uxbridge's attitude towards the conduct of his troops:

> Never was such devotion witnessed as the French cuirassiers, our cavalry (with the exception of two brigades [presumably Ponsonby's and Somerset's]) never would face them. Our cavalry on the whole disgraced the name of Englishmen. That noble fellow, Lord Uxbridge said 'I have tried every brigade in the cavalry & and I cannot get one to follow me'. He rode up to the Guards & said 'Thank God, I am now with men, who make me not ashamed of being an Englishman.'[48]

Lieutenant Colonel James Stanhope similarly states that Uxbridge congratulated the Guards whilst simultaneously decrying the role of the light cavalry. According to him, Uxbridge:

> rode up to us & said 'Well done men, by God we stand on you. If I could only get my fellows to do the same but by God they won't budge; but I'll try again' & he rode and charged ineffectually at the head of a regiment of light cavalry on our left. The heavy cavalry did wonders, but our light cavalry, partly from their being brought up in small isolated attacks instead of a great mass, in this part of the battle, near us [i.e. during the massed French cavalry attacks], did very little.[49]

Perhaps predictably, some amongst the heavies felt their lighter counterparts let down the side, such as Captain Edward Kelly, 1st Life Guards, who expressed this criticism to a fellow officer back home in a hunting metaphor: 'Some boys rode with us and others did not at the Tally ho! In the morning.'

Later, in the same vein he added: 'If you should go to town [London] you will hear at Hyde Park Barrack who were foremost and who were not.'[50] Captain Horace Churchill, 1st Foot Guards, similarly condemned the conduct of British light cavalry in response to the massed French cavalry attacks: 'Our cavalry rode round but did not charge the enemy.'[51]

The role of the Imperial Guard proved fundamentally important to the outcome of the battle. In the evening, with the Prussians debouching from Plancenoit, Napoleon had no choice but to commit part of the Guard; but whether or not he should have sent them forward when La Haye Sainte fell – and thus exploited in a timely fashion the moment when Wellington's line appeared most vulnerable – remains contentious. Napoleon should have attacked at 7 p.m.; instead, he waited until 7.30 p.m. – a vital thirty minutes in which, although his troops retook Plancenoit, he lost the opportunity to break the Allied centre. The Emperor rightly appreciated that he must retain part of the Guard in his centre while sensibly detaching a portion to hold or retake Plancenoit; but to wait until after the critical moment had passed – after his forces still retained the ability to split the Anglo-Allied centre – must figure into the long tally of missed French opportunities at Waterloo. Moreover, when they proceeded with an attack – led by Ney rather than Napoleon – the Imperial Guard ought to have gone straight up the main road past La Haye Sainte, not in the open fields between that farm and Hougoumont, where they were exposed to concentrated artillery fire over 1,000 yards of open ground.

Despite this catalogue of errors – mostly on the French side but by no means confined to it – the outcome of Waterloo must not be viewed as a foregone conclusion. The French enjoyed high morale, for Napoleon represented in their eyes a man of immense military prestige whose reputation for succeeding against the odds strongly boosted his men's spirits on the 18th, only two days since defeating the Allies at two separate engagements. The French well out-gunned Wellington and, in sharp contrast to the Anglo-Allies, were distinguished by their homogeneity, with quality consistent across all units, requiring no recourse to the process of intermingling foreign with French units to ensure a leavening between them.

Essentially, Waterloo represented little more than a slogging match in which victory to the defender depended on steadiness and discipline above all else. Henegan summed this up beautifully:

> ... the battle of Waterloo ... differed from all others in the sacrifices demanded and conceded during its long continuance, of nine hours. Wellington had taken the best position left to him. It covered the capital of Belgium – it communicated on the left with the Prussians. The undulating nature of the ground was favourable for acting on the defensive until the arrival and co-operation of Blucher, and upon strict adherence to the defensive, the safety of Wellington depended.
>
> Here then was no field for the display of skilful generalship, and tactical knowledge. The one great essential to a Commander so placed, was firmness, and fortunately for the allies, Wellington possessed that attribute in no small degree. The one great essential for soldiers so placed, was blind obedience – which is a habit rather than a principle – and was so rigidly inculcated in the British army by the Duke of Wellington, that he well knew how far he could depend upon its practice in the field.
>
> Necessity demanded that the position of the allies at Waterloo should be maintained, though rivers of blood should flow from its defenders. And more than this; necessity demanded that brave men should stand passively to be slain, nor slay in turn, until, like automatons, their faculties were put

into movement by a superior power. This it was, that made the bloody field
of Waterloo one, over which angels might have wept. No retaliation was
offered by the brave, the young, the haughty, as mutilated and bleeding, their
comrades fell in heaps around them. The flashing eye and panting heart,
told what the spirit longed to do; but confidence in their leader, and blind
obedience to his will, were stronger even than revenge, and like lambs they
stood the slaughter, until the word of command roused them to be lions.[52]

Finally, much credit accrues personally to the leadership qualities of the Duke
of Wellington, who made himself present at vulnerable points along the line
at critical periods throughout the day. Referring to Quatre Bras, though it
was a characteristic even more applicable to Waterloo, Captain Henry Grove
spoke of 'the perfect coolness with which the Duke rode about the field...',[53]
whilst Lieutenant Colonel John Fremantle, one of the Duke's aides-de-camp,
observed the day after that 'never was such a business from beginning to end,
ever known. The duke did wonders and earned well his victory, we were
near losing the day four times, and I assure you that nothing but his countenance kept the matter going.'[54] Lieutenant Colonel Sir William Gardiner
noted that the Duke 'appeared to be ever in the midst of those who were supporting the most unequal and tremendous conflict'.[55] Writing of a period of
heavy cannonade directed against his regiment around 6 p.m., Ensign Edward
Macready recorded how Wellington's presence steadied the ranks as casualties
gradually mounted:

> The Duke visited us frequently at this momentous period. He was coolness
> personified. As he crossed the rear face of our square, a shell fell amongst
> our Grenadiers, and he checked [i.e. halted] his horse to see its effect. Some
> men were blown to pieces by the explosion, and he merely stirred the rein
> of his charger, apparently as little concerned at their fate as his own danger.
> No leader ever possessed so fully the confidence of his soldiery, 'but none
> did love him'. Wherever he appeared, a murmur of 'Silence – stand to your
> front – here's the Duke', was heard through the column, and then all was
> steady as on a parade.[56]

The high regard in which the troops held their commander-in-chief naturally
lent itself to the duke's talent for steadying the ranks. An unshakeable faith in
the Duke's ability to deliver victory pervaded the army, typified by Macready's
remark that 'no British soldier could dread the result when Wellington commanded'.[57] Captain Thomas Wildman similarly asserted his belief that 'under
any other man in the world but the Duke of Wellington, even British valour
would have been unavailing, it was *vaincre ou mourir* [conquer or die] on both

sides & Wellington & England prevailed'.[58] Lieutenant John Sperling, Royal Engineers, recognised 'judgement and decision ... conspicuous in all his arrangements. One is not surprised at his fame as a General.'[59]

Nor was this view confined to officers, one rifleman of the 95th simply declaring over a drink after the battle, 'Lord Wellington don't know how to lose'.[60] Sergeant Charles Wood, like so many others, identified Wellington's inspirational qualities:

> The Duke has greatly endeared himself to the British soldier; more so in these actions [i.e. Quatre Bras and Waterloo] than in all before. I ever loved and reposed confidence in him as my commander; but the example he gave us on the 18th ... was sufficient to influence every man with that fortitude and determination 'With Wellington we will conquer, or with Wellington we will die!'[61]

Numerous officers joined the chorus, such as Ensign Samuel Barrington, who expressed faith in the commander-in-chief before the campaign and was subsequently killed at Quatre Bras: 'We are all in the highest spirits here and anxious to try our strength with the first who dare oppose us,' he wrote three months before Waterloo. 'If we do but get the Duke of Wellington we are sure to lick them.'[62] Elizabeth Ord, in Brussels, struck a chord prevalent across the army in the wake of the fighting:

> There is no difference in opinion, that the confidence both officers & men have in him, his inalterable coolness, his decision, the quickness of his eye, qualities united to such a degree in no other general, were all necessary to the event. Then his gallantry in exposing himself was surpassed by none on the field and the only miracle is how he or any one is still alive.[63]

Sir Henry Clinton, commander of the 2nd Division and therefore the voice of a senior officer, echoed these views. 'During the battle which lasted long & was well contested,' he wrote a few days after the battle:

> our situation was often critical & gave occasion for displaying the greatest qualities of a commander in a far greater degree than any in which I have seen the Duke of Wellington engaged. He must, I think, have felt this himself, for as soon as the day was fairly at an end, he remarked that he had (I think) four times said the day was his by patience & perseverance. It was a glorious day for the allied armies & more so than any in his life for the Duke of Wellington.[64]

The day after the battle Colonel Colin Campbell asserted that:

> No language of mine can do justice to the extraordinary mind and talents the Duke displayed during the whole of the action ... The Duke was all day everywhere in the thickest of it and his place of refuge was in one of the squares when the enemy's cavalry charged.[65]

Even Wellington himself – not prone to self-promotion – apparently told Thomas Creevey, a British civilian in Brussels, that much of the day's outcome rested on his own contribution to it. 'I can hardly conceive it now I think of it,' the Duke reportedly remarked. 'It was critical, I do believe that if I had not been on the ground myself it would have been lost ...'[66]

16

THE WATERLOO LEGACY:

POLITICAL AND

STRATEGIC CONSEQUENCES

Quite apart from lives lost and bodies maimed, Waterloo cost Napoleon and France as a whole dear, politically, economically and strategically. Internally, with the Bourbons restored for a second time, the French people faced a greater reversal of revolutionary reforms than in the previous year. Many Napoleonic officers were hunted down in the 'White Terror' and the mood of the nation clearly shifted, as reflected in the election of August 1815, whereby the great majority of the electorate – albeit not one chosen on anything like a democratic basis – overwhelmingly rejected liberal principles and the military clique so closely associated with Napoleonic rule. The extent of this rejection may be appreciated by the fact that in November the Chamber of Peers, by a vote of 157 to 1, condemned and executed Ney on the perfectly reasonable charge of treason – a decision that only confirmed the prevailing view across France that whatever the past sins of the monarchy, a curtain surely now had finally to be drawn across the days of Empire and the principle of *la Gloire* – the pursuit of glory through force of arms. Nor did peers merely constitute Bourbon appointees; many had come to power under the Empire, most drawn from the untitled, albeit comfortable classes, and though doubtless inclined to curry favour with the new regime in order to maintain their respective positions in society, were not unduly prevailed upon to seal the marshal's fate. In short, Ney's death reflected a fundamental change of political attitude in France, bringing about a revolt against the radical politics of the past which had brought into power, and sustained for far too long, an overambitious, self-seeking tyrant whose dictatorship – notwithstanding years of military triumph and the prestige thereby bestowed upon the nation – ultimately led a great nation to humiliation and ruin.

It is important to explain these circumstances in concrete terms – to demonstrate exactly what Allied victory and French defeat at Waterloo actually meant, practically speaking – and to stress that its consequences and legacy must not be seen in isolation; that is, as an event without a past. As the last

battle of the Napoleonic Wars Waterloo marked the culmination of events
– the end of an era which had begun at least as early as the Revolution in
1789, but certainly no later than the start of the wars which that movement
spawned, three years later. Thus, to assess the significance of Waterloo is to
assess the French Revolutionary and Napoleonic Wars as a whole.

The wars that stretched from 1792 to 1815 demonstrated that only by concerted action could the Great Powers of Europe expect to prevail against the
overwhelming strength of France, a point that ought to have been appreciated before 1941 by the United States and the Soviet Union. Moreover, by
1814 the Allies had come to the correct conclusion that peace would be
but shortlived unless they maintained a system of collaboration whereby the
rights of states were respected and force became a last resort in the exercise
of power. By adhering to these principles, peace was maintained for two
generations – an unprecedented period of tranquility in the modern era. The
arrangements reached at the Congress of Vienna, which reconvened after
Waterloo, marked the beginning of a new phase in international relations
for, although flawed, the series of decisions at Vienna produced a broadly
accepted compromise, putting paid to the complex system of temporary alliances dating back to the formation of the First Coalition in 1792 which,
owing to its failure, brought forth six more coalitions (the Waterloo campaign of course constituting the seventh) of varying strength and a host of
other minor alliances in the quest for victory over France. In this respect, the
Vienna settlement proved a panacea to the long eighteenth-century tradition of warfare waged on a regular basis between antagonists whose alliances
shifted as and when their interests dictated.

To reach that point, however, significant costs in human life were involved,
even when examining the losses of only two of the (albeit principal) combatants, Britain and France. Notwithstanding Britain's physical isolation and
the protection from invasion offered by her naval superiority – in addition to
the fact that the army, although heavily engaged in Iberia, did not suffer the
colossal losses of the long, attritional struggles endured by her Continental
counterparts – she still lost about 220,000 soldiers and sailors, only a tenth of
whom perished as a consequence of combat, the remaining falling victim to
sickness and disease. One may be surprised to learn that losses on this scale,
as a proportion of Britain's population, closely resembled those of the First
World War. Overall, the Napoleonic Wars alone are thought to have caused
over a million military deaths across Europe, translated into a mortality rate
for those males born between 1790 and 1795 of nearly 40 per cent. If to this
figure is added civilian deaths, the number rises to perhaps five million, or
roughly the same proportion of the European population lost in the conflict of 1914–18 – an extraordinary statistic when one considers the yawning

technological gaps which separate the two conflicts, albeit the First World War covering a much more confined period of time.

The French Revolutionary and Napoleonic Wars ushered in the modern state – a fact which the outcome of Waterloo simply could not reverse – for although in 1815 the ruling classes who had been divested of power restored the former style of government wherever possible, their predecessors' efforts at centralising power and fashioning a more efficient government bureaucracy remained in place and generally found favour with the new regime and its successors. Together with greater centralisation of power, a number of states in 1815 found themselves physically enlarged, for the treaties of Paris and the agreements reached at Vienna consolidated territorial holdings in far fewer hands than had been the case in 1792, greatly simplifying the political map of Europe and creating several monolithic states, such as Austria and Prussia, with very few non-contiguous territories – in sharp contrast to the pre-war era when the Austrian Netherlands and many parts of the (Prussian-controlled) Rhineland lay well beyond the immediate protection and administration of their masters. In addition, a number of the small German states of the former Holy Roman Empire were of sufficient size to become considerably more economically viable than their predecessors and could now field respectable armed forces in their own right, particularly Bavaria.

As a result of Waterloo if, in many though not all, cases, dynasties and individual rulers were restored to their former possessions – though much rationalisation of the map in light of two decades of change was required – this could not entirely alter the fact that subjects had experienced a taste of republicanism, such that the concept of 'the people' could not pass altogether ignored. Feudalism, which maintained the system of serfs owing allegiance to local landowners, and which had been abolished in France under the Revolution and in most of the rest of Europe by 1808, was not reinstated; nevertheless, the aristocracy for the most part reasserted itself socially and politically – certainly in France, but in German territories as well – despite the reforms introduced and in many cases firmly ensconced by enemy occupation. Yet at least for the next fifteen years there was no significant backlash or violent reaction, partly as a result of the growing desire of the middle classes for social mobility; in short, those of a bourgeois disposition were hardly prepared to undermine the power of the upper classes, when it was to their social, political and economic status to which the middle class aspired. Indeed, the two regarded themselves as natural allies, looking upon those socially inferior to themselves as a potential threat to the status quo, above all the stable political order ushered in by peace. So far as they were concerned the masses were not to be loathed, but certainly not trusted, and thus the forms of liberal government which had proliferated among the German states of the

Confederation of the Rhine, the Low Countries and northern and central Italy, gave way to more limited forms of representative government, to the extent that the dramatic inroads made by republicanism since the outbreak of the wars in 1792 faced powerful reactionary forces. Allied victory at Waterloo simply could not turn the clock back entirely.

Waterloo at last enabled the victorious powers to recast Europe on the basis originally sought when the Congress of Vienna first met the previous year – though in light of Napoleon's new bid for power in 1815, and in contrast to the atmosphere prevailing in the spring of 1814, the Allies were no longer seeking conciliation or to welcome France back into the community of nations on a more-or-less equal basis. Rather, theirs was to be a transparently punitive peace, with conditions far harsher than those contained in the first Treaty of Paris of 30 May 1814. Accordingly, the Allies established and fixed new frontiers in the wake of more than two decades of upheaval, with the principal decisions made – as at Versailles a hundred years later – by the principal victors: in this case Britain, Russia, Austria, and Prussia. There is no question that Britain's decisive contribution to French defeat at Waterloo immensely strengthened her hand in these affairs. Thus, what contemporaries identified as the 'Great Powers', including Britain, established a series of buffer states around France for the purpose of creating a defensive ring to discourage future forays. These included a new United Kingdom of the Netherlands, consisting of what today constitutes Holland, Belgium and Luxembourg, and a German Confederation, which greatly reduced the number of independent states in central Europe from the several hundred of the early 1790s to a much more manageable number.

To the south-east, the Kingdom of Lombardy-Venetia was established under the control of the Austrian emperor – again as a buffer against any renewed French efforts in pursuit of territorial aggrandisement. In the east, Poland, having been partitioned three times in the 1770s and '90s and making a brief revival in the form of the Napoleonic satellite state, the Duchy of Warsaw, was replaced by 'Congress Poland', a kingdom under Tsar Alexander. As Russia thus expanded west and the Austrians extended into Italy and re-established control over the Dalmatian coast, Prussia could not go uncompensated, acquiring territory in Westphalia, Pomerania and Saxony. The settlement of 1815 also rewarded Sweden with the annexation of Norway, while Britain retained the Cape of Good Hope, Ceylon, Mauritius, St Lucia, Tobago and Malta, with a protectorate over the Ionian Islands. Switzerland became officially neutral from this time and the former dynasties ousted from across Europe for the most part re-established themselves, with efforts made to restore the privileges once enjoyed by their royalist supporters. Thus, the former royalist houses resumed control in Spain, Sardinia and Naples, and Tuscany and Modena. France was reduced to her frontiers of 1790, with territorial concessions going to Prussia, Bavaria, Piedmont-Sardinia and the Netherlands in the form of part of Savoy and the whole of Philippeville, Marienburg, Saarlouis and Landau. France was to pay an indemnity of 700,000 francs and accept the military occupation of seventeen of her fortresses, at her own expense, for three years.

Quite apart from performing the task of keeping a watch along the Rhine against future French expansion, the heads of state and diplomats at Vienna inadvertently established the basis for future German unification – albeit a circumstance not realised until 1871 – not simply as a result of the simplification of central European frontiers, but as a consequence of the recently unleashed forces of nationalism, particularly those encouraged by the French occupation of Prussia between 1807 and 1813. In short, the antagonisms engendered by the conqueror went far in encouraging Germans to regard themselves as a single people rather than a disparate group who, though sharing a common language and culture (albeit divided between the Protestant north and the Catholic south), continued to adhere to regional, parochial allegiances, such as the local potentate or ecclesiastical state.

In France, while the Bourbons might once again mount the throne in Paris they could not entirely reverse what had been achieved on the political front, and thus had to settle again, as before Waterloo, for a constitutional monarchy not unlike that which existed in Britain at the time. This was broadly acceptable to the Allies, who understood that the old dynasty and a new constitution, though not entirely palatable, would have to be tolerated lest its abolition unleash the revolutionary ferment which had plunged Europe into chaos in the first place. Indeed, many of the reforms instituted during the wars remained and, in many cases, found welcoming adherents among the new elites – not least the Napoleonic Code, which greatly simplified the old, immensely complex legal system of the royalist era. Many of those new to power also embraced the machinery of the administrative structure introduced by the revolutionaries and later improved upon by Napoleon, who had also established a stable financial base for the nation. Many reforms, which championed equality before the law, the right of land ownership, and protection for private property, particularly benefited the middle classes and contributed to the sort of social and political stability sought by those newly restored to power. While trampling upon such reforms may have appealed to those of a more reactionary disposition, most of them appreciated the adoption of a pragmatic approach: a tolerance for the new order of things in recognition of the unimpeachable fact that an irreversible social revolution had taken place during their long absence in exile.

Napoleon's defeat at Waterloo – or the Allies' victory, depending on one's perspective – could not reverse the profoundly influential impact France made on the conquered states of Europe – no more so than in the territories which France had incorporated directly into the Empire, thereby ensuring that the impact of Napoleonic influence remained strong until the closing days of the Emperor's reign. In the Low Countries, the Rhineland and other small German states, and even as far away as Naples and Poland, the Napoleonic Code (Code Napoléon) persisted for many years virtually untouched or, where diluted, continued to make an impact until well into the twentieth century – and in some cases continues to prevail as the legal norm down to the present day. Other Napoleonic institutions remained substantially as the Emperor had left them upon his final exile, such as the police service, the system of taxation, and the political and religious accommodation made with the Catholic Church, known as the Concordat. Moreover, if the Napoleonic army was recast under the Bourbons to efface many of the changes undertaken during the Empire, this was less the case with France's neighbours, many of whom continued to maintain armed forces organised, trained, clothed and armed in the style of their former masters.

Finally, the wars had demonstrated that the era of manoeuvre for the sake of attaining a limited advantage over one's opponent in the quest for a negotiated settlement – such as for the acquisition of a set of fortresses or a narrow strip of territory – had come to a close. War, in the manner practised both by the revolutionaries and by Napoleon, now determined the fate of nations. Armies were to seek battle, not avoid it – with Waterloo merely the last of many dozens like it in scale, particularly since Austerlitz in 1805 – with the expressed intention of destroying the enemy's main force in pursuit of a decisive and long-term political result. Nothing marked the break between Napoleon's manner of waging war and that of his eighteenth-century predecessors more than the concept of wielding the army as a political instrument for the sake of recasting the vanquished as a vassal state or refashioning it as an ally prepared to support the conqueror's ambition of expanding his power and dominion in an endless quest for glory.

APPENDICES

Appendix I

Lieutenant Colonel John Burgoyne, Royal Engineers: 'Waterloo: Remarks made on a visit to the ground in 1816'

The field of Waterloo in front of Mont St Jean is frequently accounted as no position, and does not show to very much advantage, even on Craan's plan, although that appears to be an accurate survey. On inspection, however, without which it is impossible to have a perfect idea of ground, it is certainly favourable for giving battle on, and if a little work could have been done on it, might have been made excellent.

It was not that commanding kind of position that is sometimes found, and which strikes the eye at once; on the contrary, the ridge occupied by our army is lower than the heights a mile or two in front, from whence the French army advanced. But it still had many of the essentials of a good fighting position. The flanks were on commanding points, that discovered the ground well all round them, at a fair distance from the main road by which the enemy approached and would have required him to make a considerable detour across the country to have turned them.

The real left of the position, at a turning of the cross road, was not more than three quarters of a mile from the Genappe chausee [*chaussée*] in the centre, the right resting immediately above Goumont [Hougoumont]; the whole being about a mile and a half or two miles in extent; it, therefore, very compact. In front of the left the ground was well discovered, and with no very favourable points for the enemy's artillery. A road ran along the line in this part with thin hedges along it and a very slight bank, affording some little cover to the infantry if they laid down. This road continued along the centre and right of the position, out of sight of the enemy in those parts, but not affording any cover. The ground in front of the centre and right was more broken, but the hollows were well looked into by the château of Goumont in front of the right, and the farm of the La Haye Sainte on the high road. The whole line was on a ridge, which rounding back to the rear, covered the troops from the sight and from the direct fire of the enemy.

The château of Goumont and the Haye Sainte were strong buildings, not too far in front of the line, and situated in hollows, so as not to be much exposed to be cannonaded severely. They were both of very great consequence as posts. The first was occupied and defended so well as to be retained through the whole day, in spite of all the efforts of the enemy. The troops were put into the Haye Sainte only a short time before the action commenced. The approach to it from the position was very much exposed indeed. The men in it became a kind of forlorn hope; they fired all their ammunition away, and then, for want of communication and support, were overpowered. When the French were in possession of this point an extensive hollow was open to them, which could not be seen from any part of our line, and under favour of which, their great mass of cavalry remained for some hours within 400 yards of our line, from whence they advanced and made charges at their pleasure.

Such was the nature of our ground. Even a single company of sappers with their tools might in a few hours, have rendered most essential service in improving it, by preparing the two buildings for defence, and throwing up traverses for guns across the two chaussées. The Guards did to the château what was necessary for its defence. Had the Haye Sainte been loopholed, all its doors and approaches towards the front and flanks been strongly barricaded, and a communication made to the rear, it would probably have been held through the whole day. The traverse across the Genappe chaussées would have given our artillery the command of that road by which the enemy brought down his troops to many of the most serious attacks, and still more so had the 18-pounders been up, which had been prepared for the field.

Had there been an opportunity and means for more work, the points are clearly marked out where four or six detached works could have been placed to advantage, besides the cover that might be thrown up for the line. The Duke did not wish to have any ground entrenched beforehand which might give any clue to his intentions, but would have been glad to have had anything which could be thrown up at the time. Two companies of sappers and 3,000 men might, on the night of the 17th, in addition to the above mentioned posts, have thrown up such a line, as would have afforded great cover to our infantry and guns, have brought them more to the ridge of the hill and would have considerably checked and broken the advances of cavalry.[1]

Appendix II

Lord Uxbridge's Decision to Launch the Heavy Cavalry

I immediately galloped to the Heavy Cavalry, and ordered the Household Brigade to prepare to form line, passed on to Sir William Ponsonby's, and having told him to wheel into line when the other Brigade did, I instantly returned to the Household Brigade, and put the whole in motion.

Towards the bottom of the slope I found our Infantry mostly in line, but getting into squares to receive the Enemy's Cavalry, and making intervals for us as our Squadrons presented themselves. Thus we passed through the Infantry as fast and as well as we could (but necessarily not with exact regularity), when, again forming, we instantly charged and fell upon large masses of Cavalry and of Infantry; but these gave way in a moment, and of the latter arm 3,000 men were taken, and two Eagles sent to the rear.

The pursuit was continued until a vast number of Guns were in our possession, or rather passed, and I have been assured by Lord Lauderdale that a French General Officer at Paris, whom he named, but whose name I have forgotten (I think, however, he was of the Artillery), told him that they had more than forty Guns put *hors de combat* by that charge. Unfortunately they could not be brought off, for the pursuit had been continued without order and too far, and the second line (excepting only a small part of Sir J. Vandeleur's Brigade – in fact, I believe, only two Squadrons of the 12th, under Sir F. Ponsonby) had not followed the movements of the Heavy Cavalry, whose horses were now exhausted, and had to receive the shocks of fresh troops.

After the overthrow of the Cuirassiers I had in vain attempted to stop my people by sounding the Rally, but neither voice nor trumpet availed; so I went back to seek the support of the 2nd Line, which unhappily had not followed the movements of the Heavy Cavalry.

Had I, when I sounded the Rally, found only four well-formed Squadrons coming steadily along at an easy trot, I feel certain that the loss the first line suffered when they were finally forced back would have been avoided, and most of these Guns might have been secured, for it was obvious the effect of that charge had been prodigious, and for the rest of the day, although the Cuirassiers frequently attempted to break into our Lines, they always did it *mollement* [half-heartedly] and as if they expected something more behind the curtain.

My impression is that the French were completely surprised by the first Cavalry attack. It (our Cavalry) had been rather hidden by rising ground immediately before their position. I think the left wing of our Infantry was partially retiring, when I determined upon the movement, and then these 19 Squadrons pouncing down hill upon them so astonished them that no very great resistance was made, and surely such havoc was rarely made in so few minutes.

When I was returning to our position I met the Duke of Wellington, surrounded by all the *Corps diplomatique militaire*, who had from the high ground witnessed the whole affair. The plain appeared to be swept clean, and I never saw so joyous a group as was this *Troupe dorée* [golden troupe]. They thought the Battle was over. It is certain that our Squadrons went into and over several Squares of Infantry, and it is not possible to conceive greater confusion and panic than was exhibited at this moment.

This forces from me the remark that I committed a great mistake in having myself led the attack. The *carrière* [charge] once begun, the leader is no better than any other man; whereas, if I had placed myself at the head of the 2nd line, there is no saying what great advantage might not have accrued from it. I am the less pardonable in having deviated from a principle I had laid down for myself, that I had already suffered from a similar error in an affair at Irtragau [?], where my reserve, instead of steadily following as I had ordered, chose to join in the attack, and at the end of it I had no formed body to take advantage with.[2]

Appendix III

Private Thomas Playford, 2nd Life Guards: Account of his regiment's charge as part of the Household Brigade

After a time I saw the Earl of Uxbridge, who had been in front watching the progress of events, gallop towards us, when a slight murmur of gladness passed along the ranks. The word 'Mount' was given, and the trumpet sounded 'Draw swords': and the command followed, 'Form line on the leading squadron of the 2nd Life Guards.' This done the word 'Advance' was given, and the trumpet sounded 'Walk'. But we saw no enemy; yet there was a strange medley of shouts, musket shots, and the roar of cannon, beyond the rising ground in front of us.

Presently we met a number of English foot soldiers running for their lives: they passed between our horses, or through squadron intervals, formed behind us, and followed us. They were succeeded by a confused mixture of artillery and rifle men, hastening to get out of our way and form behind us. At the same time I noticed the soldiers of a battalion of Belgian infantry, formed under the brow of a hill, run away: and I supposed they were very young soldiers, for no veterans would have done so.

So great was the impetuosity of the various attacks, that our first line was somewhat shaken, and a body of cuirassiers was ascending the crest of our position. The First Cavalry Brigade deployed and advanced; halted a few minutes between the first and second lines [of infantry], (not one hundred yards from the enemy's ranks) and then charged in line! It was a magnificent sight. The charge of the Life Guards was tremendous! They rushed with overwhelming fury on the ranks of the enemy, and hurled them back in confusion.

The French cuirassiers came on in the pride of assumed superiority, and with all that martial bearing and daring audacity so remarkably evinced by that arm throughout the day; their advance was therefore singularly imposing; but being met in mid-onset by the British Household Cavalry, although in every respect the elite of the French army, and like the mailed warriors of chivalry, 'locked up in steel', they were completely overthrown, cut down, and driven back *l'epée dans les reins* [a sword in the kidneys]. In the pursuit the Second Regiment of Life Guards passed some columns of French infantry, and captured several pieces of cannon; but being pressed on all sides by superior numbers, and the regiment having to fight its way back, it was unable to retain possession of the guns, which were consequently dismounted and abandoned. Before the regiment could regain the position of the allies it was closely pressed by a corps of lancers, of more than treble its own strength, and was exposed to the fire of two columns of French infantry.

Our troop formed the right half of the left squadron of the brigade. In the centre of the squadron troop quarter master Beamond (who was killed) was stationed. On his right hand was Shaw, riding a very powerful horse and grasping a recently ground broad sword. Next to Shaw rode a trooper named Adamson (who was killed); on Adamson's right was seen Hilton (who was also numbered with the slain). On Hilton's right hand I was stationed; and on my right hand rode a powerful Yorkshireman named Youeson: but memory fails to retain the names of the other brave men who fought near us; they were, however, nearly all killed through penetrating too far into the French lines.

We were advancing in line at a slow pace with horses well reined in; for they were excited by the dreadful din of battle in our front; but we saw no enemy, for the scene of combat was still hidden from us by the rising ground.

The trumpet sounded 'Trot', yet we saw no enemy. The Earl of Uxbridge was in front watching for the best moment to bring us into action; and he regulated the pace we should move at accordingly. Meanwhile a few cannon shots took effect in our ranks and Shaw was hit, as we rode slowly forward Youeson gave me a nudge with his elbow and said 'Shaw is hit!' I instantly looked to my left and noticed Shaw's head had fallen from its erect position, his right hand was raised in the air, and his sword had fallen from his grasp but was held by a strap fastened to his wrist: and as his person was not injured I concluded that he had been struck by a spent ball which had knocked the breath out of him. A few moments afterwards Youeson nudged me again and said 'There goes Shaw's horse without a rider: what a splendid creature he is!' I then noticed that Shaw's horse had galloped through the squadron and was sporting in front; and with head raised and tail extended he galloped first one way and then another. I, like Youeson, thought him a magnificent beast.

The Earl of Uxbridge again approached us; he took off his hat, waved it round his head, and then passed his hat forward over his horse's head. It was a signal, and the trumpets sounded 'Charge'. Hurrah! Shouted the soldiers; Hurrah! Responded the infantry behind us; and there appeared to be a pause in the battle to look at us. And at that moment a line of French horsemen in bright armour appeared in front of us; they were shouting, waving their swords and sabring the English infantry and artillerymen who had not got out of our way. Our shouts had arrested their attention, and looking up they saw fearful ranks of red-horsemen coming galloping forward, shouting and brandishing their swords. The cuirassiers paused and looked at us as likely to prove an easy conquest. Their bearing had all the bravado and audacity of veterans accustomed to triumph and they appeared to look upon us as victims given to their superior swords. They met us in mid-onset near the brow of the hill as men confident of victory, but the shock of battle overthrew many of them; for the weight and power of our men and horses was too great for their less powerful men and weaker horses. They gave way, some fell back: but returning to the attack, hand to hand and sword to sword the work of death went on; but our weight and [the] strength of our men and horses again proved too much for them. Many fell; others fled, and were pursued towards their own lines. British valour had triumphed so far; but the French cuirassiers were also brave men and good swordsmen; only we fell upon them when their line was a little deranged, otherwise they would, doubtless, have stood their ground longer; yet I think that our charge was irresistible. As the cuirassiers fell back, and the English troopers pressed forward a melee took place in which lancers and infantry musketeers mingled in the fray.

From the moment that Shaw fell from his horse I never saw him alive afterwards; but presuming that the heroic conduct ascribed to him by journalists and historians was founded on facts witnessed by some of his companions in arms (although, perhaps, a little heightened in print), it would appear that he speedily revived from the effects produced by the spent cannon ball, regained his horse, and dashing into the thickest of the hand to hand fight, when cuirassiers, lancers, and musketeers fell beneath the broad sword wielded by his powerful arm. For he was a very strong man of impulsive temperament and determined purpose, and it is affirmed in history that he wrought wonderful execution among the opposing combatants. According to the accounts published at the time the glittering blade of this heroic swordsman was seen descending with fatal violence first upon one enemy and then upon another until his strength was exhausted, when he received a fatal wound which terminated his victorious career. In the printed records he is comrade with some of Homer's heroes. And while it may be truly said that many brave men fell at Waterloo, it may be added that Shaw was one of the bravest of the brave.

I have a painful recollection of the pursuit, of shots, of clashing swords, of mangled bodies and groaning men; yet, strange to say, no enemy confronted me. Those who first looked me in the face rode off before we crossed swords, not I suppose, from the fear of a personal conflict, but from noticing that it was impossible for them to maintain their ground against our numbers.

I pursued; my progress was arrested by a hedge, and I looked over the fence, when I saw dreadful deeds taking place in a paddock a little to my right: my blood was hot and I went to a gap in the fence, but it was choked up with horses struggling in the agonies of death. I turned to my left and saw fearful carnage taking place on the main road to Brussels; but my recollection of what I saw is confused like a frightful dream. Under a hot impulse I hurried to the scene, but the fighting there soon ceased; and all I could do was to ride after some soldiers destroying the men and horses of some French artillery. But in whatever direction I turned every Frenchman got out of my way, excepting one cuirassier who fell completely into my power. He was unhorsed, his helmet was knocked off, and I raised my hand to cleave his skull; but at that moment compassion sprung up within me, I checked the blow and let the conquered cuirassier escape with a wound on the side of his head.

We pursued the French too far, and when we returned we sustained some loss. We had galloped through wet ploughed ground, and many of our horses panted for breath; at the same time a number of fresh enemies rode down upon us, and a few single combats occurred in which Frenchmen generally had the advantage. Yet I rode among conflict and slaughter and every enemy avoided me. Those of my companions who fell at this time generally lost their lives from rash bravado; for they rode singly out of their way to attack two or three enemies, and when a greater number came against them, their horses were blown and they could not escape. They could only sell their lives as dear as possible.

…

As we rode back towards our lines, a body of French infantry intercepted us; a regiment of the King's German Legion menaced the infantry with a charge, when the French formed two squares; between these squares we had to pass, and as we approached both squares opened an oblique fire on us; but not a single man and only one horse fell. I therefore concluded that these French soldiers were not good marksmen; for as we were not much above two hundred yards from them, I considered that the greater half of our number ought to have fallen, but their balls must have struck the ground before they reached us or have passed over our heads.

…

When our regiment was again formed, I looked round to see who was there, and I found that about three out of four were not present. Many were killed, some were only wounded, and others had lost their horses; but our loss altogether was a dreadful [one]. We were only a small remnant of what we were in the morning; and some of that remnant were bleeding.[3]

Appendix IV

Captain A.K. Clark Kennedy: Account of the Charge of the Royal Dragoons

The cannon shot that passed over the crest of the ridge beginning to fall pretty fast, the Brigade was advanced slowly towards the ridge by the troops wheeling to the left, and taking ground to the right by the flank march of Threes.

On arriving very near the top of the ridge the column fronted, and halted for perhaps four or five minutes.

The Marquis of Anglesey [Uxbridge] came up at speed (apparently from the Household Brigade on the right), wheeled the Royals and Inniskillings into line, and ordered them to charge, the Greys forming a second line in support.

At this moment many of the Artillery (I believe all) were ordered to leave, or did leave, their guns, which were stationed behind the hedges, and they passed through the intervals of our Squadrons. The Infantry that, I presume, had previously lined the hedges, were wheeled by Sections to their left, and were firing on the *left flank* of the French column, the head of which had at this time *passed both hedges unchecked*, as far as I could perceive, and were advancing rapidly. From the nature of the ground we did not see each other until we were very close, perhaps eighty or ninety yards. The head of the Column appeared to be seized with a panic, gave us a fire which brought down about twenty men, went instantly about and endeavoured to regain the opposite side of the hedges; but we were upon and amongst them before this could be effected, the whole column getting into one dense mass, the men between the advancing and retiring parts getting so jammed together that the men could not bring down their arms, or use them effectively, and we had nothing to do but to continue to press them down the slope, the right Squadron of the Royals naturally outflanking them, as the centre one (which I commanded) also did to a certain degree.

We continued to press on, and went a little further than we ought to have done, perhaps, getting under the fire of fresh troops stationed on the opposite height, and losing a good many men.

About half-way between the two positions we endeavoured to collect our Squadrons as well as we could; but we were so much scattered that few could be got together, and with these few we retired slowly towards our own position, under a pretty severe fire, driving as many prisoners before us as we could.

No cavalry was opposed to that part of the Brigade with which I was; but I was told that the left suffered greatly when retiring from an attack of Lancers.

Our infantry, which we had passed at the hedge, now proved of essential service to us. They had formed small bodies or squares following in the rear of the charge, and not only checked [the French] pursuit, but without their support and assistance I am satisfied we should not have got back so well as we did, and certainly we could not have secured one-half of the prisoners taken in the charge. Many who had surrendered effected their escape, yet above 2,000 were secured and sent to the rear.

The French on this occasion behaved very ill, many of our soldiers falling from the fire of men who had surrendered, and whose lives had been spared only a few minutes before. I had a narrow escape myself. One of these men put his musket close to my head and fired, a sudden turn of the head saving my life, the ball taking off the tip of my nose instead of passing through the head, as was kindly intended …

Had the charge been delayed two or three minutes, I feel satisfied it would probably have failed … [for] there were no infantry in reserve behind that part of the position, though there were on the Brussels road.

The pause after wheeling into line did not exceed a few seconds. The left of my squadron (the centre one) being already in front of part of the enemy's left column, I brought it more so, and clear of our own infantry, by inclining a little to the left. How the others got on I cannot say. I came in contact with the head of the column on the Brussels side of the hedges as it was going about, after having given us a destructive fire at a distance of perhaps fifty yards. No preparation appeared to be made to receive cavalry, nor do I think there could have been, as there was not above a hundred yards to go over *after we saw* each other.

The line was quickly lost where I was, the two squadrons (I can only speak of the 1st and 2nd) endeavouring to keep collected to their own centres as much as possible, and getting round the column as it retired gradually, inclining and gaining ground to the front and left.

I can give no account of the 3rd Squadron. I rather think it charged the front near the enemy's right, which must naturally have brought it and the Inniskilling Dragoons round the opposite flank to where I was.

The charge took place on the crest, not on the slope of the ridge, though it was followed up to the hollow ground between the two positions.

The Greys (2nd line) must have charged immediately after the 1st line, at least, they were up and mixed with the Royals long before we got half-way down the slope. No cavalry checked the right flank of the brigade. It retired from exhaustion, and from getting under the fire of fresh troops on the opposite ridge. It was not attacked in retiring, only fired upon. The left of the Brigade, I understood, was followed and suffered severely from a body of lancers, but I did not see it.[4]

Appendix V

Captain H. W. Powell, 1st Foot Guards: Account of the Repulse of the
Imperial Guard

The Duke of Wellington had but a short time *previous* rode down to see what
was doing at Hougoumont, and in returning had ordered the 1st Brigade
of Guards *to take ground to its left and form line four deep*, which poor Frank
D'Oyley did by wheeling up the sides of the Square, putting the Grenadiers
and my Company (1st Battalion Company) in the centre of our line. What
would Dundas [author of the standard work on infantry drill] have said!!!

   This brought the Brigade precisely on the spot the Emperor had chosen for
his attack. There ran along this part of the position a cart road, on one side of
which was a ditch and bank, in and under which the Brigade sheltered themselves during the cannonade, which might have lasted three-quarters of an
hour. Without the protection of this bank every creature must have perished
[from artillery fire].

   The Emperor probably calculated on this effect, for suddenly the firing
ceased, and as the smoke cleared away a most superb sight opened on us.
A close Column of Grenadiers ... of La Moyenne Garde, about 6,000 strong,
led, as we have since heard, by Marshal Ney, were seen ascending the rise
au pas de charge [quick march] shouting '*Vive l'Empereur*'. They continued to
advance till within fifty or sixty paces of our front, when the Brigade were
ordered to stand up. Whether it was from the sudden and unexpected appearance of a Corps so near them, which must have seemed as starting out of the
ground, or the tremendously heavy fire we threw into them, *La Garde*, who
had never before failed in an attack *suddenly* stopped. Those who from a distance and more on the flank could see the affair, tell us that the effect of our
fire seemed to force the head of the Column bodily back.

   In less than a minute above 300 were down. They now wavered, and several
of the rear divisions began to draw out as if to deploy, whilst some of the men
in their rear beginning to fire over the heads of those in front was so evident a
proof of their confusion, that Lord Saltoun (who had joined the Brigade, having
had the whole of his Light Infantry Battalion dispersed at Hougoumont) holloaed out, '*Now's the time, my boys.*' Immediately the Brigade sprang forward.
La Garde turned and gave us little opportunity of trying the steel. We charged
down the hill till we had passed the end of the orchard of Hougoumont, when
our right flank became exposed to another heavy Column (as we afterwards
understood of the Chasseurs of the Garde) who were advancing in support of
the former Column. This circumstance, besides that our charge was isolated,
obliged the Brigade to retire towards their original position.

Opportunely, Sir F. Adam's Light Brigade had in the meantime come round the knoll between the position and Hougoumont, when we had been ordered to take ground to our left, and were advancing under the hedge and blind line along the northern side of the orchard at Hougoumont. As soon therefore as we had uncovered their front we halted and fronted.

The two Brigades now returned to the charge which the Chasseurs did not wait for, and we continued our forward movement till we got to the bottom of the valley between the positions. Here our Brigade halted to restore its order by calling out the covering Sergeants and forming Companies. As soon as the Column was formed we proceeded towards the *chaussée* (to Namur) [in fact to Charleroi], where we found nearly sixty pieces of Artillery jammed together and deserted. Whilst we were halted in the valley the Light Troops and Cavalry had passed us and gone in pursuit.[5]

Appendix VI

Captain Digby Mackworth, 7th Foot, Aide-de-camp to Lieutenant General Hill: The Repulse of the Imperial Guard

The cannonade continued without intermission, and about 6 o'clock we saw heavy columns of infantry supported by dragoons forming for a fresh attack, it was evident it would be a desperate and, we thought, probably a decisive one; everyone felt how much depended on this terrible moment. A black mass of the grenadiers of the Imperial Guard with music playing and the great Napoleon at their head came rolling onward from the farm of 'La Belle Alliance'; with rapid pace they descended the opposite heights, all scattered firing ceased on both sides, our little army seemed to collect within itself, the infantry deployed into line, and the artillery, charged to the muzzle with grape and canister, waited for the moment when the enemy's columns should commence the ascent of our heights; those spaces in our lines which death had opened and left vacant were covered in appearance by bodies of cavalry.

The point at which the enemy aimed was now evident; it was a re-entering angle formed by a brigade of Guards, and the light brigade of Lord Hill's corps, Lord Hill was there in person. The French moved on with arms sloped *au pas de charge* [quick march]; they began to ascend the hill, in a few seconds they were within a hundred paces of us, and as yet not a shot had been fired. The awful moment was now at hand, a peal of ten thousand thunders burst at once on their devoted heads, the storm swept them down as a whirlwind which rushes over the ripe corn, they paused, their advance ceased, they commenced firing from the head of their columns and attempted to extend their front; but death had already caused too much confusion among them, they crowded instinctively behind each other to avoid a fire which was intolerably dreadful; still they stood firm, '*La Garde meurt ne se rend pas.*' [Interesting that it should be written on the night of the battle. Cambronne may actually have said it.] For half an hour this horrible butchery continued, at last seeing all their efforts in vain, all their courage useless, deserted by their emperor, who had already flown, unsupported by their comrades, who were already beaten, the hitherto invincible Old Guard gave way and fled in every direction. One spontaneous and almost painfully animated 'Hurra' burst from the victorious ranks of England, the line at once advanced; general officers, soldiers all partaking of one common enthusiasm. The battle was over, guns, prisoners, ammunition wagons, baggage, horses successively fell into our hands; night and fatigue compelled us to halt, we halted on each side of the road ...[6]

Appendix VII

Major General Sir Hussey Vivian: Account of the Charge of His Brigade During the General Advance

We at last began to find that the shots did not come so thick, and I discovered that the Enemy were, instead of advancing to gain our position, retrograding on theirs. The moment to attack was arrived, and I received orders to advance.

...

Having cleared the smoke I observed the French retiring up the hill and along the high road covered by their Guns – two large bodies of Cavalry, and two Squares of Infantry, whilst our Infantry were gallantly moving on also after them.

I led the head of my Brigade diagonally across the ground for the left body of Cavalry. The Enemy, seeing this, opened a fire upon me from the Square, and with grape from their Guns, and I suffered some loss. But every man was at his post. We gave them a cheer in reply, and I instantly ordered the Regiments to form line on their front half-Squadrons. They did it to admiration. I led the 10th against a body of Cuirassiers and Lancers, much superior to them in force, on the French left, and having seen them fairly in, the Enemy flying and falling under their swords, I rushed to the 18th Hussars, and with them attacked the Cuirassiers and Chasseurs who formed the French right in support of the Square and Guns. They were routed by the intrepidity and gallantry of this Regiment, and the artillerymen cut down at their Guns. From this moment not another cannon shot was fired. By this time the remains of the 10th had again formed. The 1st Hussars, still in reserve, determined that the glory of ending the day should rest[?] with the Regiment of my Royal Master, I ordered the 10th to charge the Squares of Infantry still steady and close to us. This they did most gallantly, and as gallantly was the attack received.

The 10th cut down the French in their ranks, some few then escaped under cover of a hedge, but from this time every man was in retreat, and eventually every man was taken during a pursuit which lasted as long as we could see, so long, indeed, until from actually having cut down some Prussians, we were obliged to desist and give them the pursuit.[7]

Appendix VIII

Lord Uxbridge Undergoes the Amputation of His Leg

Uxbridge, mounted on his horse beside Wellington, was wounded around 8 p.m. not, as some suggest, by a round shot which shattered his leg but, contrary to popular belief, did not sever it,[8] but by a grape shot which passed immediately in front of the Duke.[9] He was lifted off his horse into a blanket and carried away to the village of Waterloo by six men, led by Captain Horace Seymour, 18th Hussars, his aide-de-camp.[10] Deputy Inspector John Hume left the following account of the remarkable amputation of his leg, conducted in an age when surgeons possessed no understanding of the importance of operating under hygienic conditions and possessed, apart from the very limited utility of alcohol and laudanum, no genuinely effective anaesthetics.

… his lordship made his appearance [in the village of Waterloo] in a gig or Tilbury supported by some of his aides-de-camp. I followed him to his quarters and found on inspection that a grape shot had struck him on the right knee to the lower edge of the patella and entered on the inside of the ligament, and having torn open the capsular ligament had made its exit behind, externally fracturing the head of the tibia end, cutting the outer hamstring in two. The capsular ligament was filled with fragments of bone and cartilage like gravel, but there was no swelling whatever of the joint or limb. His lordship was perfectly cool, his pulse was calm and regular as if he had just risen from his bed in the morning and he displayed no expression of uneasiness though his suffering must have been extreme; but what struck me as most remarkable was his excessive composure though he had been on horseback during the whole day and personally present in almost every one of the many charges made by the cavalry during the battle, he was neither heated nor did he display the least agitation. There could hardly be a doubt of the expediency of amputating the leg but as I was not personally known to his lordship I conceived it was a duty

I owed to his family and to himself to do nothing rashly or without evincing to all the world that amputation was not only necessary but unavoidable. I therefore without giving a decided opinion applied a piece of lint wet with cold water over the knee and having desired his lordship to repose himself for a little I went out to endeavour to collect as many medical officers as I could meet [with] that they might see the wound and assist me in the operation.

I could find no staff surgeon or any other surgeon of the line but I met with several surgeons of artillery who were kind enough to accompany me and from one of them I borrowed a knife that had never been used as my own had been a good deal employed during the day. We entered Lord Uxbridge's quarters together, his lordship was lying in the same posture as when I left him, and with the most placid smile I ever beheld he said 'Good evening, gentlemen!' I went up to him and... removed the piece of lint which covered the wound ... Lord Uxbridge who was attentive to everything that passed [said] 'I put myself under your charge and I resign myself entirely to your decision, at the same time whilst I observe to you that I feel as any other man would naturally do, anxious to save my limb, yet my life being of infinitely more consequence to my numerous family I request that you will without having regard to anything else act in such a way as to the best of your judgment is most calculated to preserve that.' ... There was but one opinion amongst us, so having prepared the dressings etc, we returned into the room where I announced to Lord Uxbridge that the operation being found necessary the sooner it was performed the better, He said 'Very well I am ready.' I disposed the assistants as I thought best calculated to avoid confusion and having applied the tourniquet I took the knife in my hand. Lord Uxbridge said 'Tell me when you are going to begin.' I replied 'Now, my Lord.' He laid his head upon the pillow and putting his hand up to his eyes said 'Whenever you please.' I began my incision without retracting the integument nor in the usual way with one circular sweep, but with my knife I made one cut above from within outwards describing a small segment of a circle and in the same manner below, beginning at the inner point or horn of the upper and keeping as nearly parallel as possible ... With one stroke of the knife I divided the muscles all round to the bone and having retracted them on both sides I took the saw. I had sawn nearly through the femur but the person who held the leg being over apprehensive of splintering the bone raised up the limb so that the saw being confined could not be pushed backwards or forwards. I did not perceive what was the cause and said angrily 'Damn the saw', when Lord Uxbridge lifting up his head said with a smile 'What is the matter?' These were the only words he spoke and during the whole of the operation he neither uttered groan or complaint nor gave any sign of impatience or uneasiness. I had only two arteries to tie, namely the femoral and a small cutaneous branch. The stump was dressed in the usual manner and his Lordship having drank a very small quantity of weak wine and water was undressed and made as comfortable as the miserable bed upon which he was stretched would allow him to be. His skin was perfectly cool, his pulse which I was curious enough to count gave only 66 beats to the minute, and so far was he from exhibiting any symptoms of what he had undergone in his countenance that I am quite certain had anyone entered the room they would have enquired of him where the wounded man was.[11]

Appendix IX

The Waterloo Dispatch: Wellington's Official Report to Earl Bathurst, Secretary of State for War, 19 June 1815

Ensign Charles Dallas, 32nd Foot, writing home a week after Waterloo, remarked that, 'Of the battle and the events that preceded it, Lord W.'s dispatch will give you every thing better than I can.'[12] Sir Robert Gardiner certainly thought the document more than sufficient for its purpose: 'I had prepared after the 18th and intended to have forwarded to you as usual, some extracts from my journal,' he wrote:

> but hesitated particularly after reading the Duke's dispatches from Waterloo. He has so perfectly detailed the events of that day, both his own difficulties, the fearful mass opposed to him and the success with which they were defeated, that it becomes a sort of presumption in any other person to venture any remark, or illustration to what he has so unusually well related.[13]

In fact, the dispatch offers little insofar as any genuine detail of the battle is concerned, though in fairness this did not constitute the purpose of such a report – but rather a medium describing a broad outline of the campaign and its engagements, an opportunity with which to offer thanks to various participants and to apportion credit to those whom the Duke deemed it fit to receive. If his dispatch was not fulsome of its praise, there is at least clear evidence that Wellington personally complimented various units in the field on their conduct, such as the 2nd Battalion 3rd Foot Guards.[14] Nonetheless, public recognition meant a great deal more than verbal remarks rendered at the close of fighting, not least when such an historic document as the Duke's report to the War Office was certain to appear, reprinted but almost certainly unexpurgated, in *The Times* – which it did within days of its receipt in London.

Many of those who had fought at Waterloo expressed disappointment at
both its brevity and the very general nature of the expressions employed by
the Duke, one of Wellington's aides-de-camp diplomatically describing it as
'very concise, for such an operation' – which is to say for both Quatre Bras
and Waterloo.[15] According to Elizabeth Ord, who undoubtedly conversed
with numerous officers in Brussels, Wellington:

> ... wrote the coldest and most common place dispatch that ever was writ-
> ten, neither doing justice to the army nor to individuals. The army hurt
> at it, particularly are [we] about the manner in which General Barnes is
> mentioned. Even his friend the Duke of Richmond says how bad it was
> & that the only thing that can be said is Lord W cannot write & that
> he believes his feelings stupefied him. It was not the least vanity in him
> to say he thought the day would have been lost if he had not been on
> the ground.[16]

Specifically, various officers, at least privately, complained that the Duke failed
to acknowledge what they perceived as the distinguished contribution of
either their own arm of service or their particular regiment or corps. Captain
Arthur Kennedy, 18th Hussars, is a case in point, for he explicitly denounced
the absence of a reference to the contribution made by Vandeleur's cavalry
brigade, of which his regiment formed a part:

> Our brigades of light cavalry which had been but little engaged as yet (in
> consequence of their having had so much to do the previous day) were
> brought up from the left flank of our line ... in a column of squadrons, our
> brigade leading [was] most admirably led by [Major General] Sir Hussey
> Vivian. This it was, it is said, that decided the day although not a word of it is
> mentioned in the Duke's dispatch ...[17]

A letter written by Lieutenant Henry McMillan, Scots Greys, a fortnight after
the battle, reveals his considerable disappointment at what he deemed the
Duke's failure to dispense a proper degree of recognition for the achievements of the heavy cavalry, in particular by naming distinguished individuals,
and by his mentioning what McMillan judged to be the paltry efforts of the
light cavalry:

> No regiment could behave better than the Greys, Sergeant Ewart took an
> eagle, and the Royals another, which I believe were all that were taken,
> but not one word in the Despatch by whom taken, indeed the Despatch
> is extremely cold, and which is observed as such by everyone here, that has

seen it. The heavy brigade are [only] mentioned as having done their duty … the hussars and light dragoons had little or anything to do except look on. Sergeant Ewart cut down the officer and two soldiers before he could get possession of the eagle.[18]

Sir James Kempt, who survived a musket ball striking him in the mouth, expressed considerable disappointment at the tenor of the Waterloo Dispatch:

I must … snatch a moment to thank you, which I do most cordially, for your very kind letter and hearty congratulations on the late glorious events; you have in a few words expressed yourself strongly and said everything that we all feel, both as to the nature of the battle and its mighty consequences. Would to God that our illustrious leader had expressed himself something in the same manner. His dispatches are records for history and in his accounts of the battles of the 16th and 18th, he neither does justice to himself or the army that fought under his orders in the field of Waterloo. We are all, however, quite satisfied that these services will be fully appreciated in England and throughout Europe; but you must not treat us as we do our great coats, called for when the storm approaches, but laid aside with very little ceremony when it is dispersed.[19]

Captain Arthur Kennedy of the 18th Hussars was even more scathing. 'But to relate the late wonderful occurrences,' he fumed:

I may commence with supposing you are made acquainted with the principal part of them through the medium of the newspapers in which Lord Wellington's lame account appeared, which by the bye seems to have given offence to the whole army by its coldness, will have given you some idea of our movements. Bonaparte's bulletins do much more justice to the British army than the despatch of His Grace …[20]

Wellington began writing the dispatch in the early hours of Monday morning, 19 June, at his headquarters in the village of Waterloo – hence the name was given to the battle. (It was also partly due to the fact that it was easier to pronounce than Mont St Jean.) He may not have finished it until a few hours later when he reached Brussels, where he then gave it to his only remaining unwounded aide-de-camp, Major the Hon. Henry Percy, 14th Light Dragoons, who swiftly departed for London around noon in a post chaise and four, travelling along a very muddy road to Ghent with the captured French standards and eagles protruding from the windows of his carriage. Percy carried instructions to present the dispatch to Lord Bathurst, the Secretary of

State for War, and then to proceed to the Prince Regent, at whose feet he was to lay the trophies.

Upon reaching Ostend, Percy boarded HMS *Peruvian*, a 16-gun brig, bound for Dover, only to find the vessel becalmed half way across the Channel. The crew accordingly lowered a gig, manned by four sailors, Captain White and Percy (who had rowed at Eton), and rowed for shore with the dispatch and two eagles, reaching land at about 3 p.m. on Wednesday 21 June at or near Broadstairs in Kent. White and Percy then proceeded in a chaise and four to London, changing horses at Canterbury, Sittingbourne and Rochester before reaching the metropolis at about 10 p.m. Percy stopped first at the War Office in Downing Street, where, thronged by excited crowds, he learned that Bathurst was attending a cabinet dinner at the house of cabinet member Lord Harrowby, 44 Grosvenor Square, from the doorstep of which Harrowby officially announced victory to the public.

Still wearing the same ADC uniform he had worn at the Duchess of Richmond's ball the previous Thursday – now dishevelled and bloodstained – Percy then sought out the Prince Regent, who, accompanied by his brother the Duke of York (the commander-in-chief), was preparing to dine at 16 St James's Square as the guest of a wealthy merchant. Rushing upstairs to the ballroom on the first floor, Percy knelt down on one knee, declaring, 'Victory … victory, Sire', and presented the two eagles. His task completed, the exhausted Percy went to his father's house, No. 8. Portman Square and collapsed into sleep. He was later knighted and promoted to lieutenant colonel. In 1821 Percy retired from the army on half pay, becoming MP for Beeralston in Devon two years later. He died in 1825 at the age of only 40:

My Lord,   Waterloo, 19th June, 1815.

Buonaparte [*sic*], having collected the 1st, 2nd, 3rd, 4th, and 6th corps of the French army, and the Imperial Guards, and nearly all the cavalry, on the Sambre, and between that river and the Meuse, between the 10th and 14th of the month, advanced on the 15th and attacked the Prussian posts at Thuin and Lobbes, on the Sambre, at day-light in the morning.

I did not hear of these events till in the evening of the 15th; and I immediately ordered the troops to prepare to march, and afterwards to march to their left, as soon as I had intelligence from other quarters to prove that the enemy's movement upon Charleroi was the real attack.

The enemy drove the Prussian posts from the Sambre on that day; and General Ziethen, who commanded the corps which had been at Charleroi, retired upon Fleurus; and Marshal Prince Blücher concentrated the Prussian army upon Sombref [*sic*], holding the villages in front of his position of St. Amand and Ligny.

The enemy continued his march along the road from Charleroi towards Bruxelles [*sic*]; and, on the same evening, the 15th, attacked a brigade of the army of the Netherlands, under the Prince de Weimar, posted at Frasne [*sic*], and forced it back to the farm house, on the same road, called Les Quatre Bras.

The Prince of Orange immediately reinforced this brigade with another of the same division, under General Perponcher, and, in the morning early, regained part of the ground which had been lost, so as to have the command of the communication leading from Nivelles and Bruxelles [*sic*] with Marshal Blücher's position.

In the mean time [*sic*], I had directed the whole army to march upon Les Quatre Bras; and the 5th division, under Lieut. General Sir Thomas Picton, arrived at about half past two in the day, followed by the corps of troops under the Duke of Brunswick, and afterwards by the contingent of Nassau.

At this time the enemy commenced an attack upon Prince Blücher with his whole force, excepting the 1st and 2nd corps, and a corps of cavalry under General Kellermann, with which he attacked our post at Les Quatre Bras.

The Prussian army maintained their position with their usual gallantry and perseverance against a great disparity of numbers, as the 4th corps of their army, under General Bülow, had not joined; and I was not able to assist them as I wished, as I was attacked myself, and the troops, the cavalry in particular, which had a long distance to march, had not arrived.

We maintained our position also, and completely defeated and repulsed all the enemy's attempts to get possession of it. The enemy repeatedly attacked us with a large body of infantry and cavalry, supported by a numerous and powerful artillery. He made several charges with the cavalry upon our infantry, but all were repulsed in the steadiest manner.

In this affair, His Royal Highness the Prince of Orange, the Duke of Brunswick, and Lieut. General Sir Thomas Picton, and Major Generals Sir James Kempt and Sir Denis Pack, who were engaged from the commencement of the enemy's attack, highly distinguished themselves, as well as Lieut. General Charles Baron Alten, Major General Sir C. Halkett, Lieut. General Cooke, and Major Generals Maitland and Byng, as they successively arrived. The troops of the 5th division, and those of the Brunswick corps, were long and severely engaged, and conducted themselves with the utmost gallantry. I must particularly mention the 28th, 42nd, 79th, and 92nd regiments, and the battalion of Hanoverians.

Our loss was great, as your Lordship will perceive by the enclosed return; and I have particularly to regret His Serene Highness the Duke of Brunswick, who fell fighting gallantly at the head of his troops.

Although Marshal Blücher had maintained his position at Sombref [*sic*], he still found himself much weakened by the severity of the contest in which he had been engaged, and, as the 4th corps had not arrived, he determined to fall back and to concentrate his army upon Wavre; and he marched in the night, after the action was over.

This movement of the Marshal rendered necessary a corresponding one upon my part; and I retired from the farm of Quatre Bras upon Genappe, and thence upon Waterloo, the next morning, the 17th, at ten o'clock.

The enemy made no effort to pursue Marshal Blücher. On the contrary, a patrole [*sic*] which I sent to Sombref [*sic*] in the morning found all quiet★; and the enemy's vedettes fell back as the patrole [*sic*] advanced. Neither did he attempt to molest our march to the rear, although made in the middle of the day, excepting by following, with a large body of cavalry brought from his right, the cavalry under the Earl of Uxbridge.

This gave Lord Uxbridge an opportunity of charging them with the 1st Life Guards, upon their *débouché* [emergence] from the village of Genappe, upon which occasion his Lordship has declared himself to be well satisfied with that regiment.

The position which I took up in front of Waterloo crossed the high roads from Charleroi and Nivelles, and had its right thrown back to a ravine near Merke Braine [*sic*], which was occupied, and its left extended to a height above the hamlet of Ter la Haye, which was likewise occupied. In front of the right centre, and near the Nivelles road, we occupied the house and gardens of Hougoumont, which covered the return of that flank; and in front of the left centre we occupied the farm of La Haye Sainte. By our left we communicated with Marshal Prince Blücher at Wavre, through Ohain; and the Marshal had promised me that, in case we should be attacked, he would support me with one or more corps, as might be necessary.

The enemy collected his army, with the exception of the 3rd corps, which had been sent to observe Marshal Blücher, on a range of heights in our front, in the course of the night of the 17th and yesterday morning, and at about ten o'clock he commenced a furious attack upon our post at Hougoumont. I had occupied that post with a detachment from General Byng's brigade of Guards, which was in position in its rear; and it was for some time under the command of Lieut. Colonel Macdonell, and afterwards of Colonel Home; and I am happy to add that it was maintained throughout the day with the utmost gallantry by these brave troops, notwithstanding the repeated efforts of large bodies of the enemy to obtain possession of it.

This attack upon the right of our centre was accompanied by a very heavy cannonade upon our whole line, which was destined to support the repeated attacks of cavalry and infantry, occasionally mixed, but sometimes separate, which were made upon it. In one of these the enemy carried the farm house of La Haye Sainte, as the detachment of the light battalion of the German Legion, which occupied it, had expended all its ammunition; and the enemy occupied the only communication there was with them.

The enemy repeatedly charged our infantry with his cavalry; but these attacks were uniformly unsuccessful; and they afforded opportunities to our cavalry to charge, in one of which Lord E. Somerset's brigade, consisting of the Life Guards, the Royal Horse Guards, and [the] 1st dragoon guards, highly distinguished themselves, as did that of Major General Sir William Ponsonby, having taken many prisoners and an eagle.

These attacks were repeated till about seven in the evening, when the enemy made a desperate effort with cavalry and infantry, supported by the fire of artillery, to force our left centre, near the farm of La Haye Sainte, which, after a severe contest, was defeated; and, having observed that the troops retired from this attack in great confusion, and that the march of General Bülow's corps, by Frischermont [*sic*], upon Planchenois [*sic*] and La Belle Alliance, had begun to take effect, and as I could perceive the fire of his cannon, and as Marshal Prince Blücher had joined in person with a corps of his army to the left of our line by Ohain, I determined to attack the enemy, and immediately advanced the whole line of infantry, supported by the cavalry and artillery. The attack succeeded in every point: the enemy was forced from his positions on the heights, and fled in the utmost confusion, leaving behind him, as far as I could judge, 150 pieces of cannon, with their ammunition, which fell into our hands.

I continued the pursuit till long after dark, and then discontinued it only on account of the fatigue of our troops, who had been engaged during twelve hours, and because I found myself on the same road with Marshal Blücher, who assured me of his intention to follow the enemy throughout the night. He has sent me word this morning that he had taken 60 pieces of cannon belonging to the Imperial Guard, and several carriages, baggage, &c., belonging to Buonaparte [*sic*], in Genappe.

I propose to move this morning upon Nivelles, and not to discontinue my operations.

Your Lordship will observe that such a desperate action could not be fought, and such advantages could not be gained, without great loss; and I am sorry to add that ours has been immense. In Lieut. General Sir Thomas Picton His Majesty has sustained the loss of an officer who has frequently distinguished himself in his service; and he fell gloriously leading his division to a charge with bayonets, by which one of the most serious attacks made by the enemy on our position was repulsed. The Earl of Uxbridge, after having successfully got through this arduous day, received a wound by almost the last shot fired, which will, I am afraid, deprive His Majesty for some time of his services.

His Royal Highness the Prince of Orange distinguished himself by his gallantry and conduct, till he received a wound from a musket ball through the shoulder, which obliged him to quit the field.

It gives me the greatest satisfaction to assure your Lordship that the army never, upon any occasion, conducted itself better. The division of Guards, under Lieut. General Cooke, who is severely wounded, Major General Maitland, and Major General Byng, set an example which was followed by all; and there is no officer nor description of troops that did not behave well.

I must, however, particularly mention, for His Royal Highness's [the Prince Regent's] approbation, Lieut. General Sir H. Clinton, Major General Adam, Lieut. General Charles Baron Alten (severely wounded), Major General Sir Colin Halkett (severely wounded), Colonel Ompteda, Colonel Mitchell (commanding a brigade of the 4th division), Major Generals Sir James Kempt and Sir D. Pack, Major General Lambert, Major General Lord E. Somerset, Major General Sir W. Ponsonby, Major General Sir C. Grant, and Major General Sir H. Vivian, Major General Sir J. O. Vandeleur, and Major General Count Dornberg.

I am also particularly indebted to General Lord Hill for his assistance and conduct upon this, as upon all former occasions.

The artillery and engineer departments were conducted much to my satisfaction by Colonel Sir George Wood and Colonel Smyth; and I had every reason to be satisfied with the conduct of the Adjutant General, Major General Barnes, who was wounded, and of the Quarter Master General, Colonel De Lancey, who was killed by a cannon shot in the middle of the action [in fact, he died of his wounds on the 26th]. This officer is a serious loss to His Majesty's service, and to me at this moment.

I was likewise much indebted to the assistance of Lieut. Colonel Lord FitzRoy [*sic*] Somerset, who was severely wounded, and of the officers composing my personal Staff, who have suffered severely in this action. Lieut. Colonel the Hon. Sir Alexander Gordon, who has died of his wounds, was a most promising officer, and is a serious loss to His Majesty's service.

General Kruse, of the Nassau service, likewise conducted himself much to my satisfaction; as did General Tripp, commanding the heavy brigade of cavalry, and General Vanhope, commanding a brigade of infantry in the service of the King of the Netherlands.

General Pozzo di Borgo, General Baron Vincent, General Müffling, and General Alava, were in the field during the action, and rendered me every assistance in their power. Baron Vincent is wounded, but I hope not severely; and General Pozzo di Borgo received a contusion.

I should not do justice to my own feelings, or to Marshal Blücher and the Prussian army, if I did not attribute the successful result of this arduous day to the cordial and timely assistance I received from them. The operation of General Bülow upon the enemy's flank was a most decisive one; and, even if I had not found myself in a situation to make the attack which produced the final result, it would have forced the enemy to retire if his attacks should have failed, and would have prevented him from taking advantage of them if they should unfortunately have succeeded.

Since writing the above, I have received a report that Major General Sir William Ponsonby is killed; and, in announcing this intelligence to your Lordship, I have to add the expression of my grief for the fate of an officer who had already rendered very brilliant and important services, and was an ornament to his profession.

I send with this dispatch three eagles [in fact, two], taken by the troops in this action, which Major Percy will have the honor of laying at the feet of His Royal Highness. I beg leave to recommend him to your Lordship's protection.

I have the honor to be, &c.
Wellington.

*Lieut. Colonel the Hon. Alexander Gordon was sent, escorted by a squadron of the 10th hussars, to communicate with the Prussian head quarters [*sic*], as to co-operation with the British army [which was] ordered to retire to the position in front of Waterloo.

Appendix X

Private Richard MacLaurence, 2nd Battalion Coldstream Guards: The Defence of Hougoumont

No sooner were the [Coldstream] guardsmen fairly within the chateau [*sic*] garden than the tempting ripe cherries drew their attention and the soldiers were to be seen plucking them off the wall trees by the handful quite regardless of the shot and shells which were incessantly pouring amongst them.

'You scoundrels' roared out Major [Lieutenant Colonel] James Macdonnell, the officer in command of the brigade. 'If I survive this day I will punish you all.' But alas! Before the close of the murderous struggle how few of the cherry stealers were left for punishment in this world. Out of 134, as smart young soldiers as ever drew trigger (the number of two companies), only

13 could muster when the Roll was called; and these survivors were led out of action by Corporal [James] Smith, every other officer and non-commissioned officer being either killed or wounded.

The Emperor's commands 'Carry the post', while our Duke's were 'Keep it', and a most terrible post it was to keep. Once the French broke into the courtyard and such a scene of bayonet work, I, the narrator of this article never before or since beheld. It was fairly a trial of strength, the French Grenadiers were not to be trifled with and we looked like so many butchers, red with gore, or rather like so many demons rioting against fire, for the shells had set two haystacks in a blaze and many a poor fellow lying bleeding and wounded, being unable to get out of the way, was burnt to death.

'Shut the courtyard gates' roared out our Sergeant Major [*sic*: almost certainly Sergeant] Fraser and keep them out', and a rush was instantly made to the gates, the French without and the guards within. Life and death was in the struggle, for Ney was at hand with a force that threatened destruction to the post, but the English physical strength overcame the French ardour and the gates were closed by the powerful shoulders of Major Macdonell and the giant of the Sergeant Major, with as many of ours as could get to them.

The French thus enclosed in the courtyard, surrendered by throwing down their firelocks and were ordered to fall back, but they forgot the duties of prisoners. Their countrymen again charged Hougoumont with horse and foot and partly overpowered the Nassau troops and caused them to reel a bit; and then it was that the few Frenchmen we had taken, again seized their arms, and attacked us from the rear. Fortunately the post was not carried and now vengeance stern and dreadful awaited the prisoners. They had grossly violated the articles of war by taking up their arms after surrendering as prisoners and the consequence was that every man of them was put to death, some by the bayonet, and some were thrown into the blazing haystacks by our infuriated men.

Though now 27 years have rolled away since that dreadful scene took place, yet it is fresh in my mind's eye, and my ears yet tingle with the yells of these misguided Frenchmen as they were tumbled in the fiery furnace.

Charge after charge, cannonade after cannonade were repeated on this devoted post, yet still it was not carried. During one of the charges by the French cavalry, I could not but admire the coolness of a Highlander belonging to the 92nd Regiment. Donald by some means, got separated from his regiment and could not get to it before the cuirassiers came up; he, therefore came quietly up to our post, coolly saying 'Lads I'll just f a' in wi ye a bit, our regiment is receiving cavalry I see'.

As one of the 13 guardsmen who were able to muster, being unhurt, I distinctly say that I have been in many a hard fought action and seen many an arduous struggle but to hold the post at Hougoumont was by far the most dreadful I ever witnessed. We might have given it up, for there was scarcely a man, either foreign, or English, that was not hurt, but then our Iron Duke's orders were 'Keep the post' and keep it we did, proving to the strictest letter that we knew and could do our duty.[22]

Appendix XI

Unknown Officer: The Defence of Hougoumont by One Who Was Present

The post of Hougoumont was one of considerable strength. It had been occupied on the night of the 17th by various bodies of light troops and the foreign contingent of Nassau, about 800 strong under the command of Colonel Macdonnell [*sic*]. [It is unlikely that Macdonell – the correct spelling – commanded the Nassau troops.] Something had been done by art during the night to strengthen the defences; but either from the want of entrenching tools and axes, or from some other cause, not a tenth part was done of that which might have been done, and which would have added greatly to the security and certainty of the defence. Not a spadeful of earth was moved; and although the wood in front presented very great facilities, no attempt to form an abattis, or oppose any impediment to the rush of an enemy by the felling of a few trees, was made, although this could have been done within thirty yards of the defences of the place.

The position itself consisted of the orchard on the left, containing somewhere about three acres, surrounded on all the assailable sides by a close, thick and lofty quickset hedge. The stems of the quick were thicker than the arm of a strong man, at least ten or twelve feet high, and so close that nothing larger than a cat could pass between them. Immediately behind the hedge was a deep ditch enough to shelter the troops employed, thus offering a natural and secure stockade, stronger than any artificial fortification. The orchard, had only one point by which it could be assailed in front, namely a gate leading into the wood; this gate was tolerably well secured and built up.

On the British right of the orchard, forming one of its sides, and looking into it, stood the citadel and key of the position, the garden, house, and farm offices of Hougoumont. The whole of this part of the defence was surrounded, on the side next [to] the enemy and the right flank by lofty walls, and was perfectly unassailable in front, except by artillery. The troops, being perfectly sheltered, were able to pour their fire in security from the loop holes and windows upon anything advancing in front. This part, including house, garden, and farm offices, covered nearly an acre of ground, and in conjunction with the orchard, formed an oblong parallelogram, presenting a front of somewhere about two hundred yards to the enemy.

On the French side of the house, and garden, coming close to both, was an open but thickly planted wood of about five acres. Upon this wood did the successful issue of the defence and real strength of the post entirely depend; for the house and garden, although proof against musketry, could not have stood for ten minutes against the fire of a few pieces of field artillery, but, ill built, must have tumbled down and buried its defenders in the ruins. Neither could the orchard have been kept for one moment after the fall and occupation of the house and garden; for, although the orchard was very strong; it was entirely commanded, looked into, and swept from these points; and was only defensible so long as they remained in the occupation of our troops. But the wood entirely screened the house, garden, and offices from the sight and operation of the enemy's artillery; rendering mud cemented walls, [Not so: the walls were made of brick and cement] through which their shot would have passed like brown paper, thus equal, for the purposes of defence, to the strongest fortification. Owing to the existence of this wood, the troops occupying the house and garden enjoyed a complete exemption from the storm of shot and shells which fell with such fury on the other parts of the position. Except an ill directed shell, which occasionally passed over and now and then a discharge of grape, which was lost among the branches of the trees, the attack and defence consisted entirely of musketry.

Through this wood, passing close by the offices and right flank of Hougoumont, ran a carriageway to the rear and to the Nivelles road. Still farther to the right were corn fields looking from a considerable elevation into the rear of the house, garden, and orchard, within musket range. These fields were occupied during the whole day by the enemy's troops, who were however, invisible from the chateau itself. It was in this direction that the position was principally threatened during the after part of the day, the access from this quarter being perfectly practicable, few artificial and no natural impediments existing. From the house, along the carriage way above mentioned ran a row of trees, and the remains of an old hedge and ditch to the Nivelles road, affording some shelter to the troops who covered and defended the debouche [*sic*] from the wood and the flank of the position. This line was occupied in force about an hour after the commencement of the action, by strong detachments of the Fusilier Guards [i.e. the 3rd Foot Guards, later known as the Scots Fusilier Guards], sent down from the heights in the rear.

From the above description it will be seen that the post of Hougoumont did in reality consist of three totally distinct and separate points of defence; that, although all the three might be said to be under one command, as acting in mutual support, yet that the officers on each of these points were obliged to act upon their own judgement and responsibility as circumstances arose; and that it was utterly impossible for any one officer to superintend the three points of defence at one and the same time.

When the action began about half past eleven, Colonel Macdonnell had occupied the extreme skirt of the wood nearest the enemy with the larger part of the garrison of Hougoumont. They were attacked in this open position by overwhelming numbers of tirailleurs, supported by heavy masses of infantry and after a short and gallant struggle, were driven in unavoidable confusion down the carriage way to the rear of the chateau and into the house and offices. Several Frenchmen followed up so closely that they entered along with our troops, and were taken prisoners in the courtyard; and it was only by the great personal exertions and courage of Colonel Macdonnell himself that the gates were secured and a check given to the pursuit.

It was at this moment that the post ran the greatest danger of being carried which it incurred during the day. Not only were the troops, including *the whole Nassau contingent,* who had been thus placed in advance, driven in, but they were completely dispersed. Of the Nassau contingent, the 'several foreign battalions' said to have been commanded by Colonel Hepburn, [Commander of the 3rd Foot Guards] not a man was to be found on the ground after one o'clock, with the exception of *one officer,* who made his appearance about eight at night, after the action was over, for the purpose of asking a certificate of the loss of the Colours of that corps by fire. This certificate was granted upon *his representation of the fact,* and no doubt at this moment forms a conspicuous proof and document of the *hard services* and *gallantry* of that distinguished body of troops.

By whose orders, or for what object, an open and indefensible wood had been occupied so close to the enemy's lines, or why the strong and true point of defence had been abandoned for that which was weak and of no importance, are questions which might be easily asked, but which could not be easily answered. It has always appeared to me that this exposure of the troops in the first instance showed more gallantry and animal courage than military science or judgement; and that the general issue, and subsequent more judicious defence, covered a great and dangerous mistake rashly made in the beginning, and which might have led to the most fatal results.

To reinforce the garrison weakened by all those losses, Colonel Woodford [Commander of the Coldstream Guards] was sent down from the main position with the Coldstream. After dispersing the enemy, he joined Colonel Macdonnell in the garden, to which point they henceforward confined their superintendence, and from which neither of them stirred during the subsequent operations of the day, leaving the defence on the other points entirely to the different officers commanding there.

Shortly after the above movement of the Coldstream, five or six companies of the Fusilier Guards, amounting to *above six hundred men,* were detached from the main position, and placed under the command of [Lieutenant] Colonel [Francis] Home [3rd Foot Guards], with orders to occupy the *debouches* [*sic*] of the wood, to cover and defend the right flank of the post, and put himself in communication with and report his arrival to the officers in the chateau and garden. After occupying his ground, a sergeant was sent into the house by Colonel Home, to report his arrival to Colonels Woodford and Macdonnell, and the situation occupied by the Fusilier Guards commanded by him. The sergeant shortly returned, stating that he had looked everywhere in vain for these officers, and that they were not to be found.

Soon after these dispositions had been made, the fire of the enemy considerably increased. Some small stacks of hay or straw also took fire, which produced much smoke, and these circumstances being noticed by the Duke of Wellington, he sent Major [Andrew] Hamilton, aide de camp to Sir E. Barnes [the Adjutant General] with a message and orders to the position. On arriving there he enquired for the officer in command, and was conducted to Colonel Home, with whom the following conversation passed:-

Major Hamilton – 'Do you command here?'

Colonel Home – 'I believe so. I have seen no officer superior to myself. It has been reported to me that Colonels Macdonnell and Woodford are not to be found'.

Major Hamilton – 'I am directed by the Duke of Wellington to give you the following order; You are to hold the position to the very last, and on no account to give it up or abandon it.'

Colonel Home – 'The orders of the Duke shall be obeyed.'

Major Hamilton then rode away, but shortly after returned and said – 'So you, Colonel Home, perfectly understand the full extent of the Duke's order? He holds the maintaining of this post to be essential to the success of the operations of this day. It must on no account be given up.'

Colonel Home's answer was, 'I perfectly understand the Duke's order; it shall be punctually obeyed. Tell the Duke from me, that if the enemy do not attack us much more vigorously than anything I have as yet seen, we shall continue to hold our ground without much difficulty.'

The above message was delivered by Major Hamilton to the Duke, and that a direct relation was established between his Grace and the officer to whom his orders had been delivered, and a great and fearful responsibility was thrown upon the shoulders of the latter. It is quite true that in reality, as afterwards appeared, both Colonel Macdonnell and Colonel Woodford were in the garden at the time, and that Colonel Home was led into the mistake by the report of a stupid sergeant …

The defence was thus successfully conducted on all sides, until about half past three o'clock, when the stables having taken fire, the senior officer of the Fusiliers went into the house to give the necessary directions and to remove the wounded officers and men to the rear. This having been accomplished, he proceeded to the garden and there encountered both Colonel's [*sic*] Macdonnell and Woodford, whom the sergeant had reported as nowhere to be found, and who, as it appeared, had never quitted the spot. The Duke's message was now delivered to them and on rejoining the Fusiliers in their original position, Colonel Home found himself superseded in his command by Colonel [Douglas] Mercer [3rd Foot Guards]. Up to this time, Colonel Mercer had been engaged in the defence of the orchard; but having been relieved on that point by Lord Saltoun and the light companies of the Grenadier Guards [the name given the 1st Foot Guards about a month after Waterloo], he had fallen back on the main position and from thence had been detached with the remaining companies of the 3rd Regiment to join those on the right of Hougoumont. Shortly after the arrival of Colonel Mercer, he was followed by General Hepburn, who came down, not because he was 'ordered to take the command,' but because not a man remained on the main position whom he could command. Instead of arriving early in the day, it was *past four o'clock* when he made his *first appearance*, after the principal attack had been made and failed …

From the time of General Hepburn's arrival at Hougoumont, until the termination of the battle, no event of importance in reality took place. …

It has always appeared to me that the merits of this defence have been somewhat overrated. The position, secure from the operation of artillery, at least by the points of attack adopted, was impregnable in the hands of good troops, so long as their ammunition held out … although much has been said, and much written upon the desperate attacks and resistance at this point, I must say that the resistance and exposure upon the main position itself was fully equal, at least, to anything which I saw in the more sheltered, although apparently more exposed, post of Hougoumont, and that the importance of the post itself contributed much to the score of fame, as the resistance and gallantry of the troops employed in the defence. Having participated in both, I think myself an impartial, as well as a competent, judge.[23]

Appendix XII

Ensign Edward Macready, 2/30th: His Battalion in Action

It was near seven o'clock, and our front had sustained three attacks from fresh troops, when the Imperial Guard were seen ascending our position, in as correct order as at a review. As they rose step by step before us, and crossed the ridge, their red epaulettes and cross belts, put on over their blue greatcoats, gave them a gigantic appearance, which was increased by their high hairy caps and long red feathers, which waved with the nod of their heads as they kept time to a drum in the centre of their column. 'Now for a clawing', I muttered; and I confess, when I saw the imposing advance of these men, and thought of the character they had gained, I looked for nothing but a bayonet in my body, and I half breathed a confident sort of wish that it might not touch my vitals.

While they were moving up the slope, Halkett, as well as the noise permitted us to hear him, addressed us, and said, 'My boys, you have done everything I could have wished, and more than I could expect, but much remains to be done; at this moment we have nothing for it but a charge.' Our brave fellows replied by three cheers. The enemy halted, carried arms about forty paces from us, and fired a volley. We returned it, and giving out 'Hurra!' brought down the bayonets. Our surprise was inexpressible when, pushing through the clearing smoke, we saw the backs of the Imperial Grenadiers. We halted, and stared at each other as if mistrusting our eyesight. Some nine pounders from the rear of our right poured in the grape amongst them, and the slaughter was dreadful. In no part of the field did I see carcases so heaped upon each other. I could not account for their flight, nor did I ever hear an admissible reason assigned for it. It was a most providential panic. We could not pursue on account of their cavalry, and their artillery was still shockingly destructive. About this time Baron Alten was wounded, and General Halkett went to take the command of the division.

There was a hedge in our rear, to which we were ordered to move as some cover from the fire. As we descended the declivity, the enemy thought we were flying, and according to their invariable custom, turned a trebly furious cannonade upon us. Shot, shell and grape came like a hurricane through the square, and the hurly burly of these moments can never be erased from my memory. A shriek from forty or fifty men burst forth amid the thunder and hissing of the shot. I was knocked off my legs, by the fall of a brother officer, and, just as I recovered my feet, an intimate friend, in the delirium of agony occasioned by five wounds, seized me by the collar, screaming, 'Is it deep, Mac, is it deep!' Another officer was seen to halt, as if paralysed, and stare upon a burning fuse, till it fired the powder and shattered him to pieces. At this instant the two regiments who were on our right [the joint square of the 33rd and 69th Foot] rushed amongst us in frightful confusion, and our men passed the hedge at an accelerated pace. The exertions of the officers were rendered of no avail by the irresistible pressure, and as, crying with rage and shame, they seized individuals to halt them, they were hurried on by the current. ... at this moment, someone huzza'd, we all joined, and the men halted. Major Chambers ordered me to dash out with our light bobs and Grenadiers, while the regiments marched up to the hedge and reformed. The whole brigade was within an ace of ruin. Our men were steady as rocks till the others came amongst them, when the disorder was extreme. The officers did wonders, but the shout alone saved us. I never could discover who raised it, nor can I conceive what the enemy was about during our confusion. Fifty Cuirassiers would have annihilated our brigade.

Some of them advanced when everything was remedied, and forced my party to retire; but as they did not appear inclined to charge, I was reinforced with Roe's 2nd Company, and we continued to amuse them, and the 33rd and 69th Regiments, having formed four deep, went to occupy their proper position in the line. Some Brunswickers had formed on our left, as a support; they gave way once, but were rallied, and now stood their ground famously. Cooke's and Clinton's Divisions had also to repulse attacks of the Guard.

The ground between Hougoumont and the hill was now occupied by the 2nd Division, which, on the advance of the Lancers, had moved up, and altered the original convex of the division to a concave, thus raking the advance of the French columns. There was severe fighting on this point, and the Welsh Fusiliers suffered terribly.

The Prussians had ere this [time] begun to push the enemy's right, and it was evident, from the lull which now took place near us – for cannonading and close skirmishing with columns in grey greatcoats was now all work – that affairs were altering. We were in line four deep, and the enemy's columns within one hundred and fifty yards of us, and yet neither party advanced. I lost some men while covering the regiment, but the dead horses and soldiers formed capital shelter for both sides. I was wondering at the apathetic listlessness that seemed to possess us all, when suddenly the enemy's column fired away with considerable effect. Major Chambers of ours dropped dead, General Halkett was shot through the face, and the casualties were again numerous. The fire towards the right of the French became tremendous. Our opponents rapidly and unexpectedly disappeared, and a regiment of German Hussars galloped past to our right, cheering us and swearing they'd pay 'em off for us. This is the moment mentioned in the Despatch as the general charge. I believe the Guards, Adam's Brigade and some other corps followed the cavalry, but we did not attempt it. We marched to the crest of the hill, and the noise moved rapidly from us. The enemy must have defended some of their guns well, as long after the dragoons had passed a solitary round shot whizzed through us and carried off the four men it had encountered. This must have been near eight o'clock.

Soon after we piled our arms and lay down to rest. I remember, as long as I remained awake I was thinking on the day's work, and considering whether it would be called an action or a battle. I certainly considered we had 'spilt blood enough to make our title good' to the latter honour; but I fancied that, so far as we were concerned, some grand bayoneting charge, some concluding *coup de theatre* [*sic*], or rather *coup de grace* [*sic*], was wanting to entitle us to it. It appears that when the Prussians turned the enemy's right, and carried the village of Plancenoit, all became lost. A panic seized their troops, and our united cavalry cut them down like sheep. Some regiments of the Old Guard formed square and exclaimed, to an offer of mercy, '*La Garde meurt mais ne se rend pas!*', but they were soon destroyed. Old Blucher's cooperation was grand and decisive. He deserves the thanks of legitimate Europe.[24]

Appendix XIII

Lieutenant Colonel James Stanhope, 3rd Battalion 1st Foot Guards: Account of the massed French cavalry attacks

Soon after a cry of cavalry was heard on the crest of the hill & we saw the artillerymen run from their guns & seek protection in our squares. The men stood up; we advanced a few yards & saw a mass of cuirassiers close to us with thousands of forked pennons waving behind them in all their vanity of colours. From the rain there was no dust & it was a most beautiful sight. The square on the left of the 3rd Division opened their fire first and soon from every square issued a steady well directed & destructive fire. For four hours the cavalry never left our front, sometimes retiring a little under the hill to get into order & then charging afresh with all the fury of despair; it is not possible to exaggerate their bravery. They repeatedly rode in upon & got temporary possession of our guns; the instant our fire drove them back, our brave artillerymen returned & poured fresh volleys of grape into their dense masses till successive charges drove them back into our squares. Thus continued our part of the battle & except a momentary impetuosity on first beating off the cavalry, when our men shouted & wished to charge, they were as cool as if in the park. The French cavalry at length sent skirmishers close up to us to fire pistols into our squares to tease us into a volley at these small game, whilst we saw their great masses below laying [*sic*] [in] wait to charge; but we were as cool as they were & allowed only a few of our good shots to pick these fellows off. When we drove the cavalry from the guns many came up to us & shook their sabres at us in rage & some smashed their swords on the guns they had so often ineffectively taken. The Duke frequently rode by us …[25]

Appendix XIV

Ensign Edward Macready, 2/30th: Account of the massed French cavalry charges

When Napoleon saw his columns irretrievably routed on the left, he appears to have determined on a grand and desperate push upon our centre. Infantry had alone advanced against Hougoumont and Picton's line, but they were now to be supported by the whole of his cavalry, and accompanied by a formidable artillery.

Before the commencement of this attack, our company and the Grenadiers of the 73rd were skirmishing briskly in the low ground, covering our guns and annoying those of the enemy. The line of tirailleurs opposed to us was not stronger than our own, but on a sudden they were reinforced by numerous bodies, and several guns began playing on us with canister. Our poor fellows dropped very fast, and Colonel Vigoureux, Rumley, and Pratt were carried off badly wounded in about two minutes. I was now commander of our company. We stood under this hurricane of small shot till [Major General Sir Colin] Halkett sent to order us in, and I brought away about a third of the light bobs; the rest were killed or wounded, and I really wonder how one of them escaped. As our bugler was killed, I shouted and made signals to move by the left, in order to avoid the fire of our guns and to put as good a face on the business as possible.

When I reached Lloyd's abandoned guns, I stood near them for about a minute to contemplate the scene; it was grand beyond description. Hougoumont and its wood sent up a broad sheet of flame through the dark masses of smoke that overhung the field. Beneath this cloud, the French were indistinctly visible. Here a waving mass of long red feathers could be seen; there, gleams as from a sheet of steel showed that the cuirassiers were moving. Four hundred cannon were belching forth fire and death on every side. The roaring and shouting were indistinguishably commixed – together they gave me the idea of a labouring volcano.

Bodies of infantry and cavalry were pouring down on us, and it was time to cut contemplation, so I moved towards our columns, which were standing up in square. Our regiment and 73rd formed one, and 33rd and 69th another. To our right, beyond them, were the Guards, and on our left the Hanoverians and German Legion of our division [the former under Major General Count Kielmannsegge and the latter under Colonel Baron von Ompteda].

As I entered the rear face of our square I had to step over a body, and looking down, recognised [Lieutenant] Harry Beere, an officer of our Grenadiers, who about an hour before had shook hands with me, laughing, as I left the column, I was on the usual terms of military intimacy with poor Harry, i.e. if either of us had died a natural death, the other would have pitied him as a good fellow, and smiled at his neighbour as he congratulated him on the step; but seeing his herculean frame and animated countenance thus suddenly stiff and motionless before me (I know not whence the feeling could originate, for I had just seen my dearest friends drop almost with indifference), the tears started in my eyes as I chucked up my head and sighed out, 'Poor Harry!'

The tear was not dry on my cheek when poor Harry was no longer thought of. The gallant resistance of the light battalions of the legion who occupied La Haye Sainte detained the enemy some time, but when their ammunition was expended the post was carried and, in a few minutes after, the enemy's cavalry galloped up and crowned the crest of our position. Our guns were abandoned, and they formed between the two brigades, about an hundred paces in our front. Their first charge was magnificent. As soon as they quickened their trot into a gallop the cuirassiers bent their heads, so that the peaks of their helmets looked like visors, and they seemed cased in armour from the plume to the saddle. Not a shot was fired till they were within thirty yards, when the word was given, and our boys peppered away at them. The effect was magical. Through the smoke we could see helmets falling, cavaliers starting from their seats with convulsive springs as they received our balls, horses plunging and rearing in the agonies of fright and pain, and crowds of the soldiery dismounted; part of the squadrons in retreat, but the more daring remainder hacking their horses to force them on our bayonets. Our fire soon disposed of these gentlemen. The main body reformed in our front, were reinforced, and rapidly and gallantly repeated their attacks. In fact, from this time (about four o'clock) till near six, we had a constant repetition of these brave but unavailing charges. There was no difficulty in repulsing them, but our ammunition decreased alarmingly. At length an artillery wagon galloped up, emptied two or three casks of cartridges into the square, and we were all comfortable.

The best cavalry is contemptible to a steady and well supplied infantry regiment. Even our men saw this, and began to pity the useless perseverance of their assailants, and as they advanced would growl out 'Here come these damned fools again!' one of their superior officers tried a *ruse de guerre* by advancing and dropping his sword, as though he surrendered. Some of us were deceived by him, but Halkett ordered the men to fire, and he coolly retired, saluting us. Their devotion was invincible. One officer whom we had taken prisoner was asked what force Napoleon might have in the field, and replied, with a smile of mingled derision and threatening, '*Vous verrez bientot* [sic] *sa force, Messieurs*' ['You will soon see his strength, Gentlemen']. A private Cuirassier was wounded and dragged into the square; his only cry was, '*Tuez, donc, tuez, tuez moi, soldats!*' ['Kill, therefore, kill, kill me, soldiers!'] and as one of our men dropped dead close to him, he seized his bayonet, and forced it into his own neck; but this not despatching him, he raised up his cuirass, plunged it into his stomach, and kept working it about till he ceased to breathe.

Though we constantly thrashed our steel clad opponents, we found more troublesome customers in the round shot and grape which all this time played on us with terrible effect, and fully avenged the Cuirassiers. Often, as the volleys created openings in our square, would the cavalry dash on, but they were uniformly unsuccessful. A regiment on our right seemed sadly disconcerted, and at one moment were in considerable confusion. Halkett rode out, and seizing their snow white Colour, waved it over his head, and restored them to something like order, though not before his horse was shot under him. At the height of their unsteadiness we got the order 'Right face', to move to their assistance. Some of the men mistook it for 'Right about', and faced accordingly, when old Major [Archibald] McLean, 73rd, called out, 'No, my boys, its 'right face'; you'll never hear the right about as long as a French bayonet's in front of you!' In a few moments he was mortally wounded.

A regiment of light dragoons, by their facings either 16th or 23rd [It was the 23rd], came up on our left and charged the Cuirassiers. We cheered each other as they passed us. They did all they could, but were obliged to retire after a very few minutes at the sabre. A body of Belgian cavalry [actually, Hanoverians: The Duke of Cumberland's Hussars] advanced for the same purpose, but, on passing our square, they stopped short. Our noble Halkett rode out to them and offered to charge at their head. It was of no use. The Prince of Orange came up and exhorted them to do their duty, but in vain. They hesitated till a few shots whizzed through them, when they turned about and galloped like fury, or, rather, like fear. As they passed the right face of our square the men, irritated by their rascally conduct, unanimously took up their pieces and poured in a volley among them, and 'many a good tall fellow was destroyed so cowardly'.

The enemy's cavalry were by now nearly disposed of, and as they had discovered the inutility of their charges, they commenced annoying us with a spirited and well directed carbine fire. While we were occupied in this manner it was impossible to see farther than the columns on our right and left, but I imagine most of the army was similarly situated. All the British and Germans were doing their duty.[26]

Appendix XV

Commissary Tupper Carey: Description of the Battlefield on 19 June

It was dreadful to see the numbers of the killed, both men and horses, on each side of the road. Many bodies were already stripped of their clothes. As we descended down towards La Haye Sainte, the scene of carnage was still more developed. All round the Haye Sainte and on the *chaussee* [*sic*] leading to the French position, the dead were innumerable, French and English intermixed. Those who had fallen in the road had been trampled upon by horses and wheels of artillery, into a mass of blood, flesh, and clothes, hardly to be distinguished one from the other. In the hollow between the two armies on each side of the road, there lay piles of dead Frenchmen and horses, among whom were many of the Imperial Guard. Their large bear-skin caps, which they had thrown away in the struggle, strewed the ground. To add to the numbers were many dead cuirassiers, still with their cuirasses on, some of which I could easily have brought away had I had time or someone to assist me in stripping the dead bodies. With the exception of a few parties wandering in quest of wounded men, as well as plunder, all was as quiet as a churchyard …

   We followed the *chaussee* [*sic*] in the midst of this field of death, which, in addition to men and animals, was strewed with arms of every description, until we reached the foot of the French position, where it was said Napoleon took leave of his Guard moving on to the final attack. On ascending to the top of the eminence we came upon the French guns scattered in various directions, evidently in the way of being dragged to the *chaussee* [*sic*] from different positions. This attempt had failed owing to the muddy state of the ploughed land and the rapidity of our advance, which obliged the drivers of the gun carriages to flee for their lives by cutting the horse's traces. I perceived that some of the guns had engraved on them *Egalite, Fraternite,* and others with the letter N; many of the guns had the number of the English regiments which had captured them chalked on them; a mode usually adopted in the Peninsula. The carriages were sunk in the ground almost to the axle trees.[27]

Appendix XVI

William Thomson, Deputy Commissary General of Stores: Observations on Hougoumont in 1818

The chateau stands to the left of the road among some trees and presents many confused masses of shattered walls brought down by the artillery and bomb shells of the enemy. There are several regular tiers of holes, perforated through a high brick wall which surrounds the gardens, through which the English could fire with advantage upon the numerous furious assailants.

A few regiments of the British Guards with a small detachment of Brunswickers [in fact Nassauers] kept good this important position against 30,000 of the enemy. The Chateau of Goumont was considered the key of the British right wing; it was therefore the scene of a most tremendous conflict, and reflects immortal honour upon the small force which bravely resisted the very superior numbers of the French troops who vainly attempted to storm the gardens.

Neither the house nor the gardens have been touched since the day of Waterloo, they are therefore in the highest degree interesting. Flowers, intermingled with weeds, and shattered fruit trees are growing over the graves of the brave men who were cut down by the shot and shells of the enemy so plentifully poured in upon them. A part of a house in the centre of the courtyard now alone affords a slender asylum to a poor family who show the ruins and gardens to strangers. Its shattered front is covered with a luxuriant vine and beds of mignonette, blighted violets and daisies are growing over the blood stained soil around this poor tenement.

A small chapel was shown in another part of the court which was partly burnt during the action. A crucifix is nailed upon the wall of this sanctuary, which when the fire reached, it went out entirely.

The honest folks of this quarter look upon the accidental escape of this poultry [*sic*] image and the sudden disappearance of the flames, as a heavenly interposition.

The traces amid the ruins of Goumont, of its regular appearance, commodious out houses, and well laid out gardens indicate its being formally [*sic*] a very handsome agreeable mansion ...

The ... grounds which three years ago were gored and fattened with the streaming wounds of thousands, are now clothed by stubble of the grain cut down in last autumn. The ploughman was at his peaceful labour on the same fields where so lately the mighty hosts of war were arrayed.[28]

Appendix XVII

Lieutenant William Ingilby, Royal Horse Artillery: The Charge of the Union Brigade

... a column of infantry advanced with loud shouts of *Vive l'Empereur* & drove back one of our divisions from its position, they were then charged by our cavalry & completely routed with great loss. The same cavalry then advanced against a body of French cavalry, which approached supported by another column of their cavalry, to save or sustain their broken & retiring infantry. As the two lines of cavalry neared each other, the French rather hesitated or at least slackened their pace, the English increased theirs; they met and the French were instantly overthrown and the ground which had before been clear was now covered with wrecks of the charge. Some of our dragoons, we could see, individually, or in small parties pushing on, & they had actually possession of the right of the large battery of French guns, while on the left their guns continued the fire.

Sir H[ussey] Vivian [commander of the 6th (Light) Cavalry Brigade] was extremely anxious to do something with his brigade at this charge, but I knew he was restrained by his instructions, which were by no means to quit his position & expose the left flank of the army, as both cavalries charged obliquely to the left and the French cavalry was part of their centre right & extreme right & did not move so fast as ours, it brought the charge nearly opposite the position of our brigade, Sir H. Vivian therefore took a couple of guns of the troop and proceeded with them to assist General Ponsonby & his cavalry. These were my division, but we became so completely within range of the enemy's numerous battery of superior calibre that one of the first shots directed against us blew up a limber, killed the sergeant, and passed through the shoulders of my charger exactly above my knees, & Sir H. Vivian immediately withdrew them, lest, knowing his orders, he might attract the notice of the commander in chief. The French on seeing the limber blow up gave some loud cheers, but that could not compensate for defeat with great loss of both attacks by the infantry and cavalry. General [William] Ponsonby was killed & [Lieutenant] Colonel [Frederick] Ponsonby [12th Light Dragoons] very badly wounded and left on the enemy's positions.

The French supporting column of cavalry on seeing the overthrow of its leading column, instantly put about and retired at a trot to its original ground on the extreme right of the French position; they were clothed in red. In these charges (excepting at the great charge between the two large bodies of cavalry) & repulses, the sight was perpetually interrupted by the smoke of the cannon and musketry and it was difficult at the distance to offer to each corps or regiment the part or share it took in them. Our infantry that appeared driven back were highlanders and the cavalry that immediately charged were the Scots Greys. The great charge was made by heavy cavalry supported by light.[29]

Appendix XVIII

Lieutenant George Gunning, 1st (Royal) Dragoons: An account of the charge of the Union Brigade

… the Union Brigade of heavy cavalry did not disappoint their leaders. The charge was made; and in proof of our victory, the Royals have the honour to say that the eagle of the 105th Regiment of French infantry was captured in that charge by Corporal Styles, belonging to the troop of the regiment that day under my command, for which Mr Styles was promoted to an ensigncy in the army.

The Greys have the honour to say, that the eagle of the 45th Regiment of French infantry was captured in that charge by Sergeant Ewart, for which he was also promoted to an ensigncy in the army.

The Union Brigade was in line, but by bringing up our left shoulders in the attack, we came in contact with the French nearly in a column of squadron in echelon, so that the right squadron of the Royals came in contact with the left corner of the square of the enemy, and suffered most severely in officers and men. The centre and left squadrons of the Royals did great execution against the middle of the enemy's square. I commanded the left half of the centre squadron. As a matter of course the Enniskillen's [*sic.* 6th Dragoons] did not receive so much fire from the square as first fell on the Royals; but the Greys came in contact with the right corner of the square, and also received a severe volley of musketry from the light infantry of the enemy on the extreme right of their attack; this body of troops retired in excellent order. It is impossible to say too much in praise of the steadiness of this body, and the broken regiment formed on them. After our charge the enemy were running in every direction for their own lines. I saw an eagle among a small body, I told Corporal Styles to secure it, and led the men on to the attack. At this moment I saw no officer near me. I killed the French officer who commanded the party, whose sword passed between my arm and my body at the moment my sword passed through his left breast. He was a fine looking, elegant man; his last words were '*Vive Napoleon!*' The prisoners said he was the commanding officer of the 105th Regiment. It was the work of a moment, I saw the eagle in the hands of Corporal Styles and I ordered him to leave the field, and not to give up the eagle till he had a proper receipt for it at headquarters from one of the Duke of Wellington's personal Staff.

Great difference of opinion existed in the Royals, who ought to have had the reward for taking the eagle of the 105th Regiment; and in the end, nearly a year afterwards (or more), his Royal Highness the Duke of York gave

Corporal Styles an ensigncy. If Mr Styles is still living I shall feel obliged to him to give the public his statement on this matter.

My namesake and relative, George Gunning, of the 10th Hussars, was killed at Waterloo, on the 18th June. At first it was supposed that I was killed and so it was reported; and then, with a wound both severe and dangerous, I was returned as only slightly wounded. But no matter, facts are stubborn things to get over.

At the moment Corporal Styles left me, going to the rear with the eagle, General Ponsonby rode up to me by himself, and said, 'For God's sake, Sir, collect your men, and retire on the brigade.' At this moment the French infantry on our left advanced rapidly, and fired a volley of musketry among the scattered cavalry. By this volley General Ponsonby was killed, within twenty yards of me. I saw him fall from his horse at the bottom of the hollow way, to the left of General Picton's Division. The ridiculous story about the general's horse being unmanageable was all a farce to please the lovers of the marvellous. I was severely wounded by the same volley of musketry and in a few seconds afterwards my horse had his near fore leg [hit] by a cannon ball. I then made my way into the square of the 28th Regiment of Foot (General Picton's Division), with several other dismounted men, and remained there till the evening before I could get a horse to go to the rear.[30]

ORDERS OF BATTLE

Armée du Nord

Emperor Napoleon (at Waterloo: 77,500 men and 246 guns)

Imperial Guard
Lieutenant General Comte Drouot

Général de Division Comte Friant
1st and 2nd Grenadiers

Général de Division Comte Roguet
3rd and 4th Grenadiers

Général de Division Comte Morand
1st and 2nd Chasseurs

Général de Division Comte Michel
3rd and 4th Chasseurs

Général de Division Comte Duhesme
1st and 3rd Tirailleurs

Général de Division Comte Barrois
1st and 3rd Voltigeurs

Général de Division Lefebvre-Desnöettes
Lancers and Chasseur à Cheval

Général de Division Comte Guyot
Dragoons, Grenadiers à Cheval and Gendarmerie d'Elite

Général de Division Desvaux de St Maurice
9 batteries, Guard Foot Artillery; 4 batteries, Guard Horse Artillery; Marines
of the Guard; Engineers of the Guard

I Corps
Général de Division Jean Baptiste Drouet, Comte d'Erlon

1st Division
Général de Division Baron Quiot du Passage

   1st Brigade (Général de Brigade Quiot)
   54th and 55th Légère

   2nd Brigade (Général de Brigade Bourgeois)
   28th and 105th Ligne

2nd Division
Général de Division Baron Donzelot

   1st Brigade (Général de Brigade Schmitz)
   13th Légère and 17th Ligne

   2nd Brigade (Général de Brigade Baron Aulard)
   19th and 31st Ligne

3rd Division
Général de Division Baron Marcognet

   1st Brigade (Général de Brigade Noguès)
   21st and 46th Ligne

4th Division
Général de Division Comte Durutte

   1st Brigade (Général de Brigade Pegot)
   8th and 29th Ligne

   2nd Brigade (Général de Brigade Brue)
   85th and 95th Ligne

1st Cavalry Division
Général de Division Baron Jacquinot

   1st Brigade (Général de Brigade Bruno)
   7th Hussars and 3rd Chasseurs à Cheval

2nd Brigade (Général de Brigade Baron Gobrecht)
3rd and 4th Lancers

Artillery
5 batteries, Foot Artillery; 1 battery, Horse Artillery; Engineers

II Corps
Général de Division Comte Honoré Charles Reille

5th Division
Général de Division Baron Bachelu

    1st Brigade (Général de Brigade Baron Husson)
    2nd Légère and 61st Ligne

    2nd Brigade (Général de Brigade Baron Campi)
    72nd and 108th Ligne

6th Division
Général de Division Prince Jérôme Napoleon

    1st Brigade (Général de Brigade Baron Baudouin)
    1st Légère and 3rd Ligne

    2nd Brigade (Général de Brigade Soye)
    1st and 2nd Légère

7th Division
Général de Division Comte Girard

    1st Brigade (Général de Brigade de Villiers)
    11th Légère and 82nd Ligne

    2nd Brigade (Général de Brigade Baron Piat)
    12th Légère and 4th Ligne

9th Division
Général de Division Comte Foy

    1st Brigade (Général de Brigade Baron Gauthier)
    92nd and 93rd Ligne

2nd Brigade (Général de Brigade Jamin)
4th Légère and 100th Ligne

2nd Cavalry Division
Général de Division Piré

  1st Brigade (Général de Brigade Baron Hubert)
  1st and 6th Chasseurs à Cheval

  2nd Brigade (Général de Brigade Baron Wathiez)
  5th and 6th Lancers

Artillery
5 batteries, Foot Artillery; 1 Battery, Horse Artillery; Engineers

III Corps
Général de Division Comte Vandamme (at Wavre)

8th Division
Général de Division Baron Lefol

  1st Brigade (Général de Brigade Baron Billiard)
  15th Légère and 23rd Ligne

  2nd Brigade (Général de Brigade Baron Corsin)
  37th and 64th Ligne

10th Division
Général de Division Baron Habert

  1st Brigade (Général de Brigade Gengoult)
  34th and 88th Ligne

  2nd Brigade (Général de Brigade Dupeyroux)
  22nd and 70th Ligne, 2nd Swiss Regiment

11th Division
Général de Division Baron Berthezène

  1st Brigade (Général de Brigade Dufour)
  12th and 56th Ligne

2nd Brigade (Général de Brigade Baron Lagarde)
33rd and 86th Ligne

3rd Cavalry Division
Général de Division Baron Domon

1st Brigade (Général de Brigade Baron Dommanget)
4th and 9th Chasseurs à Cheval

2nd Brigade (Général de Brigade Baron Vinot)
12th Chasseurs à Cheval

Artillery
4 Batteries, Foot Artillery; 1 Battery, Horse Artillery; Engineers

IV Corps
Général de Division Count Gérard (at Wavre)

12th Division
Général de Division Count Pêcheux

1st Brigade (Général de Brigade Rome)
30th and 96th Ligne

2nd Brigade (Général de Brigade Baron Shoeffer)
6th Légère and 63rd Ligne

13th Division
Général de Division Baron Vichery

1st Brigade (Général de Brigade Baron le Capitaine)
59th and 76th Ligne

2nd Brigade (Général de Brigade Desprez)
48th and 69th Ligne

14th Division
Général de Division Hulot

1st Brigade (Colonel Baume)
9th Légère and 111th Ligne

2nd Brigade (Général de Brigade Toussaint)
44th and 50th Ligne

7th Cavalry Division
Général de Division Baron Maurin

1st Brigade (Général de Brigade Baron Vallin)
6th Hussars and 8th Chasseurs à Cheval

2nd Brigade (Général de Brigade Berruyer)
6th, 11th and 16th Dragoons

Artillery
4 Batteries, Foot Artillery; 1 Battery, Horse Artillery; Engineers

VI Corps
Général de Division Georges Mouton, Comte de Lobau

19th Division
Général de Division Baron Simmer

1st Brigade (Général de Brigade Baron de Bellair)
5th and 11th Ligne

2nd Brigade (Général de Brigade Jamin)
27th and 84th Ligne

20th Division
Général de Division Baron Jeanin

1st Brigade (Général de Brigade Bony)
5th Légère and 10th Ligne

2nd Brigade (Général de Brigade de Tromelin)
107th Ligne

21st Division
Général de Division Baron Teste

1st Brigade (Général de Brigade Baron Lafitte)
8th Légère

2nd Brigade (Général de Brigade Baron Penne)
65th and 75th Ligne

Artillery
4 batteries, Foot Artillery; 1 battery, Horse Artillery; Engineers

I Reserve Cavalry Corps
Général de Division Count Pajol (at Wavre)

4th Cavalry Division
Général de Division Maréchal Soult

   1st Brigade (Général de Brigade St Laurent)
   1st and 4th Hussars

   2nd Brigade (Général de Brigade Ameil)
   5th Hussars

5th Cavalry Division
Général de Division Baron Subervie

   1st Brigade (Général de Brigade de Colbert)
   1st and 2nd Lancers

   2nd Brigade (Général de Brigade Merlin de Douai)
   11th Chasseurs à Cheval

Artillery
2 batteries, Horse Artillery

II Reserve Cavalry Corps
Général de Division Count Exelmans (at Wavre)

9th Cavalry Division
Général de Division Baron Strolz

   1st Brigade (Général de Brigade Baron Burthe)
   5th and 13th Dragoons

2nd Brigade (Général de Brigade Baron Vincent)
15th and 20th Dragoons

10th Cavalry Division
Général de Division Baron Chastel

1st Brigade (Général de Brigade Baron Bennemains)
4th and 12th Dragoons

2nd Brigade (Général de Brigade Berton)
14th and 17th Dragoons

Artillery
2 batteries, Horse Artillery

III Cavalry Corps
Général de Division Kellermann

11th Cavalry Division
Général de Division Baron L'Héritier

1st Brigade (Général de Brigade Baron Picquet)
2nd and 7th Dragoons

2nd Brigade (Général de Brigade Baron Guiton)
8th and 11th Cuirassiers

12th Cavalry Division
Général de Division Roussel d'Hurbal

1st Brigade (Général de Brigade Baron Blanchard)
1st and 2nd Carabiniers

2nd Brigade (Général de Brigade Donop)
2nd and 3rd Cuirassiers

Artillery
2 batteries, Horse Artillery

IV Cavalry Corps
Général de Division Comte Milhaud

13th Cavalry Division
Général de Division Wathier

> *1st Brigade (Général de Brigade Baron Dubois)*
> 1st and 4th Cuirassiers

> *2nd Brigade (Général de Brigade Travers)*
> 7th and 12th Cuirassiers

14th Cavalry Division
Général de Division Baron Delort

> *1st Brigade (Général de Brigade Baron Vial)*
> 5th and 10th Cuirassiers

> *2nd Brigade (Général de Brigade Baron Farine)*
> 6th and 9th Cuirassiers

Artillery
2 batteries, Horse Artillery

Total strength:

	At Waterloo	At Wavre	Total
Infantry	53,400	24,000	77,400
Cavalry	15,600	3,500	19,100
Artillery & Train	6,500	2,000	8,500
Others★	2,000	500	2,500
Totals	77,500	30,000	107,500
Guns	246	96	342 +8 at Ligny

★Includes HQ Staff; regimental staffs included in infantry and cavalry statistics above.

Anglo-Allied Army

Field Marshal the Duke of Wellington (at Waterloo: 73,200 men and 157 guns + 1 rocket battery)

1st Corps
The Prince of Orange

1st Division
Major General George Cooke

   1st British Brigade (Major General Maitland)
   1st and 3rd Battalions 1st Foot Guards

   2nd British Brigade (Major General Sir J. Byng)
   2nd Battalion 2nd Foot Guards; 2nd Battalion 3rd Foot Guards

   Artillery (Lieutenant Colonel Adye)
   1 Foot Battery, Royal Artillery; 1 Horse Artillery Battery, King's German Legion

3rd Division
Lieutenant General Sir Charles Alten

   5th British Brigade (Major General Sir Colin Halkett)
   2nd Battalion 30th Foot; 33rd Foot; 2nd Battalion 69th Foot; 2nd Battalion 73rd Foot

   2nd King's German Legion Brigade (Colonel von Ompteda)
   1st and 2nd Light Battalions; 5th and 8th Line Battalions

   1st Hanoverian Brigade (Major General Count Kielmannsegge)
   Field-Battalions Bremen, Verden and York; Light Battalions Lüneburg and Grubenhagen; Field-Jäger Corps

   Artillery (Lieutenant Colonel Williamson)
   1 Foot Battery, Royal Artillery; 1 Foot Battery, King's German Legion

2nd Netherlands Division
Lieutenant General Baron de Perponcher

   1st Brigade (Major General Count Bylandt)
   7th Infantry; 27th Jägers; 5th, 7th and 8th Militia

   2nd Brigade (Prince Bernhard of Saxe-Weimar)
   2nd Nassau Regiment; Regiment of Orange Nassau

   Artillery (Major van Opstal)
   1 Battery, Horse Artillery; 1 Battery, Foot Artillery

3rd Netherlands Division
Lieutenant General Baron Chassé

   1st Brigade (Colonel Detmers)
   2nd Infantry; 35th Jägers; 4th, 6th, 17th and 19th Militia

   2nd Brigade (Major General d'Aubremé)
   3rd, 12th and 13th Infantry; 36th Jägers; 3rd and 10th Militia

   Artillery (Major van der Smissen)
   1 Battery, Horse Artillery; 1 Battery, Foot Artillery

2nd Corps
Lieutenant General Lord Hill

2nd Division
Lieutenant General Sir Henry Clinton

   3rd British Brigade (Major General Adam)
   1st Battalion 52nd Light Infantry; 1st Battalion 71st Light Infantry; 2nd and
   3rd Battalions 95th Rifles

   1st King's German Legion Brigade (Colonel du Plat)
   1st, 2nd, 3rd and 4th Line Battalions

3rd Hanoverian Brigade (Colonel H. Halkett)
Landwehr Battalions Bremervörde, Osnabrück, Quackenbrück and Salzgitter

Artillery (Lieutenant Colonel Gold)
1 Battery, Foot Artillery, Royal Artillery; 1 Horse Artillery Battery, King's German Legion

4th Division
Lieutenant General Sir Charles Colville

4th British Brigade (Colonel Mitchell)
3rd Battalion 14th Foot; 1st Battalion 23rd Fusiliers; 51st Light Infantry

6th British Brigade (Major General Johnstone)
2nd Battalion 35th Foot; 1st Battalion 54th Foot; 2nd Battalion 59th Foot; 1st Battalion 91st Foot

6th Hanoverian Brigade (Major General Sir J. Lyon)
Field–Battalions Lauenberg and Calenberg; *Landwehr* Battalions Nienburg, Hoya and Bentheim

Artillery (Lieutenant Colonel Hawker)
1 Battery, Foot Artillery, Royal Artillery; 1 Battery, Foot Artillery, King's German Legion

1st Netherlands Division
Lieutenant General Stedmann

1st Brigade (Major General Hauw)
4th and 6th Infantry; 16th Jägers; 9th, 14th and 15th Militia

2nd Brigade (Major General Eerens)
1st Infantry; 18th Jägers; 1st, 2nd and 18th Militia

Artillery
1 Battery, Foot Artillery

Netherlands Indian Brigade (Lieutenant General Anthing)
5th Infantry; Battalion of Flanquers; 10th and 11th Jägers; 1 Battery, Foot Artillery Reserve

5th Division
Lieutenant General Sir Thomas Picton

8th British Brigade (Major General Sir J. Kempt)
1st Battalion 28th Foot; 1st Battalion 32nd Foot; 1st Battalion 79th Highlanders; 1st Battalion 95th Rifles

9th British Brigade (Major General Sir D. Pack)
3rd Battalion 1st Foot; 1st Battalion 42nd Highlanders; 2nd Battalion 44th Foot; 1st Battalion 92nd Highlanders

5th Hanoverian Brigade (Colonel von Vincke)
Landwehr Btns Hameln, Gifhorn, Peine and Hildesheim

Artillery (Major Heisse)
1 Battery, Foot Artillery, Royal Artillery; 1 Battery, Foot Artillery, Hanoverian Artillery

6th Division
Lieutenant General Hon. Sir Lowry Cole

10th British Brigade (Major General Sir J. Lambert)
1st Battalion 4th Foot; 1st Battalion 27th Foot; 1st Battalion 40th Foot; 2nd Battalion 81st Foot

4th Hanoverian Brigade (Colonel Best)
Landwehr Battalions Lüneburg, Verden, Osterode and Münden

Artillery (Lieutenant Colonel Brückmann)
2 Batteries, Foot Artillery, Royal Artillery

British Reserve Artillery (Major Drummond)
2 Batteries, Royal Horse Artillery; 3 Batteries, Royal Foot Artillery

Brunswick Corps
Duke of Brunswick

　Advanced Guard Battalion (Major von Rauschenplatt)

　Light Brigade (Lieutenant Colonel von Buttlar)
　Guard Battalion; 1st, 2nd and 3rd Light Battalions

　Line Brigade (Lieutenant Colonel von Specht)
　1st, 2nd and 3rd Line Battalions

　Artillery (Major Mahn)
　1 Battery, Horse Artillery; 1 Battery, Foot Artillery

Hanoverian Reserve Corps
Lieutenant General von der Decken

　1st Brigade (Lieutenant Colonel von Bennigsen)
　Field-Battalion Hoya; *Landwehr* Battalions Mölln and Bremerlehe

　2nd Brigade (Lieutenant Colonel von Beaulieu)
　Landwehr Battalions Nordheim, Ahlefeldt and Springe

　3rd Brigade (Lieutenant Colonel Bodecker)
　Landwehr Battalions Otterndorf, Zelle and Ratzeburg

　4th Brigade (Lieutenant Colonel Wissel)
　Landwehr Battalions Hanover, Uelzen, Neustadt and Diepholz

Nassau Contingent
General von Kruse

Anglo-Allied Cavalry

1st British Brigade (Major General Lord Somerset)
1st and 2nd Life Guards; Royal Horse Guards; 1st Dragoon Guards

2nd British Brigade (Major General Sir W. Ponsonby)
1st, 2nd and 6th Dragoons

3rd British Brigade (Major General Sir W. Dörnberg)
23rd Light Dragoons; 1st and 2nd Light Dragoons, King's German Legion

4th British Brigade (Major General Sir J. Vandeleur)
11th, 12th and 16th Light Dragoons

5th British Brigade (Major General Sir C. Grant)
7th and 15th Hussars; 2nd Hussars, King's German Legion

6th British Brigade (Major General Sir H. Vivian)
10th and 18th Hussars; 1st Hussars, King's German Legion

7th British Brigade (Colonel Sir F. von Arentschildt)
13th Light Dragoons; 3rd Hussars, King's German Legion

British Horse Artillery (attached to the cavalry)
5 Batteries, Royal Horse Artillery; 1 Battery, Mounted Rocket Corps

1st Hanoverian Brigade (Colonel von Estorff)
Prince Regent's Hussars; Bremen and Verden Hussars; Duke of Cumberland's Hussars

Cavalry of the Brunswick Corps
Regiment of Hussars; Regiment of Uhlans

1st Dutch-Belgian Brigade (Major General Trip)
1st and 3rd Dutch Carabiniers; 2nd Belgian Carabiniers

2nd Dutch-Belgian Brigade (Major General de Ghigny)
4th Dutch Light Dragoons; 8th Belgian Hussars

3rd Dutch-Belgian Brigade (Major General van Merlen)
5th Belgian Light Dragoons; 6th Dutch Hussars

Total strength:

	At Waterloo	At Hal and Tubize	Total
Infantry	53,850	15,000	68,850
Cavalry	13,350	1,200	14,550
Artillery	5,000	700	5,700
Others★	1,000	100	1,100
Totals	73,200	17,000	90,200
Guns	157 + 1 section of rockets		

★Sappers, Miners, Staff Corps, HQ Staff, etc.

Prussian Army of the Lower Rhine

Field Marshal Gebhard Leberecht von Blücher (at Waterloo: 49,000 men and 134 guns)

I Corps
Lieutenant General Count Hans von Ziethen

1st Brigade (General Steinmetz)
12th and 24th Infantry; 1st Westphalian *Landwehr*; 1st and 3rd Silesian *Jäger* Companies

2nd Brigade (General von Pirch II)
6th and 28th Infantry; 2nd Westphalian *Landwehr*

3rd Brigade (General von Jagow)
7th and 29th Infantry; 3rd Westphalian *Landwehr*; 2nd and 4th Silesian *Jäger* Companies

4th Brigade (General von Henkel)
19th Infantry; 4th Westphalian *Landwehr* Cavalry (Lieutenant General von Röder)

Brigade of General von Treskow
2nd and 5th Dragoons; Brandenburg Uhlans

Brigade of Lieutenant Colonel von Lützow
6th Uhlans; 1st and 2nd Kurmark *Landwehr* Cavalry; 1st Silesian Hussars; 1st Westphalian *Landwehr* Cavalry

Artillery (Colonel von Lehmann)
3 12lb Foot Batteries; 5 6lb Foot Batteries; 1 Howitzer Battery; 3 Horse Artillery Batteries

II Corps
Major General von Pirch I

1st Brigade (General von Tippelskirchen)
2nd and 25th Infantry; 5th Westphalian *Landwehr*

6th Brigade (General von Krafft)
9th and 26th Infantry; 1st Elbe *Landwehr*

7th Brigade (General von Brause)
14th and 22nd Infantry; 2nd Elbe *Landwehr*

8th Brigade (Colonel von Langen)
21st and 23rd Infantry; 3rd Elbe *Landwehr*

Cavalry
General von Jürgass

   Brigade of Colonel Von Thümen
   Silesian Uhlans; 6th Dragoons; 11th Hussars

   Brigade of Colonel Count Schulenburg
   1st Dragoons; 4th Kurmark *Landwehr* Cavalry

   Brigade of Lieutenant Colonel von Sohr
   3rd and 5th Hussars; 5th Kurmark *Landwehr* Cavalry; Elbe *Landwehr* Cavalry

Artillery (Colonel Von Röhl)
2 12lb Foot Batteries; 5 6lb Foot Batteries; 3 Horse Artillery Batteries

III Corps
Lieutenant General von Thielemann (at Wavre)

9th Brigade (General von Borcke)
8th and 36th Infantry; 1st Kurmark *Landwehr*

10th Brigade (Colonel von Kämpfen)
27th Infantry; 2nd Kurmark *Landwehr*

11th Brigade (Colonel von Luck)
3rd and 4th Kurmark *Landwehr*

12th Brigade (Colonel von Stülpnagel)
31st Infantry; 5th and 6th Kurmark *Landwehr*

Cavalry (General von Hobe)

   Brigade of Colonel von der Marwitz
   7th and 8th Uhlans; 9th Hussars

   Brigade of Colonel Count Lottum
   5th Uhlans; 7th Dragoons; 3rd and 6th Kurmark *Landwehr* Cavalry

Artillery (Colonel von Mohnhaupt)
1 12lb Foot Battery; 2 6lb Foot Artillery Batteries; 3 Horse Artillery Batteries

IV Corps
General Count Friedrich Wilhelm Bülow von Dennewitz

13th Brigade (Lieutenant General von Hacke)
10th Infantry; 2nd and 3rd Neumark *Landwehr*

14th Brigade (General von Ryssel)
11th Infantry; 1st and 2nd Pomeranian *Landwehr*

15th Brigade (General von Losthin)
18th Infantry; 3rd and 4th Silesian *Landwehr*

16th Brigade (Colonel Hiller von Gartringen)
15th Infantry; 1st and 2nd Silesian *Landwehr*

Cavalry
General Prince William of Prussia

Brigade of General von Sydow
1st Uhlans; 2nd and 8th Hussars

Brigade of Colonel Count Schwerin
10th Hussars; 1st and 2nd Neumark *Landwehr* Cavalry; 1st and 2nd Pomeranian
Landwehr Cavalry

Brigade of Lieutenant Colonel von Watzdorf
1st, 2nd and 3rd Silesian *Landwehr* Cavalry

Artillery (Lieutenant Colonel von Bardeleben)
3 12lb Foot Batteries; 5 6lb Foot Batteries; 3 Horse Artillery batteries

Total strength (approximately):

	At Waterloo	En route	At Wavre	Total
Infantry	38,000	20,300	20,000	78,300
Cavalry	7,000	3,000	3,000	13,000
Artillery	2,500	2,000	1,250	5,750
Others*	1,500	1,000	750	3,250
Totals	49,000	26,300	25,000	100,300
Guns	134	106	43	283

NOTES

Introduction

1. Ensign Edward Macready, 2nd Battalion 30th Foot, 7 July 1815, *Waterloo Archive*, vol. i, doc. 46.
2. Private John Lewis, 2nd Battalion 95th Rifles, 8 July 1815, *Waterloo Archive*, vol. i, doc. 45.
3. For an extensive list see the bibliography, but readers are particularly directed to the works of Chandler, Roberts, Weller, Barbero, Howarth, Fremont-Barnes and Black.
4. See, for instance, three books by Peter Hofschröer: *Waterloo 1815 – Ligny and Quatre Bras*; *1815 – The Waterloo Campaign: The German Victory*; *Waterloo 1815: Wavre to Plancenoit*; and Andrew Field's *Waterloo: The French Perspective*.
5. Lieutenant Colonel Sir Robert Gardiner, Royal Artillery, July 1815, *Waterloo Archive*, vol. iii, doc. 57.
6. Major General Sir Hussey Vivian, commanding 6th (Light) Cavalry Brigade, 14 February 1837, *Waterloo Archive*, vol. iv, doc. 23.
7. Captain and Lieutenant Colonel (Ensign at Waterloo) J.P. Dirom, 1st Foot Guards, *Waterloo Letters*, no. 111.
8. Captain (Lieutenant, 27th Foot at Waterloo) E.W. Drewe, 95th Rifles, 23 July 1842, *Waterloo Letters*, no. 174.
9. Mercer, *Journal,* p. 162.
10. Kincaid, *Adventures*, pp. 168–9.
11. Major (Lieutenant at Waterloo) J. Browne, 4th Foot (King's Own), 21 April 1835, *Waterloo Letters*, no. 172.
12. Lieutenant Colonel (Major, 73rd Foot and Assistant Quartermaster General at Waterloo) Dawson Kelly, 14 October 1835, *Waterloo Letters*, no. 146.
13. First Lieutenant William Ingilby, Royal Horse Artillery, 18 June 1815, *Waterloo Archive*, vol. iv, doc. 53.
14. Triangle Player John Scott, 1st Battalion 42nd Highlanders, 1889, *Waterloo Archive*, vol. vi, doc. 87.
15. Commissary Tupper Carey, undated, *Waterloo Archive*, vol. vi, doc. 100.
16. Unknown officer, 13th Hussars, undated, *Waterloo Archive*, vol. i, doc. 23.
17. Private Thomas Playford, 2nd Life Guards, undated, *Waterloo Archive*, vol. iv, doc. 12.
18. Gronow, *Reminiscences*, vol. i, p. 183.
19. Colonel (Major, 5th West India Regiment and extra aide-de-camp to Sir William Ponsonby at Waterloo) Sir George De Lacy Evans, undated, *Waterloo Letters*, no. 32.
20. Hospital Assistant John Davy, 26 July 1815, *Waterloo Archive*, vol. i, doc. 70.
21. Ross-Lewin, *With 'The Thirty-Second'*, p. 278.
22. Lieutenant Colonel Sir John May, Royal Artillery, Assistant Adjutant General, 23 June 1815, *Waterloo Archive*, vol. iv, doc. 51; vol. i, doc. 25.
23. Gronow, *Reminiscences*, vol. i., pp. 73, 74.
24. Captain Courtenay Ilbert, Royal Artillery, 17 June (1815), *Waterloo Archive*, vol. iii, doc. 123.
25. Lieutenant Standish O'Grady, 7th Hussars, 31 July 1815, *Waterloo Archive*, vol. iii, doc. 54.
26. Lieutenant Colonel Sir John May, Royal Artillery, Assistant Adjutant General, 23 June 1815, *Waterloo Archive*, vol. iv, doc. 51.

27. Lieutenant Colonel Lord Greenock, Assistant Quartermaster General to Sir Thomas Graham, 1 July 1815, *Waterloo Archive*, vol. iv, doc. 3.

28. Lieutenant Colonel James Stanhope, 3rd Battalion 1st Foot Guards, 19 June 1815, *Waterloo Archive*, vol. vi, doc. 62.

29. Lieutenant Colonel Lord Saltoun, 3rd Battalion 1st Foot Guards, 22 June 1815, *Waterloo Archive*, vol. vi, doc. 57.

30. Ross-Lewin, *With 'The Thirty-Second'*, p. 268.

31. Lieutenant Colonel Sir John May, Royal Artillery, Assistant Adjutant General, 23 June 1815, *Waterloo Archive*, vol. iv, doc. 51.

32. Colonel Sir George Wood, commanding the artillery at Waterloo, (1817), *Waterloo Archive*, vol. i, doc. 24.

33. First Lieutenant William Chapman, 1st Battalion 95th Rifles, 4 July 1815, *Waterloo Archive*, vol. i, doc. 53.

34. Ensign Thomas Wedgwood, 2nd Battalion 3rd Foot Guards, 19 June 1815, *Waterloo Archive*, vol. i, doc 38.

35. Lieutenant Colonel Sir John May, Royal Artillery, Assistant Adjutant General, 23 June 1815, *Waterloo Archive*, vol. i, doc. 25.

36. Gunner John Edwards, Royal Artillery, 14 July 1815, *Waterloo Archive*, vol. i, doc. 26.

37. Unknown sergeant, 2nd Dragoons (Scots Greys), 25 June 1815, *Waterloo Archive*, vol. i, doc. 14.

38. Colonel Sir George Wood, commanding the artillery at Waterloo (1817), *Waterloo Archive*, vol. i, doc. 24.

39. Captain George Luard, 18th Hussars, 20 June 1815, *Waterloo Archive*, vol. i, doc 21.

40. Paymaster James Cocksedge, 15th Hussars, 19 June 1815, *Waterloo Archive*, vol. iii, doc. 55.

41. Gunner John Edwards, Royal Artillery, 14 July 1815, *Waterloo Archive*, vol. i, doc. 26; Private Joseph Lord, 2nd Life Guards, 8 August 1815, *Waterloo Archive*, vol. i, doc. 6; Assistant Surgeon John Haddy James, 1st Life Guards, 9 July 1815, *Waterloo Archive*, vol. i, doc. 3; Captain Edward Kelly, 1st Life Guards, 19 June 1815, *Waterloo Archive*, vol. vi, docs. 13 and 14.

42. Lieutenant James Crummer, 1st Battalion 28th Foot, 4 July 1815, *Waterloo Archive*, vol. vi, doc. 82.

43. Lieutenant Richard Cocks Eyre, 2nd Battalion 95th Rifles, 28 June 1815, *Waterloo Archive*, vol. iii, doc. 85.

44. Captain George Barlow, 2nd Battalion 69th Foot, 19 June 1815, *Waterloo Archive*, vol. iv, doc. 75.

45. Gunner John Edwards, Royal Artillery, 14 July 1815, *Waterloo Archive*, vol. i, doc. 26; Private Joseph Lord, 2nd Life Guards, 8 August 1815, *Waterloo Archive*, vol. i, doc. 6; Assistant Surgeon John Haddy James, 1st Life Guards, 9 July 1815, *Waterloo Archive*, vol. i, doc. 3.

46. Colonel Colin Campbell, Commandant at Headquarters, 19 June 1815, *Waterloo Archive*, vol. iv, doc. 2.

47. Captain and Lieutenant Colonel Sir Henry Willoughby Rooke, 2nd Battalion 3rd Foot Guards, Assistant Adjutant General, *Waterloo Archive*, vol. i, doc. i; Captain Arthur Kennedy, 18th Hussars, 19 June 1815, *Waterloo Archive*, vol. iv, doc. 26; Colonel Colin Campbell, Commandant at Headquarters, 19 June 1815, *Waterloo Archive*, vol. iv, doc. 2; Captain Thomas Fenton, 2nd Dragoons (Scots Greys), 23 June 1815, *Waterloo Archive*, vol. vi, doc. 36.

48. Colonel Felton Hervey, 14th Light Dragoons, Assistant Quartermaster General, 20 June 1815, *Waterloo Archive*, vol. i, doc. 2.

49. Captain Thomas Wildman, 7th Hussars, aide-de-camp to the Earl of Uxbridge, 19 June 1815, *Waterloo Archive*, vol. vi, doc. 4; Chaplain George Stonestreet, 20 June 1815, *Waterloo Archive*, vol. vi, doc. 96.

50. Captain Courtenay Ilbert, Royal Artillery, 17th June (1815), *Waterloo Archive*, vol. iii, doc. 123.

51. Triangle Player John Scott, 1st Battalion 42nd Highlanders, 21 July 1889, *Waterloo Archive*, vol. vi, doc. 87.

52. Ross-Lewin, *With 'The Thirty-Second'*, p. 278; Captain the Hon. Orlando Bridgeman, 1st Foot Guards, aide-de-camp to Lord Hill, 21 June 1815, *Waterloo Archive*, vol. iv, doc. 6; Henegan, *Seven Years' Campaigning*, vol. ii, p. 326.

53. H.M. Leathes, Royal Horse Artillery, 16 March 1859, *Waterloo Archive*, vol. i, doc. 28.

54. Gronow, *Reminiscences*, vol. i, p. 198.

55. Private Thomas Patton, 1st Battalion 28th Foot, 17 July 1846, *Waterloo Archive*, vol. i, doc. 50.

56. Lieutenant General Sir Henry Clinton, commanding 2nd Division, 23 June 1815, *Waterloo Archive*, vol. i, doc. 41.

57. Ensign Thomas Wedgwood, 2nd Battalion 3rd Foot Guards, 19 June 1815, *Waterloo Archive*, vol. i, doc. 38.

58. Lieutenant Colonel Sir John May, Royal Artillery, Assistant Adjutant General, 23 June 1815, *Waterloo Archive*, vol. iv, doc. 51.

59. Lieutenant General Sir Henry Clinton, commanding 2nd Division, 23 June 1815, *Waterloo Archive*, vol. i, doc. 41.

60. Triangle Player John Scott, 1st Battalion 42nd Highlanders, 1889, *Waterloo Archive*, vol. vi, doc. 87.

61. Colonel Felton Hervey, 14th Light Dragoons, Assistant Quartermaster General, 20 June 1815, *Waterloo Archive*, vol. i, doc. 2.

62. Troop Sergeant Major James Page, 1st (King's) Dragoon Guards, 3 July 1815, *Waterloo Archive*, vol. iii, doc. 17.

63. Gunner John Edwards, Royal Artillery, 14 July 1815, *Waterloo Archive*, vol. i, doc. 26.

64. Captain B.H. Liddell Hart, ed., *The Letters of Private Wheeler*, p. 171.

65. See Appendix IX.

66. Ensign Thomas Wedgwood, 2nd Battalion 3rd Foot Guards, 19 June 1815, *Waterloo Archive*, vol. i, doc. 38.

67. Ensign Charles Short, 2nd Battalion Coldstream Guards, 19 June 1815, *Waterloo Archive*, vol. iv, doc. 67.

68. Lieutenant Colonel Sir Robert Gardiner, Royal Artillery, July 1815, *Waterloo Archive*, vol. iii, doc. 57.

69. Cornet James Gape, 2nd Dragoons (Scots Greys), June 1815, *Waterloo Archive*, vol. vi, doc. 41.

70. Sergeant William Dewar, 1st Battalion 79th Highlanders, 5 August 1815, *Waterloo Archive*, vol. vi, doc. 83.

71. Ross-Lewin, *With 'The Thirty-Second'*, p. 269.

72. Sergeant Archibald Johnston, 2nd Dragoons (Scots Greys), June 1815, *Waterloo Archive*, vol. i, doc. 15; Ensign William Thain, 2nd Battalion 33rd Foot, *Waterloo Archive*, vol. vi, doc. 81.

73. Colonel Sir George Wood, commanding the artillery at Waterloo (1817), *Waterloo Archive*, vol. i, doc. 24.

74. Private Joseph Lord, 2nd Life Guards, 3 July 1815, *Waterloo Archive*, vol. i, doc. 5.

75. De Lancey, *A Week at Waterloo*, p. 50.

76. Henegan, *Seven Years' Campaigning*, vol. ii.

77. Lieutenant General Sir Henry Clinton, commanding 2nd Division, 23 June 1815, *Waterloo Archive*, vol. i, doc. 41.

78. Sergeant William Tennant, 3rd Battalion 1st Foot Guards, 19 June 1815, *Waterloo Archive*, vol. iii, doc. 62.

79. Major General Sir Hussey Vivian, commanding 6th (Light) Cavalry Brigade, 23 June 1815, *Waterloo Archive*, vol. iv, doc. 21.

80. Lieutenant Colonel the Hon. Henry Murray, 18th Hussars, undated, *Waterloo Archive*, vol. iv, doc. 24.

81. Second Lieutenant Richard Cocks Eyre, 2nd Battalion 95th Rifles, 28 June 1815, *Waterloo Archive*, vol. iii, doc. 85.

82. Captain George Barlow, 2nd Battalion 69th Foot, 19 June 1815, *Waterloo Archive*, vol. iv, doc 76.

83. Lieutenant Colonel (Lieutenant at Waterloo) Henry Lane, 15th Hussars, 24 March 1835, *Waterloo Letters*, no. 69.
84. Colonel Colin Campbell, Commandant at Headquarters, 19 June 1815, *Waterloo Archive*, vol. iv, doc. 2.
85. Lieutenant George Gunning, 1st (Royal) Dragoons, undated, *Waterloo Archive*, vol. vi, doc. 34.
86. Captain Edward Kelly, 1st Life Guards, 19 June 1815, *Waterloo Archive*, vol. vi, doc. 13.
87. Lieutenant John Sperling, Royal Engineers, 20 June 1815, *Waterloo Archive*, vol. vi, doc. 93.
88. Major John Oldfield, Royal Engineers, July 1815, *Waterloo Archive*, vol. vi, doc. 90.
89. Lieutenant Colonel Francis Home, 2nd Battalion 3rd Foot Guards, (probably) June 1815, *Waterloo Archive*, vol. i, doc. 37; Major John Oldfield, Royal Engineers, July 1815, *Waterloo Archive*, vol. vi, doc. 90; attributed to 'Diggle' of the 52nd.
90. Captain the Hon. Orlando Bridgeman, 1st Foot Guards, aide-de-camp to Lord Hill, 21 June 1815, *Waterloo Archive*, vol. iv, doc. 6.
91. Ensign Edward Macready, 2nd Battalion 30th Foot, 7 July 1815, *Waterloo Archive*, vol. i, doc. 46.
92. Major General Lord Edward Somerset, commanding the Household Brigade, 23 June 1815, *Waterloo Archive*, vol. vi, doc. 9.
93. Captain Peter Bowlby, 1st Battalion 4th Foot, undated memoirs, *Waterloo Archive*, vol. vi, doc. 89.
94. Captain Horace Churchill, 1st Foot Guards, aide-de-camp to Lord Hill, 24 June 1815, *Waterloo Archive*, vol. vi, doc. 3.
95. Lieutenant Colonel Sir John May, Royal Artillery, Assistant Adjutant General, 23 June 1815, *Waterloo Archive*, vol. i, doc. 25.
96. Private John Marshall, 10th Hussars, 11 July 1815, *Waterloo Archive*, vol. i, doc. 20.
97. Lieutenant Colonel Sir John May, Royal Artillery, Assistant Adjutant General, 23 June 1815, *Waterloo Archive*, vol. iv, doc. 51.
98. Ensign William Thain, 2nd Battalion 33rd Foot, 19 June 1815, *Waterloo Archive*, vol. iv, doc. 69.
99. Lieutenant Colonel the Hon. Frederick Ponsonby, 'Substance of answers given to questions respecting the Battle of Waterloo put to Lieutenant Colonel Ponsonby by his particular friends', undated, *Waterloo Archive*, vol. iv, doc. 19.
100. Captain James Nixon, 1st Foot Guards, 19 June (1815), *Waterloo Archive*, vol. i, doc. 32.
101. Captain Joseph Logan, 2nd Battalion 95th Rifles, 10 July 1815, *Waterloo Archive*, vol. i, doc. 44.
102. Major (Lieutenant, 30th Regiment at Waterloo) John Pratt, late 27th Regiment, 23 March 1835, *Waterloo Letters*, no. 138.
103. Commissary Tupper Carey, 'Reminiscences', *Waterloo Archive*, vol. vi, doc. 100.
104. Private John Abbott, 1st Battalion 51st Light Infantry, 12 November 1815, *Waterloo Archive*, vol. vi, doc. 77.
105. Lieutenant Colonel Lord Saltoun, 3rd Battalion 1st Foot Guards, 22 June 1815, *Waterloo Archive*, vol. vi, doc. 57.
106. First Lieutenant William Ingilby, Royal Horse Artillery, 18 June 1815, *Waterloo Archive*, vol. vi, doc. 53.
107. Captain Henry Grove, 23rd Light Dragoons, 19 June 1815, *Waterloo Archive*, vol. vi, doc. 45.
108. Captain Thomas Wildman, 7th Hussars, aide-de-camp to the Earl of Uxbridge, 19 June 1815, *Waterloo Archive*, vol. vi, doc. 4.
109. Captain James Naylor, 1st (King's) Dragoon Guards, 16–18 June 1815, *Waterloo Archive*, vol. vi, doc. 26.
110. Captain Courtenay Ilbert, Royal Artillery, 17 June (1815), *Waterloo Archive*, vol. iii, doc. 123.
111. Kincaid, *Adventures*, p. 168.
112. Major (Lieutenant at Waterloo) Robert Winchester, 92nd Highlanders, 24 November 1834, *Waterloo Letters*, no. 168.
113. Colonel (Captain at Waterloo) A. Clark Kennedy, 1st (Royal) Dragoons, 13 April 1835, *Waterloo Letters*, no. 35.

114. Cotton, *A Voice from Waterloo*, pp. 29, 42.

115. Captain Arthur Kennedy, 18th Hussars, 2 July 1815, *Waterloo Archive*, vol. iv, doc. 28.

116. Henegan, *Seven Years' Campaigning*, p. 317.

117. First Lieutenant William Ingilby, Royal Artillery, 10 August 1815, *Waterloo Archive*, vol. i, doc. 27.

118. *Wheatley Diary*, p. 67.

119. Lieutenant John Sperling, Royal Engineers, 20 June 1815, *Waterloo Archive*, vol. vi, doc. 93.

120. Lieutenant Colonel John Woodford, 1st Foot Guards, extra aide-de-camp to the Duke of Wellington, 19 June 1815, *Waterloo Archive*, vol. iv, doc. 4.

121. Lieutenant George Horton, 1st Battalion 71st Foot, 23 June 1815, *Waterloo Archive*, vol. i, doc. 42.

122. Ross-Lewin, *With 'The Thirty-Second'*, p. 286.

123. Captain William Bowles, Royal Navy, 23 June 1815, *Waterloo Archive*, vol. vi, doc. 106.

124. Cotton, *A Voice from Waterloo*, p. 24.

125. Henegan, *Seven Years' Campaigning*, vol. ii, p. 317.

126. Lieutenant Colonel John Fremantle, aide-de-camp to the Duke of Wellington, 19 June 1815, *Waterloo Archive*, vol. vi, doc. 1.

127. Lieutenant Colonel Lord Saltoun, 3rd Battalion 1st Foot Guards, 19 June 1815, *Waterloo Archive*, vol. vi, doc. 56.

128. Private Samuel Boulter, 2nd Dragoons (Scots Greys), 23 September 1815, *Waterloo Archive*, vol. vi, doc. 42.

129. Ensign Jack Barnett, 1st Battalion 71st Light Infantry, 21 June 1815, *Waterloo Archive*, vol. vi, doc. 72.

130. Captain George Bowles, 2nd Battalion Coldstream Guards, 19 June 1815, *Waterloo Archive*, vol. vi, doc. 65.

131. Captain Henry Grove, 23rd Light Dragoons, 19 June 1815, *Waterloo Archive*, vol. vi, doc. 45.

132. Henegan, *Seven Years' Campaigning*, vol. ii, p. 318.

133. Captain George Barlow, 2nd Battalion 69th Foot, 19 June 1815, *Waterloo Archive*, vol. iv, doc 76.

134. Unknown officer, 1st Battalion 95th Rifles, undated, *Waterloo Archive* vol. iv, doc. 90.

135. Captain Arthur Kennedy, 18th Hussars, 2 July 1815, *Waterloo Archive*, vol. iv, doc. 28.

136. Colonel Colin Campbell, Commandant at Headquarters, 19 June 1815, *Waterloo Archive*, vol. iv, doc. 2.

137. Major General Peregrine Maitland, commanding 1st Brigade, 19 June 1815, *Waterloo Archive*, vol. iv, doc 54.

138. Lieutenant Colonel the Hon. James Stanhope, 3rd Battalion 1st Foot Guards, 19 June 1815, *Waterloo Archive*, vol. i, doc. 31.

139. Lieutenant Colonel Sir Henry Willoughby Rooke, 2nd Battalion 3rd Foot Guards, Assistant Adjutant General, 19 June 1815, *Waterloo Archive*, vol. i, doc. 1.

140. Captain James Nixon, 1st Foot Guards, 19 June (1815), *Waterloo Archive*, vol. i, doc. 32. The Battle of Leipzig was fought on 16–19 October 1813 between Austrian, Russian, Prussian and Swedish forces on the one hand, and those of Napoleon and his allies on the other. The largest battle in European history until the First World War, it ousted the French from Germany and contributed decisively to Napoleon's downfall the following year.

141. Elizabeth Ord, stepdaughter to Thomas Creevey, undated, *Waterloo Archive*, vol. i, doc. 73.

142. Lieutenant Colonel Sir Henry Willoughby Rooke, 2nd Battalion 3rd Foot Guards, Assistant Adjutant General, 19 June 1815, *Waterloo Archive*, vol. i, doc. 1.

143. Colonel Felton Hervey, 14th Light Dragoons, Assistant Quartermaster General, 20 June 1815, *Waterloo Archive,* vol. i, doc. 2.

144. Sergeant Thomas Critchley, 1st (Royal) Dragoons, 24 July 1815, *Waterloo Archive*, vol. iv, doc. 15.

145. Gunner John Edwards, Royal Artillery, 14 July 1815, *Waterloo Archive*, vol. i, doc. 26.

146. Captain the Hon. Orlando Bridgeman, 1st Foot Guards, aide-de-camp to Lord Hill, 21 June 1815, *Waterloo Archive*, vol. iv, doc. no. 6.

147. Lieutenant Colonel Sir John May, Royal Artillery, Assistant Adjutant General, 23 June 1815, *Waterloo Archive*, vol. iv, doc. 51.
148. Lieutenant Henry McMillan, 2nd Dragoons (Scots Greys), 3 July 1815, *Waterloo Archive*, vol. vi, doc. 40.
149. Lieutenant Colonel Sir Alexander Dickson, Battering Train, 20 June 1815, *Waterloo Archive*, vol. iv, doc. 52.
150. Lieutenant Colonel Sir John May, Royal Artillery, Assistant Adjutant General, 23 June 1815, *Waterloo Archive*, vol. i, doc. 25.
151. Elizabeth Ord, stepdaughter to Thomas Creevey, undated, *Waterloo Archive*, vol. i, doc. 73.
152. Lieutenant Donald Mackenzie, 1st Battalion 42nd Foot, undated, *Waterloo Archive*, vol. i, doc. 55.
153. Hospital Assistant Isaac James, 29 June 1815, *Waterloo Archive*, vol. i, doc. 72.

2. British Troops at Waterloo

1. See for example, Adkin, *Waterloo Companion*; Bowden, *Armies at Waterloo*; Fletcher, *Wellington's Regiments*; Haythornthwaite, *Waterloo Men*.
2. Sherer, *Recollections*, pp. 261–2.
3. Sergeant Charles Wood, 3rd Battalion 1st Foot Guards, 29 July 1815, *Waterloo Archive*, vol. vi, doc. 63.
4. Kincaid, *Adventures*, p. 172.
5. Gleig, *The Subaltern*, p. 30.
6. Quoted in Maxwell, *The Life of Wellington*, pp. 122–3.
7. Neville, *Leisure Moments*, pp. 98–9.
8. Lieutenant George Gunning, 1st (Royal) Dragoons, undated, *Waterloo Archive*, vol. vi, doc. 34.
9. Sergeant Charles Wood, 3rd Battalion, 1st Foot Guards, 29 July 1815, *Waterloo Archive*, vol. vi, doc. 63.
10. Captain Peter Bowlby, 1st Battalion 4th Foot, undated memoirs, *Waterloo Archive*, vol. vi, doc. 89.
11. Captain Thomas Wildman, 7th Hussars, aide-de-camp to the Earl of Uxbridge, 19 June 1815, *Waterloo Archive*, vol. vi, doc. 4.
12. 'Recollection of Waterloo by A Staff Officer [Basil Jackson] regarding Lt Arthur Gore, 33rd Foot', 1847, *Waterloo Archive*, vol. vi, doc. 80.
13. Gronow, *Reminiscences*, vol. ii, pp. 186, 190.
14. Hangar, *To All Sportsmen*, p. 205.
15. Gronow, *Reminiscences*, vol. ii, pp. 12–13.
16. Gleig, *The Subaltern*, p. 123.
17. *A Manual for Volunteer Corps of Infantry*, pp. 30–3.
18. Wheeler, *Letters*, pp. 171–2.
19. Kincaid, *Adventures*, p. 168.
20. Sergeant Archibald Johnston, 2nd Dragoons (Scots Greys), June 1815, *Waterloo Archive*, vol. i, doc. 15.
21. Gleig, *The Subaltern*, p. 140.
22. Kincaid, *Adventures in the Rifle Brigade*, pp. 252–3.
23. Lawrence, *The Autobiography of Sergeant William Lawrence*, p. 210.
24. Gleig, *The Subaltern*, p. 137.
25. Cornet James Gape, 2nd Dragoons (Scots Greys), June 1815, *Waterloo Archive*, vol. vi, doc. 41; Ensign Joseph St John, 2nd Battalion 1st Foot Guards, 22 June 1815, *Waterloo Archive*, vol. vi, doc. 55.
26. Gronow, *Reminiscences*, vol. i, pp. 68–9.

27. Maréchal Thomas Robert Bugeaud, *Aperçu sur quelques détails de la guerre*.
28. Gleig, *The Subaltern*, pp. 79–80.
29. Gleig, *The Subaltern*, pp., 133–4.
30. Tomkinson, *Diary*, p. 310.
31. Gleig, *The Subaltern*, p. 138.
32. Smithies, *Adventurous Pursuits* p. 86.
33. Gronow, *Reminiscences*, vol. i, p. 80.
34. Gleig, *The Subaltern*, p. 136.
35. Private Thomas Playford, 2nd Life Guards, undated, *Waterloo Archive*, vol. iv, doc. 12.
36. Gronow, *Reminiscences*, vol. i, p. 196.
37. Sergeant Matthew Colgan, 18th Hussars, undated memoirs, *Waterloo Archive*, vol. iv, doc. 33.
38. Lieutenant Colonel (Captain and Brevet Major at Waterloo) T. W. Taylor, 10th Hussars, November 1829, *Waterloo Letters*, no. 75.
39. Wellington to Hill, 18 June 1812, *The Dispatches of Field Marshal the Duke of Wellington*, compiled by Lieutenant Colonel Gurwood, vol. ix, p. 240.
40. Gronow, *Reminiscences*, vol. i, p. 5.
41. Gronow, *Reminiscences*, vol. i. pp. 79–80.
42. Gleig, *The Subaltern*, pp. 243–4.
43. Corporal John Bingley, Royal Horse Guards, 13 August 1815, *Waterloo Archive*, vol. vi, doc. 4.
44. Quoted in Adkin, *Waterloo Companion*, p. 263.
45. Gleig, *The Subaltern*, p. 240.
46. Gronow, *Reminiscences*, vol. i, p. 3.
47. Sergeant William Dewar, 1st Battalion 79th Highlanders, 5 August 1815, *Waterloo Archive*, vol. vi, doc. 83.
48. Captain (Lieutenant at Waterloo) F. Warde, Royal Horse Artillery, 27 May (1840), *Waterloo Letters*, no. 86.
49. Gleig, *The Subaltern*, p. 215.
50. George Napier, *Passages*, ed. by his son, General William Napier, p. 219.

4. Opening Moves

1. Private James Gunn, 42nd Foot, undated, *Waterloo Archive*, vol. i, doc. 57.
2. Assistant Surgeon John Haddy James, 1st Life Guards, 9 July 1815, *Waterloo Archive*, vol. i, doc. 3.
3. Major General Sir Hussey Vivian, Commander 6th (Light) Cavalry Brigade, 23 June 1815, *Waterloo Letters*, no. 70.
4. Ensign Charles Dallas, 1st Battalion 32nd Foot, 25 June 1815, *Waterloo Archive*, vol. i, doc. 51.
5. Hospital Assistant John Davy, 26 July 1815, *Waterloo Archive*, vol. i, doc. 70.
6. Elizabeth Ord, stepdaughter to Thomas Creevey, undated, *Waterloo Archive*, vol. i, doc. 73.
7. Captain Digby Mackworth, 7th Foot, aide-de-camp to Lord Hill, (16 June 1815), *Waterloo Archive*, vol. iv, doc. 5.
8. Captain John Whale, 1st Life Guards, memoir compiled by his daughter, undated, *Waterloo Archive*, vol. iv, doc. 11.
9. Private John Lewis, 2nd Battalion 95th Rifles, 8 July 1815, *Waterloo Archive*, vol. i, doc. 45.
10. Private James Gunn, 42nd Foot, undated, *Waterloo Archive*, vol. i, doc. 57.
11. Ensign Charles Dallas, 1st Battalion 32nd Foot, 25 June 1815, *Waterloo Archive*, vol. i, doc. 51.
12. Lieutenant John Black, 3rd Battalion 1st Foot, 10 July 1815, *Waterloo Archive*, vol. i, doc. 54.
13. Hospital Assistant Isaac James, 29 June 1815, *Waterloo Archive*, vol. i, doc. 72.
14. Major General Sir Hussey Vivian, commanding 6th (Light) Cavalry Brigade, 23 June 1815, *Waterloo Letters*, no. 70.

15. Apart from narratives of the battle found in all standard campaign histories of the Hundred Days, see the works specifically devoted to this subject: Robinson, *The Battle of Quatre Bras 1815* and Hofschröer, *Waterloo 1815: Ligny and Quatre Bras*.

16. As with Quatre Bras, two sources cover Ligny in greater detail than in the standard campaign histories: Uffindell, *The Eagle's Last Triumph* and Peter Hofschröer, *Waterloo 1815: Ligny and Quatre Bras*.

17. Ensign Charles Short, 2nd Battalion Coldstream Guards, 19 June 1815, *Waterloo Archive*, vol. iv, doc. 67.

18. Lieutenant George Maule, Royal Artillery, *Waterloo Archive*, vol. i, doc. 30.

19. Ensign Thomas Wedgwood, 2nd Battalion 3rd Foot Guards, 19 June 1815, *Waterloo Archive*, vol. i, doc. 38; Private John Lewis, 2nd Battalion 95th Rifles, 8 July 1815, *Waterloo Archive*, vol. i, doc. 45; Lieutenant George Maule, Royal Artillery, extract from his journal, *Waterloo Archive*, vol. i, doc. 30.

20. Major (Lieutenant at Waterloo) A. Forbes, 79th Highlanders, 3 May 1837. *Waterloo Letters*, no. 156.

21. Private Thomas Jeremiah, Royal Welch Fusiliers, *Waterloo Archive*, vol. iv, doc. 87.

22. Major General Sir Hussey Vivian, commanding 6th (Light) Cavalry Brigade, 23 June 1815, *Waterloo Archive*, vol. iv, doc no. 21.

23. Sergeant Matthew Colgan, 18th Hussars, undated memoirs, *Waterloo Archive*, vol. iv, doc. 33.

24. Lieutenant Edward Byam, 15th Hussars, 'Extracts from the Troop Order Book of Lieutenant Edward Byam, written at the time', *Waterloo Archive*, vol. i, doc. 18.

25. Sergeant Major James Page, 1st (King's) Dragoon Guards, 3 July 1815, *Waterloo Archive*, vol. iii, doc. 17.

26. Lieutenant John Black, 3rd Battalion 1st Foot, 10 July 1815, *Waterloo Archive*, vol. i, doc. 54.

27. Lieutenant Donald Mackenzie, 1st Battalion 42nd Foot, undated, *Waterloo Archive*, vol. i, doc. 55.

28. Unknown sergeant, 2nd Dragoons (Scots Greys), 25 June 1815, *Waterloo Archive*, vol. i, doc. 14; Private Thomas Playford, 2nd Life Guards, undated, *Waterloo Archive*, vol. iv, doc. 12; Troop Sergeant Major James Page, 1st (King's) Dragoon Guards, 3 July 1815, *Waterloo Archive*, vol. iii, doc. 17.

29. Unknown officer, 1st Battalion 95th Rifles, undated but June 1815, *Waterloo Archive* vol. iv, doc 90.

30. Gunner John Edwards, Royal Artillery, 14 July 1815, *Waterloo Archive*, vol. i, doc. 26.

31. Lieutenant William Turner, 13th Light Dragoons, 3 July 1815, *Waterloo Archive*, vol. i, doc. 22.

32. Lieutenant George Simmons, 1st Battalion 95th Rifles, *Waterloo Archive*, vol. iv, doc. 91.

33. Captain the Hon. Orlando Bridgeman, 1st Foot Guards, aide-de-camp to Lord Hill, 21 June 1815, *Waterloo Archive*, vol. iv, doc. 6.

34. Sergeant Archibald Johnston, 2nd Dragoons (Scots Greys), June 1815, *Waterloo Archive*, vol. i, doc. 15.

35. Lieutenant George Simmons, 1st Battalion 95th Rifles, *Waterloo Archive*, vol. iv, doc. 91.

36. Lieutenant George Simmons, 1st Battalion 95th Rifles, *Waterloo Archive*, vol. iv, doc. 91.

37. Lieutenant Richard Cocks Eyre, 2nd Battalion 95th Rifles, 28 June 1815, *Waterloo Archive*, vol. iii, doc. 85.

38. Sergeant Archibald Johnston, 2nd Dragoons (Scots Greys), June 1815, *Waterloo Archive*, vol. i, doc. 15.

39. Private Thomas Playford, 2nd Life Guards, undated, *Waterloo Archive*, vol. iv, doc. 12.

40. Private Thomas Jeremiah, Royal Welch Fusiliers, *Waterloo Archive*, vol. iv, doc. 87.

41. Private John Lewis, 2nd Battalion 95th Rifles, 8 July 1815, *Waterloo Archive*, vol. i, doc. 45.

42. Lieutenant George Maule, Royal Artillery, *Waterloo Archive*, vol. i, doc. 30; Captain George Barlow, 2nd Battalion 69th Foot, 19 June 1815, *Waterloo Archive*, vol. iv, doc. 76; Lieutenant George Blathwayt, 23rd Light Dragoons, 1865, *Waterloo Archive*, vol. iii, doc. 53.

43. Cornet Robert Bullock, 11th Light Dragoons, *Waterloo Archive*, vol. i, doc. 16.

44. Private Thomas Playford, 2nd Life Guards, undated, *Waterloo Archive*, vol. iv, doc. 12.

45. Tomkinson, *Diary*, pp. 286, 288.

46. Lieutenant George Packe, 13th Light Dragoons, 20 June 1815, *Waterloo Archive*, vol. iv, doc. 39.

47. Private George Hemingway, 33rd Foot, 14 August 1815, *Waterloo Archive*, vol. i, doc. 48.

48. Private John Marshall, 10th Hussars, 11 July 1815, *Waterloo Archive*, vol. i, doc. 20. The battle would not be affected by inclement weather during the course of the 18th, as the day remained dry throughout, though cloudy. See, Lieutenant Edward Byam, 15th Hussars, 'Extracts from the Troop Order Book of Lieutenant Edward Byam, written at the time', *Waterloo Archive*, vol. i, doc. 18.

49. Gronow, *Reminiscences*, vol. i, pp. 68–9.

50. Private Joseph Lord, 2nd Life Guards, 3 July 1815, *Waterloo Archive*, vol. i, doc. 5.

51. Captain the Hon. Orlando Bridgeman, 1st Foot Guards, aide-de-camp to Lord Hill, 21 June 1815, *Waterloo Archive*, vol. iv, doc. 6.

52. Ross-Lewin, *With 'The Thirty-Second'*, p. 266.

53. Sergeant Matthew Colgan, 18th Hussars, undated memoirs, *Waterloo Archive*, vol. iv, doc. 33.

54. Lieutenant Donald Mackenzie, 1st Battalion 42nd Foot, undated, *Waterloo Archive*, vol. i, doc. 55.

55. Troop Sergeant Major James Page, 1st Dragoon Guards, 3 July 1815, *Waterloo Archive*, vol. iii, doc. 17.

56. Sergeant Archibald Johnston, 2nd Dragoons (Scots Greys), June 1815, *Waterloo Archive*, vol. i, doc. 15.

57. Lieutenant Edward Byam, 15th Hussars, 'Extracts from the Troop Order Book of Lieutenant Edward Byam, written at the time', *Waterloo Archive*, vol. i, doc. 18.

58. Assistant Surgeon Donald Finlayson, 33rd Foot, 25 June 1815, *Waterloo Archive*, vol. iii, doc. 130.

59. Ensign Charles Short, 2nd Battalion Coldstream Guards, 19 June 1815, *Waterloo Archive*, vol. iv, doc. 67.

60. Private George Hemingway, 33rd Foot, 14 August 1815, *Waterloo Archive*, vol. i, doc. 48.

61. Lieutenant Colonel Sir George Scovell, Assistant Quartermaster General, undated, *Waterloo Archive*, vol. iii, doc. i.

62. Lieutenant George Blathwayt, 23rd Light Dragoons, 1865, *Waterloo Archive*, vol. iii, doc. 53.

63. Lieutenant Colonel the Hon. Frederick Ponsonby, 'Substance of answers given to questions respecting the Battle of Waterloo put to Lieutenant Colonel Ponsonby by his particular friends', undated, *Waterloo Archive*, vol. iv, doc. 19.

64. Triangle Player John Scott, 1st Battalion 42nd Highlanders, 1889, *Waterloo Archive*, vol. vi, doc. 87.

65. Lieutenant General Sir Henry Clinton, commanding 2nd Division, 23 June 1815, *Waterloo Archive*, vol. i, doc. 41.

66. Cotton, *A Voice from Waterloo*, p. 27, quoting Wellington, *Dispatches*, vol. xii, p. 129.

67. Tomkinson, *Diary of a Cavalry Officer*, p. 288.

68. Lieutenant Colonel Sir Robert Gardiner, Royal Artillery, July 1815, *Waterloo Archive*, vol. iii, doc. 57.

69. Cotton, *A Voice from Waterloo*, pp. 26–7.

70. Lieutenant Colonel the Hon. Frederick Ponsonby, 12th Light Dragoons, undated, *Waterloo Archive*, vol. iv, doc. 19.

71. Captain William Burney, 1/44th, 1864, *Waterloo Archive*, vol. iii, doc. 98.

72. Ensign Charles Dallas, 1st Battalion 32nd Foot, 25 June 1815, *Waterloo Archive*, vol. i, doc. 51.

73. Ensign Edward Macready, 2nd Battalion 30th Foot, (Journal, June 1815), *Waterloo Archive*, vol. vi, doc. 79.

74. Major General (Lieutenant Colonel at Waterloo) Henry Murray, 18th Hussars, *Waterloo Letters*, no. 76.

75. Cotton, *A Voice from Waterloo*, pp. 32–3.

76. Cotton, *A Voice from Waterloo*, pp. 28–9.

77. Cotton, *A Voice from Waterloo*, p. 30.

78. Lieutenant General (Lieutenant Colonel, 2nd Foot Guards and Assistant Quartermaster General to 5th Division at Waterloo) Sir William Gomm, 5 January 1837, *Waterloo Letters*, no. 13.

79. Henegan, *Seven Years' Campaigning*, vol. ii, p. 310.

80. Major General Sir Hussey Vivian, Commander 6th (Light) Cavalry Brigade, 23 June 1815, *Waterloo Archive*, vol. iv, doc. 21.

81. Major General Sir Hussey Vivian, Commander 6th (Light) Cavalry Brigade, 3 June 1839, *Waterloo Letters*, no. 71.

82. Lieutenant Colonel Francis Home, 2nd Battalion 3rd Foot Guards, (probably) June 1815, *Waterloo Archive*, vol. i, doc. 37.

83. Mercer, *Journal*, p. 163.

84. Tomkinson, *Diary*, p. 289.

85. Tomkinson, *Diary*, p. 297.

86. Lieutenant General Sir Henry Clinton, commanding 2nd Division, 23 June 1815, *Waterloo Archive*, vol. i, doc. 41.

87. Captain Digby Mackworth, 7th Foot, aide-de-camp to Lord Hill, 11 p.m. 18 June 1815, *Waterloo Archive*, vol. iv, doc. 5.

88. Lieutenant Colonel James Stanhope, 3rd Battalion 1st Foot Guards, *Waterloo Archive*, vol. vi, doc. 59.

89. Captain George Bowles, 2nd Battalion Coldstream Guards, 19 June 1815, *Waterloo Archive*, vol. vi, doc. 65.

90. Gronow, *Reminiscences*, vol. i, p. 187.

91. Tomkinson, *Diary*, pp. 296–7.

92. Major John Oldfield, Royal Engineers, July 1815, *Waterloo Archive*, vol. vi, doc. 90. The map showing Allied dispositions, partly prepared on the basis of reconnoitring and with the aid of the Ferraris & Capitaine maps of Belgium of 1797, is extant at the Royal Engineers Museum at Gillingham.

93. Lieutenant John Sperling, Royal Engineers, 13 June 1815, *Waterloo Archive*, vol. vi, doc. 92.

94. Tomkinson, *Diary*, p. 288.

95. For detailed contemporary descriptions of Allied dispositions see, Major John Oldfield, Royal Engineers, July 1815, *Waterloo Archive*, vol. vi, doc. 90; Lieutenant John Sperling, Royal Engineers, 20 June 1815, *Waterloo Archive*, vol. vi, doc. 93; Ensign Edward Macready, 2nd Battalion 30th Foot, (Journal, June 1815), *Waterloo Archive*, vol. vi, doc. 79; and Lieutenant W.B. Ingilby, Royal Horse Artillery, 18 June 1815, *Waterloo Archive*, vol. vi, doc. 53.

96. Major John Oldfield, Royal Engineers, July 1815, *Waterloo Archive*, vol. vi, doc. 90.

97. Lieutenant John Sperling, Royal Engineers, 20 June 1815, *Waterloo Archive*, vol. vi, doc. 93.

98. Major John Oldfield, Royal Engineers, July 1815, *Waterloo Archive*, vol. vi, doc. 90.

99. Lieutenant John Sperling, Royal Engineers, 13 June 1815, *Waterloo Archive*, vol. vi, doc. 92.

100. Lieutenant John Hildebrand, 2nd Battalion 35th Foot, undated, *Waterloo Archive*, vol. vi, doc. 98.

101. Cotton, *A Voice from Waterloo*, pp. 28–9.

102. Cotton, *A Voice from Waterloo*, pp. 32–3.

103. Kincaid, *Adventures*, p. 164.

104. Lieutenant George Simmons, 1st Battalion 95th Rifles, 1815, *Waterloo Archive*, vol. iv. doc. 91.

105. Kincaid, *Adventures*, p. 165.

106. Lieutenant W.B. Ingilby, Royal Horse Artillery, 18 June 1815, *Waterloo Archive*, vol. vi, doc. 53.

107. Cotton, *A Voice from Waterloo*, p. 45.

108. Ensign Edward Macready, 2nd Battalion 30th Foot, (Journal, June 1815), *Waterloo Archive*, vol. vi, doc. 79. For a detailed description of the initial placement of Anglo-Allied artillery,

see Lieutenant Colonel Sir Augustus Frazer, staff, Royal Artillery, 25 August 1815, *Waterloo Archive*, vol. vi, doc. 52.

109. Captain Digby Mackworth, 7th Foot, aide-de-camp to Lord Hill, 11 p.m. 18 June 1815, *Waterloo Archive*, vol. iv, doc. 5.

110. Cotton, *A Voice from Waterloo*, pp. 26–7, 30.

111. Lieutenant John Sperling, Royal Engineers, 20 June 1815, *Waterloo Archive*, vol. vi, doc. 91.

112. Cotton, *A Voice from Waterloo*, p. 37.

5. The Defence of Hougoumont

1. Lieutenant Colonel and Colonel (Lieutenant and Captain, 1st Foot Guards at Waterloo) Robert Ellison, Grenadier Guards, 1 March 1835, *Waterloo Letters*, no. 107.

2. Lieutenant General (Major and Colonel at Waterloo) Sir Alexander Woodford, Coldstream Guards, 9 December 1838, *Waterloo Letters*, no. 115.

3. Lieutenant Colonel and Colonel (Lieutenant and Captain, 1st Foot Guards at Waterloo) Robert Ellison, Grenadier Guards, 1 March 1835, *Waterloo Letters*, no. 249.

4. Lieutenant General (Major and Colonel at Waterloo) Sir Alexander Woodford, Coldstream Guards, 9 December 1838, *Waterloo Letters*, no. 115. Lieutenant Colonel Home, 2/3rd Foot Guards is quite incorrect in citing inadequate defensive measures: 'It (Hougoumont) formed the most important point in that day's position and yet at eleven o'clock there was not a single loop hole made in the garden wall; at no time was half the advantage taken of it which might have been done. It possessed great capabilities but the defence of that point was no ways indicated to our engineers; a few picks and irons of the pioneers formed all the tools. With these a few loop holes were made and the gate reinforced, and this formed all the additional defence of the place. The troops did the rest.' See, Lieutenant Colonel Francis Home, 2nd Battalion 3rd Foot Guards, undated, *Waterloo Archive*, vol. i, doc. 37.

5. Major (Lieutenant, 2nd Light Battalion, King's German Legion at Waterloo) G.D. Graeme, Hanoverian Service, 6 December 1842, *Waterloo Letters*, no. 179. The engineers played a comparatively small role on the 18th. See Major John Oldfield, Royal Engineers, July 1815, *Waterloo Archive*, vol. vi, doc. 90.

6. Total strength of II Corps was 20,200 men and forty-six guns, though the whole of these were not engaged at Hougoumont.

7. Major General Sir Hussey Vivian, Commander 6th (Light) Cavalry Brigade, 23 June 1815, *Waterloo Archive*, vol. iv, doc. 21.

8. Ross-Lewin, *With 'The Thirty-Second'*, p. 269.

9. Henegan, *Seven Years' Campaigning*, p. 311.

10. Gronow, *Reminiscences*, vol. i, p. 188; Ross-Lewin, *With 'The Thirty-Second'*, p. 269.

11. Lieutenant Colonel Sir John May, Royal Artillery, Assistant Adjutant General, 23 June 1815, *Waterloo Archive*, vol. i, doc. 25.

12. Captain and Brevet Major (Major at Waterloo) Robert Bull, Royal Horse Artillery, 24 June 1835, *Waterloo Letters*, no. 78; Lieutenant Colonel Sir Augustus Frazer, Staff, Royal Artillery, 25 August 1815, *Waterloo Archive*, vol. vi, doc. 52.

13. Lieutenant Colonel (Captain at Waterloo) E.Y. Walcott, Royal Horse Artillery, 18 January 1835, *Waterloo Letters*, no. 80.

14. Major (Captain at Waterloo) S. Rudyard, Royal Artillery, 6 January 1835, *Waterloo Letters*, no. 99.

15. Cleeve, Lloyd, Sandham, Kuhlman, and Beane.

16. Colonel Sir George Wood, commanding the artillery at Waterloo (1817), *Waterloo Archive*, vol. i, doc. 24; Lieutenant Colonel Francis Home, 2nd Battalion 3rd Foot Guards, (probably) June 1815, *Waterloo Archive*, vol. i, doc. 37; Ensign Thomas Wedgwood, 2nd Battalion 3rd Foot

Guards, 19 June 1815, *Waterloo Archive*, vol. i, doc. 38; Lieutenant Edward Byam, 15th Hussars, 'Extracts from the Troop Order Book of Lieutenant Edward Byam, written at the time', *Waterloo Archive*, vol. i, doc. 18; Sergeant Charles Wood, 3rd Battalion 1st Foot Guards, 29 July 1815, *Waterloo Archive*, vol. vi, doc. 63; Lieutenant Colonel James Stanhope, 3rd Battalion 1st Foot Guards, *Waterloo Archive*, vol. vi, doc. 59.

17. Mercer, *Journal,* p. 165.

18. Lieutenant General Sir Henry Clinton, commanding 2nd Division, 23 June 1815, *Waterloo Archive*, vol. i, doc. 41.

19. Captain and Brevet Major (Major at Waterloo) Robert Bull, Royal Horse Artillery, 24 June 1835, *Waterloo Letters*, no. 78.

20. Lieutenant General (Major and Colonel at Waterloo) Sir Alexander Woodford, Coldstream Guards, 9 December 1838, *Waterloo Letters*, no. 115.

21. Lieutenant Colonel Francis Home, 2nd Battalion 3rd Foot Guards (probably) June 1815, *Waterloo Archive*, vol. i, doc. 37.

22. Gronow, *Reminiscences*, vol. i, p. 188.

23. Lieutenant Colonel Francis Home, 2nd Battalion 3rd Foot Guards (probably) June 1815, *Waterloo Archive*, vol. i, doc. 37.

24. Captain and Lieutenant Colonel (Ensign at Waterloo) F.D. Standen, 3rd Foot Guards, undated, *Waterloo Letters*, no. 119.

25. Captain George Barlow, 2nd Battalion 69th Foot, 19 June 1815, *Waterloo Archive*, vol. iv, doc. 76.

26. Captain and Lieutenant Colonel (Ensign at Waterloo) F.D. Standen, 3rd Foot Guards, undated, *Waterloo Letters*, no. 118. Woodford learned after the war from Jérôme's Chef d'Etat Major that the whole of Jérôme's corps occupied the wood. Lieutenant General (Major and Colonel at Waterloo) Sir Alexander Woodford, Coldstream Guards, 14 January 1838, *Waterloo Letters*, no. 116; 9 December 1838, *Waterloo Letters*, no. 115.

27. Lieutenant General (Major and Colonel at Waterloo) Sir Alexander Woodford, Coldstream Guards, 9 December 1838, *Waterloo Letters*, no. 115.

28. Lieutenant Colonel Francis Home, 2nd Battalion 3rd Foot Guards (probably) June 1815, *Waterloo Archive*, vol. i, doc. 37.

29. Lieutenant General (Major and Colonel at Waterloo) Sir Alexander Woodford, Coldstream Guards, 9 December 1838, *Waterloo Letters*, no. 115.

30. Lieutenant General (Major and Colonel at Waterloo) Sir Alexander Woodford, Coldstream Guards, 14 January 1838, *Waterloo Letters*, no. 116.

31. Lieutenant General (Major and Colonel at Waterloo) Sir Alexander Woodford, Coldstream Guards, 9 December 1838, 14 January 1839, *Waterloo Letters*, nos. 115 and 116.

32. Lieutenant General (Major and Colonel at Waterloo) Sir Alexander Woodford, Coldstream Guards, 9 December 1838, *Waterloo Letters*, no. 115.

33. Lieutenant Colonel (Ensign at Waterloo) F.D. Standen, 3rd Foot Guards, undated, *Waterloo Letters*, no. 118. Curiously, Standen states that the barn was already on fire at this time, whereas most accounts indicate the fire occurring later. It is therefore conceivable that this represents a second incursion into the courtyard: 'During this time the whole of the barn and cart house were in flames. During the confusion three or four Officers' horses rushed out into the yard from the barn, and in a minute or two rushed back into the flames and were burnt.'

34. Lieutenant General (Major and Colonel at Waterloo) Sir Alexander Woodford, Coldstream Guards, 14 January 1838, *Waterloo Letters*, no. 115.

35. Four light companies totalling, without consideration of losses thus far sustained, about 350: 2/1, 3/1, 2/2 and 2/3 Guards, the 800 men of 1/2 Nassau, and seven companies of the 2/2 Guards. The French consisted of seven battalions from Baudin's brigade and six from Soye's. At least three British batteries – Webber-Smith's, Bull's and Ramsey's – stood in support on the ridge immediately behind Hougoumont.

36. Lieutenant Colonel Francis Home, 2nd Battalion 3rd Foot Guards, (probably) June 1815, *Waterloo Archive*, vol. i, doc. 37. This evidence revises Adkin's contention that the fire broke out at about 3 p.m.

37. The original order is in Apsley House, London, home of the Duke of Wellington.

38. Lieutenant General (Major and Colonel at Waterloo) Sir Alexander Woodford, Coldstream Guards, 9 December 1838, 14 January 1839, *Waterloo Letters*, nos. 115 and 116; Ensign Standen, 3rd Foot Guards, could not be sure how the barn caught fire, but many years after the battle he informed Siborne that an opening in the wall was large enough for a man bearing a bit of burning hay to pass through. Captain and Lieutenant Colonel (Ensign at Waterloo) F.D. Standen, 3rd Foot Guards, undated, *Waterloo Letters*, no. 118.

6. D'Erlon's Attack

1. Often referred to in contemporary correspondence as 'the *chaussée*'.

2. Major (Captain at Waterloo) S. Rudyard, Royal Artillery, 6 January 1835, *Waterloo Letters*, no. 99.

3. Lieutenant Colonel James Stanhope, 3rd Battalion 1st Foot Guards, *Waterloo Archive*, vol. vi, doc. 59.

4. Major (Lieutenant, 30th Regiment at Waterloo), John Pratt, late 27th Regiment, 23 March 1835, *Waterloo Letters*, no. 138.

5. Lieutenant Colonel (First Lieutenant at Waterloo) William Ingilby, Royal Horse Artillery, 20 November 1834, *Waterloo Letters*, no. 82.

6. Unknown officer, 1st Battalion 95th Rifles, undated but June 1815, *Waterloo Archive*, vol. iv, doc. 90.

7. Despite the advance of their three divisional columns, the French did not entirely halt their cannonade, Major Campbell of the 42nd Highlanders recalling being 'under the fire of the French Artillery the whole time'. Colonel (Captain and Brevet Major at Waterloo) J. Campbell, 42nd Highlanders, 15 March 1838, *Waterloo Letters*, no. 164.

8. Unknown officer, 1st Battalion 95th Rifles, undated but June 1815, *Waterloo Archive*, vol. iv, doc. 90; Lieutenant Colonel (First Lieutenant at Waterloo) William Ingilby, Royal Horse Artillery, 20 November 1834, *Waterloo Letters*, no. 82.

9. Tirailleurs formed the basic infantry component of French light infantry battalions, known as *Infanterie de légère*. Voltigeurs formed one company of each line infantry battalion (*Infanterie de ligne*) and were detached to form a skirmish screen in front of the battalion. Both these types of infantry served the same function.

10. A rough barricade fashioned from felled trees and sharpened branches.

11. Lieutenant General (Lieutenant Colonel and Brevet Colonel at Waterloo) Sir Andrew Barnard, 1st battalion 95th Rifles, 20 November 1834, *Waterloo Letters*, no. 158.

12. Captain J. Kincaid (Lieutenant and Adjutant at Waterloo), 1st battalion 95th Rifles, 2 May 1839, *Waterloo Letters*, no. 161.

13. The struggle for La Haye Sainte, being an affair of King's German Legion troops, will not detain us here, but it is essential to note that the contest for its possession would continue ferociously for the next several hours and would constitute one of the epic features of the battle as a whole, with the bravery of Baring's men unsurpassed.

14. Lieutenant General (Lieutenant Colonel and Brevet Colonel at Waterloo) Sir Andrew Barnard, 1st Battalion 95th Rifles, 20 November 1834, *Waterloo Letters*, no. 158.

15. Captain J. Kincaid (Lieutenant and Adjutant at Waterloo), 1st Battalion 95th Rifles, 2 May 1839, *Waterloo Letters*, no. 161.

16. If accurate, this indicates that Kincaid observed about half the strength of d'Erlon's corps.

17. The musicians of the line infantry.

18. He almost certainly means the horns of the light infantry as well as the trumpets of the cavalry.

19. Kincaid, *Adventures*, pp. 165–7.

20. Lieutenant Colonel (Captain and Brevet Major at Waterloo) J. Leach, 1st Battalion 95th Rifles, 22 November 1840, *Waterloo Letters*, no. 160.

21. Major (Lieutenant at Waterloo) Robert Winchester, 92nd Highlanders, 24 November 1834, *Waterloo Letters*, no. 168; Lieutenant General (Lieutenant Colonel and Brevet Colonel at Waterloo) Sir Andrew Barnard, 1st Battalion 95th Rifles, 20 November 1834, *Waterloo Letters*, no. 158; Jackson, *Notes and Reminiscences*, pp. 89–90.

22. Sergeant William Dewar, 1st Battalion 79th Highlanders, 5 August 1815, *Waterloo Archive*, vol. vi, doc. 83.

23. Ensign Edward Macready, 2nd Battalion 30th Foot, (Journal, June 1815), *Waterloo Archive*, vol. vi, doc. 79.

24. Lieutenant George Gunning, 1st (Royal) Dragoons, *Waterloo Archive*, vol. vi, doc. 34.

25. Ensign Edward Macready, 2nd Battalion 30th Foot, (Journal, June 1815), *Waterloo Archive*, vol. vi, doc. 79.

26. Lieutenant James Crummer, 1st Battalion 28th Foot, 4 July 1815, *Waterloo Archive*, vol. vi, doc. 82.

27. First Lieutenant James Gairdner, 1st Battalion 95th Rifles, 19 June 1815, *Waterloo Archive*, vol. vi, doc. 85.

28. Most of the Dutch-Belgians and Hanoverians wore dark blue, the Nassauers dark green, the Brunswickers black. King's German Legion units wore red like the British, apart from their light infantry, which wore dark green.

29. Kincaid, *Adventures*, p. 167.

30. Colonel (Major, 5th West India Regiment and extra aide-de-camp to Sir William Ponsonby at Waterloo) Sir George De Lacy Evans, 1 September 1839, *Waterloo Letters*, no. 31.

31. Jackson, *Notes and Reminiscences*, pp. 89–90.

32. Jackson, *Notes and Reminiscences*, pp. 89–90.

33. Unknown officer, 1st Battalion 95th Rifles, undated but June 1815, *Waterloo Archive*, vol. iv, doc. 90.

34. (Private) A. Cruickshank, 79th Highlanders, September 1839, *Waterloo Letters*, no. 157.

35. Captain (Ensign, 28th Foot at Waterloo) W.F.B. Mountsteven, 19 August 1839, *Waterloo Letters*, no. 151.

36. Major (Lieutenant at Waterloo) Robert Winchester, 92nd Highlanders, 24 November 1834, *Waterloo Letters*, no. 168.

37. Colonel (Brevet Major at Waterloo) E.C. Whinyates, Royal Horse Artillery, 10 March 1841, 20 November 1842, *Waterloo Letters*, nos. 83 and 84; Captain (Lieutenant at Waterloo) F. Warde, Royal Horse Artillery, 27 May (1840), *Waterloo Letters*, no. 86.

38. Lieutenant General (Lieutenant Colonel, 2nd Foot Guards and Assistant Quartermaster General to the 5th Division at Waterloo) Sir William Gomm, 5 January 1837, *Waterloo Letters*, no. 13.

39. Captain (Lieutenant at Waterloo) G.S. Maude, Royal Artillery, 30 December 1834, *Waterloo Letters*, no. 103.

40. General (Major General at Waterloo) Sir James Kempt, Commander 8th Brigade, undated, *Waterloo Letters*, no. 148; Captain J. Kincaid (Lieutenant and Adjutant at Waterloo), 1st Battalion 95th Rifles, 2 May 1839, *Waterloo Letters*, no. 161.

41. The two columns referred to are those of Bourgeois and Donzelot. Marcognet's was opposite Pack's brigade.

42. Jackson, *Notes and Reminiscences*, pp. 89–90.

43. Sergeant William Dewar, 1/79th, 5 August 1815, *Waterloo Archive*, vol. vi, doc. 83.

44. Captain (Ensign 28th Foot at Waterloo) W.F.B. Mountsteven, 19 August 1839, *Waterloo Letters*, no. 151.

45. Kincaid, *Adventures*, pp. 165–7.

46. Lieutenant Colonel (Captain and Brevet Major at Waterloo) J. Leach, 22 November 1840, *Waterloo Letters*, no. 160.

47. Captain (Lieutenant at Waterloo) J.W. Shelton, 28th Foot, 29 September 1839, *Waterloo Letters*, no. 150.

48. Major (Lieutenant at Waterloo) Robert Winchester, 92nd Highlanders, 24 November 1834, *Waterloo Letters*, no. 168.

49. Colonel (Captain 60th Rifles and aide-de-camp to the Earl of Uxbridge at Waterloo) Sir Horace Seymour, 30 November 1842, *Waterloo Letters*, no. 10.

50. Colonel (Captain and Brevet Major at Waterloo) T. Rogers, Royal Artillery, 9 February 1837, *Waterloo Letters*, no. 102.

51. Colonel (Captain 60th Rifles and aide-de-camp to the Earl of Uxbridge at Waterloo) Sir Horace Seymour, 21 November 1842, *Waterloo Letters*, no. 9.

52. General (Major General at Waterloo) Sir James Kempt, Commander 8th Brigade, undated, *Waterloo Letters*, no. 148. According to Kempt, 'The Enemy made three different attempts to carry the position immediately on the left of the road where my Brigade was posted, and were invariably repulsed in the same manner.' This assertion is not corroborated by any other source.

53. Ross-Lewin, *With 'The Thirty-Second'*, p. 272.

54. Unknown officer, 1st Battalion 95th Rifles, undated but June 1815, *Waterloo Archive*, vol. iv, doc. 90.

55. Ross-Lewin, *With 'The Thirty-Second'*, p. 272.

56. Unknown officer, 1st Battalion 95th Rifles, undated but June 1815, *Waterloo Archive*, vol. iv, doc. 90.

57. Lieutenant General (Lieutenant Colonel and Brevet Colonel at Waterloo) Sir Andrew Barnard, 1st Battalion 95th Rifles 20 November 1834, *Waterloo Letters*, no. 158.

58. Lieutenant Colonel (Captain and Brevet Major at Waterloo) J. Leach, 1/95th, 22 November 1840, *Waterloo Letters*, no. 160.

59. (Private) A. Cruickshank, 79th Foot, September 1839, *Waterloo Letters*, no. 157.

60. Captain J. Kincaid (Lieutenant and Adjutant at Waterloo), 1st Battalion 95th Rifles, 2 May 1839, *Waterloo Letters*, no. 161.

61. Ross-Lewin, *With 'The Thirty-Second'*, p. 274; Major (Lieutenant at Waterloo) Robert Winchester, 92nd Highlanders, 24 November 1834, *Waterloo Letters*, no.168.

62. Lieutenant Colonel (Captain and Brevet Major at Waterloo) R. Macdonald, 1st (Royals), 29 December 1838, *Waterloo Letters*, no. 162.

63. Lieutenant Colonel (Captain and Brevet Major at Waterloo) J. Leach, 22 November 1840, *Waterloo Letters*, no. 160.

7. The Charge of the Union and Household Brigades

1. According to one dragoon, Uxbridge issued an order a few days before Waterloo to be read to every cavalry regiment, which included the statement: 'His lordship expected everything from discipline, bravery, and a high sense of honour.' From Hasker's pen, in October 1843, entitled 'Waterloo; Reflections of a Dragoon on the Eve of Battle', *Waterloo Archive*, vol. i, doc. 9.

2. Paymaster (Cornet at Waterloo) W. Crawford, 2nd Dragoons (Scots Greys), 12 June 1839, *Waterloo Letters*, no. 42.

3. Sergeant Archibald Johnston, 2nd Dragoons (Scots Greys), June 1815, *Waterloo Archive*, vol. i, doc. 15.

4. General the Marquess of Anglesey (Lieutenant General the Earl of Uxbridge, commanding the Cavalry at Waterloo), 18 October 1842. *Waterloo Letters*, no. 3.

5. Colonel (Major, 5th West India Regiment and extra aide-de-camp to Sir William Ponsonby at Waterloo) Sir George De Lacy Evans, undated, *Waterloo Letters*, no. 32.

6. Colonel (Captain at Waterloo) A. Clark Kennedy, 1st (Royal) Dragoons, 18 June 1839, *Waterloo Letters*, no. 36.

7. Colonel (Captain at Waterloo) A. Clark Kennedy, 1st (Royal) Dragoons, undated, *Waterloo Letters*, no. 34; Lieutenant Colonel (Lieutenant at Waterloo) C. Wyndham, 2nd Dragoons (Scots Greys), (14 March) 1839, *Waterloo Letters*, no. 41; Captain Charles Radclyffe, 1st (Royal) Dragoons, 7 July 1815, *Waterloo Archive*, vol. i, doc. 11; Lieutenant General (known at Waterloo as Lieutenant Colonel and Colonel J. Muter) Sir Joseph Straton, 6 June 1839, *Waterloo Letters*, no. 43; Captain Charles Radclyffe, 1st (Royal) Dragoons, 4 July 1815, *Waterloo Archive*, vol. i, doc. 10. Clark Kennedy distinctly remembered Picton's infantry crossing the hedges at the time the Union Brigade was forming into line. Colonel (Captain at Waterloo) A. Clark Kennedy, 1st (Royal) Dragoons, 27 July 1839, *Waterloo Letters*, no. 38.

8. Lieutenant Colonel (Major and Lieutenant Colonel at Waterloo) F.S. Miller, 6th (Inniskilling) Dragoons, 11 June 1839, *Waterloo Letters*, no. 45.

9. Colonel (Captain at Waterloo) A. Clark Kennedy, 1st (Royal) Dragoons, 14 July 1839, *Waterloo Letters*, no. 37.

10. Colonel (Captain at Waterloo) A. Clark Kennedy, 1st (Royal) Dragoons, 13 April 1835, *Waterloo Letters*, no. 35.

11. Colonel (Major, 5th West India Regiment and extra aide-de-camp to Sir William Ponsonby at Waterloo) Sir George De Lacy Evans, 1 September 1839, *Waterloo Letters*, no. 31.

12. Colonel (Captain at Waterloo) A. Clark Kennedy, 1st (Royal) Dragoons, 14 July 1839, *Waterloo Letters*, no. 37.

13. Lieutenant Colonel (Captain and Brevet Major at Waterloo) J. Leach, 1st Battalion 95th Rifles, 22 November 1840, *Waterloo Letters*, no. 160.

14. Captain Charles Radclyffe, 1st (Royal) Dragoons, 4 July 1815, *Waterloo Archive*, vol. i, doc. 10.

15. Colonel (Captain at Waterloo) A. Clark Kennedy, 1st (Royal) Dragoons, 14 July 1839, *Waterloo Letters*, no. 37.

16. Captain (Lieutenant at Waterloo) J.W. Shelton, 28th Foot, 29 September 1839, *Waterloo Letters*, no. 150.

17. Colonel (Captain at Waterloo) A. Clark Kennedy, 1st (Royal) Dragoons, undated, *Waterloo Letters*, no. 34.

18. Colonel (Captain at Waterloo) A. Clark Kennedy, 1st (Royal) Dragoons, undated, *Waterloo Letters*, no. 34. The British infantry seen by Ponsonby's brigade reaching the hedge in apparent confusion was in fact simply returning to its former position in order to re-form. See letter no. 38 by the same officer.

19. Colonel (Captain, 60th Rifles and aide-de-camp to the Earl of Uxbridge at Waterloo) Sir Horace Seymour, 21 November 1842, *Waterloo Letters*, no. 9.

20. Major (Lieutenant at Waterloo) Robert Winchester, 92nd Highlanders, 24 November 1834, *Waterloo Letters*, no. 168.

21. Sergeant Archibald Johnston, 2nd Dragoons (Scots Greys), June 1815, *Waterloo Archive*, vol. i, doc. 15; Lieutenant Winchester confirms the cry of 'Scotland forever!' Major (Lieutenant at Waterloo) Robert Winchester, 92nd Highlanders, 24 November 1834, *Waterloo Letters*, no. 168. According to Clark Kennedy of the Royal Dragoons, elements of all three of the Highland regiments, not just the 92nd, may have made their way down the slope with the Union Brigade: 'The Brigade was most gallantly supported by the Infantry, both in advancing and in retiring, by numerous small squares or parties of from ten, to twenty, or thirty men each, who came down the slope of the hill after us. Several of those parties

were Highlanders, but whether 42nd, 79th, or 92nd, I cannot say, perhaps some of them all and other Regts, for as I mentioned in a former letter, troops of various descriptions got mingled together.' Colonel (Captain at Waterloo) A. Clark Kennedy, 1st (Royal) Dragoons, 27 July 1839, *Waterloo Letters*, no. 38.

22. Colonel (Captain at Waterloo) A. Clark Kennedy, 1st (Royal) Dragoons, 28 October 1839, *Waterloo Letters*, no. 39.

23. Lieutenant Colonel (First Lieutenant at Waterloo) William Ingilby, Royal Horse Artillery, 20 November 1834, *Waterloo Letters*, no. 82.

24. Colonel (Captain at Waterloo) A. Clark Kennedy, 1st (Royal) Dragoons, undated, *Waterloo Letters*, no. 34.

25. Captain (Lieutenant at Waterloo) R. Belcher, 32nd Foot, 27 February 1843, *Waterloo Letters*, no. 154.

26. Lieutenant Colonel (Lieutenant at Waterloo) C. Wyndham, 2nd Dragoons (Scots Greys), (14 March) 1839, *Waterloo Letters*, no. 41.

27. Unknown sergeant, 2nd Dragoons (Scots Greys), 25 June 1815, *Waterloo Archive*, vol. i, doc. 14.

28. Sergeant Charles Ewart, 2nd Dragoons (Scots Greys), undated, *Waterloo Archive*, vol. iii, doc. 26.

29. Sergeant Archibald Johnston, 2nd Dragoons (Scots Greys), June 1815, *Waterloo Archive*, vol. i, doc. 15.

30. Cornet James Gape, 2nd Dragoons (Scots Greys), July 1815, *Waterloo Archive*, vol. vi, doc. 41. See also the undated account of Lieutenant Archibald Hamilton of the same regiment, *Waterloo Archive*, vol. vi, doc. 38 and answers to detailed questions put to Lieutenant Charles Wyndham, 13 August 1839, reproduced in *Waterloo Archive*, vol. vi, doc. 37.

31. De Lacy Evans, erroneously stated that the French actually crossed the hedge: 'Our Brigade came up to one hundred yards in rear of the little sunken road and hedge. I communicated the order for this movement myself. We waited there for a few minutes till the head of the Enemy's Column had just crossed the sunken road – as I understood – to allow our Infantry to pass round the flanks of Squadrons, and also that the Enemy should be a little deranged in passing the road, instead of our being so, had we charged across the road.' Colonel (Major, 5th West India Regiment and extra aide-de-camp to Sir William Ponsonby at Waterloo) Sir George De Lacy Evans, 1 September 1839, *Waterloo Letters*, no. 31.

32. Lieutenant Colonel (Major and Lieutenant Colonel at Waterloo) F.S. Miller, 6th (Inniskilling) Dragoons, 18 June 1839, *Waterloo Letters*, no. 46.

33. Lieutenant General (known at Waterloo as Lieutenant Colonel and Colonel J. Muter) Sir Joseph Straton, 17 June 1839, *Waterloo Letters*, no. 44.

34. Colonel (Major, 5th West India Regiment and extra aide-de-camp to Sir William Ponsonby at Waterloo) Sir George De Lacy Evans, 1 September 1839, *Waterloo Letters*, no. 31.

35. General (Major General at Waterloo) Sir James Kempt, commanding 8th Brigade, undated, *Waterloo Letters*, no. 148.

36. Lieutenant General (known at Waterloo as Lieutenant Colonel and Colonel J. Muter) Sir Joseph Straton, 6 June 1839, *Waterloo Letters*, no. 43.

37. Captain Charles Radclyffe, 1st (Royal) Dragoons, 7 July 1815, *Waterloo Archive*, vol. i, doc. 11.

38. Colonel (Captain at Waterloo) A. Clark Kennedy, 1st (Royal) Dragoons, 14 July 1839, *Waterloo Letters*, no. 37. The fact that Styles carried it to the rear has led some sources to claim that he captured it jointly with Clark Kennedy. Thus, Captain Radclyffe 'saw with pride & pleasure Corporal Styles of the Royals bringing away an eagle which he had the good fortune to take'. Captain Charles Radclyffe, 1st (Royal) Dragoons, 7 July 1815, *Waterloo Archive*, vol. i, doc. 11. Captain Charles Methuen, Royal Dragoons also thought Styles and Clark Kennedy took it jointly. Captain Charles Methuen, 1st (Royal) Dragoons, not present at Waterloo, 27 June 1815, *Waterloo Archive*, vol. i, doc. 12. See also Clark Kennedy's brief letter of 26 June, in which he does not mention Styles. Captain A. Clark Kennedy, 1st (Royal) Dragoons, 26 June 1815, *Waterloo Archive*, vol. vi, doc. 33.

39. Colonel (Major, 5th West India Regiment and extra aide-de-camp to Sir William Ponsonby at Waterloo) Sir George De Lacy Evans, undated, *Waterloo Letters*, no. 32.

40. Lieutenant General (known at Waterloo as Lieutenant Colonel and Colonel J. Muter) Sir Joseph Straton, 17 June 1839, *Waterloo Letters*, no. 44.

41. Captain Gronow later wrongly claimed that this proved their undoing: 'When The Earl of Uxbridge gave orders to Sir W. Ponsonby and Lord Edward Somerset to charge the enemy, our cavalry advanced with the greatest bravery, cut through everything in their way, and gallantly attacked whole regiments of infantry; but eventually they came upon a masked battery of twenty guns, which carried death and destruction through our ranks, and our poor fellows were obliged to give way.' Gronow, *Reminiscences*, vol. i, pp. 77–8.

42. Lieutenant Colonel (Lieutenant at Waterloo) W.B. Ingilby, Royal Horse Artillery, 20 November 1834, *Waterloo Letters*, no. 82.

43. According to Wyndham the lancers attacked the wounded on the ground and those otherwise unhurt but unhorsed. Many men received ten or twelve wounds and, in one case a trooper received at least seventeen wounds, yet miraculously survived. Colonel (Captain at Waterloo) A. Clark Kennedy, Royal Dragoons, undated, *Waterloo Letters*, no. 34.

44. Ross-Lewin, *With 'The Thirty-Second'*, p. 274.

45. Colonel (Major, 5th West India Regiment and extra aide-de-camp to Sir William Ponsonby at Waterloo) Sir George De Lacy Evans, 1 September 1839, *Waterloo Letters*, no. 31.

46. Gronow, *Reminiscences*, vol. i, p. 197.

47. Ross-Lewin, *With 'The Thirty-Second'*, p. 274.

48. Colonel (Major, 5th West India Regiment and extra aide-de-camp to Sir William Ponsonby at Waterloo) Sir George De Lacy Evans, 23 August 1842, *Waterloo Letters*, no. 33.

49. Captain Charles Methuen, 1st (Royal) Dragoons, not present at Waterloo, 27 June 1815, *Waterloo Archive*, vol. i, doc. 12.

50. Sergeant Archibald Johnston, 2nd Dragoons (Scots Greys), June 1815, *Waterloo Archive*, vol. i, doc. 15.

51. Sergeant William Clarke, 2nd Dragoons (Scots Greys), 8 July 1815, *Waterloo Archive*, vol. i, doc. 13.

52. Colonel (Major, 5th West India Regiment and extra aide-de-camp to Sir William Ponsonby at Waterloo) Sir George De Lacy Evans, 1 September 1839, *Waterloo Letters*, no. 31. His body was recovered the following day.

53. Sergeant Archibald Johnston, 2nd Dragoons (Scots Greys), June 1815, *Waterloo Archive*, vol. i, doc. 15.

54. Lieutenant Colonel (Lieutenant at Waterloo) C. Wyndham, 2nd Dragoons (Scots Greys), (14 March) 1839, *Waterloo Letters*, no. 41. Cocker and Hoyle were the authors of manuals of cavalry tactics and drill.

55. Tomkinson, *Diary*, pp. 300–1.

56. Major General (Lieutenant Colonel and Colonel, commanding 12th Light Dragoons at Waterloo) Sir Frederick Ponsonby, 29 July 1836, *Waterloo Letters*, no. 57.

57. General (Major General, commanding 4th Cavalry Division at Waterloo) Sir John Vandeleur, undated but *c.* October 1836, *Waterloo Letters*, no. 51.

58. General (Major General, commanding 4th Cavalry Division at Waterloo) Sir John Vandeleur, undated but *c.* October 1836, *Waterloo Letters*, no. 51.

59. Major (Captain, 12th Light Dragoons at Waterloo) A. Barton, 12th Royal Lancers, 3 November 1834, *Waterloo Letters*, no. 58.

60. Major (Captain, 12th Light Dragoons at Waterloo) A. Barton, 12th Royal Lancers, 3 November 1834, *Waterloo Letters*, no. 58.

61. Major General (Lieutenant Colonel and Colonel, commanding 12th Light Dragoons at Waterloo) Sir Frederick Ponsonby, 29 July 1836, *Waterloo Letters*, no. 57.

62. Major (Captain at Waterloo) W. Tomkinson, 16th Light Dragoons, 2 April 1835, *Waterloo Letters*, no. 59.

63. Major (Captain, 12th Light Dragoons at Waterloo) A. Barton, 12th Royal Lancers, 3 November 1834, *Waterloo Letters*, no. 58; Major (Lieutenant and Adjutant at Waterloo) J. Luard, undated, *Waterloo Letters*, no. 61.

64. Major General Sir (Lieutenant Colonel and Colonel Commanding the 12th Light Dragoons at Waterloo) Frederick Ponsonby, 29 July 1836, *Waterloo Letters*, no. 57.

65. See pp. 276–8.

66. See the section, 'Charge of the Household Brigade' below.

67. Colonel (Captain at Waterloo) A. Clark Kennedy, 1st (Royal) Dragoons, 27 July 1839, *Waterloo Letters*, no. 38.

68. Lieutenant George Maule, Royal Artillery, *Waterloo Archive*, vol. i, doc. 30; Colonel (Captain at Waterloo) A. Clark Kennedy, 1st (Royal) Dragoons, 13 April 1835, *Waterloo Letters*, no. 35; Colonel (Major, 5th West India Regiment and extra aide-de-camp to Sir William Ponsonby at Waterloo) Sir George De Lacy Evans, 1 September 1839, *Waterloo Letters*, no. 31; Unknown officer, 1st Battalion 95th Rifles, undated but June 1815, *Waterloo Archive* vol. iv, doc. 90; Lieutenant General (known at Waterloo as Lieutenant Colonel and Colonel J. Muter) Sir Joseph Straton, 6th (Inniskilling) Dragoons), 17 June 1839, *Waterloo Letters*, no. 44; Major (Lieutenant at Waterloo) Robert Winchester, 92nd Highlanders, 24 November 1834, *Waterloo Letters*, no. 168.

69. Lieutenant Colonel (Captain and Brevet Major at Waterloo) R. Macdonald, 1st Foot (Royals), 14 February 1839, *Waterloo Letters*, no. 163; Lieutenant General (known at Waterloo as Lieutenant Colonel and Colonel J. Muter) Sir Joseph Straton, 6th (Inniskilling) Dragoons, 6 June 1839, *Waterloo Letters*, no. 43; Lieutenant Colonel (Major and Lieutenant Colonel at Waterloo) F.S. Miller, 6th (Inniskilling) Dragoons, 11 June 1839, *Waterloo Letters*, no. 45; Colonel (Major, 5th West India Regiment and extra aide-de-camp to Sir William Ponsonby at Waterloo) Sir George De Lacy Evans, 1 September 1839, *Waterloo Letters*, no. 31.

70. Ross-Lewin, *With 'The Thirty-Second'*, p. 274.

71. Lieutenant Archilbald Hamilton, 2nd Dragoons (Scots Greys), 24 June 1815, *Waterloo Archive*, vol. vi, doc. 39.

72. Lieutenant John Sperling, Royal Engineers, 20 June 1815, *Waterloo Archive*, vol. vi, doc. 93. See also, three other descriptions of the atmosphere of panic in Brussels by Edward Heeley, servant of Lieutenant Colonel Sir George Scovell, Assistant Quartermaster General, campaign journal, *Waterloo Archive*, vol. vi, doc. 102; Commissary Tupper Carey, 'Reminiscences', *Waterloo Archive*, vol. vi, doc. 100; Major John Oldfield, Royal Engineers, July 1815, *Waterloo Archive*, vol. vi, doc. 90.

73. Captain Charles Methuen, 1st (Royal) Dragoons, not present at Waterloo, 27 June 1815, *Waterloo Archive*, vol. i, doc. 12. Another source claims 3,000: Lieutenant Archibald Hamilton, 2nd Dragoons (Scots Greys), 24 June 1815, *Waterloo Archive*, vol. vi, doc. 39.

74. Major Miller of the Inniskillings relates a story that suggests the possibility that a third Eagle was taken in the charge, though no such trophy emerged after the battle as proof: 'As to Penhold taking an Eagle, I only know what I *heard* at the time, that he took an Eagle which was by some means dropped or lost, and brought off by a man of the Greys or Royals. But Penn says that Penfold *told* him that after we charged he saw an Eagle, which he rode and seized hold of; that the person who held it would not give it up, and that he dragged him by it for a considerable distance; that the pole broke about the middle and Penfold carried it off; that immediately afterwards he saw Hassard engaged by himself, and went to his assistance, giving the Eagle to a young soldier of the Inniskillings, whose name Penn now forgets; and that a Corporal of the Royals persuaded that young soldier to let him have it, and he carried it off, and Penn says he *saw* an Eagle broken as described going to Brussels with the prisoners.' Lieutenant Colonel (Major and Lieutenant Colonel at Waterloo) F.S. Miller, 6th (Inniskilling) Dragoons, 11 June 1839, *Waterloo Letters*, no. 45.

75. Sergeant Charles Ewart, 2nd Dragoons (Scots Greys), undated, *Waterloo Archive*, vol. iii, doc. 26.

76. Commissary Tupper Carey, 'Reminiscences', *Waterloo Archive*, vol. vi, doc. 100.

77. Gronow, *Reminiscences*, vol. i, p. 189. No French guns were in fact spiked.

78. Captain Charles Methuen 1st (Royal) Dragoons, not present at Waterloo, 27 June 1815, *Waterloo Archive*, vol. i, doc. 12.

79. Lieutenant Colonel (Lieutenant at Waterloo) C. Wyndham, 2nd Dragoons (Scots Greys), (14 March) 1839, *Waterloo Letters*, no. 41.

80. Tomkinson, *Diary*, p. 301.

81. Lieutenant Colonel Muter assumed command of the brigade on Ponsonby's death, but when the former was wounded around 6 p.m. command devolved upon Sir Arthur Clifton. Lieutenant General (known at Waterloo as Lieutenant Colonel and Colonel J. Muter) Sir Joseph Straton, 6th (Inniskilling) Dragoons, 6 June 1839, *Waterloo Letters*, no. 43.

82. Captain Charles Methuen, 1st (Royal) Dragoons, not present at Waterloo, 27 June 1815, *Waterloo Archive*, vol. i, doc. 12.

83. Captain Charles Methuen, 1st (Royal) Dragoons, not present at Waterloo, 27 June 1815, *Waterloo Archive*, vol. i, doc. 12.

84. Lieutenant Colonel (Lieutenant at Waterloo) C. Wyndham, 2nd Dragoons (Scots Greys), (14 March) 1839, *Waterloo Letters*, no. 41.

85. Colonel (Captain, 1st (Royal) Dragoons at Waterloo) A. Clark Kennedy, 7th Dragoon Guards, 18 June 1839, *Waterloo Letters*, no. 36.

86. Major General Sir Hussey Vivian, Commander 6th (Light) Cavalry Brigade, 18 January 1830, *Waterloo Letters*, no. 72.

87. The commanding officer of the Royal Horse Guards stated, more than twenty-five years after the battle, that his regiment fought in the front line and not in the second in support. He claims to have distinctly seen the commanding officer of the 1st Life Guards fall from a shot, which if true does suggest that these regiments were in fact aligned at the start or became so in the course of the charge, which is more likely. General (Captain and Lieutenant Colonel at Waterloo) Clement Hill, Royal Horse Guards, 14 July 1841, *Waterloo Letters*, no. 28. Still, Somerset himself states that the Royal Horse Guards stood in the second line in support. Lieutenant General (Major General, commanding Household Brigade at Waterloo) Lord Edward Somerset, 4 April 1835, *Waterloo Letters*, no. 18.

88. Lieutenant Colonel (Captain at Waterloo) Robert Wallace, 1st (King's) Dragoon Guards, 19 November 1824, *Waterloo Letters*, no. 29.

89. Lieutenant General (Major General, commanding Household Brigade at Waterloo) Lord Edward Somerset, 4 April 1835, *Waterloo Letters*, no. 18

90. Private Thomas Playford, 2nd Life Guards, undated, *Waterloo Archive*, vol. iv, doc. 12.

91. Lady Uxbridge, 26 June 1815, *Waterloo Archive*, vol. iii, doc. 6.

92. Lieutenant General (Major General, commanding Household Brigade at Waterloo) Lord Edward Somerset, 4 April 1835, *Waterloo Letters*, no. 18; Colonel (Captain, 60th Rifles and aide-de-camp to the Earl of Uxbridge at Waterloo) Sir Horace Seymour, 21 November 1842, *Waterloo Letters*, no. 9; Ensign Edward Macready, 2nd Battalion 30th Foot, Journal, June 1815, *Waterloo Archive*, vol. vi, doc. 79; Major John Oldfield, Royal Engineers, July 1815, *Waterloo Archive*, vol. vi, doc. 90. At a trial conducted at Paris, Colonel Hake was cashiered, and as punishment for their cowardice at Waterloo, his regiment was assigned duty as part of the wagon train of the Commissariat. Major (Lieutenant at Waterloo) S. Waymouth, 2nd Life Guards, 2 July 1841, *Waterloo Letters*, no. 24.

93. Major (Lieutenant at Waterloo) S. Waymouth, 2nd Life Guards, 2 July 1841, *Waterloo Letters*, no. 24.

94. Lieutenant General (Major General, commanding Household Brigade at Waterloo) Lord Edward Somerset, 4 April 1835, *Waterloo Letters*, no. 18.

95. Troop Sergeant Major James Page, 1st (King's) Dragoon Guards, 3 July 1815, *Waterloo Archive*, vol. iii, doc. 17.

96. Captain William Elton, 1st (King's) Dragoon Guards, 15 July 1815, *Waterloo Archive*, vol. iv, doc. 13.

97. Lieutenant John Hibbert, 1st (King's) Dragoon Guards, 13 July 1815, *Waterloo Archive*, vol. vi, doc. 29.

98. (Private) A. Cruickshank, 79th Highlanders, September 1839, *Waterloo Letters*, no. 157.

99. Benjamin Haydon, in London, undated, *Waterloo Archive*, vol. i, doc. 74.

100. Lieutenant General (Major General, commanding Household Brigade at Waterloo) Lord Edward Somerset, 4 April 1835, *Waterloo Letters*, no. 18.

101. Benjamin Haydon, in London, undated, *Waterloo Archive*, vol. i, doc. 74.

102. Kincaid, *Adventures*, pp. 165–7.

103. Kincaid, *Adventures*, p. 167.

104. Lieutenant General (Lieutenant Colonel and Brevet Colonel at Waterloo) Sir Andrew Barnard, 1st Battalion 95th Rifles, 20 November 1834, *Waterloo Letters*, no. 158.

105. Major (Lieutenant at Waterloo) S. Waymouth, 2nd Life Guards, 8 April 1837, *Waterloo Letters*, no. 22.

106. Major (Lieutenant at Waterloo) S. Waymouth, 2nd Life Guards, 16 March 1837, *Waterloo Letters*, no. 20.

107. Benjamin Haydon, in London, undated, *Waterloo Archive*, vol. i, doc. 74. Another civilian, also not present in the fighting, claimed that Shaw engaged seven cuirassiers on his own, of whom he killed two and wounded and dismounted the remainder. Edward Heeley, servant of Lieutenant Colonel George Scovell, Assistant Quartermaster General, *Waterloo Archive*, vol. vi, doc. 102.

108. Benjamin Haydon in London, undated, *Waterloo Archive*, vol. i, doc. 74.

109. Colonel Sir John Elley, Deputy Adjutant General, undated, *Waterloo Archive*, vol. vi, doc. 5.

110. Edward Heeley, servant of Lieutenant Colonel Sir George Scovell, Assistant Quartermaster General, *Waterloo Archive*, vol. vi, doc. 102.

111. Private Thomas Playford, 2nd Life Guards, undated, *Waterloo Archive*, vol. iv, doc. 12.

112. Benjamin Haydon, in London, undated, *Waterloo Archive*, vol. i, doc. 74.

113. Major (Lieutenant at Waterloo) S. Waymouth, 2nd Life Guards, 8 April 1837, *Waterloo Letters*, no. 22.

114. Major (Ensign at Waterloo) Thomas Marten, 2nd Life Guards, 23 February 1843, *Waterloo Letters*, no. 27.

115. Major (Lieutenant at Waterloo) S. Waymouth, 2nd Life Guards, 8 April 1837, *Waterloo Letters*, no. 22.

116. Assistant Surgeon John Haddy James, 1st Life Guards, 9 July 1815, *Waterloo Archive*, vol. i, doc. 3.

117. Benjamin Haydon, in London, undated, *Waterloo Archive*, vol. i, doc. 74.

118. Corporal Richard Coulter, 1st Life Guards, 20 July 1815, *Waterloo Archive*, vol. vi, no. 21.

119. Lieutenant General (Major General, commanding the Household Brigade at Waterloo) Lord Edward Somerset, 4 April 1835, *Waterloo Letters*, no. 18.

120. Major (Lieutenant at Waterloo) S. Waymouth, 2nd Life Guards, 16 March 1837, *Waterloo Letters*, no. 20; Lieutenant General (Major General, commanding the Household Brigade at Waterloo) Lord Edward Somerset, 4 April 1835, *Waterloo Letters*, no. 18.

121. Lieutenant General (Major General, commanding the Household Brigade at Waterloo) Lord Edward Somerset, 4 April 1835, *Waterloo Letters*, no. 18.

122. Assistant Surgeon John Haddy James, 1st Life Guards, 9 July 1815, *Waterloo Archive*, vol. i, doc. 3.

123. Major (Lieutenant at Waterloo) S. Waymouth, 2nd Life Guards, 9 May 1837, *Waterloo Letters*, no. 21.

124. Surgeon David Slow, Royal Horse Guards, 21 June 1815, *Waterloo Archive*, vol. vi, doc. 22.

125. Lieutenant General (Major General, commanding the Household Brigade at Waterloo) Lord Edward Somerset, 4 April 1835, *Waterloo Letters*, no. 18.

126. Private Joseph Lord, 2nd Life Guards, 8 August 1815, *Waterloo Archive*, vol. i, doc. 6.

127. Private Joseph Lord, 2nd Life Guards, 3 July 1815, *Waterloo Archive*, vol. i, doc. 5.

128. Major (Lieutenant at Waterloo) S. Waymouth, 2nd Life Guards, 2 July 1841, *Waterloo Letters*, no. 24.

129. Sergeant Thomas Critchley, 1st (Royal) Dragoons, 24 July 1815, *Waterloo Archive*, vol. iv, doc. 15.

8. The French Artillery Bombardment: 'Unceasing Destruction'

1. Lieutenant Colonel Sir Robert Gardiner, Royal Artillery, July 1815, *Waterloo Archive*, vol. iii, doc. 57.

2. Ensign William Thain, 2nd Battalion 33rd Foot, 19 June 1815, *Waterloo Archive*, vol. iv, doc. 69.

3. Lieutenant Colonel Sir John May, Royal Artillery, Assistant Adjutant General, 23 June 1815, *Waterloo Archive*, vol. i, doc. 25; Lieutenant Colonel Sir Augustus Frazer, commanding the Royal Horse Artillery, 25 August 1815, *Waterloo Archive*, vol. vi, doc. 52.

4. Captain and Brevet Major (Major at Waterloo) Robert Bull, Royal Horse Artillery, 24 June 1835, *Waterloo Letters*, no. 78; Colonel (Brevet Major at Waterloo) E.C. Whinyates, Royal Horse Artillery, 10 March 1841, *Waterloo Letters*, no. 83; Captain (Lieutenant at Waterloo) F. Warde, Royal Horse Artillery, 27 May (1840), *Waterloo Letters*, no. 86; Lieutenant W.M. Sharpin, Royal Artillery, 6 December 1834, *Waterloo Letters*, no. 97; Captain (Lieutenant at Waterloo) F. Wells, Royal Atillery, 13 March 1837, *Waterloo Letters*, no. 100.

5. Lieutenant Colonel Sir Augustus Frazer, commanding the Royal Horse Artillery, 19 June 1815, *Waterloo Archive*, vol. iv, doc. 50.

6. Lieutenant Colonel Sir Robert Gardiner, Royal Artillery, July 1815, *Waterloo Archive*, vol. iii, doc. 57.

7. Captain Arthur Kennedy, 18th Hussars, 2 July 1815, *Waterloo Archive*, vol. iv, doc. 28.

8. Captain Horace Churchill, 1st Foot Guards, aide-de-camp to Lord Hill, 24 June 1815, *Waterloo Archive*, vol. vi, doc. 3.

9. Lieutenant Colonel Sir John May, Royal Artillery, Assistant Adjutant General, 23 June 1815, *Waterloo Archive*, vol. iv, doc. 51.

10. Major (Lieutenant, 30th Regiment at Waterloo) John Pratt, late 27th Regiment, 23 March 1835, *Waterloo Letters*, no. n138.

11. Major John Oldfield, Royal Engineers, July 1815, *Waterloo Archive*, vol. vi, doc. 90.

12. Lieutenant Colonel (Captain and Brevet Major at Waterloo) T.W. Taylor, 10th Hussars, November 1829, *Waterloo Letters*, no. 75.

13. First Lieutenant George Simmons, 1st Battalion 95th Rifles, *Waterloo Archive*, vol. iv, doc. 91.

14. Lieutenant Colonel (Major, 23rd Light Dragoons at Waterloo) P.A. Latour, 23rd Lancers, 28 February 1835, *Waterloo Letters*, no. 49.

15. Tomkinson, *Diary of a Cavalry Officer*, p. 306.

16. Kincaid, *Adventures in the Rifle Brigade*, pp. 164–5.

17. Major (Lieutenant and Adjutant at Waterloo) J. Luard, 16th Light Dragoons, undated, *Waterloo Letters*, no. 61.

18. F.H. Pattison, Esq. (Lieutenant, 33rd Foot at Waterloo), 6 December 1842, *Waterloo Letters*, no. 142.

19. Colonel (Captain and Brevet Major at Waterloo) S. Stretton, 40th Foot, 7 February 1837, *Waterloo Letters*, no. 177.

20. Mercer, *Journal*, p. 165.

21. Captain (Lieutenant, Royal Horse Artillery at Waterloo) J.E. Maunsell, Royal Artillery, 30 November 1834, *Waterloo Letters*, no. 93.

22. Colonel (Major and aide-de-camp to The Earl of Uxbridge at Waterloo) W. Thornhill, 7th Hussars, 16 July 1839, *Waterloo Letters*, no. 8.

23. Lieutenant Colonel F.S. Tidy, 3rd Battalion 14th Foot, as told to his daughter, undated, *Waterloo Archive*, vol. i, doc. 49.

24. *Wheatley Diary*, p. 65.

25. Sergeant Archibald Johnston, 2nd Dragoons (Scots Greys), June 1815, *Waterloo Archive*, vol. i, doc. 15.

26. Major General Sir Hussey Vivian, commanding 6th (Light) Cavalry Brigade, 19 June 1815, *Waterloo Archive*, vol. iv, doc. 22.

27. Sergeant Matthew Colgan, 18th Hussars, undated memoirs, *Waterloo Archive*, vol. iv, doc. 33.

28. Private Joseph Lord, 2nd Life Guards, 3 July 1815, *Waterloo Archive*, vol. i, doc. 5.

29. Captain A.C. Mercer, G Troop, Royal Horse Artillery, 14 March 1859, *Waterloo Archive*, vol. i, doc. 28.

30. Mercer, *Journal*, p. 170.

31. Lieutenant Edward Byam, 15th Hussars, 'Extracts from the Troop Order Book of Lieutenant Edward Byam, written at the time', *Waterloo Archive*, vol. i, doc. 18.

32. Lieutenant William Sharpin, Royal Artillery 6 December 1834, *Waterloo Letters*, no. 97.

33. First Lieutenant William Ingilby, Royal Horse Artillery, 18 June 1815, *Waterloo Archive*, vol. vi, doc. 53.

34. Mercer, *Journal*, p. 176.

35. Major (Captain at Waterloo) S. Rudyard, Royal Artillery, 6 January 1835, *Waterloo Letters*, no. 99.

36. Lieutenant Samuel Phelps, Major Lloyd's Battery, Royal Artillery, 18 July 1815, *Waterloo Archive*, vol. iv, doc. 53.

37. Mercer, *Journal*, pp. 166–7.

38. Major (Lieutenant, 13th Light Dragoons at Waterloo) D. Doherty, 27th Foot, 14 November 1834, *Waterloo Letters*, no. 66.

39. *Wheatley Diary*, p. 66.

40. Sergeant Archibald Johnston, 2nd Dragoons (Scots Greys), June 1815, *Waterloo Archive*, vol. i, doc. 15.

41. Henegan, *Seven Years' Campaigning*, vol. ii, p. 332.

42. Major John Oldfield, Royal Engineers, July 1815, *Waterloo Archive*, vol. vi, doc. 90.

43. Edward Heeley, servant of Lieutenant Colonel Sir George Scovell, Assistant Quartermaster General, *Waterloo Archive*, vol. vi, doc. 102.

44. De Lancey, *A Week at Waterloo*, pp. 50, 51, 73, 74, 79–80, 84, 97–8.

45. *Wheatley Diary*, p. 66.

46. Ensign Edward Macready, 2nd Battalion 30th Foot, (Journal, June 1815), *Waterloo Archive*, vol. vi, doc. 79.

47. Lieutenant General (Lieutenant Colonel and Brevet Colonel at Waterloo) Sir Andrew Barnard, 1st Battalion 95th Rifles, 20 November 1834, *Waterloo Letters*, no. 158; Captain Peter Bowlby, 1st Battalion 4th Foot, undated memoirs, *Waterloo Archive*, vol. vi, doc. 89.

48. Edward Heeley, servant of Lieutenant Colonel Sir George Scovell, Assistant Quartermaster General, *Waterloo Archive*, vol. vi, doc. 102.

49. Major General Peregrine Maitland, commanding 1st Brigade, 19 June 1815, *Waterloo Archive*, vol. iv, doc. 54.

50. Major General Peregrine Maitland, commanding 1st Brigade, 19 June 1815, *Waterloo Archive*, vol. iv, doc. 54.

51. Captain Joseph Logan, 2nd Battalion 95th Rifles, 10 July 1815, *Waterloo Archive*, vol. i, doc. 44.

52. Private John Lewis, 2nd Battalion 95th Rifles, 8 July 1815, *Waterloo Archive*, vol. i, doc. 45.

53. Lieutenant Colonel F.S. Tidy, 3rd Battalion 14th Foot, as told to his daughter, undated, *Waterloo Archive*, vol. i, doc. 49.

54. Leeke, *History of Lord Seaton's Regiment*, pp. 221–2. One young officer attributed virtually all the 71st's casualties to shot and shell. Ensign Jack Barnett, 1st Battalion 71st Light Infantry, 31 July 1815, *Waterloo Archive*, vol. vi, doc. 73.

55. Lawrence, *Autobiography*, p. 134.

56. *Wheatley Diary*, p. 66.

57. Gronow, *Reminiscences*, vol. i, p. 69.

58. Ensign Thomas Wedgwood 2nd Battalion 3rd Foot Guards, 24 June 1815, *Waterloo Archive*, vol. i, doc. 39.

59. Lieutenant Colonel Francis Home, 2nd Battalion 3rd Foot Guards (probably) June 1815, *Waterloo Archive*, vol. i, doc. 37.

60. Lieutenant Colonel James Stanhope, 3rd Battalion 1st Foot Guards, *Waterloo Archive*, vol. vi, doc. 59.

61. Brevet Major (Captain at Waterloo) A.C. Mercer, Royal Horse Artillery, 26 November 1834, *Waterloo Letters*, no. 89.

62. Private John Smith, 1st Battalion 71st Foot, 14 July 1815, *Waterloo Archive*, vol. iii, doc. 84.

63. Major (Lieutenant at Waterloo) Robert Winchester, 92nd Highlanders, 24 November 1834, *Waterloo Letters*, no. 168.

64. Gronow, *Reminiscences*, vol. i, pp. 191–2.

65. Colonel (Captain at Waterloo) A. Clark Kennedy, 1st (Royal) Dragoons, undated, *Waterloo Letters*, no. 34.

66. Wheeler, *Letters*, p. 165.

67. Lawrence, *Autobiography*, p. 131.

68. Major General (Lieutenant Colonel at Waterloo) Henry Murray, 18th Hussars, *Waterloo Letters*, no. 76.

69. Paymaster (Cornet at Waterloo) W. Crawford, 2nd Dragoons (Scots Greys), 12 June 1839, *Waterloo Letters*, no. 42.

70. Private Joseph Lord, 2nd Life Guards, 3 July 1815, *Waterloo Archive*, vol. i, doc. 5.

71. Sergeant Archibald Johnston, 2nd Dragoons (Scots Greys), June 1815, *Waterloo Archive*, vol. i, doc. 15.

72. Captain Edward Kelly, 1st Life Guards, 3 July 1815, *Waterloo Archive*, vol. vi, doc. 19; 19 June 1815, *Waterloo Archive*, vol. vi, doc. 13.

73. Lieutenant William Turner, 13th Light Dragoons, 3 July 1815, *Waterloo Archive*, vol. i, doc. 22.

74. Sergeant Archibald Johnston, 2nd Dragoons (Scots Greys), June 1815, *Waterloo Archive*, vol. i, doc. 15.

75. Private Joseph Lord, 2nd Life Guards, 3 July 1815, *Waterloo Archive*, vol. i, doc. 5.

76. Paymaster (Cornet at Waterloo) W. Crawford, 2nd Dragoons (Scots Greys), 12 June 1839, *Waterloo Letters*, no. 42.

77. Sergeant Archibald Johnston, 2nd Dragoons (Scots Greys), June 1815, *Waterloo Archive*, vol. i, doc. 15.

78. Captain William Elton, 1st (King's) Dragoon Guards, 15 July 1815, *Waterloo Archive*, vol. iv, doc. 13.

79. Lieutenant Colonel (Captain at Waterloo) T.W. Robbins, 7th Hussars, 31 March 1835, *Waterloo Letters*, no. 63; Major (Lieutenant, 13th Light Dragoons at Waterloo) D. Doherty, 27th Foot, 14 November 1834, *Waterloo Letters*, no. 66.

80. Lieutenant Colonel (Captain and Brevet Major at Waterloo) T.W. Taylor, 10th Hussars, November 1829, *Waterloo Letters*, no. 75.

81. Private Joseph Lord, 2nd Life Guards, 3 July 1815, *Waterloo Archive*, vol. i, doc. 5.

82. Private Thomas Hasker, 1st (King's) Dragoon Guards, 18 June 1815, *Waterloo Archive*, vol. i, doc. 7.

83. Troop Sergeant Major James Page, 1st (King's) Dragoon Guards, 3 July 1815, *Waterloo Archive*, vol. iii, doc. 17.

84. Assistant Surgeon John Haddy James, 1st Life Guards, 9 July 1815, *Waterloo Archive*, vol. i, doc. 3.

85. Lieutenant Colonel (Major, 23rd Light Dragoons at Waterloo) P.A. Latour, 23rd Lancers, *Waterloo Letters*, 28 February 1835, no. 49; Captain Henry Grove, 23rd Light Dragoons, 18 June 1815, *Waterloo Archive*, vol. vi, doc. 45.

86. Private Thomas Playford, 2nd Life Guards, undated, *Waterloo Archive*, vol. iv, doc. 12.

87. Lieutenant George Packe, 13th Light Dragoons, 20 June 1815, *Waterloo Archive*, vol. iv, doc. 39.

88. Lieutenant George Blathwayt, 23rd Light Dragoons, 1865, *Waterloo Archive*, vol. iii, doc. 53.

89. Private Joseph Lord, 2nd Life Guards, 3 July 1815, *Waterloo Archive*, vol. i, doc. 5.

90. Tomkinson, *Diary*, p. 303.

91. H.M. Leathes, Royal Horse Artillery, 16 March 1859, *Waterloo Archive*, vol. i, doc. 28.

92. Lieutenant General Sir Henry Clinton, commanding 2nd Division, 23 June 1815, *Waterloo Archive*, vol. i, doc. 41.

93. Kincaid, *Adventures*, pp. 169–170.

94. Mercer, *Journal*, p. 165.

95. Mercer, *Journal*, pp. 177–9. See also, Captain A.C. Mercer, G Troop, Royal Horse Artillery, 14 March 1859, *Waterloo Archive*, vol. i, doc. 28.

9. Resisting the Massed French Cavalry Attacks: 'We Stood Like a Rock'

1. Private John Smith, 1st Battalion 71st Light Infantry, 14 July 1815, *Waterloo Archive*, vol. iii, doc. 84.

2. Henegan, *Seven Years' Campaigning*, vol. ii, p. 319.

3. Sources vary as to the timing of the massed French cavalry attacks. Phelps stated it as 2 p.m., while an unidentified officer of the 95th recorded it as 3.30 p.m. Lieutenant Samuel Phelps, Major Lloyd's Battery, Royal Artillery, 18 July 1815, *Waterloo Archive*, vol. iv, doc. 53; Unknown officer, 1st Battalion 95th Rifles, undated but June 1815, *Waterloo Archive*, vol. iv, doc. 90.

4. Mercer is probably the only source which refers to groups of skirmishers sent forward to snipe at his gunners with the intention of provoking them into firing prematurely. Captain A.C. Mercer, G Troop, Royal Horse Artillery, 14 March 1859, *Waterloo Archive*, vol. doc. 28.

5. Unknown officer, 1st Foot Guards, 22 June, *Waterloo Archive*, vol. iv, doc. 63.

6. Captain Courtenay Ilbert, Royal Artillery, 17 June (1815), *Waterloo Archive*, vol. iii, doc. 123.

7. Lawrence, *Autobiography*, p. 134.

8. Private John Lewis, 2nd Battalion 95th Foot, 8 July 1815, *Waterloo Archive*, vol. i, doc. 45.

9. General (Major General at Waterloo) Sir James Kempt, commanding 8th Brigade, undated, *Waterloo Letters*, no. 148.

10. Colonel Colin Campbell, Commandant at Headquarters, 19 June 1815, *Waterloo Archive*, vol. iv, doc. 2.

11. Captain and Lieutenant Colonel Sir Henry Willoughby Rooke, 2nd Battalion 3rd Foot Guards, Assistant Adjutant General, *Waterloo Archive*, vol. i, doc. 1. The attacks continued for about two hours, during the course of which Willoughby Rooke states that the infantry actually advanced and charged supporting columns of French infantry which upon reaching the brow of the hill were driven off by counter-charges. No other source corroborates this claim, however. The infantry remained *in situ* throughout.

12. Lieutenant General Sir Henry Clinton, commanding 2nd Division, 23 June 1815, *Waterloo Archive*, vol. i, doc. 41.

13. Lieutenant John Black, 3rd Battalion 1st Foot, 10 July 1815, *Waterloo Archive*, vol. i, doc. 54.

14. Ensign Edward Macready, 2nd Battalion 30th Foot, 7 July 1815, *Waterloo Archive*, vol. i, doc. 46; Colonel (Lieutenant Colonel at Waterloo) W.K. Elphinstone, 33rd Foot, 28 November 1834, *Waterloo Letters*, no. 140; Lieutenant General (Major General, commanding 5th Infantry Brigade at Waterloo) Sir Colin Halkett, 5 November 1835, *Waterloo Letters*, no. 135; Major (Lieutenant, 30th Regiment at Waterloo), John Pratt, late 27th Regiment, 23 March 1835, *Waterloo Letters*, no. 138.

15. Colonel (Lieutenant Colonel at Waterloo) W.K. Elphinstone, 33rd Foot, 28 November 1834, *Waterloo Letters*, no. 140; Major (Lieutenant, 30th Regiment at Waterloo), John Pratt, late 27th Regiment, 23 March 1835, *Waterloo Letters*, no. 138.

16. General the Marquess of Anglesey (Lieutenant General the Earl of Uxbridge, commanding the Cavalry at Waterloo), 8 November 1839, *Waterloo Letters*, no. 5.

17. Captain A.C. Mercer, G Troop, Royal Horse Artillery, 14 March 1859, *Waterloo Archive*, vol. i, doc. 28. Mercer disregarded Wellington's orders and stayed with his battery. This may be a unique case, for Frazer declared that 'all our guns were repeatedly abandoned but our gallant infantry formed squares, never budged, & after each repulse we returned to our guns again'. Lieutenant Colonel Sir Augustus Frazer, commanding the Horse Artillery, 19 June 1815, *Waterloo Archive*, vol. iv, doc. 50. Lieutenant John Sperling, Royal Engineers, wrote of gunners taking refuge both in the squares or by laying down under their guns: 20 June 1815, *Waterloo Archive*, vol. vi, doc. 93.

18. Lieutenant Colonel (Captain at Waterloo) E.Y. Walcott, Royal Horse Artillery, 18 January 1835, *Waterloo Letters*, no. 80. A lone source on this matter and almost certainly mistaken, Captain Horace Churchill stated a week after the battle that Smith's troop actually remanned their guns and fired at the cavalry while it proceeded between the squares. Captain Horace Churchill, 1st Foot Guards, aide-de-camp to Lord Hill, 24 June 1815, *Waterloo Archive*, vol. vi, doc. 3.

19. Ross-Lewin, *With 'The Thirty-Second'*, p. 271.

20. Colonel (Captain and Brevet Lieutenant Colonel Royal Horse Artillery at Waterloo) Sir Hew Ross, Royal Horse Artillery, 22 March 1841, *Waterloo Letters*, no. 92.

21. Gunner John Edwards, Royal Artillery, 14 July 1815, *Waterloo Archive*, vol. i, doc. 26.

22. *Wheatley Diary*, p. 67.

23. Lieutenant Samuel Phelps, Major Lloyd's Battery, Royal Artillery, 18 July 1815, *Waterloo Archive*, vol. iv, doc. 53.

24. Major (Captain at Waterloo) S. Rudyard, Royal Artillery, 6 January 1835, *Waterloo Letters*, no. 99.

25. Mercer, *Journal*, p. 169.

26. Mercer, *Journal*, pp. 171–3.

27. Mercer, *Journal*, pp. 173–4.

28. Mercer, *Journal*, pp. 174–6. Mercer's lengthy correspondence with Siborne almost twenty years after the battle presents a much-contracted version of the material which later appeared in the former officer's memoirs. See, Brevet Major (Captain at Waterloo) A.C. Mercer, Royal Horse Artillery, 26 November 1834, *Waterloo Letters*, no. 89.

29. *Wheatley Diary*, p. 65.

30. Gronow, *Reminiscences*, vol. i, p. 192.

31. Captain George Barlow, 2nd Battalion 69th Foot, 19 June 1815, *Waterloo Archive*, vol. iv, doc. 75.

32. Captain and Lieutenant Colonel Sir Henry Willoughby Rooke, 2nd Battalion 3rd Foot Guards, Assistant Adjutant General, *Waterloo Archive*, vol. i, doc. 1. The attacks continued for about two hours, during the course of which Rooke states that the infantry actually advanced and charged supporting columns of French infantry which, upon reaching the brow of the hill were driven off by counter-charges. No other source identifies infantry attacking other infantry, although Lieutenant Horton of the 1st Battalion 71st Light Infantry

claimed that his battalion shifted position: '… we advanced in square of regiments; the French cavalry charged us, & we drove them back with immense loss'. Lieutenant George Horton, 1st Battalion 71st Light Infantry, 23 June 1815, *Waterloo Archive*, vol. i, doc. 42.

33. Major General Peregrine Maitland, commanding 1st Brigade, 19 June 1815, *Waterloo Archive*, vol. iv, doc. 54.

34. Gronow, *Reminiscences*, vol. i, p. 72.

35. Kincaid, *Adventures*, p. 169.

36. Lieutenant Donald Mackenzie, 1st Battalion 42nd Foot, undated, *Waterloo Archive*, vol. i, doc. 55.

37. Sergeant Charles Wood, 3rd Battalion 1st Foot Guards, 29 July 1815, *Waterloo Archive*, vol. vi, doc. 63.

38. Ensign Jack Barnett, 1st Battalion 71st Light Infantry, 31 July 1815, *Waterloo Archive*, vol. vi, doc. 73.

39. Captain James Nixon, 1st Foot Guards, 22 June (1815), *Waterloo Archive*, vol. i, doc. 33.

40. Lawrence, *Autobiography*, p. 133.

41. Lawrence, *Autobiography*, p. 134.

42. Henegan, *Seven Years' Campaigning*, vol. ii, pp. 315–17.

43. Private John Smith, 1st Battalion 71st Light Infantry, 14 July 1815, *Waterloo Archive*, vol. iii, doc. 84.

44. Lieutenant John Black, 3rd Battalion 1st Foot, 10 July 1815, *Waterloo Archive*, vol. i, doc. 54.

45. Diary of Captain Digby Mackworth, 7th Foot, aide-de-camp to Lord Hill, 11 p.m. 18 June 1815, *Waterloo Archive*, vol. iv, doc. 5.

46. Major (Lieutenant at Waterloo) R.P. Holmes, 23rd Fusiliers, 20 April 1835, *Waterloo Letters*, no. 131.

47. Colonel (Major and Lieutenant Colonel at Waterloo) S. Rice, 51st Foot, 6 December 1834, *Waterloo Letters*, no. 132.

48. Lieutenant Colonel (Lieutenant at Waterloo) Henry Lane, 15th Hussars, 24 March 1835, *Waterloo Letters*, no. 69.

49. Lieutenant Colonel (Captain at Waterloo) E.Y. Walcott, Royal Horse Artillery, 18 January 1835, *Waterloo Letters*, no. 80.

50. Mercer, *Journal*, p. 176.

51. Wheeler, Private William, *Letters* p. 156.

52. Lieutenant Colonel the Hon. James Stanhope, 1st Foot Guards, 19 June 1815, *Waterloo Archive*, vol. i, doc. 31. Corporal Richard Coulter described Uxbridge as 'everywhere animating his men …' Corporal Richard Coulter, 1st Life Guards, 20 July 1815, *Waterloo Archive*, vol. vi, doc. 21. Captain Thomas Wildman, Uxbridge's aide-de-camp, offered econiums for his commander's conduct: 'His conduct the whole day beggars all description. His arrangements, firmness & intrepidity surpassed what had been expected of him & not in cavalry movements & attacks alone, but he frequently rendered the most judicious and timely assistance in affairs of infantry where any sudden danger was to be apprehended.' Captain Thomas Wildman, 7th Hussars, aide-de-camp to the Earl of Uxbridge, 19 June 1815, *Waterloo Archive*, vol. vi, doc. 4.

53. General the Marquess of Anglesey (Lieutenant General the Earl of Uxbridge, commanding the Cavalry at Waterloo), 8 November 1839, *Waterloo Letters*, no. 5.

54. Lieutenant General Sir Henry Clinton, commanding 2nd Division, 23 June 1815, *Waterloo Archive*, vol. i, doc. 41.

55. Colonel (Major and aide-de-camp to the Earl of Uxbridge at Waterloo) William Thornhill, 7th Hussars, 16 July 1839, *Waterloo Letters*, no. 8.

56. Unknown officer, 13th Hussars, undated, *Waterloo Archive*, vol. i, doc. 23.

57. Lieutenant Standish O'Grady, 7th Hussars, 31 July 1815, *Waterloo Archive*, vol. iii, doc. 54.

58. Brevet Major (Lieutenant, 23rd Light Dragoons at Waterloo) John Banner, 93rd Highlanders, 3 September 1835, *Waterloo Letters*, no. 48.

59. Lieutenant Colonel (Major, 23rd Light Dragoons at Waterloo) P.A. Latour, 23rd Lancers, 28 February 1835, *Waterloo Letters*, no. 49. The Earl of Portalington, Lieutenant Colonel, 23rd Light Dragoons, afflicted by 'a violent bowel attack' on the night of the 17th, was evacuated to Brussels. On recovering lightly and learning of the fighting at Waterloo, he arrived late in the day but, failing to locate his regiment, charged with the 18th Hussars, during which action his horse was severely wounded. Nevertheless, many never forgave his tardiness.

60. Lieutenant Colonel (Major General at Waterloo). J. Thackwell, on behalf of Lieutenant General (Major General at Waterloo) Sir Colquhoun Grant, 9 July 1835, *Waterloo Letters*, no. 62; Lieutenant Colonel (Lieutenant at Waterloo) S. O'Grady, 7th Hussars, 18 March 1835, *Waterloo Letters*, no. 64; Lieutenant Colonel (Lieutenant at Waterloo) A.T. Maclean, 13th Light Dragoons, 4 November 1844, *Waterloo Letters*, no. 67.

61. Lieutenant General (Major General, commanding Household Brigade at Waterloo) Lord Edward Somerset, 4 April 1835, *Waterloo Letters*, no. 18; *Wheatley Diary*, p. 65.

62. General the Marquess of Anglesey (Lieutenant General the Earl of Uxbridge, commanding the Cavalry at Waterloo) 8 November 1839, *Waterloo Letters*, no. 5.

63. Lieutenant General (Assistant Quartermaster General to the Cavalry at Waterloo) Lord Greenock, 21 January 1835, *Waterloo Letters*, no. 7.

64. Captain Arthur Kennedy, 18th Hussars, 2 July 1815, *Waterloo Archive*, vol. iv, doc. 28.

65. Ensign Charles Short, 2nd Battalion Coldstream Guards, 19 June 1815, *Waterloo Archive*, vol. iv, doc. 67.

66. Private Thomas Hasker, 1st (King's) Dragoon Guards, 18 June 1815, *Waterloo Archive*, vol. i, doc. 7.

67. Captain Courtenay Ilbert, Royal Artillery, 17 June (1815), *Waterloo Archive*, vol. iii, doc. 123.

68. Lieutenant Colonel Sir John May, Royal Artillery, Assistant Adjutant General, 23 June 1815, *Waterloo Archive*, vol. iv, doc. 51.

69. Lieutenant William Turner, 13th Light Dragoons, 3 July 1815, *Waterloo Archive*, vol. i, doc. 22.

70. Mercer, *Journal*, p. 167.

71. Lieutenant Edward Byam, 15th Hussars, 18 June 1815, *Waterloo Archive*, vol. i, doc. 18.

72. Lieutenant George Blathwayt, 23rd Light Dragoons, 1865, *Waterloo Archive*, vol. iii, doc. 53.

73. Wheeler, Letters, p. 157.

74. Private John Lewis, 2nd Battalion 95th Rifles, 8 July 1815, *Waterloo Archive*, vol. i, doc. 45.

75. A reference to the Grenadiers à Cheval, the mounted version of the Grenadiers à Pied, both units of the Imperial Guard. The former participated in the massed cavalry assaults. Many contemporary accounts wrongly connect the cuirassiers with the Imperial Guard.

76. Ensign Edward Macready, 2nd Battalion 30th Foot, 7 July 1815, *Waterloo Archive*, vol. i, doc. 46.

77. Captain Joseph Logan, 2nd Battalion 95th Rifles, 10 July 1815, *Waterloo Archive*, vol. i, doc. 44. The general to which he refers is probably Kempt.

78. Lieutenant Colonel Alexander Hamilton, 2nd Battalion 30th Foot, 26 July 1815, *Waterloo Archive*, vol. iii, doc. 86.

79. Lawrence, *Autobiography*, p. 135.

80. Lieutenant Colonel F.S. Tidy 3rd Battalion 14th Foot, as told to his daughter, undated, *Waterloo Archive*, vol. i, doc. 49.

81. Brevet Major (Captain at Waterloo) A.C. Mercer, Royal Horse Artillery, 26 November 1834, *Waterloo Letters*, no. 89.

82. Gronow, *Reminiscences*, vol. i, pp. 69–73.

83. Gronow, *Reminiscences*, vol. i, pp. 190–1.

84. Private John Smith, 1st Battalion 71st Foot, 14 July 1815, *Waterloo Archive*, vol. iii, doc. 84; Lieutenant John Sperling, accompanying Lieutenant Colonel James Carmichael Smyth, Royal Engineers on Wellington's staff, observed how the various cavalry charges required

staff officers to seek refuge in the squares. Lieutenant John Sperling, Royal Engineers, 20 June 1815, *Waterloo Archive*, vol. vi, doc. 93.

85. Gronow, *Reminiscences*, vol. i, p. 70.
86. Lieutenant Colonel (Major, 73rd Foot and Assistant Quartermaster General at Waterloo) Dawson Kelly, 26 November 1834, *Waterloo Letters*, no. 145.
87. Gronow, *Reminiscences*, vol. i, p. 190.
88. Cotton, *A Voice from Waterloo*, pp. 42–3.
89. *Wheatley Diary*, p. 66.
90. Wheeler, *Letters*, p. 162.
91. Colonel Colin Campbell, Commandant at Headquarters, 19 June 1815, *Waterloo Archive*, vol. iv, doc. 2.
92. Private Henry Swan, 3rd Battalion 1st Foot Guards, undated, *Waterloo Archive*, vol. iv, doc. 64.
93. Ensign Charles Short, 2nd Battalion Coldstream Guards, 19 June 1815, *Waterloo Archive*, vol. iv, doc. 67.
94. Ensign William Thain, 33rd Foot, 18 June 1815, *Waterloo Archive*, vol. vi, doc. 81.
95. Lieutenant Colonel James Stanhope, 1st Foot Guards, 19 June 1815, *Waterloo Archive*, vol. i, doc. 31.
96. Lieutenant Colonel Sir Augustus Frazer, commanding the Royal Horse Artillery, 19 June 1815, *Waterloo Archive*, vol. iv, doc. 50.
97. Major General Peregrine Maitland, commanding 1st Brigade, 19 June 1815, *Waterloo Archive*, vol. iv, doc. 54.
98. Lieutenant Colonel James Stanhope, 1st Foot Guards, 19 June 1815, *Waterloo Archive*, vol. i, doc. 31.
99. Captain James Nixon, 1st Foot Guards, 19 June 1815, *Waterloo Archive*, vol. i, doc. 32.

10. The Fall of La Haye Sainte and the Struggle for Plancenoit

1. Kincaid, *Adventures in the Rifle Brigade*, p. 168.
2. Lieutenant Colonel (Captain and Brevet Major at Waterloo) J. Leach, 22 November 1840, *Waterloo Letters*, no. 160.
3. Captain (Lieutenant at Waterloo) F. Warde, Royal Horse Artillery, 27 May (1840), *Waterloo Letters*, no. 86.
4. Colonel (Captain and Brevet-Lieutenant Colonel Royal Horse Artillery at Waterloo) Sir Hew Ross Royal Horse Artillery, 27 January 1835, *Waterloo Letters*, no. 91.
5. Lieutenant General (Major General, commanding 5th Infantry Brigade at Waterloo) Sir Colin Halkett, 5 November 1835, *Waterloo Letters*, no. 135.
6. Major (Lieutenant at Waterloo) Robert Winchester, 92nd Highlanders, 24 November 1834, *Waterloo Letters*, no. 168.
7. Lieutenant General (Lieutenant Colonel and Brevet Colonel at Waterloo) Sir Andrew Barnard, 1st Battalion 95th Rifles, 20 November 1834, *Waterloo Letters*, no. 158.
8. Ensign James Howard, 33rd Foot, 8 July 1815, *Waterloo Archive*, vol. i, doc. 47.
9. Tomkinson, *Diary*, p. 303.
10. Ross-Lewin, *With 'The Thirty-Second'*, pp. 275–7.
11. Lieutenant General (Major General and commander of the Household Brigade at Waterloo) Lord Edward Somerset, 4 April 1835, *Waterloo Letters*, no. 18.
12. Captain George Barlow, 2nd Battalion 69th Foot, 19 June (1815), *Waterloo Archive*, vol. iv, doc. 76.

11. The Continuing Defence of Hougoumont

1. Major General (Captain and Lieutenant Colonel at Waterloo) Lord Saltoun, 1st Foot Guards, 29 January 1838, *Waterloo Letters*, no. 106.
2. Lieutenant Colonel and Colonel (Lieutenant and Captain, 1st Foot Guards at Waterloo) Robert Ellison, Grenadier Guards, 1 March 1835, *Waterloo Letters*, no. 249.
3. Major General (Major and Lieutenant Colonel at Waterloo) Francis Hepburn, 3rd Foot Guards, 22 November 1834, *Waterloo Letters*, no. 117.
4. Lieutenant Colonel Francis Home, 2nd Battalion 3rd Foot Guards, (probably) June 1815, *Waterloo Archive*, vol. i, doc. 37.
5. These are of course approximate, as are those of the French, and do not represent the unknown numbers of casualties sustained at this point.
6. Major General (Major and Lieutenant Colonel at Waterloo) Francis Hepburn, 3rd Foot Guards, 22 November 1834, *Waterloo Letters*, No. 117.
7. Wheeler, *Letters*, p. 173.
8. Gronow, *Reminiscences*, vol. i, p. 199.
9. Major General John Byng, commanding 2nd Brigade of Guards, 19 June 1815, *Waterloo Archive*, vol. iv, doc. 65.
10. This has not been substantiated by any other known source.
11. Ensign Thomas Wedgwood, 2nd Battalion 3rd Foot Guards, 19 June 1815, *Waterloo Archive*, vol. i, doc. 38.
12. Colonel (Captain, 60th Rifles and aide-de-camp to the Earl of Uxbridge at Waterloo) Sir Horace Seymour, 21 November 1842, *Waterloo Letters*, no. 9.
13. Quoted in Adkin, *Waterloo Companion*, p. 335.
14. Clay, *Narrative*, p. 27.
15. Home wrongly asserts that this was 1,200. Lieutenant Colonel Francis Home, 2nd Battalion 3rd Foot Guards (probably) June 1815, *Waterloo Archive*, vol. i, doc. 37.

12. Repulse of the Imperial Guard and the Anglo-Allied Advance: 'The Crisis of This Eventful Day'

1. Captain George Barlow, 2nd Battalion 69th Foot, 19 June (1815), *Waterloo Archive*, vol. iv, doc. 76.
2. Lieutenant Colonel Sir Robert Gardiner, Royal Artillery, July 1815, *Waterloo Archive*, vol. iii, doc. 57.
3. Major General (Lieutenant Colonel, 2nd Foot Guards and aide-de-camp to the Duke of Wellington at Waterloo) John Fremantle, 20 November 1842, *Waterloo Letters*, no. 11; Colonel (Captain, 60th Rifles and aide-de-camp to Lord Uxbridge at Waterloo) Sir Horace Seymour, 21 November 1842, *Waterloo Letters*, no. 9; 30 November 1842, *Waterloo Letters*, no. 10.
4. Lieutenant General Sir Henry Clinton, commanding 2nd Division, 23 June 1815, *Waterloo Archive*, vol. i, doc. 41.
5. Mercer, *Journal*, pp. 177–8.
6. Ross-Lewin, *With 'The Thirty-Second'*, pp. 277–8.
7. Captain (Lieutenant and Captain at Waterloo) H.W. Powell, 1st Foot Guards, 21 April 1835, *Waterloo Letters*, no. 108.
8. Lieutenant General (Major General, commanding 3rd Infantry Brigade at Waterloo) Frederick Adam undated, possibly 1838, *Waterloo Letters*, no. 120; Lieutenant General

(Lieutenant Colonel and Colonel Sir John Colborne at Waterloo) Lord Seaton, 52nd Foot, 22 February 1843, *Waterloo Letters*, no. 123; Colonel (Major and Brigade Major, Adam's Brigade at Waterloo) Thomas Hunter Blair, 52nd Foot, 29 November 1835, *Waterloo Letters*, no. 122.

9. Lieutenant General (Major General at Waterloo) Sir Peregrine Maitland, commanding 1st Infantry Brigade, 24 November 1834, *Waterloo Letters*, no. 105.

10. Lieutenant General (Assistant Quartermaster General, Cavalry at Waterloo) Lord Greenock, 21 January 1835, *Waterloo Letters*, no. 7; Colonel (Lieutenant Colonel at Waterloo) W.K. Elphinstone, 33rd Foot, 28 November 1834, *Waterloo Letters*, no. 140.

11. Tomkinson, *Diary*, p. 310; Ross-Lewin, *With 'The Thirty-Second'*, p. 278; Lieutenant General Sir Henry Clinton, commanding 2nd Division, 23 June 1815, *Waterloo Archive*, vol. i, doc. 41; Lieutenant General (Lieutenant Colonel, 2nd Foot Guards and Assistant Quartermaster General, 5th Division at Waterloo) Sir William Gomm, 5 January 1837, *Waterloo Letters*, no. 13; Lieutenant Colonel (Lieutenant, 6th Dragoon Guards and extra aide-de-camp to the Duke of Wellington at Waterloo) George Cathcart, 8th Foot, 24 December 1835, *Waterloo Letters*, no. 16; Lieutenant General (Major General at Waterloo) Sir Peregrine Maitland, commanding 1st Infantry Brigade, 24 November 1834, *Waterloo Letters*, no. 105.

12. Unknown officer, 1st Guards, 22 June, *Waterloo Archive*, vol. iv, doc. 63; Ensign Charles Short, 2nd Battalion Coldstream Guards, 19 June 1815, *Waterloo Archive*, vol. iv, doc. 67; Captain and Lieutenant Colonel Sir Henry Willoughby Rooke, 2nd Battalion 3rd Foot Guards, Assistant Adjutant General, *Waterloo Archive*, vol. i, doc. 1; Colonel Colin Campbell, Commandant at Headquarters, 19 June 1815, *Waterloo Archive*, vol. iv, doc. 2.

13. Henegan, *Seven Years' Campaigning*, vol. ii, p. 325.

14. Colonel (Lieutenant Colonel at Waterloo) W.K. Elphinstone, 33rd Foot, 28 November 1834, *Waterloo Letters*, no. 140.

15. Captain George Barlow, 2nd Battalion 69th Foot, 19 June (1815), *Waterloo Archive*, vol. iv, doc. 76.

16. Ensign Edward Macready, 2nd Battalion 30th Foot, *Waterloo Archive*, (Journal, June 1815), vol. vi, doc. 79.

17. Lieutenant W.M. Sharpin, Royal Artillery, 6 December 1834, *Waterloo Letters*, no. 97.

18. Captain (Lieutenant at Waterloo) G. Pringle, Royal Artillery, 25 November 1834, *Waterloo Letters*, no. 96.

19. Major (Ensign at Waterloo) Edward Macready, 30th Foot, 30 November 1836, *Waterloo Letters*, no. 139.

20. Lieutenant Colonel (Major, 73rd Foot and Assistant Quartermaster General at Waterloo) Dawson Kelly, 14 October 1835, *Waterloo Letters*, no. 146.

21. Lieutenant Colonel (Major, 73rd Foot and Assistant Quartermaster General at Waterloo) Dawson Kelly, 26 November 1834, *Waterloo Letters*, no. 145.

22. Lieutenant General (Major General, commanding 5th Infantry Brigade at Waterloo) Sir Colin Halkett, 5 November 1835, *Waterloo Letters*, no. 135.

23. Lieutenant Colonel (Major, 73rd Foot and Assistant Quartermaster General at Waterloo) Dawson Kelly, 26 November 1834, *Waterloo Letters*, no. 145.

24. Colonel (Lieutenant Colonel at Waterloo) W.K. Elphinstone, 33rd Foot, 28 November 1834, *Waterloo Letters*, no. 140.

25. Captain (Lieutenant at Waterloo) F. Wells, Royal Artillery, 13 March 1837, *Waterloo Letters*, no. 100.

26. Major (Ensign at Waterloo) Edward Macready, 30th Foot, 30 November 1836, *Waterloo Letters*, no. 139.

27. Lieutenant (Lieutenant 69th Foot at Waterloo) H. Anderson, 75th Foot, 18 November 1835, *Waterloo Letters*, no. 144.

28. Quoted in Adkin, *Waterloo Companion*, p. 397.

29. Gronow, *Reminiscences*, vol. i, p. 73.

30. Captain (Lieutenant and Captain at Waterloo) H.W. Powell, 1st Foot Guards, 21 April 1835, *Waterloo Letters*, no. 108.

31. Henegan, *Seven Years' Campaigning*, vol. ii, p. 326.

32. Ensign Joseph St John, 2nd Battalion 1st Foot Guards, 22 June 1815, *Waterloo Archive*, vol. vi, doc. 55.

33. Captain (Lieutenant and Captain at Waterloo) H.W. Powell, 1st Foot Guards, 21 April 1835, *Waterloo Letters*, no. 108.

34. Major General (Captain and Lieutenant Colonel at Waterloo) Lord Saltoun, 1st Foot Guards, 29 January 1838, *Waterloo Letters*, no. 106.

35. Private Henry Swan, 3rd Battalion 1st Foot Guards, undated, *Waterloo Archive*, vol. iv, doc. 64.

36. Lieutenant and Captain James Nixon, 1st Foot Guards, 22 June (1815), *Waterloo Archive*, vol. i, doc. 33.

37. Lieutenant and Captain James Nixon, 1st Foot Guards, 19 June (1815), *Waterloo Archive*, vol. i, doc. 32.

38. Unknown officer, 1st Guards, 22 June (1815), *Waterloo Archive*, vol. iv, doc. 63.

39. Major General John Byng, commanding 2nd Brigade of Guards, 19 June 1815, *Waterloo Archive*, vol. iv, doc. 65; Captain and Lieutenant Colonel Sir Henry Willoughby Rooke, 2nd Battalion 3rd Foot Guards Assistant Adjutant General, *Waterloo Archive*, vol. i, doc. 1.

40. Captain William Walton, Acting Adjutant, 2nd Battalion Coldstream Guards, 22 June 1815, *Waterloo Archive*, vol. vi, doc. 67.

41. Captain George Bowles, 2nd Battalion Coldstream Guards, 19 June 1815, *Waterloo Archive*, vol. vi, doc. 65.

42. Major John Oldfield, Royal Engineers, July 1815, *Waterloo Archive*, vol. vi, doc. 90.

43. Lieutenant Colonel James Stanhope, 3rd Battalion 1st Foot Guards, 19 June 1815, *Waterloo Archive*, vol. vi, doc. 62.

44. Lieutenant Colonel (Lieutenant and Captain at Waterloo) H. Davis, 1st Foot Guards, *Waterloo Letters*, 19 March 1835, no. 110.

45. Ensign Charles Short, 2nd Battalion Coldstream Guards, 19 June 1815, *Waterloo Archive*, vol. iv, doc. 67.

46. Henegan, *Seven Years' Campaigning*, vol. ii, p. 326.

47. Major General Peregrine Maitland, commanding 1st Brigade, 19 June 1815, *Waterloo Archive*, vol. iv, doc. 54.

48. Gronow, *Reminiscences*, vol. i, p. 190.

49. Lieutenant Colonel Lord Saltoun, 3rd Battalion 1st Foot Guards, 22 June 1815, *Waterloo Archive*, vol. vi, doc. 57.

50. Sergeant Charles Wood, 3rd Battalion 1st Foot Guards, 29 July 1815, *Waterloo Archive*, vol. vi, doc. 63.

51. Henegan, *Seven Years' Campaigning*, vol. ii, p. 326; Major General John Byng, commanding 2nd Brigade of Guards, 19 June 1815, *Waterloo Archive*, vol. iv, doc. 65.

52. Gronow, *Reminiscences*, vol. i. pp. 73–4.

53. Captain and Lieutenant Colonel (Ensign at Waterloo) J.P. Dirom, 1st Foot Guards, *Waterloo Letters*, no. 111.

54. Major General (Captain and Lieutenant Colonel at Waterloo) Lord Saltoun, 1st Foot Guards, 29 January 1838, *Waterloo Letters*, no. 106.

55. Lieutenant General (Major General at Waterloo) Sir Peregrine Maitland, commanding 1st Infantry Brigade, 24 November 1834, *Waterloo Letters*, no. 105.

56. Lieutenant General (Major General, commanding 3rd Infantry Brigade at Waterloo) Frederick Adam, undated (1838), *Waterloo Letters*, no. 120; Lieutenant Colonel (Captain and Brevet Major at Waterloo) W. Eeles, 95th Rifles, 22 December 1834. *Waterloo Letters*, no. 129; Colonel (Major and Brigade Major, Adam's Brigade at Waterloo) Thomas Hunter Blair, 52nd Foot, 29 November 1835, *Waterloo Letters*, no. 122; (Captain) (Captain at Waterloo) T.R. Budgen, 95th Rifles, (17 December 1834), *Waterloo Letters*, no.127.

57. Lieutenant Colonel (Captain at Waterloo) E.Y. Walcott, Royal Horse Artillery, 18 January 1835, *Waterloo Letters*, no. 80.
58. (Captain) (Captain at Waterloo) T.R. Budgen, 95th Rifles, 17 December 1834, *Waterloo Letters*, no. 127.
59. Lieutenant General (Major General commanding 3rd Infantry Brigade at Waterloo) Frederick Adam, undated, possibly 1838, *Waterloo Letters*, no. 120.
60. Tomkinson, *Diary*, pp. 310–11.
61. Lieutenant Colonel James Stanhope, 3rd Battalion 1st Foot Guards, *Waterloo Archive*, vol. vi, doc. 59.
62. Lieutenant General (Lieutenant Colonel and Colonel Sir John Colborne at Waterloo) Lord Seaton, 52nd Foot, 24 February 1843, *Waterloo Letters*, no. 123.
63. Lieutenant General (Major General commanding 3rd Infantry Brigade at Waterloo) Frederick Adam undated, possibly 1838, *Waterloo Letters*, no. 120.
64. Tomkinson, *Diary*, p. 315.
65. Lieutenant General Lord Seaton (Lieutenant Colonel and Colonel Sir John Colborne at Waterloo), 52nd Foot, 22 February 1843, *Waterloo Letters*, no. 123. Colborne was sensitive to the fact that in later years the Guards received greater credit for the repulse of the Imperial ' Guard than the 52nd Foot.'... I am persuaded several absurd blunders and stories have originated from the movements of the 52nd, and General Adam's Brigade, having been misrepresented', Colborne told Siborne. See also Lieutenant Colonel G. Gawler (Lieutenant at Waterloo) 52nd Foot, 22 December 1834, *Waterloo Letters*, no. 124.
66. Colonel (Major and Brigade Major to Adam's Brigade at Waterloo) Thomas Hunter Blair, 52nd Foot, 29 November 1835, *Waterloo Letters*, no. 122.
67. Captain Joseph Logan, 2nd Battalion 95th Rifles, 10 July 1815, *Waterloo Archive*, vol. i, doc. 44.
68. Lieutenant General Sir Henry Clinton, commanding 2nd Division, 23 June 1815, *Waterloo Archive*, vol. i, doc. 41.
69. Major General (Captain and Lieutenant Colonel at Waterloo) Lord Saltoun, 1st Foot Guards, 29 January 1838, *Waterloo Letters*, no. 106.
70. (Captain) (Captain at Waterloo) T.R. Budgen, 95th Rifles, 17 December (1834), *Waterloo Letters*, no. 127.
71. Captain (Lieutenant and Captain at Waterloo) H.W. Powell, 1st Foot Guards, 21 April 1835, *Waterloo Letters*, no. 108.
72. Smith, *Autobiography*, p, 271.
73. Unknown officer, 1st Battalion 95th Rifles, undated, *Waterloo Archive*, vol. iv, doc. 90.
74. Ensign Thomas Wedgwood, 2nd Battalion 3rd Foot Guards, 19 June 1815, *Waterloo Archive*, vol. i, doc. 38.
75. Lieutenant Richard Cocks Eyre, 2nd Battalion 95th Rifles, 28 June 1815, *Waterloo Archive*, vol. iii, doc. 85.
76. Lieutenant and Captain James Nixon, 1st Foot Guards, 19 June (1815), *Waterloo Archive*, vol. i, doc. 32.
77. Ensign Thomas Wedgwood, 2nd Battalion 3rd Foot Guards, 19 June 1815, *Waterloo Archive*, vol. i, doc. 38.
78. Lieutenant General (Major General at Waterloo, Sir Peregrine Maitland, Commanding 1st Infantry Brigade, 24 November 1834, *Waterloo Letters*, no. 105; Major (Captain at Waterloo) S. Reed, 71st Foot, 10 November 1834, *Waterloo Letters*, no. 126.
79. Lieutenant Colonel (Captain and Brevet Major at Waterloo) J. Leach, 95th Rifles, 22 November 1840, *Waterloo Letters*, no. 160; Lieutenant General (Major General Commanding 10th Brigade at Waterloo) Sir John Lambert, 18 December 1834, *Waterloo Letters*, no. 170.
80. Brevet Major (Captain at Waterloo) A.C. Mercer, Royal Horse Artillery, 26 November 1834, *Waterloo Letters*, no. 89; Colonel (Captain and Brevet Lieutenant Colonel at Waterloo) Sir Hew Ross, Royal Horse Artillery, 27 January 1835, *Waterloo Letters*, no. 91; Captain

(Lieutenant, Royal Horse Artillery at Waterloo) J.E. Maunsell, Royal Artillery, 30 November 1834, *Waterloo Letters*, no. 93; Colonel (Captain and Brevet Major at Waterloo) T. Rogers, Royal Artillery, 9 February 1837, *Waterloo Letters*, no. 102; Captain (Lieutenant at Waterloo) G.S. Maude, Royal Artillery, 30 December 1834, *Waterloo Letters*, no. 103.

81. Brevet Major (Captain at Waterloo) A.C. Mercer, Royal Horse Artillery, 26 November 1834, *Waterloo Letters*, no. 89.

82. Captain and Brevet Major (Major at Waterloo) Robert Bull, Royal Horse Artillery, 24 June 1835, *Waterloo Letters*, no. 78; Lieutenant Colonel (Lieutenant at Waterloo) W.B. Ingilby, Royal Horse Artillery, 20 November 1834, *Waterloo Letters*, no. 82.

83. Kincaid, *Adventures*, pp. 170–1.

84. Ross-Lewin, *With 'The Thirty-Second'*, p. 280.

85. Lieutenant General Sir Henry Clinton, Commander 2nd Division, 23 June 1815, *Waterloo Archive*, vol. i, doc. 41.

86. Brevet Major (Captain at Waterloo) A.C. Mercer, Royal Horse Artillery, 26 November 1834, *Waterloo Letters*, no. 89.

87. Lieutenant Colonel (Lieutenant at Waterloo) W.B. Ingilby, Royal Horse Artillery, 20 November 1834, *Waterloo Letters*, no. 82.

88. Major (Captain, 12th Light Dragoons at Waterloo) A. Barton, 12th Royal Lancers, 3 November 1834, *Waterloo Letters*, no. 58.

89. Private John Smith, 1st Battalion 71st Foot, 14 July 1815, *Waterloo Archive*, vol. iii, doc. 84.

90. Colonel (Lieutenant Colonel at Waterloo) W.K. Elphinstone, 33rd Foot, 28 November 1834, *Waterloo Letters*, no. 140. Lieutenant Colonel (Major 73rd Foot and Assistant Quartermaster General at Waterloo) Dawson Kelly, 14 October, 26 November 1834, *Waterloo Letters*, nos. 145, 146; Major General (Lieutenant Colonel and Colonel Thomas Reynell at Waterloo) Sir Thomas Reynell, 71st Foot, 15 November 1834, *Waterloo Letters*, no. 125.

91. (Captain) (Captain at Waterloo) T.R. Budgen, 95th Rifles, 17 December (1834), *Waterloo Letters*, no. 127.

92. Lieutenant General (Major General, commanding 3rd Infantry Brigade at Waterloo) Frederick Adam, undated, possibly 1838, *Waterloo Letters*, no. 120.

93. Lieutenant General Lord Seaton, (Lieutenant Colonel and Colonel Sir John Colborne at Waterloo) 52nd Foot, 22 February 1843, *Waterloo Letters*, no. 123.

94. Quoted in Adkin, *Waterloo Companion*, p. 399.

95. Major (Captain at Waterloo) S. Reed, 71st Foot, 10 November 1834, *Waterloo Letters*, no. 126.

96. Other accounts claim he simply shouted, '*Merde!*' It may be of note that Ensign Macready refers to this incident in his campaign journal, i.e. a contemporary account, but this alone does not confirm the story – only that the accounts are not the invention of a later period. Ensign Edward Macready, 2nd Battalion 30th Foot, (Journal, June 1815), *Waterloo Archive*, vol. vi, doc. 79. See also Appendix XII.

97. General (Lieutenant Colonel, commanding a Hanoverian brigade at Waterloo) William Halkett, Hanoverian Service, 20 December 1837, *Waterloo Letters*, no. 130; see also Gronow, *Reminiscences*, vol. i. pp. 73, 74.

98. Undated Report of Lieutenant Colonel Sir George Scovell, Assistant Quarter Master General, undated, *Waterloo Archive*, vol. iii, doc. 1; Ensign William Thain, 2nd Battalion 33rd Foot, 19 June 1815, *Waterloo Archive*, vol. iv, doc. 69.

99. Gronow, *Reminiscences*, vol. i. p. 74.

100. Major General Sir Hussey Vivian, Commander 6th Brigade, 14 February 1837, *Waterloo Archive*, vol. iv, doc. 23; Lieutenant General (Assistant Quartermaster General to the Cavalry at Waterloo) Lord Greenock, 21 January 1835, *Waterloo Letters*, no. 7; Colonel (Captain 60th Rifles and aide-de-camp to the Earl of Uxbridge at Waterloo) Sir Horace Seymour, 21 November 1842, *Waterloo Letters*, no. 9.

101. Lieutenant General (Assistant Quartermaster General to the Cavalry at Waterloo) Lord Greenock, 21 January 1835, *Waterloo Letters*, no. 7.
102. Major (Captain, 12th Light Dragoons at Waterloo) A. Barton, 12th Royal Lancers, 3 November 1834, *Waterloo Letters*, no. 58.
103. Lieutenant Colonel (Major, 23rd Light Dragoons at Waterloo) P.A. Latour, 23rd Lancers, 28 February 1835, *Waterloo Letters*, no. 49.
104. General (Major General, commanding 4th Cavalry Division at Waterloo) Sir John Vandeleur, (undated, *c.* October 1836), *Waterloo Letters*, no. 51.
105. Lieutenant General (Lieutenant Colonel, commanding 11th Light Dragoons at Waterloo), J.W. Sleigh, 11 November 1841, *Waterloo Letters*, no. 53.
106. Major (Captain, 12th Light Dragoons at Waterloo) A. Barton, 12th Royal Lancers, 3 November 1834, *Waterloo Letters*, no. 58.
107. Major (Captain at Waterloo) W. Tomkinson, 16th Light Dragoons, *Waterloo Letters*, no. 59; Major (Lieutenant and Adjutant at Waterloo) J. Luard, 16th Light Dragoons, undated, *Waterloo Letters*, no. 61.
108. Major General Sir Hussey Vivian, commanding 6th (Light) Cavalry Brigade, 3 June 1839, *Waterloo Letters*, no. 71; also, 18 January 1830, no. 72.
109. Lieutenant Colonel Henry Murray, 18th Hussars, undated, *Waterloo Archive*, vol. iv, doc. 24.
110. Major General Sir Hussey Vivian, commanding 6th (Light) Cavalry Brigade, 23 June 1815, *Waterloo Letters*, no. 70.
111. Major General Sir Hussey Vivian, commanding 6th (Light) Cavalry Brigade, 27 November 1841, *Waterloo Letters*, no. 74.
112. Major General (Lieutenant Colonel at Waterloo) Henry Murray, 18th Hussars, *Waterloo Letters*, no. 76.
113. Lieutenant Colonel (Captain and Brevet Major at Waterloo) T.W. Taylor, 10th Hussars, November 1829, *Waterloo Letters*, no. 75.
114. Major General Sir Hussey Vivian, commanding 6th (Light) Cavalry Brigade, 23 June 1815, *Waterloo Archive*, vol. iv, doc. 21.
115. Major General Sir Hussey Vivian, commanding 6th (Light) Cavalry Brigade, 19 June 1815, *Waterloo Archive*, vol. iv, doc. 22.
116. Lieutenant Colonel Henry Murray, 18th Hussars, undated, *Waterloo Archive*, vol. iv, doc. 24.
117. Lieutenant and Adjutant Henry Duperier, 18th Hussars, 19 June 1815, *Waterloo Archive*, vol. iii, doc. 56.
118. Captain Arthur Kennedy, 18th Hussars, 2 July 1815, *Waterloo Archive*, vol. iv, doc. 28.
119. Lieutenant Colonel (Lieutenant and Brevet Major at Waterloo) T.W. Taylor, 10th Hussars, *Waterloo Letters*, no. 75.
120. Lieutenant Standish O'Grady, 7th Hussars, 31 July 1815, *Waterloo Archive*, vol. iii, doc. 54.
121. Lieutenant Colonel (Major General at Waterloo). J. Thackwell, on behalf of Lieutenant General (Major General at Waterloo) Sir Colquhoun Grant, 9 July 1835, *Waterloo Letters*, no. 62; Lieutenant Colonel (Lieutenant at Waterloo) S. O'Grady, 7th Hussars, 18 March 1835, *Waterloo Letters*, no. 64; Major (Lieutenant, 13th Light Dragoons at Waterloo) D. Doherty, 27th Foot, 14 November 1834, *Waterloo Letters*, no. 66.
122. Lieutenant Colonel (Lieutenant at Waterloo) Henry Lane, 15th Hussars, 24 March 1835, *Waterloo Letters*, no. 69.
123. Mercer, *Journal of the Waterloo Campaign*, pp. 180–1.
124. Lieutenant William Turner, 13th Light Dragoons, 3 July 1815, *Waterloo Archive*, vol. i, doc. 22.
125. Unknown officer, 13th Light Dragoons, undated, *Waterloo Archive*, vol. i, doc. 23.
126. Tomkinson, *Diary*, pp. 311–13.
127. Lieutenant General (Major General, commanding Household Brigade at Waterloo) Lord Edward Somerset, 4 April 1835, *Waterloo Letters*, no. 18; Major (Second Lieutenant at Waterloo) Thomas Marten, 2nd Life Guards, 5 December 1834, *Waterloo Letters*, no. 26.

128. Gronow, *Reminiscences*, vol. i, p. 198.

129. Sergeant Archibald Johnston, 2nd Dragoons (Scots Greys), June 1815, *Waterloo Archive*, vol. i, doc. 15.

130. Captain the Hon. Orlando Bridgeman, 1st Foot Guards, aide-de-camp to Lord Hill, 21 June 1815, *Waterloo Archive*, vol. iv, doc. 6.

13. Aftermath and Butcher's Bill: 'A Frightful Scene of Carnage'

1. Kincaid, *Adventures*, p. 173.

2. Captain William Bowles, Royal Navy, 23 June 1815, *Waterloo Archive*, vol. vi, doc. 106.

3. Assistant Surgeon Donald Finlayson, 33rd Foot, 25 June 1815, *Waterloo Archive*, vol. iii, doc. 130.

4. De Lancey, *A Week at Waterloo*, p. 77.

5. Private John Abbott, 1/51st, 12 November 1815, *Waterloo Archive*, vol. vi, doc. 77.

6. For an accurate breakdown of losses by unit, see *A Near Observer*, which lists casualties with a sufficient time lag after the battle to take into account men recovered from wounds, those who died of them, and men initially reported as missing but many of whom later returned to the ranks. Thus, the 'returns' sent to the War Office in the immediate wake of the battle and those contained in Siborne's history leave much to be desired by way of an accurate tally of Wellington's casualties.

7. Elizabeth Ord, stepdaughter to Thomas Creevey, undated, *Waterloo Archive*, vol. i, doc. 73.

8. Colonel Felton Hervey, 14th Light Dragoons, Assistant Quartermaster General, 20 June 1815, *Waterloo Archive*, vol. i, doc. 2.

9. Lieutenant Henry McMillan, 2nd Dragoons (Scots Greys), 3 July 1815, *Waterloo Archive*, vol. vi, doc. 40.

10. Sergeant William Clarke, 2nd Dragoons (Scots Greys), 8 July 1815, *Waterloo Archive*, vol. i, doc. 13.

11. Sergeant Archibald Johnston, 2nd Dragoons (Scots Greys), June 1815, *Waterloo Archive*, vol. i, doc. 15.

12. Unknown sergeant, Scots Greys, 25 June 1815, *Waterloo Archive*, vol. i, doc. 14.

13. Lieutenant Colonel Henry Murray, 18th Hussars, undated, *Waterloo Archive*, vol. iv, doc. 24; Major General (Lieutenant Colonel at Waterloo) Henry Murray, 18th Hussars, *Waterloo Letters*, no. 76.

14. Ensign Charles Short, 2nd Battalion Coldstream Guards, 19 June 1815, *Waterloo Archive*, vol iv, doc. 67.

15. Kincaid, *Adventures*, p. 172–3.

16. Captain James Nixon, 1st Foot Guards, 22 June 1815, *Waterloo Archive*, vol. i, doc. 33.

17. Lieutenant Colonel (Lieutenant at Waterloo) W.B. Ingilby, Royal Horse Artillery, 20 November 1834, *Waterloo Letters*, no. 82.

18. Corporal John Stubbings, 1st Dragoon Guards, undated, *Waterloo Archive*, vol. iii, doc. 19.

19. Captain Arthur Kennedy, 18th Hussars, 20 June (1815), *Waterloo Archive*, vol. iv, doc. 26.

20. *Wheatley Diary*, p. 72.

21. Captain George Barlow, 2nd Battalion 69th Foot, 19 June 1815, *Waterloo Archive*, vol. iv, doc. 75.

22. Tomkinson, *Diary*, p. 300.

23. Mercer, *Journal of the Waterloo Campaign*, p. 188.

24. Brevet Major (Captain at Waterloo) A.C. Mercer, Royal Horse Artillery, 26 November 1834, *Waterloo Letters*, no. 89.

25. Captain Arthur Kennedy, 18th Hussars, 2 July 1815, *Waterloo Archive*, vol. iv, doc. 28.

26. Unknown officer, undated but June 1815, 1st Battalion 95th Foot, *Waterloo Archive*, vol. iv, doc. 90.

27. Mercer, *Reminiscences*, vol. i, pp. 186–7.

28. Lieutenant Colonel Sir Alexander Dickson, Battering Train, 20 June 1815, *Waterloo Archive*, vol. iv, doc. 52.

29. Colonel Colin Campbell, Commandant at Headquarters, 19 June 1815, *Waterloo Archive*, vol. iv, doc. 2.

30. Captain Horace Churchill, 1st Foot Guards, aide-de-camp to Lord Hill, 24 June 1815, *Waterloo Archive*, vol. vi, doc. 3.

31. Captain and Lieutenant Colonel Sir Henry Willoughby Rooke, 2nd Battalion 3rd Foot Guards Assistant Adjutant General, 19 June 1815, *Waterloo Archive*, vol. i, doc. 1.

32. Elizabeth Ord, stepdaughter to Thomas Creevey, undated, *Waterloo Archive*, vol. i, doc. 73.

33. Major General John Byng, commanding 2nd Brigade, 19 June 1815, *Waterloo Archive*, vol. iv, doc. 65.

34. Captain Edward Kelly, 1st Life Guards, 25 June 1815, *Waterloo Archive*, vol. vi, doc. 15.

35. Lieutenant John Hibbert, 1st (King's) Dragoon Guards, 13 July 1815, *Waterloo Archive*, vol. vi, doc. 29.

36. Henry Paget, 24 June 1815, *Waterloo Archive*, vol. iii, doc. 5.

37. Sergeant Archibald Johnston, 2nd Dragoons (Scots Greys), June 1815, *Waterloo Archive*, vol. i, doc. 15.

38. Private John Marshall, 10th Hussars, 11 July 1815, *Waterloo Archive*, vol. i, doc. 20.

39. Lieutenant William Turner, 13th Light Dragoons, 3 July 1815, *Waterloo Archive*, vol. i, doc. 22.

40. Lieutenant John Luard, 16th Light Dragoons, 19 June 1815, *Waterloo Archive*, vol. i, doc. 17.

41. Assistant Surgeon John Haddy James, 1st Life Guards, 9 July 1815, *Waterloo Archive*, vol. i, doc. 3.

42. Captain Arthur Kennedy, 18th Hussars, 2 July 1815, *Waterloo Archive*, vol. iv, doc. 28.

43. Major General (Lieutenant Colonel at Waterloo) Henry Murray, 18th Hussars, January 1835, *Waterloo Letters*, no. 76.

44. Lieutenant Colonel (Captain at Waterloo) Robert Wallace, 1st (King's) Dragoon Guards, 19 November 1824, *Waterloo Letters*, no. 29.

45. Sergeant Thomas Critchley, 1st (Royal) Dragoons, 24 July 1815, *Waterloo Archive*, vol. iv, doc. 15.

46. Colonel (Captain at Waterloo) A. Clark Kennedy, 1st (Royal) Dragoons, 13 April 1835, *Waterloo Letters*, no. 35.

47. Ensign James Howard, 33rd Foot, 8 July 1815, *Waterloo Archive*, vol. i, doc. 47. The significance of such observations is only appreciated by an understanding of the officer rank structure for an infantry battalion which, in ascending order, is thus: Ensign, 2nd Lieutenant, 1st Lieutenant, Captain, Major, Lieutenant Colonel.

48. Ensign Thomas Wedgwood 2nd Battalion 3rd Foot Guards, 24 June 1815, *Waterloo Archive*, vol. i, doc. 39.

49. Lieutenant Colonel (Major, 73rd Foot and Assistant Quartermaster General at Waterloo) Dawson Kelly, 14 October 1835, *Waterloo Letters*, no. 146.

50. Lieutenant and Captain James Nixon, 1st Foot Guards, 19 June (1815), *Waterloo Archive*, vol. i, doc. 32. Vitoria and Albuera were particularly bloody Peninsular battles; Leipzig was the largest European battle heretofore, fought in Saxony involving half a million combatants: Russians, Austrians, Prussians and Swedes against the French and their allies, in October 1813. Waterloo did not come close to matching Leipzig in scale of numbers.

51. Leach, Captain Jonathan, *Rough Sketches*, p. 391.

52. General (Major General at Waterloo) Sir James Kempt, Commander 8th Brigade, undated, *Waterloo Letters*, No. 148.

53. Lieutenant Samuel Phelps, Major Lloyd's Battery, Royal Artillery, 18 July 1815, *Waterloo Archive*, vol. iv, doc. 53.

54. Captain Courtenay Ilbert, Royal Artillery, 17 June (1815), *Waterloo Archive*, vol. iii, doc. 123.

55. Lieutenant W.B. Ingilby, Royal Artillery, 10 August 1815, *Waterloo Archive*, vol. i, doc. 27.

56. Lieutenant Colonel Sir Robert Gardiner, Royal Artillery, July 1815, *Waterloo Archive*, vol. iii, doc. 57.

57. Lieutenant Colonel Sir John May, Royal Artillery, Assistant Adjutant General, 23 June 1815, *Waterloo Archive*, vol. i, doc. 25; vol. iv, doc. 51.

58. Captain Arthur Kennedy, 18th Hussars, 2 July 1815, *Waterloo Archive*, vol. iv, doc. 28; Colonel (Captain and Brevet Major at Waterloo) S. Stretton, 40th Foot, 7 February 1837, *Waterloo Letters*, no. 177.

59. Unknown sergeant, 2nd Dragoons (Scots Greys), 25 June 1815, *Waterloo Archive*, vol. i, doc. 14.

60. Lieutenant and Captain James Nixon, 1st Foot Guards, 22 June (1815), *Waterloo Archive*, vol. i, doc. 33.

61. Lieutenant Richard Cocks Eyre, 2nd Battalion 95th Rifles, 28 June 1815, *Waterloo Archive*, vol. iii, doc. 85.

62. Lieutenant Colonel (Captain and Brevet Major at Waterloo) R. Macdonald, 1st Foot (Royals), 29 December 1838, *Waterloo Letters*, no. 162.

63. Lieutenant John McDonald, 1st Battalion 23rd Fusiliers, 23 June 1815, *Waterloo Archive*, vol. iii, doc. 92.

64. Gronow, *Reminiscences*, vol. ii, p. 2.

65. Captain Courtenay Ilbert, Royal Artillery, 19 June (1815), *Waterloo Archive*, vol. iii, doc. 123.

66. Lieutenant Colonel the Hon. Frederick Ponsonby, undated, *Waterloo Archive*, vol. iv, doc. 19. According to Captain Gronow, Ponsonby did subsequently discover the identity of his saviour. When Ponsonby was governor of Malta, he met a French Waterloo veteran and as they exchanged stories it became obvious this was the very man, one Baron de Laussat. See Gronow, *Reminiscences*, pp. 153–4, 1964 edition.

67. Lieutenant John Hibbert, 1st (King's) Dragoon Guards, 13 July 1815, *Waterloo Archive*, vol. vi, doc. 29.

68. Lieutenant Colonel (Major, 73rd Foot and Assistant Quartermaster General at Waterloo) Dawson Kelly, 26 November 1834, *Waterloo Letters*, no. 145.

69. Lieutenant Colonel (Major, 23rd Light Dragoons at Waterloo) P.A. Latour, 23rd Lancers, 28 February 1835, *Waterloo Letters*, no. 49.

70. Lieutenant and Captain James Nixon, 1st Foot Guards, *Waterloo Archive*, vol. i, doc. 33.

71. Ensign Edward Macready, 2nd Battalion 30th Foot, 7 July 1815, *Waterloo Archive*, vol. i, doc. 46; Lieutenant Colonel (Major, 73rd Foot and Assistant Quartermaster General at Waterloo) Dawson Kelly, 26 November 1834, *Waterloo Letters*, no. 145.

72. Lieutenant General the Earl of Uxbridge, commanding the Allied cavalry, 21 June 1815, *Waterloo Archive*, vol. iii, doc. 3.

73. Lieutenant Colonel Francis Home, 2nd Battalion 3rd Foot Guards, probably June 1815, *Waterloo Archive*, vol. i, doc. 37.

74. Tomkinson, *Diary of a Cavalry Officer*, p. 315.

75. Lieutenant Colonel Sir John May, Royal Artillery, Assistant Adjutant General, 23 June 1815, *Waterloo Archive*, vol. i, doc. 25.

76. Lieutenant Colonel John Fremantle, Coldstream Guards and on Wellington's staff at Waterloo, 19 June 1815, in Fremantle, *Wellington's Voice*, p. 211.

77. Lieutenant Colonel James Stanhope, 1st Foot Guards, 19 June 1815, *Waterloo Archive*, vol. i, doc. 31.

78. Lieutenant Colonel Sir John May, Royal Artillery, Assistant Adjutant General, 23 June 1815, *Waterloo Archive*, vol. iv, doc. 51; vol. i, doc. 25.

79. Captain the Hon. Orlando Bridgeman, 1st Foot Guards, aide-de-camp to Lord Hill, 21 June 1815, *Waterloo Archive*, vol. iv, doc. 6.

80. Captain the Hon. Orlando Bridgeman, 1st Foot Guards, aide-de-camp to Lord Hill, 23 June 1815, *Waterloo Archive*, vol. iv, doc. 6.

81. Major General Sir James Kempt, commanding 8th Brigade, then 5th Division, 3 July 1815, *Waterloo Archive*, vol. iv, doc. 89.

82. Ross-Lewin, *With 'The Thirty-Second'*, p. 280.

83. Lieutenant Dixon Denham, 54th Foot, 'Journal of the Waterloo Campaign', *Waterloo Archive*, vol. iv, doc. 92.

84. Lieutenant Colonel John Fremantle, Coldstream Guards and on Wellington's staff at Waterloo, 19 June 1815, in Fremantle, *Wellington's Voice*, p. 211.

85. Lieutenant James Crummer, 1st Battalion 28th Foot, 4 July 1815, *Waterloo Archive*, vol. vi, doc. 82.

86. Captain George Bowles, 2nd Battalion Coldstream Guards, 19 June 1815, *Waterloo Archive*, vol. vi, doc. 65.

87. Kincaid, *Adventures*, p. 168.

88. Kincaid, *Adventures*, p. 170.

89. Major John Oldfield, Royal Engineers, July 1815, *Waterloo Archive*, vol. vi, doc. 90.

90. Cornet James Gape, 2nd Dragoons (Scots Greys), 1815, *Waterloo Archive*, vol. vi, doc. 41.

91. 'A Visitor Resident at Brussels', undated, *Waterloo Archive*, vol. vi, doc. 103.

92. Commissary Tupper Carey, 'Reminiscences', *Waterloo Archive*, vol. vi, doc. 100.

93. Edward Heeley, servant of Lieutenant Colonel George Scovell, Assistant Quartermaster General, campaign journal, *Waterloo Archive*, vol. vi, doc. 102.

94. H.M. Leathes, Royal Horse Artillery, 16 March 1859, *Waterloo Archive*, vol. i, doc. 28.

95. Smith, *Autobiography*, p, 271.

96. Elizabeth Ord, stepdaughter to Thomas Creevey, undated, *Waterloo Archive*, vol. i, doc. 73.

97. Lieutenant General the Earl of Uxbridge, 21 June 1815, *Waterloo Archive*, vol. iii, doc. 3.

98. Charles Grenfell, 13 July 1815, *Waterloo Archive*, vol. iv, doc. 107.

99. Lieutenant Colonel (Major General at Waterloo). J. Thackwell, on behalf of Lieutenant General (Major General at Waterloo) Sir Colquhoun Grant, 9 July 1835, *Waterloo Letters*, no. 62; another source claims only four: Lieutenant Colonel (Lieutenant at Waterloo) T. Maclean, 13th Light Dragoons, 4 November 1844, *Waterloo Letters*, no. 67; Lieutenant William Turner, 13th Light Dragoons, 3 July 1815, *Waterloo Archive*, vol. i, doc. 22.

100. Captain John Whale, 1st Life Guards, compiled by his daughter, undated, *Waterloo Archive*, vol. iv, doc. 11.

101. Cornet James Gape, 2nd Dragoons (Scots Greys), June 1815, *Waterloo Archive*, vol. vi, doc. 41; Lieutenant Henry McMillan, 2nd Dragoons (Scots Greys), 3 July 1815, *Waterloo Archive*, vol. vi, doc. 40.

102. Colonel (Captain at Waterloo) A. Clark Kennedy, 1st (Royal) Dragoons, 13 April 1835, *Waterloo Letters*, no. 35.

103. Lieutenant Colonel John Fremantle, Coldstream Guards and on Wellington's staff at Waterloo, 19 June 1815, Fremantle, *Wellington's Voice*, p. 211.

104. Lieutenant Colonel (Lieutenant at Waterloo) A.T. Maclean, 13th Light Dragoons, 4 November 1844, *Waterloo Letters*, no. 67.

105. Captain Thomas Fenton, 2nd Dragoons (Scots Greys), 19 June 1815, *Waterloo Archive*, vol. vi, doc. 35.

106. Colonel Hugh Mitchell, 1/51st, 19 June 1815, *Waterloo Archive*, vol. vi, doc. 76.

107. Lieutenant Colonel Lord Saltoun, 3rd Battalion 1st Foot Guards, 19 June 1815, *Waterloo Archive*, vol. vi, doc. 56.

108. Captain Edward Kelly, 1st Life Guards, 19 June 1815, *Waterloo Archive*, vol. vi, doc. 13.

109. Lieutenant Colonel Sir William Gomm, 2nd Battalion Coldstream Guards, Assistant Quartermaster General, 19 June 1815, *Waterloo Archive*, vol. vi, doc. 8.

110. Major General Lord Edward Somerset, commanding Household Cavalry Brigade, 23 June 1815, *Waterloo Archive*, vol. vi, doc. 9.

111. Private Thomas Playford, 2nd Life Guards, undated, *Waterloo Archive*, vol. iv, doc. 12.
112. Major John Hill, 1st Battalion 23rd Fusiliers, 7 July 1815, *Waterloo Archive*, vol. vi, doc. 75.
113. Private Thomas Playford, 2nd Life Guards, undated, *Waterloo Archive*, vol. iv, doc. 12.
114. Captain Peter Bowlby (his brother), 1st Battalion 4th Foot, undated, *Waterloo Archive*, vol. vi, doc. 89.
115. Major John Oldfield, Royal Engineers, July 1815, *Waterloo Archive*, vol. vi, doc. 90.
116. Ensign Jack Barnett, 1st Battalion 71st Foot, 21 June 1815, *Waterloo Archive*, vol. vi, doc. 72.
117. Lieutenant Colonel (Major and Lieutenant Colonel at Waterloo) F.S. Miller, Inniskilling Dragoons, 11 June 1839, *Waterloo Letters*, no. 45.
118. Lieutenant John Sperling, Royal Engineers, *Waterloo Archives*, vol. vi, doc. 91.
119. Captain Alexander Clark Kennedy, 1st (Royal) Dragoons, 26 June 1815, *Waterloo Archive*, vol. vi, doc. 33.
120. Colonel (Major, 5th West India Regiment and extra aide-de-camp to Sir William Ponsonby at Waterloo) Sir George De Lacy Evans, 23 August 1842, *Waterloo Letters*, no. 33.
121. Lieutenant Colonel David Mackinnon, 2nd Battalion Coldstream Guards, 23 June 1815, *Waterloo Archive*, vol. iv, doc. 66.
122. Mercer, *Journal*, p. 183.
123. Unknown sergeant, 2nd Battalion (Scots Greys), 25 June 1815, *Waterloo Archive*, vol. i, doc. 14.
124. H.M. Leathes, Royal Horse Artillery, 16 March 1859, *Waterloo Archive*, vol. i, doc. 28.
125. Captain Edward Kelly, 1st Life Guards, 25 June 1815, *Waterloo Archive*, vol. vi, doc. 14.
126. Captain and Lieutenant Colonel Edward Bowater, 2nd Battalion 3rd Foot Guards, 21 June 1815, *Waterloo Archive*, vol. iii, doc. 82.
127. Captain Orlando Bridgeman, 1st Foot Guards, aide-de-camp to Lord Hill, 21 June 1815, *Waterloo Archive*, vol. iv, doc. 6.

14. The Wounded and the Dead

1. Lieutenant James Gardiner, 19 June 1815, *Waterloo Archive*, vol. vi, doc. 85.
2. Mercer, *Journal*, pp. 185–6.
3. Private George Hemingway, 33rd Foot, 14 August 1815, *Waterloo Archive*, vol. i, doc. 48.
4. Lieutenant Colonel James Stanhope, 3rd Battalion 1st Foot Guards, undated, *Waterloo Archive*, vol. vi, doc. 59.
5. Lieutenant Edward Stephens, 1/32nd, 19 June 1815, *Waterloo Archive*, vol. iii, doc. 96.
6. Mercer, *Journal*, pp. 172–3.
7. Sergeant William Clarke, 2nd Dragoons (Scots Greys), 8 July 1815, *Waterloo Archive*, vol. i, doc. 13.
8. Elizabeth Ord, stepdaughter to Thomas Creevey, undated, *Waterloo Archive*, vol. i, doc. 73.
9. Charles Grenfell, 13 July 1815, *Waterloo Archive*, vol. iv, doc. 107.
10. Private Thomas Hasker, 1st (King's) Dragoon Guards, 13 December 1841, *Waterloo Archive*, vol. i, doc. 8. See also doc. 7, an extract from his journal.
11. Sergeant Archibald Johnston, 2nd Dragoons (Scots Greys), June 1815, *Waterloo Archive*, vol. i, doc. 15.
12. Private Thomas Playford, 2nd Life Guards, undated, *Waterloo Archive*, vol. iv, doc. 12.
13. Lieutenant Colonel the Hon. Frederick Ponsonby, undated, *Waterloo Archive*, vol. iv, doc. 19.
14. Lieutenant Colonel Sir Alexander Gordon, 3rd Foot Guards, aide-de-camp to Wellington, who died after an operation to amputate his leg.
15. Lieutenant Colonel Frederick Ponsonby, undated, *Waterloo Archive*, vol. iv, doc. 19.
16. Gronow, *Reminiscences*, vol. i, p. 194.
17. Simmons, *British Rifle Man*, p. 201–2.
18. Lieutenant Richard Cocks Eyre, 2nd Battalion 95th Rifles, 28 June 1815, *Waterloo Archive*, vol. iii, doc. 85.

19. Surgeon David Slow, Royal Horse Guards, 21 June 1815, *Waterloo Archive*, vol. vi, doc. 22.

20. Journal of Sergeant Archibald Johnston, 2nd Dragoons (Scots Greys), June 1815, *Waterloo Archive*, vol. i, doc. 15.

21. Gronow, *Reminiscences*, vol. i, p. 195.

22. Gleig, *The Subaltern*, p. 135.

23. There are various unconfirmed claims of the murder of some British prisoners by the French, however, specifically those taken wounded at Quatre Bras. The practice, if true, is unlikely to have been widespread, as numerous Allied prisoners were later released unharmed. See, for example, Sergeant Charles Wood, 3rd Battalion 1st Foot Guards, 29 July 1815, *Waterloo Archive*, vol. vi, doc. 63; Lieutenant George Gunning, 1st (Royal) Dragoons, undated, *Waterloo Archive*, vol. vi, doc. 34; Lieutenant John Hibbert, King's Dragoon Guards, 13 July 1815, *Waterloo Archive*, vol. vi, doc. 29.

24. Lieutenant John Sperling, Royal Engineers, 20 June 1815, *Waterloo Archive*, vol. vi, doc. 93.

25. Sergeant Charles Wood, 3rd Battalion 1st Foot Guards, 29 July 1815, *Waterloo Archive*, vol. vi, doc. 63.

26. Captain Horace Churchill, 1st Foot Guards, aide-de-camp to Lord Hill, 24 June 1815, *Waterloo Archive*, vol. vi, doc. 3.

27. Lieutenant General (Captain at Waterloo) A.C. Mercer, G Troop, Royal Horse Artillery, 12 June 1860, *Waterloo Archive*, vol. i, doc. 28.

28. Lieutenant Donald Mackenzie, 1st Battalion 42nd Foot, undated, *Waterloo Archive*, vol. i, doc. 55.

29. Private John Marshall, 10th Hussars, 11 July 1815, *Waterloo Archive*, vol. i, doc. 20.

30. Major General (Lieutenant Colonel at Waterloo) Henry Murray, 18th Hussars, January 1835, *Waterloo Letters*, no. 76.

31. Major John Oldfield, Royal Engineers, July 1815, *Waterloo Archive*, vol. vi, doc. 90

32. Captain Horace Churchill, 1st Foot Guards, aide-de-camp to Lord Hill, 24 June 1815, *Waterloo Archive*, vol. vi, doc. 3.

33. Major General Lord Edward Somerset, commanding Household Brigade, 23 June 1815, *Waterloo Archive*, vol. vi, doc. 9.

34. Lieutenant General (Major General, commanding 6th (Light) Cavalry Brigade at Waterloo) Lord Hussey, 27 November 1841, *Waterloo Letters*, no. 74.

35. Captain Horace Churchill, 1st Foot Guards, aide-de-camp to Lord Hill, 24 June 1815, *Waterloo Archive*, vol. vi, doc. 3.

36. Tomkinson, *Diary*, p. 308.

37. Captain (Lieutenant at Waterloo) F. Warde, Royal Horse Artillery, 27 May (1840), *Waterloo Letters*, no. 86.

38. Colonel Colin Campbell, Commandant at Headquarters, 19 June 1815, *Waterloo Archive*, vol. iv, doc. 2.

39. Gronow, *Reminiscences*, vol. i, p. 194.

40. Henry Paget, 24 June 1815, *Waterloo Archive*, vol. iii, doc. 5.

41. Lieutenant William Chapman, 1st Battalion 95th Rifles, 4 July 1815, *Waterloo Archive*, vol. i, doc. 53.

42. Ensign Edward Macready, 2nd Battalion 30th Foot, (Journal, June 1815), *Waterloo Archive*, vol. vi, doc. 79.

43. Lieutenant John Sperling, Royal Engineers, 20 June 1815, *Waterloo Archive*, vol. vi, doc. 93.

44. Edward Heeley, servant of Lieutenant Colonel George Scovell, Assistant Quartermaster General, June 1815, *Waterloo Archive*, vol. vi, doc. 102.

45. Edward Heeley, servant of Lieutenant Colonel Sir George Scovell, Assistant Quartermaster General, June 1815, *Waterloo Archive*, vol. vi, doc. 102.

46. Corporal Richard Coulter, 1st Life Guards, 20 July 1815, *Waterloo Archive*, vol. vi, doc. 21.

47. Lieutenant Archibald Hamilton, 2nd Dragoons (Scots Greys), undated, *Waterloo Archive*, vol vi, doc. 38.

48. Captain Edward Kelly, 1st Life Guards, 19 June 1815, *Waterloo Archive*, vol. vi, doc. 13.

49. Captain the Hon. Orlando Bridgeman, 1st Foot Guards, aide-de-camp to Lord Hill, 23 June 1815, *Waterloo Archive*, vol. iv, doc. 6.

50. Captain the Hon. Orlando Bridgeman, 1st Foot Guards, aide-de-camp to Lord Hill, 21 June 1815, *Waterloo Archive*, vol. iv, doc. 6.

51. Troop Sergeant Major James Page, 1st (King's) Dragoon Guards, 3 July 1815, *Waterloo Archive*, vol. iii, doc. 17.

52. Lieutenant Colonel James Stanhope, 1st Foot Guards, 19 June 1815, *Waterloo Archive*, vol. i, doc. 31.

53. Private Joseph Lord, 2nd Life Guards, 8 August 1815, *Waterloo Archive*, vol. i, doc. 6.

54. Lieutenant Edward Stephens, 1st Battalion 32nd Foot, 19 June 1815, *Waterloo Archive*, vol. iii, doc. 96.

55. Lieutenant Richard Cocks Eyre, 2nd Battalion 95th Foot, 28 June 1815, *Waterloo Archive*, vol. iii, doc. 85.

56. Henegan, *Seven Years' Campaigning*, vol. ii, pp. 330–4.

57. Extract from 'Some notices of my life' by John Davy, undated, *Waterloo Archive*, vol. i, doc. 71.

58. Tomkinson, *Diary of a Cavalry Officer*, p. 319.

59. Hospital Assistant George Finlayson, undated but evidently 26 June 1815, *Waterloo Archive*, vol. iii, doc. 133.

60. John Davy, extract from 'Some notices of my life', undated, *Waterloo Archive*, vol. i, doc. 71.

61. Elizabeth Ord, stepdaughter to Thomas Creevey, undated, *Waterloo Archive*, vol. i, doc. 73.

62. Hospital Assistant Isaac James, 29 June 1815, *Waterloo Archive*, vol. i, doc. 72.

63. Unknown private, 1st Battalion 42nd Foot, 24 June 1815, *Waterloo Archive*, vol. vi, doc. 86.

64. Ensign William Thain, 33rd Foot, 22 June 1815, *Waterloo Archive*, vol. vi, doc. 81.

65. Captain the Hon. Orlando Bridgeman, 1st Foot Guards, aide-de-camp to Lord Hill, 21 June 1815, *Waterloo Archive*, vol. iv, doc. 6.

66. Henegan, *Seven Years' Campaigning*, vol. ii, pp. 336–7.

67. De Lancey, *A Week at Waterloo*, pp. 51, 73, 74, 79–80, 84, 97–8.

68. Charles Grenfell, 5 July 1815, *Waterloo Archive*, vol. iv, doc. 106.

69. Charles Grenfell, 13 July 1815, *Waterloo Archive*, vol. iv, doc. 107.

70. Unknown sergeant of the Scots Greys, 25 June 1815, *Waterloo Archive*, vol. i, doc. 14.

71. Elizabeth Ord, stepdaughter to Thomas Creevey, undated, *Waterloo Archive*, vol. i, doc. 73.

72. Robert Hume, Deputy Inspector of Hospitals and Surgeon to the Commander of the Forces, 10 August 1815, *Waterloo Archive*, vol. iv, doc. 20.

73. Assistant Surgeon Donald Finlayson, 33rd Foot, 25 June 1815, *Waterloo Archive*, vol. iii, doc. 130.

74. Lieutenant General the Earl of Uxbridge, commanding of the Allied cavalry), 21 June 1815, *Waterloo Archive*, vol. iii, doc. 3. See the account of Uxbridge's surgery in Appendix VIII.

75. Lieutenant Colonel Sir George Scovell, Assistant Quartermaster General, undated, *Waterloo Archive*, vol. iii, doc. 1.

76. Major General Lord Edward Somerset, commanding the Household Brigade, 23 June 1815, *Waterloo Archive*, vol. vi, doc. 9.

77. Gronow, *Reminiscences*, vol. i, p. 193.

78. John Davy, extract from 'Some notices of my life', undated, *Waterloo Archive*, vol. i, doc. 71.

79. 'Notes by Deputy Inspector John Hume on the treatment of Sir Alexander Gordon', undated, *Waterloo Archive*, vol. i, doc. 69.

80. Hospital Assistant Henry Blackadder, 'Outline of a case: injury of the brain,' 6 August 1815, *Waterloo Archive*, vol. iv, doc. 99.

81. Cotton, *A Voice from Waterloo*, p. 29.

82. Captain William Elton, 1st (King's) Dragoon Guards, 15 July 1815, *Waterloo Archive*, vol. iv, doc. 13.

83. Lieutenant George Blathwayt, 23rd Light Dragoons (1865), *Waterloo Archive*, vol. iii, doc. 53.

84. Lieutenant Colonel Sir Augustus Frazer, Commanding the Horse Artillery, 19 June 1815, *Waterloo Archive*, vol. iv, doc. 50.

85. Lieutenant Colonel (Captain and Brevet Major at Waterloo) T.W. Taylor, 10th Hussars, November 1829, *Waterloo Letters*, no. 75.

86. Tomkinson, *Diary of a Cavalry Officer*, p. 314.

87. Private Thomas Bingham, Royal Horse Guards, 4 July 1815, *Waterloo Archive*, vol. vi, doc. 25.

88. Lieutenant John Hibbert, King's Dragoon Guards, 13 July 1815, *Waterloo Archive*, vol. vi, doc. 29.

89. De Lancey, *A Week at Waterloo*, p. 101.

90. Hospital Assistant George Finlayson, undated but evidently 26 June 1815, *Waterloo Archive*, vol. iii, doc. 133.

91. Sergeant Archibald Johnston, 2nd Dragoons (Scots Greys), June 1815, *Waterloo Archive*, vol. i, doc. 15.

92. John Sadler, Regarding Lieutenant James Carruthers, 2nd Dragoons (Scots Greys), 24 June 1815, *Waterloo Archive*, vol. iv, doc. 17; Ensign Jack Barnett, 1st Battalion 71st, 21 June 1815, *Waterloo Archive*, vol. vi, doc. 72.

93. Captain Orlando Bridgeman, 1st Foot Guards, aide-de-camp to Lord Hill, 23 June 1815, *Waterloo Archive*, vol. iv, doc. 6.

94. Private Joseph Lord, 2nd Life Guards, 3 July 1815, *Waterloo Archive*, vol. i, doc. 5.

95. Private Joseph Lord, 2nd Life Guards, 8 August 1815, *Waterloo Archive*, vol. i, doc. 6.

96. Lieutenant John Sperling, Royal Engineers, 24 June 1815, *Waterloo Archive*, vol. vi, doc. 94.

97. Lady Uxbridge, 3 July 1815, *Waterloo Archive*, vol. iii, doc. 12. Somewhat in contradiction to the foregoing account, a visiting naval officer stated that on his visit of 2 July he found all the bodies gone 'and everything except a few caps so completely cleared away, that if the corn (which was, as you may suppose, entirely destroyed) had not marked the direction of the movements, nobody would have supposed that towards 50,000 men had been killed or wounded there a fortnight before'. Captain William Bowles, Royal Navy, 6 July 1815, *Waterloo Archive*, vol. vi, doc. 107.

98. Lady Uxbridge, 3 July 1815, *Waterloo Archive*, vol. iii, doc. 12.

99. Charles Grenfell, 13 July 1815, *Waterloo Archive*, vol. iv, doc. 107.

15. Victory and Defeat

1. Captain Alexander Clark Kennedy, 1st (Royal) Dragoons, 26 June 1815, *Waterloo Archive*, vol. vi, doc. 33.

2. Captain Thomas Wildman, 7th Hussars, aide-de-camp to Lord Uxbridge, 19 June 1815, *Waterloo Archive*, vol. vi, doc. 4.

3. Mercer, *Journal of the Waterloo Campaign*, pp. 167–8.

4. Lieutenant Colonel Francis Home, 2nd Battalion 3rd Foot Guards, probably June 1815, *Waterloo Archive*, vol. i, doc. 37.

5. Ross-Lewin, *With 'The Thirty-Second'*, pp. 286–7.

6. Lieutenant Colonel James Stanhope, 3rd Battalion 1st Foot Guards, 19 June 1815, *Waterloo Archive*, vol. vi, doc. 62.

7. Tomkinson, *Diary*, p. 299.

8. Gronow, *Reminiscences*, vol. i, p. 188.

9. Wheeler, letters, p. 175.

10. Cotton, *Voices from Waterloo*, pp. 137–8.

11. Captain Horace Churchill, 1st Foot Guards, aide-de-camp to Lord Hill, 24 June 1815, *Waterloo Archive*, vol. vi, doc. 3.

12. Ensign Edward Macready, 2nd Battalion 30th Foot, (Journal, June 1815), *Waterloo Archive*, vol. vi, doc. 79.

13. Assistant Surgeon John Haddy James, 1st Life Guards, 9 July 1815, *Waterloo Archive*, vol. i, doc. 3.

14. Lieutenant Colonel James Stanhope, 3rd Battalion 1st Foot Guards, *Waterloo Archive*, vol. vi, doc. 59.

15. On this point see, however, Lieutenant John Hildebrand, 2nd Battalion 35th Foot, undated, *Waterloo Archive*, vol. vi, doc. 98.

16. Tomkinson, *Diary*, pp. 298–9.

17. Captain William Bowles, Royal Navy, 23 June 1815, *Waterloo Archive*, vol. vi, doc. 106.

18. Kincaid, *Adventures*, p. 172.

19. Ross-Lewin, *With 'The Thirty-Second'*, p. 287.

20. Lieutenant Colonel F.S. Tidy, 3rd Battalion 14th Foot, as told to his daughter, undated, *Waterloo Archive*, vol. i, doc. 49.

21. Sergeant Charles Wood, 3rd Battalion 1st Foot Guards, 29 July 1815, *Waterloo Archive*, vol. vi, doc. 63.

22. Lieutenant Colonel Sir Andrew Barnard, 1st Battalion 95th Rifles, 23 June 1815, *Waterloo Archive*, vol. vi, doc. 84.

23. Tomkinson, *Diary*, p. 289.

24. Tomkinson, *Diary*, p. 318.

25. Captain Arthur Kennedy, 18th Hussars, 2 July 1815, *Waterloo Archive*, vol. iv, doc. 28.

26. Lieutenant Colonel James Stanhope, 3rd Battalion 1st Foot Guards, *Waterloo Archive*, vol. vi, doc. 59.

27. Tomkinson, *Diary*, pp. 282–3.

28. Lieutenant General Lord Vivian (Major General Sir Vivian Hussey at Waterloo, Commander 6th (Light) Cavalry Brigade), 3 June 1839, *Waterloo Letters*, no. 71.

29. Lieutenant Colonel James Stanhope, 3rd Battalion 1st Foot Guards, 19 June 1815, *Waterloo Archive*, vol. vi, doc. 62

30. Captain Henry Grove, 23rd Light Dragoons, 18 June, *Waterloo Archive*, vol. vi, doc. 45.

31. Major General Lord Edward Somerset, Commander of the Household Brigade, 23 June 1815, *Waterloo Archive*, vol. vi, doc. 9.

32. Kincaid, *Adventures*, pp. 168, 172.

33. Major General Sir Hussey Vivian, Commander 6th (Light) Cavalry Brigade, 3 June 1839, *Waterloo Letters*, no. 71.

34. Ross-Lewin, *With 'The Thirty-Second'*, p. 269.

35. Tomkinson, *Diary*, p. 306.

36. Ross-Lewin, *With 'The Thirty-Second'*, p. 288.

37. Lieutenant Colonel James Stanhope, 3rd Battalion 1st Foot Guards, undated (morning of 19 June 1815), *Waterloo Archive*, vol. vi, doc. 61.

38. Lieutenant Colonel Lord Saltoun, 3rd Battalion 1st Foot Guards, 22 June 1815, *Waterloo Archive*, vol. vi, doc. 57.

39. Ensign William Thain, 33rd Foot, 18 June 1815, *Waterloo Archive*, vol. vi, doc. 81.

40. Ross-Lewin, *With 'The Thirty-Second'*, p. 287.

41. Colonel Colin Campbell, Commandant at Headquarters, 19 June 1815, *Waterloo Archive*, vol. iv, doc. 2.

42. Major General Lord Edward Somerset, Commander Household Brigade, 23 June 1815, *Waterloo Archive*, vol. vi, doc. 9.

43. Kincaid, *Adventures*, pp. 172–3.

44. Tomkinson, *Diary*, pp. 303–4.

45. Gronow, *Reminiscences*, vol. i, p. 79.

46. Gronow, *Reminiscences*, vol. i, p. 78.

47. Gronow, *Reminiscences*, vol. ii, p. 3.
48. Captain Horace Churchill, 1st Foot Guards, aide-de-camp to Lord Hill, 24 June 1815, *Waterloo Archive*, vol. vi, doc. 3.
49. Lieutenant Colonel James Stanhope, 3rd Battalion 1st Foot Guards, *Waterloo Archive*, vol. vi, doc. 59.
50. Captain Edward Kelly, 1st Life Guards, 25 June 1815, *Waterloo Archive*, vol. vi, doc. 15.
51. Captain Horace Churchill, 1st Foot Guards, aide-de-camp to Lord Hill, 24 June 1815, *Waterloo Archive*, vol. vi, doc. 3.
52. Henegan, *Seven Years' Campaigning*, vol. ii, pp. 312–13.
53. Captain Henry Grove, 23rd Light Dragoons, 16 June 1815, *Waterloo Archive*, vol. vi, doc. 45.
54. Lieutenant Colonel John Fremantle, Coldstream Guards, aide-de-camp to the Duke of Wellington, 19 June 1815, *Waterloo Archive*, vol. vi, doc. 1.
55. Lieutenant Colonel Sir Robert Gardiner, Royal Artillery, July 1815, *Waterloo Archive*, vol. iii, doc. 57.
56. Ensign Edward Macready, 2nd Battalion 30th Foot, (Journal, June 1815), *Waterloo Archive*, vol. vi, doc. 79.
57. Ensign Edward Macready, 2nd Battalion 30th Foot, (Journal, June 1815), *Waterloo Archive*, vol. vi, doc. 79.
58. Captain Thomas Wildman, 7th Hussars, aide-de-camp to Lord Uxbridge, 19 June 1815, *Waterloo Archive*, vol. vi, doc. 4.
59. Lieutenant John Sperling, Royal Engineers, 20 June 1815, *Waterloo Archive*, vol. vi, doc. 93.
60. Edward Heeley, servant of Lieutenant Colonel Sir George Scovell, Assistant Quatermaster General, journal, June 1815, *Waterloo Archive*, vol. vi, doc. 102.
61. Sergeant Charles Wood, 3rd Battalion 1st Foot Guards, 29 July 1815, *Waterloo Archive*, vol. vi, doc. 63.
62. Lieutenant Colonel John Fremantle, Coldstream Guards and on Wellington's staff at Waterloo, 19 June 1815, in Glover, ed. *Wellington's Voice*, p. 211.
63. Elizabeth Ord, stepdaughter to Thomas Creevey, undated, *Waterloo Archive*, vol. i, doc. 73.
64. Lieutenant General Sir Henry Clinton, Commander, 2nd Division, 23 June 1815, *Waterloo Archive*, vol. i, doc. 41.
65. Colonel Colin Campbell, Commandant at Headquarters, 19 June 1815, *Waterloo Archive*, vol. iv, doc. 2.
66. Elizabeth Ord, stepdaughter to Thomas Creevey, undated, *Waterloo Archive*, vol. i, doc. 73.

Appendices

1. Lieutenant Colonel John Burgoyne, Royal Engineers (not at Waterloo), 'Waterloo: Remarks made on a visit to the ground in 1816', *Waterloo Archive*, vol. iv, doc. 100.
2. General (Lieutenant General the Earl of Uxbridge, commanding the Cavalry at Waterloo), the Marquess of Anglesey, 8 November 1839, *Waterloo Letters*, no. 5.
3. Private Thomas Playford, 2nd Life Guards, undated, *Waterloo Archive*, vol. iv, doc. 12.
4. Lieutenant Colonel (Captain, 1st (Royal) Dragoons at Waterloo) A.K. Clark Kennedy, 7th Dragoon Guards, 18 June 1839, *Waterloo Letters*, no. 36.
5. Captain (Lieutenant and Captain at Waterloo) H.W. Powell, 1st Foot Guards, 21 April 1835, *Waterloo Letters*, no. 109.
6. Diary of Captain Digby Mackworth, 7th Foot, aide-de-camp to Lord Hill, 18 June 1815, *Waterloo Archive*, vol. iv, doc. 5.
7. Major General Sir Hussey Vivian, Commanding Officer, 6th (Light) Cavalry Brigade, 23 June 1815, *Waterloo Letters*, no. 70.

8. Lieutenant and Adjutant Henry Duperier, 18th Hussars, 19 June 1815, *Waterloo Archive*, vol. iii, doc. 56. This proves the oft-repeated supposed exchange between Wellington and Uxbridge about the latter's missing leg to be apocryphal.

9. Captain Horace Churchill, 1st Foot Guards, aide-de-camp to Lord Hill, 24 June 1815, *Waterloo Archive*, vol. vi, doc. 3.

10. Lieutenant Colonel Lord Greenock, Assistant Quartermaster General to Sir Thomas Graham, 1 July 1815, *Waterloo Archive*, vol. iv, doc. 3; Lieutenant Archibald Hamilton, 2nd Dragoons (Scots Greys), undated, *Waterloo Archive*, vol. vi, doc. 38.

11. Deputy Inspector John Hume, undated, *Waterloo Archive*, vol. i, doc. 68.

12. Ensign Charles Dallas, 1st Battalion 32nd Foot, 25 June 1815, *Waterloo Archive*, vol. i, doc. 51.

13. Lieutenant Colonel Sir Robert Gardiner, Royal Artillery, July 1815, *Waterloo Archive*, vol. iii, doc. 57.

14. Ensign Thomas Wedgwood, 2nd Battalion 3rd Foot Guards, 19 June 1815, *Waterloo Archive*, vol. i, doc. 38.

15. Lieutenant Colonel John Fremantle, Coldstream Guards, aide-de-camp to Wellington, 19 June 1815, *Waterloo Archive*, vol. vi, doc. 40.

16. Elizabeth Ord, stepdaughter to Thomas Creevey, undated, *Waterloo Archive*, vol. i, doc. 73.

17. Captain Arthur Kennedy, 18th Hussars, 2 July 1815, *Waterloo Archive*, vol. iv, doc. 28.

18. Lieutenant Henry McMillan, 2nd Dragoons (Scots Greys), 3 July 1815, *Waterloo Archive*, vol. vi, doc. 40.

19. Major General Sir James Kempt, Commander 8th Brigade, then 5th Division, 3 July 1815, *Waterloo Archive*, vol. iv, doc. 89.

20. Captain Arthur Kennedy, 18th Hussars, 2 July 1815, *Waterloo Archive*, vol. iv, doc. 28.

21. The National Archives, PRO 30/22/1A/32. Wellington, *Dispatches*, vol. xii, pp. 478–84.

22. Private Richard MacLaurence, 2nd Battalion Coldstream Guards, 12 January 1843, *Waterloo Archive*, vol. vi, doc. 69.

23. Unknown officer, 2nd Battalion 3rd Foot Guards, July 1836, *Waterloo Archive*, vol. vi, doc 70. Written in the third person, but probably Lieutenant Colonel Francis Home.

24. Ensign Edward Macready, 2nd Battalion 30th Foot, (Journal, June 1815), *Waterloo Archive*, vol. vi, doc. 79.

25. Lieutenant Colonel James Stanhope, 3rd Battalion 1st Foot Guards, *Waterloo Archive*, June 1815, vol. vi, doc. 59.

26. Ensign Edward Macready, 2nd Battalion 30th Foot, (Journal, June 1815), *Waterloo Archive*, vol. vi, doc. 79.

27. Commissary Tupper Carey, 'Reminiscences', *Waterloo Archive*, vol. vi, doc. 100.

28. William Thomson, Deputy Commissary General of Stores, 2 November 1818, *Waterloo Archive*, vol. vi, doc. 104.

29. First Lieutenant William Ingilby, Royal Horse Artillery, 18 June 1815, *Waterloo Archive*, vol. vi, doc. 53

30. Lieutenant George Gunning, 1st (Royal) Dragoons, *Waterloo Archive*, vol. vi, doc. 34.

BIBLIOGRAPHY

Published Primary Sources

Adye, Ralph Willett, *The Bombardier, and Pocket Gunner*, London, 1827.

A Manual for Volunteer Corps of Infantry, London, 1803,

Anonymous, *The Battle of Waterloo ... From a Variety of Authentic and Original Sources ... by a Near Observer*, Edinburgh, 1816.

Anonymous, *Journal of T.S. of the 71st Highland Light Infantry, in Memorials of the Late Wars*, Edinburgh, 1828.

Anonymous, *Life of a Soldier by a Field Officer*, London, 1834.

Anonymous, *Military Memoirs of an Infantry Officer, 1809–1816*, Edinburgh, 1833.

Anonymous, *The Nineteen Movements as Ordered for the British Army*, Calcutta, 1809.

Anonymous, *Rules and Regulations for the Manual and Platoon Exercise Formation, Field Exercise, and Movement of His Majesty's Forces*, London, 1807.

Anonymous, *The Waterloo Medal Roll*, Dallington, 1992.

Anonymous, *Waterloo Memoirs*, 1817.

Anton, J., *Retrospect of a Military Life*, Edinburgh, 1841.

Blackman, Captain John Lucie, *'It All Culminated at Hougoumont': The Letters of Captain John Lucie Blackman, 2nd Battalion Coldstream Guards, 1812–15*, ed. Gareth Glover, Cambridge, 2009.

Blathwayt, Colonel, *Recollections of My Life including Military Service at Waterloo, by Colonel Blathwayt, 23rd Light Dragoons, 1814–17*, ed. Gareth Glover, Cambridge, 2004.

Booth, John, *A Near Observer: Additional Particulars to the Battle of Waterloo*, 2 vols, London, 1817.

Bowles, Captain George, *A Guards Officer in the Peninsula and at Waterloo: The Letters of Captain George Bowles, Coldstream Guards, 1807–1819*, ed. Gareth Glover, Cambridge, 2008.

Bridgeman, Captain Orlando, *A Young Gentleman at War: The Letters of Captain Orlando Bridgeman, 1st Foot Guards, in the Peninsula and at Waterloo, 1812–15*, ed. Gareth Glover, Cambridge, 2008.

Bunbury, Thomas, *Reminiscences of a Veteran, Being Personal and Military Adventures in Portugal, Spain, France, Malta ... and India*, 3 vols, London, 1861.

Carr-Gomm, Francis Culling, *Letters and Journals of Field-Marshal Sir William Maynard Gomm, G.C.B.*, London, 1881.

Chad, George William, *Conversations of the First Duke of Wellington*, Cambridge, 1956.

Clay, Matthew, *A Narrative of the Battles of Quatre Bras and Waterloo; with the Defence of Hougoumont, by Matthew Clay*, ed. Gareth Glover, Cambridge, 2006.

Costello, Edward, *Adventures of a Soldier; or Memoirs of Edward Costello ... Comprising Narratives of the Campaigns in the Peninsula under the Duke of Wellington*, London, 1852.

Cotton, Sergeant Major Edward, *A Voice from Waterloo*, London, 1889.

Creevey, Thomas, *The Creevey Papers*, ed. L. Gore, London, 1963.

Croker, John Wilson, *Correspondence and Diaries*, 3 vols, edited by Louis Jennings, London, 1885.

Dalton, Charles, *The Waterloo Roll Call*, London, 1904.

De Lancey, Lady, *A Week at Waterloo in 1815: Lady De Lancey's Narrative*, ed. Major B.R. Ward, London, 1906.

De Rottenburg, Colonel, *Regulations for the Exercise of Riflemen and Light Infantry, and Instructions for their Conduct in the Field*, London, 1798.

Dundas, Colonel David, *Principles of Military Movements, Chiefly Applied to Infantry, etc.*, London, 1788.

Eaton, Charlotte, *Narrative of a Residence in Belgium During the Campaign of 1815; and of a Visit to the Field of Waterloo*, London, 1817.

Facey, Sergeant Peter, *The Diary of a Veteran: The Diary of Sergeant Peter Facey, 28th (North Gloucestershire) Regiment of Foot, 1803–19*, ed. Gareth Glover, Cambridge, 2007.

Fenton, Captain Thomas, *Campaigning in Spain and Belgium: The Letters of Captain Thomas Charles Fenton, 4th Dragoons and Scots Greys, 1809–15*, ed. Gareth Glover, Cambridge, 2010.

Fielding, Lieutenant Colonel William, *A Memoir of the Waterloo Campaign, 1815, by Lieutenant Colonel William Fielding, Coldstream Guards*, ed. Gareth Glover, Cambridge, 2011.

Franklin, John, *Waterloo: Hanoverian Sources – Letters and Reports from Manuscript Sources*, 2010.

Franklin, John, *Waterloo: Netherlands Correspondence – Letters and Reports from Manuscript Sources*, 2010.

Frazer, Augustus, *Letters of Colonel Sir Augustus Frazer, KCB Commanding the Royal Horse Artillery in the Army Under the Duke of Wellington, Written During the Peninsular and Waterloo Campaigns*, ed. E. Sabine, London, 1859.

Frazer Augustus, *Remarks on the Organization of the Corps of Artillery in the British Service*, London, 1818.

Fremantle, Lieutenant Colonel John, *Wellington's Voice: The Candid Letters of Lieutenant Colonel John Fremantle, Coldstream Guards, 1808–1837*, ed. Gareth Glover, London, 2012.

Gavin, Ensign William, *The Diary of William Gavin, Ensign and Quarter-Master, 71st Highland Regiment, 1806–1815*, ed. Gareth Glover, Cambridge, 2013.

Gleig, George Robert, *Personal Reminiscences of the First Duke of Wellington*, Edinburgh and London, 1904.

Gleig, George Robert, *The Subaltern*, London, 1825.

Glover, Gareth, ed., *Letters from the Battle of Waterloo: Unpublished Correspondence by Allied Officers from the Siborne Papers*, London, 2004.

Glover, Gareth, ed., *The Waterloo Archive, Volume I: British Sources*, London, 2010.

Glover, Gareth, ed., *The Waterloo Archive, Volume II: German Sources*, London, 2010.

Glover, Gareth, ed., *The Waterloo Archive, Volume III: British Sources*, London, 2011.

Glover, Gareth, ed., *The Waterloo Archive, Volume IV: British Sources*, London, 2012.

Glover, Gareth, ed., *The Waterloo Archive, Volume V: German Sources*, London, 2013.

Glover, Gareth, ed., *The Waterloo Archive, Volume VI: British Sources*, London, 2014.

Gomm, William Maynard, *Letters and Journals of Field-Marshal Sir William Maynard Gomm, GCB*, London, 1881.

Gore, Captain Arthur, *An Historical Account of the Battle of Waterloo, etc.*, London, 1817.

Greville, Charles Cavendish Fulke, *The Greville Diary*, ed. Philip Wilson, 2 vols, London, 1927.

Griffiths, Captain F.A. Royal Artillery, *The Artillerist's Manual and British Soldier's Compendium*, Woolwich, 1847.

Gronow, Captain Rees Howell, *The Reminiscences and Recollections of Captain Gronow, 1810–1860*, 2 vols, London, 1900.

Hangar, George, *To All Sportsmen*, London, 1814.

Hardman, F., *Peninsular Scenes and Sketches*, London, 1846.

Hay, Captain William, *Reminiscences, 1808–1815 Under Wellington*, edited by his daughter, London, 1901.

Henegan, Sir Richard, *Seven Years' Campaigning in the Peninsula and the Netherlands; from 1808 to 1815*, 2 vols, London, 1846.

Hibbert, Christopher, ed., *The Wheatley Diary*, London, 1964.

Hibbert, Lieutenant John, *Waterloo Letters: The 1815 Letters of Lieutenant John Hibbert, 1st King's Dragoon Guards*, ed. Gareth Glover, Cambridge, 2007.

Hope, Lieutenant James, *Letters from Portugal, Spain and France, etc.*, Edinburgh, 1819.

Hope Pattison, F., *Personal Recollections of the Waterloo Campaign*, Glasgow, 1870.

Jackson, Lieutenant Colonel Basil, *Notes and Reminiscences of a Staff Officer Chiefly Relating to the Waterloo Campaign and to St Helena Matters During the Captivity of Napoleon*, ed. R.C. Seaton, London, 1903.

Jarry, General John, *Instructions Concerning the Duty of Light Infantry*, London, 1803.

Jeremiah, Private Thomas, *A Short Account of the Life and Adventures of Private Thomas Jeremiah, 23rd or Royal Welch Fusiliers, 1812–37*, ed. Gareth Glover, Cambridge, 2008.

Kennedy, Sir James Shaw, *Notes on the Battle of Waterloo*, London, 1865.

Keppel, George, *Fifty Years of My Life*, 1876.

Kershaw, Robert, ed., *24 Hours at Waterloo, 18 June 1815: Eyewitness Accounts from the Battle*, London, 2014.

Kincaid, Captain Sir John, *Adventures in the Rifle Brigade and Random Shots from a Rifleman*, London, 1835.

Lawrence, William, *The Autobiography of Sergeant William Lawrence*, ed. G.N. Bankes, London, 1886.

Leach, Lieutenant Colonel Jonathan, *Rough Sketches of the Life of an Old Soldier*, London, 1831.

Leeke, William, *History of Lord Seaton's Regiment at the Battle of Waterloo*, London, 1866.

Leslie, Major John, ed., *The Dickson Manuscripts Being Diaries, Letters, Maps, Account Books, with Various Other Papers of the Late Major-General Sir Alexander Dickson, 1809–1818*, Woolwich, 1905.

Low, E.B., *With Napoleon at Waterloo*, London, 1911.

McGrigor, Sir J., *Autobiography and Services with Notes, etc.*, London, 1861.

Mercer, Alexander, *Journal of the Waterloo Campaign*, ed. Cavalié Mercer, London, 1870.

Morris, Sergeant Thomas, *Recollections of Military Service in 1813, 1814, and 1815*, London, 1845.

Müffling, Carl von, *Passages From My Life*, London, 1853.

Mullen, A.L.T., *The Military General Service Roll, 1793–1814*, London, 1990.

Naylor, Captain James, *The Waterloo Diary of Captain James Naylor, 1st (King's) Dragoon Guards, 1815–16*, ed. Gareth Glover, Cambridge, 2008.

Neville, J.F., *Leisure Moments in the Camp and Guard-Room*, York, 1812.

Owen, E., *The Waterloo Papers: 1815 and Beyond*, Tavistock, 1997.

Playford, Sergeant Thomas, *A Lifeguardsman in Spain, France and at Waterloo: The Memoirs of Sergeant Thomas Playford, 2nd Life Guards, 1810–30*, ed. Gareth Glover, Cambridge, 2007.

Robertson, D., *Journal of Sergeant D. Robertson, Late 92nd Foot*, Perth, 1842.

Robinson, H.B., *Memoirs of Lieutenant General Sir Thomas Picton, GCB*, London, 1836.

Ross-Lewin, Harry, *With 'The Thirty-Second' in the Peninsular and other Campaigns*, ed. John Wardell, Dublin, 1904.

Saltoun, Lord Alexander *Waterloo Campaign Letters written by Lieutenant Colonel Alexander, Lord Saltoun, 1st Foot Guards, 1815*, ed. Gareth Glover, Cambridge, 2010.

Siborne, Herbert, ed., *The Waterloo Letters*, London, 1891. Reprinted, London, 1983.

Simmons, George, *A British Rifle Man: The Journals and Correspondence of Major George Simmons During the Peninsular War and Campaign of Waterloo*, ed. Willoughby Verner, 1899.

Smirke, R.J., *Review of a Battalion of Infantry Including the Eighteen Manoeuvres*, London, 1799.

Smith, Sir Harry, *The Autobiography of Lieutenant General Sir Harry Smith*, ed. G.C. Moore Smith, London, 1902.

Smithies, Private, *Adventurous Pursuits of a Peninsular War and Waterloo Veteran: The Story of Private James Smithies, 1st (Royal Dragoons), 1807–15*, ed. Gareth Glover, Cambridge, 2012.

Sperling, First Lieutenant John, *The Letters of First Lieutenant John Sperling, Royal Engineers*, ed. Gareth Glover, Cambridge, 2012.

Stanhope, Earl, *Notes of Conversations with the Duke of Wellington*, London, 1888.

Stanhope, Lieutenant Colonel James Hamilton, *Eyewitness to the Peninsular War and the Battle of Waterloo: The Letters and Journals of Lieutenant Colonel James Hamilton Stanhope, 1803–25*, ed. Gareth Glover, Barnsley, 2010.

Stanhope, Lieutenant Colonel James, *A Staff Officer in the Peninsula and at Waterloo: The Letters of the Honourable Lieutenant Colonel James H. Stanhope, 1st Foot Guards, 1809–15*, ed. Gareth Glover, Cambridge, 2007.

Surtees, William, *Twenty-five Years in the Rifle Brigade*, London, 1833.

Taylor, Thomas William, *Letters of Captain Thomas William Taylor*, Tetbury, 1895.

Temple, Henry John, 3rd Viscount Palmerston, *Private Journals of Tours in France in 1815–1818*, London, 1871.

Tomkinson, Lieutenant Colonel William, *The Diary of a Cavalry Officer in the Peninsular and Waterloo Campaigns, 1809–1815*, London, 1895.

Verner, William, *The Reminiscences of William Verner (1782–1871)*, ed. R.W. Verner, London, 1965.

Vivian, Hon. Claud, *Richard Hussey Vivian, First Baron Vivian: A Memoir*, London, 1897.

Waterloo Medal Roll, Dallington, 1992.

Waters, Lieutenant Colonel J., Assistant-Adjutant General, *The Morning State: Strength of the British Army on the morning of the Battle of Waterloo 18th June 1815, Dispatches of Field-Marshal the Duke of Wellington*, vol. xiii, 1838.

Wellington, Arthur Wellesley, 1st Duke of, *The Dispatches of Field Marshal the Duke of Wellington During his Various Campaigns, in India, Denmark, Portugal, Spain, the Low Countries and France*, compiled by Lieutenant Colonel Gurwood, London, 1837–38.

Wellington, Arthur Wellesley, 1st Duke of, *Supplementary Dispatches and Memoranda of Field-Marshal Arthur, Duke of Wellington*, ed. by Arthur Richard Wellesley, 2nd Duke of Wellington, London, 1858–72.

Wheeler, William, *The Letters of Private Wheeler, 1809–1828*, ed. B.H. Liddell Hart, London, 1951.

Secondary Sources

Adkin, Mark, *The Waterloo Companion: The Complete Guide to History's Most Famous Land Battle*, London, 2001.

Balen, Malcolm, *A Model Victory: Waterloo and the Battle for History*, London, 2005.

Bamford, Andrew, *Gallantry and Discipline: The 12th Light Dragoons at War with Wellington*, London, 2014.

Bamford, Andrew, *Sickness, Suffering, and the Sword: The British Regiment on Campaign, 1808–1815*, Tulsa, 2013.

Barbero, Alessandro, *The Battle: A New History of the Battle of Waterloo*, London, 2005.

Barthorp, Michael, *Wellington's Generals*, Oxford, 1978.

Beamish, North Ludlow, *History of the King's German Legion*, London, 1837.

Bernard, Giles and Lachaux, Gérard, *Waterloo*, Paris, 2005.

Black, Jeremy, *The Battle of Waterloo: A New History*, London, 2010.

Blanco, Richard, *Wellington's Surgeon-General Sir James McGrigor*, Durham, 1974.

Bowden, Scott, *Armies at Waterloo*, Arlington, 1983.

Brett-James, Antony, *The Hundred Days*, London, 1964.

Brett-James, Antony, *Life in Wellington's Army*, London, 1972.

Brett-James, Antony, *Wellington at War, 1794–1815*, London, 1961.

Burnham, Robert and McGuigan, Ron, *The British Army Against Napoleon: Facts, Lists, and Trivia, 1805–1815*, London, 2010.

Buttery, David, *Waterloo Battlefield Guide*, Barnsley, 2013.

Cantlie, Neil, *A History of the Army Medical Department*, vol. i, London, 1974.

Chalfont, Lord, ed., *Waterloo: The Hundred Days*, London, 1979.

Chandler, David, *The Campaigns of Napoleon*, London, 1995.

Chandler, David, ed., *Napoleon's Marshals*, London, 2000.

Chandler, David, *Waterloo: The Hundred Days*, New York, 1981.

Chesney, Colonel Charles, *Waterloo Lectures: A Study of the Campaign of 1815*, London, 1907.

Colby, Reginald, *The Waterloo Despatch: The Story of the Duke of Wellington's Official Despatch on the Battle of Waterloo and its Journey Back to London*, London, 1995.

Corrigan, Gordon, *Wellington: A Military Life*, London, 2001.

Coss, Edward, *All for the King's Shilling: The British Army Under Wellington, 1808–1814*, Oklahoma, 2010.

Crumplin, Michael, *The Bloody Fields of Waterloo: Medical Support at Wellington's Greatest Battle*, Cambridge, 2013.

Crumplin, Michael, *Guthrie's War: A Surgeon in the Peninsula and Waterloo*, Barnsley, 2010.

Dalton, Charles, *Waterloo Roll Call*, London, 1904.

Davies, Huw, *Wellington's Wars: The Making of a Military Genius*, New Haven, CT, 2012.

Elting, John, *Swords Around a Throne: Napoleon's Grande Armée*, London, 1997.

Esposito, Vincent J. and Elting, John, *A Military History and Atlas of the Napoleonic Wars*, London, 1990.

Field, Andrew, *Waterloo: The French Perspective*, Barnsley, 2012.

Fletcher, Ian, *A Desperate Business: Wellington, the British Army and the Waterloo Campaign*, Staplehurst, 2003.

Fletcher, Ian, *Gentlemen's Sons: The Foot Guards in the Peninsula and at Waterloo, 1808–1815*, Tunbridge Wells, 1992.

Fletcher, Ian, *Galloping at Everything: The British Cavalry in the Peninsular War and at Waterloo, 1808–15: A Reappraisal*, Stroud, 2008.

Fletcher, Ian, *Wellington's Regiments: The Men and their Battles from Roliça to Waterloo, 1805–15*, Staplehurst, 1994.

Forrest, Alan, *Napoleon's Men: The Soldiers of the Revolution and Empire*, New York, 2002.

Fortescue, Sir John, *A History of the British Army*, vol. 10, London, 1920.

Foster, R.E., *Wellington and Waterloo: The Duke, the Battle and Posterity, 1815–2015*, The History Press, 2014.

Foulkes, Nicholas, *Dancing into Battle: A Social History of the Battle of Waterloo*, Phoenix, 2007.

Franklin, John, *Hanoverian Correspondence: Letters and Reports from Manuscript Sources*, London, 2010

Franklin, John, *Netherlands Correspondence: Letters and Reports from Manuscript Sources*, London, 2010Fremont-Barnes, Gregory, ed., *Armies of the Napoleonic Wars*, Barnsley, 2011.

Fremont-Barnes, Gregory, ed., *The Encyclopedia of the French Revolutionary and Napoleonic Wars*, 3 vols, Oxford, 2006.

Fremont-Barnes, Gregory, *The French Revolutionary Wars*, Oxford, 2001.

Fremont-Barnes, Gregory, *Napoleon Bonaparte*, Oxford, 2010.

Fremont-Barnes, Gregory, *The Napoleonic Wars, Vol. III: The Peninsular War, 1807–1814*, Oxford, 2002.

Fremont-Barnes, Gregory, *The Napoleonic Wars, Vol. IV: The Fall of the French Empire, 1813–1815*, Oxford, 2002.

Fremont-Barnes, Gregory, *Battle Story – Waterloo 1815*, The History Press, 2012.

Gawler, George, *The Crisis and Close of the Action at Waterloo*, Dublin, 1833.

Gawler, Lieutenant Colonel George, 'The Crisis and Close of the Action at Waterloo', *United Service Journal*, July 1833, Part 2, pp. 299–309.

  Vivian, Lieutenant General Sir Hussey, 'Reply to Major Gawler, on his "Crisis of Waterloo"', *United Service Journal*, July 1833, Part 2, pp. 310–24.

  Gawler, Lieutenant Colonel George, 'A Correction to Some Points in the "Crisis of Waterloo"', *United Service Journal*, 1835, Part 1, pp. 303–4.

Gillespie-Payne, *Jonathan, Waterloo: In the Footsteps of the Commanders*, London, 2004.

Glover, Michael, *Wellington's Army*, Newton Abbot, 1977.

Glover, Richard, *Peninsular Preparation: The Reform of the British Army, 1795–1809*, Cambridge, 1963.

Guedalla, Philip, *The Duke*, London, 1931.

Guy, Alan J., ed., *The Road to Waterloo: The British Army and the Struggle against Revolutionary and Napoleonic France, 1793–1815*, London, 1990.

Hamilton-Williams, David, *Waterloo: New Perspectives, the Great Battle Reappraised*, London, 1993.

Harvey, Robert, *The War of Wars: The Epic Struggle Between Britain and France, 1789–1815*, London, 2007.

Haythornthwaite, Philip, *The Armies of Wellington*, London, 1996.

Haythornthwaite, Philip, *The Napoleonic Source Book*, London, 1990.

Haythornthwaite, Philip, *Red Coats: The British Soldiers of the Napoleonic Wars*, Barnsley, 2012.

Haythornthwaite, Philip, *Napoleon's Military Machine*, Staplehurst, 1995.

Haythornthwaite, Philip, *Uniforms of Waterloo*, London, 1996.

Haythornthwaite, Philip, *The Waterloo Armies: Men, Organisation and Tactics*, Barnsley, 2007.

Haythornthwaite, Philip, *Waterloo Men: The Experience of Battle, 16–18 June 1815*, Ramsbury, 1999.

Haythornthwaite, Philip, *Weapons and Equipment of the Napoleonic Wars*, Poole, 1979.

Haythornthwaite, Philip, *Wellington's Military Machine*, Staplehurst, 1997.

Herold, Christopher, *The Battle of Waterloo*, London, 1967.

Hibbert, Christopher, *Waterloo: Napoleon's Last Campaign*, Blue Ridge Summit, 2004.

Hofschröer, Peter, *Waterloo 1815 – Ligny and Quatre Bras*, London, 2005.

Hofschröer, Peter, *Waterloo 1815: Wavre to Plancenoit*, London, 2006.

Hofschröer, Peter, *1815 – The Waterloo Campaign – The German Victory*, London, 1999.

Hofschröer, Peter, *Wellington's Smallest Victory: The Duke, the Model Maker and the Secret of Waterloo*, London, London, 2004.

Holmes, Richard, *Wellington: The Iron Duke*, London, 2003.

Houssaye, Henry, *Napoleon and the Campaign of 1815: Waterloo*, London, 1900.

Howarth, David, *Waterloo: A Near Run Thing*, London, 2003.

Hughes, B.P., *Firepower*, London, 1974.

Keegan, John, *The Face of Battle*, London, 1976.

Kennedy, General Sir James Shaw, *Notes on the Battle of Waterloo*, Staplehurst, 2003.

Knight, Roger, *Britain against Napoleon: The Organization of Victory, 1793–1815*, London, 2013.

Lachouque, Henry and Browne, Anne S., *The Anatomy of Glory*, London, 1978.

Lachouque, Henry, *Waterloo*, London, 1972.

Lawford, James, *Napoleon: The Last Campaigns, 1813–15*, London, 1977.

Leach, Captain Jonathan, *Rough Sketches of the Life of an Old Soldier*, London, 1831, reprinted 2005

Linch, Kevin, *Britain and Wellington's Army: Recruitment, Society and Tradition, 1807–15*, London, 2011.

Lipscombe, Nick, *Wellington's Guns: The Untold Story of Wellington and his Artillery in the Peninsula and at Waterloo*, Oxford, 2013.

Longford, Elizabeth, *Wellington: The Years of the Sword*, London, 1973.

Martin, Howard, *Wellington's Doctors: The British Army Medical Services in the Napoleonic Wars*, Stroud, 2002.

Maxwell, Sir Herbert, *The Life of Wellington*, London, 1899.

Müffling, Baron F.K.F. von, *History of the Campaign of the British, Dutch, Hanoverian and Brunswick Armies … in the Year 1815*, London, 1816.

Muir, Rory, *Britain and the Defeat of Napoleon, 1807–1815*, New Haven, CT, 1996.

Muir, Rory, *Tactics and the Experience of Battle in the Age of Napoleon*, New Haven, CT, 2000.

Muir, Rory, *Wellington: The Path to Victory, 1769–1814*, New Haven, CT, 2013.

Muir, Rory; Burnham, Robert; Muir, Howie and McGuigan, Ron, *Inside Wellington's Peninsular Army, 1808–1814*, Barnsley, 2006.

Naylor, John, *Waterloo*, London, 1960.

Neillands, Robin, *Wellington and Napoleon: Clash of Arms, 1807–1815*, London, 1994.

Nofi, Albert, *The Waterloo Campaign: June 1815*, New York, 1998.

Nosworthy, Brent, *Battle Tactics of Napoleon and His Enemies*, London, 2001.

Oman, Sir Charles, *Wellington's Army*, London, 1912.

Paget, Henry, Marquess of Anglesey, *One-Leg: The Life and Letters of Henry William Paget*, London, 1961.

Paget, Julian, *Hougoumont*, London, 1992.

Pericolli, Ugo, *1815: The Armies at Waterloo*, London, 1973.

Pivka, Otto von, *The King's German Legion*, Oxford, 1974.

Roberts, Andrew, *Napoleon and Wellington: The Long Duel*, London, 2003.

Roberts, Andrew, *Waterloo: Napoleon's Last Gamble*, London, 2005.

Robinson, Mike, *The Battle of Quatre Bras 1815*, Stroud, 2010.

Rogers, Colonel H.C.B., *Wellington's Army*, Shepperton, 1979.

Rothenberg, Gunther, *The Art of Warfare in the Age of Napoleon*, London, 1977.

Schom, Alan, *One Hundred Days: Napoleon's Road to Waterloo*, Oxford, 1993.

Sherer, Moyle, *Recollections of the Peninsula*, London, privately published, 1823.

Siborne, William, *History of the War in France and Belgium 1815*, 2 vols, London, 1848.

Smith, Digby, *Charge! Great Cavalry Charges of the Napoleonic Wars*, London, 2003.

Summerville, Christopher, *Who Was Who at Waterloo: A Biography of the Battle*, Harlow, 2007.

Swiney, G.C., *Historical Records of the 32nd (Cornwall) Light*, Uxfield, 2003.

Uffindell, Andrew, *The Eagle's Last Triumph: Napoleon's Victory at Ligny, June 1815*, London, 2006.

Uffindell, Andrew, *The National Army Museum Book of Wellington's Armies: Britain's Campaigns in the Peninsula and at Waterloo, 1808–1815*, London, 2005.

Uffindell, Andrew and Michael Corum, *On the Fields of Glory: The Battlefields of the Waterloo Campaign*, London, 1996.

Uffindell, Andrew, *Waterloo: The Battlefield Guide*, Barnsley, 2003.

Urban, Mark, *Rifles: Six Years with Wellington's Legendary Sharpshooters*, London, 2004.

Ward, S.G.P., *Wellington's Headquarters*, Oxford, 1957.

Weller, Jac, *Wellington at Waterloo*, London, 1992.

Weller, Jac, *On Wellington: The Duke and his Art of War*, London, 1998.

Wood, Sir Evelyn, *Cavalry in the Waterloo Campaign*, London, 1897.

Wooten, Geoffrey, *Waterloo 1815*, Oxford, 1992.

Young, Peter, *Blücher's Army, 1813–15*, Oxford, 1972.

Forthcoming Publications

Clayton, Tim, *Waterloo: Four Days that Changed Europe's Destiny*, London 2014.

Cornwell, Bernard, *Waterloo: The History of Four Days – Three Armies, Three Battles*, London 2014.

Corrigan, Gordon, *Waterloo: A New History of the Battle and its Armies*, London, 2014.

Franklin, John, *Waterloo 1815 (1): Quatre Bras*, Oxford, 2014.

Franklin, John, *Waterloo 1815 (2): Ligny*, Oxford, 2015.

Franklin, John, *Waterloo 1815 (3): Mont St Jean and Wavre*, Oxford, 2015.

Glover, Gareth, *Waterloo: Myth and Reality*, Barnsley, 2014.

Lipscombe, Col. Nick, ed., *Waterloo: The Decisive Victory*, Oxford, 2014.

Sale, Nigel, *The Lie at the Heart of Waterloo: The Battle's Hidden Last Half Hour*, Stroud, 2014.

Simms, Brendan, *The Longest Afternoon: The 400 Men Who Decided the Battle of Waterloo*, London, 2014.

ACKNOWLEDGEMENTS

I wish to extend my grateful thanks to Gareth Glover, who kindly provided, prior to its publication, a copy of the sixth volume of his *Waterloo Archive*, thus enabling me to draw upon the invaluable primary sources contained in his complete series. To my father-in-law, Ivan Barnes, who kindly read the manuscript and offered very helpful advice and corrections, I am much indebted. Three members of the staff at The History Press deserve my particular thanks: Jo de Vries, Senior Commissioning Editor, for assenting to the particular perspective I proposed on Waterloo when she commissioned this work; Sophie Bradshaw, Publisher, who not only expertly oversaw the writing phase of the book, but generously granted me both an extended date of submission and an enhanced word limit; and Lauren Newby, Editor, who worked tirelessly, accepting my corrections, identifying errors which I overlooked and remaining stoic and cheerful even in the face of my numerous requests for eleventh-hour alterations. Naturally, any errors which remain are my own.

To my father, A. C. Fremont MD, who spent his childhood, several years of it in wartime, living near Waterloo, I owe enormous thanks for instilling in me a lifelong passion for history. Greatest thanks belong to my wife, Judith, who demonstrated exceptional forbearance while I madly immersed myself in the affairs of another age.

INDEX